# HISTORY OF WOMEN IN THE UNITED STATES

# HISTORY OF WOMEN IN THE UNITED STATES
## Historical Articles on Women's Lives and Activities

*Edited by Nancy F. Cott*

Series ISBN 3-598-41454-4

1. Theory and Method in Women's History
ISBN 3-598-41455-2 Part 1
ISBN 3-598-41477-3 Part 2

2. Household Constitution and Family Relationships
ISBN 3-598-41456-0

3. Domestic Relations and Law
ISBN 3-598-41457-9

4. Domestic Ideology and Domestic Work
ISBN 3-598-41458-7 Part 1
ISBN 3-598-41475-7 Part 2

5. The Intersection of Work and Family Life
ISBN 3-598-41459-5 Part 1
ISBN 3-598-41476-5 Part 2

6. Working on the Land
ISBN 3-598-41460-9

7. Industrial Wage Work
ISBN 3-598-41461-7 Part 1
ISBN 3-598-41693-8 Part 2

8. Professional and White-Collar Employments
ISBN 3-598-41462-5 Part 1
ISBN 3-598-41694-6 Part 2

9. Prostitution
ISBN 3-598-41463-3

10. Sexuality and Sexual Behavior
ISBN 3-598-41464-1

11. Women's Bodies: Health and Childbirth
ISBN 3-598-41465-X

12. Education
ISBN 3-598-41466-8

13. Religion
ISBN 3-598-41467-6

14. Intercultural and Interracial Relations
ISBN 3-598-41468-4

15. Women and War
ISBN 3-598-41469-2

16. Women Together: Organizational Life
ISBN 3-598-41470-6

17. Social and Moral Reform
ISBN 3-598-41471-4 Part 1
ISBN 3-598-41695-4 Part 2

18. Women and Politics
ISBN 3-598-41472-2 Part 1
ISBN 3-598-41697-0 Part 2

19. Woman Suffrage
ISBN 3-598-41473-0 Part 1
ISBN 3-598-41696-2 Part 2

20. Feminist Struggles for Sex Equality
ISBN 3-598-41474-9

# HISTORY OF WOMEN IN THE UNITED STATES

## Historical Articles on Women's Lives and Activities

# 15. Women and War

Edited with an Introduction by

Nancy F. Cott
Yale University

K · G · Saur
Munich · New Providence · London · Paris · 1993

**Publisher's Note**

The articles and chapters which comprise this collection originally appeared in a wide variety of publications and are reproduced here in facsimile from the highest quality offprints and photocopies available. The reader will notice some occasional marginal shading and text-curl common to photocopying from tightly bound volumes. Every attempt has been made to either correct or minimize this effect.

Copyright information for articles reproduced in this collection appears at the end of this volume.

**Library of Congress Cataloging-in-Publication Data**

History of women in the United States : historical articles on
women's lives and activities / edited with
an introduction by Nancy F. Cott.
p. cm.
Includes bibliographical references and indexes.
Contents: 1. Theory and method in women's history -- 2. Household constitution and family relationships -- 3. Domestic relations and law -- 4. Domestic ideology and domestic work -- 5. The intersection of work and family life -- 6. Working on the land -- 7. Industrial wage work -- 8. Professional and white-collar employments -- 9. Prostitution -- 10. Sexuality and sexual behavior -- 11. Women's bodies -- 12. Education -- 13. Religion -- 14. Intercultural and interracial relations -- 15. Women and war -- 16. Women together -- 17. Social and moral reform -- 18. Women and politics -- 19. Woman suffrage -- 20. Feminist struggles for sex equality.
ISBN 3-598-41454-4 (set)
1. Women--United States--History. 2. Women--United States--Social conditions. I. Cott, Nancy F.
HQ1410.H57 1992
305.4'0973--dc20 92-16765
CIP

Die Deutsche Bibliothek - CIP - Einheitsaufnahme

**History of Women in the United States:** historical articles
on women's lives and activities / ed. with an introd. by Nancy F. Cott.
- Munich ; New Providence ; London ; Paris : Saur.
ISBN 3-598-41454-4
NE: Cott, Nancy F. (Hrsg.)
Vol. 15. women and war - (1993)
ISBN 3-598-41469-2

Printed on acid-free paper/Gedruckt auf säurefreiem Papier



Printed in the United States of America
Printed/Bound by Edwards Brothers Incorporated, Ann Arbor

ISBN 3-598-41469-2 (vol. 15)
ISBN 3-598-41454-4 (series)

# Contents

CONTENTS

CONTENTS

# Series Preface

In the space of one generation, women's history has become the fastest-growing area of scholarship in U.S. history. Since the resurgence of feminism in the late 1960s and 1970s, insistent questions about the historical meanings of "woman's place" have sowed and reaped a garden of scholarship. Where scholarly works used to be bare of mention of women, academic enterprise has now produced a vigorous growth of books and articles, bringing to light diverse women of every region, race, class and age. This research is marked by a renovating intent that refuses to accept as "human" history a history of men. Interest is lively and debate is stimulating and sought after: attendance at the Berkshire Conference on the History of Women rivals the size of the annual convention of the American Historical Association.

While books in women's history are daily increasing in numbers and strength, as in any fast-developing field the scholarly literature in the form of articles is most expansive and up-to-the-minute. All the history journals now publish articles on women's work, domestic settings, family relations, household matters, female politics and organizations and so forth, and new journals have sprung into being to concentrate on such topics. Women's historians publish in numerous regional and thematic history journals as well as in feminist outlets and in journals of other social science disciplines. This series brings together a collection of outstanding articles from the field, almost all written in the past twenty years and more than half published during the 1980s. It brings together, in volumes organized by topic, essays otherwise widely dispersed. These volumes reprint only articles that originally appeared in journals, not chapters of books; review articles are not included. Articles have been chosen for overall quality and for range. Each one was chosen for one or more of the following reasons: because it is the standard authority on its subject matter; represents an important statement on a topic by a recognized scholar; presages an important book to come; provides a first look at new evidence or new methods; or opens an untapped area or new controversy. Older articles have been reprinted if their data or interpretation have not been surpassed or if they marked an important stage in the historiography, even if since superseded.

The historical coverage of the series extends from the Revolutionary era to the 1960s. The articles themselves are dated from the 1940s through 1988. Volumes are organized by topic rather than time period. Within each volume, the articles are ordered chronologically (with respect to substance), so that the whole can be read as an historical overview. The only exception to this ordering principle is Volume One, on Theory and Method, in which the contents are arranged in order of publication. Within each volume there is an attempt to include articles on as diverse kinds of women as possible. None of the volume topics is regionally or racially defined; rather, all volumes are topically designed so as to afford views of women's work, family lives, and public activities which cut across races and regions. Any volume in the series stands on its own, supplying as full a treatment of a designated subject matter as the scholarly literature will provide. Several groupings of volumes also make sense; that is, volumes two through five all center around domestic and family matters; volumes five through nine consider other varieties of women's work; volumes nine through eleven concern uses and abuses of women's bodies; volumes twelve through fourteen look at major aspects of socialization; and volumes fifteen through twenty include organizational and political efforts of many sorts.

As a whole, the series displays in all its range the vitality of the field of women's history. Aside from imbuing U.S. history with new vision, scholarship in this area has informed, and should continue to inform, current public debate on issues from parental leave to the nuclear freeze. By bringing historical articles together under topical headings, these volumes both represent accurately the shape of historical controversy (or consensus) on given issues and make historians' findings most conveniently available for current reference.

# Introduction

Despite formal exclusion from enlistment in military service until the twentieth century, women have participated in and contributed to all four major wars undertaken by the U.S., on the home front and on the battlefield. In this there is nothing nationally unique, since through human history, while men have been the recognized warriors, no war has ever been fought (and certainly none won) without women's supportive efforts. Examining evidence from the Revolution, the Civil War, and both World Wars, the collection of articles in this volume consider women's wartime roles and the impact of wars in bringing subsequent burdens or opportunities to women. Two articles also consider women's initiatives in peace advocacy. This collection reveals a great deal not only about gender roles but also about the modernization and bureaucratization of the state along with changes in work and social values.

Exclusion or inclusion in military service has been always associated with the qualities of citizenship, or of belonging to the polity, in Western political theory and in fact in American political practice. A central although often unspoken part of the definition of citizenship—for the male—is his obligation and ability to serve his country as a soldier in war. By the same token, the exclusion (or protection) of women from the need to fight has warranted seeing the quality of their citizenship as lesser. Thus there has been considerable reason for women interested in equal rights to pursue military service of one description or another. During the long campaign for the vote for women, one frequently-invoked justification for denying the ballot to women was that they were not called upon to defend their country by arms. Conversely, the tremendous service to the nation which women provided during World War I, both in the military service and outside it, became a persuasive reason for much public opinion to turn to endorse female suffrage. Although the reasons for the success of the Nineteenth Amendment shortly after World War I were much more complex than the simple reason of war service, that did play a role in shifting long-resistant public and Congressional opinion toward majority approval of women's voting.

Women's relation to war has always been ambiguous. Cultural assumptions about women and war have traditionally been double-edged: on the one side, the female role in creating and nurturing life has brought along with it the notion that women are naturally pacific and opposed to war; on the other, the heroic mother who dedicates her sons to battle has also been set up as a cultural icon, and twentieth-century states at war—whether democratic, fascist or communist—have explicitly championed the woman who serves her country "behind the lines."[1] Women have been signal leaders in twentieth-century peace movements. Sometimes female pacifists have believed and relied on the claim that the maternal role destines them to preserve life and therefore oppose war. At other times female opponents of war have developed the more sophisticated argument that women can imagine diplomatic means of alternatives to war more clearly than men, for the very reason that women have traditionally and historically been excluded from statecraft reliant on war-making as a solution to disputes. Pacifist movements in the U.S., most notably during the decades from 1915 to 1940, have drawn a majority of female adherents. The National Conference on the Cause and Cure of War, an umbrella organization founded by former woman suffrage leader Carrie Chapman Catt in 1925 to present alternatives to militarism and to lobby for peace, had, by assembling the major women's organizations under its aegis, a membership of five million women when it started. By 1930 it claimed to speak for more than one out of five adult women in the U.S.[2] Yet the still larger experience of American women has been necessary and sometimes quite willing support for war efforts.

Historians have inquired into women's roles during wartime not only to find out about women's relation to the state but also to see if, or how, the sexual division of labor changes under the exigencies of war. This would not be so central a question were work tasks not so generally defined and limited by sex. In the U.S. economy, sex-segregation in occupations has been the general rule; yet when men are called to war, the likeliest candidates to take up their ordinary and necessary occupations are women. Of course not all men are soldiers, and not all men's occupations need be replaced; on the other hand, war creates economic and production demands outside military service itself, which also require staffing.

The dimensions and intensity of shifts in gender allocation of work roles during wartime varies according to the scale of the conflict and the specialization and diversification of the economy at the time. During the Revolutionary War when the economy was very predominantly agricultural, the planting and harvesting that women shouldered in addition to their household production did not change their location, although it increased their hardships and, often, their self-respect. By the time of the Civil War, the U.S. economy was sufficiently diversified that certain structural results of men's being diverted to war service could be seen. Women were hired into white-collar work in federal departments for the first time, for example; women's employment in the mass production of clothing greatly expanded (to clothe to army); and in the chartering of a national organization, the U.S. Sanitary Commission, the voluntary efforts of Northern women were organized along with men's in the war effort.

Industrialization and economic specialization and diversification were so far advanced by the time of the two World Wars that war-induced dislocations of the economy were visible in myriad and repeated ways, including urgent calls for women to serve in capacities formerly thought possible only for men. Because U.S. participation in the first World War was relatively brief, its impact was smaller than that of World War II. With regard to both of these world conflicts, however, historians have asked similar questions: how far did the demands of wartime catapult women into new occupations and positions? What did this mean for their earnings, their self-assessments, their positions in their families and communities. their relationships with men? What was the long-term result of women's wartime roles? Much historical investigation has focused on the greatly expanded federal government's role in fostering women's opportunities or rights during wartime, and actively manipulating public views of appropriate womanhood, in the attempt to gain the most of women's services. Overall, historians have found the war periods to serve as a kind of magnifying lens, revealing in larger detail the gender system of the surrounding era; for this reason as well as for the intrinsic usefulness of highlighting women's civic roles, these essays command special attention.

## Notes

[1] *See Behind the Lines: Gender and the Two World Wars*, ed. Margaret Higonnet et al. (New Haven, CT Yale Univ. Press, 1987).

[2] *See* Merle Curti, *Peace or War* (N.Y., Norton, 1936), 272.

# Women and War

# WOMEN IN THE AMERICAN REVOLUTION

ELIZABETH COMETTI

WAR was very real to the women of the Revolutionary period. Along the extended frontier there hung a perpetual threat of Indian incursions with their attendant acts of savagery. On the coast and by navigable rivers the British fleet and army kept the inhabitants in an intermittent state of alarm. In the interior sporadic fighting and foraging raids left their victims shaken and impoverished. Yet with the exception of those whom the exigencies of war forced to become refugees, women generally remained at home ministering to the needs of their households, assuming their absent husbands' responsibilities, meeting as best they could the inevitable wartime scarcities, taking over jobs compatible with their physical limitations and conventions, and longing always for the return of their men and for peace.

As if loneliness and sorrow were not enough, war brought privation and destitution to many wives and widows of men in the military service. Even before the continental currency started on its disastrous toboggan slide, soldiers' pay had not been uniform, prompt, or sufficient, despite various bounties offered to encourage enlistments. As there was no general provision for allotments to dependents of fighting men, the latter were often forced to see their loved ones become objects of local charity. Neither were widows and orphans of fighting men adequately or uniformly pensioned, with the result that many of them had to petition the government for relief.[1] When the full month's pay of an officer was required to meet his traveling expenses for one day, how could bereaved dependents exist on the half pay allotted them by a law which had no general application until 1780, five years after the outbreak of hostilities?[2]

[1] *Minutes of the Council of Safety of the State of New Jersey* (Jersey City, 1872), 280-283, 287. Research for this paper was made possible by a Southern-Grant-in-Aid from the Social Science Research Council.

[2] Allen Bowman, *The Morale of the American Revolutionary Army* (Washington, 1943), 23-25; Otto G. Eckstein, *The History of the Law of Pensions* (Philadephia, 1890), 32-33.

Some women bore their difficulties in silence; others, however, complainingly enumerated them to the men at camp, thereby causing the latter to increase their clamors for pay adjustments. "... Four months' pay of a private will not procure his wretched wife and children a single bushel of wheat. . . ." indignantly exclaimed a soldier. "Few of us have private fortunes: many have families who already are suffering everything that can be received from an ungrateful country. Are we then to submit to all the inconveniences, fatigue, and dangers of a camp life, while our wives and children are perishing for want of common necessaries at home . . . ?" asked others.[3] Young Joshua Huntington, who had left Yale just before graduation to join the army, could scarcely contain himself: "You Resolved in your Last Session, [of Connecticut] that the Soldiers family should be Supplied, whether they sent Money or not, but it is not done, nor will it be done—not a Day Passes my head, but some Soldier with Tears in his Eyes, hands me a letter to read from his Wife Painting forth the Distresses of his Family in such strains as these 'I am without bread, & cannot get any, the Committee will not supply me, my Children will Starve, or if they do not, they must freeze, we have no wood, neither Can we get any—*Pray Come Home.*' "[4]

Despairing of relief, some wives took their problems straight to the authorities. One woman complained that her husband had received no pay for four years and that she had "three small children to maintain & for want of assistance . . . her Household Goods, even her Bed was seiz'd and sold for Rent which brought her & Children to very great Distress, having neither Wood nor Bread . . . ."[5] The revolutionary committees and state legislatures were not wholly insensible to these justifiable entreaties, and sought remedies in a variety of resolutions and acts providing for distribution of money and food to soldiers'

[3] *Selections from the Correspondence of the Executive of New Jersey from 1776 to 1786* (Newark, 1848), 143-145, 164-166.

[4] Ebenezer Huntington to Ja. Huntington, December 21, 1778, in G. W. F. Blanchfield, editor, *Letters Written by Ebenezer Huntington during the American Revolution* (New York, 1915), 77-78.

[5] Papers of the Continental Congress, III, 42, 52, Library of Congress.

families, for limiting prices, for rationing essential commodities, and for state purchasing and marketing of goods. Frequently, however, the negligence and indifference of local officials nullified the results anticipated from these measures. In order to preclude this, New Hampshire passed a law which stated that if any town refused or neglected to make provisions "to the amount of such Sums as shall be lodged by such Non-commissioned Officers and private Soldiers . . . not exceeding the one Half Part of their Wages respectively," its selectmen should administer relief all the same, and later assess the town for whatever was expended.[6]

The distress of dependents was not always chargeable to officialdom; for example, the removal of families from places where their men had enlisted, the wide differences in terms of enlistments, and the inflation, which required periodic adjustments in pay and benefits, all complicated the handling of allotments.[7] Moreover, when treasury receipts were insufficient to meet the cost of war and government, pensioners were among the first to suffer. Thus Virginia repealed an act empowering the county courts to support soldiers' families on the ground that it had "created an expenditure greatly exceeding the expectations of the legislature . . . ." The law, however, excepted those who were too poor to maintain themselves, but their allowance was limited to "one barrel of corn and fifty pounds of nett pork, for each person . . . annually."[8] Fortunately, these niggardly allotments were supplemented with contributions from church congregations, societies, and individuals. Affluent John Hancock donated a hundred and fifty cords of wood to the poor of Boston, many of whom had men in the service.[9]

Whether they liked it or not, women in straitened circum-

[6] *Acts and Laws of the State of New-Hampshire in America* (Exeter, 1780), 96-97.

[7] New Hampshire Broadside, December 28, 1779. Broadside in Library of Congress Broadside Collection, Portfolio 88, 20.

[8] William W. Hening, editor, *The Statutes at Large* (Richmond, 1821), x, 212; xii, 262.

[9] *A Report of the Record Commissioners of the City of Boston* (Boston, 1895), xviii, 291, 293-294.

stances had to accept relief, for there were few remunerative jobs available to them under existing industrial conditions. The home, with its garden and barn, was woman's workshop; outside the home, her productive potentialities were only dimly suspected and meagerly utilized. The textile industry, one of the first to feel the impact of industrialization, employed women in some number, partly because the nature of the work and the tradition surrounding it made adjustment from home to factory relatively easy. The adoption of non-intercourse acts created a textile scarcity which the extraordinary demands of war rendered still more acute. Clearly, only increased industrial and domestic production coupled with curtailed consumption could ease the situation. In a mildly ridiculous fashion the non-intercourse agreement tried to encourage the latter by prescribing the use of black crepe bandeaus in lieu of the usual mourning dresses complete with black gloves and scarves ordinarily worn at funerals, a provision which the Tory press mischievously parodied:

> And when a Son dies, we will take no more Notice,
> Than as if one should say, I know nor care who 'tis
> With a piece of black Crape, we will sit down content;
> When all our old Cloaths are quite tatter'd and rent;
> The giving of Gloves and of Scarfs we'll decry,
> When we've got none to give, faith, let who will die.[10]

Among the largest of the new enterprises was the American Manufactory of Philadelphia, which installed a spinning "jenny" and employed about four hundred women in spinning and other work.[11] The company's advertisement in the *Pennsylvania Packet* for August 1775 carried this special message for women: "In this time of public distress you have each of you an opportunity not only to help to sustain your families, but likewise to call your mite into the treasury of the public good." In order to stimulate domestic production women were

10 "Bob Jingle," "The Association of the Delegates (1774)," in *The Magazine of History with Notes and Queries* (Tarrytown, 1927), XXXIII, no. 4, 47.

11 J. Leander Bishop, *A History of American Manufactures from 1608 to 1860* (Philadelphia, 1864), I, 387-388, 394.

everywhere enjoined to "cease trifling their time away [and] prudently employ it in learning the use of the spinning wheel."[12]

Aside from the textile industry the opportunities for gainful employment were limited. One woman took over the management of a large tanning yard following the death of her husband. Another was employed as jailor by Isle of Wight County, Virginia. In the same state, some ladies, largely in fun, once assisted in making munitions. Work stoppage was the usual recourse for women against industrial exploitation, hence in Virginia several seamstresses refused to make shirts for fifteen inflated dollars apiece paid in certificates of doubtful value.[13]

On the farms of New England and the Middle States, women raised foodstuffs, often with only the assistance of boys and old men. "I find it necessary to be the directress of our husbandry," wrote the indomitable Abigail Adams. "I hope in time to have the reputation of being as good a *farmeress* as my partner has of being a good statesman,"[14] she flatteringly told her husband in Philadelphia.

Volunteer services as well as remunerative work took women outside the home, where they could forward their patriotic endeavors in the pleasant sociability of the group. Many of them employed their leisure in making shirts for the ragged Continentals, who were all too often the victims of official neglect. When the observant Chevalier de Chastellux visited Benjamin Franklin's daughter, Mrs. Bache, he was conducted into "a room filled with work, lately finished by the ladies of Philadelphia." "This work," he noted approvingly, "consisted neither of embroidered tambour waistcoats, nor net work edging, nor of gold and silver brocade—it was a quantity of shirts for the soldiers of Pennsylvania. The ladies bought the linen

[12] *Pennsylvania Packet*, August 7, 1775; December 19, 1774.

[13] William P. Palmer, editor, *Calendar of Virginia State Papers and Other Manuscripts* (Richmond, 1881), 440, 416, 608-609. *Virginia Gazette* (P), November 21, 1777.

[14] Abigail Adams to John Adams, April 7, September 29, 1776. Charles F. Adams, editor, *Familiar Letters of John Adams and his Wife Abigail Adams, During the Revolution* (Boston, 1875), 150-153; 229-230.

from their own private purses, and took a pleasure in cutting them out and sewing them themselves. On each shirt was the name of the married, or unmarried lady who made it, and they amounted to 2200."[15]

Frequently women organized drives for collecting money, clothing, food, and scarce materials. In Philadelphia some prominent ladies canvassed the city to obtain money for soldiers in the Pennsylvania regiments. So great was the ladies' enthusiasm for their philanthropic task that one who was still too weak from her recent confinement to participate in the drive offered to nurse the child of a canvasser. Since by their own modest admission the ladies "knew nothing of affairs of State," they forwarded the money collected to General Washington for disposal as he saw fit.[16] Women in other cities followed the example of their sisters in Philadelphia, even to the extent of selecting the most prominent among themselves for key positions in the drives.[17] The consequent bustle and publicity tickled the men, to whose quips the ladies replied: ". . . some persons have amused themselves with the importance which we have given [the drive]. . . . We have made it a serious business, and with great reason—an object so interesting was certainly worthy an extraordinary attention."[18]

Shortages of paper and hospital supplies occasioned numerous and ingenious appeals to women for the salvage and collection of their cast-off sheets and garments. A paper manufacturer in North Carolina reminded young ladies that in "sending to the Paper Mill an old Handkerchief, no longer fit to cover their snowy Breasts, there [was] a Possibility of its returning to them again in the more pleasing Form of a Billet

[15] Marquis de Chastellux, *Travels in North America in the Years 1780-81-82* (New York, 1827), 98. To a group of Baltimore belles who had invited him to a ball, Lafayette once said: "You are very handsome; you dance very prettily; your ball is very fine—but my soldiers have no shirts." Quoted in Bishop, *History of American Manufactures*, I, 395.

[16] *Independent Chronicle and Universal Advertiser* (Boston), July 27, August 10, 1780.

[17] *Pennsylvania Packet*, July 8, November 4, 1780.

[18] *Independent Chronicle and Universal Advertiser*, August 10, 1780.

Deaux from their Lovers. . . ."[19] A Hartford paper concern warned matrons that the "Schools will be essentially affected, and all writing business cease unless the Ladies will exert themselves and shew their patriotism on this occasion."[20] Equally urgent and frequent were appeals for rags and lint to make bandages and compresses for use in military hospitals. Leaden household articles and ornaments were also in demand; for them the patriotic housewife was offered six pence per pound.[21]

Women experienced their greatest difficulties with shortages and high prices while trying to meet the requirements of their own households. One anonymous Molly Gutridge doubtless spoke for many harassed members of her sex when she versified:

It's hard and cruel times to live,
Takes thirty dollars to buy a sieve
To buy sieves and other things too,
To go thro' the world how can we do?

. . . . . . . . . . . . . .

For salt is all the Farmer's cry,
If we've no salt we sure must die.
We can't get fire nor yet food,
Takes 20 weight of sugar for two foot of wood,
We cannot get bread nor yet meat,
We see the world is nought but cheat.

. . . . . . . . . . . . . .

All we can get it is but rice
And that is of a wretched price.

. . . . . . . . . . . . . .

These times will learn us to be wise,
We now do eat what we despis'd.
I now have something more to say,
We must go up and down the Bay.
To get a fish a-days to fry,
We can't get fat were we to die.[22]

19 *North Carolina Gazette*, November 14, 1777.

20 *Connecticut Courant*, September 22, 1777; *New Jersey Gazette*, January 20, 1779. Some newspapers had to reduce their size because of the paper shortage.

21 *Pennsylvania Packet*, May 13, July 22, 1776.

22 Ola Elizabeth Winslow, editor, *American Broadside Verse* (New Haven, 1943), 190-191.

Scarcer and much higher in price than domestic foodstuffs were the commodities formerly imported from England—medicines, spices, sugar, coffee, tea, pins, to name only a few. The prospect of seeing their families without the customary necessities and small luxuries induced even high-minded ladies to lay in "a small stock of West India articles" against the day when they would be off the market.[23] The poorer sort, prevented from hoarding by lack of cash, used more irregular means to stock their empty larders. Thus in East Hartford "a corps of female infantry, of 20 rank and file . . . marching westward about one mile, in martial array and excellent order, saving stride and gabble, there attacked and carried without opposition from powder, law or conscience, Mr. Perkin's store, in which was lodged a quantity of sugar designed for the army of which they plundered and bore away in triumph 218 lb.—A travelling gentleman falling in with their rear, who they mistook for the owner of the spoils, was attacked and drove with great fury; but being well mounted made his escape."[24] These and similar antics of the female "mobility" disgusted and alarmed their more restrained, but also less hungry sisters.

As a scarce commodity, tea was in a class by itself; because it symbolized the hated imperial policy, tea-drinking became synonymous with disaffection. At the outbreak of the Revolution patriots urged the banishing of India tea from the tables and substituting various aromatic herbs. But this was easier recommended than done, for the ladies loved their tea and its voluntary discontinuance entailed considerable will-power. When the designated moment of sacrifice came, groups of ladies would sometimes assemble over a last ceremonial cup of tea to pledge farewell to the "pernicious weed." And they were vigilant in seeing that others should not have what they had given up, going so far as to denounce those who dared to relapse from their resolutions; for it was possible to obtain tea by such

[23] Abigail Adams to John Adams, July 16, September 8, 1775, in *Familiar Letters*, 78-83, 96.

[24] *Independent Chronicle and Universal Advertiser*, October 9, 1777.

strategems as whispering across the merchant's counter and obtaining falsely labelled packages of tea.[25] Eventually tea re-appeared on the market openly and in abundance, particularly after the doughty privateers increased their activities, but its price remained excessively high.

In spite of the appeals of good Whigs, there is little evidence of herbs ever having been substituted for India tea, though sage tea, balm tea, and teaberry were tried. Few, indeed, were the substitute materials introduced because of war scarcity. To be sure, a meat pickle was made by mixing that scarce commodity with lye from walnut ashes to take the place of pure salt.[26] In Rhode Island, "An American Woman" published her recipe for soap which could be easily carried by soldiers.[27] The greatest success was achieved in the use of corn stalks for making a syrup reputed to be nearly as good as West India molasses, the basic ingredient of rum. According to the investigations of Dr. Ezra Stiles, president of Yale College, distillers succeeded in making a fine grade of rum from this juice.[28] Because of the popularity of rum, the production of this syrup received wide publicity in contemporary newspapers. The textile scarcity caused some talk of using buckskin and doeskin instead of woolen cloth, but the general public was reluctant to change materials. Only occasionally did patriotic women urge their sisters to abandon British extravagances and, like "the Matildas, the Elizabeths, the Maries, the Catherines," to wear simple clothing of home manufacture.[29] But judging from the notoriety given a wedding in which "the bride and two of her sisters appeared in very genteel-like gowns, and others of the family in handsome apparel, with sundry silk handkerchiefs,

[25] *Connecticut Courant*, March 6, April 24, 1775; John F. Watson, *Annals of Philadelphia, and Pennsylvania, in the Olden Time* (Philadelphia, 1898), II, 327-328.

[26] Jedediah Huntington to Andrew Huntington, December 20, 1777, in *Huntington Papers—Connecticut Historical Society Collection* (Hartford, 1923), 389.

[27] *Providence Gazette*, August 5, 1780.

[28] Franklin B. Dexter, editor, *The Literary Diary of Ezra Stiles* (New York, 1901), II, 209, 229.

[29] *Virginia Gazette*, August 9, 1780.

&c., entirely of their own manufacture," it would seem that weddings in homespun were the exception and not the rule among people who could afford a choice.[30]

Women showed their attachment to the Revolution not only in works and sacrifices but also in their personal relations with those whose loyalties they suspected or who were indisputably inimical to independence. Once a generous hostess was meanly and publicly labelled a Tory by her former guests because she had refused to drink a second toast to Washington.[31] At a quilting frolic a group of young ladies stripped their lone male guest to the waist and covered him with molasses and the "downy tops of flags" because he had cast aspersions on Congress.[32] In New England a ladies' battalion, nearly two hundred strong, set out to tar and feather the mother of a new-born baby who had been christened Thomas Gage, and only the pleas of the distracted father restrained the mob.[33] In Philadelphia, the ladies were singularly unkind to poor Grace Galloway, whose husband, Joseph Galloway, came and went from Philadelphia with the British army. Her health, family, and position gone, her petitions denied, her property confiscated, poor Mrs. Galloway did not even have the consolation of loyal friendship. The same women who had once been her neighbors and companions were now "cold" to her pathetic importunities for the loan of their carriage to enable her to take some much-needed exercise. "I am Declineing for [want of] exercise," she wrote, "yet no one will take me out or give me a Meal if I was perishing all Ye Notice taken of Me is to come & pump Me for News & talk Me almost to Death. Oh ye time servers how I despise ye."[34]

30 Quoted in Frank Moore, *Diary of the American Revolution* (New York, 1860), I, 267.

31 *Maryland Gazette*, July 3, 24, August 7, 1777.

32 *Connecticut Courant*, October 2, 1775.

33 *Virginia Gazette* (P), April 20, 1776.

34 Raymond C. Werner, editor, "Diary of Grace Growden Galloway, Kept at Philadelphia, July 1, to September 30, 1779," *Pennsylvania Magazine of History and Biography*, LXVII, 164 (April, 1934).

Worse still was the treatment of beautiful Madame de Riedesel, who endured with dignity and courage the dangers of camp, the hardship of the march, and the humiliations of the prison in order to be with her husband, the Hessian general, Baron de Riedesel. In their days of adversity, following the surrender of Saratoga, the gentle "frolicksomeness," unfailing optimism, and ready adaptability of the Baroness contrasted sharply with the pessimism and moodiness of her husband. At the same time, her generous understanding and sense of propriety appeared to a greater advantage in juxtaposition to the vindictiveness and discourtesy of some American women. For instance, the wife of a Boston barrack-master in charge of the German prisoners chose to "comb out her children's heads, which were full of vermin" whenever the Riedesels sat down to eat. Small wonder that the Baroness concluded that Boston was "inhabited by violent patriots, and full of wicked people. The women, especially, were so shameless, that they regarded [her] with repugnance and even spat at [her] when [she] passed them."

The prisoner was to learn that the women of Boston were not alone in their detestation of the enemy, particularly the Hessians. More than once the inhabitants along the route to Virginia refused to sell food to the hungry German lady and her three pinched little girls. With irrefutable logic, if not humanitarianism, they replied to her appeals for food: "You shall not have a morsel of it. Why have you come out of your land to kill us, and waste our goods and possessions? Now you are our prisoners; it is, therefore, our turn to torment you." But the *lex talionis,* at least when applied by women, usually broke down before the mute appeal of the children, a bribe of tea, or even a song, though once an implacable countrywoman said: "Not for a hundred [guineas] would I give you any; and should you all die of hunger, it will be so much the better." But nothing shocked the Baroness more than the wish of a pretty fourteen-year-old, who cried: "Oh, if I only had the king of England here, with what satisfaction I could cut his body in pieces, tear out his heart, dissect it, put it upon these coals, and consume it!"[35]

After such unreasonable outbursts, how wonderfully surprising and comforting was the spontaneous courtesy and magnanimous hospitality of Thomas Jefferson, the first citizen of Albemarle County, where the prisoners were at length interned. When Baron Riedesel sought to thank him, he responded: "The little attentions you are pleased to magnify so much, never deserved a mention or thought. My mortification was, that the peculiar situation in which we were, put it out of our power to render your stay here more comfortable."[36] Women of prominent families, like the Schuylers and Washingtons, accustomed to the amenities, were also inclined to be courteous to the gentlewoman whom the accidents of war had marked as their enemy and prisoner.

Usually, however, women's patriotism took commendable forms, especially toward men in service. Here and there ebullient young ladies associated for the purpose of pledging their hearts to patriots only, or met to sew regimental colors for their beaux.[37] Older women satisfied their patriotic impulses by sending packages of food to soldiers and by showing them other small attentions. With all due respect to the ladies' motives, the latter were not always in the best interests of the soldiers; for example, a doctor's wife persuaded an unsuspecting soldier to take a barbarous prescription for kidney stones: one quart of gin, a tea dish of mustard seed, and a handful of horseradish roots steeped together.[38] During the occupation of Charleston the ladies of that city defiantly refused to frat-

[35] Mrs. General [Friederike Charlotte Louise] Riedesel, *Letters and Journals Relating to the War of the American Revolution and the Capture of the German Troops at Saratoga* (Albany, 1867), 135-140, 146-148, 151-153.

[36] Jefferson to General de Riedesel, May 3, 1780, in Andrew A. Lipscomb and Albert E. Bergh, editors, *The Writings of Thomas Jefferson* (Washington, 1903-1904), IV, 85-86.

[37] Moore, *Diary of the American Revolution*, I, 464; *Pennsylvania Packet* (Lancaster), June 17, 1778; Hezekiah Niles, *Principles and Acts of the Revolution in America* (New York, 1876), 211.

[38] Elijah Fisher, *Journal While in the War for Independence* (Augusta, Maine, 1880), 5.

ernize with British officers and to buy British goods. In place of the imported frills and the silver buckles they had been forced to sell, these Southern ladies wore bright cockades in the colors of their flag.[39] For largeness of heart, no patriotic gesture surpassed that of a free Negro woman in Philadelphia who spent two dollars earned by laundering to purchase ingredients for a wholesome soup and some bread which she delivered to the American prisoners. Richly did this deserve the *Packet's* comment: "Humanity is the same thing in rich or poor, white or black."[40]

Yet war was not all severity; for some women it had a bright, exciting side which they would likely remember long after its dreary aspect was forgotten. Even danger brought compensations, or so thought young Sally Wister, whose home was temporarily turned into a miniature headquarters swarming with smart officers. ". . . Our dress and lips were put in order for conquest," she wrote shortly after the men arrived, "and the hopes of adventure gave brightness to each passive countenance." The din of battle in the distance held no terrors for her. "Tis amazing how we get reconciled to such things. Six months ago the bare idea of being within ten, aye twenty miles, of battle wou'd almost have distracted me. And now, tho' two such large armies are within six miles of us, we can be cheerful and converse calmly of it."[41]

The thrilling clamor of marching soldiers never failed to bring women to windows and fences; from here they waved to the men and occasionally offered them food and drink—cold milk, red apples. On their part the soldiers took note of the ladies: those of Salem were "handsome and genteely dressed"; in Virginia they "muffled [themselves] with linnen in order to prevent the sun from burning their fair faces."[42] Among

[39] Moore, *Diary of the American Revolution*, II, 279, 430.

[40] *Pennsylvania Packet* (Lancaster), April 22, 1778.

[41] Albert C. Myers, editor, *Sally Wister's Journal* (Philadelphia, 1902), 76-77, 113-114.

[42] See "Journal of Major Ennion Williams" and "Journal of Lieutenant William McDowell" in *Pennsylvania Archives*, IX, second series (Harrisburg, 1893), 12-17, 299, 330.

the most interested observers of American women were the French allies, who found them pretty enough; a few, indeed, were real beauties even by international standards. Yet in their dress, their coiffures, their dancing and singing, American ladies lacked the taste, the charm, the grace and verve of French women. To be unkindly frank, added the allies, the former were somewhat monotonous. There were exceptions, of course, like the incredibly gentle and friendly Quakeresses dressed in "silvery drab poplin," with little frills at the sleeves and neat gauze caps on their heads, their quiet charm captivating both enemies and friends.[43]

At the beginning of the Revolution many forms of pleasure were discouraged as unpatriotic and extravagant; but in time austerity gave way to gaiety. Dancing, in particular, became increasingly popular after the arrival of the French. With the principal ladies setting the fashion—Mrs. Nathanael Greene, Martha Washington herself—the young girls determined to make the most of what war had to offer by way of diversion. In Newport they were disconsolate on hearing of the imminent departure of the French army. Tearfully they declared it meant the end of their fun and their balls. As was expected, this poignant show of regret touched the sensitive foreigners; they would arrange a farewell ball for the girls. The bustle of preparation was nearly as wonderful as the festive event itself, which went off with many toasts and many whispered compliments and goodbyes.[44]

To the horrified disapproval of pure and respectable Whigs, the love of pleasure led some young ladies to the very arms of the enemy, who, by the way, could be disarmingly suave. During the British occupation of Philadelphia no one was surprised to hear of Quaker ladies consorting with the enemy; but that Whig ladies should do likewise, well, that was too

[43] The best of the Frenchmen's comments on American women are in Chastellux, *Travels in North America* and in *Melanges Publiés Par la Société de Bibliophiles François*, Deuxieme Partie (Paris, 1903).

[44] Duc de Broglie, "Deux François Aux États-Unis et dans La Nouvelle Espagne en 1782," in *Melanges*, 69-70.

much. Aware of the censure and gossip elicited by their unpatriotic sociability, the latter begged that "proper allowances" be made "for young people in the bloom of life & spirits . . . so long deprived of the gaieties and amusements of life, which their ages and spirits called for." "Plays, concerts, balls, assemblies, in rotation courted their presence," continued the counsel for the defense. "Politics never intruded; the known Whig ladies were treated with equal politeness and attention with the Tory ladies. I myself, though a noted one, was at last prevailed on to partake some of the amusements, though nothing could have made me believe, at the beginning of the winter, that such a thing was possible. I am generally styled, in raillery, with several other ladies, 'rebel,' but I had always effrontery enough to declare that I gloried in the name. . . . They never failed collecting the Whig news for me and from them I received the glorious news of Burgoyne's defeat. . . ." Indeed, so complaisant was the gallant enemy toward the spirited behavior of the Philadelphia girls, that little Poll Redman could warble the line "Cooped up in a town," from the then popular "Burgoyne's Defeat," with "the most particular emphasis" and the sauciest of countenances.[45]

Shortly after the liberation of the city, American and French officers were a little slow in inviting to their dances the belles who had so recently been the guests of enemies. But when the American commander of Philadelphia, General Benedict Arnold, began to pay suit to Peggy Shippen, one of the youngest and prettiest of these belles, it looked as if the army's policy, at least, was to let bygones be bygones.[46] The patriots, however, did take exception to the elaborate head-dress, of London origin, which both poor and rich women had adopted during the occupation. On the Fourth of July, 1778, eye-witnesses reported: "A very high Head-dress was exhibited thro' ye streets this afternoon, on a very dirty Woman, with a mob after her,

[45] "From a lady in Philadelphia" to Mrs. Theoderick Bland, 1778, in Charles Campbell, editor, *The Bland Papers* (Petersburg, 1840), 90-94.

[46] Watson, *Annals of Philadelphia*, II, 297, III, 364-365; John R. Young, editor, *Memorial History of Philadelphia* (New York, 1895), II, 52-57.

with Drums, &c. by way of ridiculing that very foolish fashion."[47] Incidents like this spelled bankruptcy for the several London coiffeurs who had gone into business with infatuating stocks of beauty aids including scented waters, powders, creams, curls, wigs, pins, and combs. Such symbols of frivolity had no place in the capital of the struggling Republic. Consequently the hair-dressers who chose to remain in the city following its liberation were forced to seek less interesting employment as gentlemen's valets.[48]

The American Revolution produced no great heroine in council, pulpit, or field; women were barred from the first two, and their activities in the latter were limited to nursing, cooking, laundering, and to the questionable rôle of camp-followers. To be sure, Martha Washington, Catherine Greene, and other wives of military leaders were frequent and honored visitors at camp, but their position differed greatly from that of the anonymous women who followed their soldier husbands and lovers to war. The camp-followers were a source of annoyance to Washington, who complained of their riding on military wagons and eating at public expense instead of working in the country at what he regarded "most extravagant" wages. The commander-in-chief, however, encouraged them to act as nurses in the pitiably equipped field hospitals.[49] As if to adjust a claim to honor due to the unknown women who thus served their country, legend chose one of them to represent the intrepid qualities of the women of the Revolution. Appropriately enough, this heroine was called by the meaningful sobriquet of "Molly Pitcher," not by one of her rightful names of Mary Ludwig, Mary Hayes, or Mary McCauley, the last two acquired by marriage. It was as Mary Hayes that she carried pitchers full of water to the tired and grateful soldiers during

[47] Henry D. Biddle, editor, *Extracts from the Journals of Elizabeth Drinker from 1759 to 1807* (Philadelphia, 1889), 107.

[48] *Pennsylvania Ledger*, November 26, 1777, February 28, 1778, May 2, 1778; *Pennsylvania Evening Post*, March 7, 1778; *Pennsylvania Packet*, July 16, 1778.

[49] General Orders, May 13, June 19, 1778, John C. Fitzpatrick, editor, *The Writings of George Washington* (Washington, 1934), XI, 497-498, XII, 94; Washington to Brigadier General John Stark, August 5, 1778, XII, 283-284.

the battle of Monmouth, and later took her fallen husband's place at the cannon. Why Molly did not share honors for the latter feat with Margaret Corbin who was "wounded and disabled in the attack on Fort Washington," remains a mystery. But at least Margaret received some recognition from her contemporaries, for she was cited for her courage by the Continental Congress and awarded half-pay.[50]

Actually the Revolution produced only one bona fide female soldier, Deborah Sampson, who enlisted and served in the army under the name of Robert Shurtleff. After her discharge, marriage, and motherhood, the now famous Mrs. Gannett took to the lecture platform, where she sometimes appeared in uniform to apologize for and to exult over her youthful adventure.[51]

The last and not altogether deserving addition to the album of revolutionary heroines was Mrs. Betsy Ross of Philadelphia, whose grandson in 1870 claimed for her the distinction of having made the first stars-and-stripes at General Washington's bidding. Alas for the pretty story, Washington was not in Philadelphia at the time Congress adopted the stars-and-stripes as the national flag, nor do the records show that Mrs. Ross was ever paid for making such a flag, though it is true that she was a good needle-woman and did make flags.[52]

In their unobtrusive, eighteenth-century way, the women of '76 served well the cause of independence. Plagued by scarcities and high prices, they managed to feed and clothe their families and to render important volunteer services. Even women in affluent homes were obliged to be industrious, since the war provided a path to freedom for many indentured servants, both

[50] C. P. Wing, "Moll Pitcher," *Pennsylvania Magazine of History and Biography* (Philadelphia, 1879), III, 109-110; William S. Stryker, *The Battle of Monmouth* (Princeton, 1927), 188-192; Worthington C. Ford, editor, *Journals of the Continental Congress* (Washington, 1909), XIV, 805.

[51] John Adams Vinton, editor, *Life of Deborah Sampson* (Boston, 1866); Eugene Tappan, editor, *An Address Delivered in 1802 in Various Towns in Massachusetts, Rhode Island and New York* (Boston, 1905).

[52] "Betsy Ross," *Dictionary of American Biography* (New York, 1935), XVI, 174-175; Theodore D. Gottlief, *The Origin and Evolution of the Betsy Ross Flag Legend or Tradition* (Newark, 1938).

male and female. Only among the very rich in the South did Chastellux note any sign of indolence among women, and here the critical Frenchman had to acknowledge "their magnificance and hospitality."[53] Although women often complained about the sacrifices exacted by war, few ever questioned the merits of the cause or faltered in the fulfillment of their stern, monotonous duties.

[53] Chastellux, *Travels in North America*, 297.

# Eighteenth-Century American Women in Peace and War: The Case of the Loyalists

Mary Beth Norton

In recent years historians have come to recognize the central role of the family in the shaping of American society. Especially in the eighteenth century, when "household" and "family" were synonymous terms, and when household manufactures constituted a major contribution to the economy, the person who ran the household—the wife and mother—occupied a position of crucial significance. Yet those who have studied eighteenth-century women have usually chosen to focus on a few outstanding, perhaps unrepresentative individuals, such as Eliza Lucas Pinckney, Abigail Smith Adams, and Mercy Otis Warren. They have also emphasized the activities of women outside the home and have concentrated on the prescriptive literature of the day. Little has been done to examine in depth the lives actually led by the majority of colonial women or to assess the impact of the Revolution upon them.[1]

Such a study can illuminate a number of important topics. Demographic scholars are beginning to discover the dimensions of eighteenth-century households, but a knowledge of size alone means little without a delineation of roles filled by husband and wife within those households.[2] Historians of

Ms. Norton is a member of the Department of History, Cornell University. She wishes to thank Carol Berkin, Carl Kaestle, Pauline Maier, Robert Wells, and Peter Wood for their comments on an earlier version of this article. A portion of it was read at the Second Berkshire Conference on the History of Women, held at Radcliffe College, Oct. 1974.

[1] See, for example, such works as Mary Sumner Benson, *Women in Eighteenth-Century America: A Study of Opinion and Social Usage* (New York, 1935); Elisabeth Anthony Dexter, *Colonial Women of Affairs*, 2d ed. (New York, 1931); and Joan Hoff Wilson, "Dancing Dogs of the Colonial Period: Women Scientists," *Early American Literature*, VII (1973), 225-235. Notable exceptions are Julia Cherry Spruill, *Women's Life and Work in the Southern Colonies* (Chapel Hill, N.C., 1938), and Eugenie Andruss Leonard, *The Dear-Bought Heritage* (Philadelphia, 1965). On the importance of the early American family see David Rothman, "A Note on the Study of the Colonial Family," *William and Mary Quarterly*, 3d Ser., XXIII (1966), 627-634.

[2] Two recent works that deal with family size, among other topics, are Robert V. Wells, "Household Size and Composition in the British Colonies in America, 1675-1775," *Journal of Interdisciplinary History*, IV (1974), 543-570, and Daniel Scott

nineteenth-century American women have analyzed the ideology which has been termed the "cult of true womanhood" or the "cult of domesticity," but the relationship of these ideas to the lives of women in the preceding century remains largely unexplored.[3] And although some historians of the Revolution now view the war as a socially disruptive phenomenon, they have not yet applied that insight specifically to the study of the family.[4]

Fortunately, at least one set of documents contains material relevant to an investigation of all these aspects of late eighteenth-century American family life: the 281 volumes of the loyalist claims, housed at the Public Record Office in London. Although these manuscripts have been used extensively for political and economic studies of loyalism, they have only once before been utilized for an examination of colonial society.[5] What makes the loyalist

---

Smith, "Population, Family and Society in Hingham, Massachusetts, 1635-1880" (Ph.D. diss., University of California, Berkeley, 1973). Internal household relationships in 17th-century New England have been analyzed by Edmund S. Morgan, *The Puritan Family: Religion & Domestic Relations in Seventeenth-Century New England* (Boston, 1944), and John Demos, *A Little Commonwealth: Family Life in Plymouth Colony* (New York, 1970).

[3] Barbara Welter, "The Cult of True Womanhood, 1820-1860," *American Quarterly*, XVII (1966), 151-174, was the first to outline the dimensions of this ideology. For writings dealing with some of the implications of the "cult of domesticity" see Carroll Smith-Rosenberg, "The Hysterical Woman: Sex Roles and Role Conflict in 19th-Century America," *Social Research*, XXXIX (1972), 652-678; Ann Douglas Wood, "Mrs. Sigourney and the Sensibility of the Inner Space," *New England Quarterly*, XLV (1972), 163-181; Kathryn Kish Sklar, *Catharine Beecher: A Study in American Domesticity* (New Haven, Conn., 1973); and Nancy Falik Cott, "In the Bonds of Womanhood: Perspectives on Female Experience and Consciousness in New England, 1780-1830" (Ph.D. diss., Brandeis University, 1974), esp. chap. 6. An explicit assertion that women were better off in 18th-century America than they were later is found in Dexter, *Colonial Women of Affairs*, vii, 189-192, and in Page Smith, *Daughters of the Promised Land* (Boston, 1970), 37-76. But two European historians have appropriately warned that it may be dangerous to assume the existence of a "golden, preindustrial age" for women, noting that the "goldenness is seen almost exclusively in terms of women's work and its presumed relationship to family power, not in terms of other vital aspects of their lives, including the physical burdens of work and child bearing." Patricia Branca and Peter N. Stearns, "On the History of Modern Women, a Research Note," *AHA Newsletter*, XII (Sept. 1974), 6.

[4] For example, John Shy, "The American Revolution: The Military Conflict Considered as a Revolutionary War," in Stephen G. Kurtz and James H. Hutson, eds., *Essays on the American Revolution* (Chapel Hill, N.C., 1973), 121-156; John Shy, "The Loyalist Problem in the Lower Hudson Valley: The British Perspective," in Robert A. East and Jacob Judd, eds., *The Loyalist Americans: A Focus on Greater New York* (Tarrytown, N.Y., 1975), 3-13; and Ronald Hoffman, *A Spirit of Dissension: Economics, Politics, and the Revolution in Maryland* (Baltimore, 1973), esp. chaps. 6, 8.

[5] Catherine S. Crary, "The Humble Immigrant and the American Dream: Some

claims uniquely useful is the fact that they contain information not only about the personal wartime experiences of thousands of Americans but also about the modes of life the war disrupted.

Among the 3,225 loyalists who presented claims to the British government after the war were 468 American refugee women. The analysis that follows is based upon an examination of the documents—formal memorials, loss schedules, and private letters—submitted by these women to the loyalist claims commission, and on the commission's nearly verbatim records of the women's personal appearances before them.[6] These women cannot be said to compose a statistically reliable sample of American womanhood. It is entirely possible that loyalist families differed demographically and economically, as well as politically, from their revolutionary neighbors, and it is highly probable that the refugee claimants did not accurately represent even the loyalist population, much less that of the colonies as a whole.[7] Nonetheless, the 468 claimants included white women of all descriptions, from every colony and all social and economic levels: they were educated and illiterate; married, widowed, single, and deserted; rural and urban; wealthy, middling, and poverty-stricken. Accordingly, used with care, the loyalist claims can tell us much about the varieties of female experience in America in the third quarter of the eighteenth century.[8]

---

Case Histories, 1746-1776," *Mississippi Valley Historical Review*, XLVI (1959), 46-66.

[6] For a detailed examination of the claims process see Mary Beth Norton, *The British-Americans: The Loyalist Exiles in England, 1774-1789* (Boston, 1972), 185-222. More than 468 women appear in the claims documents; excluded from the sample selected for this article are all female children, all English women who never lived in America (but who were eligible for compensation as heirs of loyalists), and all American women who did not personally pursue a claim (that is, whose husbands took the entire responsibility for presenting the family's claims). In addition to those requesting reimbursement for property losses, the sample includes a number of women—mostly the very poor, who had lost only a small amount of property, if any—who applied solely for the subsistence pensions which were also awarded by the claims commissioners. On the allowance system see *ibid.*, 52-61, 111-121, and 225-229.

[7] On the statistical biases of the loyalist claims see Eugene Fingerhut, "Uses and Abuses of the American Loyalists' Claims: A Critique of Quantitative Analyses," *WMQ*, 3d Ser., XXV (1968), 245-258.

[8] This approach to women in the Revolutionary era differs from the traditional focus on their public contributions to the war effort. See, for example, Elizabeth F. Ellet, *The Women of the American Revolution* (New York, 1848-1850); Walter Hart Blumenthal, *Women Camp Followers of the American Revolution* (Philadelphia, 1952); Elizabeth Cometti, "Women in the American Revolution," *NEQ*, XX (1947), 329-346; and Linda Grant DePauw, *Four Traditions: Women of New York during the American Revolution* (Albany, 1974).

One aspect of prewar family life that is systematically revealed in the claims documents is the economic relationship of husband and wife within the household. All claimants, male and female alike, had to supply the commission with detailed estimates of property losses. Given the circumstances of the war, documentary evidence such as deeds, bills of sale, and wills was rarely available in complete form, and the commission therefore relied extensively upon the sworn testimony of the claimants and their witnesses in assessing losses. The claimants had nothing to gain by withholding information, because the amount of compensation they received depended in large part on their ability to describe their losses. Consequently, it may be assumed that what the loyalists told the commission, both orally and in writing, represented the full extent of their knowledge of their families' income and property.[9] The women's claims thus make it possible to determine the nature of their participation in the financial affairs of their households.

Strikingly, although male loyalists consistently supplied detailed assessments of the worth of their holdings, many women were unable to place precise valuations on the property for which they claimed compensation. Time after time similar phrases appear in the records of oral testimony before the commission: "She cant say what the Houses cost or what they woud have sold for" (the widow of a Norfolk merchant); "Says she is much a Stranger to the state of Her Husband's Concerns" (the widow of a storekeeper from Ninety-Six, South Carolina); "It was meadow Land, she cannot speak of the Value" (a New Jersey farmer's widow); "Her husband was a Trader and had many Debts owing to him She does not know how much they amounted to" (a widow from Ninety-Six); "She can't speak to the Value of the Stock in Trade" (a Rhode Island merchant's widow); "It was a good Tract but does not know how to value it" (the widow of a Crown Point farmer).[10]

[9] Only if they intended to commit fraud could loyalists gain by withholding information from the commission; two refugees, for example, requested compensation for property they had already sold during the war. But the commissioners found deliberately fraudulent only 10 of the claims submitted to them, and although they disallowed others for "gross prevarication," none of the claims falling into either category were submitted by women. See Norton, *British-Americans*, 217-219, on the incidence of fraud, and 203-205, 216-217, on the importance of accurate testimony.

[10] Joyce Dawson, testimony, May 5, 1787, A.O. 12/56, 330, Public Record Office; Isabella McLaurin, testimony, Nov. 27, 1784, A.O. 12/47, 233; Margaret Hutchinson, testimony, Aug. 10, 1786, A.O. 12/16, 34; Margaret Reynolds, testimony, Dec. 9, 1783, A.O. 12/46, 168; case of Mrs. Bowers, Feb. 24, 1783, A.O. 12/99, 48; Elizabeth Campbell, testimony, n.d., A.O. 12/26, 267. For other similar statements see A.O. 12/10, 254, A.O. 12/48, 233, A.O. 12/50, 390-391, and A.O. 13/68, pt. 1, 183.

Even when women submitted detailed loss schedules in writing, they frequently revealed at their oral examinations that they had relied on male relatives or friends, or even on vaguely recalled statements made by their dead husbands, in arriving at the apparently knowledgeable estimates they had initially given to the commission. For example, a New Jersey woman, questioned about her husband's annual income, referred the commissioners to her father and other male witnesses, admitting that she did not know the amount he had earned. Similarly, the widow of a Charleston saddler told the commissioners that "she does not know the Amount of Her husband's Property, but she remembers to have heard him say in the year 1777 that he was worth £2,000 sterling clear of all Debts." Such statements abound in the claims records: "She is unable to speak to the value of the Plantn herself, but refers to Mr. Cassills"; "Says she cannot speak to the Value—the Valuatn was made by Capt McDonald and Major Munro"; "Says her Son in Law Capt Douglas is better acquainted with the particulars of her property than herself and she refers to him for an Account thereof."[11]

Although many female claimants thus lacked specific knowledge of their families' finances, there were substantial variations within the general pattern. The very wealthiest women—like Isabella Logan of Virginia (who could say only that she and her husband had lived in "a new Elegant, large double Brick House with two wings all finish'd in the best taste with Articles from London") and Mrs. Egerton Leigh of South Carolina (who gave it as her opinion that her husband had "a considerable real Estate as well as personal property . . . worth more than £10,000 . . . tho' she cannot herself speak to it with accuracy")—also tended to be the ones most incapable of describing their husbands' business affairs.[12] Yet some wealthy, well-educated women were conversant with nearly every detail of the family finances. For the most part, this latter group was composed of women who had brought the property they described to their husbands at marriage or who had been widowed before the war and had served as executrixes of the estates in question for some time. A case in point is that of Sarah Gould Troutbeck, daughter, executrix, and primary heir of John Gould, a prosperous Boston merchant. Her husband John, an Anglican clergyman, died in 1778, and so

[11] Frances Dongan, testimony, Dec. 6, 1784, A.O. 12/13, 267-272; case of Charlotte Pollock, June 27, 1783, A.O. 12/99, 336; Mary Ann Balfour, testimony, Mar. 13, 1786, A.O. 12/48, 242; Janet Murchison, testimony, July 26, 1786, A.O. 12/34, 405; Mary Kearsley, testimony, Apr. 28, 1785, A.O. 12/38, 282. Cf. Mrs. Kearsley's testimony with her written memorial, A.O. 13/102, 324-329. And see, for other examples, A.O. 12/4, 220, A.O. 12/14, 265, A.O. 12/47, 239, A.O. 13/63, 342, and A.O. 13/94, 318-326.

[12] Isabella Logan, loss schedule, Feb. 17, 1784, A.O. 13/32, 129; case of Lady Leigh, July 1, 1783, A.O. 12/99, 313. See also the claim of Mary Auchmuty, A.O. 12/24, 114-117, 264-266, and A.O. 13/63, 133-140.

she carried the full burden of presenting the family's claim to the commission. Although she deprecatingly described herself to the board as "a poor weak Woman unused to business," she supplied the commissioners with detailed evidence of her losses and unrelentingly pursued her debtors. "Your not hearing from me for so long a time may induce you to think I have relinquishd my claim to the intrest due on your note," she informed one man in 1788. "If you realy entertain any such thoughts I must beg leave to undeceive you." In addition, she did what few loyalists of either sex had the courage to attempt—return to the United States to try to recover her property. When she arrived in 1785, she found her estates "in the greatest confusion" but nevertheless managed within several months to repossess one house and to collect some debts. In the end she apparently won restoration of most of her holdings.[13]

Yet not all the female loyalists who had inherited property in their own right were as familiar with it as was Sarah Troutbeck. Another Massachusetts woman admitted to the commissioners that she did not know the value of the 550 acres left her by a relative, or even how much of the land was cultivated. "Her Brother managed everything for her and gave her what Money she wanted," she explained. In the same vein, a New Yorker was aware that her father had left her some property in his will, but "she does not know what property." A Charleston resident who had owned a house jointly with her brother commented that "it was a good House," but the commission noted, "she does not know the Value of it." And twice-widowed Jane Gibbes, claiming for the farms owned by her back-country South Carolina husbands, told the commission that she had relied on neighbors to assess the worth of the property, for "she can't speak positively to the value of her Lands herself."[14]

But if Jane Gibbes could not precisely evaluate the farms she had lived on, she still knew a good deal about them. She described the total acreage, the amount of land under cultivation, the crops planted, and the livestock

[13] Sarah Troutbeck to commissioners, June 5, 1787, A.O. 13/49, pt. 2, 565; Troutbeck to Samuel Peters, May 22, 1788, Peters Papers, III, fol. 83 (microfilm), New-York Historical Society, New York City; Troutbeck to commissioners, Jan. 3, 1785, A.O. 13/137, 609. Her total claim covers fols. 539-590 in A.O. 13/49, pt. 2, and fols. 726-740 in A.O. 13/74. On the recovery of her property see A.O. 12/81, 47. For other examples of well-to-do women with a good knowledge of the family property see A.O. 13/134, 571-574, and A.O. 12/54, 61-71 (Mary Rothery), A.O. 13/64, 81-99, and A.O. 13/97, 344-348 (Henrietta Colden), and A.O. 12/13, 311-314 (Mary Poynton). Mary Winslow knew her own property in detail but was not so familiar with her husband's (A.O. 13/79, 757-758).

[14] Case of Mrs. Dumaresq, Mar. 31, 1783, A.O. 12/99, 134; case of Margaret Smithies, Nov. 13, 1783, A.O. 12/100, 66; case of Barbara Mergath, May 8, 1783, A.O. 12/99, 234; Jane Gibbes, testimony, Dec. 15, 1783, A.O. 12/46, 245-247.

that had been lost. In this she was representative of most rural female loyalists with claims that were not complicated by the existence of mortgages or outstanding debts. Although they did not always know the exact value of the land for which they requested reimbursement, they could supply the commission with many important details about the family property: the number of cattle, horses, sheep, and hogs; the types of tools used; the acreage planted, and with what crops; the amounts of grain and other foodstuffs stored for the winter; and the value of such unusual possessions as beehives or a "Covering Horse." It was when they were asked about property on which they had not lived, about debts owed by their husbands, or about details of wills or mortgages that they most often admitted ignorance.[16]

A good example is Mary McAlpin, who had settled with her husband on a farm near Saratoga, New York, in 1767. She did not know what her husband had paid for some unimproved lands, or the acreage of another farm he had purchased, but she was well acquainted with the property on which they had lived. The farm, she told the commissioners, "had been wholly cleared and Improved and was in the most perfect State of Cultivation." There were two "Log Houses plaistered and floored," one for them and one for their hired laborers, and sufficient materials on hand to build "a large and Commodious Brick House." Her husband had planted wheat, rye, peas, oats, barley, corn, turnips, potatoes, and melons; and "the Meadows had been laid down or sown with Clover and Timothy Grass, the two kind of Grass Seeds most Valued in that Country." The McAlpins had had a kitchen garden that produced "in great abundance every Vegitable usually cultivated in that part of America." Moreover, the farm was "well Provided" with such utensils as "a Team waggon, Carts sledges Carwls [*sic*] Wheels for Waggons, Wheels for Carts, Wheelbarrows, drags for Timber Ploughs, Harrows Hay Sythes Brush Sythes Grubbling Harrows, and all sorts of Carpenters Tools Shoemakers Tools Shovels, Spades, Axes Iron Crow Barrs etc."

After offering all these details, however, Mrs. McAlpin proved unable to assess the value of the property accurately. She gave the commission a total claim of £6,000, clearly an estimate, and when asked to break down a particular item on her schedule into its component parts she could not do so, saying that "She valued the Whole in the Lump in that Sum." Moreover,

[16] Jane Gibbes, testimony, Dec. 16, 1783, A.O. 12/46, 247-249; Widow Boyce, loss schedule, Oct. 16, 1783, A.O. 13/90, 181; Elizabeth Hogal, loss schedule, n.d., A.O. 12/27, 37. Typical examples of claims submitted by rural women may be found in A.O. 13/56, 91-93, A.O. 13/138, 475, A.O. 12/4, 72-74, A.O. 12/20, 270-271, A.O. 12/26, 14-16, and A.O. 12/29, 79. Cf. claims from rural men in A.O. 13/79, 73-77, 211-216. For a claim involving property owned elsewhere see that of Elinor Maybee, A.O. 12/28, 343-346, and A.O. 12/64, 1; for one involving both a mortgage and a misread will see that of Margaret Hutchinson, A.O. 12/16, 33-37, and A.O. 12/63, 61.

she proved ignorant of the terms of her husband's will, confusedly telling the commissioners that he had "left his real personal Estate to his Son—This she supposes was his Lands" (the board's secretary noted carefully, "This is her own Expression"), when in fact she had been left a life interest in the real estate plus half the personal estate.[16] In short, Mary McAlpin typifies the rural female claimant, though her husband's property was substantially larger than average. She knew what he had owned, but she did not know exactly how much it was worth. She was well acquainted with the day-to-day operations of the farm but understood very little about the general family finances. And she knew nothing at all about legal or business terminology.

The pattern for urban dwellers was more varied. In the first place, included in their number were most of the wealthy women mentioned earlier, both those who knew little or nothing about their husbands' estates and those who, like Sarah Troutbeck, were conversant with the family holdings. Secondly, a higher percentage of urban women engaged directly in business. Among the 468 female claimants there were forty-three who declared either that they had earned money on their own or that they had assisted their husbands in some way. Only three of these forty-three can be described as rural: a tavernkeeper's wife from Ticonderoga, a small shopkeeper from Niagara, and the housekeeper for the family of Col. Guy Johnson. All the other working women came from cities such as Boston, Philadelphia, Charleston, and New York, or from smaller but substantial towns like Williamsburg, Wilmington, N.C., and Baltimore. The urban women's occupations were as varied as the urban centers in which they resided. There were ten who took lodgers, eighteen shopkeepers and merchants of various sorts, five tavernkeepers, four milliners, two mantua makers, a seamstress, a midwife, an owner of a coffeehouse, a schoolteacher, a printer, one who did not specify an occupation, and two prostitutes who described themselves as owners of a small shop and declared that their house had been "always open" to British officers needing "aid and attention."[17]

As might be expected, the women who had managed businesses or assisted their husbands (one wrote that she was "truly his Partner" in a "steady Course of painfull Industry") were best informed about the value of their property. Those who had been grocers or milliners could usually list in

[16] Mary McAlpin, loss schedule, n.d., A.O. 13/131, 10-11, and testimony, Nov. 14, 1785, A.O. 12/21, 51-65.

[17] The list totals more than 40 because some women listed two enterprises. The women divided as follows: 10 each from New York City and Charleston, 7 each from Boston and Philadelphia, 2 from Baltimore, and 1 each from Savannah, Williamsburg, Wilmington, N.C., and St. Augustine. Twenty-eight were long-time widows or single, or were married but operated businesses independently of their husbands; 8 assisted their husbands; and 7 took over businesses after the death or incapacitation of their husbands.

detail the stock they had lost; the midwife had witnesses to support her claim to a high annual income from her profession; the boardinghouse keepers knew what they had spent for furniture and supplies; and the printer could readily value her shop's equipment.[18] But even these working women could not give a full report on all aspects of their husbands' holdings: the widow of a Boston storekeeper, for example, could accurately list their stock in trade but admitted ignorance of the value of the property her husband had inherited from his father, and although the widow of another Boston merchant had carried on the business after her husband was wounded at Bunker Hill, she was not familiar with the overall value of their property.[19]

It is therefore not surprising that women claimants on the average received a smaller return on their claims than did their male counterparts. Since the commissioners reimbursed only for fully proven losses, the amounts awarded are a crude indicator of the relative ability of individual refugees to describe their losses and to muster written and oral evidence on their own behalf. If women had known as much as their husbands about the family estates, there would have been little or no difference between the average amounts granted to each sex. But of the claims heard in England for which complete information is available, 660 loyalist men received an average return of 39.5 percent, while for 71 women the figure was 34.1 percent. And this calculation does not take into account the large number of women's claims, including some submitted by businesswomen, which were entirely disallowed for lack of proof.[20]

In the absence of data for other time periods and populations, it is difficult to assess the significance of the figures that show that slightly less than 10 percent (9.2 percent, to be exact) of the loyalist refugee women worked outside the home. Historians have tended to stress the widespread participation of colonial women in economic enterprise, usually as a means of

[18] The quotation is from Rachel Wetmore, claims memorial, Mar. 25, 1786, A.O. 13/16, 271. For a milliner's claim see Margaret Hutchinson's, A.O. 13/96, 601-602; for a grocer and boardinghouse keeper's see Sarah Simpson's, A.O. 12/25, 25-28. The midwife, Janet Cumming, claimed to have made £400 sterling annually, and her witnesses confirmed that estimate (A.O. 12/50, 347-348). See also Margaret Draper's original and revised loss estimates, A.O. 13/44, 342-344, 387, and Mary Airey's schedule, A.O. 12/24, 79.

[19] Hannah Pollard, claims memorial and testimony, A.O. 13/49, pt. 1, 158-159, 166; testimony re: claim of Mary Campbell, Oct. 24, 1786, A.O. 12/50, 103-105. The detailed schedule presented by the tavernkeeper Rachel Brain had been prepared by her husband before his death; see A.O. 12/26, 308-310.

[20] For a general discussion of claims receipts see Norton, *British-Americans*, 216-220. Property claims submitted by 10 of the businesswomen were disallowed, and at least another 10 of them apparently did not pursue a claim for lost property. (Because of the destruction and disappearance of some of the claims records it is impossible to be more precise.)

distinguishing them from their reputedly more confined nineteenth-century counterparts.[21] The claims documents demonstrate that some women engaged in business, either alone or with their husbands, but 9.2 percent may be either a large or a small proportion of the total female population, depending on how one looks at it. The figures themselves must remain somewhat ambiguous, at least until additional data are obtained.[22] What is not at all ambiguous, however, is the distinctive pattern of the female claimants' knowledge.

For regardless of whether they came from rural or urban areas, and regardless of their background or degree of participation in business, the loyalist women testified almost exclusively on the basis of their knowledge of those parts of the family property with which their own lives brought them into regular contact. What they uniformly lacked were those pieces of information about business matters that could have been supplied only by their husbands. Evidently, late eighteenth-century American men, at least those who became loyalists, did not systematically discuss matters of family finances with their wives. From that fact it may be inferred that the men—and their wives as well, perhaps—accepted the dictum that woman's place was in the home. After all, that was where more than 90 percent of the loyalist women stayed, and their ignorance of the broader aspects of their families' economic circumstances indicates that their interest in such affairs was either minimal or else deliberately thwarted by their husbands.[23]

It would therefore appear that the 9 percent figure for working women is

[21] This emphasis appears to have resulted from the influence of Dexter's *Colonial Women of Affairs*. Although she was careful to explain that she had searched only for examples of women who worked outside the home, and although she did not attempt to estimate the percentage of such women in the female population as a whole, historians who draw upon her book invariably stress the wide-ranging economic interests of colonial women. See, for example, Gerda Lerner, *The Woman in American History* (Reading, Mass., 1971), 15-19, and Carol Ruth Berkin, *Within the Conjuror's Circle: Women in Colonial America* (Morristown, N.J., 1974), 8-10.

[22] If anything, the loyalist claimants tended to be more urban than other loyalists and the rest of the American population, and therefore would presumably over-represent working women. See the analysis in Norton, *British-Americans*, 37-39, and Fingerhut, "Uses and Abuses of Loyalists' Claims," *WMQ*, 3d Ser., XXV (1968), 245-258. Further, the method of choosing the sample—including only those women who themselves submitted claims and pension applications—would also tend to bias the result in favor of working women, since they would be the most likely to act on their own.

[23] The failure of 18th-century men to discuss finances with their wives is also revealed in such letters as that of Jane Robbins to her daughter Hannah Gilman, Sept. 1799, Gilman Papers, Massachusetts Historical Society, Boston. Mrs. Robbins declared that, although her husband had made his will some years before, "I never saw it till after his death." Further, she informed her daughter, on his deathbed he told her, "I should have many debts to pay that I knew nothing about."

evidence not of a climate favorable to feminine enterprise but rather of the opposite: women were expected to remain largely within the home unless forced by necessity, such as the illness or death of their husbands, to do otherwise. The fact that fewer than one-half (seventeen, to be precise) of the working women enumerated earlier had healthy, living husbands at the time they engaged in business leads toward the same conclusion. The implication is that in mid-eighteenth-century America woman's sphere was rigidly defined at all levels of society, not merely in the wealthy households in which this phenomenon has been recognized.[24]

This tentative conclusion is supported by evidence drawn from another aspect of the claims, for a concomitant of the contention that colonial women often engaged in business endeavors has been the assertion that colonial men, as the theoretical and legal heads of household, frequently assumed a large share of domestic responsibilities.[25] Yet if men had been deeply involved in running their households—in keeping accounts and making purchases, even if not in doing day-to-day chores—they should have described household furnishings in much the same detail as their wives used. But just as female claimants were unable to delineate their husbands' business dealings accurately, so men separated from their wives—regardless of their social status—failed to submit specific lists of lost household items like furniture, dishes, or kitchen utensils. One such refugee observed to the commission in 1788, "As Household Furniture consists of a Variety of Articles, at this distance of time I cannot sufficiently recollect them so as to fix a Value on them to the Satisfaction of my mind."[26] It is impossible to imagine a loyalist woman making a comparable statement. For her, what to a man was simply "a Variety of Articles" resolved itself into such familiar and cherished objects as "1 Compleat set blue and white Tea and Table China," "a Large new Goose feather Bed, bolster Pillows and Bedstead," "a Small painted Book Case and Desk," "1 Japan Tea Board," "2 smoothing Irons," and "1 old brass Coffee Pott." Moreover, although men usually noted losses of clothing in a general way, by listing a single undifferentiated sum, women frequently claimed for specific articles of jewelry and apparel. For example, Mary Swords of Saratoga disclosed that she had lost to rebel plunderers a "Long Scarlet Cloak" and a "Velvet Muff and Tippett," in addition to "One pair of Ear

[24] Berkin, *Conjuror's Circle*, 12-14, and Nancy F. Cott, ed., *Root of Bitterness: Documents of the Social History of American Women* (New York, 1972), 8-10, link sex role differentiation specifically to the upper classes that were emerging in the process which has been called "Europeanization" or "Anglicization."

[25] See, for example, Spruill, *Women's Life and Work*, 78-79.

[26] David Ingersoll to commissioners, July 30, 1788, A.O. 13/74, 288. For rare cases of men who did list household furnishings see A.O. 13/98, 431-432, and A.O. 13/73, 140-155.

Rings French paste set in Gold," "One small pair of Ear Rings Garnets," and "one Gold Broatch with a small diamond Top."[27]

The significance of such lists lies not only in the fact that they indicate what kinds of property the claimants knew well enough to describe accurately and in detail, but also in the insight they provide into the possessions which claimants thought were sufficiently important to mention individually. For example, a rural New York woman left no doubt about her pride in "a fine large new stove"; a resident of Manhattan carefully noted that one of her lost beds was covered in "Red Damask"; and a Rhode Islander called attention to the closets in her "large new dwelling house."[28] The differentiated contents of men's and women's claims thus take on more importance, since the contrasting lists not only suggest the extent of the claimants' knowledge but also reveal their assessments of the relative importance of their possessions. To men, furniture, dishes, and clothing could easily be lumped together under general headings; to women, such possessions had to be carefully enumerated and described.

In the end, all of the evidence that can be drawn from the loyalist claims points to the conclusion that the lives of the vast majority of women in the Revolutionary era revolved around their immediate households to a notable degree. The economic function of those households in relation to the family property largely determined the extent of their knowledge of that property. In rural areas, where women's household chores included caring for the stock and perhaps occasionally working in the fields, women were conversant with a greater proportion of the family estates than were urban women, whose knowledge was for the most part confined to the furnishings of the houses in which they lived, unless they had been widowed before the war or had worked outside the home. The wealth of the family was thus a less significant determinant of the woman's role than was the nature of the household. To be sure, at the extreme ends of the economic scale, wealth and education, or the lack of them, affected a woman's comprehension of her family's property, but what the women displayed were relative degrees of ignorance. If the loyalist claimants are at all representative, very few married colonial women were familiar with the broader aspects of their families' financial affairs. Regardless of where they lived, they were largely insulated from the agricultural and business worlds in which their husbands engaged daily. As a result, the

[27] Martha Leslie, loss schedule, Mar. 25, 1784, A.O. 13/91, 2-3; Frances Dongan, inventory, [Nov. 1, 1783], A.O. 13/109, 45; Catherine Bowles, loss schedule, May 10, 1783, A.O. 13/90, 175-176; Mary Swords, "Things Plundered from me by the Rebels," n.d., A.O. 13/67, 311.

[28] Mary Gibbins, loss schedule, n.d., A.O. 13/80, 167; "Estimate of Losses sustained at New York by Hannah Foy in the year 1775" [1782], A.O. 13/54, 431; Elizabeth Bowers, loss schedule, n.d., A.O. 13/68, pt. 1, 64.

Revolutionary War, which deprived female loyalists of the households in which they had lived and worked, and which at the same time forced them to confront directly the wider worlds of which they had had little previous knowledge, was for them an undeniably traumatic experience.

At the outbreak of the war, loyalist women expected that "their Sex and the Humanity of a civilized People" would protect them from "disrespectfull Indignities." Most of them soon learned otherwise. Rebel men may have paid lip service to the ideal that women and children should be treated as noncombatants, but in practice they consigned female loyalists to much the same fate as their male relatives. Left behind by their fleeing husbands (either because of the anticipated difficulties of a journey to the British lines or in the hope that the family property might thereby be preserved), loyalist wives, with their children, frequently found themselves "stripped of every Thing" by American troops who, as one woman put it, "not contented with possessing themselves of her property were disposed to visit severity upon her person and Those of her friends."[29] Female loyalists were often verbally abused, imprisoned, and threatened with bodily harm even when they had not taken an active role in opposing the rebel cause.[30]

When they had assisted the British—and many aided prisoners or gathered intelligence—their fate was far worse. For example, the New Yorker Lorenda Holmes, who carried letters through the lines in 1776, was stripped by an angry band of committeemen and dragged "to the Drawing Room Window . . . exposing her to many Thousands of People Naked." On this occasion Mrs. Holmes admitted that she "received no wounds or bruises from them only shame and horror of the Mind," but a few months later, after she had shown some refugees the way to the British camp, an American officer came to her house and held her "right foot upon the Coals until he had burnt it in a most shocking manner," telling her "he would learn her to carry off Loyalists to the British Army."[31]

[29] Sarah Stuart, memorial to Lords of Treasury, Jan. 22, 1786, A.O. 13/135, 702; Elizabeth Phillips, affidavit, Oct. 9, 1788, A.O. 13/67, 303; Phebe Stevens, claims memorial, Mar. 23, 1784, A.O. 13/83, 580. For accounts of rebel looting see, for example, A.O. 12/56, 326-327, A.O. 13/73, 485, A.O. 13/91, 190, A.O. 13/93, 556, A.O. 13/102, 1278, A.O. 13/109, 43, A.O. 13/121, 478, and A.O. 13/126, 589.

[30] See, for example, A.O. 12/21, 53-54, A.O. 13/110, 351, A.O. 13/112, 55, A.O. 13/123, 240-241, A.O. 13/128, 7, and A.O. 13/135, 698. Two women said they suffered miscarriages as a result of scuffles with Revolutionary troops (A.O. 13/81, 59, and A.O. 13/64, 76-77), and a third was raped by a rebel soldier. The latter incident is discussed in Thomas Goldthwait to his daughter Catherine, Aug. 20, 1779, J. M. Robbins Papers, Mass. Hist. Soc.

[31] Lorenda Holmes, claims memorial, n.d., A.O. 13/65, 529-530. Similar though less graphic tales were recounted by other women whose assistance to the British was also discovered by the Revolutionaries. See A.O. 12/49, 56-58, A.O. 12/102, 80,

As can readily be imagined, the women did not come through such experiences emotionally unscathed. One Massachusetts mother reported that her twelve-year-old daughter suffered from "nervous Fits" as a result of "the usage she met with from the Mobs"; and another New England woman, the wife of a merchant who was an early target of the local committee because he resisted the nonimportation movement, described to a female friend her reaction to a threatening letter they had received: "I have never injoyed one hours real Sattisfaction since the receipt of that Dreadfull Letter my mind is in continual agitation and the very rustling of the Trees alarms me." Some time later the same woman was unfortunate enough to be abused by a rebel militiaman. After that incident, she reported, "I did not recover from my fright for several days. The sound of drum or the sight of a gun put me into such a tremor that I could not command myself."[32] It was only natural for these women to look forward with longing to the day when they could escape to Canada or, better still, to England, "a land of peace, liberty and plenty." It seemed to them that their troubles would end when they finally left America. But, as one wrote later with the benefit of hindsight, their "severest trials were just begun."[33]

Male and female refugees alike confronted difficult problems in England and Canada—finding housing, obtaining financial support, settling into a new environment. For women, especially widows with families, the difficulties were compounded. The Bostonian Hannah Winslow found the right words: it was a "cruell" truth, she told her sister-in-law, that "when a woman with a family, and Particularly a large one, looses her Husband and Protector People are afraid to keep up the Acquaintance least they may ask favrs."[34] Many of the men quickly reestablished their American friendship

---

A.O. 13/45, 530, A.O. 13/67, 192, A.O. 13/68, 125, A.O. 13/96, 263, and A.O. 13/102, 1107.

[32] Mary Serjeant, loss schedule, Feb. 19, 1783, A.O. 13/49, pt. 1, 285; Christian Barnes to Elizabeth Smith, July 13-28, 1770, Christian Barnes Letterbook, Library of Congress; Barnes to Elizabeth Smith Inman, Apr. [2]9, [1775], in Nina Moore Tiffany, ed., *Letters of James Murray, Loyalist* (Boston, 1901), 187-188.

[33] Louisa Susannah Wells Aikman, *The Journal of a Voyage from Charlestown, S.C., to London undertaken during the American Revolution* . . . (New York, 1906), 52; Catherine Goldthwait to Elizabeth [Inman], Mar. 27, 1780, Robbins Papers, Mass. Hist. Soc. For a discussion of the loyalists' initial optimism and subsequent disillusionment see Mary Beth Norton, "The Loyalists' Image of England: Ideal and Reality," *Albion*, III (1971), 62-71.

[34] Hannah Winslow to [a sister-in-law], June 27, 1779, Winslow Papers, Mass. Hist. Soc. See also Rebecca Dolbeare to John Dolbeare, Aug. 30, 1780, Dolbeare Papers, Mass. Hist. Soc.; Polly Dibblee to William Jarvis, Nov. 1787, A.O. 13/41, 248. For a general discussion of the exiles' financial problems see Norton, *British-Americans*, 49-61. For another similar observation by a single woman see Louisa Oliver to Andrew Spooner, Mar. 1, 1788, Hutchinson-Oliver Papers, Mass. Hist. Soc.

networks through the coffeehouses and refugee organizations; the women were deprived not only of the companionship such associations provided but also of the information about pensions and claims that was transmitted along the male networks. As a result, a higher proportion of female than male loyalists made errors in their applications for government assistance, by directing the memorials to the wrong officials and failing to meet deadlines, often because they learned too late about compensation programs. Their standard excuses—that they "had nobody to advise with" and that they "did not know how to do it"—were greeted with skepticism by the claims commission, but they were undoubtedly true.[35]

On the whole, female loyalists appear to have fared worse in England than their male counterparts, and for two major reasons. In the first place, the commissioners usually gave women annual pensions that were from £10 to £20 lower than those received by men, apparently because they believed that the women had fewer expenses, but also because in most cases the women could not claim the extra merit of having actively served the royal cause.[36] Second, fewer women than men found work to supplement the sums they received from the government. To the wealthier female refugees work seemed so automatically foreclosed as an option that only a small number thought it necessary to explain to the commission why they could not contribute to their own support. Mary Serjeant, the widow of a Massachusetts clergyman, even regarded her former affluence as a sufficient reason in itself for her failure to seek employment. In 1782 she told the commissioners, "Educated as a Gentlewoman myself and brought up to no business I submit it to your [torn], Gentlemen, how very scanty must be the Subsistence which

[35] The quotation is from the case of Mary Hind, Feb. 1783, A.O. 12/99, 35. For examples of other women who claimed ignorance of proper forms and application procedures see A.O. 12/46, 165, A.O. 12/99, 238, A.O. 13/24, 284, A.O. 13/26, 63, 199, 282, 360, A.O. 13/113, 88, A.O. 13/131, 65, and A.O. 13/137, 150. Of course, a few men also made similar claims; see, for example, A.O. 12/43, 322-325, 328-331, and A.O. 12/46, 63. On the male networks see Norton, *British Americans*, 63-79, 162-164, 186-196, 206-216. The memorials submitted by women were not only more prone to error but also more informal, less likely to be written in the third person, less likely to contain the sorts of ritualistic phrases and arguments used by the men, and consequently more likely to be personally revealing.

[36] Norton, *British-Americans*, 52-61, 111-121, discusses the bases for pension decisions. It was standard practice for the commission to lower a family's allotment immediately after the death of the husband, regardless of the fact that the widow usually had to meet medical and funeral expenses at exactly that time. The pension records (A.O. 12/99-105, and T. 50/11ff, Public Record Office) show that women's pensions were normally smaller than men's. In addition, T. 50/11 reveals a clear case of discrimination: in 1789 the Charleston midwife Janet Cumming (see note 18 above) was, under the commission's rules, entitled to an annual pension of £200 for loss of profession (she was the only woman to qualify for one in her own right); instead, she was granted only a £50 widow's allowance.

my Own Industry [can] procure us." Those who did try to earn additional income (many of whom had also worked outside the home in America) usually took in needlework or hired out as servants or housekeepers, but even they had trouble making ends meet. One orphaned young woman reported, "I can support myself with my needle: but not my two Sisters and infant Brother"; and another, who had learned the trade of mantua making, commented, "I now got Work for my selef [*sic*]—but being oblidged to give long credit and haveing no Money of my one [*sic*] to go on with, I lived Cheifly upon tea which with night working brought me almost into the last stadge of a Consumtion so that when I rec'd my Money for work it went almost [all] to dockters."[37]

Many of the loyalist women displayed a good deal of resilience. Some managed to support themselves, among them the Wells sisters of Charleston, who in 1789 opened a London boardinghouse for young ladies whose parents wished them to have a "suitable" introduction to society. Others survived what might seem an overwhelming series of setbacks—for example, Susannah Marshall of Maryland, who, after running taverns in Baltimore and Head of Elk and trying but failing to join Lord Dunmore off Norfolk in 1776, finally left the United States by sea the following year, only to have her chartered ship captured first by the Americans and then by the British. In the process she lost all the goods she had managed to salvage from her earlier moves, and when she arrived in England she not only learned of her husband's death but was unsuccessful in her application for a subsistence pension. Refusing to give up, she went to work as a nurse to support her children, and although she described herself to the commission in 1785 as "very Old and feeble," she lived long enough to be granted a permanent annual allowance of £20 in 1789.[38]

Susannah Marshall, though, had years of experience as a tavernkeeper

[37] Mary Serjeant to John Wilmot and Daniel P. Coke, Dec. 1, 1782, A.O. 13/49, pt. 1, 283; Ann Asby to commissioners, Apr. 14, 1788, A.O. 13/43, 147; Susanna Sandys, memorial, n.d., A.O. 13/84, 613. (Sandys was English, though the daughter of a refugee, and is quoted here because of the detailed nature of her comments.) For a statement similar to Mrs. Serjeant's see Margaret Smythies to Lords of Treasury, Jan. 23, 1782, A.O. 13/67, 230. For two women who did explain why they could not work see A.O. 13/75, 627, and A.O. 13/53, 193. Information about nearly all the loyalist women who worked in England may be located in the following documents: A.O. 12/30, 230, A.O. 12/99, 50, 244, 264, A.O. 12/101, 137, A.O. 12/102, 87, 136, 164, 165, 175, 187, A.O. 13/43, 661, A.O. 13/44, 427, A.O. 13/71, 156, and A.O. 13/131, 359.

[38] On the Wells sisters' enterprise see Steuart Papers, 5041, fol. 123, National Library of Scotland, Edinburgh; Ann Elmsley to James Parker [1789?], Parker Papers, Pt. IV, no. 15, Liverpool Record Office, England; and Aikman, *Journal of a Voyage*, 71. Susannah Marshall's story may be traced in A.O. 13/62, 4, 7, A.O. 12/6, 257-263, and A.O. 12/99, 244.

behind her and was thus more capable of coping with her myriad difficulties than were women whose prewar experience had been restricted to their households. Such women recognized that they were "less able than many who never knew happier days to bear hardships and struggle with adversity." These women, especially those who had been, as one of them put it, "*born to better expectations*" in America, spoke despairingly of encounters with "difficultys of which she had no experience in her former life," of "Adversities which not many years before she scarcely thought it possible, that in any situation, she should ever experience."[39]

For women like these, exile in England or Canada was one long nightmare. Their relief requests have a desperate, supplicating tone that is largely absent from those submitted by men. One bewailed the impending birth of her third child, asking, "What can I do in my Condishtion deprived of helth with out Friends or mony with a helpless family to suffer with me?" Another begged the commission's secretary for assistance "with all humility" because "the merciless man I lodge with, threatens to sell the two or three trifling articles I have and put a Padlock on the Room unless I pay him the Rent amounting to near a Pound." By contrast, when a man prepared a memorial for the exceptionally distressed Mrs. Sarah Baker, he coolly told the commissioners that they should assist her because her children "as Soldiers or Sailors in his Majesty's Service may in future compensate the present Expence of saving them."[40]

The straits to which some of the female refugees were driven were dramatically illustrated in early 1783 when a South Carolina woman appeared before the commission "in Rags," explaining that she had been "obliged to pawn her Goods." It was but the first incident of many. Time and again women revealed that they had sold or pawned their clothes—which were usually their most valuable possessions—to buy food for themselves and their children. One was literally "reduced to the last shift" when she testified before the commission; another, the New Yorker Alicia Young, pawned so much that "the want of our apparel made our situation very deplorable"

[39] Harriet, Mary, Sarah, and Elizabeth Dawson and Ann Dawson Murray to commissioners, n.d., A. O. 13/113, 195; Mary Muirson to Lords of Treasury, May 28, 1784, A.O. 13/56, 342; Isabella Logan, claims memorial, Feb. 17, 1784, A.O. 13/32, 126; Patience Johnston, claims memorial, Dec. 21, 1785, A.O. 13/26, 196. For similar statements see A.O. 13/40, 93, A.O. 13/75, 354, 603, A.O. 13/132, 257, and A.O. 13/134, 504.

[40] Mary Lowry to [Samuel Remnant], n.d., A.O. 13/31, 202; Mary Curtain to Charles Monro, July 7, 1789, A.O. 13/137, 98; Samuel Peters to Daniel P. Coke, Nov. 20, 1784, A.O. 13/43, 352. Cf. the statements in the text with those of men; for example, Samuel Porter to Lords of Treasury, Feb. 23, 1776, T. 1/520, 27; Thomas Banks to Lords of Treasury, Feb. 9, 1779, T. 1/552, 3; John Saunders to Lords of Treasury, Mar. 31, 1785, F.O. 4/1, 248, Public Record Office.

until friends helped her to redeem some of her possessions. Strikingly, no man ever told the commission stories like these. Either male refugees were able to find alternatives to pawning their clothes, or, if they did not, they were too ashamed to admit it.[41]

Such hardships took a terrible mental as well as physical toll. Evidence of extreme mental stress permeates the female loyalists' petitions and letters, while it is largely absent from the memorials of male exiles. The women speak constantly of their "Fear, Fatigue and Anxiety of Mind," their "lowness of Spirit," their "inexpressable" distress, their "accumulated anguish." They repeatedly describe themselves as "desolate and distressed," as "disconsolate, Distressed and helpless . . . with a broken Spirit Ruined health and Constitution," as "Oppressed in body and distressed in mind."[42] "I am overwhelm'd with misfortunes," wrote one. Poverty "distracts and terrifies me," said another; and a third begged "that she may not be left a Prey to Poverty, and her constant companons [*sic*], Calamity and Sorrow." "My pen is unable to describe the horrors of My Mind—or the deploreable Situation of Myself and Infant family," Alicia Young told a member of the commission. "Judge then Dr Sir what is to become of me, or what we are to exist upon—I have no kind of resource. . . . oh Sir the horrors of my Situation is almost too much for me to bear." Most revealing of all was the wife of a Connecticut refugee: "Nature it self languishes," Mary Taylor wrote, "the hours that I should rest, I awake in such an aggitation of mind, as though I had to suffer for sins, that I neaver committed, I allmost shudder when I approache the Doone [doom?]—as every thing appears to be conspired against me, the Baker, and Bucher, seams to be weary of serving me oh porvity what is its Crime, may some have Compassion on those who feeals its power—for I can doo nothing—but baith my infant with my tears—while seeing my Husbands sinking under the waight of his misfortuens, unable to afford me any release."[43]

[41] Case of Margaret Reynolds, Mar. 26, 1783, A.O. 12/99, 116; Charlotte Mayne to—[Aug. 1783], H.O. 42/3, Public Record Office; Alicia Young to Robert Mackenzie, June 3, 1789, A.O. 13/67, 641. Mrs. Young gave the commissioners a detailed list of the items she had pawned (A.O. 13/67, 646). For other similar accounts of women pawning or selling their goods see A.O. 12/99, 13, 56, 60, A.O. 12/101, 196, 364, A.O. 13/43, 350, A.O. 13/64, 76, and A.O. 13/135, 81, 426.

[42] "Mrs Derbage's Narrative," Mar. 1789, A.O. 13/34, 298; Penelope Nicoll, deposition, July 6, 1787, A.O. 13/68, 267; Mary Broadhead to commissioners, Nov. 12, 1788, A.O. 13/125, 626; Margaret Draper to John Robinson, June 27, 1777, A.O. 13/44, 345; Rose Brailsford to Lords of Treasury, Dec. 29, 1779, A.O. 13/125, 580; Joyce Dawson to Lord Dunmore, July 24, 1781, A.O. 13/28, 220; Charlotte Pollock to Lords of Treasury, n.d., A.O. 13/133, 442.

[43] Lucy Necks to Lady North, Aug. 14, 1781, A.O. 13/32, 155; Elizabeth Barkesdale to commissioners, Nov. 24, 1786, A.O. 13/125, 402; Lydia Doty to Lords of Treasury, May 8, 1782, A.O. 13/113, 328; Alicia Young to Robert Mackenzie,

Even taking into account the likelihood that it was more socially acceptable for women to reveal their emotions, the divergence between men's and women's memorials is too marked to be explained by that factor alone. It is necessary to probe more deeply and to examine men's and women's varying uses of language in order to delineate the full dimensions of the difference.[44] As C. Wright Mills pointed out in an influential article some years ago, actions or motives and the vocabularies utilized to describe them cannot be wholly separated, and commonly used adjectives can therefore reveal the limitations placed on one's actions by one's social role. Mills asserted that "the 'Real Attitude or Motive' is not something different in kind from the verbalization or the 'opinion,'" and that "the long acting out of a role, with its appropriate motives, will often induce a man [or, one is compelled to add, a woman] to become what at first he merely sought to appear." Furthermore, Mills noted, people perceive situations in terms of specific, "delimited" vocabularies, and thus adjectives can themselves promote or deter certain actions. When adjectives are "typical and relatively unquestioned accompaniments of typal situations," he concluded, "such words often function as directives and incentives by virtue of their being the judgements of others as anticipated by the actor."[45]

In this theoretical context the specific words used by female loyalists may be analyzed as a means of understanding the ways in which they perceived themselves and their circumstances. Their very phraseology—and the manner in which it differs from that of their male counterparts—can provide insights into the matrix of attitudes that helped to shape the way they thought and acted. If Mills is correct, the question whether the women were deliberately telling the commission what they thought it wanted to hear

---

June 6, 1789, A.O. 13/67, 643; Mary Taylor to commissioners, Apr. 12, 1783, A.O. 13/42, 590. In sharp contrast to such statements, Andrew Allen, a male refugee, wrote in Feb. 1783, "Notwithstanding what has happened I have the Satisfaction to feel my Spirits unbroken and my Mind prepared to look forwards without Despondency." Allen to James Hamilton, Feb. 3, 1783, Dreer Collection, Historical Society of Pennsylvania, Philadelphia.

[44] Recent articles by linguists raise provocative questions about sex differences in speech. Most of them are concerned with 20th-century oral expression, however, and it is difficult to determine how accurately they apply to 18th-century documents. Among the most interesting are Nancy Faires Conklin, "Toward a Feminist Analysis of Linguistic Behavior," *University of Michigan Papers in Women's Studies*, I (1974), 51-73; Mary Ritchie Key, "Linguistic Behavior of Male and Female," *Linguistics: An International Review*, LXXXVIII (1972), 15-31; Cheris Kramer, "Women's Speech: Separate but Unequal?," *The Quarterly Journal of Speech*, LX (1974), 14-24; and Robin Lakoff, "Language and Woman's Place," *Language in Society*, II (1974), 45-79.

[45] C. Wright Mills, "Situated Actions and Vocabularies of Motive," *American Sociological Review*, V (1940), 904-913, esp. 906-909.

becomes irrelevant: it is enough to say that they were acting in accordance with a prescribed role, and that that role helped to determine how they acted.[46]

With these observations in mind, the fact that the women refugees displayed an intense awareness of their own femininity assumes a crucial significance. The phrases permeate the pages of the petitions from rich and poor alike: "Though a Woman"; "perhaps no Woman in America in equal Circumstances"; "being done by a Woman"; "being a poor lame and infirm Woman." In short, in the female loyalists' minds their actions and abilities were to a certain extent defined by their sex. Femininity was the constant point of reference in measuring their achievements and making their self-assessments. Moreover, the fact of their womanhood was used in a deprecating sense. In their own eyes, they gained merit by not acting like women. Her services were "allmost Matchless, (being done by a Woman)," wrote one; "tho' a Woman, she was the first that went out of the Gates to welcome the Royal Army," declared another. Femininity also provided a ready and plausible excuse for failures of action or of knowledge. A South Carolinian said she had not signed the address to the king in Charleston in 1780 because "it was not posable for a woman to come near the office." A Pennsylvanian apologized for any errors in her loss estimate with the comment, "as far as a Woman can know, she believes the contents to be true." A Nova Scotian said she had not submitted a claim by the deadline because of "being a lone Woman in her Husband's Absence and not having any person to Advise with." A Vermonter made the ultimate argument: "had she been a man, Instead, of a poor helpless woman—should not have faild of being in the British Servace."[47]

The pervasive implication is one of perceived inferiority, and this implication is enhanced by the word women used most often to describe them-

[46] The only woman claimant who appears to have manipulatively assumed a "feminine" role was Sarah Troutbeck. It is also difficult to determine, first, what it was that the commission "wanted" to hear from female loyalists and, second, how the women would know what the commission wanted, given their isolation from the male information networks. It could perhaps be argued that every 18th-century woman "knew" what every 18th-century man expected of her, but the fact is that the women claimants had a great deal to gain by displaying a very "unfeminine" knowledge of their husband's estates and by demonstrating their competence to the commission. See, for example, A.O. 12/101, 186, A.O. 12/40, 40-44, and A.O. 12/66, 6.

[47] The long quotations: Margaret Hutchinson, claims memorial, Feb. 23, 1784, A.O. 13/96, 601; Eleanor Lestor, claims memorial, n.d., A.O. 12/48, 359; Elizabeth Thompson to John Forster, Dec. 21, 1785, A.O. 13/136, 8; Mary Kearsley, testimony, Apr. 28, 1785, A.O. 12/38, 282; Mary Williams, affidavit, Dec. 21, 1785, A.O. 13/26, 535; Catherine Chilsom, claims memorial, Mar. 11, 1786, A.O. 13/24, 90. The shorter phrases: A.O. 13/16, 271, A.O. 13/24, 357, A.O. 13/26, 357.

selves: "helpless." "Being a Poor helpless Widow"; "she is left a helpless Widow"; "a helpless woman advanced in life"; "being a helpless woman": such phrases appear again and again in the claims memorials.[48] Male loyalists might term themselves "very unhappy," "wretched," "extremely distressed," or "exceedingly embarrassed," but *never* were they "helpless." For them, the most characteristic self-description was "unfortunate," a word that carried entirely different, even contrary, connotations.[49] Male loyalists can be said to have seen their circumstances as not of their own making, as even being reversible with luck. The condition of women, however, was inherent in themselves; nothing they could do could change their circumstances. By definition, indeed, they were incapable of helping themselves.

It should be stressed here that, although women commonly described themselves as "helpless," their use of that word did not necessarily mean that they were in fact helpless. It indicates rather that they perceived themselves thus, and that that perception in turn perhaps affected the way they acted (for example, in seeking charitable support instead of looking for work). Similarly, the fact that men failed to utilize the adjective "helpless" to refer to themselves does not mean that they were not helpless, for some of them surely were; it merely shows that—however incorrectly—they did think that they could change their circumstances. These two words, with all their connotations, encapsulate much of the divergence between male and female self-perceptions in late eighteenth-century America, even if they do not necessarily indicate much about the realities of male-female relationships in the colonies.[50]

There was, of course, more to the difference in sex roles than the sex-related ways in which colonial Americans looked at themselves. The claims documents also suggest that women and men placed varying emphases on

[48] A.O. 13/118, 488, A.O. 13/67, 234, A.O. 13/73, 586, A.O. 13/81, 59. Men also described women in the same terms; for examples see A.O. 13/28, 215, and A.O. 12/101, 235. The widows of Revolutionary soldiers also called themselves "helpless"; see, for example, Papers of the Continental Congress, V, 16 (M-41), Roll 50, V, 37, 122 (M-42), Roll 55, National Archives.

[49] T. 1/612, 157, A.O. 13/53, 62, A.O. 13/137, 574, A.O. 12/8, 124. For a few "unfortunate" men see A.O. 12/46, 104, A.O. 12/51, 208, A.O. 12/13, 188, and A.O. 12/42, 132.

[50] The women who were most definitely not helpless (for example, Susannah Marshall, Janet Cumming, and Sarah Troutbeck) did not use that word to describe themselves. Consequently, it appears that the term was not simply a formulaic one utilized by all women indiscriminately, but rather that it represented a real self-perception of those who did use it. At least one 18th-century woman recognized the sex-typed usage of the word "helpless." In her book of essays, Judith Sargent Murray noted that she hoped that "the term, *helpless widow,* might be rendered as unfrequent and inapplicable as that of *helpless widower.*" See Judith Sargent Murray, *The Gleaner*, III (Boston, 1789), 223.

familial ties. For women, such relationships seemed to take on a special order of magnitude. Specifically, men never said, as several women did, that after their spouses' deaths they were so "inconsolable" that they were unable to function. One woman declared that after her husband's execution by the rebels she was "bereft of her reason for near three months," and another described herself as "rendred almost totally incapable of Even writing my own Name or any assistance in any Shape that Could have the least Tendency to getting my Bread."[51] Furthermore, although loyalist men expressed concern over the plight of the children they could not support adequately, women were much more emotionally involved in the fate of their offspring. "Your goodness will easily conceive, what I must feel for My *Children,*" Alicia Young told a claims commissioner; "for myself—I care not—Misfortunes and distress have long since made me totally indifferent to every-thing in the World but *Them*—they have no provision—no provider—no protector—but God—and me." Women noted that their "Sorrows" were increased by the knowledge that their children were "Partners in this Scene of Indigence." Margaret Draper, widow of a Boston printer, explained that although she had been ill and suffering from a "disorderd Mind," "what adds to my affliction is, my fears for my Daughter, who may soon be left a Stranger and friendless." In the same vein, a New Jersey woman commented that she had "the inexpressible mortification of seeing my Children in want of many necessaries and conveniencies. . . . and what still more distresses me, is to think that I am obliged by partaking of it, to lessen even the small portion they have."[52]

The women's emphasis on their families is entirely compatible with the earlier observation concerning the importance of their households in their lives. If their menfolk were preoccupied with the monetary consequences of adhering to the crown, the women were more aware of the human tragedy brought about by the war. They saw their plight and that of their children in much more personal terms than did their husbands. Likewise, they personalized the fact of their exile in a way that male loyalists did not, by almost invariably commenting that they were "left friendless in a strange Country."

[51] Isabella Logan, claims memorial, Feb. 17, 1784, A.O. 13/32, 126; Jane Hilding, claims memorial, July 30, 1788, A.O. 13/46, 315; Joyce Dawson to Lord Dunmore, July 24, 1781, A.O. 13/28, 220. Also of interest is Jane Constable to Lords of Treasury, n.d., A.O. 13/73, 374.

[52] Alicia Young to Robert Mackenzie, June 6, 1789, A.O. 13/67, 643; Jane Roberts, claims memorial, Mar. 17, 1784, A.O. 13/71, 245; Margaret Draper to Lord ——, Oct. 15, 1782, A.O. 13/44, 349; Elizabeth Skinner to commissioners, Aug. 28, 1786, A.O. 13/112, 61. Mrs. Draper lived to see her daughter well married (Margaret Draper to the Misses Byles, June 21, 1784, Byles Papers, I, 134, Mass. Hist. Soc.). Cf. men's attitudes toward their children and other dependents in A.O. 13/75, 556, A.O. 12/105, 115, A.O. 13/131, 399, and A.O. 13/137, 2.

Refugee men, though they might call themselves "strangers," rarely noted a lack of friends, perhaps because of the coffeehouse networks. To women, by contrast, the fact that they were not surrounded by friends and neighbors seemed calamitous. "I am without Friends or Money," declared one; I am "a friendless, forlorn Woman . . . a Stranger to this Country, and surrounded by evils," said another. She is "far from her native Country, and numerous Friends and Relations where she formerly lived, much respected," wrote a third of her own condition.[53]

When the female refugees talked of settling elsewhere or of returning to the United States, they spoke chiefly of the friends and relatives they would find at their intended destinations. Indeed, it appears from the claims that at least six women went into exile solely because their friends and relatives did. A loyalist woman who remained in the United States after the war explained that she did so because she chose "to reside near my relations [rather] than to carry my family to a strange Country where in case of my death they would be at the mercy of strangers." And Mary Serjeant's description of her situation in America as it would have been had her husband not been a loyalist carried the implication that she wished she too had stayed at home: "His poor Children and disconsolate Widow would now have had a House of their own and some Land adjoining to it And instead of being almost destitute in a Land of Strangers would have remained among some Relatives."[54]

In sum, evidence drawn from the loyalist claims strongly suggests that late-eighteenth-century women had fully internalized the roles laid out for them in the polite literature of the day. Their experience was largely confined

[53] Elizabeth Putnam to Thomas Dundas, Nov. 7, 1789, A.O. 13/75, 309; Elizabeth Dumaresq to Lord Shelburne, Sept. 14, 1782, A.O. 13/44, 429; Elizabeth Barkesdale to commissioners, Nov. 24, 1786, A.O. 13/125, 402, Rachel Wetmore, claims memorial, Mar. 25, 1786, A.O. 13/16, 272. Other comments on neighbors and relatives may be found in A.O. 12/3, 231, A.O. 12/56, 339, A.O. 13/25, 275, A.O. 13/32, 595, A.O. 13/44, 345, A.O. 13/75, 544, 641, and A.O. 13/107, 271. Mr. and Mrs. James Parker had an interesting exchange of letters on the subject of whether she would join him in England, in which her ties to her American friends figured strongly. "Tho I would not hesitate one moment to go with you my Dearest friend to any place on earth, yet I cannot think of parting forever with my Dear and valuable friends on this side the atlantick, without many a heart felt sigh," she wrote on July 24, 1783. His response (Mar. 5, 1784) recognized her concern: "I realy sympathize with you on this trying scene of leaving of your Country and all our friends." Parker Papers, Pt. VIII, nos. 26, 31, Liverpool Record Office.

[54] Elizabeth Macnair to John Hamilton, Dec. 27, 1789, A.O. 13/131, 400; Mary Serjeant to John Wilmot and Daniel P. Coke, Dec. 1, 1782, A.O. 13/49, pt. 1, 283. See also A.O. 13/34, 471, and A.O. 13/70B, 145, on resettlement. For women who followed friends and relatives into exile see A.O. 13/116, 468, A.O. 13/114, 662, A.O. 12/102, 24, and A.O. 13/37, 3.

to their households, either because they chose that course or because they were forced into it. They perceived themselves as "helpless"—even if at times their actions showed that they were not—and they strongly valued ties with family and friends. When the Revolution tore them from the familiar patterns of their lives in America, they felt abandoned and adrift, far more so than did their male relatives, for whom the human contacts cherished by the women seemed to mean less or at least were more easily replaced by those friendships that persisted into exile.

The picture of the late-eighteenth-century woman that emerges from the loyalist claims, therefore, is of one who was almost wholly domestic, in the sense that that word would be used in the nineteenth-century United States. But at the same time the colonial woman's image of herself lacked the positive attributes with which her nineteenth-century counterpart could presumably console herself. The eighteenth-century American woman was primarily a wife and a mother, but America had not yet developed an ideology that would proclaim the social value of motherhood. That was to come with republicanism—and loyalist women, by a final irony, were excluded by their political allegiance from that republican assurance.[55]

[55] On the development of republican ideology pertaining to women see Linda K. Kerber, "Daughters of Columbia: Educating Women for the Republic, 1787-1805," in Stanley Elkins and Eric McKitrick, eds., *The Hofstadter Aegis* (New York, 1974), 36-59.

## New Leaves

Editor's Note: *The past two issues of* Carolina Comments *have featured articles by Jean Bradley Anderson and Paul D. Escott on the views of a southern planter and of slaves respectively. This article by Terrell Armistead Crow concentrates on the distaff side of the plantation South. It was first presented in a slightly different form to the Historical Society of North Carolina on March 30, 1979, at Greensboro. Mrs. Crow, who helped see the Edmondston diary through press, wishes to thank Mrs. Graham A. Barden, Jr., of New Bern who generously allowed her full access to the rich family documents on which this paper is based. Mrs. Crow is currently editorial assistant with the North Carolina Colonial Records Project.*

# "As Thy Days, So Shall Thy Strength Be": North Carolina Planter Women in War and Peace

Terrell Armistead Crow

The Devereux family of Halifax County sprang from a long line of planter-aristocrats in North Carolina. Descendants of a colonial governor and other prominent political and social leaders, the Devereuxs by 1860 occupied an affluent, privileged position in southern society. Owners of vast holdings in land and slaves, they prized stability and the continuation of the status quo. Imbued with the conservative, aristocratic values of the planter South and reared to be autocratic in nature, the Devereuxs exhibited distinct class and cultural biases toward people whom they considered social inferiors (black and white), toward political issues, and toward social problems. Rigid class prerogative characterized the Devereuxs' response to any challenge from within or without southern society. The women of the family, no less than the men, subscribed to these beliefs and dutifully played the roles assigned them.

The Civil War and Reconstruction came as stunning blows to the six Devereux sisters and produced irreversible changes in their lives. The cataclysm of war and defeat tested the strength of each sister, a process reflected in the Biblical verse Catherine Ann Devereux Edmondston frequently cited in her diary: "As thy days, so shall thy strength be." Faced with the reality of a crumbling plantation society, these women began the slow and painful adjustment to a new world.

The letters, poems, and notes of Kate Edmondston and her five sisters—Frances Devereux Miller, Elizabeth Devereux Jones, Mary Bayard Devereux Clarke, Nora Devereux Cannon, and Sophia Devereux Turner—reveal graphically the widening gulf between the antebellum ideal of southern womanhood and the stark realities of their lives. That southern ideal was instilled early. During her adolescence each of the Devereux women received instructions on the behavior expected of her. Submissiveness and domesticity, attributes highly esteemed in southern culture, predominated, but the demands of organizing and running a large household smoothly—how to manage slaves, how to preserve and prepare food and medication, and the ubiquitous necessity of sewing and needlework—were also drilled into the Devereux women.

Besides this traditional training the Devereux women received a classical education that allowed them to use their minds and to expand their outlook beyond the plantation's boundary. Though the sisters incorporated into their own thinking elements of the South's conservative values regarding woman's place in the home, the sanctity of southern culture, and white supremacy, their education, ability to reason, and sense of personal independence combined to produce conflict between social expectations and personal ambitions and desires. Mary Bayard Clarke, a talented woman actively engaged in writing, publishing, and editing, summed up her dilemma in a letter she wrote in 1872: "Live your own life is my motto, but I was brought up to think I ought to live somebody else's life and must take my opinions and feelings as I did my clothes when a child. They were cut and made properly and I must wear them."

Mary Bayard's distrust of enforced conformity incited her to rebellion on more than one occasion when her personal freedom was suppressed. She insisted on establishing a literary career for herself, much against the advice of sister Kate, who enjoyed composing her own poetry. Though she herself had anonymously published a poem, Kate cautioned: "beware of stepping out of your sphere & publishing them [poems]. Then indeed you would forget a woman's first ornament, modesty. Women have no business to rush into print; so wide an arena does not become them."

## A Woman Warrior

Mary Bayard also championed freedom of speech and action for herself, eventually to the injury of her own reputation. During the war her husband, William J. Clarke, served as colonel of the Twenty-fourth North Carolina Regiment, which was usually stationed in Virginia. Mary Bayard briefly contented herself with staying at the homes of relatives, but she soon rejected a passive role during the war and by 1862 joined her husband in Virginia. In ambulances, wagons, and occasionally on horseback at the head of the regiment she accompanied him across the Virginia countryside for several months. These experiences stirred her to compose patriotic poems and songs that were quite popular at the time. Other members of the Devereux family, however, were moved by entirely different emotions. Surprisingly, straitlaced Kate understood Mary Bayard's wish to be close to her husband and approved her going " 'tho Father and Mother go mad.' " Frances Miller, the eldest of the Devereux women and Mary Bayard's favorite sister, was appalled, however. Strong-willed Frances, who herself had run counter to the wishes of the family in 1862 by opening a boardinghouse in Raleigh after the death of her husband in order to meet his debts and support her children, minced no words with Mary Bayard: "It is not respectable my dear Sister that you should be following your husband to the seeming neglect of your children as it now stands." Frances approved of careers for women only if they did not interfere with household duties. To complicate matters, Mary Bayard had left her children at Frances's boardinghouse in the care of Jane, a free Negro woman who had been with the Clarkes in Texas before the war. Mary Bayard, no liberal where the caste system was concerned, entertained a strong affection for Jane as an individual and refused to dismiss her despite the insistence of her family who could not tolerate Jane's independence and freedom of manner with the Clarke children. Mary Bayard finally resolved the problem by bringing Jane to Virginia to tend to the needs of William Clarke and his officers and turned her children over to Frances—much to Frances's relief. Conditioned by the patterns of plantation etiquette, Frances candidly admitted distaste for a Negro "whom I could not govern. . . ." She further explained to Mary Bayard, "I do believe I am as forbearing towards my inferiors as any one but Jane I could not stand any longer. . . . We aint used to such my dear sister so do take Jane and welcome. . . ." Mary Bayard's decision to consider her own wants and needs over those of the family continued to embroil her in disputes,

Mary Bayard Clarke briefly followed her husband to the battlefields of Virginia during the Civil War; later she shed the role of retiring southern woman to pursue a full-time literary career. Her husband, William J. Clarke, was a Confederate officer who became a Republican judge after the war.

culminating in a rupture with Frances and Sophia Devereux Turner by the 1870s.

Despite her own independent strain, Mary Bayard remained extremely conservative in attitude toward those she deemed socially beneath her, toward blacks, toward woman's rights, and toward politics. During Reconstruction she wrote countless magazine and newspaper articles that derided "Rad-i-kills" and their policies. In one series of articles, penned under the pseudonym Betsey Bittersweet, she satirized individual political personalities involved in Reconstruction and their policies and aggressively attacked them through somewhat absurd situations. In one article dated January 1, 1868, she ridiculed Radical reforms by suggesting that Christmas too be reconstructed: "It was a very good thing in the old time when we had servants and money and could keep it like ladies and gentlemen, but it don't suit these times. And, while we are reconstructing, I vote to reconstruct Christmas, and appint [*sic*] that hereafter it shall fall on the twenty-ninth day of February instead of the twenty-fifth day of December. Thanksgiving belongs to the Yankees, fourth of July to the niggers, and Christmas ought to belong to the white folks."

Courageous enough to demand the personal freedom of "live your own life," Mary Bayard remained unsympathetic to the growing agitation for woman's rights and woman suffrage. Coyly asking as Betsey Bittersweet, "What does a woman want to vote for, when at the very least she can always, if she understands her rights, make at least one man vote as she pleases?" Mary Bayard then went on to state bluntly her own formula for getting things done her way: "I ain't of opinion that she has a right to be a man or even pretend she's one; if she is obliged to wear the britches for the good of the family, her skirts ought to be long enough to hide 'em."

## Woman's Three Rights

Another Devereux sister, Nora Cannon, echoed similar sentiments while discussing what she termed woman's three rights: namely, the right to be "bewitching," the right to serve good meals, and the right to keep the buttons sewn on men's shirts. Almost as an afterthought she amplified woman's first right—the bewitching stage—to include physical attractiveness and also intelligence and a good disposition. "God help the man whose wife lets her mind go to waste and shelters herself behind ***housekeeping duties***," intoned Nora. In a reference to her own life as a working widow, Nora pointed out that where necessity required it, a woman should be encouraged to "take on herself part of the man's work and rights and resign her own."

Nora was gradually forced to assume many of the duties traditionally reserved for men in order to provide for her family. When her two oldest daughters entered St. Mary's School in Raleigh, Nora helped in various phases of teaching at the academy and sewed clothes for extra income. And Nora loved it. Writing to a nephew in 1872, she exulted, "You do not know the pride I feel in the fact that last year I supported, clothed and educated my children & boarded and clothed my self without one cent from any of my relatives except your Father who sent me twice a present of $10.00." Nora indirectly shed light on the disapproving reaction of sister Kate to the new job by describing her own pleasure in telling Kate of the success: "when she asked 'how' it was as good as a play. 'By my sewing machine. I often sewed til 12 o'clock at night.' "

Nora rearranged the course of her life when outside events forced her to do so. This was true to a lesser or greater extent for the other Devereux sisters as well.

Frances opened her boardinghouse because of economic necessity and the determination not to be dependent on her father and brother for money. Even Kate changed although she ostensibly agreed with the sentiments of one male member of the family who said, "A modest diffident and soothing style as well in writing as in conversation when combined with simplicity of character and truth are among the finest ornaments of the female mind. A bold, self-assured and positive manner is the very reverse and ought to be avoided. . . ."

Kate never left the farm but she assumed a greater and greater proportion of its management during the war and Reconstruction. Happily married and devoted to Patrick M. Edmondston, Kate discussed how her husband's belief that the "first duty of woman was to attend to the cooking . . . pained and mortified" her to the point of tears in the first years of their marriage. She well recalled asking herself, " 'Was it for *this* that you had been educated? Was it for *this* that such tastes had been cultivated in you?' " Years later, when Patrick died suddenly, Kate refused to succumb to either her tremendous personal grief or to the incredible complications involved in continuing plantation operations. The Edmondstons had begun a battle with creditors over their Looking Glass plantation in 1865, a battle that lasted nearly ten years. Three of those years Kate carried on the struggle alone, determined to keep the property she regarded as being rightfully her own. When the land was finally confiscated and placed on public auction in December, 1874, Kate doggedly and triumphantly placed the highest bid, $6,000, despite her precarious health and financial situation. Less than a month later Catherine Edmondston was dead, but she had retained possession of her property.

Significantly, the two Devereux sisters who not only shared Kate's verbal allegiance to the "proper sphere" of women but actually continued clinging to this southern stereotype and the memory of their past grandeur were the two sisters who suffered the greatest mental anguish after the war. Sophia, married to Josiah Turner, the eccentric Democratic editor of the Raleigh *Sentinel*, turned to morphine for the support she could not find in her husband or her domestic duties. She died a lonely death in the Raleigh insane asylum. Elizabeth, unable to imagine or create a new life for herself, allowed her daughter to earn a living for the two of them while she retired from the world and submissively waited at home for whatever fate held in store for her.

In sharp contrast to Sophia and Elizabeth was Nora, who perhaps received the roughest lesson of any of the Devereux women although it was not an atypical one for planters in the vortex of war. Living close to Memphis, Tennessee, Nora and her husband endured Federal raids and early in the war lost their slaves. Admittedly displeased over emancipation and bitter toward favored slaves who were among the leaders of the black exodus from the South's plantations, Nora discovered in 1863 that household work was not as bad as she had feared: "Robert worked in the garden, fed the cows, & pigs . . . whilst I cooked, milked, & scoured, and we both thrived and fattened on it. My health was never so good."

After her husband's death around 1867, Nora and her four daughters returned to North Carolina to live until the two eldest girls finished their education. Nora, to repay the generosity of family members who sheltered her during the first rough years of transition, assumed control of household tasks in addition to teaching her children during the day. Although she bridled at the monotony of her existence, she enjoyed the work and the chance to be useful to other family members. Detailing the uneventful course of a hot July day in 1871 while staying with Kate, she discovered that she looked forward with the greatest delight to retiring to her room to "slip on the thinnest blouse I can find [,] light my pipe and take a novel or open

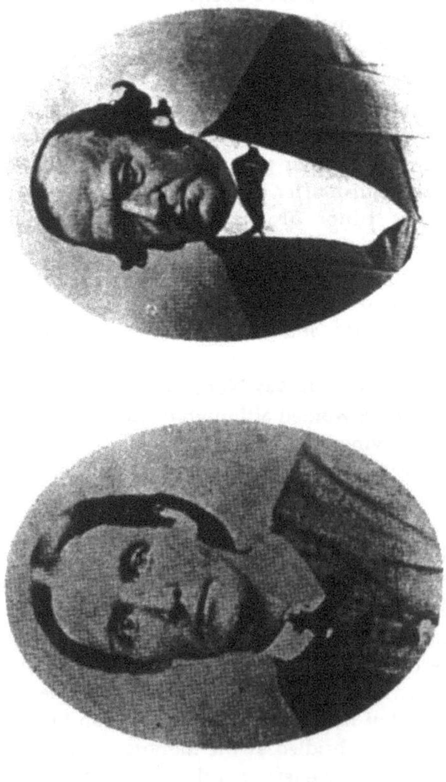

Sophia Turner was married to the strident Democratic editor of the Raleigh *Sentinel*, Josiah Turner. Unable to cope with the catastrophic changes in her life, she turned to morphine and died in a Raleigh asylum.

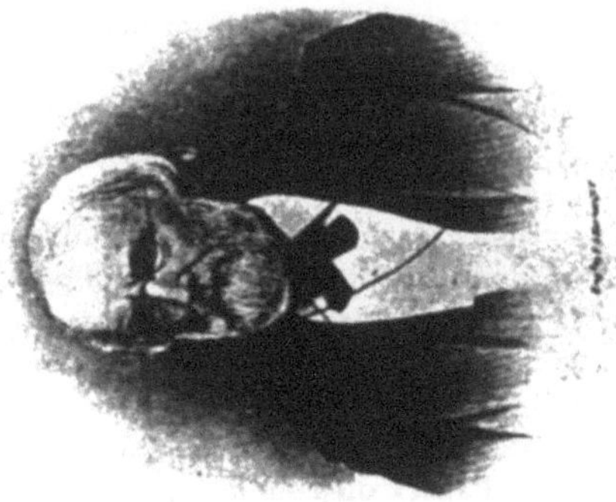

Mary Bayard Clarke's association with Justice Edwin G. Reade of the state supreme court, who had been a prominent Whig before the war and a Republican after, scandalized her family and led to a permanent rupture with her oldest sister.

my desk . . . & smoke, & read or write till it gets cool. . . ." Nora also assumed charge of the Edmondston plantation when Patrick and Catherine were absent on business. On one such occasion in 1870 "a most fearful religious excitement broke out among the poor ignorant negroes." The "two grand rascals" leading the revival directly challenged Nora's authority and control over the other field laborers. She wasted little time addressing the problem. She began by confronting the leaders and ordering them off the plantation with the promise that " 'if they were seen on the place they should have a quick trip to the next world for I should shoot them down as if they were mad dogs.' " She added pointedly: "I am a bag shot." Her reactions toward emancipated and assertive blacks was a reflection of her planter background but her method of dealing with the situation was definitely not meek or submissive. Nora had adopted, in her own words, "man's work and rights" with a vengeance.

Her growing poise and self-confidence ultimately led Nora back to Tennessee along with three of her daughters. There she owned a small farm and, in effect, championed woman's rights when she assumed elective office as superintendent of public instruction in Fayette County, Tennessee. She served two years, beginning in 1881, and won reelection to office in 1886—a nontraditional role indeed for the woman who once claimed that woman's place was in the home.

## "A Person Who Makes Revolutions"

Mary Bayard, a woman described by one male acquaintance as "a person who makes revolutions" because of her "natural garniture of right-thinking independence," continued to evolve and change, partly as a result of her personality and partly because of her suffering from "so much intolerance on every subject. . . ." An ardent Confederate, a belligerent foe of the conquering Yankee, Mary Bayard could not contain her curiosity about people. In 1866 she resumed correspondence with an old friend then serving as a colonel in the United States Army. She never failed to chide him on "Yankee rud[e]ness," but neither did she divorce herself from corresponding with him. In 1865, while living with Frances and awaiting the release of her husband from a Federal prison, Mary Bayard again indulged her penchant for creating revolutions by conversing with some of the Union officers stationed in occupied Raleigh. Publicly and privately chastised by Frances and other relatives for this offense, Mary Bayard immediately pursued a similar policy with regard to carpetbaggers and scalawags in Raleigh to the mortification and anger of her other sisters. (Remember, this was the period of her Betsey Bittersweet articles and venomous attacks on Reconstruction politics.) What propelled her into subsequent "offenses" was the disapprobation of family members seeking to coerce her into their limited spheres. Frances actually threatened Mary Bayard, married and the mother of four children, with disciplinary action by their father. She warned Mary that she would not permit a recurrence of Mary's conversations with Yankees in her boardinghouse because, "It is against my taste, an outrage to my children, & above all in my view . . . an insult to Bro. William while he is in a Northern prison to have his wife entertain for four hours one of his jailers. . . ." Frances promised to "write to Father, & tell him that you were his daughter, & he must take you under his eye till you could be restored to the protection of your husband as your conduct was compromising me." Frances should have known that she was only adding fuel to the fire.

Mary Bayard not only refused to be "guided," but she ultimately broke completely with the politics of her family. Unwilling to restrict herself because society required it, she studied opposing viewpoints and grew to believe "that God intended men to think differently" and not to "think that because people don't agree with you they are necessarily wrong. . . ." Suiting her actions to her words, Mary Bayard became friends with many Radical Republicans in North Carolina and served as private secretary to Judge Edwin G. Reade of the North Carolina Supreme Court—a scalawag and a boarder in Frances Miller's establishment. The Devereux family universally condemned the friendship and the job and insinuated that the money was too dearly earned at the expense of Mary Bayard's reputation. In actuality the income she earned was essential to her family, for William Clarke, suffering from some form of mental depression after his release from prison, failed to hold a steady job until he became a Republican and received a judgeship.

Mary Bayard continued to experiment with her literary and professional career for the rest of her life, with varying success. Besides continuing her poetry and newspaper articles, she wrote short stories, librettos for opera, Sunday school hymns, and book reviews—anything to provide for her family and fulfill her need for a career. She also attempted in 1868 "to inaugurate the system of female clerks" in the state's supreme court because she believed she "could be the means of opening such a field of labor for our women. . . ." She shrewdly added that "people who at first would say it was a piece of my excentricity [*sic*] and independence would in a few weeks be seeking places."

Her most daring effort to expand her opportunities as a woman involved her bid to become the librarian of the state supreme court. Unfortunately, this gambit did not go well, for it brought the final rupture with her family and she failed to obtain the job. The Devereux family quietly sabotaged her nomination for the job and deeply offended the Clarke family by impugning the reputation of Mary Bayard and Judge Reade. Strong enough to accept this defeat, Mary Bayard carried her literary talents to the North, well beyond the reach of meddling family members, and continued to thrive in a competitive and demanding career.

The experience of Mary Bayard Clarke may have been atypical, but the process that made her transformation possible must have been repeated thousands of times throughout the South. The Civil War demonstrated the inadequacy of the traditional role for southern women. If the war liberated Mary Bayard Clarke, it also forced each of the other five sisters in varying degrees to cope with a new social order and to test traditional boundaries. For all its upheaval and suffering, the war allowed each sister to explore her own capacity to grow and to survive by dint of her own efforts. Perhaps only Mary Bayard and Nora recognized the full implications of the war's impact on southern womanhood, but discontent with the South's romantic view of women, though guarded, had surfaced in the correspondence and lives of all the sisters. In the end those sisters least wed to the confining role imposed by southern culture before the war were the ones who weathered best the drastic changes thereafter.

# Emily Lyles Harris: A Piedmont Farmer During the Civil War

*Philip N. Racine*

Emily Harris, a South Carolina farmer's wife of the last century, might well have been missed as far as history is concerned except for the fact that she married a man who kept a journal. Her husband, David Harris, started his journal in 1855 to keep an accurate record of his farm work so he could eventually learn the very best time and method for undertaking his various tasks. With his wife, Emily Jane Lyles, his many children, and his ten slaves, he worked one hundred acres of a five-hundred-acre farm located eight miles southeast of the village of Spartanburg, South Carolina. In addition to recording his daily work, David often used his journal to comment on current affairs, family life, and his own state of mind. His records tell us much about farm life in the county, for he was a diligent and perceptive witness.

Yet, any investigation of the state of mind of people in Spartanburg District during the Civil War must also pay particular attention to Emily Harris. When David eventually went off to war, he asked his wife to carry on with his journal. He did us a great favor, for Emily made the journal her confidante. To it she confided her feelings, her opinions, and her fears. Through the entries in her journal we catch a glimpse of what it was like in the middle of the nineteenth century to be the wife of a farmer and of a soldier. There is no better contemporary record of life in Spartanburg District and not many its equal for the region. Throughout the literature on women in the Confederacy, including the recent work of Bell Wiley, Mary Elizabeth Massey, and the diary kept by another South Carolinian, Mary Boykin Chesnut, there is no more introspective and brutally honest commentator than Emily Harris. Some women who left us records were closer to battle, some were closer to the government, most were richer, but none looked at themselves and their world as unsparingly as did this farm wife in Spartanburg.

In 1860 Spartanburg County was an overwhelmingly agricultural area with few industries outside of small grist and saw mills and cotton gins. The county population was 18,500 whites and 8,100 slaves. The

Philip Racine *teaches history at Wofford College in South Carolina. He is at present writing a history of Spartanburg County.*

village had about one thousand inhabitants, eighteen stores, a couple of hotels, four churches, and five schools. There were no troops in the county during the war outside of the wounded and men on furlough, and no battles were fought there. The first Union soldiers who officially came to Spartanburg were chasing Jefferson Davis after the war's end. They stayed only a few days. So, for the most part, Spartanburg was a backwater of the war, but, nonetheless, its residents felt the war's effects. This was the setting in which David and Emily Harris recorded their perspectives on the county in wartime.

Born in 1827, Emily Jane Lyles Harris grew up in Spartanburg village until 1840 when her parents moved to the country. Her father, Amos Lyles, was intent on educating his only daughter, and Emily soon found herself boarding in the village so she might attend Phoebe Paine's school. Phoebe Paine was a Yankee schoolmarm who believed that women should be educated to use their intellectual gifts. In later years Emily recalled Phoebe Paine admonishing her to remember her "buried talent."[1] Historians of Spartanburg owe Phoebe Paine much, if for no other reason than for preparing Emily Lyles to write well, with feeling and understanding about herself and her times.

Emily Harris had nine children. When war broke out a set of twins had died and her seven remaining children were ages one year and nine months, four, six, eight, ten, twelve, and fourteen. She was thirty-three years old. Since her marriage in 1846, Emily's life had been filled with giving birth to and raising children, sometimes teaching them, making their clothes, and tending a garden from which much of the food for the family was taken; she had at least one house servant to help her. Although she enjoyed church, attended some social functions, and at times received relatives at home, she did not often go to the village or much of anywhere else. Her elderly mother lived with her for a few years in the late 1850's. With all these responsibilities she stayed at home, and there is evidence that she was not altogether content. Her husband, David, often complained of her temper, which irritated him; they seem to have quarreled often. Emily's temper was appreciated by all on the farm, for she was sometimes angry enough to whip her female slaves, and at least once, she whipped a male slave.

Such frequent outbursts of temper may have been partly a response to the physical isolation of the farm which denied David and Emily adequate diversion to relieve the monotony of their rural existence. It was ironic that this isolation, of which both Harrises complained, did not afford them any personal privacy. In 1862 David Harris wrote:

1. Reminiscence of Mrs. Laura L. Harris, typescript in private hands. Unless otherwise noted all quotations are from the David Golightly Harris Farm Journals, 1855–1870, a microfilm copy of which is in the Southern Historical Collection at the University of North Carolina, Chapel Hill.

Solitude sometimes is my most pleasant companion. How nice it is to sit in a quiet room by a glowing fire of shining embers, and to live over the past and to mark out pleasant plans for the future. This is a pleasure almost entirely denied me. So many children, and many cares. Oftentimes I would sit by the fire, and read and wright and dream. But children will be children, and children will make a noise. Then my resort is the bed. To find rest for my wearied limbs, and my diseased boddy. Wife often asks me to remain up with her, but I am compelled to take refuge in the bed, until I have become so accostomed to retiring early, that I cannot well do otherwise.

David wrote this entry at a time when Emily was also feeling overburdened and depressed, but he made no mention of her need for the same privacy and solitude that he craved. Nor did he seem to understand her need for his adult company. He was shutting her out, isolating her even more, and finding his peace, such as it was, partly at her expense. In the war's later years Emily confided to the journal that she "craved a few quiet days and for several weeks they have been denied me. I may as well give it up and resign myself to live in hub-bub all my life." A few days later Emily spoke a general human complaint when she lamented that her seven "children have all been at home. I have been much troubled by their noise and confusion which has caused me to ask myself what I should do with them when the school was out, and then what I should do with myself if I had no children." Farm life was a paradox. These two adults did not seem to be able to find sufficient companionship in each other to fill their individual needs for adult society, and the press of humanity which resulted from nine people living in a small house only added to their frustration and anxiety. The farm was isolated, but the people were never alone.[2]

When David Harris learned that his departure for service with the state volunteers was imminent he worried about leaving his family. He was sure Emily would care for the children, that she would work conscientiously and hard, but he also knew she would "be much at a loss with the management of the farm and the negroes." She had never had to assume the responsibility for the operation of everything and now, all of a sudden, it was dropped in her lap. He knew she would try, and he was ready to accept the consequences, whatever they might be. Emily was not quite so reconciled.

The trial has come at last, my husband has gone to the war, he left me yesterday afternoon. I thought I would rather not go with him to the depot but after he had gone I felt an almost irresistable impulse to follow him and keep his beloved countenance in my sight as long as possible. It was a hard parting, a bitter farewell. Ninety days, how long to be without him, how long for him to bear the privations and hardships of the camp and . . . how I shudder to think I may

2. July 1862, David suffered from severe headaches; 16 and 18 Oct. 1864.

never see him again. A load of responsibilities are resting upon me in his absence but I shall be found trying to bear them as well as I can.[3]

Among her difficulties was that faced by all mothers whose husbands are away for long periods of time—how to deal with the children. These were farm children used to having both their parents with them, or nearby, almost all the time. The younger children did not understand David Harris's long absence; one child, his father's namesake, in anger about something ran from the house to the gate "expecting to be taken up by his father. The tears would come a little in spite of one but I choked them down because the children seem sad enough. . . ." Emily controlled her emotions to help her children adjust, but the sensitivity, good nature, and deep feelings for people she showed in doing so rewarded her unkindly. Troubled and unsettled as she was, others among her relatives and friends turned to her for support; to them she was a strong woman, a realistic woman, a woman who could cope. Such had always been her role, and she was sought out, ironically, for the very comfort and advice, the very intimate sharing she herself so desperately needed. During a visit by a relative grieving a husband off to war, Emily had to "laugh and be gay on her account. . . ." She was the one to whom many turned, and thus "it has always been my lot to be obliged to shut up my griefs in my own breast." As it turned out she could manage the farm better than she could manage her griefs.[4]

Even when Emily felt she had things under control her journal entries are marked with sadness and a depressing sense of foreboding and loss:

All going well as far as I can judge but tonight it is raining and cold and a soldier's wife cannot be happy in bad weather or during a battle. All the afternoon as it clouded up I felt gloomy and sad and could not help watching the gate for a gray horse and its rider but he came not, though all his family are sheltered and comfortable the one who prepared the comfort is lying far away with scanty covering and poor shelter.

Most of the time she did not feel under control but rather overwhelmed. Her days were full ones; she felt almost crushed by the myriad things she had to do:

It has rained all day, the children have been cross and ungovernable. Old Judah and Edom [slaves] were both sick. Ann is trying to weave, and a poor weave it is, the sewing must be done, everything must be attended to, Laura is coughing a rough ominous cough, has scarcely any shoes on her feet, and no hope of getting any this week, West has the croup. I am trying to wean the baby and the cows laid out last night, and last and worst of all I know my husband is somewhere miserably cold, wet, and comfortless.[5]

3. 13 and 20 Nov. 1862.
4. 23 Nov. 1862.
5. 2 and 4 Dec. 1862.

No matter how badly things went for her, Emily always thought of David, and she took some comfort in the fact that he wrote her every day.

Emily did settle into the routine of running the farm, and some of her journal entries sound much like those of her husband. She planted, complained of the weather, meticulously recorded all the data of farm life her husband so cherished, constantly berated her slaves and, unlike her husband, always recorded the health of the children. "Family not well, negroes doing nothing but eating, making fires and wearing out clothes," was a typical entry. But she did grow crops, and grow them well. She had to hire extra field hands to help her bring in the harvest, although hiring was difficult; no one wanted money, everyone wanted food. Her record crop of oats—the best in her area of the district—almost went to ruin in the field because she had to pay her hired hands in wheat and she almost ran out. She exhausted everyone including herself in getting the oats in.

Yet, even her successes took their toll. Her persistence was in spite of herself: "I shall never get used to being left as the head of affairs at home. The burden is very heavy, and there is no one to smile on me as I trudge wearily along in the dark with it. I am constituted so as to crave a guide and protector. I am not an independent woman nor ever shall be." Emily felt insecure and incompetent, but to everyone around her she appeared just the opposite. She did get everything done but despaired of the life it meant she had to lead and the strength it meant she had to conjure up: "I am busy cutting our winter clothing, every thing is behind time and I'm tired to death with urging children and negroes to work."[6]

The pressures of farm, slaves, and family were almost too much. By late 1863 Emily was beginning to hate the farm, despair of her life, and fear herself: "If I am always to live as I have lived the last few months I shall soon tire of life and be willing to die. It seems that I have to think for every one on the place. . . . Every little thing has to pass through my hands in some way." Assailed as she was by self-doubt, lack of privacy, and burdens of responsibility, it is not surprising that the war itself began to take on an evil aspect for her. She blamed her husband's absence on the government, a government which she came to hate. In the spring of 1864 David Harris tried to get out of the army by securing an exemption as a farmer, but he was turned down. "Now of course there is no hope but for him to remain and fight our foes," she wrote, but as for herself she felt as much "like fighting our men who, standing at the head of affairs, are the cause of keeping such as him in the field, as I do the Yankees." This is self-pity; there were thousands like him and thousands like her. Her skepticism about the

6. 28 Jan., 7 Nov. 1863, 8 July 1864.

war grew until in 1865 she was openly hoping for a quick defeat. When she heard of a battle that was won by the Confederates she commented that it "will only prolong the struggle and do us no good I fear." She once remarked that she wished "the government would take all we've got and then call out the women and children and see if that would not rouse this people to a sense of their condition."[7]

These were lucid comments which reflected realities. But at times, she did tend to be a bit melodramatic: "There is no pleasure in life and yet we are not willing to die. I do not know how it might be but I feel like I should welcome the *Messenger* if it were not for those who need my services. . . ." And at another time she complained that "the great trouble is, there is no one on this place that has the welfare and prosperity of the family at heart but me. No one helps me to care and to think. . . . Losses, crosses, disappointments assail me on every hand. Is it because I am so wicked?"[8]

Yet, she was not self-centered. In addition to worrying about her own state of mind, she often thought and wrote of all the people who suffered around her. She might have been speaking for the whole of the county in 1864 when she wrote:

How we pity the brave men who are engaged in these battles. How we sympathize with the anxious hearts which almost stand still with suspense as they turn and listen in every direction for the last scrap of news from the battle. These hearts are more to be pitied than those that lie cold and still on the bloody field.

Every body is anxious and gloomy. Constantly we are hearing of some brave man who has fallen and whether an acquaintance or not he is somebody's son, somebody's friend. Some face will grow pale at news of his death, perchance some heart break, some soul pray, in its anguish, for death.[9]

As the year 1864 closed, Emily did become increasingly theatrical, yet there was a note of genuine desperation in her comments and a growing sense of self-doubt, a sense that there was something wrong with her. In late 1864 she confronted her depression:

It is seldom I stop to think of how I feel, much less write about it, but tonight I feel so unnaturally depressed that I cannot help casting about in my mind to see what is the matter. I left home . . . with Mary and Quin . . . to celebrate the anniversary of their marriage. I forgot all I wanted to carry with me. I lost some money. I felt unwell. I came home and found my sick ones not so well, I heard that the troops [with David] . . . were ordered *to sleep with their shoes and cartridge boxes on*. After supper the topic of conversation was Death. Our faithful dog, Boney, has howled ever since dark. What ails me, I do wonder?

7. 24 Nov. 1863, 31 May 1864, 5 and 27 Jan. 1865.
8. 27 Aug. and 1 Oct. 1864.
9. 18 May 1864.

Then late one night her husband returned on furlough. "After we all had hugged and kissed our best friend, we raised a light to gaze upon and scrutinize the beloved features which had begun to be something belonging to the past." David looked well and "his arrival has dispelled all gloom for the present."[10] David was well pleased with what Emily had done; by all measures she had managed the farm and the slaves with skill, making enough money and trading wisely enough for all to have lived fairly well. From the journal entries during his furlough it is difficult to know if Harris sensed his wife's state of mind. If he did sense the need and the fear, he did not record it, and in two weeks he was once again gone.

David's departure brought on all the old anxieties and fits of depression. Before he would come home again Emily would have to face two new problems, both of which might frighten even the most steadfast personality. By war's end slaves would grow impudent and rebellious, and desperate men—some soldiers and some deserters—would blanket the countryside; and Emily would have to face them both alone.

The war posed special problems for the Harris family and their Negroes. The very prospect of war had raised the remote possibility of Negro rebellion in David's mind, and there had been one case of alleged planned insurrection in the district in 1860. The fear that war would trigger a Negro uprising was general throughout the South, but the fears were unfounded. David Harris remained skeptical of the possibility of a general slave uprising in Spartanburg District for much of the war as we see in this late 1863 description of a sortie prompted by an alleged black conspiracy. A friend came to the house "and warned me to take guns and equipment to repair at dusk to Cedar Spring to watch a big negro-frolick that was to take place. . . . I went according to request (but without my gun) and bravely charged upon the house. But it was dark, silent and quiet, so we charged home again."[11] Otherwise, until the summer of 1864, Harris's relations with his slaves did not change. Every once in a while a Negro ran off for a short period, usually because of a flogging, but that was not so unusual.

When David went off to war he was concerned about his wife's ability to manage his slaves. Running the farm was one thing, managing its labor was another. Emily was nervous about the prospect seemingly without much cause. Then the war turned decidedly sour, and an ominous series of strange events began to plague her. Her field hands began to find hogs butchered on her place. By the summer of 1864 a good many had been killed, by white renegades she at first believed, but then

10. 20 and 29 Oct. 1864.
11. 26 Dec. 1863.

she was given cause to suspect blacks. Slaves from the neighborhood had been selling pork for some time, and whites were in such need as not to raise many questions about the source. Also, rumor among her own blacks had it that runaways hiding in the neighborhood were killing her stock. With the help of two neighbors she interrogated her slaves, but all they could agree upon was that one certain Negro, whose name was Pink, was selling pork. Pink said he had bought the pork from her own slave named Eliphus. She did not believe him and let the matter drop. Emily came to believe that her hogs were being killed "for revenge as well as gain. We have insulted a negro who is too smart to be detected in his villainy."[12] If true, it was the first sign that she could be the object of rebellion.

If the first, this was not the last sign, for by 1864, the relationship between masters and slaves was changing in ominous ways. Either because of the news that the war was going badly for the South (Negroes kept informed) or because they considered Emily less a master than David, or both, the Harris slaves began to take liberties. At Christmas in 1864 several of her blacks left the farm without her permission and stayed away at length, and others to whom she had given permission overstayed their time. The same was going on elsewhere in the district. Even more worrisome, for it showed where the sympathy of these "faithful blacks" lay, was the news she accidentally learned from slaves not her own: "I have learned through negroes that three Yankee prisoners have been living for several days in our gin house and have been fed by our negroes. The neighbors are seen watching for them with their guns." After putting together a surprise raid on her own slave quarters, Emily was disappointed that "the search for Yankee prisoners on our premises ended without success or information except the unmistakeable evidence that some one or more had been lodged and fed in and about our gin for some days. We tried to get the negroes to tell something about it but in vain. We could hear of their telling each other about it, but they wouldn't tell us nothing."[13] The slaves were not rising up, but they were harboring the enemy, and they were keeping things to themselves.

As Emily began to lose control over her slaves, she started to fear them. Negroes were aware that the Yankees were coming and some began to act on that knowledge, or at least, on that hope. In early 1865 "old Will came to me and asked me to give him 'a paper' and let him go and hunt him a home. York [the Harris's Negro overseer] has given him a whipping and he wishes to leave the place." This was the first request for freedom ever made by a Harris slave. Emily denied it,

12. 13 June, 25 Nov., and 7 Dec. 1864.
13. 16 and 18 Dec. 1864.

but the altercation between the two Negroes created a crisis, for Emily was put in a position where she realized the actual limits of her authority, limits which were an outcome of the times. "I'm in trouble," she wrote; "York must be corrected for fighting the old negro and there is no one willing to do it for me. It seems people are getting afraid of negroes."[14]

But the loss of authority hurt two ways. The white leadership, which before 1861 had sought some justice for slaves in special Negro courts, was off to war, and wives found that there were severe limits on what they could do to protect their chattels from the irresponsible exercise of power. As whites grew more fearful of blacks late in the war, arbitrary punishments became more frequent and severe. In crises the niceties tend to get trampled. Emily Harris again:

> NEGRO TRIAL, great trouble
> Today some runaway negroes were caught. One of them, Sam, who once belonged to Dr. Dean confessed a good deal and implicated others who were accordingly severely whipped without giving them a chance to prove their innocence. Eliphus [a Harris slave] and Guinn Harris' Pink were both whipped without proof of their guilt. I never will allow another negro of mine punished on suspicion. I understand that on next Monday the const[ables] are to go in search of evidence against Eliphus. Things are reversed. People used to be punished when found guilty, now they are punished and have their trial afterward.
> Eliphus has cause to deplore the absence of his master as well as I. If he had been here it would not have been managed in this way.[15]

Whether Emily gave Eliphus cause to know her feelings on the matter we do not know, but her indignation was a little late to help him. It is worth noting, however, that she did expect her slave to receive justice.

In 1865, as the weeks of winter and spring passed, Emily lost more and more control over her slaves. She found it "a painful necessity that I am reduced to the use of a stick but the negroes are becoming so impudent and disrespectful that I cannot bear it." In March she set down the plain fact that "the negroes are all expecting to be set free very soon and it causes them to be very troublesome." David Harris reflected white reaction to the emerging Negro attitude when he said, on hearing of a Negro who had been shot, that the dead man was "a bad boy & I am glad that he is killed. There is some others in this community that I want to meet the same fate."[16]

The last few months of the war were among the most traumatic for Spartanburg district. When General William T. Sherman captured Savannah in December 1864, South Carolinians realized that he would

14. 3 Jan. 1865.
15. 20 Jan. 1865.
16. 22 Feb., 6 and 27 March 1865.

soon invade their state. They also knew that, as the first southerners to secede, they were blamed by Union soldiers for the war and that their state stood as a symbol of rebellion. They expected the worst Sherman's army could dish out, and by reputation that could be pretty bad. Knowing that the end was near, some people in the village openly rejoiced at the prospect of peace and even flew a peace flag. There was little adverse reaction even to such a blatant act, for, as Emily put it, "every one seems to think we are to have peace soon and no one seems to care upon what terms." But peace was some months off. Word came to Spartanburg that Sherman was burning Columbia with thousands of women and children fleeing that part of the state. After hearing about Columbia, Emily Harris described her neighbors and herself as "in a dreadful state of excitement, almost wild. The Yankee army are advancing upon Spartanburg we fear. They are now destroying Alston and Columbia. . . . It has been impossible for me to sit or be still or do any quiet thing today. I am nearly crazy."[17] Emily had no need to fear, for Sherman turned toward Camden and never came near Spartanburg.

The Union army proved a chimeric threat but not so the deserters and renegades who plagued the northern part of the district. These desperadoes became bolder as the Confederate and state forces grew increasingly weak and ineffective. In the middle of 1863, that bad time for the Confederacy in general, the deserters became a serious problem. Their numbers, estimated at anywhere from six hundred to one thousand, were growing and many of them were "armed; are bold, defiant and threatening. Nothing but extreme measures can accomplish anything," wrote the officer in charge of the Greenville district requesting advice on how to control these marauders. The South Carolina troops were detailed to hunt down the deserters, but they were almost bribed into doing so. "By arresting a notorious deserter . . . ," David Harris recorded in his journal, "I was granted a twenty days furlough." Most deserters eluded capture largely because they were aided by local citizens who had never been in favor of the war or who were disgusted with it.[18]

By 1864 the deserters and others were getting bolder and stealing food and goods all over Spartanburg District. Food was disappearing from front yards of farms very close to the village. When Emily Harris heard that a barrel of molasses was stolen from under the bedroom window of her very close neighbor, Dr. Dean, she exclaimed of the

17. 8 and 20 Feb. 1865.

18. John Durant Ashmore to [unknown], Greenville, S.C., 30 Aug. 1863, John Durant Ashmore Papers, South Caroliniana Library, University of South Carolina; The South Caroliniana Library will hereafter be cited as *SCL*; 6 Dec. 1863.

thieves that "shooting them is the only remedy." Her husband, frustrated by the imminent defeat of the Confederacy, railed at "the thieves about me [who] are troubling me as much as the war. It seems that they will steal all we have got, and leave us but little for my family." By March of 1865 state soldiers who were assigned for local defense despaired of providing adequate protection; one of them wrote to his comrade that "from what I can hear, in the Districts of Union, Spartanburg & Greenville the citizens have been almost overrun by Deserters and absentees from the Army."[19]

The absentees presented a special problem of their own. Throughout the war, the spring had been a time when men simply walked away from their units. Worried about crops and about their families running out of food, they suffered a special homesickness. In the spring of 1865 all was made worse by the obvious futility of continuing the war, and soldiers set off for home on foot by the thousands. Such movement by strangers through the district posed problems for Emily Harris: "Late this afternoon a cavalry soldier came and begged to stay all night. I allowed him to stay but shall do so no more. . . . There are hundreds of soldiers passing to and fro. This is a little dangerous for women and children and fine horses to trust themselves on the road." The fear was well founded, but it created pangs of conscience for women who were also loyal citizens and distressed wives. Emily Harris worried that "there are thousands of soldiers now passing through the District on their way to join Gen. Lee near Richmond. Two have just asked to spend the night but I sent them away. In the same way my poor *husband* will be turned away to sleep in the rain and mud. . . ." These soldiers were dirty, raggedly dressed, and had not been paid in months. They found themselves thrown onto the mercy of farm and village people who, in turn, felt threatened by these strangers.[20]

Throughout all of her trials—the burden of raising children by herself, of managing a farm, of handling quarrelsome slaves, and the fear of the dislocation of defeat and the imminence of privation—Emily Harris constantly fought her personal war against depression. More than anything else she feared herself; she believed that her emotions and her mind threatened her world most immediately. In February of 1865, in the midst of rebellious slaves and national defeat, she got the answer to a desperate question she had put to herself months before, "What ails me, I do wonder?" One evening in February she recorded her answer:

19. 25 Oct. and 8 Nov. 1864; J. A. Keller to Col. John M. Obey, [place unknown], 16 March 1865, J. A. Keller Papers, *SCL*.

20. 6 and 3 March 1865.

A Presentiment

When Mrs. Harris, my esteemed mother in law, among her various objections to her son's alliance with me mentioned that of insanity being an hereditary affliction of my family I laughed at the idea of ever being in any danger of it. But the years which have intervened since then have left upon me the imprint of the trials and sufferings they in passing listerred [carved] on me. I sometimes have days of misery for which I cannot give, even to myself, a cause. These spells are periodical and today for the first time I have thought perhaps they were the transitory symptoms of insanity. It is a dark dream to dread. I wonder if the hopelessly insane do suffer much. If it is to be so who can arrest the fate. . . .[21]

Emily Jane Lyles Harris faced the ordeal of increasing slave arrogance and the fear of wandering soldiers with the realization that she might be losing her mind. Luckily, her husband came home unhurt within a month. He took over the journal once again, and Emily faded from view, for David hardly mentioned her. However, we do know she did not go insane. Her ordeal stemmed not from insanity, but rather from overwhelming burdens, loneliness, and sensitivity. What is especially striking about her entries in the journal is not that she was depressed, but that her depression made her feel so guilty and incompetent. Indeed, her life gave her ample reason to be fearful and anxious, yet her society expected her to react to her burdens otherwise; being unable to meet society's expectations, she felt compelled to seek some unnatural explanation, such as her mother-in-law's comment on insanity, for her self-doubts. Emily's anguish stemmed from the unrealistic self-perception fostered in women during the nineteenth century, a self-perception which even an education by Phoebe Paine could not significantly alter. Emily's reaction to her condition was probably more typical of most women, and especially farm women, caught up in this Civil War than the bombast of men would have us believe. And in her remarks about the tedious work, the isolation, and the trouble of daily life, she spoke truly of what much of an ante-bellum farm existence was like.

David Harris died at age fifty-four in 1875. Emily lived with her children until her death in 1899 from a stroke suffered, according to family tradition, in a dentist's chair. The dentist reportedly was badly unsettled by the possibility that he might have brought on the attack; poor fellow, had he read the journal he would have known that Emily had always had a flair for the dramatic.

21. 17 Feb. 1865. Emily's maternal grandparents were first cousins, which may have been what her mother-in-law objected to.

# THE WAR WITHIN A WAR:
## Women Nurses in the Union Army

*Ann Douglas Wood*

Dr. A. Curtis, president of the Botanico-Medical College of Ohio and author of *Lectures on Midwifery* published in 1836, lamented the passing of women midwives, and the take-over of their occupation by men. "The destruction of scores of modern women and infants, and the miserable condition of multitudes that escape immediate death" testified all too clearly, he believed, that the change was "not made for the better."[1] For better or worse, the change was very real. In 1646, as Gerda Lerner tells us, a man had been prosecuted in Maine for practicing as a midwife. One hundred and thirty years later, Dr. William Shippen started to lecture on midwifery in Philadelphia. In the next half century, medical schools proliferated, and state after state legislated that a physician had to be licensed to practice. Professionalization served to drive women from medicine as it automatically excluded them from formal training, licenses, and hence practice.[2] As Victor Robinson, the historian of nursing in America, sums it up, "in the change from colonial to national medicine, the casualty was woman: woman was not ignored, she was expelled."[3] This expulsion was hardly an unforeseen result of professionalization; rather, it was a desired and sought-after end. One Boston doctor boasted in 1820:

> It was one of the first and happiest fruits of improved medical education in America that females were excluded from practice, and this has only been effected by the united and persevering efforts of some of the most distinguished individuals of the profession.[4]

Women continued to play a role in the healing process, but it was a totally unprofessional one. Any sister, daughter or mother was expected to be able to nurse the sick of her household: indeed, she was idealized and glorified as a bedside watcher. Catharine Beecher's comparison of woman's role as healer to that of Jesus Christ was a com-

[1] A. Curtis, *Lectures on Midwifery and the Forms of Disease Peculiar to Women and Children* (Columbus, 1841), p. 9.

[2] Gerda Lerner, "The Lady and the Mill Girl: Changes in the Status of Women in the Age of Jackson," *Midcontinent American Studies Journal*, X (Spring, 1969), 7-8.

[3] Victor Robinson, *White Caps: The Story of Nursing* (Philadelphia and New York, 1946), p. 139.

[4] *Ibid.*

monplace.[5] Woman's silent, long-suffering ministry was the subject of countless poems and tales, but it was to hold sway principally in the home, usually her own, and never in any circumstance to come into competition with the professional doctor's role. William A. Alcott, a Boston physician and author of many books on women's health, proposed that all women should be trained to care for the sick at home. Women needed a little occupation to save them from "ennui," "disgust," and even "suicide," and they were by nature better qualified as nurses than men: self-sacrificing and self-forgetful, "they are formed for days and nights and months and years of watchfulness." Not only capable of such marathons of selflessness, women also "more readily anticipate our wants." Naturally, given such altruistic natures, the women nurses who are to be employed officially outside of their homes, "can be employed much cheaper" than men.[6] The essence of professionalism in nineteenth-century America was competition, and competition should clearly be anathema to the womanly watcher Alcott paints.

A rough bargain was being struck here as in so many other occupational fields at the turn of the nineteenth century. Women were exchanging some kind of professional expertise and official recognition for a domesticated version of the occupation in question, a version fed by official veneration but sapped by its distance from technological, scientific advance and its closeness to the hearth.[7] In other words, women, told that they had been third-rate professional doctors, were promised that they could be first-rate amateur nurses. They could no longer be midwives, but they could be madonnas. One can even speculate that the sentimental adulation granted the mother watching at the sickbed was a kind of guilty, if unconscious compensation for the hostility which drove the female doctor from her paying patient. Be that as it may, it is clear that in the mid-nineteenth century, American women were to use this new mystique as an important weapon in an attack against the very professionalism which had exiled them to a domestic shrine, and as the basis for a renewed claim on their own part to active professional life.

Lerner and other historians who have treated the subject agree that the American Revolution hastened the professionalization of medicine by vastly increasing the need for medical skill and providing a battle-

[5] See Catharine Esther Beecher and Harriet Beecher Stowe, *The American Home: or Principles of Domestic Sicence* (New York, 1869), pp. 335-347. This attitude and the related practice were so prevalent throughout the nineteenth century that the famous Philadelphian physician S. Weir Mitchell attacked prolonged familial nursing as in itself a prominent source of ill-health in women. See his *Doctor and Patient* (Philadelphia and London, 1888), pp. 125-7 and *Fat and Blood and How to Make Them* (Philadelphia, 1877), pp. 29-30.

[6] W. A. Alcott, "Female Attendance on the Sick," *Ladies' Magazine*, 7 (1834), 303-4.

[7] This applies to all kinds of industrial occupations (see Lerner, "Lady and the Mill Girl", 6, 9) and, in a different but related way, to the writing profession, see Ann D. Wood, "The 'Scribbling Women' and Fanny Fern: Why Women Wrote," *American Quarterly*, XXIII (1971), 3-24.

field on which to gain it.[8] Hence, the Revolution was the death-knell of the woman physician. The Civil War, almost a hundred years later, also dramatically changed the medical picture. The study of gun-shot wounds led to important discoveries, anesthetics were developed, and the basic principles of sanitation slowly became apparent if only because they were so terribly violated. But as important as any of these was the opportunity this war offered women to return to the medical ranks from which they had been ejected at the time of the Revolution.

Wartime nursing, newly elevated and glamorized in the 1850's by the work of Florence Nightingale in the Crimea, not only provided wider outlets for feminine skills, but afforded women a way to debunk the officialdom which had been their enemy. In coming on to the battlefield, they brought with them the myth of the bedside Madonna, still resplendent with her healing maternal power, and pitted its potency against masculine authority. As northerners, the nurses who followed the Union Army reckoned the Confederacy to be the enemy, but in daily practice their battles were more often with the ponderous war machine of their own menfolk and with the bureaucratic professionals —military and medical—who struggled to maintain it.

Of course, the majority of American women, as contemporary feminine observers delighted to stress, stayed home during the war and suffered. Mary Livermore, a leader in the Sanitary Commission, pointed out rather proudly that the pain of men in battle, inspired by martial enthusiasm or at least distracted by military necessities, was as nothing next to the agony that women feel sending forth their loved ones to war, "knowing full well the risks they run—this involves exquisite suffering, and calls for another kind of heroism."[9] Elizabeth Stuart Phelps, author of the best-selling novel *Gates Ajar*, designed to comfort the thousands of mourning women left in the war's wake, almost seemed to see the war as an act of hostility committed by men against the all-too-delicate sensibilities of their women-folk. She never worried greatly about the men who lost loved ones in the war, for the war, she implied, was their choice, their doing. It was rather "the women,—the helpless, outnumbering, unconsulted women; they whom war trampled down, without a choice at protest"[10] who were her concern. These anxious, grieving women were very much performing their madonna-function, the selfless sickbed watchers, taking all the suffering of their ill husbands and brothers on their slender shoulders.

But the efforts of the women at home to aid their men were not all so passive. They formed some ten thousand Soldier's Aid Societies, they made countless bandages, they held huge Sanitary Fairs that together netted three million dollars.[11] And not all of them confined their

[8] See Lerner, "Lady and the Mill Girl", 8.

[9] Mary A. Livermore, *My Story of the War* (Hartford, Conn., 1889), p. 110.

[10] Elizabeth Stuart Phelps, *Chapters from a Life* (Boston and New York, 1897), p. 98.

[11] Agatha Young, *The Women and the Crisis: Women of the North in the*

labors to the home-front. George A. Sale, a British journalist, wrote with some wonder that no conflict in history was so much "a woman's war" as the Civil War.[12] These ladies would not let go. Mary Livermore proudly advertised their indomitability as they "refused to release their hold upon the men of their households although the government had taken them out of the home and organized them into an army."[13] Waging their own war on military professionalism and on the masculine establishment that tried to exclude them, they simply refused to let this be the old kind of war, fought by men, with the wounded tended by men.[14] They came along in a multitude, some on a single trip to care for a wounded or dying son or husband, but thousands "enlisted for the war" as volunteer nurses.

Their backgrounds ranged from blue-blood society to poor white communities, but they all had one thing in common. Whether they worked under Dorothea Dix, appointed by the government as Superintendent of Nurses, or later for the Sanitary Commission, or appeared, as many did, sent by themselves and God, they were all without formal training. No schools for nurses opened until after the Civil War,[15] and so these volunteers had no experience beyond caring for the sick at home. Their ideal was, consequently, not the hospital, and certainly not the barracks, but the home. Indeed, many of them apparently were determined to turn the army camp with its masculine military code into the home, dominated by the maternal creed. This was a way of keeping their hold on the men who had just left the fireside for the campfire, but it was also a dramatic claim for greatly extended power. Woman's "influence," the genteel word favored by *Godey's Lady's Book*, was recognized as supreme within the sacred realm of home and family:[16] not surprising, then, that these women seemed bent, with Clara Barton, in making the "mother earth" of the

---

*Civil War* (New York, 1959), pp. 67, 312. Another, although less good, book on the same subject is Marjorie Barstow Greenbie, *Lincoln's Daughters of Mercy* (New York, 1944).

[12] Quoted in Mary Elizabeth Massey, *Bonnet Brigades* (New York, 1966), p. 25.

[13] Livermore, *My Story of the War*, p. 470.

[14] In the War of 1812 most of the nursing had been done by men. See Robinson, *White Caps*, pp. 140-2.

[15] On the history of nursing and its organization, see Mary M. Roberts, *American Nursing: History and Interpretation* (New York, 1955), Robinson, *White Caps*, and Lucy Ridgely Seyner, *A General History of Nursing* (New York, 1949). For a detailed and valuable discussion of Florence Nightingale's role, see Cecil Woodham-Smith, *Florence Nightingale 1820-1910* (New York, 1951). On the Sanitary Commission, see *The United States Sanitary Commission: A Sketch of Its Purposes and Its Work* (Boston, 1863); George Fredrickson, *The Inner Civil War: Northern Intellectuals and the Crisis of the Union* (New York, 1965), pp. 98-113; William Quentin Maxwell, *Lincoln's Fifth Wheel: The Political History of the United States Sanitary Commission* (New York, London, and Toronto, 1956).

[16] To understand fully the doctrine of female "influence," one must look through the ten volumes of the *Ladies' Magazine* (1828-1837) edited and largely written by Sarah J. Hale, who later edited *Godey's Lady's Book*.

battlefield into their "kitchen hearth"[17] and the soldiers into their sons. If the world was a home, where would their "influence" end? This subtle, yet sweeping question was posed by the actions of a minority. Most northern women, as we have seen, suffered patiently at home, sending only prayers, letters or bandages to wounded soldiers; but some moved to participate more directly in the Union effort, refusing to let sympathetic healing be outdistanced by destructive conflict. The progression from feminine self-abnegation to competitive involvement is clear, and it was all done under the maternal banner and the flags of the home fireside.

Many of the boys in blue were just that—boys, and they missed their homes and sang their songs not about their sweethearts, but about their mothers.[18] The women who came to nurse them kept voicing a sense, however, that *all* these men, young and old, playing at war with such terrible earnestness, were just children, children, moreover, who had not quite known what they were doing when they put themselves so far from home. Sophronia Bucklin, a talented volunteer nurse explained sagely:

> Woman's help had not been counted upon, when, in the first tremultuous rush of excited feeling, the citizen enlisted to serve under the banner of the soldier. And when her hand with its softer touch pressed on the aching forehead, and bathed the fevered face, words failed in the attempt to express the gratitude of a full heart.

Miss Bucklin clearly had a sense that these men, whose "universal childishness" she stressed, were like little boys who had run away from home, heedless of the consequences, and were only too grateful when mother appeared.[19] There is pity, but there is an undernote of I-told-you-so in the tone of these nurses when they describe, as Mary Livermore did, mutilated men, deliriously screaming, "'Mother! Mother!'"[20] Intent on rescuing such orphans, Clara Barton called the soldiers her "boys," and Emily E. Parsons, a handicapped but courageous nurse, wrote about the patients in her ward as her "forty-five children."[21]

Re-establishing the rule of mother on the battlefield meant fighting loose military morals with hometown ethics. As Mary Elizabeth Massey has noted, "stories of drinking, gambling, and immorality in camp spread like wildfire,"[22] and they were not without foundation. E. W. Locke, the popular song-writer and temperance reformer who was constantly with the Union troops, devoted his chapter on "Women in the

[17] Percy H. Epler, *The Life of Clara Barton* (New York, 1917), p. 352.

[18] Emily Elizabeth Parsons notes this allegiance in the *Memoir of Emily Elizabeth Parsons* (Boston, 1880), p. 68, published by her family.

[19] Sophronia E. Bucklin, *In Hospital and Camp: A Woman's Record of Thrilling Incidents Among the Wounded in the Late War* (Philadelphia, 1869), pp. 32-3.

[20] Livermore, *My Story of the War*, pp. 188-9.

[21] Parsons, *Memoir*, pp. 19, 21, 27, 52, 79.

[22] Massey, *Bonnet Brigades*, p. 213.

Army" in his war memoirs not just to the mothers and nurses, but also to "the Delilahs and Magdalenes" who followed the soldiers everywhere.[23] When duty called, the nurses could act like fierce watchdogs for the domestic virtues. " 'What, my boy, playing checkers on Sunday?' " one nurse reproved a wounded patient, offering him a New Testament.[24] But the real guardian was the legendary Dorothea Dix herself, pioneer in insane asylum and prison reform, now official Superintendent of Nurses, and determined to clean up the army as she had cleaned up the jails and asylums. Backed by her troops of nurses (by her own absolute requirement "plain-looking women," over thirty, dressed in black or brown, "with no bows, no curls, no jewelry, and no hoop-skirts"), she was a vigilance committee in herself. She did not take one day off in the entire course of the war.[25]

Opening a branch of the American Home at the front was not the only way these women found to extend their power. Coupled with their maternal lust to care for the soldier was a desire to compete with him, even to outdo him. Historians now estimate that approximately four hundred women joined the ranks disguised as men.[26] One, unmasked before Annie Wittenmeyer, a temperance leader prominent in the Sanitary Commission, when asked why she had done it, replied succinctly, " 'I thought I'd like camp-life, and I did.' "[27] The adventures of Pauline Cushman, actress and Federal spy, who disguised herself as a man, became the subject of two popular biographies.[28] These pretenders to masculinity occasionally came rather frighteningly close to the real thing. Emma Edmonds, another spy and male impersonator, who wrote up her wartime adventures under the catchy title of *The Female Spy of the Union Army*, narrated with relish shooting a southern woman, and then, Achilles-like, dragging her prey behind her horse.[29] Even some of the women at home waxed warrior-like, and one member of the fair sex complained that "the gentle-hearted ladies [were] admiring swords, guns, and pistols."[30]

The actual Amazons were few, but many of the volunteer nurses showed sparks of the same martial fire. Katharine Wormeley, a nurse

[23] E. H. Locke, *Three Years in Camp and Hospital* (Boston, 1870), p. 195.

[24] Young, *Women and the Crisis*, p. 227.

[25] Helen E. Marshall, *Dorothea Dix: Forgotten Samaritan* (Chapel Hill, 1937), pp. 206, 210. Young, *Women and the Crisis*, pp. 62-3, 75-6, 98-104, 193-6, 308-9 also covers Dix's war efforts skillfully.

[26] Young, *Women and the Crisis*, p. 43.

[27] Annie Wittenmeyer, *Under the Guns: A Woman's Reminiscences of the Civil War* (Boston, 1895), p. 18.

[28] See V. L. Sarmiento, *Life of Pauline Cushman the Celebrated Union Spy and Scout* (Philadelphia, 1865).

[29] S. Emma E. Edmonds, *The Female Spy of the Union Army: the Thrilling Adventures, Experiences and Escapes of a Woman, a Nurse, Spy, and Scout in Hospitals, Camps and Battlefields* (Boston, 1864), p. 94. Interestingly enough, the book was also published as *Nurse and Spy: or Unsexed, the Female Soldier*. It had tremendous popularity.

[30] Quoted in Massey, *Bonnet Brigades*, p. 259.

working for the Sanitary Commission, wrote a letter on board a hospital ship describing the chaos and confusion and activity around her and closed it, "Good-bye! *This is life*."[31] These women were getting a taste of a larger life; they were entering the masculine world of hard work and struggle, and many of them loved it. "I am in the army just as Chauncey [her brother] is, and I must be held to work just as he is," Emily Parsons explained proudly to her anxious parents. For the first time in her sheltered life, she senses she has become a participant in American history:

I feel now as if I had really entered into the inner spirit of the times,—the feeling which counts danger as nothing, but works straight on as our Puritan forefathers worked before us.[32]

Even though she knows her parents will worry, she cannot refrain from telling them how hard her bed is, how she is rained on at night, how poor the food is: these hardships are her badge of honor.

Many of the women leaders in the war were fighters from birth. A contemporary described Dix as "a general on a battlefield" long before the Civil War, and she herself knew that "the tonic I need is the tonic of opposition."[33] But her best battles had already been fought elsewhere. Not so with Clara Barton. Forty when the war began, after two decades of teaching and civil service work, she was inwardly restless and deeply melancholy. Raised by a "soldier-father" as she loved to call him, she had grown up riding fast horses and listening "breathlessly to his war stories."[34] When Fort Sumter was fired on, she went out to a rifle-range and shot at a target, "putting nine balls successively within the space of six inches at a distance of fifty feet."[35] She obtained her father's blessing, and then promptly went to war. Only Dr. Mary Walker, surgeon and suffragist, outdid her: she joined the ranks in pants,—but *not* disguised as a man—shot at the first soldier who was insolent with her, and retired from action dressed in an officer's uniform.[36]

Such strongly aggressive, not to say belligerent gestures, conspicuous in the careers of not a few of the most famous nurses during the war, seem to unmask the element of competitive attack in their volunteer crusade. They said they wanted to take care of the men: but did not they also want to take them over? Onlookers may have wondered.

31 Quoted in Young, *Women and the Crisis*, p. 177.

32 Parsons, *Memoir*, pp. 44, 54. Barton felt this sense of expanded activity strongly and wrote a poem about it. See "The Women Who Went to the Field," in Epler, *Clara Barton*, pp. 399-401.

33 Francis Tiffany, *Life of Dorothea Lynde Dix* (Boston and New York, 1890), pp. 163, 161.

34 Epler, *Clara Barton*, p. 6.

35 Young, *Women and the Crisis*, p. 45.

36 For an account of Dr. Walker's rather amazing career, see Charles McCool Snyder, *Mary Walker: the Little Lady in Pants* (New York, Washington, and Hollywood, 1962).

This unspoken anxiety perhaps accounts for the ambivalent feelings expressed by American men about the invasion within an invasion taking place before their eyes. Despite popular tributes from the troops, the nurses received little monetary compensation and less government recognition. Compilations of laudatory sketches like Frank Moore's *Women of the War: Their Heroism and Sacrifice* (1866) sold immensely,[37] but unpublished criticism of the women nurses was also current. Dr. Samuel Howe, although himself one of the original leaders of the Sanitary Commission, forbade his restless and patriotic wife, Julia Ward Howe, to be a nurse during the war. "If he had been engaged to Florence Nightingale," he explained, "and had loved her ever so dearly, he would have given her up as soon as she commenced her career as a public woman."[38] No wonder that women like Mary Livermore felt compelled to stress how reluctant they were to leave cherished home duties even for the pressing obligations that wartime presented.[39]

The hostility towards the female ranks was strongest, however, not at home, but in the army and at the front. Effort after effort was made by various officials to drive women out of the army,[40] and even the most powerful of the nurses had to deal with constant challenges to their presence and their authority. Once, when Clara Barton was in the midst of heroic labors after a terrible battle, an officer remarked to her, " 'Miss Barton, this is a rough and unseemly position for you, a woman, to occupy.' " She quickly and unanswerably retorted, "Is it not as rough and unseemly for these pain-racked men?' " But she did not always come off as easily. In 1863, she was rudely ousted from her post by the officials, and spent the winter in depressed inactivity before she was again allowed to return to the troops.[41] At the same time Dorothea Dix, originally given complete control over the appointment of nurses, was gently pushed aside, and her authority became permanently subordinate to that of the Surgeon-General's.

This resistance to the women volunteers was apparently not shared by the men in the ranks, as the nurses typically got plenty of unofficial appreciation. The problem centered on their official professional status, and their opponents were principally, and predictably, the army officials and doctors. In Nurse Bucklin's opinion, these two groups were

[37] For the nurses' poor pay, see Massey, *Bonnet Brigades*, pp. 63-4. Other popular tributes to the volunteers were L. P. Brockett and Mary C. Vaughan, *Woman's Work in the Civil War: A Record of Heroism, Patriotism, and Patience* (Philadelphia, Chicago, St. Louis, and Boston, 1867), and Mary A. Gardner Holland, *Our Army Nurses: Interesting Sketches and Photographs of Over One Hundred of the Noble Women Who Served in Hospitals and on Battlefields During Our Late Civil War 1861-1865* (Boston, 1897).

[38] Quoted in Young, *Women and the Crisis*, p. 61.

[39] Mary Livermore, *The Story of My Life: or, the Sunshine and Shadows of Seventy Years* (Hartford, Conn., 1898), p. 471.

[40] See Young, *Women and the Crisis*, pp. 120-1, 319-20.

[41] Ishbel Ross, *Angel of the Battlefield: The Life of Clara Barton* (New York, 1956), pp. 35, 61 ff.

"determined by a systemmatic course of ill-treatment . . . to drive women from the service."[42] Of course, some of the women volunteers were undoubtedly incompetent, ineffectual, and even harmful, but the skillful ones, as we have seen, had almost equal trouble establishing their position. They aroused official hostility precisely because they were challenging the male authorities directing the war, calling for credentials from men who thought they had left such tests decades of professional life behind, and then implicitly comparing the worth of such testimonies with that of the sources of their own vaunted authority as women and as mothers. Naturally the military officials were antagonized and threatened by this challenge, but the medical officials, directly dealing with these nurses in the wards, and supposedly having double authority over them as officers and as doctors, were especially threatened. And contemporary evidence suggests that they were especially antagonistic.

Indeed, many of these doctors apparently took an attitude of no-holds-barred in their resistance. Mary Phinney von Olnhausen, a protégé of Dorothea Dix's, summed up her impression of her male colleagues simply if sharply: surgeons were "the most brutal men I ever saw."[43] Another nurse, Georgeanna Woolsey, bore eloquent witness to the sufferings inflicted by doctors on nurses. Explaining that the surgeons "determined to make their [the nurses'] lives so unbearable that they should be forced in self-defense to leave," she elaborates:

> [no-one knows] how much opposition, how much ill-will, how much unfeeling want of thought these women nurses endured. Hardly a surgeon of whom I can think, received or treated them with even common courtesy. . . . I have known women, delicately cared for at home, half fed in hospitals, hard worked day and night, and given, when sleep must be had, a . . . closet, just large enough for a camp bed to stand in.

Only the knowledge that they were "pioneers," blazing a trail for those to come, sustained the first volunteers.[44]

Perhaps the doctors so fiercely defended their position because it was a particularly vulnerable one. The Medical Department of the Army consisted of the Surgeon General, an Assistant Surgeon General, and a number of short-term "contract surgeons." It was this latter group who received most criticism. They deserved it, but it is hardly surprising that they should have done a bad job. One of their more sympathetic critics, Jane Woolsey, a war-time nurse, explained their dilemma:

> Contract surgeons were more or less victims of a system which made them an anomalous civil element in a military establishment, with but little military re-

[42] Bucklin, *In Hospital and Camp*, pp. 124-5.

[43] Sylvia G. L. Dannett (ed.), *Noble Women of the North* (New York and London, 1959), p. 95. It should be remembered that these women were coming in contact principally with surgeons, rather than doctors, and were horrified by the sights of the amputation-table. See *ibid.*, pp. 99-104.

[44] *Ibid.*, pp. 88-9.

strictions, and no military incentive in the shape of promotion. They had no position, small pay, and mere nominal rank. They were a temporary expedient in the first place. . . . They served their little term, made their little experiments, and disappeared. The class was bad; it was under no obligations to be anything else.[45]

As a result of this incentive problem, the men who became surgeons in the army were either talented physicians, patriotically donating their talents to the war effort at considerable loss to themselves, or men who had failed in their home practice, "to whose care," as one commentator ruefully noted, "we would not be willing to intrust a sick or disabled horse."[46] Not surprisingly, *medical*—not war—casualties were such that one historian has calculated that a soldier's safety was more imperiled if he had to undergo medical treatment in an army hospital for an injury than if he fought all three days at Gettysburg.[47]

Of this rather mixed crew of doctors, moreover, complicated demands were made. As E. W. Locke remarked, their medical knowledge, while absolutely necessary, was not all-sufficient as it might be in peacetime. In an age when few people, no matter how sick, went to hospitals, the doctor customarily drew for his nursing help chiefly on the amateur feminine nurses in his patients' homes. Now on the front, dealing with wounded or sick men who were far from their homes, he was asked to supply not only his professional skill, but this almost familial care as well. He must, in Locke's words, "stand in the place of parent, wife, or sister." As a result, Locke concludes, the best doctors were those with "heart-power," which goes far "deeper" than medicine, and they were "almost like mothers."[48] Maternity had nearly become a professional requirement.

Locke's analysis, backed up by the motherly role a man like Walt Whitman chose to assume at the bedside of the wounded, casts the doctors and volunteer nurses in a competitive double contest for maternal and medical pre-eminence, a contest whose potential the women were quick to grasp. They were not officials of any kind. Poorly paid volunteers attached to various military hospitals, they had no regular professional status. But they *were* mothers or potential ones, and this apparently could now provide the basis for a professional claim. Not surprisingly, they proceeded to attack the errors and false professionalism of the surgeons and of the military authorities who backed them up with all the dignity and force lent them by their consecrated maternal natures.

Basic to these women's complicated urge to make the front truly a home-front, to replace the captain with the mother, the doctor with the nurse, and even to out-soldier the soldiers, was their sense that

[45] *Ibid.*, p. 98.

[46] Locke, *Three Years in Camp and Hospital*, p. 73. For a recent account of doctors in the Civil War, see George Worthington Adams, *Doctors in Blue* (New York, 1952).

[47] Robinson, *White Cap*, p. 153.

[48] Locke, *Three Years in Camp and Hospital*, pp. 71-2.

they were being kept out, of medicine, of war, of *life itself*, by a complicated professional code that simply boiled down to men's unwillingness to let anyone—including themselves—know what a mess they had made. And the first thing the volunteers wanted to reveal was the mess in all its enormity. Eliza Howland, an energetic nurse, wrote her husband about her herculean labors in a veritable Augean stable of a hospital. She and her fellow nurses cleaned the floors, covered with dust, nails, and shavings, taking up the "rubbish" with shovels and putting it in barrels. But the plight of the patients, "crowded in upon us" was less easily rectified: they were "soaked with malignant malarial fever, from exposure night after night, to drenching rain." She could only damn the prevalent "murderous, blundering want of prevision and provision" which caused their plight.[49]

These women had little hesitation in calling a spade a spade and in marshalling their forces against the (in their view) heedless men in local positions of command. Annie Wittenmeyer was shocked to find an acting medical director of a military hospital on the job "reeling drunk." No wonder he ordered such a right-minded and astute woman off the premises, drunkenly insisting, " 'I'm boss here.' " Calmly but grimly thinking, "One or the other of us must certainly leave that hospital,' " she arranged for his dismissal. When she found another surgeon putting logwood in the coffee intended for the wounded, a "righteous indignation" burned in her heart, and another head rolled.[50] Dorothea Dix, astonished by the laxities and lapses perhaps inevitable in the early stages of an unforeseen war, irritated military authorities by being in a perpetual state of "breathless excitement," as one exasperated official called it. Cynically, George Templeton Strong, a Sanitary Commissioner, could seize on the absurd and hysterical aspects of her over-concern:

> She is disgusted with us because we do not leave everything else and rush off the instant she tells us of something that needs attention. The last time we were in Washington she came upon us in breathless excitement to say that a cow in the Smithsonian grounds was dying of sunstroke, and she took it very ill that we did not adjourn instantly to look after the case.[51]

What Strong understandably failed to note was that her anxiety, like Annie Wittenmeyer's strong-minded indignation, rose from her horror, here focused on a petty detail, that all these *men*, not just professing Christians (women were that, after all), but wage-earners and professionally trained, might be incompetent—incompetent despite the reassuring tokens of self-confidence, responsibility, training, in sum, of masculinity, which she and all her world were accustomed to accept as some kind of seal of approval. After she had opened the first door of her first state-run jail and seen the enormities of neglect and maltreat-

[49] Dannett, *Noble Women*, p. 82.
[50] Wittenmeyer, *Under the Guns*, pp. 75, 193 ff.
[51] Young, *Women and the Crisis*, p. 104.

ment there, she *doubted*. She enjoyed the doubts, because they implied that if men were apparently not helped, were even *disabled* by their training for the task of running the world right, the burden fell on her, and her apparent (and feminine) lack of qualifications became a positive asset for the task. Yet the intense reactions and distorted, but oppressive sense of responsibility which resulted from her frightening conclusion that she was the only wakeful passenger on a ship headed for certain wreck,[52] were real too. When the Civil War came, thousands of other American women put themselves in a position to open the same door (or raise the equivalent tent-flap), and they saw similar sights and felt the same complex mingling of hysterical fear and righteous elation.

If this nightmare of untended men, dirty wards, overworked and sometimes incompetent doctors was military professional medicine, there was only one resource for these ladies: opposition. The necessary force and authority came from many different sources, as did the women volunteers themselves; some had or made friends in power, some had the backing of Dix's organization, some were acting for the increasingly powerful Sanitary Commission, some used personal charm. In the more belligerent line, Dix, who demanded no professional training of her nurses (she had seen enough to know what good *that* did!), simply told them to disregard the surgeons and obey her.[53] In a different fashion, young and delicate Mary Safford, finding all "surgeons and authorities everywhere" opposed to her presence, disarmed the opposition by "her sweetness and grace and beauty." Hailed like Clara Barton as an "angel," she was also "the most indomitable little creature living." According to a contemporary report, "*She did just what she pleased*."[54]

And what these women wanted to do was to cut through the "red tape,"—a phrase they used over and over again to signify what they were fighting against. They wanted to destroy the professionalism, the bureaucracy that was keeping them out and keeping the wounded uncared for, and they hoped to replace it by the new and better professionalism at their command. Georgeanna Woolsey, in a witty mood, characterized "that sublime, unfathomed mystery—'Professional Etiquette'" as an "absolute Bogie," a Bogie "which puts its cold paw on private benevolence . . . which kept shirts from ragged men, and broth from hungry ones."[55]

The past-mistress of the art of defying and outwitting this omnipresent Bogie was a little-educated but superbly shrewd Illinois woman in her forties named Mary Ann Bickerdyke. She was soon called

[52] It seems no chance similarity that both she and Clara Barton were chronic insomniacs. Barton in fact slept with a lighted candle and pen and pad by her bed, ready to write down any important thoughts that occurred to her in the night.

[53] Young, *Women and the Crisis*, p. 134.

[54] Brockett and Vaughan, *Women's Work in the Civil War*, pp. 359-60.

[55] Dannett, *Noble Women*, p. 89.

"Mother" Bickerdyke by the troops, and became the heroine of women like Annie Wittenmeyer and Mary Livermore. Both devote more space to her in their war memoirs than to any other single person, and their adoration is extremely significant. Leaders in the male-dominated, highly organized Sanitary Commission with its quickly developing professional code, Wittenmeyer and Livermore showed their true colors in their adulation of such a maverick as Bickerdyke. Totally unprofessional by any conventional standard, she made a profession of the calling both these women also exploited: motherhood. Wittenmeyer, who set up special sanitary diet kitchens in military hospitals was cooking for a vastly extended family. "Mother" Bickerdyke, who had practiced before the war informally as a botanic doctor, was doing home nursing on an equally vast scale. The fact that all three women left families behind them to join the war effort indicates that they went to war not so much to satisfy their maternal urges as to use their maternal status as the basis for a play for a professional one. But the profession (nursing) they evolved was intended to share none of the weaknesses of its masculine rival. "Mother" Bickerdyke's work in the war represents the clearest example of this effort on the part of the volunteer nurses to put to shame the male bureaucratic professional organization behind the military hospitals by the shining example of a militant motherhood, which outdid its rival in efficiency but showed the heart its competitor so conspicuously lacked.

Bickerdyke's husband, whom, she privately stated, would have lived twenty years longer "had he not worn himself into the grave trying to boss her,"[56] was dead when she agreed in 1861 to accompany medical supplies for the boys to Cairo, Illinois. Her words on that occasion were a battle cry:

> I'll go to Cairo, and I'll clean things up there [she promised]. You don't need to worry about that, neither. Them generals and all ain't going to stop me. This is the Lord's work you're calling me to do.[57]

She kept her pledge. The Lord's was the only authority she ever did accept, and He generally sounded a good deal like Mother Bickerdyke. Even General Sherman toed her line. An admirer of Bickerdyke's, he told one furious officer that he could not help him against this formidable foe: " 'She ranks me,' " he explained.[58] She brought in countless supplies, she nursed thousands, and, as Annie Wittenmeyer said, she "cut red tape." She explained to one of many irate doctors as she calmly sidestepped medical protocol in her customary fashion: " 'It's of no use for you to try to tie me up with your red tape. There's too much

[56] Livermore, *My Story of the War*, p. 479.

[57] Quoted in Nina Brown Baker, *Cyclone in Calico: the Story of Mary Ann Bickerdyke* (Boston, 1952), p. 11.

[58] Young, *Women and the Crisis*, p. 266. General Butler was reported to have used the same phrase about Clara Barton in a similar situation (see Ross, *Angel of the Battlefield*, p. 78). Clearly the line had a significance which made it dwelt-upon and even transferable.

to be done down here to stop for that.' "[59] The underlying reproach to the dangerously silly men in command around her, unwilling to stop playing the games they have been trained to play even when life and death are at stake, is clear. Men can be allowed to play at authority in peacetime, she implies, but when a war comes, it's time to obey the women. In such a crisis, Mother Bickerdyke, an Admirable Crichton in the Union army, simply must assume her natural place of leadership. Bringing the primitive justice of the frontier and the ready kindness of what her biographers liked to call her "great maternal heart" to the front, she moved always to the point. When she discovered that an officer was stealing clothes reserved for sick soldiers, she stripped him publicly, "leaving him nude save his pantaloons."[60]

Clara Barton too had a way of kicking over regulations to get to the men and their needs. Working alone, outside the Sanitary Commission and Dix's organization, she was the first woman, and one of very few, to take the actual front as her territory, turning up during battles with medical supplies and her own considerable nursing skill before any organized help could arrive. This was the absolute essence of her tactics: not to cut through red take so much as to anticipate, and hence to forestall it, to appear at the actual moment of crisis when officialdom is always irrelevant. Many of the most prominent nurses saw their role in similar terms and loved to tell stories of how they provided some desperate or dying soldier, not with the standard treatment, so little susceptible of being bent to individual needs, but with precisely that thing which they, with lightning quick feminine intuition, knew he needed most.[61]

Clara Barton's mssion was to bring this instinct to a kind of perfection on the battlefield itself. She knew when to obey the doctors, but she had feuds with certain military medics and distrusted medicine to the point of being a near Christian Scientist in later life. At the core of her being was a profound suspicion of all organizations, and it seems significant that the great organization she helped to found, the Red Cross, was in key ways an anti-institution, at least as she ran it. Like the special kitchens run by Wittenmeyer, it was an effort which drew complex and double strength from implicitly attacking existing professional efforts in the same field even while endowing its own anti-institutional unprofessionalism with the forces of a profession—money, publicity and organized labor.[62] The Red Cross was, in other words, an extension of

[59] Livermore, *My Story of the War*, 509.

[60] *Ibid.*, p. 481.

[61] Adelaide Smith, another nurse, is very explicit on this point. See Robinson, *White Caps*, p. 162.

[62] Epler, *Clara Barton*, p. 204. Epler also charts the course of her struggle to retain power over the Red Cross and to prevent it from becoming the kind of bureaucratic organization it became after her forced retirement. For her own account of the Red Cross, see Clara Barton, *The Red Cross: A History of This Remarkable International Movement in the Interest of Humanity* (Albany, N.Y., 1898). Note how even in her title she avoids calling it an organization or an insti-

the principles behind Barton's and Bickerdyke's work in the Civil War. As she explained it, its purpose was to deal with the damage wrecked by the forces "that red tape is not strong enough to hold . . . in check."[63] It was "unlike any other organization in the country" because, in her words,

> It is an organization of physical action, of instantaneous action, at the spur of the moment; it cannot await the ordinary deliberations of organized bodies if it would be of any use to suffering humanity; . . . it has by its nature a field of its own.[64]

The Red Cross as it began in America was organized feminine intuition, anti-professional and anti-institutional in nature, the logical culmination of the spirit of woman's efforts in the Civil War.

Clara Barton, with Mother Bickerdyke and many others, felt that she had the right to break through official medical protocol because she had the healing touch. Her thinking, like that of Dorothea Dix, in many ways paralleled that of Mary Baker Eddy. Dix had tremendous faith in what her first biographer called "the renovating power over bodily infirmity of a great purpose":[65] it was this which gave her her fabled "divine magnetism," as Horace Mann reverently called it. In her work with the insane, she was given to rather expansive, not to say Messianic, statements about her power. Considering herself "the Hope" of all "poor, crazed beings" and "the Revelation" to them,[66] she promised, "I shall see their chains off, I shall take them into the green fields . . . and a little child shall lead them."[67] One of Barton's early biographers felt compelled to make similar claims for her: she had "magnetic power," the "magnetism of mercy."[68] It is not far from here to the primitive healing power, originally allied to "animal magnetism," which Mary Baker Eddy advertised as her own.[69]

At the start of the twentieth century, Robert Herrick would write a novel called *The Healer* (1911) about a brilliant young doctor who possessed this almost magical gift, but could keep it only if he disavowed totally the corrupt professionalism of modern medicine. The women nurses of the Civil War were believers in this creed: *because* they had been excluded from the ranks of the official medical world, they had found the healing power which their male colleagues had perhaps forever lost. Time after time, the diaries, letters and biographies of wartime nurses assert that what the wounded men need is not just medicine and food (which the nurses of course bring), but

---

tution. For an unfavorable view of her connection with the Red Cross, see Robinson, *White Caps*, pp. 219 ff.

[63] Quoted in Epler, *Clara Barton*, p. 235.

[64] Quoted in Ross, *Angel of the Battlefield*, p. 239.

[65] Tiffany, *Dorothy Lynde Dix*, p. 262.

[66] Marshall, *Dorthea Dix*, pp. 140-115.

[67] Tiffany, *Dorothy Lynde Dix*, p. 266.

[68] Epler, *Clara Barton*, p. 381.

[69] For an account of Mrs. Eddy, see Edwin Franden Dakin, *Mrs. Eddy: The Biography of a Virginal Mind* (New York and London, 1929).

the *presence* of a woman, the touch of her hand. They seem to insinuate that if manhood brought on a war, womanhood was in itself healing. E. H. Locke makes clear the tremendous regenerating effect the simple appearance of two women actually had on a group of sick men in an army hospital: "Their very few words were woman's words, but they had a power man's do not." Unwilling or unable to explain this effect, Locke can only say that they seemed like beings from "another sphere," "representative" of all the women "at home."[70] The magical perfume they exude is clearly the aura of home, and this aura was the secret weapon all the volunteer nurses possessed, a weapon both powerful in its effects and safe for its user.

Women had been told that the precincts of home were sacred and assured by men desirous of keeping them there that *they* were sacred because they stayed at home. Barred from professional medical ranks, they were encouraged to believe they could be healers by the hearth. Who could argue, then, when, at the imperious call of a land battling with itself, of a country engaged in *family* strife, some women charitably shared with the nation the precious powers they had lavished on their kin—the maternal gifts of protection and healing? And in doing so, they accomplished a great deal. Their work in improving sanitary conditions in Civil War hospitals has never been questioned, but they did more. In bringing home virtues to witness against "professional" methods, they did not so much make the world a home, as they helped to make themselves at home *in the world*. Nursing the troops in the Civil War had not only offered them a chance to criticize the imprisoning professional code of the military medical corps from the perspective of their maternal natures; it had also given them the opportunity to make a profession, and a competitive one, out of their maternity. Significantly, after the war accredited schools for nurses opened their doors and women doctors began to appear in small but increasing numbers.[71] The wartime nurses, it seems, had joined a bigger army than they knew.

[70] Locke, *Three Years in Camp and Hospital*, p. 184.

[71] On the progress of nursing, see Roberts, *American Nursing*, and Robinson, *White Caps*. On women doctors, see Kate Campbell-Hurd, *Medical Women in America: A Short History of the Pinoeer Medical Women of America and of a Few of Their Colleagues in England* (Fort Pierce Beach, Fla., 1933), and Esther Pohl Lovejoy, *Women Doctors of the World* (New York, 1957). The women pioneers of medicine in America appeared in the decade before the Civil War, most notably the Blackwell sisters in New York and Marie Zakrewska in Boston, but their numbers did not reach any significant count until after the war.

# THE ROMANCE AND REALITY OF DEFEAT: SOUTHERN WOMEN IN 1865

BY NANCY T. KONDERT*

"The last day of '64, and much coveted peace seemingly as distant as ever. . . . Although woe and desolation stare at us every way we turn, the heart of the patriot is as firm as ever, and determined that, come what may, he will never yield. . . ."[1] Thus, despite the overwhelming evidence of the collapse of morale in the winter of 1864-1865, a great many Southern women did refuse to yield to the apparently inevitable fate of their cause. In Midway, Georgia, Anna Maria Green mourned, "But we were despondent our heads bowed and our hearts crushed – The Yankees in possession of Milledgeville. The Yankee flag waved from the Capitol – Our degradation was bitter but we knew it could not be long, and we never desponded, our trust was still strong. No, we went through the house singing, 'We live and die with Davis.' How can they hope to subjugate the South? The people are firmer than ever before."[2] And although some perceived, "Blue-black is our horizon.", and felt ". . . we are at the last gasp, . . . It is too late. There is no help for us now, in God or

*Mrs. Kondert is a doctoral student at the University of Southwestern Louisiana. This article is adopted from her master's thesis written at McNeese State University.

[1]Kate Cumming, *The Journal of a Confederate Nurse*. Richard Barksdale Harwell, ed. (Baton Rouge, 1959), December 31, 1864, p. 246. Hereinafter cited as *Confederate Nurse*.

[2]Anna Maria Green, *The Journal of a Milledgeville Girl 1861-1867*. James C. Bonner, ed. (Athens, Georgia, 1964), November 25, 1864, p. 63. Hereinafter cited as *Milledgeville Girl*.

men.",[3] the faith in the Confederate cause and the determination to succeed would not die easily.

Even as late as April, 1865, after the surrender of General Robert E. Lee's army, there were those Southern women who simply refused to accept defeat. In Richmond, Mrs. Mary Custis Lee would not recognize a victorious North, stating that " 'General Lee is not the Confederacy,' and that there is 'life in the old land yet.' "[4] Elsewhere, Emma LeConte described Columbia as "dark and gloomy. I do not despair as many do, but I feel very sad and bitter. . . . The South *will* not give up — I can not think that — but I look forward to years of suffering and grief, years of desolation and bloodshed." When news of Appomattox reached Columbia, Miss LeConte "was so overwhelmed by the thought of Lee's surrender that there seemed no ground under my feet. . . . But something *must* turn up — help *must* come — 'The darkest hour's before the dawn.' If there should be no dawn!"[5]

With such fierce belief in the righteousness of their cause and an iron will to win, it was with great difficulty that Southern women recognized the final collapse of the Confederacy. Deep remorse and sadness swelled their hearts as they acknowledged defeat. Upon confirmation of Lee's surrender, Anna Maria Green wrote, "Ah! this is the darkest page in the book of time. . . . But God's will must be done and yet in His appointed time and way He will deliver us."[6] And Kate Cuming

[3]Mary Boykin Chesnut, *A Diary From Dixie*. Ben Ames Williams, ed. (Boston, 1961), April 7, 1865, February 26, 1865, pp. 518, 488. Hereinafter cited as *Diary From Dixie*.

[4]*Diary of a Southern Refugee*, April 16, 1865, as cited in Matthew Page Andrews, *The Women of the South in War Times*. (Baltimore, 1927), pp. 411-412. Hereinafter cited as Andrews, *Women of the South*.

[5]Emma LeConte, *When the War Ended: The Diary of Emma LeConte*. Earl Schenck Miers, ed. (New York, 1957), April 13, 1865, April 23, 1865, pp. 85, 96-97. Hereinafter cited as *Diary of Emma LeConte*.

[6]*Milledgeville Girl*, April 25, 1865, p. 73.

again exhibited her deep faith as she prepared to meet the victors. "Well, we are all ready for the enemy. . . . I see no way of escape, and am making the best of it. . . . I will do what I can, and leave the rest to God. . . . My faith is strong in the belief that there is an unseen hand directing all our ways."[7] In North Carolina, Mrs. Catherine Edmondston revealed the despondency which the terms of Appomattox pressed upon her, "How can I write it! How find words to tell what has befallen us! *General Lee has surrendered.* . . . Surrendered the remnant of his noble army to an overwhelming horde of mercenary Yankee knaves and foreigners!"[8] And a young Virginia girl despaired, "Then came the blow. We heard that Lee had surrendered. Lee surrendered! that couldn't be true! . . . Hope was dead at last."[9]

On April 18, in Macon, Georgia, Eliza Frances Andrews recorded the dejection and apathy around her concerning Lee's surrender, "No one seems to doubt it, and everybody feels ready to give up hope. 'It is useless to struggle longer,' seems to be the common cry, and the poor wounded men go hobbling about the streets with despair on their faces." As preparations were made for evacuating Macon, Miss Andrews drove her rig from the station to the hotel. ". . . when I saw what a wild commotion the approach of the Yankees created, I lost all hope and gave up our cause as doomed. We made a brave fight but the odds against us were too great. The spell of invincibility has left us and gone

[7] *Confederate Nurse*, April 18, 1865, p. 273.

[8] Looking Glass Plantation, April 16, 1865, as cited in Clarence Poe, ed., *True Tales of the South at War How Soldiers Fought and Families Lived, 1861-1865.* (Chapel Hill, 1961), p. 138. Hereinafter cited as Poe, *True Tales*.

[9] Myrta Lockett Avary, ed., *A Virginia Girl in the Civil War, 1861-1865.* (New York, 1910), pp. 373-374. Hereinafter cited as Avary, *Virginia Girl*.

over to the heavy battalions of the enemy."[10]

Reactions to the surrender were by no means consistent. The mistress of Burge Plantation near Covington, Georgia, wrote, "General Lee has surrendered to the victorious Grant. Well, if it will only hasten the conclusion of this war, I am satisfied." She continued her journal entry, criticizing Southern leaders and blaming them for the death and destruction which had occurred. Quoting Robert Toombs, she lamented: " 'I will drink every drop of blood they will shed.' Oh, blinded men! Rivers deep and strong have been shed, and where are we now? — a ruined, subjugated people!"[11] The poor, backwoods Southern women were generally glad to see the end of the war. Kate Cumming, commenting upon the Confederate defeat, recorded evidence of this when she made the following entry in her journal, "It seems that before the surrender of Richmond the dead-letter bag was opened, and on reading the letters from the soldiers' wives, nearly all were begging the men to desert!" Miss Cumming noted that because of this many gentlemen were blaming the women for the failure of the South. She, however, defended the women, and felt "the rich people who remained at home and did nothing for the soldiers' families, are greatly to blame."[12]

Despair, dejection, hopelessness swept across the South destroying all other human emotions. "The demoralization is complete. We are whipped, there is no doubt about it. Everybody feels it, . . . though none of us like to say so." On April 21, 1865, Eliza Andrew

[10]Eliza Frances Andrews, *The War-Time Journal of a Georgia Girl*. Spencer Bidwell King, Jr., ed. (Macon, 1960), April 18, 1865, pp. 153-155. Hereinafter cited as *Journal of a Georgia Girl*.

[11]Dolly Sumner Lunt, *A Woman's Wartime Journal*. (Macon, 1927), April 29, 1865, pp. 57-60. Hereinafter cited as Lunt, *Journal*.

[12]*Confederate Nurse*, May 29, 1865, p. 296.

continued, "It is all over with us now, and there is nothing to do but bow our heads in the dust and let the hateful conquerors trample us under their feet. . . . We fought nobly and fell bravely, overwhelmed by numbers and resources, with never a hand held out to save us. I hate all the world when I think of it."[13] Perhaps Emma LeConte's sad discourse, expressing disbelief and horror, yet still seeking avoidance of the fate seemingly destined for the South, best revealed the sentiment of many women.

> The South lies prostrate — their foot is on us — there is no help. . . . who could have believed who has watched this four years' struggle that it could have ended like this! They say *right* always triumphs, but what cause could have been more just than ours? Have we suffered all — have our brave men fought so desperately and died so nobly for *this?* For four years there has been throughout this broad land little else than the anguish of anxiety — the misery of sorrow over dear ones sacrificed — for nothing! Is all this blood spilled in vain — will it not cry from the ground on the day we yield to these Yankees! *We* give up to the *Yankees!* . . . Why does not the President call out the women if there are [not] enough men? We would go and *fight*, too, — we would better all die together.
>
> . . . oh God! It is too horrible. . . . It seems dreadful to see anyone smile. . . . It is so terrible as to be unthinkable. . . . I am too sick at heart to write any more.[14]

Everyone waited in despondency and suspense to learn what indignities would be forced upon them. Despair to the depths of their souls was shown in these lines: "Till it [subjugation] comes, 'Let us eat, drink and be merry, for to-morrow we die.' Only we have

[13]*Journal of a Georgia Girl*, April 18, 1865, April 21, 1865, pp. 153, 171.
[14]*Diary of Emma LeConte*, April 20, 1865, pp. 90-91.

almost nothing to eat, and drink, and still less to be merry about." And added to the tragedy everywhere there was a new pathos in the visible signs of past struggle and sacrifice, for now ". . . we know it was all for nothing."[15]

The period immediately following surrender was a time of transition from war to occupation in which anxiety reigned supreme. All was in a state of disorganization and tumult, and there existed no law ". . . save the primitive code that might makes right." Many women felt that the war, with all its cruelty and destruction, had been better than the crumbling society left by the degrading peace. "The props that held society up are broken. . . . The suspense and anxiety in which we live are terrible."[16] "It is cruel — it is *unjust*. I used to dream about peace, to pray for it, but this is worse than war."[17]

Yet despite the "hunger and nakedness and death and pestilence" everywhere, a Virginia girl described a spirit still present in the South as she ". . . laughed and sang and played on the piano — and never believed in actual defeat and subjugation."[18] And if Southern women felt "crushed and bowed down to earth" by their defeat, it was "in sorrow, but not in shame. No! I am more of a rebel to-day than ever I was when things looked brightest for the Confederacy."[19] Mrs. Mary Boykin Chesnut, viewing the destruction left by General William T. Sherman's army, found it difficult not to curse him; she "wept incessantly at first." Then as her husband commented that the roses were already hiding the

[15]*Journal of a Georgia Girl*, April 25, 1865, April 18, 1865, pp. 185, 155.
[16]*Ibid.*, May 2, 1865, p. 90.
[17]*Diary of Emma LeConte*, April 20, 1865, p. 90.
[18]Avary, *Virginia Girl*, p. 356.
[19]*Journal of a Georgia Girl*, April 21, 1865, p. 172.

ruins, Mrs. Chesnut, reconciling in her mind the circumstances of the world in which she lived, vowed, "If we are a crushed people, I will never be a whimpering, pining slave."[20]

Poverty, destruction, desolation met the searching gazes of Southerners attempting to begin anew. Yet Miss Andrews, in Washington, Georgia, characterized well the spirit in which the challenge of the present was met. "It seems strange to think how we laugh and jest now, over things that we would once have thought it impossible to live through. We are all poor together, and nobody is ashamed of it. We live from hand to mouth like beggars."[21] And Mrs. Susan P. H. Drake, writing to her son from her home at Magnolia Springs plantation, revealed her faithful reliance upon Providence even in the face of so much disaster: "In some cases indolence induces poverty — at present poverty compels us to vigorous exertion — . . . But I do not believe the Lord will forsake the seed of the rightious *[sic]* — Though for a season we may walk in poverty & darkness let us wait patiently & trustfully for the leadings of Providence & doubtless a way will be made for us to support ourselves."[22]

However, the dark political future of the South did settle a deep and heavy gloom across the land. The women mourned the fall of the Confederacy, and even more intensely feared the oppression which might be brought to bear by the conquering North. By May of 1865, many felt, "The military men, who do the hard and cruel things in war, seem to be more merciful in

[20]*Diary From Dixie*, May 2, 1865, p. 527.
[21]*Journal of a Georgia Girl*, June 5, 1865, p. 286.
[22]Letter, Susan P. H. Drake to H. Winbourne Drake, June 23, 1865: in Claribel Drake Collection in possession of Dr. W. Magruder Drake, Lafayette, Louisiana. Hereinafter cited as Drake Collection.

peace than the politicians who stay at home and do the talking." Even Christian feelings were overcome by the actions and attitudes of the Yankees in the North. ". . . I can't believe that when Christ said, 'Love your enemies,' he meant Yankees. Of course I don't want their souls to be lost, . . . but as they are not being punished in this world, I don't see how else they are going to get their deserts." And by June of 1865, emotions had intensified so that as a means of expressing the hatred felt these "wretches," some harsh descriptive phrases were used before the term Yankee, such as "hateful Yankee," "thieving Yankee," and so on, ". . . but even this is too mild for me. I feel sometimes as if I would just like to come out with a good round 'Damn!' "[23]

The hatred and contempt Southern women felt for the Yankees was most often released full force upon the closest representatives, the Northern soldiers. Emma LeConte admonished:

> These Yankee officers who behave like gentlemen — if Yankees *can* be gentlemen — take it rather hard that they are treated so coldly and allowed no social intercourse with the citizens. . . . Great Heavens! What do they expect? They invade our country, murder our people, desolate our homes, conquer us, subject us to every indignity and humiliation — and then we must offer our hands with pleasant smiles . . . ! Are they crazy? What do they think we are made of?[24]

And Eliza Andrews revealed further explanation of the contempt in which these troops were held. ". . . these 'conquering heroes' have the face to complain because they are not admitted to our homes — as if we would

[23]*Journal of a Georgia Girl*, May 5, 1865, April 17, 1865, June 21, 1865, pp. 217, 149, 305.

[24]*Diary of Emma LeConte*, May 29, 1865, pp. 108-109.

stoop to share their attentions with our negro maids, even if there was not a yawning gulf of blood between us and them."[25]

Indeed the association of the Northern soldiers with the Southern Negroes repulsed the women of the South and even led some to theorize on the future results of this interaction. "The negroes throng around them [Northern soldiers] and they affiliate pleasantly with their colored brethren — even affectionately. . . . and why not? Doubtless they recognize in them not only their equals, but their superiors. *Perhaps* negroes *may* come in contact with them without being degraded, but I doubt it, for the negro is an imitative race. He has been elevated to some extent but will quickly retrograde in associating with such white people as these. . . . These men seem to be the meanest type of the mean nation."[26]

The fall of the Confederacy completed the freeing of the Negro slaves throughout the South. The attitudes and reactions of Southern women toward these Negroes and toward their newly acquired freedom were generally ones of sympathy and pity. Miss Emma Mordecai recorded the departure of a number of servants in May of 1865, "What an uprooting of social ties, and tearing asunder of almost kindred associations and destruction of true loyalty, this strange, new state of things produced!! The disturbance to the whites and the privations it will at first entail upon the poor, improvident Negroes is incalculable."[27] In Georgia, Eliza Andrews expressed her feelings and fears, ". . . I don't think I can ever cherish any very hard feelings towards the poor, ignorant blacks. They are like grown up children

[25] *Journal of a Georgia Girl,* June 5, 1865, p. 288.
[26] *Diary of Emma LeConte,* May 18, 1865, pp. 102-103.
[27] Mordecai Letters and Diary, May 6, 1865, as cited in Poe, *True Tales,* p. 198.

turned adrift in the world. . . . Poor creatures, I shudder to think of what they must suffer in the future, and of what they are going to make this whole country suffer before we are done with them." [28] Mrs. Judith McGuire, living in Virginia, lamented the departure of ". . . the respectful and respectable servants, born in the family and brought up with an affection for the household which seemed a part of their nature, and which so largely contributed to the happiness both of master and servant." [29]

The bonds broken by the freeing of the Negroes were much more than merely economic. In many instances, Southerners, often women, felt the need to provide some form of security for their freed slaves.

> What I shall do with mine is a question that troubles me day and night. It is my last thought at night and the first in the morning. I told them several days ago they were free to do as they liked. But it is my duty to make some provision for them. I thank God that they are freed, and yet what can I do with them? They are old and young, not profitable to hire. What provision can I make? [30]

Truly, many believed, "Poor darkeys, they are the real victims of the war, after all." [31]

Southern women shared with their men apprehension and distrust of what the freedmen might do. Jane R. Drake acknowledged this distrust in a letter to her sister-in-law in Louisiana. "The state in which our country now is, especially the spirit that influences the negros is most harrassing & enough to destroy all patience; it has already totally annihilated my confidence

[28] *Journal of a Georgia Girl*, June 21, 1865, p. 340.
[29] *Diary of a Southern Refugee*, April 24, 1865, as cited in Poe, *True Tales*, p. 184.
[30] Lunt, *Journal*, May 29, 1865, p. 63.
[31] *Journal of a Georgia Girl*, May 31, 1865, p. 277.

in the whole race —"[32] And looking toward the future, Eliza Andrews voiced the fear that, "A race war is sure to come, . . . the Yankees . . . are sowing the wind, but they will leave us to reap the whirlwind. No power on earth can raise an inferior, savage race above their civilized masters and keep them there. . . . The higher above his natural capacity they force the negro in their rash experiments to justify themselves for his emancipation, the greater must be his fall in the end, and the more bitter our sufferings in the meantime."[33] Additionally, economic pressures increased the tensions between the races. Mother Hyacinth, in describing the economic results of the war around Presentation Convent, Louisiana, exposed a source of increasing tensions for the future. "Our people here have been financially ruined by the war and by the emancipation of their slaves. . . . Until now, the slaves were the only ones who worked. Now, the white people will have to work. O, how this humiliates their pride!"[34]

The Civil War was ended; the Confederacy was gone. The women of the South had endured much of the horror that the war brought. They had met great difficulties, had overcome great obstacles; but the greatest task of all lay before them. That was the task of facing the future and living in spite of it. Kate Cumming expressed well the attitude which many women had developed by the end of May, 1865.

> This year has developed the fate of the South. Time has revealed the utter loss of all our hopes. A change must pass over every political and social idea, custom,

[32]Letter, Jane R. Drake to Lizzie (Mrs. H. W.) Drake, June 23, 1865. Drake Collection.

[33]*Journal of a Georgia Girl*, June 27, 1865, p. 316.

[34]Letter, Mother Hyacinth to her family in France, September 15, 1865 in Sister Dorothea Olga McCants, trans, and ed., *They Came to Louisiana Letters of a Catholic Mission 1854 - 1882* (Baton Rouge, 1970), p. 176.

> and relation. The consummation makes the year just passed ever memorable in our annals. In it gathers all the interest of the bloody tragedy; from it begins a new era, midst poverty, tears, and sad memories of the past. O, may we learn the lesson that all of this is designed to teach; . . . . And forgetting the past, save the lessons which it teaches, let us . . . redeem the time, live humbly, and trust God for future good.[35]

But many other Southern women, with their eyes aglow and their cheeks burning, though ". . . overwhelmed, overpowered, and trodden underfoot . . . ," kept the fires of passion lit with " 'immortal hate and study of revenge' . . . ." And revealing a widespread sentiment, Eliza Frances Andrews once again displayed the spirit and fire of Southern women by her thoughts. We can ". . . go into voluntary slavery, or resist and be thrown into chains. I don't suppose it will make much difference in the end which course we take, but it has always been my doctrine that if you have got to go to the devil anyway, it is better to go fighting, and so keep your self-respect."[36]

[35] *Confederate Nurse*, May 29, 1865, p. 307.
[36] *Journal of a Georgia Girl*, May 15, 1865, June 23, 1865, pp. 254, 311.

# Black Women and the Great War: Mobilization and Reform in the South

By WILLIAM J. BREEN

HISTORIANS HAVE DEVOTED RELATIVELY LITTLE ATTENTION TO THE study of grassroots America during World War I. Little is known about how national policies were implemented at the local level and how the American population in general, and American women in particular, were brought into the war effort.[1] Practically nothing has been written concerning the attitude of black women, particularly southern black women, toward the war or about the attempt of the national administration to incorporate them into the general war effort.[2] This paper explores some aspects of the little-

[1] The most encyclopedic coverage of domestic America during World War I remains Frederic L. Paxson, *America at War, 1917–1918* (Boston, 1939), which is Volume II of his *American Democracy and the World War* (3 vols., Boston and Berkeley, 1936–1948). Some of the state studies do attempt to come to grips with the question of how national policies were implemented at the state and local levels. Examples of the better studies include Franklin F. Holbrook and Livia Appel, *Minnesota in the War with Germany* (2 vols., St. Paul, Minn., 1928–1932); Benjamin F. Shambaugh, ed., *Chronicles of the World War* (7 vols., Iowa City, Iowa, 1920–1923); Marguerite E. Jenison, comp., *The War-Time Organization of Illinois* (Springfield, Ill., 1923), Volume V of Theodore C. Pease, ed., *Illinois in the World War* (6 vols., Springfield, Ill., 1921–1923). A brief account of the role of women in the war is contained in William L. O'Neill, *Everyone Was Brave: The Rise and Fall of Feminism in America* (Chicago, 1969), 169–224. The best contemporary accounts of the role of women in the war are Ida C. Clarke, *American Women and the World War* (New York, 1918), and Emily N. Blair, *The Woman's Committee, United States Council of National Defense: An Interpretative Report, April 21, 1917, to February 27, 1919* (Washington, 1920).

[2] The best contemporary account of the role of black women in World War I is Alice Dunbar-Nelson, "Negro Women in War Work" in Emmett J. Scott, ed., *Scott's Official History of the American Negro in the World War* ([Chicago], 1919), 374–97. A more personal account of wartime work in a government department and organizational work on behalf of southern black women and girls for the War Camp Community Service in the immediate aftermath of the Armistice is Mary C. Terrell, *A Colored Woman in a White World* (Washington, D. C., 1940), Chaps. 25, 32. For a discussion of the administration's attempt to mobilize the black male population see Jane L. Scheiber and Harry N. Scheiber, "The Wilson Administration and the Wartime Mobilization of Black Americans, 1917–18," *Labor History*, X (Summer 1969), 433–58.

MR. BREEN is a senior lecturer at La Trobe University, Melbourne, Australia. He is indebted to the Council of La Trobe University and the American Council of Learned Societies for research support for this project.

known effort made by the Committee on Women's Defense Work of the Council of National Defense (also known as the Woman's Committee) to achieve this aim. Southern black women responded patriotically to the war, and, in addition, many saw the possibilities for social reform that the wartime situation offered.[3] This reformist thrust is reflected both in the quiet struggle over the appropriate form of wartime organization for black women and in the actual programs adopted. The Woman's Committee maintained a constant, if discreet, pressure on the southern states to integrate black women into the civilian war effort on terms that made many white southerners balk. The war ended too soon for the reform impetus to come to fruition, but the direction of the change was clear.

Little or no thought had been given by the administration to the potential role of women in the event of America's becoming involved in the European war. Once war was declared, the national women's organizations deluged Washington with patriotic offers of assistance. Not quite knowing what to do with these offers, the administration decided to establish a Woman's Committee under the general aegis of the Council of National Defense, a planning body created in 1916 primarily concerned with the problems of industrial mobilization. The major national women's associations were represented on the Woman's Committee, and it was believed that this body would somehow serve as a point of contact between the national government and the general war effort on the one hand and the women of the nation on the other.[4] Once organized, the Woman's Committee divided the work to be done into departments or subcommittees and began to build a nationwide network of state committees.[5]

Although the Council of National Defense, acting in cooperation with the various state governors, had already established men's committees called Councils of Defense in each state, the Woman's Committee insisted on separate state women's organizations in the belief that there was, in fact, some unique role for the women of the

[3] On the question of domestic reform see Allen F. Davis, "Welfare, Reform and World War I," *American Quarterly*, XIX (Fall 1967), 516–33; and Otis L. Graham, Jr., *The Great Campaigns: Reform and War in America, 1900–1928* (Englewood Cliffs, N.J., 1971), 97–114.

[4] For general accounts of the establishment of the Woman's Committee see O'Neill, *Everyone Was Brave*, 169–224; and Blair, *The Woman's Committee*, Chap. 1. The National Association of Colored Women was represented on the general committee of the Woman's Committee.

[5] By July 1918 the Woman's Committee had the following departments of work: Registration for Service; Food Production and Home Economics; Food Administration; Women in Industry; Child Welfare; Maintenance of Existing Social Service Agencies; Health and Recreation; Educational Propaganda; Liberty Loan; Home and Allied Relief. See Blair, *The Woman's Committee*, 20–21.

country to play in the wartime crisis. As the war progressed both the men's and the women's state committees gradually expanded through the creation of county, township, and eventually community organizations.[6] The ultimate aim was to involve the entire population in the domestic war effort. The anomaly of this objective and the almost totally white membership of these various state committees became increasingly obvious. This was especially so in the southern states, and as time went on groping efforts began to be made to incorporate the black community, both men and women, into the organizational structure.

The pressure to incorporate the black population into the war effort in an organized and systematic way came from several directions. In the Woman's Committee there had been an increasing sense of this need, and many of the state and local organizations had begun to take some faltering steps in that direction by the winter of 1917–1918.[7] In addition, the men's Section on Cooperation with States (later the State Councils Section of the Council of National Defense) began to put pressure on the various state Councils of Defense, particularly in the South, to organize the black population in a systematic manner.[8] In February 1918 the State Councils Section circularized the southern state Councils of Defense with a suggested plan for the establishment of a statewide Negro council as an auxiliary to each state council.[9] Washington followed up this circular with various other communications on the same topic throughout 1918, and this pressure began to bear fruit as more and more of the state councils in the South decided to organize the black male population.[10] By mid-1918 other federal

[6] It was not until the very end of the war, in mid-September 1918, that these dual organizations in the states finally merged and formed the Field Division of the Council of National Defense.

[7] Woman's Committee, Minutes, Meeting of January 29, 1918, p. 278, 13A-C5, Box 570, Records of the Committee on Women's Defense Work, Records of the Council of National Defense, Record Group 62 (National Archives, Suitland Federal Record Center, Md.); hereinafter cited as WC Minutes with date and page number. Except for one citation in note 65, all manuscript materials are from the Records of the Council of National Defense, RG 62.

[8] See "Increasing the Patriotic Efforts of the Negroes in the Southern States," January 7, 1918 (unsigned memorandum: Dorothy Pope?), Reports of State Councils of Defense, Records of the Field Division, 15-C1, Box 908, folder marked "State Councils Section: Negro Organization"; cited hereinafter as Repts. SCD with category and box number.

[9] See "General Letter No. 44, February 23, 1918," *ibid.* This circular, issued by the State Councils Section of the Council of National Defense, stressed the valuable assistance that the Negro community, if organized, could give to the war effort in the states and suggested the establishment of Negro county Councils of Defense which would work under the direction of the white county councils. See also Dorothy Pope memorandum, "Response to General Letter No. 44 Calling for Organization of the Negroes," March 15, 1918, *ibid.*

[10] See "Organization of Negroes as Conducted by the Southern State Councils" (n.d.: circa July–August 1918. 24 pp. typed memorandum, unsigned), *ibid.*

agencies with machinery in the southern states had begun to incorporate the blacks. The Food Administration, the Department of Labor, and the speakers among the Four-Minute Men of the Committee of Public Information all took steps in this direction.[11]

As this pressure to incorporate the black population began to mount, the War Department helped to crystallize the attitude of the Woman's Committee and to force some positive action. In July 1918 Emmett Jay Scott, special assistant to the secretary of war, approached the Woman's Committee because of concern about reports of unrest among the black population stemming mainly from discrimination practiced by whites in war work.[12] He also approached the Woman's Division of the Committee on Public Information over the same matter.[13] Recommending the appointment of a black field representative to work among the black women in the various states, Scott argued that it "would do much to build up the morale" of the black women of the country.[14] He also pressed for the establishment of a separate black woman's council at the national level as a subcommittee of the Woman's Committee in Washington, or, at least, the establishment of councils composed of black women as subcommittees of, and directly responsible to, each state Woman's Committee. Such organizations, he thought, would give the black women of the country some national, or statewide, recognition and encourage active participation in the war effort. In response, the Woman's Committee decided to appoint Alice Dunbar Nelson as a field representative to undertake a trip through the southern states to report on the

[11] Ernest T. Attwell of Tuskegee Institute was appointed by the Food Administration as a field worker among the Negroes in the South. He later went to Washington and directed the Negro Section of the Food Administration. See John H. Franklin, *From Slavery to Freedom: A History of Negro Americans* (New York, 1969), 471. Dr. George Edmund Haynes of Fisk University was appointed to the specially created post of Director of Negro Economics in the Department of Labor in May 1918. See Scheiber and Scheiber, "The Wilson Administration," 448–49. The Scheibers emphasize (pp. 449–50) that all these efforts by the government agencies were exhortative and patriotic only. There was no emphasis on reform. By contrast, the Woman's Committee made one of the most serious efforts and one that did have more overtly reformist overtones. Alice Dunbar-Nelson believed that "The Council of National Defense made the best organized attempt at mobilizing the colored women of all the war organizations." See Dunbar-Nelson, "Negro Women in War Work," 383.

[12] WC Minutes, July 8, 1918, p. 505. For comments on Negro unrest and anxiety see Franklin, *From Slavery to Freedom*, 474–75; and Dunbar-Nelson "Negro Women in War Work," 394.

[13] WC Minutes, July 8, 1918, p. 505.

[14] The quotation is from Miss Patterson's report of Scott's conversation. See Hannah Jane Patterson to Walter S. Gifford, July 8, 1918, Central Correspondence File, 1918, Records of the Committee on Women's Defense Work, 13A-A2, Box 496, File 79 (cited hereinafter as Corr. CWDW with category, box, and file numbers); WC Minutes, July 8, 1918, pp. 505-506.

situation and help stimulate organization among the black women.[15]

Born and educated in New Orleans, Alice Ruth Moore taught literature and published her first book of poems and short stories in 1895. Two years later she moved to New York, began teaching in the Brooklyn schools, and became involved in the National Association of Colored Women, serving as recording secretary between 1897 and 1899. In 1898 she married Paul Laurence Dunbar, a young black poet and literary figure. After her husband died of tuberculosis in 1906, Mrs. Dunbar moved to Wilmington, Delaware, and began to teach at the Howard High School, where she remained for eighteen years, eventually becoming head of the English Department. In 1916 she married Robert John Nelson, editor and publisher of the weekly Wilmington *Advocate* and an activist in the fight for Negro civil rights. During American involvement in the World War Mrs. Nelson was given a year's leave of absence to work as a field representative among the black women for the Woman's Committee.[16]

On her trip through the South Mrs. Nelson was on the alert for signs of disaffection and kept the Washington office informed of what she learned. Predictably, it was a fairly depressing picture. In New Orleans she found the grievance was quite specific "because government employment bureaus here recognize in every colored girl who applies for work only a potential scrub woman, no matter how educated and refined the girl may be."[17] In Alabama and Mississippi the local Red Cross had refused the black women permission to do canteen work at the railroad stations "because they would not permit the colored women to wear the canteen uniform."[18] Understandably, this had caused "some feeling among the colored women."[19] Mrs. Nelson noted that Vicksburg, in particular, "has not been exactly a hot-bed of patriotism among the colored people." The attitude of the black community in the city had been further embittered by a tar-and-feather episode that had occurred a few weeks before Mrs. Nelson's arrival: one of the victims was a black woman whose husband was fighting in France. "Since that time the colored brass band will not lead the colored draftees to the

[15] WC Minutes, July 8, 1918, p. 505.

[16] For biographical details see Nick A. Ford, "Alice Dunbar Nelson," in Edward T. James, *et al.*, eds. *Notable American Women 1607–1950: A Biographical Dictionary* (3 vols., Cambridge, Mass., 1971), II, 614–15.

[17] Nelson to Patterson, August 14, 1918, Corr. CWDW, 13A-A2, Box 512, File 131.

[18] Nelson to Patterson, August 23, 1918, *ibid.*

[19] Nelson to Patterson, August 26, 1918, *ibid.* Mrs. Nelson referred to this grievance concerning the Red Cross, specifically in Montgomery, Alabama, and Vicksburg, Mississippi.

station, seeing no cause for making music."[20] The black women had other causes for complaint in Mississippi. When the Hoover pledge cards for food conservation were distributed, "the white people would not let the colored ministers give them to their congregations. Said colored people needn't sign them, it wasn't necessary. Too much like social equality."[21]

Mrs. Nelson believed that among the Negro community in Mississippi "even the most ignorant, are doing a lot of bitter thinking. . . . It isn't German propaganda either, it's American propaganda, that is working harm among the people."[22] Nevertheless, even though discontented over the deliberate exclusion from official participation in the more important aspects of the war effort, southern black women remained anxious to demonstrate their patriotism when given the opportunity. In Tennessee, for example, Mrs. Nelson found the black women "eager, interested, but not sure of their ground"[23] Even in Mississippi she reported that, overall, "the colored women are alive and anxious to work . . . ."[24]

Mrs. Nelson's reception in the southern states indicated the different perceptions held by the various white state chairmen of the urgency of the problem. Most of the chairmen were polite and quite willing to discuss the problem with her, though many thought the proposed organization to be unnecessary. The chairman of the South Carolina Woman's Committee, for example, saw "no necessity for her [Nelson's] visiting South Carolina at this time to organize," though she was perfectly willing to talk over the matter with Mrs. Nelson.[25] The latter spent "quite an interesting hour discussing problems and threshing out difficulties."[26] In North Carolina, Mrs. J. Eugene (Laura Holmes) Reilley approved the idea of a field representative to work among the black women and was quite willing to discuss the matter with Mrs. Nelson.[27] In Louisiana the state chairman took Mrs. Nelson's visit very personally: "But she is hurt, thinking that I've come to find fault with her work or to spy upon her . . . . will you try to disabuse her mind of the idea that the Committee at Washington thinks she isn't giving the colored

[20] Nelson to Patterson, August 23, 1918, *ibid.*
[21] Nelson to Patterson, August 21, 1918, *ibid.*
[22] *Ibid.*
[23] Nelson to Patterson, September 10, 1918, *ibid.*
[24] Nelson to Patterson, August 19, 1918, *ibid.*
[25] Mrs. J. Otey Reid to Patterson, August 20, 1918, Corr. CWDW, 13A-A2, Box 522, File 162.
[26] Nelson to Patterson, September 5, 1918, Corr. CWDW, 13A-A2, Box 512, File 131.
[27] Mrs. Eugene Reilley to Mrs. Joseph R. Lamar, July 18, 1918; Reilley to Patterson, September 7, 1918, Corr. CWDW, 13A-A2, Box 512, File 132; Nelson to Patterson, September 7, 1918, Corr. CWDW, 13A-A2, Box 512, File 131.

women a square deal?"[28] Georgia was the only state where Mrs. Nelson was rebuffed by the state chairman.[29]

If her reception had been cool or lukewarm elsewhere, Mrs. Nelson was overwhelmed by the enthusiasm of her welcome in Florida and Mississippi. Here the white state chairmen were fully aware of the problem and were anxious to do everything in their power to incorporate the black women into the patriotic war effort. In Florida the state chairman even arranged for publicity about Paul Laurence Dunbar and his literary work in order to interest the general public in Mrs. Nelson's arrival and invited "a number of prominent white people to come to this meeting to assure the negroes of our interest in their development, and our cooperation in their work."[30] In addition, a speaking itinerary was arranged for Mrs. Nelson throughout the state. Her reception in Mississippi was similarly enthusiastic. There the state chairman, Mrs. Edward McGehee, reported that if she had known the exact date of Mrs. Nelson's arrival, she would have organized a statewide meeting for her, "but as it was I got busy with the long distance phone and telegraph, and made engagements for her in three of the principal cities in the state."[31] Mrs. McGehee was impressed with Mrs. Nelson: "I found her very capable, very intelligent and with good judgement to carry on the work as planned."[32] Mrs. Nelson was equally impressed with the state chairman: "She is delightfully alive, eager and interested. Would keep me in Mississippi indefinitely and feels quite put out that I can spend only a week."[33]

The most contentious issue was not whether to organize the black women in the southern states but what form this proposed organization should take. Only Missouri, a border state, actually thought there was no need at all to organize the black women.[34] Most southern states favored some form of minimal organization of the black population that would ensure a degree of cooperation and coordination with the least likelihood of upsetting existing social relations. Formal, statewide organizations that entailed official rec-

[28] Nelson to Patterson, August 15, 1918, Corr. CWDW, 13A-A2, Box 512, File 131.

[29] For details of the incident see Nelson to Patterson, September 3, 1918 (telegram); see also Patterson to Nelson, September 3, 1918, *ibid.*; Patterson to Mrs. Samuel M. Inman, September 3, 1918; Inman to Patterson, September 6, 1918, Corr. CWDW, 13A-A2, Box 494, File 73; Nelson to Patterson, September 7, 1918, Corr. CWDW, 13A-A2, Box 512, File 131.

[30] Mrs. Frank Jennings to Patterson, August 20, 1918, Corr. CWDW, 13A-A2, Box 493, File 63.

[31] McGehee to Patterson, August 26, 1918, Corr. CWDW, 13A-A2, Box 509, File 123.

[32] *Ibid.*

[33] Nelson to Patterson, August 19, 1918, Corr. CWDW, 13A-A2, Box 512, File 131.

[34] Lamar to Patterson (memorandum), July 23, 1918, Corr. CWDW, 13A-A2, Box 505, File 116.

ognition of southern black women seemed to imply an unnecessary threat to the existing pattern of race relations in the region.

The central office of the Woman's Committee always acted with extreme caution in discussing the role of Mrs. Nelson and the nature of her trip through the South. The Woman's Committee relied on voluntary cooperation, and there was no possibility of coercing the various state committees into taking a position they did not wish to adopt. Miss Hannah Jane Patterson, the resident director of the Woman's Committee, in writing to the Georgia state chairman made clear that Mrs. Nelson "understands that she is to follow whatever plans you may have, and is to undertake only whatever propaganda and organization work you consider wise at this time."[35] In correspondence with Mrs. Reilley of North Carolina Miss Patterson stressed that "It is, of course, understood that whatever Mrs. Nelson does will be under the direction of the State Chairman."[36] After Mrs. Nelson had left North Carolina Miss Patterson reassured the state chairman that the Washington office was not trying to force a new policy on the state: "The Woman's Committee has adopted no policy with regard to organizing the negroes, but has left the matter to each state to determine. . . . The work which we had in mind is an experiment. We wish to carry it out in accordance with the policies of the State Divisions . . . ."[37]

Organization of the black population was a touchy issue in the southern states and, even though Mrs. Nelson was concerned only with black women, it was important that this undertaking have, if not the support, then at least the acquiescence of the men's state organizations. Writing to Mrs. Samuel Martin (Mildred McPheeters) Inman, state chairman in Georgia, Miss Patterson queried: "I presume that you have already consulted with the State Council of Defense, so that any work undertaken among colored women will be in harmony with the work of the State Council in its work among colored men."[38] Other states were likewise reminded to inform the men's state councils of the proposal to work among the black women.[39] In no way was Mrs. Nelson's visit allowed to appear to threaten the status quo in the southern states.

Despite such deference to the views of the southern chairmen, the national Executive Committee did have a fairly clear idea of the

[35] Patterson to Inman, August 15, 1918, Corr. CWDW, 13A-A2, Box 494, File 73.
[36] Patterson to Reilley, September 3, 1918, Corr. CWDW, 13A-A2, Box 512, File 132.
[37] Patterson to Reilley, September 13, 1918, *ibid.*
[38] Patterson to Inman, August 15, 1918, Corr. CWDW, 13A-A2, Box 494, File 73.
[39] See for North Carolina example Patterson to Reilley, September 3, 1918, Corr. CWDW, 13A-A2, Box 512, File 132.

type of organizational structure it believed most desirable. "It is the thought of the [Executive] Committee that the plan . . . of having a section of colored women organized under . . . and responsible to the State Division, would be the best form of organization. This is the plan which has worked out so well in Maryland and Florida."[40] The resident director of the Woman's Committee made these views perfectly clear to Mrs. Nelson in correspondence, adding that these black councils "carry on the same work as the white women and are constantly in consultation with the leaders of the Woman's Committee in their respective districts, whether they be state, county or local."[41] Mrs. Nelson herself considered this type of state organization for the Negro women to be "the only way they would ever become self-reliant."[42]

The views of the Washington office coincided with the aspirations of many of the black women Mrs. Nelson interviewed in her travels through the South. It became increasingly obvious to her that what these black women needed, and wanted, was a semi-independent, statewide organization of their own which would parallel the organization of the white women. For example, in North Carolina Mrs. Nelson commented that Miss Mamie McCullough, chairman of the black war workers at Charlotte, "agreed with me that a separate state organization among the colored people, that is, a colored state chairman, with county chairmen, and local chairmen, would accomplish the best good for the colored people of the state, since it would throw them on their own responsibility and at the same time enable them to reach down into all classes." In a concluding comment on the North Carolina situation Mrs. Nelson wrote: "Miss McCullough and one or two other women whom I saw last evening, tell me that the colored people are simply aching to be put in touch in an official way with the situation."[43]

The southern states exhibited remarkable diversity both in the degree and the type of organization among the black women. Florida stood at one end of the spectrum. It was the only state where Mrs. Nelson considered her visit to have been superfluous:

[40] Patterson to Gifford, July 8, 1918, Corr. CWDW, 13A-A2, Box 496, File 79. In January 1918 the men's State Council Section had suggested that black councils in the southern states be composed of both men and women. The Woman's Committee discussed the matter but decided to leave the exact form and composition of such state and local organizations to be determined at the state level. See WC Minutes, January 29, 1918, p. 278.

[41] Patterson to Nelson, August 19, 1918, Corr. CWDW, 13A-A2, Box 512, File 131.

[42] See comment in Reilley to Patterson, September 7, 1918, Corr. CWDW, 13A-A2, Box 512, File 132.

[43] Nelson to Patterson, September 7, 1918, Corr. CWDW, 13A-A2, Box 512, File 131.

"Florida is so well organized I told them they hardly need me at all." By the time of her visit in August 1918 the black women had a complete organization, which included a black state chairman, black chairmen in each county, and a complete set of committees in each county.[44] Miss Eartha M. White, who had worked with the state labor commissioner, had been appointed state chairman of the black woman's department of the state Woman's Committee. The white state chairman, Mrs. Frank E. Jennings, could not praise her work highly enough.[45] Maryland, which Mrs. Nelson did not visit on her trip, was the only other southern state that had a comparable statewide organization for black women.[46] These two states set an example, but not one enthusiastically emulated in the South as a whole.

Mississippi approximated the Florida model in intention, if not in actual performance. There the energetic white state chairman, Mrs. Edward McGehee of Como, was completely in sympathy with the need for the thorough organization of the black women and had even given up her summer vacation for the first time in her life to stay in Como and push the work.[47] Shortly before Mrs. Nelson's arrival, Mrs. McGehee had appointed a black state chairman to organize the women throughout the state. The woman appointed, Miss Sally Green, was a native of Mississippi, had been a student at Hampton Institute, had taught school for some years, and was currently a county agent for the blacks in Panola County.[48] Mrs. McGehee was so keen to get the black women organized that she paid the salary and expenses of Miss Green out of her own pocket.[49] Mrs. McGehee told the Washington office that she wanted the black women in the state organized "along the same lines that we are," and she circularized her county chairmen asking them to select "the best negro woman you know in your county to work

[44] Nelson to Patterson, August 30, 1918, *ibid.*

[45] "A History of the Activities of the Women of Florida for Service in the World War, 1917–1919. Compiled by the Woman's Committee of Florida, Council of National Defense," signed by Mrs. Frank E. Jennings, state chairman, 11, Reports from State Divisions, State Organization Department, 13L-A1, Box 635; cited hereinafter as Repts. SD with category and box number. Mrs. Frank E. Jennings had succeeded Mrs. William Hocker as state chairman of the Florida Woman's Committee. The Woman's Committee in Florida was infinitely superior to the men's state Council of Defense, which remained a rather lackluster organization.

[46] See Patterson to Nelson, August 19, 1918, Corr. CWDW, 13A-A2, Box 512, File 131.

[47] McGehee to Patterson, August 12, 1918, Corr. CWDW, 13A-A2, Box 509, File 123.

[48] For details on Sally Green see Nelson to Patterson, August 20, 1918, Corr. CWDW, 13A-A2, Box 512, File 131; McGehee to Patterson, August 12, 1918, 13A-A2, Box 509, File 123; McGehee to "My Dear Madam Chairman" (mimeograph), August 26, 1918, Corr. CWDW, 13A-A2, Box 509, File 123.

[49] Nelson to Patterson, August 20, 1918, Corr. CWDW, 13A-A2, Box 512, File 131

under your supervision, and to assist Sally Green."[50] Miss Green was to work under the joint supervision of Mrs. McGehee and the local county chairman, but the object was to establish a thorough statewide organization of black women. Miss Green began a tour of Mississippi on September 1, 1918.[51] By early October Mrs. McGehee was reporting "great results."[52]

But Mrs. Nelson found that Florida and Mississippi were the exception rather than the rule. Most southern states tended to approximate the South Carolina model, known as the Sumter County Plan. This did not really go much beyond appointing a local black to cooperate, when needed, with the local county council, and in no sense did it call for a separate black organization. The chairman of the South Carolina Woman's Committee did not see any need to go beyond this form of cooperation.[53] However, Mrs. Nelson's visit to South Carolina spurred on the effort to organize the black women and also altered the views of the white state chairman. She agreed to a plan involving the appointment of a black woman state chairman, with black chairmen in each county, who would establish black units to work with their white counterparts. Although this would take some time to organize, Mrs. Nelson could report that "They hope to get these plans under way for the colored women by the winter."[54]

Most other southern states could boast only a few sporadic examples of black organization concentrated in the major urban areas. In Louisiana, for example, only New Orleans had any organization among the black women. Mrs. Nelson found that the feeling between the races was ideal but, as she remarked, "There isn't any organization, just a lovely cooperation, and general foggy feeling of good-will and sisterly love . . . ." When she inquired about the lack of organization in the state, especially in cities like Baton Rouge, Shreveport, and Alexandria with large black populations, she was told, "Everyone seems to think that the difficulties of accommodation [and] hard travel precluded any 'delicate lady's' going into the

[50] McGehee to Patterson, August 12, 1918; McGehee to "My Dear Madam Chairman" (mimeograph), August 26, 1918, Corr. CWDW, 13A-A2, Box 509, File 123.

[51] McGehee to Patterson, August 26, 1918, *ibid.*

[52] McGehee to Patterson, October 12, 1918, *ibid.*

[53] Mrs. J. Otey Reid to Patterson, August 20, 1918, Corr. CWDW, 13A-A2, Box 522, File 162. A three-page letter outlining the Sumter County Plan from the secretary of the Sumter County Council of Defense to George F. Porter, chief, Section on Cooperation with States, CND, dated October 10, 1917, was mimeographed and circulated to the state councils and state Woman's Committees by the Washington office in late 1917. Reports of the State Councils, Records of the Field Division, 15-C1, Box 908; cited hereinafter as Repts. SCD with category and box numbers.

[54] Nelson to Patterson, September 5, 1918, Corr. CWDW, 13A-A2, Box 512, File 131.

hinterland."[55] This was in sharp contrast to the adjoining state of Mississippi, where the indefatigable Mrs. McGehee, the white state chairman, had no fear of distance. There, Mrs. Nelson reported; "The colored women are alive and anxious to work—Mrs. McGehee has seen to that. Little details of 100 or 200 miles have no terrors for her."[56] However, if Louisiana was poorly organized as a state, Mrs. Nelson found the organization in the city of New Orleans to be a model for the rest of the country.

The state Woman's Committee had appointed a special city chairman for New Orleans, Mrs. William Porteour. She appointed a white and a black chairman in each of the seventeen wards in the city and relied on them to develop appropriate local organizations.[57] On discovering that some of the black chairmen she had initially appointed did not reside in the wards they represented, she insisted on a reorganization to ensure that each ward chairman actually lived in her ward. Mrs. Nelson, who had been invited to the reorganization conference, commented that "I feel more encouraged than at any time since I left Washington . . . . It is, without doubt, one of the finest bits of organization I've ever seen anywhere, and it works."[58] Mrs. Porteour had the additional advantage of excellent cooperation with city officials and departments, including use of the City Council Chamber for one of her organizational meetings—"the first time in the history of the city that a colored or mixed audience ever met in that sacred hall."[59]

The situation in Alabama and Tennessee was uneven but encouraging. The black women in Birmingham, and surrounding Jefferson County, seemed to be quite well organized. Mrs. Nelson described the Jefferson County Woman's Committee as "more thriving, active and alert than any that I have come across anywhere thus far—I mean so far as its work among the colored women is concerned."[60] The situation in other parts of the state was disappointing. In Selma, for example, "It seems there has been no organization there of the colored women—some have been working at the sale of stamps and making sporadic efforts but undirected."[61] In Mobile she found no official organization, but she did discover an independent black women's "War Service Club," which appeared to operate in the same manner as the Woman's Committee,

[55] Nelson to Patterson, August 14, 1918, *ibid.*
[56] Nelson to Patterson, August 19, 1918, *ibid.*
[57] Nelson to Patterson, August 15, 1918, *ibid.*
[58] Nelson to Patterson, August 17, 1918, *ibid.*
[59] *Ibid.*
[60] Nelson to Patterson, August 28, 1918, *ibid.*
[61] Nelson to Patterson, August 26, 1918, *ibid.*

and with all the various departments under the direction of a county chairman. Although she talked with the chairman and other members of the club, Mrs. Nelson reported that she "was unable to elicit any definite information as to their activities. I fear their work is to be done, not accomplished."[62] In Tennessee there were black women's organizations only in Knoxville, Nashville, and Memphis. But the white state chairman was anxious to extend the organization to cover the state. Mrs. Nelson reported that the chairman "is extremely anxious to get the work under way and would keep me in Tennessee indefinitely. I promised to come back."[63]

A slightly different procedure, similar to that followed in Maryland, had been used in Kentucky. There the men's State Council of Defense had organized the black men into a state committee, and, once organized, this committee added two black women to its number. The state Woman's Committee thought this "a very happy solution of the problem, as it is one that can be much better handled by the State than Nationally."[64]

In early 1918 the executive committee of the North Carolina Woman's Committee had discussed the question of a separate state organization for the black women. All agreed, however, that the best results would be obtained by incorporating the blacks into the existing county organizations on the Sumter County Plan, and they adopted a motion to "strenuously advise against setting up separate organization of negroes for Council of Defense work in any Southern State."[65] However, the state chairman, Mrs. Reilley, was anxious to mobilize the black community: "I decidedly approve of a woman coming to work and talk to our colored population and each community can decide just how they prefer to work."[66] Moreover, she was willing to bring the matter of organization of the black community before her committee again in the light of her discussion with Mrs. Nelson.[67]

[62] Nelson to Patterson, August 29, 1918, *ibid.* This independent black women's organization paraleled the semi-independent men's organizations, the Negro Patriotic League and the Saturday Service League, that Mrs. Nelson found in Mississippi. See Nelson to Patterson, August 25, 1918, *ibid.*

[63] Nelson to Patterson, September 10, 1918, *ibid.*

[64] Mrs. Helm Bruce to Patterson, August 20, 1918, Corr. CWDW, 13A-A2, Box 502, File 103.

[65] "Minutes of Executive Meeting, North Carolina Woman's Committee, February 14, 1918," Woman's Committee File, Box 39, Records of the North Carolina Council of Defense, Military Collection, World War I Records, Pt. II (North Carolina Division of Archives and History, Raleigh, N. C.). See also Reilley to Lamar, February 20, 1918, Corr. CWDW, 13A-A2, Box 512, File 132.

[66] Reilley to Lamar, July 18, 1918, Corr. CWDW, 13A-A2, Box 512, File 132.

[67] Reilley to Patterson, September 7, 1918, *ibid.*

Mrs. Nelson found Georgia to be the most disappointing of the southern states. Although the state Woman's Committee had appointed a subcommittee on black affairs early in 1918, this had not led to the development of a statewide black women's organization. Mrs. Nelson found the attitude of the white state chairman uncooperative and aloof; Georgia was the only state where she did not meet and talk with the white chairman of the state Woman's Committee.[68] However, while in Atlanta, she did manage to get in touch with Mrs. Alice Dugged Cary, president of the State Federation of Colored Women of Georgia and the chairman of the black subcommittee of the state woman's committee. Mrs. Cary conveyed the impression that the state was relatively well organized as far as the black women were concerned, although more by cities than by counties.[69] Not satisfied with this report—"it was too roseate and indefinite"—Mrs. Nelson stopped at Augusta overnight on her way to South Carolina and talked with Miss Lucy C. Laney, the principal of the Haines Institute and "the best and strongest colored woman in Georgia." Miss Laney's impressions were more critical. She knew of occasional, sporadic bits of war work among the black women in the state but, to her knowledge, no serious organized effort was being made. She was not even aware of the appointment of a black state chairman. Miss Laney introduced Mrs. Nelson to a Mrs. Harrington, the white county chairman of Richmond County, who said the work among the black women in that county was "at a standstill." In summing up the situation in the state Mrs. Nelson commented: "Such is the situation in Georgia—stultified by self-satisfaction in Atlanta."[70]

Mrs. Nelson found that those women actively involved in the effort to organize the black community mirrored their white counterparts. In New Orleans, for example, Mrs. Nelson noted that the black women who were active and anxious to organize a black woman's committee were "for the most part, teachers and college women, with a keen sense of responsibility."[71] In New Orleans the registration of women suggested by the Woman's Committee was put in the hands of a Mrs. Williams, "a colored school principal."[72] In North Carolina Miss McCullough, the black woman Mrs. Reilley

[68] See footnote 29 above. The failure to develop a genuine black woman's organization in Georgia was attributed to class distinctions among the black women themselves. See "Report on State Organization, January 28, 1918" (Mrs. Joseph R. Lamar), attached to WC Minutes, January 29, 1918, p. 286.

[69] Nelson to Patterson, September 3, 1918, Corr. CWDW, 13A-A2, Box 512, File 131. See "Plan of Work, Atlanta Colored Women's War Council" in Gerda Lerner, ed., *Black Women in White America: A Documentary History* (New York, 1972), 498–500.

[70] Nelson to Patterson, September 4, 1918, Corr. CWDW, 13A-A2, Box 512, File 131.

[71] Nelson to Patterson, August 15, 1918, *ibid.*

[72] Nelson to Patterson, August 14, 1918, *ibid.*

relied upon, was a schoolteacher on leave of absence.[73] In Mississippi Mrs. McGehee selected Miss Sally Green, another schoolteacher, who had additional experience as a county agent.[74] In Florida the black state chairman was Miss Eartha M. White, a woman "of unusual ability," who had worked with the state labor commissioner. She was also known as "a leading negro club woman."[75] Naturally enough, educated women with organizational experience formed the core around which the bulk of the black women were organized.

The patriotic programs and achievements of the black women during the war paralleled those of the white women. The work tended to fall into two categories. The initial activities followed the traditional, well-defined patterns of women's roles in war. Guided by the programs of the Woman's Committee, a second level of activity sought to go beyond this passive, traditional role and use the wartime crisis to improve social conditions in the nation. The first programs concentrated on the soldier going into battle and on a general display of patriotism on the home front. In the industrial town of Bessemer, Alabama, for example, the black women had an active Council of Defense unit which "made comfort kits for soldiers—with Bibles in each kit. . . . They found wives of soldiers who had gone to camp and helped them, particularly in making layettes for expectant mothers."[76] In Cobb County, on the northern outskirts of Atlanta, Georgia, the black women reported in a similar vein: "The organization was started with 27 women and has seen to it that every colored soldier from Cobb County has a bible to carry with him to the battle front. We fitted up a rest room for our soldiers from Camp Gordon. We showed our patriotism in the grand parade in Atlanta, April 27th., being there with our flags and banners to represent Cobb County."[77] As Mrs. Nelson remarked in discussing the war work among the black women in Birmingham, Alabama, "Most units have concentrated on comfort kits for soldiers and care of soldiers families."[78] Another area of concern for

[73] Nelson to Patterson, September 7, 1918, *ibid.*

[74] For references to biographical details on Sally Green see footnote 48 above.

[75] Quotation "of unusual ability" is from "A History of the Activities of the Women of Florida," Repts. SD, 13L-A1, Box 635. Information about working for the state labor commissioner in "Report of Florida Division, July 15 to September 15, 1918" (By Mrs. Frank E. Jennings), 8 pp., *ibid.* She is undoubtedly the clubwoman referred to in "Increasing the Patriotic Efforts of the Negroes in the Southern States" (January 7, 1918), 4, Repts. SCD, 15-C1, Box 908.

[76] Nelson to Patterson, August 28, 1918, Corr. CWDW, 13A-A2, Box 512, File 131.

[77] Excerpt from report of black women of Cobb County, Ga., included in "Bi-monthly Report of the Woman's Committee, Council of National Defense, Georgia Division, March 15–May 15, 1918" (By Mrs. Samuel M. Inman, chairman), 10, Repts. SD, 13L-A1, Box 635.

[78] Nelson to Patterson, August 28, 1918, Corr. CWDW, 13A-A2, Box 512, File 131.

the soldiers was the staffing of canteens at the railroad stations. These canteens were generally run by the Red Cross, and sometimes there was friction between that organization and the black women who wanted to assist. In Alabama and Mississippi, for example, the Red Cross refused to give the black women permission to do canteen work at the railroad stations.[79]

In addition to its concern for the men in uniform, the Woman's Committee pressed its members throughout the states to do everything in their power to conserve and enlarge the existing food supply. This was in response to an obvious wartime need. However, the program went further and constituted an important aspect of the drive for social reform by the women. It offered the long-term hope of a better and more nutritious diet for the population as a whole. From the beginning, the Woman's Committee emphasized the need to produce more food and to conserve existing supplies, especially seasonal produce, with the new canning techniques. The unit of black women in Bessemer, Alabama, for example, canned over one thousand quarts of perishable foodstuffs.[80] In Cobb County, Georgia, the idea of increasing food production and conservation was eagerly accepted: "The motion picture on gardening for the school children was seen by 300 most of whom immediately went to work with war gardens. Prizes have been offered for the best gardens, chickens, pigs and vegetables. We have a knitting class. We are organizing canning clubs. We have now 60 members and an organization of boys, also one of girls."[81] Black women appreciated the importance of this work and actively sought help to implement it. In North Carolina, for example, Mrs. Reilley, the white state chairman of the woman's committee, commented: "We have had big county rallies and talks on well balanced meals and demonstrations by the girls of the county in the way to can—the most approved methods. We are taking the work to the colored people and the other day when I was in Anson County organizing, the colored people heard of it and requested that I speak in the Methodist Episcopal Church, so I did—my first experience but I never had a more attentive audience."[82]

In Florida the food-conservation work was pushed by Miss White, the Negro state chairman and organizer for the state

[79] Nelson to Patterson, August 23, 26, 1918, *ibid.*; see also Dunbar-Nelson, "Negro Women in War Work," 376–77.

[80] Nelson to Patterson, August 28, 1918, Corr. CWDW, 13A-A2, Box 512, File 131.

[81] Excerpt from report of Negro women of Cobb County, included in "Bi-monthly Report of the Woman's Committee, Council of National Defense, Georgia Division, March 15–May 15, 1918," p. 10, Repts. SD, 13L-A1, Box 635.

[82] Reilley to Miss Ida Tarbell, July 24, 1917, Corr. CWDW, 13A-A1, Box 468, File 132.

Woman's Committee. In Duval County, with the assistance of the county commissioners, she established a Liberty Kitchen "in the basement of the Negro High School, to teach food substitutes and economy of fuel and a registration bureau was conducted for washerwomen and cooks."[83] In Tampa the black Baptist preacher and his wife, both college graduates, turned their own kitchen into a demonstration unit for similar work.[84] In September 1918 the chairman of the Florida Woman's Committee reported that "Leon County is doing good Home Demonstration work among the negroes, due to the fine Home Economics Department of the State College for Women, working with the Agricultural Extension Department of the Government."[85] Much of this work built on foundations laid by the home economics extension service of the various state agricultural colleges, which in the previous seven years had helped organize thousands of canning and home demonstration clubs throughout the country. The Department of Agriculture paid the salary of county home demonstration agents in counties that complied with the provisions of the Smith-Hughes Act of 1917.[86]

In addition to such conventional patriotic work, a good deal of the program advanced by the Woman's Committee and taken up by the black women centered on improving the general social conditions of the black community. The war was seen as an opportunity to push social-welfare programs that had been talked about before the war but had received little positive encouragement. Probably the most important area of reform was in the field of public health. A great effort was made by the Woman's Committee, in conjunction with the Children's Bureau of the Department of Labor, to draw attention to the very high infant mortality rate in the United States and to publicize the need for better health services in the community. This was a continuation of a program launched in 1916 under the auspices of the General Federation of Women's Clubs and the Children's Bureau which sought to publicize the need for baby clinics, public nurses, accurate birth registration, purer milk supplies, and the like. The program centered on the baby weighing and measuring program, which the Woman's Committee vigorously supported throughout the country. Mrs. Nelson noted that the program seemed to have worked well in Jackson, Mississippi. She spoke to the black public-health nurse in

[83] "A History of the Activities of the Women of Florida," 11, Repts. SD, 13L-A1, Box 635.

[84] "Report of Florida Division, May 15 to July 15, 1918" (Mrs. William [Elizabeth] Hocker, retiring chairman), 4, *ibid.*

[85] "Report of Florida Division, July 15 to September 15, 1918" (Mrs. Frank E. [Minerva P.] Jennings, chairman), 4, *ibid.*

[86] Blair, *The Woman's Committee*, 76.

that city, "who has been doing some excellent work here. The colored babies in Jackson are being weighed and a milk and ice fund is under way."[87]

Not all areas could report such good results. In South Carolina, where very little organization of the black women had been effected, there had been no activity in this area. However, as a direct result of Mrs. Nelson's visit there was agreement that this matter would be taken up as soon as practicable and would begin in Columbia, the state capital.[88] In New Orleans the program ran into some opposition, and Mrs. Nelson reported that there had been some "quiet agitation" among the Negro mothers themselves. Their concern centered around the fact that nothing was done after the babies were weighed and measured, and the mothers therefore regarded it as a waste of time and effort. "If they [babies] are subnormal and home conditions are poor no effort is made to supply them with Pasteurized milk."[89] In Birmingham Mrs. Nelson found three separate black units working in different sections of the city. Although more was being done there than in New Orleans, some of the complaints were the same: "Babies weighed, but have not been followed up. There is a great deal of misunderstanding about this—some units seeming to think the weighing is an end in itself."[90]

Allied to the baby weighing and measuring program was the related drive to improve recreational facilities for children. In Atlanta Mrs. Nelson found that the Georgia State Federation of Colored Women, working in conjunction with the state woman's committee, had arranged for the establishment in the city of two playgrounds for black children.[91] In Jacksonville, Florida, Mrs. Nelson reported that "the colored women are interested in a playground for colored children, and the men have interested themselves and raised $600 for apparatus and equipment."[92] In the speeches she made to groups of black women throughout the South Mrs. Nelson did not hesitate to stress these aspects of the war program of the Woman's Committee. In Birmingham, before a big evening meeting in the largest black church in the city, she stressed the importance of the nurses' drive, the need for adequate playgrounds for the children, and the need to take measures to safeguard women in industry.[93]

[87] Nelson to Patterson, August 22, 1918, Corr. CWDW, 13A-A2, Box 512, File 131; see also Dunbar-Nelson, "Negro Women in War Work," 385. For more details on the social programs of the Woman's Committee see Blair, *The Woman's Committee*, 77–85.

[88] Nelson to Patterson, September 5, 1918, Corr. CWDW, 13A-A2, Box 512, File 131.

[89] Nelson to Patterson, August 15, 1918, *ibid.*

[90] Nelson to Patterson, August 28, 1918, *ibid.*

[91] Nelson to Patterson, September 3, 1918, *ibid.*

[92] Nelson to Patterson, August 30, 1918, *ibid.*

[93] Nelson to Patterson, August 28, 1918, *ibid.*

Just as the war opened up job opportunities for white women, so it did on a lesser scale for black women. The central Woman's Committee and the various state committees began to push for nurses' training for black women. The Washington office sent out a list of hospitals where black women could receive training in nursing and the state chairmen usually publicized this information. In Mississippi Mrs. McGehee used the opportunity to encourage the organization of black women in the state, asserting, "I want to enroll them as nurses, as they are so anxious for that training right now. I did not do this in our own enrollment, because I knew I was going to organize them, and they would like so much better to see something that their organization had done at once to give them an opportunity to serve. I thank you for the list of hospitals where they can get training."[94] In New Orleans Mrs. Nelson heard that "colored nurses are 'under way' for city work."[95] In mid-1918 the retiring chairman of the Florida Woman's Committee reported that "They have done specially good service in cities as practical nurses, releasing graduate nurses for overseas service."[96]

There were other areas in which the war opened up new opportunities for black women. In Jacksonville, Florida, for example, the Negro state organizer "supplied a dozen office buildings with negro girls for elevator service to release men. Elevator girls are also being supplied for the hotels and stores, under her direction."[97] Florida went one step further. Under the energetic direction of Miss White, a Mutual Protection League for Working Girls was established for the benefit of those "who had take up the unfamiliar work of elevator girls, bell girls in hotels, and chauffeurs. From this it was not far to a Union of Girls in Domestic Service . . . ."[98]

Mrs. Nelson's southern trip as field representative of the Woman's Committee was a valuable exercise. Although, with a few notable exceptions, she found relatively little formal organization of black women, she did find that, contrary to some rumors, they were patriotic and anxious to be incorporated in a formal way into the domestic war effort. Her reception among the white southern chairmen of the state Woman's Committees was, on the whole, polite and receptive, and in some cases she was able to influence their views on the matter of black organization. Most of the state com-

[94] McGehee to Patterson, August 12, 1918, Corr. CWDW, 13A-A2, Box 509, File 123.

[95] Nelson to Patterson, August 15, 1918, Corr. CWDW, 13A-A2, Box 512, File 131. A black nurse was already working among the city poor in New Orleans, but she was working independently of the state Woman's Committee, being "hired by a Catholic priest doing settlement work in his parish." Nelson to Patterson, August 15, 1918, *ibid.*

[96] "Report of Florida Division, May 15 to July 15, 1918," Repts. SD, 13L-AI, Box 635.

[97] "Report of Florida Division, July 15 to September 15, 1918," p. 4, *ibid.*

[98] Dunbar-Nelson, "Negro Women in War Work," 384.

mittees were aware of the need to take concrete steps to incorporate the black community into the war effort, and some were genuinely impressed with the possibilities of the project. Traveling between Alabama and Florida in August 1918, Mrs. Nelson caught that mood in her comment—"Trains slow, distances tremendous, state chairmen importunate."[99] As she journeyed from state to state it was obvious how much the success of the Woman's Committee organization in the states depended on the personal attitudes and organizational abilities of the state chairmen. It varied from state to state and made generalization difficult. In organizing the black women, the problems of the chairmen were compounded by the attitudes of the state governors and the men's state Councils of Defense, who tended to be conservative on that particular issue.[100]

By mid-1918 the war had begun to create pressures for profound social change in domestic America. Chief among these pressures was the need for a more rational approach to the utilization of all resources, including human resources. The potential for social reform inherent in the situation was grasped by southern black women. Their quiet struggle over organization was an important aspect of this battle for social reform. It formed part of the effort to erode the southern caste system and to gain more responsibility and self-respect. Similarly, in the drives for greater food production and conservation, for improved employment opportunities, and particularly in the different aspects of the child-welfare program, southern black women like their white counterparts had an opportunity both to demonstrate their patriotism and to advance social reforms that would have long-term significance for the entire community. The war ended too soon to allow any substantial or permanent social change to take place in the South, but the direction of the change was clear. The white state chairman of Mississippi recognized the opportunity the war offered the black population of her state. In commenting on the need to get the black women organized and involved in the war effort, she wrote: "I am vitally interested in this, and can see its far reaching effect—not alone now—but after the war, when we will need trained hands and brains, for the great work awaiting."[101]

[99] Nelson to Patterson, August 29, 1918, Corr. CWDW, 13A-A2, Box 512, File 131. The Scheibers argue that the general black community cooperated wholeheartedly in the war effort for reasons of "deeply-felt patriotism" coupled with the hope that this cooperation would help in the battle against discrimination in the postwar period. Scheiber and Scheiber, "The Wilson Administration," 452. My evidence shows that the southern black women, although no less patriotic, hoped to use the wartime cooperation itself to alleviate their position.

[100] Emily Newell Blair regarded the organization of black women as "One of the most difficult matters that certain parts of the country had to handle . . . ." Blair, *The Woman's Committee*, 106.

[101] McGehee to Patterson, August 12, 1918, Corr. CWDW, 13A-A2, Box 509, File 123.

# Southern Women in the War: The North Carolina Woman's Committee, 1917-1919

BY WILLIAM J. BREEN*

Very little has been written on the role of women in American society during World War I. What has been published tends to concentrate on the national level or on major social campaigns like suffrage and prohibition. There is scant material on what women accomplished at the state and local levels or on their aspirations and motivations.[1] This study explores some aspects of the work of North Carolina women during the war and tries to evaluate the contribution made both to the war effort and to the thrust of domestic reform. The mystique of the "southern lady" and the accompanying idealization of her role in the home may have inhibited the general reform movement among women in the South, but it did not extinguish it.[2] The behavior of North Carolina women suggests, if in a roundabout way, the changing position of women in that society and indicates some of the ways in which the war was used to promote social reform south of the Potomac.

The outbreak of the war produced an outpouring of patriotic offers of help from women's organizations throughout the country. Pres. Woodrow Wilson's administration had no policy on how to deal with these offers and referred them

---

* Dr. Breen is a senior lecturer, History Department, La Trobe University, Bundoora, Victoria, Australia. The author wishes to acknowledge the financial assistance of the Council of La Trobe University and the American Council of Learned Societies.

[1] See, for example, James H. Timberlake, *Prohibition and the Progressive Movement, 1900-1920* (Cambridge, Mass.: Harvard University Press, 1963), and Aileen S. Kraditor, *The Ideas of the Woman Suffrage Movement, 1890-1920* (New York: Columbia University Press, 1965). A recent survey of the role of women in the war which remains fairly much at a national level is William L. O'Neill, *Everyone Was Brave: The Rise and Fall of Feminism in America* (Chicago: Quadrangle Books, 1969), especially chapter 6, 169-224, hereinafter cited as O'Neill, *Everyone Was Brave*. The best contemporary accounts, which do try to get below the national level, are Ida Clyde Clarke, *American Women and the World War* (New York: D. Appleton and Company, 1918), and Emily Newell Blair, *The Woman's Committee, United States Council of National Defense: An Interpretative Report, April 21, 1917, to February 27, 1919* (Washington: Government Printing Office, 1920, hereinafter cited as Blair, *The Woman's Committee*.

[2] On the general question of domestic reform and the World War see especially Allen F. Davis, "Welfare, Reform and World War I," *American Quarterly*, XIX (Fall, 1967), 516-533; see also the same author's *Spearheads for Reform: The Social Settlements and the Progressive Movement, 1890-1914* (New York: Oxford University Press, 1967), Chapter XI. For a more general discussion of the issue of reform in World War I see Otis L. Graham, Jr., *The Great Campaigns: Reform and War in America, 1900-1928* (Englewood Cliffs, N.J.: Prentice Hall, 1971), Part 3. On the mystique of the "southern lady" see Anne Firor Scott, *The Southern Lady: From Pedestal to Politics, 1830-1930* (Chicago: University of Chicago Press, 1970).

Official badge of the national Woman's Committee, Council of National Defense. From document labeled "Woman's Committee, Council of National Defense, North Carolina Division," Military Collection, World War I Papers, Part II: North Carolina Council of Defense, Box 39.

to the recently organized Council of National Defense. The latter body decided to establish a special Woman's Committee, under its auspices, to act as a central "clearing house" for the patriotic work of women in the war. Of the women appointed to the new national committee, all but one were representatives of the various national women's organizations and could speak with some authority for organized women.[3] Once established, the new body took two important initial steps. It first divided the work to be done into ten separate departments or divisions;[4] it then decided to organize Woman's Committees in every state of the Union. These divisions were to be the agencies of the central Woman's Committee in Washington and would be able to elicit the support of the women in the states for the domestic programs of the government.

In North Carolina the national Woman's Committee asked Mrs. James Eugene (Laura Holmes) Reilley of Charlotte to act as temporary chairman. Mrs. Reilley called a meeting of the organized women of the state to establish a permanent state division of the Woman's Committee. This meeting was held on June 7 and 8, 1917, in the Senate chamber of the State Capitol in Raleigh. Sixty-eight women attended, elected the permanent officers of the organization, decided to divide into twelve different departments (adding Finance and Publicity to the list suggested by the parent organization), elected chairmen for these departments, and decided to organize a subcommittee in each of the 100 counties in the state.[5]

---

[3] Blair, *The Woman's Committee*, Chapter I. The Woman's Committee was comprised of the chairman, Dr. Anna Howard Shaw, honorary president, National American Woman Suffrage Association; Mrs. Philip North Moore, president, National Council of Women of the United States; Mrs. Josiah Evans Cowles, president, General Federation of Women's Clubs; Miss Maude Wetmore, chairman, National League for Women's Service; Mrs. Carrie Chapman Catt, president, National American Woman Suffrage Association; Mrs. Stanley J. McCormick, vice-president, National American Woman Suffrage Association; Mrs. Joseph R. Lamar, president, National Society of Colonial Dames; Mrs. Antoinette Funk, lawyer; Miss Ida M. Tarbell, publicist and writer; Miss Agnes Nestor, vice-president, International Glove Workers Union; and Miss Hannah J. Patterson, head of the Pennsylvania Woman Suffrage party and resident director of the Woman's Committee.

[4] The ten departments were Registration for Service; Food Production and Home Economics; Food Administration; Women in Industry; Child Welfare; Maintenance of Existing Social Service Agencies; Health and Recreation; Educational Propaganda; Liberty Loan; and Home and Allied Relief. Blair, *The Woman's Committee*, 20-21.

[5] For details on the organization and activities of the North Carolina Woman's Committee see Laura Holmes Reilley, "[Final Report of] Woman's Committee, Council of National Defense, North

Mrs. Reilley was elected permanent head of the state women's committee. An active clubwoman and former president of the North Carolina Federation of Women's Clubs, vice-president of the General Federation, and charter member of the state Equal Suffrage League, she threw herself into the new task with enthusiasm.[6] Her family was thoroughly involved in war work. In late July, 1917, she wrote:

> I have a son thirty-one who will go into the next officers' training camp, one twenty-four, who is in Dr. Brenizer's Hospital Corps and a third will graduate at Virginia Military Institute next year and get his commission. He is too young now, just twenty. One daughter is emphasizing on food conservation and keeping house for me and another has gone to Blue Ridge to take a course in Y.W.C.A. for training in war service, so you see as a family we are doing our bit. My husband is just as patriotic, but unfortunately he thinks, but fortunately for us, there is an age limit.[7]

She was to need every last ounce of patriotism and administrative skill that she possessed in the task of organizing the women of North Carolina. By mid-June she was writing an average of twenty-five letters per day—the entire operation being run from her own typewriter on the dining table of her home.[8] But this lack of an office and secretarial assistance, although frustrating, was of minor significance compared with other difficulties she had to face.

Of the various problems confronting the new president and her organization, perhaps the most irritating was the condescending attitude of the men in the state. The response of the governor, Thomas W. Bickett, to Mrs. Reilley's query concerning responsibilities was to suggest that all the work contemplated by her committee could be done, and indeed should be done, by the North Carolina

---

Carolina Division: Organized June 8, 1917, Senate Chamber, Raleigh, N.C., Disbanded February 15, 1919," typescript (16 pages) in Military Collection, World War I Papers; Part II: North Carolina Council of Defense, Box 39, File "Woman's Committee," Archives, Division of Archives and History, Raleigh, hereinafter cited as Reilley, "Final Report of Woman's Committee." The collection will be hereinafter cited as NCCD Records.

The officers and department chairmen of the North Carolina Woman's Committee and the various societies and associations represented on the state council of the Woman's Committee are listed in the appendix following the text of this paper.

[6] Mrs. Reilley (1861-1941), a native of St. Louis, attended the women's institute associated with Washington University there. Her husband's business interests took her to New Mexico, Chicago, and Baltimore before settling in Charlotte. She was elected president of the Charlotte Woman's Club in 1896, president of the state Federation of Women's Clubs in 1910, and one of the vice-presidents of the General Federation in 1916. She was also a charter member of the Westminster Church in Charlotte. When the N.C. Equal Suffrage League was founded in 1913, she was elected vice-president and was active in promoting the suffrage cause in the South. Mrs. Reilley was the only woman on the State Council of Defense, the official state mobilization agency appointed by Gov. Thomas W. Bickett. For biographical details concerning Mrs. Reilley see the 5-page typescript biography by Mrs. H. P. Shumway and Mrs. Philip N. Moore in Charles Van Noppen Papers, Manuscript Department, Duke University Library, Durham, hereinafter cited as Van Noppen Papers; for some information on her role in the suffrage fight see A. Elizabeth Taylor, "The Woman Suffrage Movement in North Carolina," Parts I and II, *North Carolina Historical Review*, XXXVIII (January, April, 1961), 45-62, 173-189. The N.C. Equal Suffrage Association in 1914 adopted a nonmilitant stand, appealing to "reason and fair play." Mrs. Reilley's obituary is in the *Charlotte Observer*, February 26, 1941.

[7] Reilley to Ida Tarbell, July 24, 1917, Records of the Council of National Defense, Record Group 62, 13A-A.1, Box 468, File 132, Federal Records Center, Suitland, Maryland, hereinafter cited as RG 62. Mrs. Reilley also had a married daughter living in New York.

[8] Reilley to Anna Howard Shaw, June 15, 1917, RG 62, 13A-A.1, Box 468, File 132.

Mrs. James Eugene (Laura Holmes) Reilley (1861-1941) of Charlotte. Photograph from *The North Carolina Federation of Women's Clubs* [Year Book], *1912-1913* (N.p.: North Carolina Federation of Women's Clubs [?], 1913 [?]), frontispiece.

chapter of the Red Cross Society which had the advantage of an existing organization that spanned most of the state and whose work "seems to cover every possible activity in which women can engage." Bickett thought that the Red Cross could, if necessary, appoint a subcommittee on the national defense.[9] Mrs. Reilley was discouraged but not deterred by this negative response and went ahead with the organization of the state Woman's Committee.

The position of the state Woman's Committee was always complicated by the existence of the parallel men's State Council of Defense which had been appointed by the governor, at the suggestion of the Council of National Defense, as the official civilian mobilization agency of the state. The existence of the women's organization implied some degree of duplication. This feeling was clearly expressed at the annual meeting of the Woman's Committee in July, 1918, when Mrs. William N. Reynolds, the second vice-chairman, declared that "most of the work is being done by the Men's Committee"; and she felt that the status of the Woman's Committee was not at all clear.[10] Mrs. Reilley was the only woman member of the State Council of Defense and could act to try to prevent obvious overlapping, but it was not until 1918 that the two organizations began to merge.[11]

---

[9] Thomas W. Bickett to Reilley, May 18, 1917, RG 62, 13A-A.1, Box 468, File 132.

[10] Minutes of Executive Meeting of N.C. Woman's Committee, July 11, 1918, NCCD Records, Box 39. For the work of the men's state council see William J. Breen, "The North Carolina Council of Defense during World War I, 1917-1918," *North Carolina Historical Review*, L (January, 1973), 1-31, hereinafter cited as Breen, "The North Carolina Council of Defense."

[11] The merger of the two organizations began at the local level in February, 1918. It was not until October, 1918, that the two state organizations finally merged completely. See Reilley to Anna Howard Shaw, February 20, 1918, RG 62, 13A-A.2, Box 512, File 132; Reilley, "Final Report of Woman's Committee," 14. For the story of the amalgamation at the federal level see Blair, *The Woman's Committee*, Chapter X.

The men's organization did propose amalgamation shortly after the two organizations were established.[12] However, Mrs. Reilley evaded amalgamation, fearing the conservative tenor of the men's committee; she felt, for example, that Dr. D. H. Hill, the chairman of the State Council of Defense, was "simply a gentleman of the old school and is slow and unprogressive."[13] The women of the state, she believed, had a definite role to play in the wartime mobilization effort.[14] Many of the men throughout the state remained opposed to the women's organization, believing it to be synonymous with woman suffrage; Duplin County, for example, had no local woman's committee until December, 1917, because, as the local chairman of the Woman's Committee explained:

> First we had to go slow as the men in this section were opposed to women doing public work, thinking it meant suffrage, and I have had to use tact, diplomacy, and even straight out politics. . . .[15]

It was an uphill battle throughout the war to convince the men of the worth of the work done by the women.[16]

Lack of adequate financial support, which plagued the women's organization, further illustrated the disdainful attitude of the men. Mrs. Reilley's initial action was to ask Governor Bickett for state funds to finance her committee. This appeal was summarily rebuffed by Bickett, who declared that "there are no state funds that can be applied to the payment of any expenses of the organization you suggest."[17] The governor was, moreover, opposed to calling an extra session of the General Assembly to discuss finance, and the regular session did not meet until January, 1919.[18] In reply to a questionnaire sent out by the federal Woman's Committee, in July, 1917, Mrs. Reilley described the financial situation of the organization as being supported

> From chairman's bank account so far. Finance Committee intends asking the wealthiest women of the state to contribute for a year in monthly subscriptions or as they desire. Forlorn hope with all the voluntary contributions asked for . . . I have given all day or most of it to the work since my appointment. We have a big business and no capital to run it on. . . .[19]

---

[12] Reilley to Mrs. Ira Couch Wood, July 14, 1917, RG 62, 13A-A.1, Box 468, File 132. The Council of National Defense, in addition to establishing the Woman's Committee, had already established a State Councils Section to coordinate and set up state councils of defense, which were expected to become the major vehicles for mobilizing the civilian population. Each state council was appointed by the state governor and was dominated by men (sometimes to the exclusion of women altogether, although usually with one woman representative).

[13] Reilley to Mrs. Ira Couch Wood, July 26, 1917, RG 62, 13A-A.1, Box 468, File 132.

[14] See especially Reilley to Mrs. Ira Couch Wood, July 14, 26, 1917, RG 62, 13A-A.1, Box 468, File 132. For the conservative tenor of the men's state council see pages 274-275 of this paper.

[15] Mrs. H. Faison Peirce, Warsaw, N.C., to Ida Tarbell, December 15, 1917, RG 62, 13B-A.2, Box 584.

[16] See especially Mrs. R. H. Latham to Miss Rodman, October 16, 1918, in Military Collection, World War I Papers; Part IV: Liberty Loan Campaign, Woman's Liberty Loan Committee, Box 2, State Archives.

[17] T. W. Bickett to Reilley, May 18, 1917, RG 62, 13A-A.1, Box 468, File 132.

[18] Reilley to Anna Howard Shaw, June 15, 1917, RG 62, 13A-A.1, Box 468, File 132.

[19] Reply to questionnaire sent out by central Woman's Committee (undated, but done July 6, 1917), RG 62, 13A-A.1, Box 468, File 132.

Mrs. William N. (Kate Bitting) Reynolds (ca. 1868-1946) of Winston-Salem. Photograph from *Everywoman's Magazine*, I (January, 1917), p. 17.

The state Woman's Committee was thrown entirely onto its own resources which the members felt was unfair; they believed that its work should have been financed either by the state or the federal government.[20]

Funds had to be found somehow. At the initial meeting of the organization Mrs. William N. Reynolds of Winston-Salem, the second vice-chairman, gave $100 to begin the work, but this obviously did not meet the need.[21] The state committee selected a finance committee which decided to ask each of the county committees to donate $2.00 per month to the state office. This plan was not very successful. By late October, 1917, the chairman of the Finance Department reported that "a few of the Counties . . . are sending this amount; some refused to contribute, and others have not been heard from."[22] An appeal to the members of the executive committee realized donations ranging from $1.00 to $50.00, "but the aggregate was disappointingly small."[23] By October, 1917, the Finance Department estimated that it needed $200 per month and asked the assistance of the men's committee.[24] This appeal for help did finally receive some attention. In February the men's committee voted that some funds should be made available to the woman's division. Eventually, the amount was fixed at $50.00 per month.[25] In all, the State Council contributed the sum of $677 to the woman's division which, coupled with the donations of generous individuals and the amounts contributed from the counties, constituted the total financial backing of the Woman's Committee.[26] As Mrs. Reilley stated in her final report:

---

[20] Reilley to Anna Howard Shaw, June 15, 1917, RG 62, 13A-A.1, Box 468, File 132.

[21] Reilley to Anna Howard Shaw, June 11, 1917, RG 62, 13A-A.1, Box 468, File 132.

[22] Mrs. C. F. Harvey to State Council of Defense, October 25, 1917, in J. Bryan Grimes Papers, Southern Historical Collection, University of North Carolina Library, Chapel Hill, hereinafter cited as Mrs. Harvey to State Council of Defense.

[23] Mrs. Harvey to State Council of Defense, October 25, 1917.

[24] Mrs. Harvey to State Council of Defense, October 25, 1917.

[25] Minutes of the North Carolina State Council of Defense, meeting of February 1, 1918, typescript (24 pages) in NCCD Records, Box 27, hereinafter cited as Minutes, NCCD, Box 27.

[26] Minutes, NCCD, Box 27. The financial report of the State Council of Defense from its formation to November 30, 1918, is included with the meeting of December 5, 1918.

> North Carolina having made no appropriation for State Defense, the Woman's Committee has had a difficult time to accomplish the work expected of us at the hands of the Government. Coming in competition with states that had millions of dollars appropriated for war work, it has been no small embarrassment to North Carolina to undertake so great a work with so little at her command.[27]

Both the attitude of the men and the problems of finances retarded the development of county organizations. Although the initial organizational meeting on June 8, 1917, provided an opportunity for a display of enthusiasm and patriotism by the women present and the organizations they represented, by early July Mrs. Reilley reported that of the 100 counties in North Carolina she had been able to organize committees in only twenty. In September, 1917, there were still thirty counties without chairmen. To help the organization, the committee adopted the plan of dividing the state into congressional districts and assigning a member of the executive committee as chairman to organize the counties in each district.[28] However, as late as mid-1918 there were a dozen or so counties that were still unorganized and did not respond to letters. Mrs. Reilley believed that

> If we had the means to go over the state all the counties would be organized. . . . Some of the states have a Field Secretary and it is what we need in North Carolina as well as a bulletin such as most of the states send out. I am at a loss [to know] how to get the messages I want to give over to the women of our state. . . .[29]

Another problem that dogged the Woman's Committee in North Carolina, although it was not confined to that state, was the lack of an exact definition of its role in the war mobilization effort. The question was whether the state Woman's Committee was essentially a coordinating body, overseeing and stimulating the work of other women's organizations, or whether it was an initiating body in its own right, responsible for carrying out various programs. There was no clear-cut answer to this query. At the organizational meeting the problem was raised more precisely. Mrs. Palmer Jerman of Raleigh asked if the work of the county committees was "not more of a general survey of the work being done rather than initiating new work." This suggestion was rejected as too narrow by Mrs. Reilley, who replied that "organized work should be coordinated, but that it was just as essential to initiate new work to include every woman."[30] Mrs. Reilley stressed the need for cooperation among the various women's groups in order that "no energies would be wasted."[31] Such a vague guideline was bound to lead to problems.

---

[27] Reilley, "Final Report of Woman's Committee," 12.

[28] Report of State Woman's Committee to North Carolina State Council of Defense, September 21, 1917, typescript (6 pages, unsigned), NCCD Records, Box 39.

[29] Reilley to D. H. Hill, June 10, 1918, NCCD Records, Box 39.

[30] Minutes of the Preliminary Meeting to form the permanent organization of the Woman's Committee of the Council of National Defense, North Carolina Division, June 8, 1917, typescript (9 pages), NCCD Records, Box 39, hereinafter cited as Minutes of the Preliminary Meeting . . . June 8, 1917. (This typescript includes the minutes of the executive committee meeting held on June 9, 1917.)

[31] Minutes of the Preliminary Meeting . . . June 8, 1917.

The issue came to a head as the North Carolina Woman's Committee began to organize formally. By mid-June, with the committee organized into twelve different departments on the model of the Washington parent committee, Mrs. Reilley asked the federal office to send the program for each department as soon as possible because "the women are all anxious to know just what the Government desires of them."[32] The work of the Home and Foreign Relief Department involved relations with the Red Cross and was obviously quite crucial because, as Mrs. Reilley observed, "this is the work that appeals to most women."[33] In her first letter to Dr. Anna Howard Shaw, chairman of the national Woman's Committee, in May, 1917, Mrs. Reilley questioned this aspect of the plan of organization that she had received:

> I note what you say that all work that properly comes under the Red Cross shall be referred thereto, but does this mean that we shall have nothing to do with it, or does it mean that those working under the Red Cross shall be directed by it and we shall keep a record of the work through the Medical Section? Perhaps the intent of the National Council of Defense is to include all work except Red Cross. . . .[34]

A reply from the central office emphasized the need to find "a harmonious working basis" that would involve stimulating the formation of Red Cross groups in every town, but the exact working connection between the two organizations was not made clear.[35] The problem of finding this "harmonious" working relationship was more difficult in practice than was at first imagined. Eventually, harmony between the Red Cross and the state Woman's Committee was achieved but at the price of the latter organization's acting in a supportive role only and referring all Home and Foreign Relief work to the Red Cross. This body received the entire credit for work done and left the Home and Foreign Relief Department with no recognition. In her final report Mrs. Reilley, trying to salvage some recognition for the work done by her committee, stated: "This department has a long list of accomplishments as reported through the counties of the state to the chairman."[36]

Like the work of the Home and Foreign Relief Department, the work of the Liberty Loan Department was tangible, clearly related to the war effort, and appealed to a large number of women, but it also received scant recognition for its work in the state.[37] The Liberty Loan Department of the state committee was effectively taken over by the Women's Liberty Loan Committee in Washington, D.C., a separate body from the national Woman's Committee and directly responsible to the Treasury Department. The Women's Liberty Loan Committee used the state machinery established by the Woman's Committee in their periodic drives to sell Liberty Loans. This rather complicated administrative arrangement led to a good deal of confusion concerning responsibility and

[32] Reilley to Anna Howard Shaw, June 15, 1917, RG 62, 13A-A.1, Box 468, File 132.

[33] Reilley to Anna Howard Shaw, May 18, 1917, RG 62, 13A-A.1, Box 468, File 132.

[34] Reilley to Anna Howard Shaw, May 18, 1917, RG 62, 13A-A.1, Box 468, File 132.

[35] Ira Couch Wood to Reilley, May 24, 1917, RG 62, 13A-A.1, Box 468, File 132.

[36] Reilley, "Final Report of Woman's Committee," 12.

[37] The Liberty Loan Department was first headed by Mrs. R. J. Reynolds of Winston-Salem and later by Mrs. R. H. Latham, also of Winston-Salem.

recognition: By mid-1918, the Women's Liberty Loan Committee, with the backing of the Treasury Department, insisted on a clearer administrative demarcation which had the effect of pushing the Woman's Committee and the state divisions of the Woman's Committee out of the field altogether.[38] Mrs. Reilley was very disappointed at this development:

I regret to sever my connections with my state Chairman [of Liberty Loan] for many reasons. It was one of the definite pieces of work which the Woman's Committee could point to as work accomplished. It is like the Red Cross in this respect one can see the demand and the supply. Many people cannot believe in work of a different character, as there is nothing tangible. Then too, it is just as much a part of woman's war work as anything else and to my mind should be included. . . .[39]

In fact, in North Carolina, in spite of the pressure from Washington to sever all connections, very amicable relations continued between Mrs. Reilley and Mrs. Rowland H. Latham, and the latter's name remained on the official stationery of the state Woman's Committee as it had in the past.[40] Mrs. Reilley's letterhead, of course, implied a formal relationship that, technically, no longer existed; but it did recognize the close working relationship between the two bodies and the continued support given by her organization to the state Liberty Loan Committee.

Frustration at the anomalous position of the state Woman's Committee was clearly reflected in the discussions at the annual meeting of the state committee in mid-1918. Mrs. William N. Reynolds provoked a spirited controversy with her comment that "we do not know exactly where we come in." Miss Mary G. Shotwell, of Oxford, who had made a report on the assistance given to the War Savings Stamp campaign, grumbled, "We are doing the work, why not get the credit for it[?]"[41] The YWCA campaign in the state had relied heavily on the Woman's Committee organization, but the latter body got no official recognition of its contribution, and this irritated Mrs. Reilley:

The reason I want it recognized is not for any glory, but some say: "Wouldn't the work be done without the Woman's Committee." They get the information through the publicity work we do, not considering that it starts with us. . . .[42]

Confusion and frustration over the exact role of the state Woman's Committee was exacerbated by the fact that many individual women throughout the state

[38] Blair, *The Woman's Committee*, 31-32.

[39] Reilley to Mrs. Joseph R. Lamar, June 11, 1918, RG 62, 13A-A.2, Box 512, File 132.

[40] Reilley to Mrs. Joseph R. Lamar, August 12, 1918, RG 62, 13A-A.2, Box 512, File 132. (Note also the reply from Mrs. Lamar, undated, in the same folder.) For a comment on this general relationship see Blair, *The Woman's Committee*, 32.

[41] Minutes of Meeting of N.C. Woman's Committee, July 12, 1918, NCCD Records, Box 39. After taking B.S. and M.A. degrees from Teachers College, Columbia University (1925-1927), Miss Mary Graves Shotwell held a number of posts in the field of public welfare with both state and federal governments. She also served as state chairman, International Women's Clubs, district governor of Altrusa Clubs, and first vice-president of the N.C. Division of the American Association of University Women. William S. Powell, *North Carolina Lives: The Tar Heel Who's Who* (Hopkinsville, Ky.: Historical Record Association, 1962), 1105.

[42] Reilley to Mrs. Joseph R. Lamar, August 12, 1918, RG 62, 13A-A.2, Box 512, File 132.

Mrs. James N. (Katie Hawkins) Gudger, Jr. (d. 1943), of Asheville. Photograph from *Everywoman's Magazine*, III (May, 1919), p. 21.

were involved in various activities in overlapping roles. The many hats worn by one Asheville woman suggest the problem of allocating credit:

> Mrs. James M. Gudger Jr., chairman of the Tenth Congressional District of the North Carolina Division [Woman's Committee], Council of National Defense, organized the thirteen counties comprising this district. As chairman of the Buncombe County Division, thoroughly organized the entire county and enrolled more nurses in the student nurse reserve than any other county in the State. Assisted in every line of activities for Relief work, in the Red Cross drives, Armenian, Jewish, and Belgian Relief drives. Chairman of the Buncombe County Division—Woman's Committee, National War Savings Campaign. As president of the Asheville Chapter of U.D.C., organized a Red Cross unit under the local Red Cross chapter which rendered invaluable service in making surgical supplies and dressings. Was an active member of the Buncombe County Division of the National League for Service and assisted in the establishment of a Community Cannery in Asheville.[43]

Many other women throughout the state were similarly involved.[44] The problem of ensuring that the umbrella organization, the state Woman's Committee, got its share of the credit for the various activities undertaken was a difficult and well-nigh impossible task.

One of the first assignments of the North Carolina Woman's Committee was to carry out a statewide registration of women for service. This was meant to

---

[43] Mrs. L. E. (Ethel Harris) Fisher, registrar, United Daughters of the Confederacy, North Carolina Division, "Report to R. B. House on the War Record of Members of the United Daughters of the Confederacy," dated July 26, 1920 (6 pages), Military Collection, World War I Papers; Pt. XIII: Miscellaneous, Women and the War, Box 17, State Archives. This report is mainly a record of the war activities of the Woman's Club of Asheville; Mrs. Fisher was secretary of the club and chairman of the War Record Committee. The report illustrates the considerable overlap of war activities among the members of the club. Mrs. Gudger was also president of the Asheville Club for Women and second vice-president of the N.C. Federation of Women's Clubs. Her activities form only one example of the many hats that women in the club wore and the consequent difficulty in assessing institutional responsibility.

[44] For illustrations of the same problem affecting women from other towns in the state see *News and Observer* (Raleigh), May 26, 1918, hereinafter cited as *News and Observer*

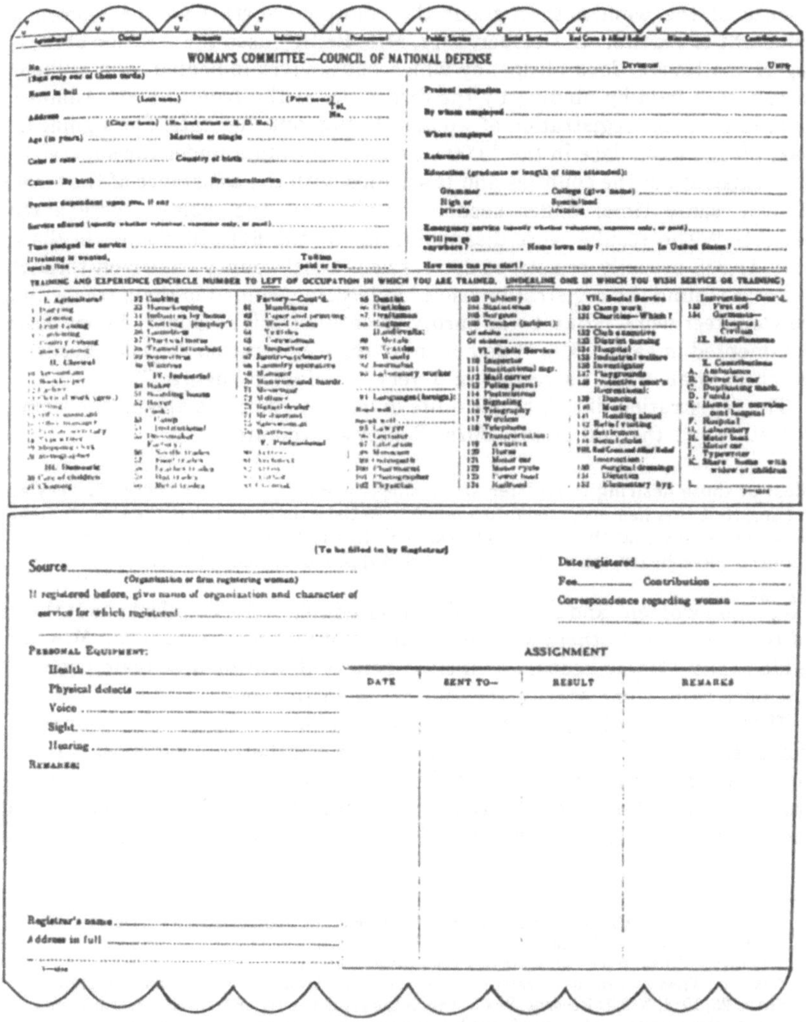
WOMAN'S COMMITTEE—COUNCIL OF NATIONAL DEFENSE

(To be filled in by Registrar)

Source

(Organization or firm registering woman)

If registered before, give name of organization and character of service for which registered

Date registered

Fee Contribution

Correspondence regarding woman

PERSONAL EQUIPMENT:

Health

Physical defects

Voice

Sight

Hearing

REMARKS:

Registrar's name

Address in full

ASSIGNMENT

| DATE | SENT TO— | RESULT | REMARKS |
|---|---|---|---|

This form was used by the North Carolina Woman's Committee to register women for national service. The form sought information concerning previous experience and training received by North Carolina's women and directed them to specify an occupation in which they would like to serve or be trained. From NCCD Records, Box 39.

parallel the registration for national service of the men and would make available to the national government an inventory of the available skills and talents of the women throughout the country. North Carolina women were reluctant to register. In October, 1917, Mrs. Reilley used the occasion of the signing of the Hoover food pledge, by which housewives indicated their willingness to conserve food by abiding by the directions of the federal Food Administration, to push the registration of women throughout the state. The signing of the food pledge took place in the 7,000 schools in the state under the supervision of the registrars of the counties and townships with the assistance of the teachers. At the same time, under separate registrars, the women were asked to register.[45] The results were disappointing. Of the 641,666 women in the state only 11,358 actually registered for service. Local county chairmen throughout the state found the registration useful in locating women in their area willing to do volunteer work.[46] But it was hardly an enthusiastic response. As one observer commented in early 1918, "I do not think this registration has been pushed very much or that it has succeeded in a very satisfactory degree."[47]

The registration did highlight quite divergent emotions among the women of the state. At the end of 1917 Mrs. Reilley commented:

> Most of those desiring to register are business women. . . . Again there is a very strong feeling that this has been given to women to satisfy them and that the Government will never use it and that the card is not practical. Really I am astonished to hear some of the things I have heard from women who are supposed to know better. . . .[48]

"Business women" and other middle-class women were skeptical about the value of the project, but others were afraid that it might be too practical. Mrs. Reilley added that: "Home-keepers as a class believe it will involve their husbands or themselves in some service they do not wish to render. . . ."[49]

If the concept of registration was foreign to the majority of women in the state, the idea of increased food production and better food conservation was not. Perhaps the most successful of the various departments established by the state Woman's Committee were the Department of Food Production and Home Economics and the Department of Food Administration. In fact, the exact divi-

---

[45] Reilley to North Carolina women county chairmen (mimeographed letter), October 17, 1917, RG 62, 13A-A.1, Box 468, File 132.

[46] Reilley, "Final Report of Woman's Committee," 10-11.

[47] W. S. Wilson, legislative reference librarian, to Woman's Committee, Washington, D.C., January 25, 1918, NCCD Records, Box 3. This is the reply to a letter from the central Woman's Committee to the secretary of state of North Carolina asking about the registration of women in that state.

[48] Reilley to Mrs. Lindsay Patterson, December 15, 1917, RG 62, 13A-A.1, Box 468, File 132. See also Reilley to Mrs. Joseph R. Lamar, March 15, 1918, RG 62, 13A-A.2, Box 512, File 132. Mrs. Ira Couch Wood, field agent for the national Woman's Committee, commented: "The women in the country districts seem to have a great fear that they will be drafted through these cards for something, or that if they say they will be able to do any kind of work themselves, it may give the Government the occasion for drafting their husbands into the army. I have done all I could to remove that misconception stating the matter as clearly as I could, but the opinion seems rather wide-spread, and it will take some time to live it down. . . ." Mrs. Ira C. Wood to Mrs. D. W. Mulvane, Topeka, Kansas, September 2, 1917, RG 62, 13A-A.2, Box 477, File 195.

[49] Reilley to Mrs. Lindsay Patterson, December 15, 1917, RG 62, 13A-A.1, Box 468, File 132.

In October, 1917, the North Carolina Woman's Committee conducted a statewide effort to encourage housewives to sign the Hoover food pledge, by which they agreed to conserve food by following the directives of the federal Food Administration. This cartoon, which appeared in the October 31, 1917, issue of the *News and Observer* (Raleigh), characterized the food pledge as "American Womanhood's Blow To Kaiserism."

sion of function between the two departments, either at the state or at the federal level, was never entirely clear. As Emily Newell Blair noted of the federal Woman's Committee:

So closely allied was the work of the two food departments . . . that it is impossible to divide them in discussing their scope or achievements. Loosely speaking, that of the former [i.e., Food Production and Home Economics] was to provide an avenue between the Department of Agriculture and the housekeepers of this country, and the latter was to promote the activities for women proposed by the Food Administrator. The Department of Food Production, however, found itself closely allied with the Food Administration of the States. In fact, a certain type of work undertaken in one State by the Food Production Department, in another would be done by the Food Administration Department.[50]

However, this work had a clear purpose, did not challenge social mores, and was accomplished with positive and very tangible results. The women of North Carolina responded with enthusiasm to this call from the government.

The Food Production Department was headed by Mrs. Lindsay Patterson of Winston-Salem who was also state chairman of the National League for Women's Service and interstate chairman of the Southern Gardeners. She was an avid gardener and one anxious to pass on these skills:

I raise three crops a year on the same ground—have 34 varieties of vegetables in summer in my garden and 12 hardy varieties in January—I am not a professional gardener—I just love it and know how. That knowledge is worth passing on. . . .[51]

[50] Blair, *The Woman's Committee*, 76.

[51] Mrs. Lindsay Patterson to Miss Hannah J. Patterson, resident director, Woman's Committee, May 5, 1918 (handwritten), RG 62, 13A-A.2, Box 512, File 132. Mrs. Lucy Bramlette Patterson was founding president of the N.C. Federation of Women's Clubs, wrote extensively for newspapers on a variety of subjects, and participated actively in the Daughters of the American Revolution. Obituary, *Journal and Sentinel* (Winston-Salem), June 21, 1942.

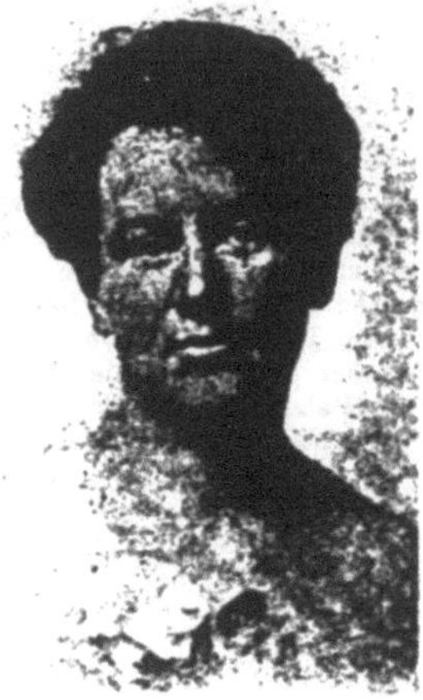

Mrs. Lindsay (Lucy Bramlette) Patterson (1865-1942) of Winston-Salem. Photograph from Gertrude S. Carraway, *Carolina Crusaders: History of North Carolina Federation of Women's Clubs* (New Bern: Owen G. Dunn Company, 1941), p. 12.

She managed to convey this enthusiasm for gardening to the women of North Carolina. The aim of the department was a garden at every home the year 'round.[52] Food production in the state quadrupled between 1917 and 1918.[53] Mrs. Patterson worked through existing societies and clubs to encourage the establishment of "Victory Gardens" and intelligent vegetable crop rotation. In Wilmington alone 3,000 Victory Gardens were reported. "She gave innumerable talks on practical gardens for summer and winter, food demonstrations and war work for women, as well as carrying on a tremendous correspondence with inquirers."[54] This work of exhortation and practical advice dovetailed with the work of the central Woman's Committee Food Administration Department which stressed the curtailment of waste and the effective use of conservation methods.

[52] Report of state Woman's Committee to national Woman's Committee, October 5, 1917, NCCD Records, Box 39.

[53] Reilley, "Final Report of Woman's Committee," 11.

[54] Reilley, "Final Report of Woman's Committee," 11. Victory Gardens antedated the war. A program of using vacant-lot cultivation as a relief measure for the poor began in 1893 when the mayor of Detroit originated the idea. In 1904 over 800 people were cultivating gardens in Philadelphia's vacant lots alone. By 1906 over thirty cities had established school gardens, and many normal schools had courses in gardening. Paul K. Conkin, *Tomorrow a New World: The New Deal Community Program* (University Microfilms, Ann Arbor, Michigan, Doctoral Dissertation Series, Publication No. 22,009), 25. This program paralleled and reinforced state government policy. In March, 1917, Governor Bickett had announced a program to make North Carolina self-sufficient in foodstuffs and to reduce the $80 million spent annually on foodstuffs imported from the Midwest. He organized the N.C. Food Conservation Commission the following month, with a unit in every county to encourage the production of foodstuffs within the state. By November it was reported that 12,000 conferences and meetings had been held, 168 newspapers had received propaganda, and the central state office had mailed out 21,000 pieces of literature on the subject. The results were spectacular—although 25 million bushels of corn were imported in 1916, virtually none was imported in 1917, and less than 20 percent of the 1916 quantity of canned goods was needed. S. R. Winters, "Food Conservation in North Carolina," *Review of Reviews* (New York), 56 (November, 1917), 504-506; reprinted in the *News and Observer*, November 5, 1917.

The Department of Food Administration operated under the chairmanship of Mrs. Jane Simpson McKimmon, a native of Raleigh, who, as her family grew older, had been drawn into a public career as an apostle of the better life for rural women. Beginning in 1908 she lectured across the entire state for the woman's division of the Farmers' Institutes, urging better housekeeping practices, particularly better gardening and canning techniques. She was made director of the Women's Institutes in 1911. In the same year she was appointed state home demonstration agent responsible for promoting the same type of program among the country women. Spectacularly successful in this work, she became a loved and respected figure throughout the state. In 1917 she was described as:

> a remarkable woman about forty or forty-five years old, of great charm, an excellent, inspiring speaker. She has apparently accomplished remarkable work. Starting about six years ago a Canning Campaign, they put up under 10,000 cans; in the summer of 1916 this increased to 400,000; in 1917 it was increased to over 7,000,000. . . .[55]

The war gave the home demonstration service a great boost as patriotism helped overcome inertia and rural conservatism.

In selecting Mrs. McKimmon as chairman of the Food Administration Department, the state Woman's Committee effectively co-opted her existing machinery under its umbrella organization. Herbert Hoover's Food Administration, when it was organized in 1917, also selected Mrs. McKimmon as the logical person to head the state woman's division of the Food Administration. The work underwent spectacular expansion during the war years, and by the end of the war 74 counties were organized for food work among the women, 7 cities in the state employed city food supervisors, 142 canning clubs were in operation, with a total of 12,000 women and girls enrolled. Twenty mill villages asked for trained supervisors; 5 full-time, trained home economics women were supplied, plus 15 part-time trained women who instructed in gardening, canning, and hygiene.[56] Demonstrations were held throughout the state. The work was pushed in every way possible: "The county Demonstrators are giving lessons to club women free and they in turn are expected to go into their several neighbourhoods and instruct classes. . . ."[57] In Forsyth County the local woman's committee was in charge of the supervision of home economics demonstrators and the conduct of the Community Cannery:

> The work of the home demonstrator was far reaching in its results; she not only taught the cookery of conservation dishes, but gave lessons in up-to-date gardening, and assumed the management of the domestic part of the emergency hospital during the epidemic. The cannery was a distinct success from every viewpoint. Besides figuring

---

[55] [George F. Porter], "Report on Trip to North Carolina," n.d. [October, 1917], typescript (6 pages), RG 62, 14-E.1, Box 787. For general biographical details concerning Mrs. Jane McKimmon (1867-1957) see typescript biographical sketch by Nell Battle Lewis (7 pages), Van Noppen Collection. See also the brief laudatory reference to the work of Mrs. McKimmon in James A. B. Scherer, *The Nation at War* (New York: George H. Doran Company, 1918), 70. Obituary in *News and Observer*, December 2, 1957.

[56] Reilley, "Final Report of Woman's Committee," 11.

[57] Reilley to Ida Tarbell, July 24, 1917, RG 62, 13A-A.1, Box 468, File 132.

A North Carolina Canning Club demonstration (ca 1914) under the direction of Mrs Jane Simpson McKimmon (1867-1957) of Raleigh Photograph from *Community Service Week in North Carolina* (Raleigh: Office of the Superintendent of Public Instruction, 1914). [p 32]

largely in saving much fruit and vegetable produce that otherwise would not have been utilized, specially with the country people, many housewives learned standard methods of canning at home.[58]

The state Woman's Committee, through its two food departments, made an important contribution to the development of better dietary habits and a more varied and interesting life for women, especially rural women. Indirectly, the entire population of the state benefited.

The contribution of the two food departments was probably the most significant example of the progressive reform impulse coming to fruition through the war work of the state Woman's Committee. But it was not the only one. Useful contributions were made by the three departments of Health and Recreation, Maintenance of Existing Social Agencies, and Child Welfare. It was in these areas that the drive for social reform was most evident. A fourth department, Women in Industry, never had the opportunity to test its reformist bent because of circumstances largely out of its control.

Long delays over the ratification of the state committee's choice of chairman for the Department of Women in Industry effectively ruined any potential for social reform that the department might have exercised. The first choice for chairman of this department was Mrs. F. C. Abbott of Charlotte who was the president of the YWCA in the state.[59] Mrs. Reilley felt that this was adequate

[58] Mrs. Louis F. Owen, "Community Service of Winston-Salem Women," typescript (7 pages) attached to note from Mrs. H. E. (Katharine B.) Rondthaler, president of the Woman's Club of Winston-Salem, to R. B. House, January 16, 1920, Military Collection, World War I Papers, Part XIII: Miscellaneous, Box 17, State Archives.

[59] Mrs. Abbott, a native of Ohio, went to Charlotte with her husband in 1897. She was one of the founders and the second president of the Charlotte Woman's Club, and she was for ten years presi-

Mrs. Frederick C. Abbott (1859-1935), left, of Charlotte was Mrs. Reilley's first choice to serve as chairman of the Department of Women in Industry. The position was ultimately filled by Miss Harriet Morehead Berry (1877-1940), right, of Chapel Hill. Photograph of Mrs. Abbott from Mrs. Sam Presson, "Charlotte Reminiscences," *Charlotte Observer*, January 29, 1939; of Miss Berry from *Southern Good Roads* (Lexington), January, 1919, p. 9.

qualification because that organization was "the only Industrial organization in North Carolina" related to women.[60] However, Mrs. Abbott waited for twelve months without getting official recognition of her position. In desperation, Mrs. Reilley decided to accept the resignation of Mrs. Abbott and asked Miss Harriet M. Berry of Chapel Hill to undertake the work. Miss Berry was the secretary of the state Geological and Economic Survey, and Mrs. Reilley thought her to be "most efficient."[61] This appointment was confirmed in late July, 1918.[62] Miss

---

dent of the Charlotte Young Women's Christian Association. See biographical sketch in *Charlotte Observer*, January 29, 1939; obituary, *Charlotte Observer*, May 1, 1935.

[60] Reilley to Mrs. James A. Field, executive secretary, Women in Industry Department, Woman's Committee, July 3, 1918, RG 62, 13A-A.2, Box 132. For a general description of this department see Blair, *The Woman's Committee*, especially 83-85.

[61] Reilley to Mrs. James A. Field, July 3, 1918, RG 62, 13A-A.2, Box 512, File 132; see also Reilley to Mrs. Joseph R. Lamar, June 21, 1918, RG 62, 13A-A.2, Box 512, File 132. For a brief description of the travails of the Women in Industry Department see O'Neill, *Everyone Was Brave*, 195-198. He describes it (p. 196) as "little more than a paper organization throughout the war."

Harriet Morehead Berry (1877-1940), a native of Hillsborough and an 1897 graduate of the State Normal and Industrial College (now the University of North Carolina at Greensboro), was also secretary of the Good Roads Association. In 1915 "Miss Hattie" helped draft the law which established the North Carolina Highway Commission; and in 1919-1921 she lobbied and lectured in the General Assembly and across the state to secure passage eventually of what the *News and Observer* described as "one of the most stupendous pieces of legislation in the history of the state"—a bill which provided that the state take over the construction, maintenance, and management of its highway system. Jeffrey J. Crow, "People in Public Works: Harriet M. Berry," *APWA Reporter*, 44 (November, 1977), 4-5.

[62] Mrs. Samuel B. Harding, executive chairman, Department of Women in Industry, Woman's Committee, to Mrs. Reilley, July 23, 1918, RG 62, 13A-A.2, Box 512, File 132. In her earlier reply on

Miss Gertrude Weil (1879-1971) of Goldsboro was active in social, civic, religious, and political affairs and was an internationally known humanitarian. During World War I she served as chairman of the Department for the Maintenance of Existing Social Service Agencies. Photograph (ca. 1915) from unidentified newspaper clipping in Gertrude Weil Papers, Miscellaneous Materials, Newspaper Clippings, etc., State Archives.

Berry began to promote the idea of young educated women going back to college to take special training in "chemistry, biology, botany, pharmacy, medicine, and allied sciences" which she felt would be in demand in the absence of men who were serving in the military.[63] The Committee on Women in Industry of the Advisory Commission of the Council of National Defense raised no objection to her scheme, although making clear the main thrust of work of the committee was "cooperation with the Department of Labor and other governmental departments in upholding the federal standards for women in industry. . . ."[64] With such a late start, it is not surprising that the work of this department was, to use Mrs. Reilley's term, "retarded."[65]

The Department for the Maintenance of Existing Social Service Agencies was put in charge of Miss Gertrude Weil of Goldsboro. A college graduate and an activist in the suffrage cause, she was also an active clubwoman and served on the boards of the North Carolina Federation and the General Federation of Women's Clubs.[66] Her first task was to organize department chairmen in the

---

July 5, 1918, Mrs. Harding had apologized for the delay and misunderstandings concerning the appointment of Mrs. Abbott, adding: "Perhaps an explanation of the routine of such appointments will be an extenuation of the delay. We have an agreement with the Committee of Women in Industry of the Advisory Commission of the Council of National Defense, whereby we agree upon one person in each State as our common representative. For this reason appointments must be approved by the Executive Committee of the Committee of Women in Industry of the Advisory Commission, and then by Mr. Gompers, before we can ask our State Chairmen to confirm the appointment finally. . . ." Harding to Reilley, July 5, 1918, RG 62, 13A-A.2, Box 512, File 132.

[63] Harriet M. Berry to Agnes Nestor, August 26, 1918, RG 62, 13A-A.2, Box 512, File 132.

[64] Mrs. Samuel B. Harding to Harriet M. Berry, August 29, 1918, RG 62, 13A-A.2, Box 512, File 132.

[65] Reilley, "Final Report of Woman's Committee," 10.

[66] Gertrude Weil (1879-1971), a native and lifelong resident of Goldsboro, was a graduate of Smith College (1901). She was active in social, civic, religious, and political projects and was an internationally known humanitarian. Her papers, totaling more than 4,200 items, do not contain

various counties. By early December, 1917, she reported that her organization covered thirty-four of the state's counties.[67]

The objective of the committee was straightforward—the Woman's Committee was determined to prevent the collapse of social services that had occurred in Great Britain in the early years of the war. Broadly speaking, the object was to see that:

> the associated charities, the orphans home, the hospitals and all philanthropic institutions in the state are not suffering in consequence of liberal contributions in other directions.[68]

The central committee in Washington sent various suggestions to Miss Weil which she then adapted to local circumstances. As she noted in replying to one of the circulars:

> Being a state of rural communities and small towns and cities, our social service agencies are in no case highly organized. . . . In many cases our women lack initiative, so I tried to make our program as definite as possible with the "Suggestions for Carrying out the Aims of the Department" and the suggested newspaper articles. . . .[69]

The work of the department, like the work of most of the other departments, involved continuous liaison with existing organizations. "It is not our intention to organize new associations," Miss Weil stated, "but to secure the support and cooperation necessary for the furthering of this object."[70] The overall effect of the work of the Department for the Maintenance of Existing Social Service Agencies was hard to measure. In her final report Mrs. Reilley emphasized the publicity that had been given to the problem by the department: "Through every means of publicity we endeavored to put before the women that their charities must not be the first item of expense to cut down and that their charities are not a luxury."[71]

The Health and Recreation Department had a more specific objective. It was concerned with the environment of the military camps that were being established across the nation and reflected the profoundly moral emphasis of the work of the Woman's Committee. The original title of this department, "Safeguarding of Moral and Spiritual Forces," best captures this orientation. Concern for the welfare of the soldiers in the camps led the department to offer its services to local authorities, civic groups, and to the government-sponsored Commission on Training Camp Activities (Fosdick Commission) which was

---

anything of relevance to her activities in World War I. This fact was confirmed following final processing of the collection by Mrs. Ellen Z. McGrew, State Archives. Mrs. McGrew to the author, January 22, 1976, letter in author's files.

[67] Gertrude Weil to Mrs. Philip N. Moore, December 6, 1917, RG 62, 13A-A.1, Box 468, File 132.

[68] Report of state Woman's Committee to North Carolina State Council of Defense, September 21, 1917, NCCD Records, Box 39.

[69] Gertrude Weil to Mrs. Philip N. Moore, December 6, 1917, RG 62, 13A-A.1, Box 468, File 132.

[70] Miss Weil's circular letter to her county chairmen of the Department for the Maintenance of Existing Social Service Agencies, December 6, 1917, attached to Gertrude Weil to Mrs. Philip N. Moore, December 6, 1917, RG 62, 13A-A.1, Box 468, File 132.

[71] Reilley, "Final Report of Woman's Committee," 11.

organized to provide healthy recreational activities inside the army camps and a decent environment surrounding them. The Health and Recreation Department mobilized the organized women in support of the effort "to foster clean moral conditions" in the area surrounding the military camps in the state, especially the major one, Camp Greene at Charlotte.[72] An investigation by the national Woman's Committee revealed considerable scope for the work of the department. The Washington office kept pressure on the North Carolina department to try to ensure that there were regular police inspections of dance halls, picture shows, and the like in the area surrounding Camp Greene and that the sanitary arrangements at the dance halls fulfilled the health regulations. It also wanted matrons assigned to the Charlotte city jail, especially as women and children were sometimes confined in them:

> Matrons should be provided in the jails and should be on duty at all hours. . . . It is a blot on the government of any state or city to permit children to be confined in jails with adult criminals. This seems to be the most important matter to be righted and anything the Woman's Committee can do to give publicity to the fact that children are being exposed to such great moral danger would surely be of value in bettering conditions. . . .[73]

The department was urged to lobby for the establishment of a separate home for juvenile delinquents and for camp followers:

> We cannot afford to let these women go from one town to another or from one state to another, and the only way to deal with them is to have a proper place to put them as soon as they are apprehended. . . .[74]

The department also aimed at a wider survey of the state in the interest of preventive work among young women who were being affected by the dislocation caused by the war. It sought data on:

> Such facts as the number of new girls who are coming in, specially where new industries are opening up—the boarding accommodations for gorls [*sic*]—the amusements, good and bad—the work and resources of every organization interested in the welfare of girls and women. Such information will be helpful to decide where lies the greatest need and how it can best be met.[75]

---

[72] Report of state Woman's Committee to North Carolina State Council of Defense, September 21, 1917, NCCD Records, Box 39. The Health and Recreation Department had two vice-chairmen responsible for conditions at the two major military installations in the state, Mrs. A. H. Washburn, Camp Greene, Charlotte, and Mrs. M. L. Stover, Ft. Caswell, Wilmington.

[73] Secretary, Department of Health and Recreation, Woman's Committee, to Mrs. Leonard Tufts, May 27, 1918, RG 62, 13A-A.2, Box 512, File 132. The work of this department exemplifies that stream of progressive thought discussed by Roy Lubove in "The Progressives and the Prostitute," *Historian*, XXIV (May, 1962), 308-330. The emphasis is very much on social control.

[74] Secretary, Department of Health and Recreation, Woman's Committee, to Mrs. Leonard Tufts, May 27, 1918, RG 62, 13A-A.2, Box 512, File 132. On the position of juvenile delinquents within the state see Joseph F. Steelman, "The Progressive Era in North Carolina, 1884-1917" (unpublished doctoral dissertation, University of North Carolina, Chapel Hill, 1955), 637-638, hereinafter cited as Steelman, "The Progressive Era in North Carolina."

[75] Report of state Woman's Committee to North Carolina State Council of Defense, September 21, 1917, NCCD Records, Box 39.

Mrs. Leonard (Gertrude Sise) Tufts (1870-1940) of Pinehurst was chairman of the Health and Recreation Department of the state Woman's Committee until August, 1918, when she was succeeded by Mrs. Katherine M. Davis Krause. Photograph courtesy Tufts Archives, Given Memorial Library, Pinehurst.

Mrs. Lucy (Owen) Robertson (1850-1930), a native of Warrenton and a longtime resident of Greensboro, was named chairman of the Child Welfare Department at the inaugural meeting of the state Woman's Committee in June, 1917. Engraving from Samuel A. Ashe and others (eds.), *Biographical History of North Carolina: From Colonial Times to the Present* (Greensboro: Charles L. Van Noppen, 8 volumes, 1905-1917), IV, facing p. 375.

One of the objects of the department was to discourage girls from going to the vicinity of the war camps, fearing a danger both to their moral and physical well-being. In a related effort, it was active in trying to clean up centers of vice in cities and towns throughout the state.[76] In August, 1918, Mrs. Katherine M. Davis Krause of Charlotte succeeded Mrs. Leonard Tufts of Pinehurst as chairman of the Health and Recreation Department of the state Woman's Committee.[77] Mrs. Reilley had engineered the new appointment. Mrs. Krause was a trained worker with the Girls' Division of the Fosdick Commission at Charlotte and was delighted to have the Woman's Committee organization to support her work.[78] Mrs. Reilley was equally delighted to have a trained person as chairman of such an important department.

The work of the Child Welfare Department proved to be at once the most progressive and the most divisive undertaken by the North Carolina Woman's

---

76 Reilley, "Final Report of Woman's Committee," 12.

77 Reilley to Mrs. Joseph R. Lamar, August 12, 1918, RG 62, 13A-A.2, Box 512, File 132. Mrs. Leonard (Gertrude Ware Sise) Tufts left no papers concerning her activities during World War I. Mrs. Mildred B. McIntosh, archivist, Given Memorial Library, Pinehurst, to the author, April 7, 1976, letter in author's files. Mrs. Tufts (1870-1940), a native of Boston, was the daughter-in-law of the founder of Pinehurst. She and her husband went to North Carolina in 1897. Mrs. Tufts was vitally interested in the Red Cross and was, in fact, working for that organization when she died suddenly in 1940. She also worked actively in behalf of the Girl Scouts, the Boy Scouts, the Parent-Teachers Association, the local health clinic, and the Community Church of Pinehurst. Obituary, *Pilot* (Southern Pines), June 21, 1940, supplied by Mrs. McIntosh.

78 Reilley to Mrs. Joseph R. Lamar, August 12, 1918, RG 62, 13A-A.2, Box 512, File 132. On Mrs. Krause's activities as secretary of the Girls' Protective Bureau of Charlotte see Mrs. K. M. D. Krause, "Work of the North Carolina State Board of Charities and Public Welfare," *Bulletin of the North Carolina State Board of Charities and Public Welfare*, 1 (July-September, 1918), 7-9.

Committee. Mrs. Lucy Robertson of Greensboro, representative of the statewide Woman's Missionary Society (Methodist), was chosen to head this department at the inaugural meeting of the committee in June, 1917.[79] This department had the advantage of close cooperation with the Children's Bureau of the Department of Labor, headed by Miss Julia Lathrop at the national level. The tasks facing this department were wide-ranging. A national program known as "Children's Year," designed to improve the standard of child welfare, was instituted:

> This program included public protection of maternity and infancy; mothers' care for elder children; enforcement of all child-labor laws; and full schooling for all children of school age; recreation for children and youth, abundant, decent, and protected from any form of exploitation. . . .[80]

The program was divided into three big drives: the Weighing and Measuring Drive, the Recreation Drive, and the Back-to-School Campaign. The national program set itself "the aim of preserving the lives of 100,000 children that might otherwise have died. . . ."[81]

The Weighing and Measuring Drive involved weighing and measuring all infants in the United States and the establishment of a permanent record of these statistics in Washington. Over 7 million record cards were issued by the Child Welfare Department of the Woman's Committee in conjunction with the Children's Bureau.[82] The objectives of this drive, of course, went far beyond simple weighing and measuring of infants. The aim was to force communities throughout the country to consider their responsibilities toward children. These obviously included the establishment of careful statistics of births, care of defective children, the establishment of child welfare stations, and the increase in the number of public health nurses.[83] The Children's Bureau and the federal Child

---

[79] Reilley, "Final Report of Woman's Committee," 3.

[80] Blair, *The Woman's Committee*, 82.

[81] Blair, *The Woman's Committee*, 82-83. The Children's Year program of 1918 brought together the efforts and aspirations of various groups and individuals. The General Federation of Women's Clubs, for example, had been interested in this work prior to American involvement in the war. In 1916 and 1917 it had held nationwide "Baby Weeks" to stimulate interest in child welfare and the related issues of nursing services, children's clinics, better milk supplies, better enforcement of birth registration, and the like. The English experience of a sharp rise in infant mortality after the war began and then a sharp decline following the institution of a government program of child welfare was cited as proof of the value of the scheme. The British infant mortality rate was only half that of the United States. See "Monthly Report of Child Welfare Department," n.d., appended to national Woman's Committee Minutes, meeting of January 29, 1918, 300-302, RG 62, 13A-C.5, Box 570.

[82] "Monthly Report of Child Welfare Department, September 11, 1918," appended to national Woman's Committee Minutes, meeting of September 13, 1918, p. 530, RG 62, 13A-C.5, Box 570, hereinafter cited as "Monthly Report of Child Welfare Department, September 11, 1918."

[83] "Monthly Report of Child Welfare Department, September 11, 1918." Because of the good work of the Vital Statistics Department of the state Board of Health, North Carolina—unlike most southern states—kept fairly good birth registration records. They were estimated to be 90 percent accurate in 1917. North Carolina was admitted as the thirteenth state to the U.S. Birth Registration area on January 1, 1917, by the U.S. Director of the Census. Virginia and Kentucky were also admitted in 1917. These were the only three states in the South with nationally accepted birth registration procedures. *News and Observer*, November 25, 1917, Section III.

Welfare Department both firmly stressed the need to establish a permanent network of public health nurses over the entire country.[84]

The Wake County branch of the North Carolina Woman's Committee did some of the most valuable work in the state in this field. In January-February, 1918, its Child Welfare Department conducted an elaborate baby-saving campaign in Raleigh in conjunction with the *Delineator* magazine's Seventh Baby Campaign.[85] Guided by a trained nurse, the members of the department undertook a detailed survey of 1,200 homes in Raleigh: one third were the homes of "the families called rich," one third were the homes of the "moderately successful," and the remaining 400 homes were of the "very poor."[86] This last group included a good deal of the Negro section of the city. The death rate among Negro children in the city was double that of white children, and it was obvious that some drastic action was needed to clean up the environment.[87] Mrs. Adelia L. Harrison, chairman of the department, commented:

> There are whole squares of houses that should be burned. There are food stores where meat and milk are sold and that should be summarily closed, and there are old and shallow wells which should be sealed. . . . We need an all-time health officer, one to whom instant report can be made of flagrant infringements of sanitary laws, and who holds full power to close up disease producing dairy or store, reeking open well or surface closets. . . .[88]

An analysis of the data produced by the survey suggested that as many as a quarter, or even a third, of all deaths that occurred in Raleigh were avoidable. The report recommended the establishment of a full-time city health officer, employment of more public health nurses, the establishment of a city health clinic, and the city-wide extension of the water and sewerage systems.[89] The Child Welfare Department of the Wake County Woman's Committee printed 500 copies of the report for circulation in an effort to influence the city commission to take action in this area. The *News and Observer* supported the campaign.[90]

---

[84] "Monthly Report of Child Welfare Department, September 11, 1918."

[85] *News and Observer*, February 20, 1918. The *Delineator*, a monthly women's magazine published in New York City, began a "Save the Seventh Baby" campaign in 1917 to publicize the infant mortality rate. It offered to send to any city of between 10,000 and 40,000 population trained personnel who would direct and coordinate a survey of the overall health facilities and make recommendations about needed reforms. The magazine required that the invitation come from the combined women's clubs, businessmen's organizations, and the local doctors and health officer of the participating city. *Delineator*, XCI (July, 1917), 14. For the development of this program see C. E. Terry, "Intensive and Constructive Journalism in Health Education: An Example," *Proceedings of the National Conference of Social Work, 44th Annual Session, Pittsburgh, Pa., June 6-13, 1917*, 206-214. In North Carolina the need was very real. The State Board of Health estimated in 1918 that of the 72,000 babies born each year in the state approximately 10,000 died in infancy. *News and Observer*, September 8, 1918.

[86] *News and Observer*, February 17, 1918, Section I.

[87] *News and Observer*, February 11, 1918.

[88] *News and Observer*, February 6, 1918.

[89] *News and Observer*, February 20, 1918.

[90] *News and Observer*, March 17, 1918, editorial. Following on these revelations, both the Chamber of Commerce and the Rotary Club of Raleigh began a campaign for a general survey of the city

Both the Back-to-School Drive and the Recreation Drive were aimed at improving the lot of older children. The Recreation Drive was designed to interest communities in providing wholesome recreational opportunities for children, particularly over the summer vacation. More than a score of national organizations cooperated with the national Woman's Committee in this effort. As the chairman of the national committee commented: "Play, helpful play, is as necessary to a child's life as air and food."[91] The Back-to-School Drive in the fall of 1918 had been preceded by the related campaign to help enforce the provisions of the new federal Child Labor Law which became effective on September 1, 1917. The law prohibited the employment of children under fourteen years in "any mill, cannery, workshop, factory or manufacturing establishment which ships interstate or in foreign commerce."[92] The central committee urged state chairmen to concentrate on the schooling of the children affected by the legislation. Dr. Anna Howard Shaw regarded it as a matter of "our first consideration."[93] North Carolina had passed legislation forbidding children under twelve years of age from working in mills and factories but had provided very inadequate enforcement machinery. The state in 1913 required only four months of schooling per year for eight-to-fourteen-year-olds, and this legislation was also not really enforced. One historian labeled this act "a sham and a fraud."[94] In 1915 over 10,000 children under sixteen years were working in manufacturing plants, and many more were employed in unregulated industries. The National Child Labor Committee surveyed the state in 1918 and urged more adequate enforcement machinery. In 1919 the state legislature made fourteen years the legal minimum working age.[95]

It was the issue of child welfare that most sharply divided the North Carolina Woman's Committee from the men's State Council of Defense. Mrs. Reilley was

---

to be conducted by the U.S. Public Health Service. In mid-1918 the city commissioners finally authorized such a survey, but the federal agency could not spare the experts. *News and Observer* September 19, 1918. For a brief discussion of public health work in North Carolina up to this time see Steelman, "The Progressive Era in North Carolina," 642-650.

[91] Anna Howard Shaw to Mrs. Reilley, August 1, 1918, RG 62, 13A-A.2, Box 512, File 132

[92] Julia Lathrop to State Chairmen, mimeographed circular, August 17, 1917, RG 62, 13A-A 1, Box 476, File 192.

[93] Anna Howard Shaw to State Chairman, mimeographed circular, August 17, RG 62, 13A-A 1, Box 476, File 192.

[94] Steelman, "The Progressive Era in North Carolina," 522.

[95] North Carolina textile men were the most adamant of all the opponents of child labor legislation. See Katharine DuPre Lumpkin and Dorothy Wolff Douglas, *Child Workers in America* (New York: International Publishers, 1937), 200-201; George Brown Tindall, *The Emergence of the New South, 1913-1945*. Volume X of *A History of the South*, edited by Wendell Holmes Stephenson and E. Merton Coulter (Baton Rouge: Louisiana State University Press and the Littlefield Fund for Southern History of the University of Texas [projected 10 volumes, 1948—], 1967), 322-323, hereinafter cited as Tindall, *Emergence of the New South*; Walter I. Trattner, *Crusade for the Children: A History of the National Child Labor Committee and Child Labor Reform in America* (Chicago: Quadrangle Books, 1970), 137-138. The North Carolina opponents of child labor legislation—from expedient motives—accepted the 1919 state law with a fourteen-year minimum-age standard for industrial employment. See Stephen B. Wood, *Constitutional Politics in the Progressive Era: Child Labor and the Law* (Chicago: University of Chicago Press, 1968), 223-224. Details of the National Child Labor Committee survey of child labor conditions in North Carolina were published in the *News and Observer*, December 8, 15, 22, 1918; editorial in issue of January 21, 1919.

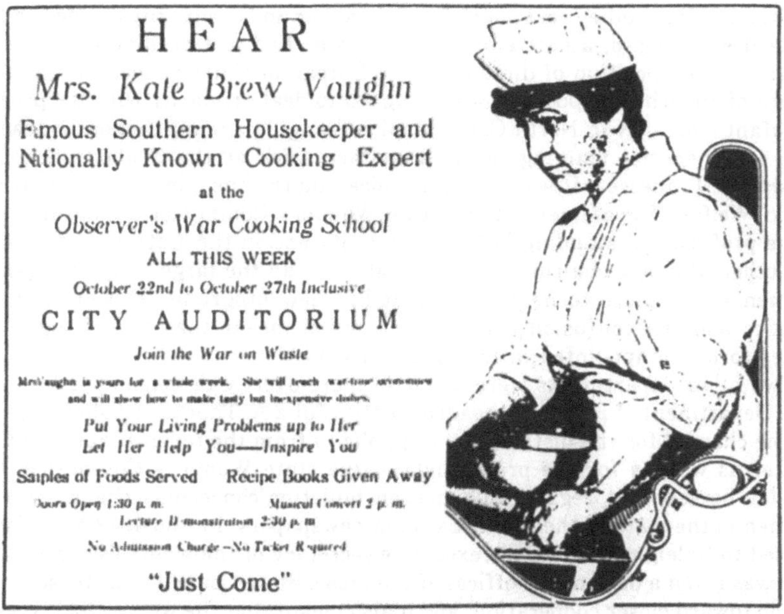


Just as the war was coming to a close Mrs. Reilley recommended Mrs. Kate Brew Vaughn, a native of Tennessee and a home economics teacher, to succeed Mrs. Lucy Robertson as chairman of the Child Welfare Department. Because of the confusion surrounding the war's end, however, Mrs. Vaughn was never formally appointed to this position. Prior to this abortive appointment Mrs. Vaughn had toured the South and conducted a "war cooking school" for the benefit of southern homemakers. Advertisement from *Charlotte Observer*, October 22, 1917.

the only woman member of the latter body. The men's council had supported the efforts of the Woman's Committee to improve the physical and moral conditions in the environs of the military camps in the state, presumably because this was clearly related to the war effort. But on the issue of child labor there was a divergent opinion. As one observer remarked:

Women are also interested in caring for children who will be thrown out of work by the Federal Child Labor Law. The men are all antagonistic to the law, and feel that it is unfair and unwise, and most of them go so far in their antagonism that they do not desire to assist in caring for the people thrown out of work. The Child Labor Law is a touchy subject and it is best not to mention it. . . .[96]

On this issue the men remained adamant.

Just as the war was ending the chairman of the state Child Welfare Department, Mrs. Lucy Robertson of Greensboro, resigned to take up a teaching

---

[96] E. D. Smith, "Memorandum for Mr. Porter for a Trip to North Carolina," typescript (October 3, 1917, 3 pages), RG 62, 14-E.1, Box 787. See also Breen, "The North Carolina Council of Defense," 25.

position.[97] Mrs. Reilley cast about for a successor and eventually decided on Mrs. Kate Brew Vaughn, a native of Tennessee who had just been appointed to the newly created position of director of the Bureau of Child Hygiene in the State Board of Health. The position was designed to deal primarily with the problem of infant mortality in North Carolina. Mrs. Vaughn, a home economics teacher, had taken special training in child welfare work at the Peabody School in Nashville, Tennessee. It was an ideal choice—on the one hand, it would give the Child Welfare Department of the state Woman's Committee a chairman with some professional standing in the community and in the state government; on the other, the new chairman would be able to tap the large body of organized women in the state to help implement her new programs. However, the armistice and the confusion over reconstruction meant that Mrs. Vaughn was never formally appointed in this dual capacity.[98]

Two other departments were active in more overtly propagandist activities. The Department of Publicity, headed by Miss Julia A. Thorns of Asheboro, acted as the channel for the distribution of publicity from the federal Woman's Committee as well as for the propaganda of the state Woman's Committee. Mrs. Reilley herself sent regular information bulletins concerning the activities of women in the state to the North Carolina newspapers. In mid-1918 Miss Thorns moved to Raleigh to act as the executive secretary of the woman's organization and was given a desk at the offices of the men's State Council of Defense. It was a step toward closer cooperation, and it also meant that the women had access to the mimeographing facilities available for the men's council.[99] The work of the Educational Propaganda Department concentrated on promoting patriotic speaking by high school girls and women throughout the state. It also conducted a survey of available classes for women in skills such as shorthand, typing, and telegraphy and contemplated establishing such classes if needed.[100] Neither

---

[97] Reilley to D. H. Hill, October 24, 1918, NCCD Records, Box 39. Mrs. Robertson (1850-1930) represented the N.C. Woman's Missionary Society (Methodist) on the Woman's Committee. Mrs. Robertson (née Lucy Henderson Owen) was a native of Warrenton and began her teaching career at Greensboro Female College in 1878. She was for nine years professor of history at State Normal and Industrial College (now the University of North Carolina at Greensboro) and served from 1902 to 1913 as president of Greensboro College for Women. Obituary, *Greensboro Daily Record*, May 28, 1930.

[98] For biographical details on Mrs. Vaughn see *News and Observer*, September 8, 1918, and editorial, September 9, 1918, congratulating the Board of Health on its choice of Mrs. Vaughn. Mrs. Vaughn wrote a weekly column for women in the *News and Observer*. Mrs. Reilley expressed her opinion to Dr. D. H. Hill, chairman of the men's State Council of Defense, thusly: "I have felt that she [Vaughn] was not only the logical one, but the most competent to take up the work. I have sounded her and also the Health Department as to their attitude and find both most cordial toward such an adjustment. Of course the invitation has not been given, but simply sent out a feeler, pending our meeting, when these questions must be adjusted." Reilley to D. H. Hill, November 17, 1918, NCCD Records, Box 39.

[99] Julia A. Thorns to D. H. Hill, July 1, 1918, NCCD Records, Box 39; Reilley to Mrs. Joseph R. Lamar, August 12, 1918, RG 62, 13A-A.2, Box 512, File 132; Reilley, "Final Report of Woman's Committee," 12. Miss Thorns (1864-1939), a native of New York, was a charter member of the Asheboro Woman's Club. In 1917-1918 she was chairman of the Conservation Department of the N.C. Federation of Women's Clubs; her interest in beautification and the welfare of the needy continued throughout her lifetime. Obituary, *Greensboro Daily News*, August 17, 1939.

[100] Report of state Woman's Committee to North Carolina State Council of Defense, September 21, 1917, NCCD Records, Box 39; Reilley, "Final Report of Woman's Committee," 12.

Miss Julia A. Thorns (1864-1939), a native of Brooklyn, New York, and a longtime resident of Asheboro, was head of the Department of Publicity of the state Woman's Committee. Photograph from advertisement in *Leslie's Weekly*, April 13, 1918, in the possession of Mrs. Marion Stedman Covington, Asheboro; reproduced by courtesy of Mrs. Covington.

department really managed to seize fully the opportunities that presented themselves; after a promising start, both seemed to flounder in comparison with the majority of other departments.

While the issue of child welfare struck a positive chord among the members of the Woman's Committee, the response to the question of patriotic organization and participation in the war effort by the black community was more ambivalent. The issue arose in early 1918 as a result of pressure from the central Woman's Committee in Washington.[101] The suggestion from Washington was that the state Woman's Committee help organize the black women into a separate woman's council to assist in the war effort. The issue was discussed at an executive meeting of the state Woman's Committee held in Raleigh on February 14, 1918. Dr. Hill, chairman of the men's State Council, was present for the discussion. The men's State Council had also been under pressure from the central office in Washington on the matter of black organization in the state, and Hill was anxious to create a united front with the state Woman's Committee on this issue. Dr. Hill expressed the opinion that to establish a separate council composed of black women would be "fatal to good policy" and would be detrimental to the whole council idea.[102] The women of the executive committee agreed with this opinion and passed a motion to "strenuously advise against

[101] The issue had been formally raised in November, 1917, when Dr. Hill had asked Mrs. Reilley to appoint three women to cooperate with three men to make a recommendation concerning Negro organization within the state. The committee never met. Reilley to Mrs. Joseph R. Lamar, February 20, 1918, RG 62, 13A-A.2, Box 512, File 132. Anne F. Scott, "After Suffrage: Southern Women in the Twenties," *Journal of Southern History*, XXX (August, 1964), 298-318, refers to the racial work of southern women in the 1920s as the "most intriguing" of all their public activities. The same expression might be applied to the complex wartime relationship between white and Negro women in the South. See William J. Breen, "Black Women and the Great War: Mobilization and Reform in the South," *Journal of Southern History*, XLIV (August, 1978).

[102] Minutes of Executive Meeting of N.C. Woman's Committee, February 14, 1918, NCCD Records, Box 39, hereinafter cited as Minutes of Executive Meeting, Woman's Committee, February 14, 1918. For a more detailed discussion of the attitude of the men's State Council of Defense on this issue see Breen, "The North Carolina Council of Defense," 25-29.

Mrs. Thomas W. (Fannie Yarborough) Bickett (1870-1941), wife of the governor and honorary cochairman of the state Woman's Committee. Photograph from Mrs. Bryan Wells Collier [Margaret Wooten Collier] (comp.), *Biographies of Representative Women of the South, 1861-1923* (N.p.: n.p., 4 volumes, 1923[?]), II, [p. 72].

setting up a separate organization of negroes for Council of Defense work in any Southern State. . . ."[103] There was no real opposition to the motion. Everyone felt that the existing plan of occasional consultation with blacks at the county level, or even the appointment of selected individuals as consultants on Negro matters, "results in benefit not only to work but to negroes as well."[104]

Yet, to suggest a simple consensus of opinion on the place and role of the black in the war effort in the state would be wrong. In July, 1918, Mrs. Reilley wrote of the "perplexing" nature of the question and admitted that "there is a difference of opinion in the state as to the best way of handling the question."[105] The general agreement on the inadvisability of separate statewide black organizations masked wide differences in approach as to how best to ensure the support of black women. Mrs. T. W. Bickett, the wife of the governor, had been opposed to any separate organization of black women at the February meeting of the executive committee of the state Woman's Committee but had "brought the colored women into the Mansion in order to enlist their interest in the child welfare campaign."[106] On the other hand, in Charlotte such personal cooperation between the races was actively discouraged. Mrs. Reilley wrote:

> in Charlotte, Mrs. Krause, representative of the Women's and Girls' Division on Training Camp Activities and with whom I am cooperating, tells me that she has a splendid woman who is working under her direction with the negroes, but such a prejudice exists that she takes her into her own room, where she lives and has a desk there for her, because she cannot do so in the office on Training Camp Activities. This leads me to believe that each section must work the question out locally and that we cannot have any concerted movement in the state along this line.[107]

[103] Minutes of Executive Meeting, Woman's Committee, February 14, 1918.
[104] Minutes of Executive Meeting, Woman's Committee, February 14, 1918.
[105] Reilley to Mrs. Joseph R. Lamar, July 18, 1918, RG 62, 13A-A.2, Box 512, File 132.
[106] Reilley to Mrs. Joseph R. Lamar, July 18, 1918, RG 62, 13A-A.2, Box 512, File 132.
[107] Reilley to Mrs. Joseph R. Lamar, July 18, 1918, RG 62, 13A-A.2, Box 512, File 132.

Mrs Alice (Moore) Dunbar-Nelson (1875-1935), a native of New Orleans, author and teacher, served during the war as black field agent of the national Woman's Committee. Her first husband was Paul Laurence Dunbar (d. 1906), noted American poet. Photograph courtesy Schomburg Center for Research in Black Culture, New York Public Library, Astor, Lenox, and Tilden foundations; reproduced by permission. The editors were unable to obtain a photograph of or biographical information concerning Miss Mamie McCullough.

In spite of the perplexities of the problem the Washington office kept pressure on state organizations to organize the black women.

When she visited North Carolina in September, 1918, Mrs. Dunbar-Nelson, the black field agent of the national Woman's Committee, had the opportunity for a lengthy discussion about the situation with Miss Mamie McCullough, a young black schoolteacher on leave of absence, working among the women of Charlotte and connected with the War Camp Community Service. She was the leading black woman war worker in the state.[108] Reporting on a conference with Mrs. Reilley, Mrs. Dunbar-Nelson wrote:

> Miss McCullough, who was present at the conference, agreed with me that separate state organization among the colored people, that is, a colored state chairman, with county chairmen, and local chairmen, would accomplish the best good for the colored people of the state, since it would throw them on their own responsibility and at the same time enable them to reach down into all classes. . . .[109]

Although Mrs. Reilley did not feel at liberty to make any drastic change in the existing organization herself, "she [Mrs. Reilley] did see that if anything is to be done, and tangible results secured, some method other than that now employed must be used."[110] Mrs. Reilley promised to raise the matter at the next meeting of her state committee in late September with a view to reorganizing the war

---

[108] Mrs. Dunbar-Nelson to H. J. Patterson, September 7, 1918, RG 62, 13A-A.2, Box 512, File 131.

[109] Mrs. Dunbar-Nelson to H. J. Patterson, September 7, 1918, RG 62, 13A-A.2, Box 512, File 131. This feeling was, of course, shared by the Negro men. It found very clear expression at the United War Work Convention at Raleigh in September, 1918, when Arch Traywick "insisted that many campaigns of like nature among the colored people have failed for the reason that the real leaders of the race were not selected to lead it. He advocated the opportunities of real leaders—the men who are recognized by the colored themselves as their leaders rather than those who are chosen by the white people of the community—to organize the race for the United War Work. . . ." *News and Observer*, September 22, 1918, Section II.

[110] Mrs. Dunbar-Nelson to H. J. Patterson, September 7, 1918, RG 62, 13A-A.2, Box 512, File 131.

work.[111] Had the war lasted longer, this pressure from the center would most likely have forced a far-reaching reorganization of the method by which the black female population was drawn into the war effort.

The signing of the armistice on November 11, 1918, put the North Carolina Woman's Committee into a quandary. The initial response of the leadership was to try to keep the organization alive to work during the reconstruction period. However, the central office in Washington, receiving no guidance from the Wilson administration, was in turn unable to offer any guidance to the state organizations. The attitude of the North Carolina state government was as discouraging at the end as at the beginning. In reply to a query from Mrs. Reilley, Governor Bickett said that he did not believe that the next state legislature would make any appropriation for the work of her committee; and he added that, in his own view, any further personal expenditure to keep the organization alive would not be justified in the circumstances.[112] Consequently, in February, 1919, Mrs. Reilley felt obliged to give the members of her state Woman's Committee an "honorable discharge"—"As we have no disposition to duplicate work or endeavor to do work which does not mean real service, our organization naturally vanishes. . . ."[113]

Final evaluation of the work of the North Carolina Woman's Committee is difficult. It was among the weakest in the Union. One commentator observed:

> In the Southern states, class lines made a really representative organization difficult. The condescension with which women were regarded by their political and economic masters, the men, also contributed to the comparative failure of women's work south of Mason and Dixon's line. Naturally the poverty of the South accounted to some extent for this condition of things, as it did in the case of the State Councils. . . .[114]

However, if most women in North Carolina saw their wartime role primarily in conventional and limited terms that emphasized Red Cross work, the knitting of comfort kits for the soldiers, manning canteens at railroad stations and the like, there were others with a wider social vision. The women who directed the activities of the North Carolina Woman's Committee drew on a wide experience in reform causes espoused by organized women over the previous decade. Their efforts helped educate women in the state to broader social issues and, in so doing, helped to nurture a growing social consciousness that would in the 1920s lead to

---

[111] Mrs. Dunbar-Nelson to H. J. Patterson, September 7, 1918, RG 62, Box 512, File 131.

[112] Reilley to Members of N.C. Woman's Committee (mimeographed circular), February 15, 1919, NCCD Records, Box 39.

[113] Reilley to Members of N.C. Woman's Committee (mimeographed circular), February 15, 1919, NCCD Records, Box 39.

[114] Frederick Lewis Allen, "The Council of Defense System: A History Submitted to the Director of the Council of National Defense, May, 1919," typescript (392 pages), 271, in RG 62, 17-B.1. Mrs. Reilley's organization did operate on a shoestring budget, and it is perhaps not surprising that its accomplishments were limited. By contrast the Illinois Woman's Committee operated on a scale that surpassed Mrs. Reilley's wildest dreams. Its central quarters occupied an entire floor of a city office building, supplied rent-free by the men's State Council of Defense, along with telephones, heat, and light. The men, "in addition, furnished the services of two stenographers, postage and office supplies amounting to about $1,000 a month." See Mrs. Joseph T. Bowen, "The War Work of the Women of Illinois," *Transactions of the Illinois State Historical Society, 1919*, 93; this same article appeared in the *Illinois State Historical Society Journal*, XII (October, 1919), 317-329.

North Carolina's being labeled "the Wisconsin of the South."[115] The chairman of the state Woman's Committee was herself very much alive to the possibilities for domestic reform that the war had created. Comparing the work of the state Woman's Committee with that of the men's State Council of Defense, one observer from the Washington office commented:

> It seems to me that the women's work is at least as well done as the men's except perhaps in the matter of organization, and that she [Mrs. Reilley] is the only person on the council [N.C. State Council of Defense] really alive to the welfare of the common people, and to the fact that war work might be made of permanent benefit to the community. . . .[116]

---

[115] Tindall, *Emergence of the New South*, 225, citing Nell Battle Lewis, *News and Observer*, January 20, 1924.

[116] "Report on Trip to Raleigh, N.C., to attend the second meeting of the North Carolina Council of Defense" (unsigned, but probably E. D. Smith), September 24, 1917, typescript (8 pages), RG 62, 14-E.1, Box 787.

APPENDIX

WOMAN'S COMMITTEE
COUNCIL OF NATIONAL DEFENSE
North Carolina Division
As of February 15, 1919

Executive Committee

*Chairman:* Mrs. James Eugene Reilley, Charlotte

*Honorary Chairmen:*
Mrs. Thomas W. Bickett, Raleigh
Mrs. R. R. Cotten, Bruce

*First Vice-Chairman:*
Mrs. Palmer Jerman, Raleigh

*Second Vice-Chairman:*
Mrs. William N. Reynolds, Winston-Salem

*Secretary:*
Miss Julia A. Thorns, Asheboro

*Treasurer:*
Mrs. E. Sternberger, Greensboro

Department Chairmen

*Registration for Service:*
Mrs. W. B. Waddill, Henderson

*Food Production and Home Economics:*
Mrs. Lindsay Patterson, Winston-Salem

*Food Administration:*
Mrs. Jane S. McKimmon, Raleigh

*Women in Industry:*
Miss Harriet M. Berry, Chapel Hill

*Child Welfare:*
Mrs. Lucy O. Robertson, Greensboro

*Maintenance of Existing Social Agencies:*
Miss Gertrude Weil, Goldsboro

*Health and Recreation:*
Mrs. Leonard Tufts, Pinehurst

*Vice Chairmen:*
Mrs. A. H. Washburn, Camp Greene, Charlotte
Mrs. H. L. Stover, Ft. Caswell, Wilmington

*Educational Propaganda:*
Miss Harriet W. Elliott, Greensboro

*Liberty Loan:*
Mrs. R. J. Reynolds, Winston-Salem, Second Loan
Mrs. R. H. Latham, Winston-Salem, Third Loan

*Publicity:*
Miss Julia A. Thorns, Asheboro

*Finance:*
Mrs. Felix Harvey, Kinston

Organizations Affiliating with the Woman's Committee

*North Carolina Nurses Association:* Miss Eugenia Henderson, Charlotte
*Southern Association of Collegiate Alumnae:* Mrs. Ernest Cruikshank, Raleigh
*Daughters of the American Revolution:* Mrs. T. S. Morrison, Asheville
*N.C. Federation of Women's Clubs:* Mrs. Clarence Johnson, Raleigh
*Grand Chapter Eastern Star:* Mrs. Agnes Hamlin, Southern Pines
*N.C. Suffrage Association:* Mrs. John Cunningham, Durham
*Parents and Teachers Association:* Mrs. David Yates, Charlotte
*N.C. Federation of Musical Clubs:* Mrs. Bertha Orndoff, Charlotte
*N.C. League for Women's Service:* Mrs. Lindsay Patterson, Winston-Salem
*N.C. WCTU:* Mrs. Adelaide Goodno, Raleigh
*N.C. Society of Colonial Dames:* Mrs. A. M. Waddell, Wilmington
*N.C. Society United Daughters of 1812:* Miss Mary Hilliard Hinton, Raleigh
*Daughters of the Revolution:* Mrs. Marshall Williams, Faison
*Woman's Department National Civic Association:* Mrs. Wm. N. Reynolds, Winston-Salem
*Woman's Missionary Society* (Methodist): Mrs. Lucy Robertson, Greensboro
*Woman's Missionary Union* (Baptist): Mrs. Wesley Jones, Raleigh
*The Synodical* (Presbyterian): Mrs. W. B. Ramsay, Hickory
*United Daughters of the Confederacy:* Mrs. Jacksie Thrash, Tarboro
*State Association of Home Economics:* Mrs. Shay, Charlotte
*United Farm Women:* Mrs. W. N. Hutt, Raleigh
*State Primary Association:* Mrs. E. C. Gerriessen, Goldsboro
*Grammar Grades Association:* Mrs. C. P. Blaylock, Raleigh
*State Library Association:* Mrs. A. F. Griggs, Durham
*N.C. Children's Aid Society:* Mrs. R. L. Justice, Greensboro
*Woman's Section Navy League:* Mrs. Lyman Cotten, Salisbury

♦

Affiliating Groups Having No State Organization

*YWCA:* Mrs. F. C. Abbott, Charlotte
Mrs. Whiteford Smith, Asheville
Mrs. H. L. Stover, Wilmington

*Medical Woman's National Association:*
Dr. Delia Dixon Carroll, Raleigh

*Red Cross:* Mrs. Ralph Van Landingham, Charlotte
Mrs. Joseph Patton, Charlotte
Mrs. John Sprunt Hill, Durham
Mrs. William Grimes, Raleigh
Mrs. Max Gardner, Shelby

Woman's Committee North Carolina Division County Chairmen

| County | Chairman | County | Chairman |
|---|---|---|---|
| Alamance | Mrs. Lawrence Holt | Johnston | Mrs. F. H. Brooks |
| Alexander | Mrs. W. R. Pritchard | Jones | Mrs. W. M. Foscue |
| Alleghany | Mrs. W. L. Cooper | Lee | Mrs. John P. Monroe* |
| Anson | Mrs. Eugene Little | Lenoir | Miss Mary Shotwell |
| Ashe | Miss Eula Todd | Lincoln | Miss Annie Wise |
| Avery | Mrs. Edgar Tufts* | McDowell | Mrs. D. E. Hudgins |
| Beaufort | Mrs. W. P. Baughan | Macon | Mrs. George Biddell |
| Bertie | Mrs. Francis Winston | Madison | Mrs. W. E. Reynolds |
| Bladen | Miss Marion Whitted* | Martin | Mrs. C. H. Godwin |
| Brunswick | Mrs. Jackson Johnson | Mecklenburg | Miss Cornelia Shaw |
| Buncombe | Mrs. J. M. Gudger, Jr. | Mitchell | ______ |
| Burke | Miss Sue Tate | Montgomery | Mrs. Boring |
| Cabarrus | Mrs. J. P. Cooke* | Moore | Mrs. S. P. McConnell |
| Caldwell | Mrs. J. W. Self | Nash | Miss Leyta Carter |
| Camden | Miss Mary L. Stevens | New Hanover | Mrs. J. D. Bellamy, Jr. |
| Carteret | Mrs. W. M. Webb* | Northampton | Mrs. David H. Brown* |
| Caswell | Miss Emma Watkins | Onslow | Mrs. R. P. Hinton |
| Catawba | Mrs. Fannie R. Williams | Orange | Mrs. J. P. Webb |
| Chatham | Mrs. Arthur London | Pamlico | Mrs. George Farnell |
| Cherokee | Mrs. J. W. Coover | Pasquotank | Mrs. C. H. Robinson |
| Chowan | Mrs. W. D. Pruden | Pender | Miss Maggie Williams* |
| Cleveland | Mrs. Hull | Perquimans | Mrs. Robert M. Smith |
| Clay | Miss Ellen Scroggs | Person | Mrs. R. Y. Teague |
| Columbus | Mrs. Joe Brown | Pitt | Mrs. Mark Quimerly |
| Craven | Mrs. T. John Hollister | Polk | Mrs. W. E. Cobb |
| Currituck | Miss Bray | Randolph | Mrs. T. I. Fox |
| Cumberland | Mrs. Hunter Smith | Richmond | Mrs. W. N. Everett |
| Dare | Mrs. C. A. Griffin | Robeson | Mrs. A. W. McLean |
| Davidson | Mrs. George Montcastle | Rockingham | Mrs. Frank Mebane |
| Davie | Miss Mary Hoitman* | Rowan | Mrs. Edwin Overman |
| Duplin | Mrs. H. F. Pierce | Rutherford | Mrs. Ed Beam |
| Durham | Miss Caroline Fuller | Sampson | Mrs. W. B. Lamb |
| Edgecombe | Mrs. James Pender | Scotland | Mrs. Peter John* |
| Forsyth | Mrs. W. J. Conrad | Stanly | Mrs. G. V. D. Reynolds |
| Franklin | Mrs. A. L. Joyner | Stokes | Miss Annie Jones |
| Gaston | Mrs. F. P. Hall | Surry | Mrs. Will Sparger |
| Gates | Mrs. Tom Costin | Swain | Mrs. A. M. Frye |
| Granville | Mrs. A. H. Powell | Transylvania | Miss Annie Jean Gash |
| Graham | Mrs. Bruce Slaughter | Tyrrell | Mrs. Charles McKeel |
| Greene | Mrs. W. B. Murphy | Union | Mrs. Frank Laney |
| Guilford | Mrs. R. L. Justice | Vance | Mrs. A. J. Cheek |
| Halifax | Mrs. J. L. Patterson* | Wake | Mrs. J. R. Chamberlain |
| Harnett | Mrs. Charles Ross | Warren | Mrs. S. P. Arrington |
| Haywood | Mrs. J. W. Ferguson | Washington | Miss Alice McQueen |
| Hertford | Miss Gertrude Lawrence | Watauga | Mrs. B. J. Councill |
| Henderson | Mrs. J. L. Rose | Wayne | Mrs. W. D. Creech |
| Hoke | Mrs. J. W. Moore* | Wilkes | Mrs. T. Finley |
| Hyde | Mrs. Lewis H. Swindell | Wilson | Mrs. Henry Connor, Jr. |
| Iredell | Miss Celeste Hinkle | Yadkin | Miss Ila Wagner* |
| Jackson | Mrs. S. N. Enloe | Yancey | Mrs. T. W. Cheseborough |

* Resigned

SOURCE: Military Collection, World War I Papers; Part II: North Carolina Council of Defense, Box 39, File "Woman's Committee."

# "THE MOTHERS OF THE RACE" IN WORLD WAR I: THE NATIONAL WAR LABOR BOARD AND WOMEN IN INDUSTRY

By VALERIE J. CONNER

MARGUERITE MARTYN: Well, do you think street car conductoring and traffic officering and such jobs really are suitable woman's work?
ANNA HERKNER: I think the only question as to what constitutes woman's work is given a certain work, does she do it as well as a man? [1]

In the 1960s, two Federal steps against sex-based discrimination—the Civil Rights Act and the "Equal Pay" amendment to the Fair Labor Standards Act—signaled victory for the heirs of the women who had fought for both equal pay and equal employment opportunities during World War I. The wartime government had embraced cautiously the demand for equal pay, had equivocated on the rights of working women, and in the end, had left a checkered legacy.

Among the government's most important agencies which dealt with women workers was the National War Labor Board. The NWLB administered America's first comprehensive experiment in labor-government-management relations. Chaired jointly by former President William Howard Taft and Frank P. Walsh—chairman of the Industrial Relations Commission of 1913-1915, the twelve-man Board was created by Woodrow Wilson in April 1918 to settle disputes in war-related in-

[1] Interview with NWLB examiner Anna Herkner by reporter Marguerite Martyn, "Woman's Work Is Whatever She Can Do As Well As Man, Says Woman Member of the Federal War Labor Board," St. Louis *Post-Dispatch*, n.d. [Oct., 1918], in National Archives, Records of the National War Labor Board, RG 2 (hereafter cited as NWLB Records), Entry 13: Interstaff Communications.

dustries. The American Federation of Labor named five labor leaders to represent employees, and the National Industrial Conference Board (NICB) selected five industrialists to speak for the nation's employers. From the outset, the NWLB employee members urged sweeping reforms and the employer representatives stood firm against change. The board's principles, which had been drafted in an effort to reconcile the two groups' conflicting demands, were themselves ambiguous. By one construction, they affirmed the status quo; by another, they augured its destruction. In the summer of 1918, as the principles were slowly hammered into specific awards, their ultimate definition depended heavily on the leadership exercised by Taft and Walsh, the men appointed by the NICB and the AFL to represent the public. Only because Taft sided more often than not against the employer interests responsible for his appointment did the board move toward what Walsh called "a new deal for American Labor."[3]

The NWLB's principle of equal pay for equal work when women worked at jobs ordinarily filled by men pleased both feminists and the labor movement; but just as important was the principle of the living wage, the right of men and women to live in "health and reasonable comfort." In 1918, women still earned only one-half to two-thirds as much as men, and frequently less than boys not yet eighteen. Part of the wage imbalance had developed because women prior to the war had worked in industry's lowest paying and least prestigious jobs. Yet even when they performed similar tasks in jobs usually held by men, they remained underpaid. Traditionalists rationalized the disparity by holding that woman's pay was "personal" or supplementary and that family considerations mandated the higher wage-scale for men. In these circumstances, the sudden unregulated introduction into the war industries of 1,500,000 women, many of whom performed as efficiently as men, resulted in changes of attitude. As early as

[3] US, Dept. of Labor, "Report of the War Labor Conference Board to the Secretary of Labor, March 29, 1918," printed in Bureau of Labor Statistics, *National War Labor Board*, Bulletin No. 287, Labor as Affected by the War Series (Washington, D.C.: Government Printing Office, 1922), 32-33; Frank P. Walsh, "A New Deal for American Labor," *Irish World and American Industrial Liberator*, June 1, 1918, New York Public Library, The Papers of Frank P. Walsh (hereafter cited as Walsh Papers), Scrapbook No. 39. For a friendly study of Taft's work as Joint Chairman, see Henry F. Pringle, *The Life and Times of William Howard Taft* (2 vols., NY: Farrar and Rinehart, 1939), II, Chapt. 43.

March 1917 the AFL had joined the women's wartime fight for equal pay. Eight months later in convention it even urged women to organize, announcing that only through organization could men and women effect wage equality. Elated, feminists had united with organized labor to protect men's wage levels and to prevent women from superseding men by underbidding them.[8]

The NWLB promise of equality suggested a new status for women in industry which the protective legislation of the pre-war years had militated against. The minimum wage legislation passed in twelve states after 1912 had never reached most working women, either because the legislation was drawn too narrowly or because it was ignored. Nor was equality ever implied. None of the laws, for example, ordered women's pay scales raised to the level normally accorded men. Furthermore, the value of such legislation was diminished by the reasoning which generally sanctioned protective laws. Justice Brewer in the *Muller* decision, for example, had approved the invasion of woman's contract rights because something in her "disposition and habits of life" prevented her full assertion of them. Even if woman stood, "so far as the statutes are concerned, upon an absolutely equal plane with [her brother]," explained Brewer, she was "so constituted" that she relied upon his aid. Beyond that, "her physical structure and a proper discharge of her maternal functions—having in view not merely her own health, but the well-being of the race—" justified state action on her behalf. Hours limitation laws, while rarely sustained for men when Brewer spoke in 1908, were thus acceptable for women because women had little bargaining power, and more precisely, because women it was believed were inherently unequal.

The wartime government's measures to protect working women reflected those pre-war attitudes. As NWLB Secretary Jett Lauck later remarked, "Women are the mothers of the race . . . and can not be dealt with on the same terms as men workers." Although the board itself merely cautioned against allotting women tasks "disproportionate to their strength," The War Labor

[8] "Report," Bureau of Labor Statistics, *National War Labor Board,* 32-33; John O'Grady, *A Legal Minimum Wage* (Washington, D.C.: National Capitol Press, 1915), see Chapt. 8; Samuel Gompers, "American Labor's Position in Peace or in War," *American Federationist,* 24 (April, 1917), 279; Gompers, "America's Labor Convention in War Time," *Ibid.,* 25 (Jan. 1918), 34.

Policies Board went farther. The Policies Board worried over "what kinds of work women should perform, how they should best be introduced, under what conditions they should be employed, and what work should be prohibited." The WLPB barred women from certain hazardous work and from places of employment for which they were "clearly unfit," such as saloons and poolrooms, and it bound employers to existing protective measures.[4]

The NWLB's detailed explanation of its equal pay principle revealed a similar inability to break free of accepted conventions about women's roles and functions and a potentially troublesome indecision on the permanent status of women in industry. While the NWLB did go a half-step beyond the protective legislation by accepting the feminist cry for "abstract justice" (asserting that women deserved payment commensurate with service), the board basically clung to a more traditional approach (maintaining that women deserved consideration because temporarily they took "the place of some men" in supporting a family). Indeed, the board virtually admitted that the real purpose of the principle was to protect working men by keeping women at home:

> It is not economically sound or socially desirable that women should be brought into industry at a faster rate or in greater numbers than the needs of production actually demand, and the only check is to make it no more profitable to employ women than men.[5]

The application of the equal pay principle, the board soon discovered, was "not so simple as it looks." In matters unrelated to pay, the NWLB awarded women equal rights with little publicity and few internal disagreements. Women, like men, gained shorter workdays and the right to join unions—when the unions would have them. But when the board set wages, it sometimes made women's pay merely three-quarters equal to the going rate for men. In the summer of 1918 the board in four of the five awards which called for equal pay also set women's min-

[4] W. Jett Lauck and Claude S. Watts, *The Industrial Code* (NY: Funk & Wagnalls Company, 1922), 170; "Report," Bureau of Labor Statistics, *National War Labor Board,* 32; United States Committee on Public Information, *Official Bulletin* No. 15, July 12, 1918, in NWLB Records, Entry 14: General Correspondence.

[5] National War Labor Board, "Industrial Justice for Women," n.d., 3, typescript in NWLB Records, Entry 24: General Subject File.

imums at 30 to 33 cents an hour, some ten to twelve cents below the minimums it fixed for men in the same plants. The lower minimums were meant to apply when women either produced less than men or worked at tasks categorically unequal, that is, at jobs which men had never held. The awards guaranteed men $21 a week, and women, about $15, a figure which Taft and Walsh considered a living wage for a woman in a small city and without dependents. Thus the NWLB despite its announced principles only amended convention: a woman it was held needed a smaller wage than a man with a family, unless of course, she broke precedent by holding a man's job. And even then, when the board offered the alternative of lower minimums, it unwittingly offered unscrupulous employers a means to evade the principle altogether.[6]

Nevertheless, the board set far higher standards than either the state and local regulators or the Federal government. In early 1919, eight months after the NWLB had begun to translate principle into policy, the average minimum weekly wage for adult, experienced women in states which regulated women's rates was just $10. Only the District of Columbia, at $16, came close to meeting the $16.50 that Frank Walsh considered a living wage for women in large cities.[7]

One case, in particular, made news throughout the country. As Taft and Walsh drafted an award for the General Electric plant at Schenectady, Taft noticed that the scrub women there, who worked four hours a day between the hours of 5:00 and 9:00 a.m., earned a mere $5.00 a week. That mean they had to work the rest of the day elsewhere to supplement their income. Although the scrub women were outside the board's jurisdiction because they had made no complaint, Taft uncharacteristically ignored legal technicalities and became their "knight errant" when he suggested a wage increase of more than 100 percent. The new

[6] *Ibid.*, 4, 5 (see also "Findings in re Employees v. General Electric Company, Pittsfield Works," July 31, 1918, Docket No. 19; "Employees v. Manufacturers of Newsprint Paper," June 27, 1918, Docket No. 35; "Findings in re Employees v. General Electric Co., Schenectady Works," July 31, 1918, Docket No. 127; "Findings in re Employees v. Employers in Munition and Related Trades, Bridgeport, Conn.," Aug. 28, 1918, Docket No. 132, all in National War Labor Board, *National War Labor Board Docket* [Washington, D.C.: Bureau of Applied Economics, 1919, 5 vols.]). Letter, Walsh to George Creel, Aug. 20, 1918, Walsh Papers, Box 22.

[7] "Women's Wages," *The Nation*, Feb. 22, 1919, 271.

$10.50 weekly minimum was of special importance, the Newark *Ledger* reported, because the charwomen for the executive departments in Washington, D.C., earned less than $8.75 a week for a six-hour workday beginning at 7:00 a.m.[8]

At the same time a newspaperman informed Walsh that women in the New York City mailrooms of the Committee on Public Information earned $8.00 per week addressing envelopes. Their superintendent's apologetic explanation that $6.00 or $7.00 was the New York average for such work "almost put me to bed," Walsh later told Public Information director George Creel as he urged him to raise the weekly wages to $16.50. The Federal government should "set the mark in decent wages and conditions," Walsh wrote angrily, yet the government was itself "the worst offender in this respect." Moreover, an irate Walsh told Creel that his New York subordinate when confronted with the situation had parroted the argument "offered by private employers every place." The incident, Walsh wrote in disgust, "made me remark, for the millionth or two time, 'what's the use?' "[9]

To raise the living standard of women who were frequently unaware of their rights obviously required more than such chance discovery or haphazard correction of inequities. In August 1918, therefore, the board created two women's divisions within its staff. Elisabeth Christman of the Women's Trade Union League came from Chicago to lead a team of field investigators. Like the teams of male staffers already at work, they were to counsel their clients before NWLB hearings. Marie Obenauer, hired as Chief Examiner of the Women's Division, would direct eight women in studies of conditions at various plants. Her staff's greatest contribution, like that of the men examiners assigned the same duties, could be in recommending and administering awards.[10]

While Christman's investigators moved smoothly into the working NWLB bureaucracy, Marie Obenauer and her examiners

[8] Pringle, II, 921-922; clipping, unidentified Chicago newspaper, enclosed with letter, Wirt. W. Hallam to Taft, Sept. 10, 1918, Library of Congress, the Papers of William Howard Taft (hereafter cited as Taft Papers), Series 3, Box 422; "Among Trade Union Women," Newark *Ledger*, Sept. 15, 1918, NWLB Records, Entry 20: Newspaper Clippings.

[9] Letter, Francis J. Reilly to Walsh, July 30, 1918, Walsh Papers, Box 21; letter, Walsh to Creel, August 20, 1918.

[10] "To Consider Problems of Women's Work," Washington *Star*, Aug. 12, 1918; "War Board Aids Working Women," *Washington Post*, Aug. 28, 1918, both in NWLB Records, Entry 20.

challenged it. Obenauer wanted to administer awards so "that the standards set up thereunder will have a cumulative influence" on industries which employed women; and while she recognized the difficulty of determining equal work, she nevertheless meant to apply the equal pay principle systematically and to improve the means used to set women's wages in the NWLB's awards. A capable labor analyst, Obenauer moved quickly to give female industrial workers a role in wage determination. In early September one of her examiners arranged a settlement for the General Electric plants in Schenectady and in Pittsfield, Massachusetts, which had been directed that summer to pay women equally, but also had been provided with alternate lower minimums. The examiner's ruling specified that women would receive the piece and hourly rates given men working at the same jobs. Reasonable deductions for "additional assistance" or "special equipment" were to be decided by agreement between board-ordered shop committees and committees representing the plant managements. Simultaneously, at Obenauer's suggestion the board ordered the election of a proportional number of women to the shop committees.[11]

Obenauer was also prompt to criticize recent awards affecting women, especially in the wake of a precedent-shattering decision by the NWLB in mid-July at Waynesboro, Pennsylvania. There, under prodding by Walsh, the NWLB had launched its reputation as an adjustment agency interested more in justice than in splitting the difference between worker and management proposals. Nowhere had the award called for equal pay, but because it made no distinction between male and female employees, the 40 cents per hour minimum for common laborers had applied to both sexes. To Obenauer, the board's subsequent establishment of lesser minimums for women in larger towns where living costs were higher had been ill-conceived. Furthermore, apprenticeship and age qualifications attached to those minimums sometimes provided experienced workers lower wages than older,

[11] Memo, Marie L. Obenauer, Bertha M. Nienburg, Agnes V. O'Mahoney, Caroline E. Wilson, Anna Herkner, Sarah Yeats Whrlen, and Mary R. Bacon, to Lauck, Nov. 11, 1918; NWLB Records, Entry 13; interview with Marie Obenauer, Oct. 28, 1918, in National Archives, Records of the Women's Bureau (Women in Industry Service), RG 86, Box 5; Memorandum Concerning Awards Affecting Women, Obenauer to Lauck, Sept. 9, 1918, Taft Papers, Series 3, Box 426; "Industrial Justice," 4, NWLB Records, Entry 24.

inexperienced women. Such infelicities convinced Obenauer of the need to professionalize the data upon which awards were based through local cost of living surveys, budget analyses, and careful scrutiny of working conditions.[12]

More important still, Marie Obenauer demanded freedom of action and broad investigatory powers for her division. The division, she believed, could be a catalyst for change only if she maintained a virtually autonomous organization. But Lauck intended a different role for Obenauer's small force. As coordinator of the NWLB's 250 employees, he wanted a cohesive staff directed by Hugh Hanna of the Division of Examiners and E. B. Woods of the Division of Administration of Awards, and planned to integrate Obenauer's force with theirs. Failing to understand that the grievances of the women examiners were symptomatic of the problems of working women, Lauck was both unwilling to restructure the staff and anxious to avoid a direct confrontation with the fiery Obenauer. On September 9, he asked Obenauer for her opinion on the best method of procedure following his impending abolition of her division. Her response made future cooperation between them impossible.[13]

Obenauer prefaced her reply with a stinging statement of ideals which boldly set forth her differences with Lauck. She was most angered by his conclusion that the NWLB had no more need of women examiners than of Negro or Indian examiners. With "the extended draft on man power forcing thousands of women to take the places of men both as producers in the factory and providers in the home," she wrote, and "with the thoughts of men centered principally upon the effect of this woman invasion upon the status of men in industry, a woman problem and not a negro or an Indian problem has been created." An "intelligent consideration of the resulting difficulties which confront women," she continued, "demands that women as well as men shall be on the force

[12] Common laborers, who made as little as 22 cents an hour, had asked for a new minimum of 30 cents, a figure which the board considered inadequate (See "Findings in re Employees v. Frick Co., Emerson-Brantingham Co., Landis Tool Co., Landis Machine Co., Bostwick-Lyons Bronze Co., Shearer Machine Co., Victor Tool Co., and Cashman Tool Co., all of Waynesboro, Pa.," July 11, 1918, Docket No. 40, in National War Labor Board, *Docket;* memorandum, Obenauer to Lauck, Sept. 9, 1918; [Obenauer] Memorandum Concerning Awards Affecting Women, n.d. [Oct., 1918], both in Taft Papers, Series 3, Box 426.

[13] Alluded to in separate Memorandum, Obenauer to Lauck, Sept. 9, 1918, NWLB Records, Entry 13.

of examiners." Her examiners should be allowed to confer with Christman's investigators and representatives of women workers and management in order to clarify unanswered questions during NWLB hearings. They should also be given the same opportunities as male examiners to discuss the contents of pending awards with board members.[14]

Lauck's persistent refusal to clarify the responsibilities of the women examiners, coupled with his veiled threat to eliminate their jobs, hampered her staff's work for several more weeks. By September 25, following a conference with Lauck, Obenauer realized that her function was to reflect, not to make, policy. She was to "keep in close touch with" Woods concerning the administration of awards, and future first-hand investigations by women examiners were to be subject to prior approval by Hugh Hanna. Although her staff could continue to analyze briefs and testimony, an informal order from Lauck to send women examiners to no more hearings until "procedure was settled" diminished the sources for analysis. As Obenauer complained, this new directive effectively stymied her work: "Although a number of cases involving women are now set before men examiners, I am unable to get the data required as a basis for an appropriate award for women.[15]

On October 28, Lauck officially abolished the Division of Women Administrative Examiners, but Marie Obenauer refused to be silenced. In early November she sought a conference with Lauck. Although "keenly disappointed" that he denied women a voice in defining policies which affected women, she wrote on behalf of her staff that "the girls" felt no personal hostility toward him. Indeed, they wanted to prevent *"needless"* destruction of friendships. Lauck's willingness to confer, however, resulted only in a reiteration of Obenauer's demands for independence and for equal time before the board. To help control the growing conflict of interest which she perceived between men and women workers, she insisted further on appointment to Lauck's Committee on Awards.[16]

[14] *Ibid.*
[15] Memo, Obenauer to Lauck, Sept. 26, 1918, Taft Papers, Series 3, Box 426.
[16] Letter, Obenauer to Lauck, Nov. 5, 1918, Taft Papers, Series 3, Box 426; memo, Obenauer, Nienburg, O'Mahoney, Wilson, Herkner, Whrlen, and Bacon to Lauck. Nov. 11, 1918.

Lauck's rejection of Obenauer's ultimatum ended the women's struggle for equal status on the NWLB staff. Any woman examiner who agreed to work as an integral part of Woods' force, Lauck promised, would be "given the fullest opportunity to be of service," but under no circumstances would he permit the continuance of Obernauer's division. Her repeated attempts to distinguish the duties of the women from those of the men examiners, he wrote on November 13, had "been our chief cause of trouble and misundertanding in the past." Her purpose defeated, Obenauer then resigned, taking with her three colleagues. She left behind a condemnation of the board's unconcern and a bitter expression of hopes dashed: cases involving women had been "submitted, heard, decided and, administered" without her knowledge; awards were sloppy; and Lauck's orders resorted to "the old method of securing harmony by making woman's work absolutely subordinate to the man's viewpoint."[17]

During Marie Obenauer's protracted battle within the staff, women from the outside had launched a compelling campaign for the appointment of two women to the NWLB itself. And understandably so. Women already served on community war labor boards throughout the country, and representatives from the Women in Industry Service of the Labor Department met regularly with the War Labor Policies Board. Mary Harriman Rumsey of New York and six others organized the Temporary Committee to Urge Representation of Women on the National War Labor Board. Among Rumsey's confederates was Margaret Dreier Robins—president of the National Women's Trade Union League, who was a Chicago confidant of board member Victor Olander and of Elisabeth Christman. Mary Dreier, Margaret Robins' sister and another committee organizer, spoke for the Women's Joint Legislative Conference of New York. The committee used publicity well and found champions both among women trade unionists dissatisfied with widespread abuse of the equal pay principle and among members of organizations eager to enhance the cause of women's rights. In September and October supporters of these two groups flooded the NWLB with

[17] Letter, Lauck to Obenauer, Nov. 13, 1918, NWLB Records, Entry 13; letter, Obenauer, Nienburg, Herkner, and Wilson, to Lauck, Nov. 12, 1918, NWLB Records, Entry 13.

wires, letters, and resolutions.[18]

University of Wisconsin Professor John R. Commons asked the board to give women representation, Theodore Roosevelt endorsed the idea, and Rabbi Stephen S. Wise offered a candidate for the post. Cornelia Byrne Pinchot, Gifford's wife, wired Secretary of Labor William B. Wilson that the appointment of women members was a "matter of vital importance," and brother-in-law Amos asked William B. Colver of the Federal Trade Commission to nominate *her* to the NWLB. "If, as he [Amos Pinchot] says, Mrs. Pinchot would back you up," Colver noted while passing on the letter to Walsh, "I am for her. I am for anybody that will back you up." The Conference of Trade Union Women, called in October by the Women in Industry Service, wanted a woman on the board to redress wage grievances. Like Marie Obenauer, it also anticipated that women employees would need protection during the post-war readjustment.[19]

Among NWLB members, Walsh alone supported the addition of women colleagues and repeatedly promised their petitioners his strong endorsement when the issue came up for discussion. Both employer and employee members opposed the modification of the board's "conventional character," Taft wrote to Theodore Roosevelt. Further, Taft himself denied that the NWLB had the legal power to augment its membership. Then, in a unanimous action taken while Walsh was out of town, the board without comment referred the question to its founding fathers—the National Industrial Conference Board and the American Federation of Labor. With that action, Walsh knew, his colleagues intended an end to the matter, but on October 30, he asked President Wilson to intercede.[20]

[18] Letter, Mary Harriman Rumsey to George Creel, n.d., [Sept., 1918], Walsh Papers, Box 23; *The Survey*, Oct. 5, 1918, 3.

[19] Letter, John R. Commons to National War Labor Board, Oct. 1, 1918, NWLB Records, Entry 14; letter, Stephen S. Wise to Walsh, Sept. 30, 1918, Walsh Papers, Box 23; letter, Theodore Roosevelt to Taft in Kansas City *Star*, Sept. 27, 1918, Taft Papers, Series 4A, Reel 322; telegram, Mrs. Gifford Pinchot to William B. Wilson, Oct. 17, 1918, NWLB Records, Entry 14; letter, Amos Pinchot to William B. Colver, Sept. 15, 1918; letter, Colver to Walsh, Sept. 17, 1918, final two entries in Walsh Papers, Box 23; proceedings of Conference of Trade Union Women, Oct. 4 and 5, 1918, 9, 18, 20, 22-24, NWLB Records, Entry 24.

[20] Letter, Walsh to Colver, Sept. 20, 1918, Walsh Papers, Box 23; letter, Walsh to Agnes Nester, Oct. 4, 1918, NWLB Records, Entry 14; letter, Walsh to Mrs. James Leeds Laidslaw, Oct. 10, 1918, NWLB Records, Entry 14; letter, Walsh to Stephen S. Wise, Oct. 15, 1918, Walsh Papers, Box 24; letter, Walsh to Estelle Lauder, Oct. 17, 1918, NWLB Records, Entry 14; letter, Walsh to Mary An-

Walsh's letter to Wilson might have been written by Marie Obenauer. The women taking jobs in war-related industries had been met with hostility from their co-workers, he began, and those unaware of their rights had been abused by their employers. When cases affecting women came before the board, moreover, the female employees had been poorly represented by the men examiners—partly from ignorance and partly from prejudice. "I feel sure," he wrote Wilson, "that our Board could act with much more intelligence if we had the advice and cooperation of two women who could act with us in the settlement of controversies constantly coming before us in which conditions surrounding women workers are among the principal issues." Accordingly, he asked Wilson to intimate to the presidents of the NICB and the AFL "that if the nominations are not promptly made you may, on account of the urgency of the matter, feel compelled to make the appointments by executive order." President Wilson did not respond. Nor, as Walsh had anticipated, did the NICB or the AFL submit nominations.[21]

If the board had a woman policy before the armistice on Nov. 11, 1918, it was a policy of convenience. The women's demands for higher wages had dovetailed neatly with the goals of organized labor. Private employers frequently found ways to avert equal pay, and their representatives on the board had made little issue of the principle. Furthermore, the board had excluded women altogether from policy-making. The board's confusion about women's status after the armistice resulted because its prior awards had been drawn to accommodate the two interest groups within its membership: organized labor and management. As the nation began its transformation from war to peace, the needs of these groups changed, and women were caught in the cross-fire. The board, whose awards required its unanimous approval and depended upon moral suasion for enforcement, floundered. Appeals from women streetcart conductors who faced summary dismissal during the fall of 1918 put squarely before the Board the critical question which Obenauer, the Temporary Committee to Urge Representation on the War Labor Board, and

derson, Asst. Director, Women in Industry Service, Oct. 21, 1918, Walsh Papers, Box 24; letter, Taft to Theodore Roosevelt, Oct. 2, 1918. Taft Papers, Series 3, Box 424 (see also letter, Taft to Issac Ullman, Oct. 30. 1918, Taft Papers, 8 Yale 78); letter, Walsh to Woodrow Wilson, Oct. 30, 1918, Walsh Papers, Box 24.

[21] Letter, Walsh to Woodrow Wilson, Oct. 30, 1918, Walsh Papers, Box 24.

the Women in Industry Service had all anticipated: Did women have a basic right to work once the war emergency had passed? The equal pay principle, read strictly, applied only in cases in which it had become "necessary" to hire women to do men's jobs. Did the principle really mean that women had the right to fill those jobs only so long as no men were available to assume them?[22]

The answer from the street railways, where women conductors did undeniably equal work, depended on whether locals of the Amalgamated Assoc. of Street and Electric Railway Employees agreed with the AFL statement that women should be organized. In Kansas City, for example, men conductors had welcomed women into the union, supported their demands for equal treatment, and united with them against the Kansas City Railways Co. The NWLB's settlement of their case in October had reflected the harmony between the sexes by granting absolute wage equality, in uncompromising and direct language which the board had never used before and would not use again: women conductors, whose hours were limited by state law and who had been guaranteed only $60 a month, were to receive the same $75 monthly minimum accorded men. Every other "adult employee" was to get a 42½¢ hourly minimum, and under no circumstances was "he or she" to be denied the minimum when the award was put into effect. But the situation was different in Cleveland and in Detroit; in these cities the male conductors had barred women from the union locals, insisted that "necessity" be interpreted literally, and demanded that the women conductors be removed.[23]

In Cleveland, 150 women conductors had been hired in August and September 1918 because the NWLB sanctioned their employment in the absence of qualified men. A Labor Department investigation, initiated at the company's request when the men threatened a strike, had persuaded the department to order the women replaced by November 1. There was no shortage of men in Cleveland, the investigators found, provided the company lowered its standards "somewhat." Instantly, the local

---

[22] "Report," Bureau of Labor Statistics, *National War Labor Board*, 32.

[23] "Findings and Award in re Amalgamated Association of Street & Electric Railway Employees of America, Division No. 764 v. The Kansas City Railways Co.," Oct. 24, 1918, Docket No. 265, in National War Labor Board, *Docket;* Report of Hearing Before Examiners, Sept. 16, 1918, Docket No. 265, NWLB Records, Entry 10, Group I: Examiners Reports, Street Railway Cases.

press denounced the investigators' conclusions. Rose Moriarty, a feisty activist who had fought for women's rights in Ohio for almost twenty years, organized local suffragists and the Cleveland Chamber of Commerce in a campaign to reverse the removal order. Meanwhile, A. L. Faulkner, Cleveland's Commissioner of Conciliation, was unable to reconcile the decision with the reported 4,000 advertised vacancies in Cleveland industries and sent news clippings about the vacancies along with his suggestion for reconsideration to Secretary of Labor Wilson. When the women conductors protested that the investigators had given them no hearing, the NWLB on October 31 ordered their retention on the cars until it could review the facts. Five weeks later the 2,400 men on the Cleveland railway walked out while the women conductors awaited board action.[24]

On December 3, 1918, the day the men struck, the mayor of Cleveland appeared before the board to demand action. The men had grown tired of waiting, he said, and both he and the city law director wanted the Labor Department ruling enforced immediately. With 600 unemployed men recently back from the front, with thousands more expected, and with increasing layoffs prompted by the termination of war contracts, the men in Cleveland needed the women conductors' jobs. "Quite a number" of the returning soldiers, the mayor testified, had worked on the street railway. The women could return to whatever they had done before the war. As for the board's award, the union had promised to ignore it if it contradicted the department's decision.[25]

In the absence of the joint chairmen, who were closeted privately on Walsh's last day on the job, the board groped for an answer. Taft appeared only long enough to regret that, legal-

[24] Bureau of Labor Statistics, *National War Labor Board*, 70-71; United States Committee on Public Information, Official Bulletin, Nov. 6, 1918, NWLB Records, Entry 15: Administrative Files; quoted in "Women Barred," editorial, Cleveland *News*, Sept. 24, 1918, Washington National Records Center, Suitland, Md., NWLB Records, Casefile No. 491; "Battles Long for Women," "Conductorets Will Appeal," "Conductorets Get Support," unidentified Cleveland news clippings, n.d. [Sept. 1918], NWLB Records, Casefile, No. 491; letter, A. L. Faulkner to W. B. Wilson, Sept. 25, 1918, NWLB Records, Casefile No. 491; United States Committee on Public Information, *Official Bulletin*, Nov. 6, 1918, NWLB Records, Entry 15.

[25] National War Labor Board, Minutes of Executive Sessions (hereafter cited as NWLB, Minutes), typescripts in Univ. of Virginia, Alderman Library, the Papers of W. Jett Lauck (hereafter cites as Lauck Papers), afternoon meeting of Dec. 3, 1918, 27-30, 39, 42-45.

ly, the women had no case; the labor members agonized as they argued for the first time against the interests of fellow employees; the board's management members watched labor's strained logic unfold. Behind the logic lay unspoken fears. Organized labor had sometimes resented women on the cars, where they received equal pay, because it believed that women rarely agitated for increased wages. Labor worried, too, that their presence would convince arbiters that conducting was "woman's work" and was thus already adequately compensated. Therefore, board member Fred Hewitt of the International Association of Machinists and colleague William Hutcheson, president of the United Brotherhood of Carpenters and Joiners, intimated that the company had had no right to hire the women and the Labor Department ruling confirmed that.[26]

Loyall A. Osborne, a Westinghouse vice-president and the board's most virulent defender of employer prerogatives, ultimately proposed the award intended to end the dispute. The women had been wronged, he explained, by the Labor Department and by the company which called it in. For the labor members, self-interest and fear of setting precedents had destroyed principle. "I have sat here for nine months and heard great arguments about the rights of employees," Osborne chided. "Just because these people are women, you are not giving them rights." Having thus embarrassed labor, he deserted the women and hid behind "necessity." The board at his suggestion considered the

[26] *Ibid.*, 41. James H. Vahey, spokesman for the carmen's union, intimated such fears at the preliminary hearing on the Cleveland case, Nov. 8, 1918; and on Dec. 5, Joint Chairmen Taft and Manly narrowly allayed them by granting women collectors on the Boston Elevated 40 cents an hour and the few men who worked with them 42½ cents. The men collectors, apparently, deserved higher pay when they worked at what the company considered a "woman's position." Ironically, because the women were unionized, Vahey had argued unsuccessfully for equal pay 42½ cents) for equal work in Boston. In Cleveland, the city law director implied, the company had hired the women as a punitive measure after the men had agitated for higher wages (see Transcript of Proceedings, Nov. 8, 1918, 90, Docket No. 491, WNRC, Suitland, Md., NWLB Records, Entry 5: Transcripts of Hearings: "Employees vs. The Boston Elevated Railway Company," Nov. 13, 1918, 2-5, 18, NWLB Records, Casefile No. 181; "Decision of Arbitrators on Appeal in re Women Collectors on Lines of Boston Elevated Railway Co.," Dec. 5, 1918, Docket No. 181, in National War Labor Board, *Docket;* NWLB, Minutes, afternoon meeting of Dec. 3, 1918, 42). NWLB, Minutes, afternoon meeting of Dec. 3, 1918, 13-17, 24-26, 31-33. It is worth noting that while Hewitt's Machinists Union allowed female membership under reduced dues and benefits, Hutcheson's Carpenters barred women from their ranks. See US, Dept. of Labor, Women's Bureau, "The New Position of Women in American Industry," Bulletin No. 12 (Washington, D.C.: Government Printing Office, 1920), 157.

employment of women conductors an obsolete war measure: men were "becoming immediately available by virtue of the reduction in the forces of industry in Cleveland and the return of men from the camps." It ordered the women paid their December wages and replaced by January 3.[27]

The award prompted considerable public criticism. It was denounced in Congress. The New York *Telegram* printed the order side by side with excerpts from a Presidential address on the equality of women and asked if President Wilson had no influence with the NWLB. The Washington *Times* predicted serious new industrial adjustment problems. And the *Nation* suggested that it might now become necessary for women to fight "simply for the right to work." The Cleveland decision, it stated, was part of a campaign by labor unions to "oust women from war-time positions . . . through the Labor Department and the War Labor Board." Already, the *Nation* pointed out, the Secretary of the AFL was talking of "the problem of disposing of women in overalls and in uniform."[28]

In response to various pressures, the NWLB at its December 19 meeting assigned the case for reconsideration to Taft and to Walsh's successor as Joint Chairman, Basil Manly, the former director of field work for the Commission on Industrial Relations. The *Survey* attributed this startling action to the public outcry, but other forces had been at work. On reflection, Taft had questioned his tacit acquiescence in the December 3 ruling. Lauck, too, had been affected by pleas from groups like the National Women's Trade Union League. Also disturbed by the award's import, Mary Van Kleeck and Mary Anderson of the Women in Industry Service had written him a personal letter. The case must have been settled, they wrote, "with reference to immediate local needs rather than in the light of its far-reaching implications," for it directed the "dismissal of an entire group of women from an occupation as a means of settling an industrial dispute." Throughout the country, Lauck suddenly understood,

[27] NWLB, Minutes, afternoon meeting of Dec. 3, 1918, 22-27, 38-39, 44-46; "Opinion in re Employees (Women Conductors) v. Cleveland Railway Co.," "Findings and Recommendation," Dec. 3, 1918, Docket No. 491, in National War Labor Board, *Docket*.

[28] National War Labor Board, Division of Information and Files, Press Clipping Report, Dec. 7-10, 1918, Taft Papers, Series 3, Box 431; The *Nation*, Dec. 21, 1918, 760-61.

women had interpreted the Cleveland order as an NWLB statement on postwar conversion.[29]

The Cleveland case, along with a similar case pending before Joint Chairmen Taft and Manly in Detroit became a *cause celebre* among persons committed to women's economic advancement in the post-war era. Each dispute provided the opportunity for a clear-cut governmental statement against sex-based discrimination. Detroit thus attracted national attention as dress-rehearsal for the second Cleveland decision. In Detroit the lines of conflict were sharply drawn. The Detroit United Railway, unlike the Cleveland Railway Company, operated under a closed union shop—one of those existing conditions which the board's principles bound it to uphold. After the armistice in November, the Detroit local not only had protested the continued service of the women conductors whose employment it had sanctioned in September, but also had reneged on its promise to issue them union cards, forcing the women to open the closed shop.[30]

When Theresa Doland, attorney for the Detroit women conductors, appeared before the board in Washington on January 18, 1919, she argued John Marsall's classic broad definition of "necessity," pled for employment opportunities on the basis of ability, and introduced information on a subject she rarely heard discussed—the relative contributions of the fathers of the race. This she considered important despite Joint Chairman Taft's admonition at the preliminary hearing five weeks earlier that "necessity" constituted the only relevant issue. At the preliminary hearing, she had sat stunned while a union spokesman condemned the employment of the women as "a fester and a disgrace upon the fair name of Detroit." He called them not only unnecessary, but also inefficient, immoral homewreckers who—along with the company—took further advantage of the collective efforts of the men because no other firm in Detroit paid men and women the same wages for the same work. This crude-

[29] "Woman's Right to Choose Her Job," *The Survey*, Dec. 21, 1918, 380; letter, Taft to J. W. Marsh, Dec. 15, 1918, Taft Papers, 8 Yale 78; letter, Margaret Dreier Robins, *et al.*, National Women's Trade Union League of America, to National War Labor Board, Dec. 11, 1918, NWLB Records, Casefile No. 491; letter, Mary Van Kleeck and Mary Anderson to Lauck, Dec. 10, 1918, NWLB Records, Casefile No. 491, quoted in NWLB, Minutes, morning meeting of Dec. 19, 1918, 26-27; NWLB, Minutes, morning meeting of Dec. 19, 1918, 20.

[30] "Report," Bureau of Labor Statistics, *National War Labor Board*, 32; transcript of Proceedings, Dec. 13, 1918, 25-28, Docket No. 444, NWLB Records, Entry 5.

ness had outraged Taft—who later suggested the union spokesman belonged in a cage. But in Washington, Doland could capitalize on no such behavior from the carmen union's smoothest and most respected attorney, the gallant James H. Vahey of Boston.[31]

Vahey, champion of street railway workers in countless NWLB cases and defender of the unionized Kansas City women conductors, apologized for what he was about to do. He denied a strict necessity for the women conductors, and then argued the ultimate traditional defense for the union: streetcar conducting was unfit work for a woman. This had been a standard argument during the war years,voiced by some of the same men and women who had promoted protective legislation in the progressive era. Streetcar conducting endangered the women's health, he explained, gave good women a bad reputation, and threatened their safety. Certainly, he would not want his daughter to conduct a streetcar, but would hope for something "better and higher and . . . larger" for American working women. Besides, if a woman wanted to fulfill "the loftiest function in the world, to be the mother of the human race," surely, she should avoid jostling cars.[32]

For almost four hours Basil Manly silently watched Doland build her case. The women conductors wanted their jobs partly because conducting was the most pleasant paid work these onetime factory workers, laundresses, and waitresses had ever done. More importantly, they had doubled, trebled, or quadrupled their incomes. Arguing that motherhood and fatherhood conveyed equal responsibilities, she used the women conductors to prove her point. One hundred twenty of them provided, in whole or in part, for 154 minors. None of the men who worried about the women's health and lofty functions, she added, had offered to support those children. Then came the moment Manly had waited for, as Doland introduced Mary Van Kleeck's four page report on a nineteen-volume study of the pre-war conditions of working women and children. This study

---

[31] Transcript of Proceedings, Jan. 18, 1919, 85-87, 90, 110, 129-136, Docket No. 444, Transcript, Dec. 13, 1918, 17-22, 44-47, 174, Docket No. 444, both in NWLB Records, Entry 5.

[32] Transcript, Jan. 18, 1919, 95-117, Docket No. 444, NWLB Records, Entry 5.

of four major industries showed that while the fathers of the race were still at home, they had been able to earn only 34 to 56 percent of the family income. "The percentage of the total income of the family?" Manly questioned. "I believe that is correct," Doland answered. "I know that is correct," said Manly, "because I wrote that report." Neatly, Doland and Manly had shattered the myth of an all-providing father in peacetime.[33]

The award, which discounted the question of suitability and was said to be based on the interpretation of contracts and "necessity," brought victory to the women conductors. They had no contracts, they were not necessary, they would probably be considered "not well adapted to the service" in peacetime, and the company was ordered to hire only men in the future. But since the women already employed had been warned of their temporary status by neither the company nor the union, "equity" and "fair dealing" demanded their retention. The union "must be content with" that. For Doland, Van Kleeck, Ethel M. Smith of the National Women's Trade Union League—and no doubt for their behind-the-scenes confidant, Basil Manly—the victory was marred by the women's failure to extract an NWLB commitment to equal employment opportunities. Instead, the award had effectively blocked their continued entrance into a field of employment. For Taft—who encouraged the expansion of occupations for women that spring in *The Ladies' Home Journal*—the NWLB's narrow jurisdiction permitted no broader statement. Even had he believed that it did, no award so radical could have won the full board's approval.[34]

[33] Such testimony from and about women conductors was frequent at NWLB hearings (see, for example, Transcript, Nov. 8, 1918, 39-40, Docket No. 491; Transcript, Dec. 13, 1918, 38, 175-180, Docket No. 444; Transcript of Proceedings, Mar. 13, 1919, 13-19, 23-24, Docket No. 491, all in NWLB Records, Entry 5; US, Dept. of Labor, Women's Bureau, "Women Street Car Conductors and Ticket Agents," Bulletin No. 11 [Washington, D.C.: Government Printing Office, 1921]), transcript, Jan. 18, 1919, 129-136, Docket No. 444, NWLB Records, Entry 5.

[34] "Opinion and Order in re Employees of Detroit United Railway, Members of Amalgamated Association of Street Railway Employees of America, v. Detroit United Railway, and Women Conductors Association v. Amalgamated Association of Street & Electric Railway Employees of America," Jan. 18, 1919, Docket No. 444, in National War Labor Board, *Docket;* letter, Ethel M. Smith to Walsh, Jan. 6, 1919, Walsh Papers, Box 27; Transcript, Jan. 18, 1919, 89-91, Docket No. 444, NWLB Records, Entry 5. In his article, "As I See the Future of Women," *The Ladies' Home Journal*, 36 (Mar. 1919), 27, 113, Taft doubted the suitability of women for streetcar conducting and voiced other protective concerns, but nonetheless endorsed the concept of economic equality between the sexes.

At the Cleveland re-hearing two months later, the women's supporters launched a last assault against tradition. Under sharp questioning from Taft, James Vahey presented his case both quickly and half-heartedly. Rose Moriarty, meanwhile had prepared a long brief for the women's new attorney, Frank Walsh. His appearance constituted a self-described "penance" for the board's December 3 ruling. Walsh had resigned as Joint Chairman, believing he could do more for employees, and for organized labor, as a private attorney. Now, as organized labor in Cleveland denounced him, he shrugged. His conversion to the cause of the women conductors, although late, had been complete. "I just cannot see any justice in the stand taken by these men against the Cleveland women," he explained to a friend.[35]

Walsh put Ethel Smith on the stand to remind the board of the women conductors' contributions to the Kansas City local and to cite new medical evidence which showed that accepted woman's work like waitressing was even more strenuous than streetcar conducting. Anna Howard Shaw, Chairman of the Women's Committee of the Council of National Defense, then made the most eloquent plea on behalf of women's rights ever delivered before the board. The women of America, Shaw said, had believed that the war was fought to extend liberty to people and that women were "equally with men people." To deprive them of the right to a livelihood in whatever work they could do, was to deprive them of liberty. As for protecting women, Shaw continued, "I have never known any body of people who sought to impose an injustice upon another group of people who did not do it for the benefit of the people upon whom they imposed it." The time had come when it was neither right nor duty nor justice for men to decide what was correct for women: "if we fail, then let us fail, but do not let us fail by the direction of men." [36]

The Cleveland award of March 17 ordered the women conductors reinstated. But it addressed none of the larger issues

[35] Letter, Ethel M. Smith to Walsh, Jan. 11, 1919; letter, Rose Moriarty to Walsh, Jan. 20, 1919, both in Walsh Papers, Box 27; letter, Walsh to Ethel M. Smith, Mar. 8, 1919, letter, Ethel M. Smith to Walsh, Mar. 10, 1919, both in Walsh Papers, Box 29; Transcript, Mar. 13, 1919, 32, 37-38 Docket No. 491, NWLB Records, Entry 5; letter, Walsh to A. A. Johannsen, Dec. 30, 1918, Walsh Papers, Box 26.

[36] Transcript, Mar. 13, 1919, 19-28, Docket No. 491, NWLB Records, Entry 5.

raised at the hearing. Rather, it mirrored the Detroit decision. "Of course, I was pleased" at the reversal of the December 3 ruling, Walsh wrote Manly, but "what a busting decision could have been made along the right of all women and men to live their own lives. . . . Anyway, the legalistic jinx was put on that Board months ago." Ultimately, the award itself was but a hollow victory for the Cleveland women. The NWLB, progressively enfeebled since the armistice, had reached its nadir. President Wilson, who had once nationalized companies which rejected NWLB awards, had lost interest in its work. Employers and employees defied it at will. When the Cleveland Railway Company declined to put the award into effect because of a threatened union walkout, the women remained off the cars.[37]

The Federal commitment to equal pay for equal work, voiced through the National War Labor Board in 1918-1919, implied a revolutionary step in the evolution of governmental policy toward women in industry. Both recent state protective legislation and long-standing American tradition had subordinated women's economic status to men's. Moreover, tradition held that men needed a higher wage than women. So shocked were Joint Chairmen Taft and Walsh at the extent to which women were underpaid, however, that four months after the board began its operations, it had hired two teams of professional women analysts to help bring women a living wage as well as equal pay when they worked at men's jobs. Before the board dissolved itself in August, 1919, it awarded women equal pay in forty-eight cases, sixteen of which involved women streetcar conductors. Among the forty-eight were also fourteen cases which set lower minimums for women than for men but even these awards reduced somewhat the vast discrepancy between male and female pay scales.[38]

Nevertheless, the NWLB failed to escape the dual heritage of law and tradition. It was unable to accept women as responsible partners in the formation and administration of policy because, fundamentally, it rejected the basic equality of women

[37] "Opinion in re Employees (Women Conductors) v. Cleveland Railway Co.," Mar. 17, 1919, Docket No. 491, in National War Labor Board, *Docket;* letter, Walsh to Basil Manly, Mar. 21, 1919, Walsh Papers, Box 29.

[38] Figures taken from study of final caseload as reflected in pages of National War Labor Board, *Docket.*

in industrial matters. Chief Women's Examiner Marie Obenauer struggled in vain to lead the NWLB toward a deeper commitment to working women because she demanded equality at a time when women, politically disfranchised and economically depressed, had little power as an interest group.

After the armistice, the consequences of Obenauer's defeat and the simultaneous rejection of feminist efforts for representation on the NWLB became obvious: women, supported in theory by labor during the emergency, threatened the status of working men during postwar reconversion. The result was the Cleveland ruling of December 3 which appeared to label women in the war industries as expendable, temporary help to whom neither the government nor private employers had further obligations. It took external stimuli for the board even to realize that it had acted insensitively.

Indecision was evident even in the Detroit award and the second Cleveland ruling in early 1919. At Detroit, the award which parenthetically called for an end to prejudice also warned against the headlong rush of women into heretofore unacceptable occupations:

> He is, however, no friend of the wise advance of women into the much to be desired independence of self-support, who does not exercise discretion by a prudent discrimination between the work which women can do without injury to health or subjection to unfavorable environment and that from which they have been heretofore excluded solely by unreasonable custom or convention or the ignorance and prejudice of men.[39]

Thus while the NWLB denounced mindless preconceptions, it remained trapped in the morass of the protective language which men used, often in good faith, to control women's economic opportunities. The most it could offer working women after the war was an endorsement of their right to retain, at equal pay, the jobs which they had been lucky enough to secure during the emergency. The NWLB denied that its cases dealt with women's rights to work at jobs of their own choosing. In the streetcar rulings, therefore, it omitted a call for equal employment opportunities for potentially employable women.

[39] "Opinion and Order in re Employees of Detroit United Railway," Docket No. 444, in NWLB, *Docket*.

The board's denunciation of ignorance and prejudice, nonetheless, seemed a long stride forward in upheaval-ridden 1919; and certainly the war experience did yield some results which suggested a better future for women at work. Van Kleeck's wartime Women in Industry Service eased into permanence as the Women's Bureau in the Department of Labor. A few progressive state legislatures in 1919 translated the NWLB's equal pay principle into law, but not until the late 1960s and 1970s did the courts begin to uphold equal pay and to rule it unconstitutional to deny anyone a job because of heretofore assumed physical weakness, unsuitability, or other sex-based characteristics.[40]

The National War Labor Board had declined to lead a revolution, but ultimately its awards had set potentially important moral precedents which leaders of the women's cause hoped to use in the post-war era. As Ethel Smith wrote Frank Walsh after the Board's second Cleveland ruling, even if the women conductors were not reinstated, the NWLB reversal had meant "a great deal in this fight to have established the principle of equal rights through a national agency. . . . " Yet even as the ink dried on that award, other contemporary observers distinguished between rhetoric and reality. In March 1919, for example, the New York State Department of Labor estimated that two-thirds of the women who replaced men in that state received less than the $15 weekly "living wage" which Taft and Walsh had awarded fulltime female employees at G. E.'s Schenectady plant. After examining the New York study and others, A. B. Wolfe and Helen Olson of the University of Texas reached the grim conclusion that:

> If the scattering investigations which have been made are a safe guide, it is certain that outside of government plants and the relatively few cases where the . . . Board or other agencies forced employers to raise

[40] US, President's Commission on the Status of Women, *American Women* (Washington, D.C.: Government Printing Office, 1963), 37; Important equal pay cases include Shultz v. Wheaton Glass Co., 421 F. 2d 259 (3d Cir.), cert. denied 398 U.S. 905, 90 Sup. Ct. 1696, 26 L. Ed. 2d 64 (1970) and Corning Glass Works v. Brennan, 417 U.S. 188, 94 Sup. Ct. 2223, 41 L. Ed. 2d 1 (1974). Protective legislation which deemed women unfit for certain jobs because of environmental or physical strictures has been nullified by the courts in Sail'er Inn, Inc. v. Kirby, 5 Cal. 3d 1, 485 P. 2d 529, 95 Cal. Rptr. 329 (1971) and Rosenfeld v. Southern Pacific Railroad Co., 444 F. 2d 1219 (9th Cir. 1971). The protective laws, the courts held, contravened the Civil Rights Act because they denied women jobs on the basis of characteristics generally attributed to their sex.

> wages, even the pressure of war demand for labor failed to bring the wages of a vast number of women up to the level necessary to "maintain the worker in health and reasonable comfort." That other ideal of justice sponsored, in theory at least, by the . . . Board—equal pay for equal work—does not appear to have appealed to more than a limited percentage of employers.

High sounding principles and moral precedents alone, it seemed, had been unable to effect widespread reform, even temporarily for an interest group which throughout the period of the war had remained at odds with far more powerful political, economic, and historic forces.[41]

[41] Letter, Ethel M. Smith to Walsh, Mar. 21, 1919, Walsh Papers, Box 29; Helen Olson and A.B. Wolfe, "War-Time Industrial Employment of Women in the United States," *Journal of Political Economy*, 27 (1919), 658-659.

## NOTES AND DOCUMENTS

# "UNCLE SAM JUST LOVES THE LADIES": SEX DISCRIMINATION IN THE FEDERAL GOVERNMENT, 1917

By WILLIAM GRAEBNER

Early in 1917, the United States Civil Service Commission posted its regular notice of an examination for *male* stenographers for service in Federal agencies. A committee of women, assembled from offices in the capitol and each known for the ability to press a grievance, took the women's case to Senator W. L. Jones. With the energy and directness for which he was known, Jones challenged Secretary of Interior Franklin K. Lane to justify sex discrimination in his department. "What special reason is there," wrote Jones, "for filling stenographic positions entirely or almost entirely by men in the government service? Why should there be any discrimination against women solely upon the ground of their sex?" Lane handed the matter over to Chief Clerk E. J. Ayers, who turned directly to the department's thirteen chief administrative officers.[1]

The letters which follow, most written within a day after the request for information was received, do more than document the position of women in the Federal bureaucracy in 1917.[2] The confidence and authority with which their male authors both deny the existence of discrimination and define it away reveal how guiltlessly inequities may be perpetuated once the rationale is established, the needs of the system defined, and expertism

[1] *Washington Post*, Feb. 11, 1917, 14.

[2] The letters are in Record Group 48, "Records of the Department of the Interior," Office of the Secretary, Personnel Supervision and Management, 1907-1942, File 15-15-35, National Archives, Washington, D.C.

harnessed to the service of the *status quo*. The *Washington Post*, in possession of several replies, brought an appropriately amazed tone to its coverage. Its headline read: "Uncle Sam Just Loves the Ladies."[3] Of the letters I have discovered, only that of William C. Taylor, Deputy Register of Wills, acknowledges the existence of sex discrimination (and then not in his own agency) and offers suggestions. His interest in retirement, while here uniquely tied to the relations between the sexes, was a staple of the efficiency-oriented Progressive era and was to come to fruition in 1920 with the Civil Service Retirement Act.

The protest responsible for these documents was vitiated in an atmosphere which assumed an enlarged role for women should the United States enter the World War. Even as women clerks and stenographers sought to bring public attention to their treatment in the Federal bureaucracy, the War Department announced plans to employ women in the manufacturing of munitions in government arsenals.[4] The *Post*, the only daily which had thought the issue newsworthy in the first place, failed to keep its readers informed of further developments. One of its reporters, however, may have captured the essence of the larger story of discrimination in a mid-February interview with eighty-six year old Elizabeth Hyde, a clerk in the division of revenue of the Treasury Department. Hyde had come to the District of Columbia in December 1864 and taken a job at $800 per year. Twenty years later her salary was raised to $1200 and in 1889 to $1400. In the second week of February 1917, after fourteen years without an absence and possibly in deference to the recent accusations of sex discrimination, clerk Hyde was informed of her promotion to $1600.[5]

[3] *Washington Post*, Feb. 11, 1917, 14.
[4] *Washington Times*, Feb. 16, 1917, 1.
[5] *Washington Post*, Feb. 18, 1917, 10.

## WASHINGTON, D.C.

February 1st, 1917.

Dear Sir:

I have the honor to acknowledge the receipt of your letter of the 30th ultimo, calling my attention to the communication from Hon. W. L. Jones, requesting information pertaining to the alleged practice of discriminating against women in the Federal Civil Service because of their sex.

It affords me pleasure to state that there is no discrimination against the employment of women in this office, the pay roll for the current month showing that sixty-two per centum of the employees are women.

I find that women are more amenable to discipline than men, and during my long experience in superintending employees, I can recall but two cases of women refusing to obey the rules or to improve the character or extent of their work.

What is the cause of the alleged discrimination against women?

It is with extreme reluctance and hesitation that I enter into a discussion of this subject, owing to the adverse criticism which is likely to be evoked by my views in this matter. However, you have asked for a frank statement, and in my opinion, the causes are as follows:—

1. The failure to put women on an absolute equality with men in so far as the Government Service is concerned.

2. The failure to install a proper system of work reports, showing the character and extent of the work performed by each individual, and to base promotions strictly on ability as shown by said work reports.

3. The proverbial cowardice of men when dealing with women. How many men can find courage to reprimand a woman? Science fails to give any data on this matter, and I do not find that even the renowned Hugo Münsterberg had time to settle this interesting subject.

4. How many superintendents or so-called chiefs are above the age of sixty-four? Should not the well tested rules of the Army and Navy, the warring nations of Europe, and industrial con-

cerns, to the effect that men over sixty-four should be retired from positions of direct responsibility of the management of employees, be adopted in the Civil Service?

Very respectfully,
William C. Taylor
Deputy Register of Wills.

* * * * *

## DEPARTMENT OF THE INTERIOR

### BUREAU OF MINES

January 31, 1917.

My dear Mr. Ayers:

Replying to your note of January 30th, transmitting a copy of Senator W. L. Jones' letter of January 18th addressed to Secretary Lane:

There is, as you know, no discrimination on the part of the Bureau of Mines against the employment of women because of their sex. In the Washington office of the Bureau the number of women stenographers, typewriters, and clerks is 15, and the number of male stenographers, typewriters, and clerks is 27.

At the principal field station of the Bureau of Mines, Pittsburgh, Pa., where the Bureau conducts most of its coal mining investigations, the laboratories and other work of the Bureau are located in a poor part of town in old buildings that lack proper sanitary and other accommodations. The Bureau has, therefore, never employed any women at this station. The Bureau's new half million dollar building near the Carnegie Technical School, is nearing completion, and as soon as the Bureau occupies these new quarters, due consideration will be given in filling vacancies to the selection of women for those positions in which it will be to the best interests of the service to employ them.

The personnel of the mine safety cars of the Bureau, which

travel about from one place to another training miners in the use of breathing apparatus and first aid methods, includes a stenographer and clerk, and from the nature of the surroundings and work to be done, it is obvious that these positions should be filled, as they have been, by male employees only.

With the exceptions of the positions in the Pittsburgh station of the Bureau and on the mine safety cars, women duly qualified for appointment are given the same consideration as men in the filling of vacant positions in the Bureau of Mines.

Very truly yours,
Van H. Manning
Director

* * * * *

## DEPARTMENT OF THE INTERIOR

### UNITED STATES PATENT OFFICE

January 31, 1917.

The Honorable
The Secretary of the Interior.

Sir:—

The Office is in receipt of a copy of a letter, dated the 18th instant, from Honorable W. L. Jones, United States Senate, asking to be advised as to the reasons for discrimination in sex in making appointments to positions in the civil service.

In reply thereto, upon the part of the Patent Office, I have to say that this Office is not informed as to any reasons which the Civil Service Commission may have for holding certain examinations open to men only, further than that the examinations are generally shaped to meet the requirements of the public service.

There is no sex discrimination upon the part of the Patent Office. There are, however, certain positions in the public service which can not be filled by women, and women, therefore, will not be selected for appointment to such positions.

Four classes of appointments to positions in the Patent Office, namely, assistant examiners at $1500, copyists at $720, laborers at $540 and messenger boys at $420, are made from lists of eligibles furnished by the Civil Service Commission.

The examinations for assistant examiner are open to both sexes, and no discrimination is made in the matter of appointments.

Stenographers and typewriters are selected from the male or female registers, in accordance with the needs of the service. During the year 1916, 20 males and 18 females were appointed copyists at $720, by selection from the civil service lists of eligibles. The score, therefore, has been quite evenly divided in the appointments to the 38 positions.

Women are not suitable for performing the duties pertaining to the positions of laborer, nor are they adapted to the position of messenger boy.

The following table shows the distribution of the clerical force of the Patent Office, according to sex:

| | | | | | | |
|---|---|---|---|---|---|---|
| Clerks, | Class 4, | $1800, | Male | 9 | Female | — |
| Clerks, | " 3, | 1600, | " | 5 | " | 4 |
| Clerks, | " 2, | 1400, | " | 8 | " | 9 |
| Clerks, | " 1, | 1200, | " | 23 | " | 107 |
| Clerks, | | 1000, | " | 27 | " | 63 |
| Copyists, | | 900, | " | 58 | " | 31 |
| Copyists, | | 720, | " | 30 | " | 20 |
| | | | Total | 160 | | 234 |

Respectfully,
Thomas Ewing
Commissioner of Patents.

* * * * *

## DEPARTMENT OF THE INTERIOR

### UNITED STATES GEOLOGICAL SURVEY

January 31, 1917.

My dear Mr. Ayers:

In reply to your notation on the copy of the letter from Senator Jones, requesting information as to whether any discrimination against women solely upon the grounds of their sex was made by the Geological Survey:

As you are doubtless aware, much of the work carried on by the Survey requires field ability for which it is necessary to employ men rather than women. In the field branches, therefore, women necessarily are unable to meet the strain attendant upon constant exposure in all kinds of weather and in the strenuous physical exertions that are required of the geologists, topographers, and hydrographic engineers. There are on the rolls of the Survey 417 men, distributed as follows among the different field branches: geologists, 188; topographers, 140; water resources engineers, 74; Alaskan geologists, 15.

In the Division of Engraving and Printing, the work is necessarily of a man's type, requiring the handling of machinery, heavy lifting, dirty work and various trades to which men are especially adapted. The conditions under which much of the engraving and printing work is done is such as to preclude the employment of women. There are 126 men employed in the various non-clerical jobs in the Division of Engraving and Printing and no women.

The force of laborers, messengers, mechanics, etc., consists of 130 men and one woman. The character of the work performed is such as to practically preclude the possibility of employing women for the various duties.

From the above enumeration it will be seen that there are 646 positions in which, from the character of the work, the employment of men is necessitated.

Turning to the distinctly clerical jobs, the following table shows the distribution among the sexes of the different clerks:

| Branches | Males | Females |
|---|---|---|
| Field | 28 | 111 |
| Engraving | 3 | 0 |
| Administrative | 53 | 28 |
| Total | 84 | 139 |

It should be noted in the above table that the great number of males in the administrative branch is due to the inclusion of all the various administrative officers not attached to the field service, as for instance, the Chief Clerk, the Chief Disbursing Officer, the Chief of the Accounts Division, the Chief of the Executive Division, the Chief of the Division of Distribution, etc.

As throwing further light on this question, I have had the requests for appointment for the calendar year 1916 examined, and find that 128 appointments were requested. Of these, 35 were for females and 93 were for males. Of the requests for males, however, 14 were for geologists, chemists, topographers or hydrographic engineers; 23 were for laborers, messenger boys, mechanics, firemen, etc.; 38 were for assistant map printers, apprentices, compositors and others needed for the work of the Division of Engraving and Printing. As already stated, the work of these various positions requires the employment of men only. There were, therefore, of the clerical type of employee, 35 appointments of women and 18 appointments of men.

I think the above tables will clearly show that women are chosen for the clerical positions, in general, in preference to the men at a rate of about two to one and that so far as the Geological Survey is concerned, the spirit, as well as the letter of the law, regarding equal chance to both sexes is lived up to.

Yours very truly,
George Otis Smith
Director.

* * * * *

## DEPARTMENT OF THE INTERIOR
### OFFICE COMMISSIONER OF INDIAN AFFAIRS

January 31, 1917.

My dear Mr. Secretary:

I have received by your reference carbon copy of a letter from Hon. W. L. Jones, dated January 18, 1917 with which he enclosed a copy of a notice from the Civil Service Commission of an examination for male stenographers and typewriters. The Senator asks what special reason there is for filling the stenographic positions entirely or almost entirely by men, in the Government service, and why there should be any discrimination against women solely on the ground of their sex.

In this Office there are 65 stenographers and typewriters, of whom 33 are male and 32 female. This is about the proportion which has been maintained in this Bureau since my incumbency, and I am advised that it is about the same ratio as existed for a number of years.

It is true, however, that male stenographers sometimes resign, but it is seldom or never that a female stenographer has resigned except in cases where they have married after coming into the service. We are, however, continually losing male stenographers through resignation, and they seem to be in demand in the outside business world. To keep up the present ratio between male and female stenographers, it would almost be necessary where resignations occur to call for male stenographers. I am not suggesting, however, that it is desirable to keep up this ratio, but we do find that the young men coming into the Office as a rule pursue courses of study in the educational institutions here in the city, which qualify them for high class clerical work. This is not the case with the female stenographers except in rare instances.

Answering specifically the inquiry as to why there should be any discrimination against women solely upon the ground of their sex, I can say positively that there has been no such discrimination in this Office.

Sincerely yours,
Cato Sells
Commissioner

DEPARTMENT OF THE INTERIOR

BUREAU OF EDUCATION

January 31, 1917.

My dear Mr. Ayers:

In reply to the letter from Senator W. L. Jones, dated January 28, 1917, which has been referred to this bureau, I beg to advise you that there are in the Bureau of Education subject to the Civil Service rules and regulations seventy-three employees. Of this total number there are:

| Men | Women |
| --- | --- |
| 39 | 34 |

Of the above number fifteen are stenographers and typewriters classified as follows:

| Men | Women |
| --- | --- |
| 4 | 11 |

I believe the above statement will show that there is no discrimination against women in the Bureau of Education.

Cordially yours,
P. P. Claxton
Commissioner

* * * * *

DEPARTMENT OF THE INTERIOR

UNITED STATES RECLAMATION SERVICE

February 5, 1917.

Dear Mr. Ayers:

I have received copy of letter of January 18 by your reference of January 30, from Hon. W. L. Jones, regarding an alleged practice of discrimination against women in the Federal civil service when making appointments.

In the Reclamation Service preference has been given to male eligibles for appointment in stenographic positions on account of conditions that are found on many of the projects in the field. In the majority of appointments an understanding is had with eligibles before their employment that an assignment to any part of the field may, and frequently does, follow initial employment. The crude quarters on some projects render it inadvisable to assign women to those places as in many cases there is little privacy possible, or consideration given by the labor element to that sex, and embarrassment and discomfort would result. Whenever it is possible to foresee the permanency of locations and where either sex would be satisfactory requests for eligibles are made accordingly and selection without regard to sex is made.

Very truly yours,
A. P. Davis
Director and Chief Engineer

# Women Workers and World War I: The American Railroad Industry, A Case Study[1]

*Maurine Weiner Greenwald*

> "Women's sphere" bade fair to become a thing of the past. The old line "motherhood occupations" gave way to jobs to be done by available help or "hands." Industry became quite sexless in ideology as well as reality.
> Theresa Wolfson, *The Woman Worker and the Trade Unions.*[2]

Despite American expectations and hopes that World War I would radically alter the sex-segregated organization of work and break down prejudices concerning women's appropriate work roles, the crisis had the opposite effect of strengthening both. Women's wartime employment opportunities ultimately depended more on national economic factors than on the women's collective proficiency in their jobs. Individual initiative could benefit only a statistically negligible number of women in their ability to retain their jobs after the wartime emergency, let alone give them an even chance for upward mobility through their work. Whether, when, where, and how women worked during the war depended almost solely on preexisting economic trends. Modern industrial organization had in effect prescribed the wartime work women would do decades before the crisis began. The increasing bureaucratization and rationalization of the American economy, the tendency toward specialization of work, and the differentiation between men's and women's jobs, as well as the feminization of certain kinds of work shaped the wartime pattern of women's employment. Some change did occur during the war, but the *nature* of the change followed lines established long before the second draft call of 1918 increased the number of women workers. The war merely accelerated former trends in women's work, in the composition of the female labor force, and in attitudes toward women as workers.

An examination of women's wartime experience in the American railroad industry attests to the war's accelerating function in previously established labor patterns. The railroad industry is significant for women's labor history in several important respects. a) To a large extent, it was a microcosm of women's employment generally. Women's railway work before, during, and after the war corresponded to national trends in women's employment in office work, personal service, and manufacturing. b) The work relations between male and female railway employees typified coworker relations in other industries. c) The wartime railroads reveal the problems of women workers with unusual clarity because of the federal government's assumption of direct control over America's private railroads from 1918 until 1920. The takeover was intended to establish an economically and militarily efficient, rationalized continental rail system, but at labor's insistence the federal wartime management introduced some fundamental improvements in the industry's working conditions, most notably a national standardization of wages and hours. In an effort to insure that women benefited equally with male employees from those policies, the government's Railroad Administration created a Women's Service Section to oversee all matters which affected female employees. As the excesses of wage inequalities were minimized, the more enduring difficulties which confronted women became glaringly apparent.[3]

The following analysis proceeds along several lines. A numerical picture of women's railroad work before, during, and after the war illuminates the temporary and permanent effects of the war on women's employment. The next section examines separately the wartime interaction of women railway office, yard, and shop workers with male supervisors, foremen, and employees. Some light is also thrown on the treatment accorded women by railway unions. The final section relates women's wartime railway experiences to other sectors of women's work.

I

Occupational and personal data on women railway workers from 1917 to 1919 reflected national changes in the patterns of women's work from 1910 to 1930. Women continued to make headway in office work, but they tended to perform jobs that had previously been considered solely women's clerical work. They also continued to work in traditional common-labor and personal-service jobs. Some limited movement away from time-honored occupations for women did occur during the war, but a detailed analysis of the employment figures according to separate job classifications in railroad work clearly demonstrates the narrow scope of women's permanent gain, outside the fields where they had already established preponderance. The few new kinds of jobs which did open to women, especially late in the war, terminated with its end, while the older female occupations retained their concentration of women.

Quarterly statistics on the number of women employees in 21

railroad occupational classifications from January 1918 through October 1920 provide a numerical measure of the war's effect on women's railroad work.[4] Women's employment increased from 61,162 in January 1918 to 90,052 in October 1920, a 67 percent increase for the 34-month period. The number of women employees rose continually until October 1918, when a total of 101,785 women were engaged in railroad work. This figure represents a gain of approximately 321 percent over the 1917 employment level of 31,400 women.[5] Significantly, the employment peak for women coincides very closely with the war's end.

Most women railway workers performed clerical and semiclerical tasks. Of the 101,785 women employed on October 1, 1918, 72 percent (73,620) worked as clerks of all kinds, stenographers, typists, comptometer operators, accountants, ticket sellers, and information agents. Only the last two positions were totally new to women. Generally, women performed routine, unskilled, or semiskilled office work of the variety that they had performed before the war. While a few women obtained supervisory positions during the war through apprenticeships in routine office work, women expert in low-level secretarial skills tended to remain in such positions.[6]

The second largest group of women wartime railway workers in October 1918 were the 5,600 women (5 percent of the total) who toiled in the traditional female occupation of cleaning. Women worked as common laborers in stations, offices, coaches, and Pullman cars. During the war the scope of this occupation widened somewhat to include work on scrap docks, in freight transfer stations, and supply departments. As relatively heavy labor, the latter positions accordingly paid higher wages.[7] With demobilization and the introduction of protective legislation, however, women lost these new jobs.

Personal service in dining rooms and kitchens as matrons, janitresses, laundresses, and hospital nurses comprised the third most numerous group of female railway employees. Only 2.8 percent (2,830) of the railroad women were working in these traditionally female roles as of October 1, 1918.

Telephone and telegraph operators composed the fourth and fifth largest groups of women railway employees. Telegraph operators constituted 2.4 percent (2,409) of women workers as of October 1, 1918 while the telephone operators numbered 2,613 or 2.6 percent of the women employees. Of the two fields, railroad telegraphy presented the greater challenge for women to enter because it had formerly been almost exclusively male. The employment of women in this field was nonetheless quite short-lived. By October 1920 women in telegraphy constituted fewer than 1 percent of all women employed in railway work. Information collected by the Women's Service Station indicates that women telephonists and telegraphers rapidly became "extra" workers after the Armistice and worked only irregularly.[8]

During the war some limited movement away from traditional occupations did occur. Outside the clerical, semiclerical, and common-labor categories, women worked at an impressive *variety* of new railroad positions. They labored as turntable operators, packers of journal boxes, and attendants in toolrooms and storerooms. They worked as level adjusters in signal towers, checkers in freight houses, and as car clerks. Other women became operators of bolt-threading, nut-tapping, and car-bearing machines as well as turret lathes, angle-cock grinders, hammers, and cranes. Women also widened their employment by becoming air-brake cleaners, repairers, and testers as well as electric welders, oxy-acetylene cutters and welders, and core makers.[9] But the actual *number* of such new positions was small. Although 5,000 women could be counted in wartime shop work, 4,500 of these were common laborers. These women had gained access to a new work place, but the type of work they performed there was mostly unskilled. Moreover, many of the women performing semiskilled labor such as welding were outside the normal avenue of advancement through apprenticeship.

Although proportionally few women gained access during the war to new railroad positions, as a whole, women preferred railroad office, shop, and yard work to similar employment elsewhere because of the special labor benefits provided by the Railroad Administration. Federal control of the railroads, which ended a particularly bitter chapter in the long history of strained relations between railroad workers and owners, brought extensive changes in working conditions, including the recognition of collective bargaining; the enforcement of an eight-hour day with time-and-a-half pay for overtime; elaborate provisions for promotions, seniority, and grievances; elimination of piecework; standardization of pay scales; and recognition of the equal rights of women and black workers.[10]

The available fragments of personal data about wartime women railway workers suggest that most of them had previously been employed. This finding corresponds to the national pattern in which the war occasioned a shift of women workers from one type of work to another, while drawing only a minority of new women into the labor force. According to information collected by the Women's

Service Section of the Railroad Administration in 1919 on 1500 female clerks in 11 offices throughout the country, about half of the clerks had formerly worked in offices and had chosen the railroads during the war in preference to performing similar work elsewhere. A little over an eighth of the women clerks entered the railroad industry during the war from manufacturing and service work in other industries. The personal data also suggest that one-fifth of the women employed as railway clerks during the war had never before worked.[11]

The WSS study found that 36.5 percent of the 1500 women clerks were under 21 years of age. Of the 676 clerks who offered information about their educational backgrounds, almost 50 percent had had only an elementary education, 47 percent had some high school, and 3 percent had some college training. More than 50 percent had worked previously as typists and stenographers, while 20 percent reported no prior work. Former saleswomen constituted slightly less than 10 percent, whereas former telegraph and telephone operators, seamstresses, milliners, and factory workers each composed only about 1 to 2 percent of the clerical employees. Thus about 12 percent of the women clerical workers had switched from other female employment to office work during the war.[12] The federal censuses on occupations for 1910 and 1920 lend credence to the railroad data insofar as the census figures show only a 6 percent increase in the number of women workers in the ten-year period, while female clerical workers increased more than 50 percent.

Data about other groups of women railroad workers are relatively sparse, but they also suggest that they had worked in similar jobs before the war. A Women's Service Section study of Pennsylvania found that women working as common laborers for the railroad during the war had formerly worked as laborers in laundries, hotels, restaurants, and in domestic day work. The economic exigencies of the war accounted for the presence of a small number of newly employed women, who were classified as widows, deserted wives, wives whose husbands were in military service, and women forced to work because of the increased cost of living.[13] Another source of increase, related to this last group, was composed of young women who normally would have entered the labor force but for whom work briefly assumed increased importance because of the war-induced decline in marriage rates.

A preliminary evaluation of the war's effect on women's railroad employment could be tallied with the demobilization which followed quickly upon the Armistice of November 11, 1918. Women made net employment gains only in their jobs as clerical workers and cleaners, while the female work force as a whole was reduced. Women lost their jobs after the Armistice when servicemen formerly employed by the railroads were reinstated and the Railroad Administration inaugurated a drastic austerity program. Both factors especially decreased the ranks of women because they generally had less railroad seniority than male workers. By early 1919, the female work force had been reduced 19.6 percent, although clerical workers and car and station cleaners suffered relatively less than other classes of labor. The number of female shop workers dropped 33 percent, whereas the ranks of women clerical workers were thinned by only 12.2 percent, and those of cleaners by 15.4 percent.[14] Of the 74,745 women office workers employed on January 1, 1919, 71,637 were still at their jobs in October 1920. Between 1920 and 1930, however, the number of female clerical workers decreased by 32 percent and the number of female common laborers decreased by 52 percent.[15]

A longer-term evaluation of women's railroad employment suggests that women did make some lasting gains. Between 1917 and 1930 the number of women railroad employees increased by 42 percent.[16] Obviously, however, this gain would have been even greater had demobilization and the 1921-22 economic depression not combined to diminish the rapid wartime increase in women workers. The continued concentration of women in clerical and common-labor jobs suggests once again that the war accelerated trends already underway.

Some women affected adversely by demobilization expressed disappointment about losing their jobs. Even though economic necessity and the prospect of decent wages had induced them to take railroad jobs, they felt that they had done their "bit" for the war and had therefore earned job security. They accepted the practice by which returning soldiers might rightfully replace them, but they felt outraged when men with no prior service on the roads were hired to do their work. Sensitive to the labor market's manipulation of their lives, they expressed their resentment at being first courted and then discarded.[17]

## II

The larger significance of this information can be best developed in the context of women's total work experience. The inner dynamic of the wartime work relations and the more enduring problems that women faced are revealed by an analysis of the women's treatment by their local supervisors and fellow employees, and the reaction of the railway unions to the women's increased employment. The women's own perceptions form a vital part of this analysis. Records from the Women's Service Section provide insight into the work experiences of 13,000 employees in 23 states and the District of Columbia.

Daily relations between men and women employed in railroad offices, yards, and shops varied considerably from one kind of work to another and from one place to another. Some common aspects of this experience can, however, be identified. Prewar patterns of women's work determined women's wartime experience more than any other factor. The wartime crisis laid bare prewar structural developments in the organization of men's and women's work, prevailing social ideas about women's proper work roles, and underlying economic considerations which shaped male workers' wartime response to women workers and women's perceptions of and reactions to their experience. The varying importance of these economic and social concerns can be seen in the separate situations of women as railroad office workers, common laborers, and semiskilled laborers.

The significance of women's wartime work in railroad offices can only be understood against the background of prewar, nationwide changes in American business practices, office technology, and education. Business consolidation and expansion after 1900 increasingly demanded larger secretarial staffs, while a technological revolution in office equipment, particularly the widening use of the typewriter and numerous mathematical machines; dramatically transformed the speed and methods for performing office work. Lastly, the spread of public-school education, especially high-school training, created a growing supply of persons, particularly women, who were eligible for office employment. These developments resulted in turn in the gradual replacement of the all round clerk by executive secretaries, stenographers, typists, bookkeepers, and office-machine operators.[18]

The shift toward specialization was accompanied by a change in the sex composition of persons employed in clerical work. What had formerly been almost exclusively men's work became increasingly shared by women after 1890. While men comprised 94 percent of all clerical workers in the United States in 1880, their majority decreased to 65.8 percent by 1910. It fell further to 54.4 percent by 1920.[19] All the while, women's employment in offices increased dramatically as did the total number of clerical workers in the labor force. Employers welcomed women into clerical work because they offered the readiest supply of educated labor and worked for lower wages.

The change in sex composition could also be seen in the growing rigidity of sex-role differentiation around the turn of the century within the field of clerical work. In most American offices men worked predominantly as the general clerks, accountants, shipping clerks, weighers, and messengers, while women accounted for a majority of the bookkeepers, cashiers, stenographers, machine operators, and filing clerks. In addition, a rigid job standardization accompanied the trends in specialization and gender differentiation. Increasingly after 1900, college-trained experts defined the content of office work as based on time-motion studies. Experts in office management also introduced new methods of payment. Piece work and bonus systems came to replace hourly or weekly wage scales. The speed with which clerical workers, particularly machine operators, performed their work determined their salaries.[20] Mechanization and scientific organization resulted in a trilevel stratification of the office labor force: a small group of men trained to deal with matters involving judgment, experience, and responsibility; a large group of semiskilled female machine operators; and a mass of unskilled women assigned routine tasks.[21]

Although office work relegated women to a status inferior to men's, in comparison to women's limited employment options, clerical work constituted a promotion. In other words, the male standard of comparison is not the only one to use, as contemporaries of both sexes recognized. The new white-collar office work offered women a higher social status, better working conditions, and more remuneration than domestic service, sales, or factory work.[22] Moreover, unlike teaching or nursing, which demanded extended professional training, specialized clerical skills could be acquired in a relatively brief time. In the hierarchy of women's work, office employment assumed a middle position between blue-collar and professional jobs.

To a large extent, these structural changes in business operations defined women's and men's jobs and relations in railroad offices before, during, and after the war. The crisis marked a major reinforcement of a long process of sex-role channeling. While men and women worked side by side, they each continued to perform different tasks. Additionally, the war brought into the open the otherwise unspoken attitudes of male supervisors and workers toward women. The evaluation of one chief clerk typifies the prevailing male view that women deserved only dead-end jobs at low wages. The chief clerk told a Women's Service Section investigator that he saw "no special difference" between men's and women's work. He explained,

> I prefer young women to young men and I am going to continue to

> employ them. We have employed women since the '80's. For our class of work they are steadier than boys. They are not so damned anxious to get out and rustle around. Women are more content with the detailed monotonous work because they are filling in between school and marriage. They never think of themselves as General Managers of a railroad and are content to work along. Boys want to move on too quickly to do our work well.[23]

The WSS field agent reported that this clerk "has so narrowed each person's opportunities that there is not much to learn and not far to advance. . . . Ease in breaking people in and getting the work [done] today seem to be his standards." The women in this office spent their work week "hanging little pieces of paper on pegs day after day."[24] Never did it cross the chief clerk's mind that women's limited employment opportunities and their boss's low expectations served to reinforce their lack of initiative.

Male supervisors sometimes complained that women loafed on the job and feigned illness in order to avoid working. It is noteworthy that the clerical workers whom the men criticized often operated office machines eight or more hours each day. Since they were subject to "speed-ups," they used their rest rooms as a refuge from increased pressure of the work routine and as a place to socialize briefly.[25] Their work habits were far more a function of production pressures than an inherent lack of ambition.

The prevailing notion that women were docile, unambitious workers found expression in the supervisors' treatment of women, in the words of one woman clerk, as "either jokes or pets."[26] Abusive personal treatment of women by male supervisors and foremen ranged from verbal discourtesy and incivility to physical assaults. In the Cincinnati auditor's office of the Southern Railroad one supervisor is reported to have assumed the privilege of pulling up dresses, pinching breasts, and verbally abusing his female subordinates. This man misused his authority by giving wage increases to those women who submitted to his molestations, while refusing raises to those who protested.[29]

In contrast to the often strained relations between male supervisors and female clerical employees, coworker relations were generally relaxed. This was especially true because the differentiation of work along male-female lines did not place women and men in direct competition. Under certain circumstances, however, men and women office workers became adversaries. When the wartime labor shortage occasioned the introduction of women into skilled positions ordinarily reserved for men, coworker relations deteriorated, especially when women received preferential treatment to help them quickly obtain the necessary job expertise. For example, in the Chicago office of the Loss and Damage Department of the Chicago, Burlington and Quincy Railroad, women began to obtain excellent advanced training. During the war the shortage of skilled male claims adjusters prompted the federal auditor to devise a training program for women. Considered a "railroad trade," the investigators' work was highly skilled, since it demanded comprehensive knowledge of freight construction and transport. In groups of 5 or 6 a total of 38 women received a month's training in all aspects of claims work. They attended lectures about their new duties, travelled to different railroad yards, acquainted themselves with types of freight cars, visited stations, and followed in detail the work involved in shipping freight. They even visited the car shops in Aurora to witness the construction of freight cars. The women also observed packing and shipping procedures in furniture factories, bottling works, and mail-order houses. Under the supervision of a skilled investigator, they spent a second month preparing actual claims of a simple nature. In this latter instance, the women received more training than regular male investigators who usually learned on the job.

Of the 38 trained women, all between the ages of 25 and 35, only 18 were employed as investigators at the time of the field-agent's report in September 1919. More than half typified a common female pattern: some had dropped out of the training program because they felt unqualified; others had married and according to the mores of the time left their employment. Those who stayed, however, voiced satisfaction with their work and hoped to advance in the department. Helen Ross noted that these women had "never thought railroad work could be so interesting."

The male employees reacted jealously, dampening this otherwise positive experiment. While the usual discriminatory situation entailed the underpayment of poorly trained women, in this instance, men doing similar work complained that the women earned more money and had received more training than they had. This resentment was formalized in a protest to Washington. Although the women maintained their positions, local officials discontinued training women as soon as male trainees again became available.[28]

In some local offices the hostility of male clerks toward women was rooted in prewar work experience. Because women had on occasion been hired at lower wages and used as strikebreakers and scabs, their increased employment under federal control made some men apprehensive. They feared that large numbers of women would underbid them and prove resistant to union membership. Under such circumstances, the men reasoned that their status would be severely weakened upon the return of the roads to private control. While the Railroad Administration's wage orders and policy of union recognition decreased the likelihood of these possibilities, local officials sometimes fanned male fears by using special agents to discourage union organizing among women.[29] The memory of strikebreakers being rewarded with promotions by private owners before the war certainly did not help to create congenial relations between the men and women who were subsequently obliged to work together during the period of federal control.[30] In situations where formal bars against women's membership in unions existed, women could be influenced by their superiors' informal comments against unions. There could be a fine line between "friendly advice" and reprisals.[31]

Despite the worries of some unionized male railway clerks, female clerks demonstrated an acute consciousness of themselves as workers, not least through their union activities. In the Brotherhood of Railway Clerks, where female membership had been negligible in 1910, women accounted for approximately 35,000 members in 1920, about 50 percent of all female railway clerks and more than 20 percent of the total 186,000 organized railway clerks. Some women even became officers of their locals, while a few held positions on railroad system boards. The female clerks' ability to sustain their gains was an entirely separate matter, however, as the dramatic wartime increase in trade-union organization among women railway clerks proved to be short-lived. As a result of the postwar demobilization and the industrial depression of 1921-22, female membership in the Brotherhood of Railway Clerks dropped to 4,420 in 1924. Although male membership also dropped dramatically during this period, the women fared much worse.[32]

There is good evidence to suggest that women union members handled the violations of their personal and occupational rights much better than women who did not join the union. According to WSS field-agent reports, it was much more common for young women new to railroad service to join a union and use the channels available to adjudicate their complaints than it was for women who had been employed by the railroad for some time and who remembered the bitter antiunion sentiment that characterized private ownership of the roads. While the Railroad Administration offered ample machinery for dealing with grievances, women who were not union members showed reluctance to fight their cases through proper channels. Instead, they complained in private to the WSS field agents about the many abuses they suffered, but at the same time pleaded with the field agents not to take any action. They feared vindictive treatment from their male superiors. In contrast, women union members felt much more secure about pursuing their grievances to some resolution.[33]

The Brotherhood of Railway Clerks gave women emotional support as well as expertise in dealing with the government's bureaucratic procedures. The locals assisted women employees in obtaining redress for discriminatory treatment on the part of railroad authorities in a number of cases that came to the attention of the Women's Service Section. When necessary, the Grand President of the Brotherhood, J.J. Forrester, intervened on a woman's behalf. In the postwar period this interest continued in instances where it was alleged that the seniority rights of women had not been recognized. When the employment situation became critical in the first part of 1919 and the union's primary concern centered on the reemployment of men who had been laid off or who had returned from active military service, the locals nonetheless persisted in their efforts to help women clerks (and occasionally car cleaners) to cope with the extreme cutbacks in the work force. Such union endeavors educated women about their rights as workers. Those who lost their jobs could at least retain a favorable view of trade unionism.[34]

Problems facing female common laborers employed in the railroad industry during the war differed in kind and degree from the difficulties facing clerical workers. Ironically, objections from the Women's Service Section, rather than from male workers or supervisors, curtailed women's wartime employment opportunities in railroad yards. Additionally, racial and sex discrimination in the labor movement frustrated these women's efforts to obtain trade union protection.

Common laborers employed in offices, shops, roundhouses, and yards were mostly assigned the task of cleaning and sweeping. A small number of women wiped engines while others operated electric lift trucks at freight transfer stations and docks, moving lumber in lots of one to two hundred pounds. They would also lift large heaps of scrap iron. Previously employed as unskilled labor in hotels, laundries, restaurants, and private homes, these women eagerly sought railroad work for its relatively better working conditions, steady employment, and higher wages. For the same class of labor these women earned about twice their former income.

Black women who had worked before the war as coach cleaners gained admittance during the war to work on scrap docks and in freight transfer stations and supply departments. As employees of the Missouri Pacific Railroad in Kansas City, for example, black women employed at an hourly rate of 35½ cents sorted and put away supplies dumped in the yards. The women picked up 25-pound forgings and castings and moved them in their arms or in wheelbarrows to supply bins. They also swept the storerooms and yards. This work sometimes involved moving 250-pound couplers and heavy oil barrels.[35]

Whether women's common labor involved excessive physical exertion is difficult to assess. According to WSS field-agent reports, some women acknowledged that they did not perform all the heavy tasks expected of them, but rather that some male workers regularly helped them.[36] The Women's Service Section decided that the work demanded more physical strength than women could easily offer. In September 1919, the Director General of the Railroad Administration accordingly ordered the roads to discontinue the employment of women as section hands and truckers. One railroad alone transferred or dismissed 223 laborers and 193 truckers as a result of this order.[37]

Despite the physical demands of the manual labor, the relatively high pay and the absence of viable alternatives made black and white women resistant to the protective regulations which would deny them employment in particular jobs. Black women often stressed the importance of keeping their jobs. The youngest woman employed as a railroad trucker was Pearl Jones, age 21. She had had three years of high school and listed her previous employment as domestic service. She explained to a field agent the severe ramifications of the discontinuance order as it affected black unskilled workers:

> All the colored women like this work and want to keep it. We are making more money at this than any work we can get, and we do not have to work as hard as at housework which requires us to be on duty from six o'clock in the morning until nine or ten at night, with might little time off and at very poor wages. . . . What the colored women need is an opportunity to make money. As it is, they have to take what employment they can get, live in old tumbled down houses or resort to street walking, and I think a woman ought to think more of her blood than to do that. What occupation is open to us where we can make really good wages? We are not employed as clerks, we cannot all be school teachers, and so we cannot see any use in working our parents to death to get educated. Of course we should like easier work than this if it were opened to us, but this pays well and is no harder than other work open to us. With three dollars a day, we can buy bonds. . . , we can dress decently, and not be tempted to find our living on the streets. . . . Please don't take this work away from us.[38]

The anxiety to retain their jobs was particularly strong among all black women, not only those subject to transfer or dismissal. Black women's work habits, particularly their regularity and their meticulous character, impressed WSS field agents. Described by their superiors as dependable, the women tried their best to retain their common-labor jobs. One scrap-dock worker who had been brought from Atlanta with her husband and children to work in the Cleveland shops of the New York Central Railroad eagerly explained to a field agent her motives for working so hard. She said that her husband worked as an ashpit man in the roundhouse. With their four children they lived in a three-room boxcar supplied by the railroad in a boxcar community of twenty other similarly employed black families. Speaking as a concerned parent, she said, "I am working with my husband so we can get along. You know the children have to be dressed better than most people who live in boxcars."[39] The second salary provided the margin of respectability.

Some women were nonetheless dismissed from jobs which the new federal regulations deemed unsuitable for females, and they protested vigorously to the Railroad Administration and their unions. The companies often did not have alternate work available, so enforcement of the federal regulation effectively meant dismissal. When 72 female truckers employed by the Minnesota Transfer Company were dismissed, the women searched elsewhere for jobs with the aid of the state employment service. It appears that only 12 received permanent positions elsewhere, while 5 found temporary jobs. According to a supervisor, others returned to their homes in the country. Some of the women received adequate support from husbands and stopped working. For those who found new employment, their new wages averaged about 48 dollars per month, which compared unfavorably with the 60- to 90-dollar salaries they had earned in railroad work. Despite the supposed intent of protecting the women's persons, the new federal regulations in practice adversely affected their income.[40]

Women employed as common laborers were also subject to special work pressures and penalties. Railroad personnel strictly supervised women's behavior and placed almost the entire burden for moral rectitude on them. The Women's Service Section sanctioned this policy because it viewed the substitution of women for men workers as an important, though fragile, wartime experiment that could potentially provide new postwar job opportunities for women throughout the economy. Since local railroad managers were often ambivalent, if not hostile, to the employment of women in men's jobs, the WSS staff feared that the hasty selection or poor supervision of women workers might have negative consequences for working women after the wartime labor shortage would end. To train women to a higher standard of work, the WSS stressed the need for strict controls over workers and the periodic evaluations of women's performance and character. The WSS hoped to mold women into model workers while entrusting to management's good will the provision of a physically and morally wholesome work environment. The agency, therefore, exhorted women to be punctual, enthusiastic, trustworthy, accurate, tactful, cooperative, able, pleasing, and proper.[41] The WSS field agents regularly commented on women's behavior and the quality of supervision provided by the roads. A case in point concerned workers employed by the Santa Fe in its Topeka, Kansas railroad yards. One WSS field agent wrote approvingly in October 1918 that

> men and women work together in the warehouse, but all seemed orderly and businesslike about their work. A foreman keeps strict supervision over them. When the women were first employed, the General Foreman talked to all the men telling them that the women were to be regarded as equals and that no intimacy was to be tolerated. Several of the first women were dismissed because their conduct was not proper, and this had a wholesome effect on the rest of the women as well as on the men. So many women have applied for the work that a vacancy is filled easily. Both the men and women recognize therefore that their employment depends on good behavior. No woman is allowed to go into a box car except to take her load if so required. If she is found there for any [other] purpose she is dismissed.[42]

The women newly hired in common-labor jobs did not complain about the daily social controls and double standard of morality imposed upon them by their supervisors. They wanted above all to keep their jobs. Aware of the precarious tenure, which resulted directly from the wartime labor shortage, they were accordingly quite careful to avoid jeopardizing their positions by some inadvertent infringement of a work rule. Most of them tolerated the constant supervision without overt complaint.

Opportunities for women in railroad yards were defined not only in terms of their presumed physical strength or social behavior but also by racial considerations. Car cleaning, for example, was divided not only between male and female tasks, but also along color lines. In the Long Island Yards of the Long Island Railroad, black women were barred from cleaning dining cars and restricted to coaches. Even in their time off the women shared identical but segregated quarters in a new locker-room facility.[43]

Racial and sex discrimination merged in the carmen's attempts to organize car cleaners. The Brotherhood of Railway Carmen attempted to increase its economic strength by claiming jurisdiction over car cleaners in many railroad yards during the war. The Brotherhood nonetheless failed to offer equal representation to two groups the black men and women on the one hand and the white women on the other. The union cared most about white male car cleaners.[44]

Moreover, instead of supporting women's right to employment after the war, as the Brotherhood of Railway Clerks had done, the Carmen directly requested the replacement of women workers by men. In June 1919, the General Chairman of the Brotherhood announced his union's objections to the employment of 22 women as car oilers, storehouse attendants, and laborers in the Greenville yards in Jersey City, and requested that the Pennsylvania Railroad dismiss them. The union leader charged that the women workers were inefficient, that they kept men out of the positions, and that they were really in need of their earnings. In February 1919, 104 men and women were temporarily laid off at the Greenville yards because of demobilization. In April, as workers were recalled according to seniority, 10 women were rehired. The local chairman of the Brotherhood complained that this procedure amounted to giving women an unfair preference over "his" men. When the union chairman's requests went unheeded by the local foremen and the General Manager of the Pennsylvania Railroad, the union took its request to the Division of Labor of the federal Railroad Administration. The Women's Service Section investigated the case and found no evidence to support the union's complaints. The final WSS report on this matter instead charges the Carmen with sex discrimination.[45]

Despite such incidents, women common laborers continued to demonstrate their commitment to the labor movement. Problems with male supremacists were seen as intramural, within the labor movement, rather than as between insiders and outsiders. Women workers gave their wholehearted support, for example, to the postwar strike of shopmen from 1922 to 1923. As a consequence of the strike's long duration, many women were forced to seek other employment.[46]

The substitution of women for skilled male workers in railroad shops and roundhouses brought considerable resistance from male railway employees, so that the pattern that developed among carmen was even more pronounced despite the absence of additional racial considerations. Although even at the peak of their railroad employment in October 1918 there were relatively few women in skilled-labor categories, they were nonetheless regarded by men as interlopers. The shopmen interpreted women's employment as a direct threat to their craft because women's introduction into the shops was accompanied by the dilution of skilled labor and the subdivision of production processes. The men therefore actively attempted to discourage the hiring of women. They harassed their female coworkers, refused them admittance to the machinists' union, and sought to make their employment as temporary as possible.

Most women hired for shop work during the war performed the work of helpers within the larger occupational designations, which credit women throughout the country with 35 blacksmiths, 6 boilermakers, 14 coppersmiths, sheet-metal workers, and pipe fitters, 14 electricians, and 370 machinists.[47] The challenge that women presented to the traditional training of the machinist can be seen particularly well in the case of female welders. Ordinarily, welding had been one stage in the apprenticeship of a machinist. During the war, however, the process was separated from this larger training process and was given to women with no prior machine-shop experience. Of 12 women investigated at the Mt. Clare Shops of the B&O in Baltimore, 11 had worked in typical female jobs before the war. One had run a power sewing machine, another had worked in a button factory, a third in a cigarette factory, and a fourth in a silk mill. Others had variously worked as time-keeper, telephone operator, cashier, spooler and spinner in a cotton mill, home dressmaker, and weaver. Two had worked in munition factories before coming to the railroad. Like other women in new wartime railway work, they uniformly liked welding and the income it provided.[48]

The male machinists in Baltimore expressed their hostility toward the women welders by opposing their union membership and refusing to help or work alongside them. Some of the women testified to the investigating field agent that "the men had tried to drive them off the jobs with their torches or with the riveting." In the case of one woman welder who had been put on boiler work, the men refused to work with her, had her taken off the job, and protested her employment to the local secretary of the International Association of Machinists.[49]

The constitution of the machinists' International permitted women to organize with men or in separate locals as specialists or helpers. In fact, national union officials sympathetically expressed the opinion that women should be organized to help insure the maintenance of standard wages for men. Nevertheless, at the workplace shopmen often discouraged women from joining the union.[50] At the Mt. Clare shops in Baltimore, women gained admittance to the union only infrequently and in the face of great reluctance on the part of the male machinists.[51]

Despite the male opposition, the female shop employees wanted to keep their jobs in the railroad industry. After the Armistice, some master mechanics attempted to get rid of the women shop workers without illegally dismissing them. In the Jersey City Erecting Shop of the Erie Railroad, the master mechanic attempted to make women resign by creating an uncomfortable work atmosphere. A visiting field agent noted the hostility among the shopmen and the "ugly spirit" of the male apprentices. In the same shop the assistant master mechanic reportedly threated to fire a woman who intended to report her misclassification as a common laborer when she was performing the work of a machinist's helper.[52]

The shopmen's bitter reaction against the women's employment in railroad shops and roundhouses reveals the complexity with which craft protection and discrimination against women combined during the war. The machinists reacted with hostility against women both because women's employment brought with it a dilution of skilled labor and a subdivision of production processes *and* because the new wartime workers happened to be women instead of men. In such a situation, the men's acceptance of women workers would have implied as well an acceptance of the accompanying changes in their craft. The machinists could conceivably have fought the dilution of their skills and also admitted women to railroad machine shops by opening the machinists' apprenticeship program to women. The men's unwillingness to pursue such a strategy suggests the degree to which they perceived of their craft in exclusively male terms.

III

The different wartime experiences of women railway clerical, common-labor, and semiskilled workers reflected similar developments in other sectors of women's work. Generally, women's new wartime jobs fell victim to demobilization while the concentration of women in particular fields and kinds of work continued. The patterns of women's work in 1930 did not markedly differ from those of 1910. Although the number of female domestics, for example, declined between 1910 and 1920 because of new wartime opportunities, the number of domestic workers dramatically increased in the next decade. During the same twenty-year period women in manufacturing gained most in the textile, clothing, food, and leather industries which had long been strongholds of women's work. Also, an increase in the number of women employed in trade as sales-women and clerks in stores continued unabated, as did the concentration of female professionals in teaching and nursing. Lastly, the most important increment in women's employment in the field of communications between 1910 and 1930 took place in telephone operating where women held the vast majority of positions even before the war.[53]

The varied response of railway unions to women's employment also corresponded to women's relations with organized labor in other fields. Two patterns appear common. In industries characterized by sex-differentiated work, unions recruited women members in an effort to extend and strengthen collective bargaining. In occupations where women were introduced for the first time during the war, unions either allowed women to join only for the duration of the crisis or resisted their employment altogether. Women responded accordingly. When they were welcomed into unions, they accepted the invitation and cooperated with men in obtaining better working conditions. Women's typically short-lived tenure and their inability to obtain trade-union protection in new wartime jobs had a particularly profound effect on their attitudes toward themselves as workers and as women. Exposure to better-paying occupations offered them a new reference point from which to evaluate their traditional employment and made them discontent with their usually limited options. When faced with union opposition, therefore, women defended their special interests. Their resistance ranged from individual refusals to be intimidated by fellow workers to collective mobilization against hostile unions. Ironically, the war brought many women their first contact with highly organized, militant male workers from whom they might have learned about the advantages of trade-union protection. Instead, the opposition of organized labor taught these women to think of trade unionism and sex discrimination synonymously.

Wartime developments in the telephone and streetcar industries further illustrate these different patterns of women's wartime relations with organized labor. In the telephone industry women worked almost solely as telephone operators while men worked in the skilled trades. Since women did not threaten men's jobs, cooperation between the two groups arose naturally as they each tried to improve their working conditions. The enrollment between 1917 and 1920 of thousands of telephone operators into the International Brotherhood of Electrical Workers strengthened the women's and men's alliance. When telephone operators struck throughout the war on the New

England and Pacific Coasts and in the South and Midwest, the repairmen, male telephone installers, line splicers, and switchboard workers gave their full support. Together they fought for and often won union recognition, improved wages and hours, and replacements of individual supervisors.[54]

In contrast, the street-transit industry was marked by intraclass struggle during and after the war. When hundreds of women became conductors for the first time during 1917 and 1918 in such cities as New York, Chicago, Cleveland, and Detroit, locals of the Amalgamated Street and Electric Railway Employees fought against the women's introduction. The women, in turn, formed associations of their own to cope with the dilemma of favorable employment amidst male backlash. Although their efforts proved unequal to the forces which led to the termination of their employment, the women refused to surrender their better-paying jobs silently.[55]

Taken together, then, the developments in the railroad industry, the long-term patterns in women's work, and the different relations between women and organized labor demonstrate the war's accelerating effect in terms of previous trends, but the crisis did not render the "woman's sphere" and the "old line motherhood occupations" a "thing of the past." The war at once exposed the formidable barriers to women workers' equality and served to harden the previous definitions and structure of women's work. The delineation of this argument suggests the need for further study of the particularities of women's work within different industries, the complications of protective legislation, and the varying nature of male-female relations outside and inside the labor movement.

*University of Pittsburgh* Maurine Weiner Greenwald

FOOTNOTES

1. This essay has benefited from the criticisms of Martin A. Greenwald, David Montgomery, John Thomas, Barbara Rosen, Peter Stearns, and Linda Pritchard. Its limitations remain my own.

2. (New York, 1926), p. 29.

3. As a byproduct of federal control, considerable documentation was created on the conditions, practices, and policies of American railroading. As a legacy of the government's takeover of the roads, the historian is afforded a close-up view of the nature of work and male-female relations on the job during the wartime crisis. Unlike other documentation on women's wartime experience, the Railroad Administration papers have survived the periodic disposal of wartime

records. The Women's Service Section reports, which are now housed in the National Archives, preserve a record of contemporary attitudes toward women railway workers by government officials, male supervisors, and male employees. These records fortunately also shed light on the women's own perceptions of and responses to their jobs, bosses, and fellow workers.

4. The author has yet to find detailed information about women's railway work for the period before or after the termination of the Railroad Administration and the Women's Service Section.

5. *Annual Report of Walter B. Hines, Director General of Railroads, 1919* (Washington, D.C., 1920), p. 61. The number of women employed by the railroads in 1917 was obtained by the Women's Service Section from 106 roads employing 25,428 women.

6. For similar information about early twentieth-century changes in office work, see Grace Coyle, *Present Trends in Clerical Occupations* (New York, 1928), pp. 11, 14, 33, and Elizabeth Kemper Adams, *Women Professional Workers* (Chautauqua, N.Y., 1921), pp. 233-5.

7. *Annual Report of W.G. McAdoo, Director General of Railroads, 1918* (Washington, D.C., 1919), p. 17.

8. *Annual Report, 1919*, p. 73.

9. *Annual Report, 1918*, p. 18.

10. W.S. Carter, "Effect of Federal Control on Railway Labor," *Proceedings of the Academy of Political Science* 8 (1918-1920): 198-210; Walter Hines, *War History of American Railroads* (New Haven, 1928), pp. 152-91; K. Austin Kerr, *American Railroad Politics*, 1914-1920 (Pittsburgh, 1968), pp. 91-101.

11. *Annual Report, 1919*, pp. 77-9.

12. *Ibid.*

13. RG 14 WSS File 273 National Archives (NA). Interestingly, three of the four WSS designations identify or classify the women by reference to marital status. Only one category is economic.

14. *Annual Report, 1919*, pp. 62-4.

15. The 1930 occupational census records 48,517 women clerical workers. In 1920 women common laborers numbered 6,586 while they numbered only 3,111 in 1930.

16. In 1917 the railroads employed 31,400 women. By 1930 the roads had a force of 54,994.

17. RG 14 WSS Complaints 51, 66, 77 (NA). Formal complaints handled by the Women's Service Section were issued by women and locals of the Brotherhood of Railway Clerks as well as government agencies. An examination of the complaints submitted by women workers indicates that their primary concern was over job retention. Complaints about dismissal comprised 25 percent of the 99 cases. Wage disputes made up 14 percent, while complaints about protective legislation and abusive treatment by male supervisors composed respectively 6

and 7 percent of the cases. While these complaints should not be given more weight than their limited number merits, they provide some insight into the women's feelings about demobilization.

18. See footnote 5, Lee Holcombe, *Victorian Ladies at Work* (Hamden, Conn., 1973), pp. 142-9, and Margery Davies, "Woman's Place is at the Typewriter: The Feminization of the Clerical Labor Force," *Radical America 8*, no. 4 (July-August 1974): 1-28.

19. Coyle, *Present Trends*, p. 13.

20. *Ibid.*, pp. 13-14; 19-25.

21. See Michel Crozier, *The World of the Office Worker* (New York, 1973), p. 17, for a similar observation about the impact of mechanization and scientific organization on French clerical workers in the 1950s.

22. *Ibid.*, p. 18.

23. Florence Clark, Report on Inspection of General Offices and Car Accountant's Office, Santa Fe Railroad, Topeka, Kansas, September, 1919 (RG 14 WSS File 61c [NA]). See also RG 14 WSS Files 66b, 74, and 75a (NA).

24. *Ibid.* See also RG 14 WSS Complaint 99 (NA). Complaint 58 offers insight into the difficulty encountered by women who attained supervisory positions.

25. Digest of a Discussion of the WSS with Supervisors of Women Employees of the Railroads, Chicago, October 20-21, 1919 (RG 14 WSS File 273 [NA]); Edith Hall, Report on Inspection of Office of Auditor Merchandise Receipts, Baltimore and Ohio Railroad, Baltimore, August 22, 1919 (RG 14 WSS File 75b [NA]); Edith Hall, Report on Inspection of Auditor of Disbursements, Baltimore and Ohio Railroad, Baltimore, August 20, 1919 (RG 14 WSS File 75a [NA]).

26. Rose Yates, Report on Inspection of General Offices, Baltimore and Ohio Railroad, Baltimore, November 6, 1918 (RG 14 WSS File 74 [NA]).

27. RG 14 WSS Complaint 82 (NA).

28. Helen Ross, Report on Inspection of Freight Claim Agents in Loss and Damage Department, Chicago Burlington and Quincy Railroad, Chicago, September 1919 (RG 14 WSS File 86 [NA]). For the official account of this training program, see *Annual Report, 1919*, pp. 76-7. Interestingly, the conflict between the male and female workers is omitted from the published WSS annual report. All of the WSS publications offer an optimistic evaluation of women workers' experience in the railroad industry.

29. Edith Hall to Pauline Goldmark, DuBois, Pa., November 20, 1919 (RG 14 WSS File 242 [NA]).

30. Rose Yates, Report on Inspection of Master Mechanic's Office, Baltimore and Ohio Railroad, Keyser, West Virginia, December 6, 1918 (RG 14 WSS File 70 [NA]).

31. Helen Ross, Report on Inspection of Office of Car Accountant, Belt Railway, Chicago, April 11, 1919 (RG 14 WSS File 77 [NA]); Florence Clark to Pauline Goldmark, August 22, 1919 (RG 14 WSS File 241 [NA]) concerns the

Cleveland, Ohio situation of the New York Central Railroad; Florence Clark to Pauline Goldmark, September 20, 1919 (RG 14 WSS File 241 [NA]) concerns Topeka, Kansas.

32. Leo Wolman, *The Growth of American Trade Unions, 1880-1923* (New York; 1924), pp. 22-3; Wolfson, *Woman Worker*, p. 214; Harry Honig, *Brotherhood of Railway Clerks* (New York; 1937), Appendix D, p. 284. Male membership declined from 151,000 in 1920 to 84,000 in 1924.

33. See footnote 38. See also RG 14 WSS Complaint 87 (NA).

34. Complaints involving the aid of the Brotherhood of Railway Clerks include RG 14 WSS Complaints 14, 19, 20, 22, 23, 28, 34, 40, 45, 60, 63, 65, 67, 73, 74, 77, 78, 87, 99 (NA).

35. Helen Ross, Report on Inspection of Supply Department, Missouri Pacific Railroad, Kansas City, Missouri, October 29, 1918 (RG 14 WSS File 148 [NA]).

36. *Ibid.*

37. *Annual Report, 1918*, p. 21.

38. Helen Ross, Report on Inspection of Freight House, Santa Fe Railroad, Topeka, Kansas, October 28, 1918 (RG 14 WSS File 55 [NA]).

39. Florence Clark, Report on Inspection of Cleveland, Ohio Collingwood Shops, New York Central Railroad, June 10-11, 1919 (RG 14 WSS File 152a [NA]).

40. Florence Clark, Report on Procedure in the Investigation of Women Truckers Employed by the Minnesota Transfer Company, St. Paul, Minnesota, December 2, 1918 (RG 14 WSS File 147 [NA]).

41. Helen Ross, Report on Inquiry of Methods Used by the Railroads in Employing and Training Railroad Office Workers, Chicago and Northwestern Railroad, Ravenswood Station, n.d. Other reports on this road are dated October 11-12, 1919 (RG 14 WSS File 105 [NA]). Memo from Pauline Goldmark to Field Agents, April 14, 1919 (RG 14 WSS File 239 [NA]); Report 42, Conference with Railroad Officials about Women Employees, Southern Pacific Railroad, June 28, 1919 (RG 14 WSS File 239 [NA]).

42. Helen Ross, Report of Inspection of Santa Fe Railroad, Topeka, Kansas, October 17, 1918 (RG 14 WSS File 55 [NA]). See also Edith Hall, Memo on Moral Situation in Regard to Women Operators, Allegheny Division, Pennsylvania Railroad, November 6, 1919 (RG 14 WSS File 174b [NA]).

43. RG 14 WSS Complaint 59 (NA).

44. In the St. Paul, Minnesota district the Carmen specifically proposed in the spring of 1919 to organize three separate groups of white men, white women, and blacks of both sexes. According to the WSS field-agent's report on the situation, neither group of women nor the group of black men was to have the same protection as the white male car cleaners. This proposal was offered at a time when demobilization was making more white men available for work, and it constituted a way of pushing women and black men out of their jobs and

replacing them with white men. Although the American Federation of Labor had no information about the situation in Minnesota, the office informed the field agent that it was not customary for the white and black car cleaners to belong to the same locals. Florence Clark, Report on Inspection of Pullman Company, Chicago, Milwaukee, and St. Paul Yards, November 21, 1919 (RG 14 WSS File 93 [NA]) and Helen Ross, Report on Coach Cleaners, Chicago, Minneapolis, Columbus, Pittsburgh, and Pitcarin Yards, n.d. Other reports in the file are dated April, May, and June 1919 (RG 14 WSS File 82b [NA]).

45. RG 14 WSS Complaint 75 (NA).

46. Alice Henry, *Women and the Labor Movement* (New York; 1923), pp. 62-3.

47. *Annual Report, 1918*, p. 27.

48. Florence Clark, Memo on Electric Welders, Mt. Clare Shops, Baltimore and Ohio Railroad, Baltimore, October 31, 1918 (RG 14 WSS File 66b [NA]).

49. *Ibid.*

50. RG 14 WSS Complaint 54 (NA).

51. Florence Clark, Report on Inspection of Riverside Yards, Baltimore and Ohio Railroad, Baltimore, October 17, 1918 (RG 14 File 66a [NA]); Edith Hall to Pauline Goldmark, February 8, 1919 (RG 14 WSS File 242 [NA]).

52. Edith Hall, Report on Complaint of Electric Welder in Jersey City Erecting Shop, Erie Railroad, December 30, 1918 (RG 14 WSS File 118 [NA]).

53. Mary V. Dempsey, *The Occupational Progress of Women 1910 to 1930*, U.S. Department of Labor Women's Bureau, Bulletin 104 (Washington, D.C.; 1933), pp. 1-53.

54. Julia O'Connor, "History of the Organized Telephone Operators' Movement," *The Union Telephone Operator* (January-March, May-July 1921).

55. U.S. Department of Labor Women's Bureau, *Women Streetcar and Ticket Agents*, Bulletin 11 (Washington, D.C.; 1921), p. 38.

# Searching for the Antecedents of Affirmative Action: The National War Labor Board and the Cleveland Women Conductors in World War I

*RONALD M. BENSON**

The development of affirmative action policies and guidelines in the late 1960's has been interpreted by most proponents and critics as either a logical or an ideological extension of the Civil Rights movement and the Second Reconstruction.[1] As social and economic barriers limiting mobility and opportunity for blacks were challenged, and minorities began successfully to assert their social and economic rights, feminists demanded a parallel extension of these rights and privileges to women. Indeed, this was the historical pattern. Post-Civil War suffragists found it difficult to accept black

---

* Professor of History, Millersville State College, Millersville, Pennsylvania; B.A., Texas Tech University; M.A., University of Iowa; Ph.D., University of Notre Dame. This paper was first read at the Midwest Conference on the History of Women sponsored by St. Catherine's College for Women, and Women Historians of the Midwest in St. Paul Minnesota, October 21-23, 1977.

1. *See generally*, Foner, *Bakke Reconstructed*, THE CHRONICLE OF HIGHER EDUCATION 48 (March 13, 1978); M. CANTOR & B. LAURIE, CLASS, SEX AND THE WOMAN WORKER (1977); Kessler-Harris, *Women, Work and the Social Order*, LIBERATING WOMEN'S HISTORY (1976); Bridenthal, *Towards a Feminist Marxism: The Dialectics of Production and Reproduction in Conceptual Frameworks for Studying Women's History*, A Sarah Lawrence College Women's Studies Publication (no date).

male suffrage in the South while at the same time continuing to suffer the disenfranchisement of women. Elizabeth Cady Stanton expressed that discontent during the debate over the fifteenth amendment: "[I]t is an open, deliberate insult to American womanhood to be cast down under the iron-heeled peasantry of the Old World and the slaves of the New, as we shall be in the practical working of the Fifteenth Amendment. . . ."[2]

The historical identification of the Civil Rights movement and the women's movement has sometimes obscured the independent efforts of women, other than those in the suffrage movement, to win recognition for the extension of their civil rights. This is particularly true in the area of the right to work. The result has been a prolonged neglect of the historical antecedents of affirmative action to combat sex discrimination in employment. This historical gap has left the impression that the recent development of guidelines for equal employment, full seniority rights, and job advancement for women derived simply from the creative minds of judges and legislators, and occurred in a historical vacuum. Such was not the case.

A search for relevant antecedents need go no farther into the nation's past than World War I. The mobilization of American women for war production work began well before April 1917. By late summer of that year, as the available pools of surplus male workers disappeared, many employers were forced to recruit women for work in industries not directly involved in war-related production. The drive to recruit women was intensified as a result of several factors: 1) European

---

2. E. DuBois, Feminism and Suffrage: The Emergence of an Independent Women's Movement in America, 1848-1869 at 173 (1978).

immigration drastically declined; 2) the Conscription Act of 1917 depleted the supply of male workers; and 3) employers were forced to replace workers drawn from less attractive to better-paying jobs. When employers could not fill positions with experienced female workers, they turned to recruitment campaigns to mobilize so-called "wageless" women for wartime work.[3]

One of the industries normally dominated by male workers which expanded its workforce to include women workers during the war was the urban transit industry. During the 1890's, horse-drawn trolleys had given way to the new electric trolleys. Following the depression years 1893-1895, urban street car companies rapidly consolidated by merger or receivership to achieve more efficient operation and economy of scale. By 1900, many urban transit systems operated a combination of routes which included surface streetcars, elevated railroads, and subway trains. The urban transportation workforce was clearly stratified, reflecting status and prestige as defined and limited by skill and sex. Pay scales reflected this stratification and ostensibly rewarded proportionately, by skill-level, seniority, and ability. The motorman and conductor positions represented the highest skill-levels, the most prestigious positions, and were therefore the best paid jobs on the streetcar or traction systems. Below these positions were the clerks, track and section men, ticket sellers, cashiers, car barn workers, and car service workers who cleaned and maintained the equipment.[4]

---

3. *See* Electric Railway Journal July 27, 1918; July 5, 1919; The Statistical History of the United States (1976); Motorman and Conductor, November 1917, at 21.

4. *See* U.S. Dept. of Commerce and Labor, Bureau of the Census, Special Reports, Street and Electric Railways (1902); Bureau of the Census, Special Reports, Street and Electric Railways 195, 201 (1907).

The jobs to which women had been admitted before World War I were ticket sellers, cashiers, and car cleaners. Motorman and conductor were classified as jobs open only to males and were guarded jealously with the aid of a collective male psychology which extolled virility and peculiarly male physical stamina as bona fide occupational necessities for the work.[5] During the last months of 1917, streetcar managers in the larger urban centers began to explore the possibility, male ideology notwithstanding, of recruiting women workers to fill vacancies on the applicant lists for the car crews, where women had not been employed, and to employ women as "extras" to replace motormen and conductors who volunteered or were drafted.[6]

Employers initiated concerted efforts to recruit women for work on the car platforms as conductors in January 1918. The Manhattan and Queens Traction Company announced that it would add women conductors, immediately dubbed "conductorettes," on two of its Long Island runs.[7] The Kansas City Street Railway Company initially approved the employment of twenty women conductors for its city lines.[8] By January 1919, women were working as conductors on the streetcars of New York, Detroit, St. Louis, Brooklyn, Baltimore, Cleveland, Duluth, Indianapolis, and Camden, among the nation's larger cities, and on the urban

---

5. *See* U.S. Dept. of Labor, Women's Bureau, Women Street Car Conductors and Ticket Agents, Bulletin No. 1T (1921), 8-9; Motorman and Conductor, November 1918, at 29-33.

6. Motorman and Conductor, November 1917, at 21.

7. Electric Railway Journal, January 19, 1918, at 119 [hereinafter cited as ERJ].

8. ERJ, June 15, 1918, at 1147-48; October 5, 1918, at 603, 609, 613, 617-18, 637; January 26, 1918, at 178.

traction lines in smaller cities such as Charles City and Keokuk, Iowa, and Vancouver, Washington.[9] The Pacific Electric Railway of Los Angeles prepared emergency plans for the employment of women conductors should ". . . the draft needs of the country for army and war purposes bring about a condition where women will have to take up the work ordinarily done by men."[10] By May 1918, the Kansas City Railway Company acknowledged a shortage of 200 men for its car service and informed its riders that the only way efficient service could be maintained was by adding women conductors to the cars as "a war measure," which meant the employment of women for at least the duration of the war.[11]

Slightly more than half of the workers in urban transportation were organized, and the major collective bargaining agent was the Amalgamated Association of Street, Electric Railway and Motor Coach Employees of America (AASERMCE), whose president was William D. Mahon.[12] The only other "organized" workers were those represented by company unions or employee representation plans.[13]

---

9. ERJ, August 3, 1918, at 119; January 25, 1919, at 178; March 2, 1918, at 416-17; June 15, 1918, at 147-48; December 28, 1918, at 1150; June 22, 1918, at 1193-94.

10. ERJ, June 8, 1918, at 1117.

11. ERJ, June 15, 1918, at 1147-48.

12. L. Wolman, The Growth of American Trade Unions, 1880-1923 at 135 (1924); *see* William D. Mahon in Biographical Dictionary of American Labor Leaders 227 (1974).

13. U.S. Dept. of Labor, Bureau of Labor Statistics, Monthly Labor Review at 1030-32 (April 1978). The Brotherhood of Interurban Trainmen represented workers on the interurbans, but few women were added to those lines during the war. Some urban traction lines, such as the Brooklyn Rapid Transit, maintained company unions.

In May 1918, the executive board of the Amalgamated Association held "that the Association is unalterably opposed to the employment of women in the occupation as either motormen or conductors. . . ." [14] Not only was the union hostile to the immediate employment of women on the cars, but also to any protective legislation which would modify working conditions in such a way as to open the positions to women workers.[15] A Union official complained that street car managers who sought to employ women conductors did so with the express intention of holding wages down in order to maximize profits under the guise of wartime emergency conditions.[16]

At the beginning of August 1918, the United States Employment Service (USES) announced a shortage of 36,000 skilled workers for northern Ohio.[17] The Cleveland Street Railway Company (CSR), whose president was John J. Stanley, hired 190 women to begin work as conductors on the cars at the end of August, based on USES's estimated shortage of workers.[18] The official explanation issued by the company was that there were insufficient male workers to fill the vacancies. The women conductors were hired as substitutes for male workers under emergency provisions im-

---

14. THE UNION LEADER, May 25, 1918.
15. *Id.*, December 21, 1918.
16. *Id.*, November 30, 1918. Report on the General Executive Board meeting of the Amalgamated Association.
17. LIFE AND LABOR, January 1919, at 15.
18. Report of the Cleveland Railway Company for the Fiscal Year Ended December 31, 1918, Submitted to the Stockholders on the Last Wednesday of January, 1919, Cleveland, Ohio, January 29, 1919, at 22.

**Greene, in *The New York Telegram*,**
***Woman's Work is Never Done.***

***Courtesy Life and Labor***

posed for the duration of the war.[19] The women were given a brief training period and were placed on the seniority list as "extras" to fill the car crews as needed. This action was immediately challenged by the male membership of Local 268 of the Amalgamated Association.[20]

The union's drive against the women in Cleveland focused on the company's claim that employable male workers were unavailable in 1918 and women were therefore hired out of "necessity." To refute the company's claim, the union asked for the submission of the hiring order to fact-finding by the Department of Labor. The CSR agreed.[21] The Labor Department dispatched two investiga-

19. THE UNION LEADER, August 31, 1918. Locals of the Amalgamated Association were asked to accept women and blacks, even though they were not union members, "if it is necessary, during the period of war." The assumption, then, was that once the wartime emergency ended, women and blacks would be dismissed under the "closed shop" provision of the contract and their places taken by male union members returning from military service. Secretary of Labor, William B. Wilson, requested the unions to make just such provisions for women workers under "necessity" agreements. The typical "necessity" clause read as follows: "It is understood that no discrimination shall prevail against the employment of any sex, or colored men, if the necessity arises."

20. Report of the Cleveland Railway Company, *supra*, n. 18, at 23. The first threat to strike against the company unless the women conductors were removed from the cars was delivered to the company on September 4th. The company promised that "No man is to be replaced by a woman, and all men will retain their seniority rights and positions with this company so long as they are qualified and give proper attention to their duties."

21. National War Labor Board, Record Group 2 (National War Labor Board, World War I), Laura Prince, Chairman, Association of Women Street Railway Employees v. Cleveland Railways Company and Local 263, Amalgamated Association, Transcript Proceedings, Docket 491, The National Archives, Washington [hereinafter cited as Docket 491]. Docket entries were not numbered and the insertion of documents followed no particular order.

tors, Henry B. Dielmann and Margaret Russanowska, to Cleveland, with instructions to confer with the company and Local 268, but apparently not with the women workers.[22] After reviewing company records and meeting with officials of the local, the investigators issued the first of two controversial, even contradictory, reports.

Writing to Stanley on September 9, Dielmann and Russanowska recommended the retention of the women conductors pending issuance of the final report of their investigation. They added: "[T]he removal of the women now in service . . . would even more seriously cripple the present inadequate transportation of the vast number of workmen dependent upon the streetcar service."[23] An estimate prepared for the National War Labor Board (NWLB) at a later date indicated that there were one million daily passengers on the city's streetcars, one-third of whom were directly involved in war production.[24] On September 21, however, the two investigators reversed their position and without explanation ordered ". . . that no woman shall be employed on the cars of the company on or after November 1, 1918." At the same time, it was admitted that the company would have to *lower* its efficiency to replace the women with less qualified males.[25] *The Cleveland News*

22. Formal Complaint, "Laura Prince. . . .," November 1, 1918, Article V, 4, Docket 491; Women Street Car Conductors and Ticket Agents, 8-9; N.Y. Times, September 24, 1918.

23. Letter, Dielmann and Russanowska to John J. Stanley, September 9, 1918, Docket 491.

24. In Re Mediation Proceedings Between Division 268 of the Amalgamated Association of Street and Electric Railway Employees of America and the Cleveland Railway Company (June 1918), RC 2, filed with Docket 491.

25. Letter, Dielmann and Russanowska to Stanley, September 21, 1918, Docket 491.

described this change of mind as "a minor mystery."[26]

A careful reading of the two reports suggests the persuasive influence of Local 268 and the Amalgamated Association in bringing about the shift in recommendations. The Department of Labor, in this instance and in several others related to the women conductors, revealed a particular sensitivity to the wishes of organized labor on the employment of women. The second report noted that suitable male workers could be recruited by the company if the men were paid for the ten-day training session, if the training program instituted for the women were extended to men, and if greater efforts were made by the company to find acceptable male workers.[27] Local 268 read the second report of the investigators as a final vindication of its demand that the women be removed from the cars at once. The company and the women proved more resistant.

The request for the investigation by the Department of Labor set the pattern for negotiations between the company and the union on the fate of the women. Local 268 refused to admit the women conductors into the union, or permit them to join in any discussion to determine future employment. The union insisted on dealing exclusively with the officers of the Cleveland Street Railway, the mayor of Cleveland, or the Department of Labor, and ignored, as much as possible, the presence of the women.[28] While company officials were eager to

26. Undated clipping, The Cleveland News, Docket 491.

27. Dielmann and Russanowska to Stanley, September 21, 1918, Docket 491.

28. All negotiations were conducted by the executive committee of Local 268 composed of Fred Telschow (president), Fred J. Schultz (business agent), and W. M. Rea (secretary). At no time did they agree to direct negotiations with the women conductors' association, or its lawyer, Florence E. Allen, since they refused to recognize in any way the legitimacy of the women's grievances.

experiment with the employment of women, they were hestitant to antagonize the union. Indeed, by the start of World War I, the Cleveland Street Railway had earned a reputation for innovative and "reform-minded" business operations which it did not wish to jeopardize by a protracted struggle over the women conductors.[29]

The major argument against the women circulated by the union was that their employment by the CSR and other companies was part of a concerted employer offensive to break the union and reduce wages across the board, while the nation was distracted by its involvement in the war. The placing of women on the cars marked the return of industrial "squawdom." It was "all part of the plan to oust car men from their jobs and put women in their places."[30] William D. Mahon, international president of the Amalgamated, suggested that the hiring of the women was directed against older male workers the company wished to dismiss.[31] The Amalgamated openly charged that working men in due time would be replaced by women unless the employment of the women conductors were checked. Indeed, the union threatened, if the companies began a large scale replacement of men by women, violence might well

---

29. For a description of traction operations under the Progressive reformers of Cleveland, *see* T. JOHNSON, MY STORY (1913), at 222-23; C. LORENZ, TOM L. JOHNSON, MAYOR OF CLEVELAND (1911), at 140, 152, 157, 176; Cleveland adopted one of the first "service at cost" urban transit plans in the nation. *See* Flexible Fares, Service at Cost as Applied to the New York Transit Lines, The City Club of New York, January 1921, at 46.

30. THE UNION LEADER, November 30, 1918.

31. *Id.*

follow.[32] James M. Lynch, member of the New York State Industrial Commission, criticized the addition of women conductors on the New York Interborough for just that reason. "How do you think a man will feel who, unable to find a job, boards a car and is obliged to hand his nickle to a woman? That is the problem in a nutshell. There is dynamite in it." [33] The hiring of women for the car crew thus appeared to threaten not only the job security of the male worker, but also his ego and his traditional position as head of the family.

The women employed by the Cleveland Street Railway organized quickly to fight for their jobs which were now in jeopardy by virtue of the Department of Labor's order for their dismissal by November 1 and because of the opposition of the union to their retention. Responding to this threat, the women conductors formed the Association of Women Street Railway Employees of Cleveland and elected Laura Prince, one of the first to be hired, as president. They elected an executive board of twelve women conductors to speak for the women and to formulate strategy to defend their jobs. They selected as their attorney Florence Allen, who had represented the union in several labor cases, and Rose Moriarty as their organizer and chief negotiator. Both women were well-known Cleveland feminists.[34]

---

32. The threats of violence were largely ignored. At the time of the December strike, militant activity was confined to picketing the carbarns, refusal to move the streetcars, and petty harassment, such as name-calling. This was in contrast to some streetcar strikes where power lines had been cut and one car dynamited. *See, e.g.*, Zeigler, *The Limits of Power: The Amalgamated Association of Street Railway Employees in Houston, Texas, 1897-1905*, 18 LABOR HISTORY, 71-90 (1977).

33. THE UNION LEADER, April 27, 1918.

34. ERJ, March 9, 1918 at 474; October 5, 1918, at 603, 630, 617-18.

Rose Moriarty was an articulate Irish Catholic suffragist from Elyria, Ohio. In her early career, she had held numerous municipal jobs ranging from membership on the Safety Department Board to Clerk of the Civil Service Board, and was popularly known as the "petticoat mayor of Elyria." She studied law, gained admission to the bar, and in 1917 moved to Cleveland to become an officer of the Champion Stove Company. She was a staunch Republican, the first elected head of the Ohio Republican State Committee, chairwoman of Women for Warren G. Harding in 1920, and the first female member of the Ohio Industrial Commission. In addition to being deeply committed to women's political action, she was an early advocate of greater female participation in business leadership. Moriarty was the chief strategist for the Cleveland women conductors and worked closely with attorney Florence Allen (who later became the first female prosecutor in Cleveland), in preparation of the briefs argued before the National War Labor Board.[35]

In conformity with the Wilson Administration's war-time guidelines which set forth a "no strike, no lock-out" policy, the women conductors association appealed to Secretary of Labor William B. Wilson for a revocation of the dismissal order on the ground that they were to be "locked-out" of their jobs on November 1. The Secretary of Labor refused to order a rehearing on the dismissal order, but under the mandate establishing the National War Labor Board, he referred their appeal to the secretary of the Board for review.[36] On November 1, the women conductors formally filed a complaint with the National War Labor Board charging that their dismissal violated their

35. The Cleveland Plain Dealer, March 25, 1919, at 15.

36. Monthly Labor Review (June 1918), at 55-57.

rights to secure and hold jobs subject to competent performance and that their dismissal had been ordered for no reason other than the fact that they were women. The complaint charged that Local 268 of Cleveland "demanded a monopoly for men of the said employment, and demanded that the said women streetcar conductors should be discharged. . . ."[37]

Five specific charges formed the core of the complaint. The women conductors alleged that the order for their dismissal: 1) violated the call for women to fill non-essential jobs so that men could be released for essential jobs and the draft; 2) violated a valid contract between the company and the women for their employment as conductors; 3) violated "the right of women to labor and remain employed when hired while performing satisfactory service;" 4) was an illegal "restriction of trade and commerce . . . to secure a monopoly of certain jobs in street railway service, eminently suitable for women to perform, for men only;" and 5) violated the provisions of the Taylor Plan which stipulated that the Cleveland Street Railway provide "efficient public service," which the traction company could not provide without the service of women employees during the war emergency.[38] The complaint also pointed out that the Department of Labor investigators, Dielmann and Russanowska, had held no public meeting, called no witnesses, and had not conferred with the women conductors before the two orders were issued. Rejecting the implication that the job was unsuited to women, Allen and Moriarty argued that the job of conductor was primarily "one of responsibility rather than one of skill." In con-

37. Original complaint, November 1, 1918, Docket 491, 4.

38. *Id.*

clusion, the Association of Women Street Railway Employees of Cleveland asked that the National War Labor Board (NWLB) overrule the Department of Labor and order that their retention be subject to continuous satisfactory performance.[39]

The argument of the women conductors that the addition of women to the car platforms was essential to efficient public service on Cleveland's street railways was reinforced by the testimony of Fielder Sanders, Cleveland's Street Railroad Commissioner. Writing to Florence Allen on October 26, 1918, he acknowledged a steady deterioration of traction service following the declaration of war. Over 500 half-trips per day were not run because of a scarcity of crews. The need for women conductors was pressing, he added, "on account of the prevalence of the influenza sickness," which affected Cleveland severely and which further heightened the psychological tension of the streetcar workers who were forced into contact with thousands of commuters daily.[40] Sanders also noted that few women had been approved as apprentices, implying that unionized instructors were deliberately obstructing the training of the women.

The November appeal to the War Labor Board was prepared in part with the guidance of the Social and Economic Reconstruction Committee of the National Women's Trade Union League, whose chairwoman was Margaret Dreier Robins.[41] The NWTUL's national publication, *Life and Labor*, immediately began extensive coverage of the

39. *See* letter from Jett Lauck to Laura Prince, October 31, 1918.

40. Letter, Fielder Sanders to Florence Allen, October 26, 1918, Docket 491.

41. LIFE AND LABOR, January 1919, 14-16; March 1918, at 52, 58; April 1919, at 98.

appeal before the NWLB, and this organization of women trade unionists, through both its middle-class and working-class members, became a major source of support for the Cleveland women. The most rankling aspect of the controversy for the NWTUL was the refusal of Local 268 to admit the women conductors into the union. Union membership would have given them protection against arbitrary dismissal.

The sexist obstructionism of the local was illustrated by the testimony before the NWLB of Laura Prince, president of the women conductors' association. She had been a waitress before the war and a member of Local Union 107 of the Hotel and Restaurants International Alliance for ten years.[42] The union segregated waitresses into separate locals and over the years had made only tentative gestures toward the admission of blacks. Prince's husband had been overseas, and, to support her two sons, she had applied for the better-paying job of conductor as soon as the Cleveland Street Railway began hiring women. Her first instructor, a union member, had refused to train her after the first day:

> [They] sent me out with a conductor and the conductor sat down and turned his back to me so I couldn't see anything he was doing. I stood up beside him. He got real peavish [*sic*] and went in the barn that night and wasn't going to take the car out if I worked on the car with him.[43]

Prince managed to learn her job well enough to be put on the car platform through the assistance

42. Testimony of Laura Prince before the NWLB, hearing of March 13, 1919, Docket 491.

43. *Id.; see* Report of the Cleveland Railway Company, 1918, 26.

of a friendly dispatcher, an older conductor, who had been warned not to teach her the bell system for stopping and starting the cars. In an effort to gain admission to the union, she had gone to the Local's office in October to secure an application only to be turned away by W. M. Rea, secretary of Local 268, who had told her "the union did not allow women in its membership. . . ."[44]

The NWTUL viewed the controversy as a crucial test of the right of women to hold jobs previously closed to them, and a vital test of organized labor's willingness to include women as a part of its new social reconstruction plans for the postwar period.[45] Ethel M. Smith, executive secretary of the NWTUL and member of Federal Employees Local 2 of Washington, D.C., explained that women trade unionists had intervened because "we regarded the attitude of the men . . . as one infringement on women's fundamental rights. We saw no reason why the women should not have a right to the streetcar jobs as well as the men."[46] Her sentiments were repeated by Mary Van Kleeck of the Women in Industry Service of the Department of Labor. She wired the NWLB from Des Moines, Iowa: "[It is] [i]mpossible to exaggerate the importance of this case to American women. No more critical issue in labor problems is before the country at this moment than to give women freedom to choose their occupation."[47]

The Amalgamated Association pursued a Janus-faced policy on equal employment. Ostensibly, the union supported the policies devised by the

44. Testimony of Rose Moriarty before the NWLB, March 13, 1919, Docket 491.

45. LIFE AND LABOR, March 1919, 58.

46. Testimony of Ethel M. Smith before the NWLB, hearing of March 13, 1919, Docket 491.

47. Testimony of Mary Van Kleeck before the NWLB, March 13, 1919, Docket 491.

Wilson Administration to insure full production and industrial peace, but at the same time the national union defended a local which ignored its own admission policies. The national union, bending to public pressure, agreed in principle to admit women "if it is necessary, during the period of the war."[48]

The executive board of the union established a number of restrictions to be followed when women were employed during the emergency. Female workers were to enter employment on the same basis as men, except that women were to take their places at the bottom of the "extras" seniority

48. Motorman and Conductor, September 1918, at 31.

list, giving them the least seniority in the work force.[49] Women were to receive the same wages as men and enjoy the same working conditions. Where they were employed in a closed or union shop, they were to be given apprentice permits, which allowed them to work ninety days without belonging to the union. Also, the executive board ruled, "when women do enter the service they shall become members of the organization, being entitled to the same protection, benefits and conditions that men are entitled to, coming under the working conditions and provisions of the agreement in the same manner."[50] Local 268 disregarded these instructions and refused to admit the Cleveland women, and it did so with impunity. The Local claimed to have had a previous agreement with the Cleveland Street Railway which prohibited the hiring of women and blacks and it insisted on the maintenance of the agreement.[51]

Women's groups were quick to perceive this duplicity, as they moved to gather support for the women conductors. Suffrage clubs, feminists within and without the labor movement, and men sympathetic to the women eagerly lent their support to the women conductors' association. The move to dismiss the Cleveland women workers was seen "as a crisis in the women's struggle for

49. Four vertical seniority lists were established by union contract. A worker moved from the temporary to the permanent list as an "extra", and then from the temporary to the permanent "regular" seniority lists. The women conductors were started at the bottom of the temporary "extra" list and thus had the least seniority of all employees. The women conductors were not used on all runs, nor as a rule, on night crews.

50. MOTORMAN AND CONDUCTOR, September 1919, 31.

51. The company refused to acknowledge an agreement with the union not to hire women, or blacks for that matter. Report of the Cleveland Railway Company, 1918, at 23-24.

economic independence—a fight for the right to work, and their equal opportunity with men."[52]

The entrance of feminists and suffragists added to the complexity of the dispute and certainly changed its immediate outcome. While the Amalgamated Association supported the suffrage amendment, the union clearly did not endorse all suffragists.[53] "This controversy has been taken advantage of by sensationalists, sentimentalists, anti-unionists, and low wage advocates, who have shed oceans of tears over a 'denial of women's rights.'" *The Union Leader* complained.[54] This distorted clamor over women's rights was the work of the "half-baked equality chanter" and the "inexperienced social reformer" who, if the truth were known, had no roots in the working class at all.[55]

Local 268 refused to modify its demand that the women conductors be dismissed as the November 1 deadline approached. Since it was not known when the NWLB would reach a final decision on the women conductors, the local stepped up its pressure against the company for their immediate removal. The union threatened a second time to strike if the women were not dismissed. The first of November arrived without a decision from the Board. Local 268 then delivered an ultimatum to President Stanley of the CSR—fire the women or the union would halt the cars. On November 29, the NWLB issued an interlocutory order restraining the company from dismissing the women until a decision was issued. On December 1, the union announced a partial walk-out, and on December 2, service was interrupted on a limited number of cars. On December 3, the union announced that

52. LIFE AND LABOR, January 1919, at 14.
53. THE UNION LEADER, May 25, 1918.
54. *Id.*, December 21, 1918.
55. *Id.*

2,400 motormen and conductors would strike, halting all service on all the cars.[56]

When the three-day strike began, President John Stanley of the Cleveland Street Railway appealed to Mayor Harry L. Davis to secure an immediate ruling from the NWLB. Davis rushed to Washington, accompanied by the city's Law Director, W.S. Fitzgerald, to seek an immediate order from the NWLB to end the strike.[57] On December 3, 1918, the NWLB released its findings and recommendations in the case and ordered the streetcar workers back to work. The National War Labor Board upheld the company's argument that women conductors had been hired as a "necessity" during the "hostilities," but since the Armistice of November 11, the war-time emergency no longer existed. Male workers were already returning

---

56. *See* N. Y. Times, December 4, 1918, at 8; Cleveland Plain Dealer, December 4, 1918, at 1-2, 12; December 5, 1918, at 1; December 6, 1918; December 7, 1918, at 5; December 8, 1918, at 8.

The interlocutory order issued by the NWLB on November 29, 1918, halting the announced dismissal of the women conductors, to which the union objected, and which prompted the strike, was primarily the work of Frank P. Walsh, labor's chairman on the National War Labor Board. He sought to protect their jobs pending a hearing before the Board. Walsh wired Joint Chairman, William Howard Taft, who was then in Butler, Pennsylvania, on November 27: "It seems to me these women should be protected until we can dispose of their case. If you agree please authorize me by wire to sign your name to an order restraining the company until we have disposed of the case." Taft agreed and the order was issued two days later. Telegram copy, Walsh to Taft, November 27, 1918, Docket 491. *See also* Cleveland Plain Dealer, December 3, 1918, at 1; December 4, 1918, at 1-2, 12; December 5, 1918, at 1; December 6, 1918, at 1, 12; December 7, 1918, at 5; December 8, 1918, at 8.

57. Cleveland Plain Dealer, December 4, 1918, at 1.

from military camps to reclaim their former jobs. The Board's finding continued:

> [W]e recommend that the Cleveland Railway Company employ no more women for this service and that within the next 30 days they shall replace the present force of women by competent men; that during the 30 days no women shall be discharged except for cause. . . .[58]

The women were to be removed from all car platforms by January 3, 1919. In order to moderate the anticipated outcry from the suffrage and women's trade union forces, on December 4 the Board issued an addendum to its ruling which urged President Stanley to find jobs for the women from the car crews elsewhere in the company if possible.[59] The women conductors were suddenly faced with the threat of being demoted from the car platform to the car barn, from ticket taker to car cleaner.[60]

The NWTUL, the feminists, and the women conductors' association rejected the arbitration finding of the NWLB, and refused to consider it binding. On December 14, the women filed a petition for a new hearing, charging that the NWLB had heard only one major witness, the mayor of Cleveland, and had refused to meet with the women or their representatives.[61] They had been deprived of their day in court. The decision against them,

---

58. Serial No. A-109, Docket 491, Findings and Recommendations in Employees v. Cleveland Railway Co., December 3, 1918, at 1, Docket 491; *see also* Cleveland Plain Dealer, December 4, 1918, at 12.

59. Addendum to the findings of December 3, 1918, dated December 4, 1918, Docket 491; *see also* Cleveland Plain Dealer, December 7, 1918, at 5.

60. Cleveland Plain Dealer, December 8, 1918, at 8.

61. Application for order to show cause, December 14, 1918, Docket 491.

moreover, affirmed a sexist "Jim Crowism" which threatened all gains made by women during the war. The 1921 report on the women conductors issued by the Women's Bureau drew special attention to the significance of the ruling:

> [I]t seemed to be a very dangerous precedent to deny to women the right to work in any occupation for no other reason than that their dismissal was demanded by the men, and without giving the women a hearing so that they might present their case.[62]

By ignoring the women and denying them the right to plead the merits of their case, the NWLB had in fact acted in a prejudicial and discriminatory manner. The Board took the new petition under advisement, agreed to set a date for a rehearing early in March 1919, and assured the women they would be permitted to appear to argue their case. The company agreed not to dismiss the women, despite pressure from Local 268, until March 1.[63] The association of women conductors then retained Frank P. Walsh, one of the most respected labor lawyers in the country, and a former joint-chairman of the NWLB, as its counsel.

In preparation for the new hearing on the dismissal order, Walsh relied on the women conductors' association and its supporters to prepare the major arguments for the brief. He told Ethel Smith of NWTUL that he expected the women "to have the matter fully prepared." If they prepared the case, he would plead it.[64] Rose Moriarty, Organizer, and President Laura Prince assumed the

---

62. Women Street Car Conductors and Ticket Agents, *supra* note 5, at 9.

63. Transcript proceedings, 30, Docket 491; Cleveland Plain Dealer, March 19, 1919, at 1.

64. Letter, Frank P. Walsh to Ethel Smith, Frank P. Walsh Papers, New York Public Library, Manuscript Division [hereinafter cited as Walsh Papers].

major responsibility for preparing for the new hearing, in cooperation with the Reconstruction Committee of the Women's Trade League. Rose Moriarty wrote Walsh shortly before Christmas 1918 that the 100,000 members of the Women Suffrage Clubs of Cleveland had pledged their complete support for the struggle to "make America safe for working women." [65] Joining the defense were Margaret Dreier Robins, Ethel Smith, Emma Steghagen, and Elizabeth Christman of NWTUL, Mary Anderson and Mary Van Kleeck of the Women in Industry Service, and Dr. Anna Howard Shaw of the National American Woman's Suffrage Association. The simple principle of justice that drew this formidable defense together was the conviction "that a government that demands universal service from its citizens in time of war should provide universal employment at a living wage for its citizens in time of peace. . . ." [66]

Walsh's decision to represent the women conductors drew the expected criticism from male union-Federation of Labor, wrote Walsh warning him that the unions in Cleveland were "very hostile" to the news that he was to defend the women. A meeting of the city's business agents almost succeeded in passing a resolution declaring Walsh's action "unfair to Labor." [67] Fitzpatrick, however, expressed his support for Walsh and admitted that the women's case had its merits. Labor's representatives and alternates on the NWLB were all men and were not expected to be sympathetic to the plight of the women conductors, as the dismissal order demonstrated.[68]

65. Letter, Rose Moriarty to Frank P. Walsh, December 23, 1918, Walsh Papers.

66. LIFE AND LABOR, March 1919, 52.

67. Letter, John Fitzpatrick to Frank P. Walsh, December 26, 1918, Walsh Papers.

68. *Id.*

The case prepared by Rose Moriarty, Florence Allen, and the feminist supporters of the women conductors emphasized the issues raised during the months the women struggled to keep their jobs: 1) the women conductors were efficient and capable workers in their own right, and their abilities were documented by the personnel records of the company; 2) the women had tried to join the union, Local 268, membership in which would have given them protection against arbitrary dismissal, but the union refused to admit them; 3) the work of the conductors was "primarily a clerical job, at which they may be seated," therefore it was not a strenuous or hazardous occupation for women; 4) the real reason for their dismissal was the simple fact that they were women, and the male members of the union were prejudiced against them; 5) there were enough vacancies on the cars of the Cleveland Street Railway to accommodate the women and the returning veterans, so there was no economic reason to dismiss them; 6) Local 268 had violated the NWLB's interlocutory order by striking against the women, so the union was in violation of the Board's ruling; 7) the Armistice did not end the jurisdiction of the NWLB, for the Labor Department's order to replace the women had been appealed before November 1918, and the Board was within its competence to order the company to retain the women on the cars.[69]

The second hearing on the case took place in Washington on March 14, 1919. Laura Prince was the major witness for the women conductors. She recounted her difficulties with the union and informed the Board that all remaining women conductors had been dismissed by March. Not only did she no longer have a job as a conductor, but by

69. Testimony, transcript proceedings, March 14, 1918, Docket 491.

a strange twist of events she could not rejoin her old waitresses' local: "I have been refused recognition by the waitresses' union because I took a man's job."[70] Testimony was also presented, under Walsh's direction, by Rose Moriarty, Dr. Shaw, and Mary Van Kleeck. The union's position, represented by its attorney, James H. Vahey of Boston, was simple and to the point: the NWLB had no jurisdiction in the case, since its mandate expired with the Armistice.[71]

The National War Labor Board issued its second and final decision in the case on March 17. Reversing itself, the Board overturned the dismissal order of December 3, 1918. The Board admitted that "the women were not given any opportunity to be heard on the subject. . . . No opening hearing was had."[72] The first hearing had not taken cognizance of the "merits" of their case:

> After a full consideration, the Board as now constituted feels that an injustice was done to the women applicants in making the order of December 3, 1918; that it was made upon the application of the mayor of Cleveland and in the absence of the women who were affected, and who had not understood that the issue was before the Board and on its merits. In other words, the women did not have their day in court. That requires that this Board should reestablish the status which existed before the order was made.[73]

---

70. Testimony of Laura Prince, transcript proceedings, March 14, 1918, Docket 491.

71. Transcript proceedings, March 14, 1918, Docket 491, at 41.

72. Serial No. A-280, National War Labor Board, Docket 491; Employees (Women Conductors) v. Cleveland Railway Co., March 17, 1919, at 1.

73. *Id.*, at 2.

The NWLB then ordered that all of the approximately sixty-four women conductors released by the company since March 1, be rehired with full "seniority and other privileges." The *contractual* understanding between the company and the women conductors, the NWLB noted, "justified them in believing that their employment would continue until normally ended by their voluntary withdrawal or the failure on their part to render proper service. . . ." [74]

Rose Moriarty was particularly cheered by the new order for which she and the women worked so hard. "Wasn't it a great victory?," she told Walsh. "And to think the opinion was rendered on St. Patrick's Day. I was so pleased at the combination that I have not gotten down to a normal state yet." [75]

The victory proved to be ephemeral. On March 19, Elizabeth Christman and Ethel Smith telegraphed Walsh to inform him that the union threatened to strike again if the Board's second ruling was accepted by the Cleveland Street Railway.[76] Local 268 would not recognize the reinstatement order. Smith and Christman urged Walsh to telegraph President William D. Mahon of the Amalgamated Association to press for the rehiring of the women and their admission to the union.[77] Ethel Smith wrote Walsh two days later, on March 21

---

74. *Id.*, at 2-3.

75. Telegram, Rose Moriarty to Frank P. Walsh, March 20, 1919, Walsh Papers.

76. Telegram, Elizabeth Christman and Ethel Smith to Frank P. Walsh, March 19, 1919, Walsh Papers.

77. Letter, Ethel Smith to Frank P. Walsh, March 21, 1919, Walsh Papers.

From "Union Maids"

thanking him for his efforts and expressing the hope that he might succeed in repairing relations with Mahon and the Amalgamated. She continued: "It means a great deal in this fight to have established the principle of equal rights through a national agency, even though we fall short of success as to the actual reinstatement of the Cleveland women." [78]

On March 21, President John Stanley of the Cleveland Street Railway announced that the NWLB's ruling would not be recognized by the company, that the women would not be rehired, and that the union's objections to women on the car crews would stand.[79] The company could not afford another strike. Determined in their cause, victorious before the NWLB, the women and their allies were defeated by the hard realities of prejudice, discrimination, and the clout of returning veterans who took up the cry "the women must go" as they demanded the return of their former jobs.

One of the real tragedies of demobilization was the total failure to protect the gains secured by women workers during the war.[80] Women, Mary Anderson noted years after the war was over, "were the 'forgotten men' of that time." [81] The view at the time, observed Mary Van Kleeck, was that women should step aside to give their jobs to returning soldiers, for women had been nothing more than surrogates for male workers all along. Mary McDowell, speaking as Vice President of the Chicago Women's Trade Union League, noted sorrow-

78. *Id.*

79. Cleveland Plain Dealer, March 19, 1919, at 1, 4.

80. U.S. Council of National Defense, Reconstruction Research Division, Readjustment and Reconstruction Information, Readjustment and Reconstruction in the States (1919).

81. M. N. Winslow, Woman at Work: The Autobiography of Mary Anderson (1951), at 94.

fully that "[D]uring the war they called us heroines —but they throw us on the scrap-heap now. . . ." [82]

The case of the Cleveland women conductors involved the right of women to work in occupations of their own choosing. Within this case, one can discern the evolution of employment programs which only later came to be called "affirmative action." From its inception, the National War Labor Board was pledged to uphold equal wages for women and a "living wage" for all workers.[83] There was never a question of wage differentials based on sex, for the Board consistently held that women conductors were to be paid according to the same wage scales as male conductors. The NWLB upheld the right of women to advance to jobs traditionally defined as "male" and to hold those jobs subject to satisfactory performance. In this regard, the Board heard a case argued primarily on equitable grounds and agreed with the women conductors that sex was an impermissible obstacle to occupational mobility. The NWLB ruled that the women conductors had been unjustly dismissed by the company after March 1, 1919, and ordered them restored to their jobs with seniority and other privileges intact. The Board ruled in effect that neither employer nor union could discriminate against them because they were women.[84]

---

82. LIFE AND LABOR, March 1919, at 58.

83. NWLB, Findings and Award in Employees v. Portland Railway, Light and Power Company, Portland, Oregon, Docket No. 72, October 24, 1918.

84. The decision of the NWLB in the case of the Cleveland Women Conductors anticipated Title VII of the Civil Rights Act of 1964 as amended by the Equal Employment Opportunity Act of 1972 and the Equal Pay Act as amended, 1972, which prohibit a union from pressuring an employer to discriminate on the basis of sex. *See* § 703(a)(1) and (2), and (c) (3) (codified at 42 U.S.C. § 2000 e-1 and 2).

This case is important in yet another respect. William Howard Taft's role as joint-chairman of the War Labor Board has been largely ignored by scholars who have concentrated either on his presidency or his tenure on the Supreme Court. Was Taft as "conservative" during this period of his career as he appears in his later years? The answer to this question invites further legal scholarship.

The struggle of the Cleveland women to retain their jobs was a vigorous display of political unity among women which in turn reflected a deeply-held determination to advance the cause of women's rights through legal action. The women conductors were supported throughout the dispute by the NWTUL, the Woman in Industry Service, NAWSA, and suffrage groups. This moral and financial support indicated how committed women were to securing recognition for the right of women to work in any occupation, and to overcoming traditional socio-economic patterns of job segregation. Because struggles such as this take place in a larger historical context, the search for precedent and historical roots ought not to be restricted to narrow and conventional sources of jurisprudential and legal history. The rich history of the American labor movement may well prove a particularly fertile source.

# *"Peace is a woman's job . . ."* Jeannette Rankin and American Foreign Policy: The Origins of Her Pacifism

by Joan Hoff Wilson

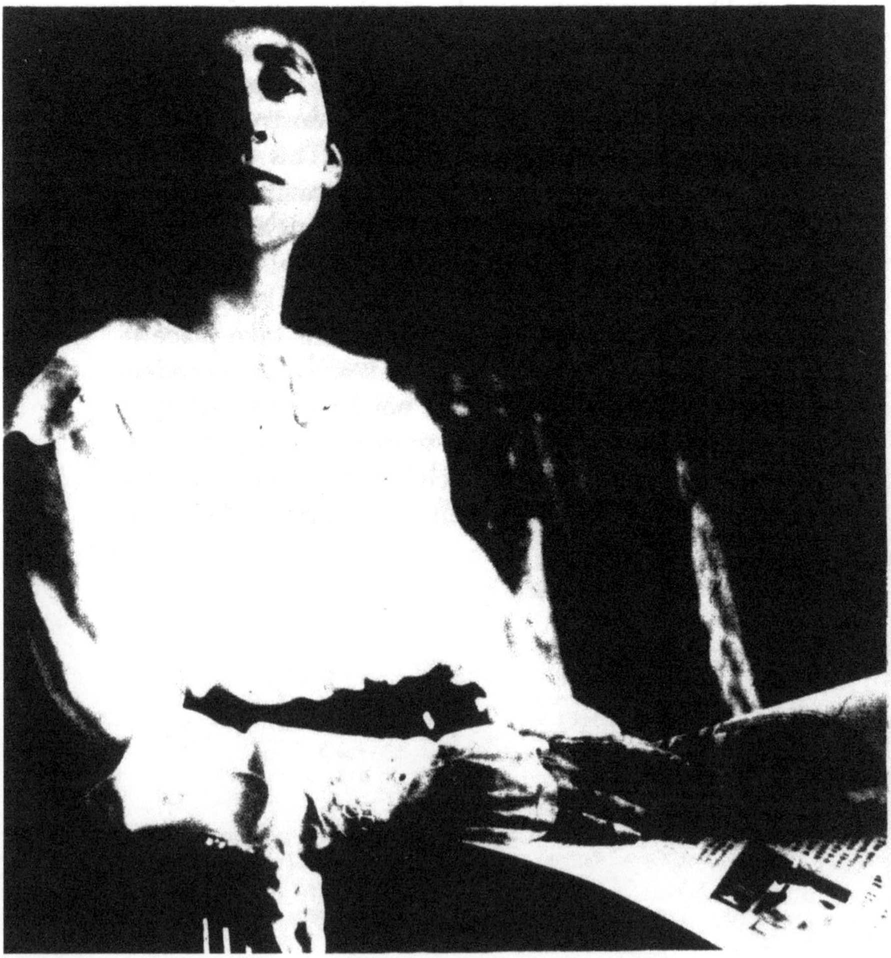

All photographs in this article from Montana Historical Society

Jeannette Rankin remains best known as the first woman elected to the House of Representatives, a feat she achieved in 1916, and as the only member of Congress to have opposed American entrance into both World Wars. Montanans have reason to be proud of her accomplishments. Yet for all of the prominence those two antiwar votes brought her, it remains difficult to piece together how she transformed a basically timid and insecure personality and several early career setbacks into a charismatic public personage. No conclusive evidence exists about the exact origins of her early ideas or about the long and indirect path that led first to her career as a suffragist and later as a pacifist. She was careless in the preservation of her private papers, leaving only a spotty record which is frustrating to the historian. Some individuals who knew her personally believe that this neglect reflected Rankin's preoccupation with the present and the future. She was a pragmatist, not a philospher; a participant, not a preserver.

Even those who remember her strong stands against war forget that she played an important, if sporadic, role in the state's Republican party politics, that she suggested major electoral reforms which have become more popular and relevant with the passage of time, and that she criticized U.S. diplomacy between the World Wars and throughout the Cold War period as well. She was a most remarkable politician, reformer, political organizer, pacifist and conscientious critic. Although the public record documents her achievements and Montanans remember much of her career, the origins of her ideas about American foreign policy remain obscured.

We know that she became an ardent advocate of peace, but we do not know when or why. Why did she adopt pacifism when none of the other members of her family were pacifists? How did she come to take an antiwar position when her brother Wellington, the family member who influenced her most and shared her reform goals during the Progressive Era, opposed his sister's pacifism? Why do people with similar backgrounds, even with the same family environment, perceive the word so differently? And how significant is the fact that Rankin's formative years coincided with the rise of female political leadership in suffrage and other reform movements?

Montanans may never be able to reconstruct Jeannette Rankin's past well enough to answer these questions, but they are questions to be asked. What partial answers emerge give us a new view of Rankin. Tracing the development of her thinking on peace and the central role she saw women playing in achieving a world free from war takes us from her youth in western Montana to her position as a national pacifist leader in the 1920s. What we discover is that Rankin's vote against war in 1917 was more than a singular action; it influenced her political thinking for the rest of her life. The pioneer ideals she accepted in her Montana youth—hard work, honesty and perseverance—blended with her perceptions of women, international conflict and the destructiveness of war to make Jeannette Rankin one of the most unique female figures in American political history.

## Rankin's Personality Traits

Born on June 11, 1880, at Grant Creek Ranch six miles from Missoula, Jeannette Pickering Rankin was the oldest of seven children—six girls and one boy. Because her father John Rankin (1841-1904) was a successful rancher and Missoula businessman, the family atmosphere in which she grew up represented an amalgam of western informality and upper middle-class expectations. As a child, therefore, Rankin exhibited seemingly contradictory personality traits stemming in part from this relatively unusual environment. She displayed a capacity for hard work, strong convictions, frontier independence of spirit tempered by the necessity to cooperate. Yet sibling rivalry and insecurity about her intellectual ability also made shyness and stubbornness hallmarks of her personality.

At best these characteristics made Rankin tolerant and innovative when dealing with new situations and ideas; at worst, they produced temper tantrums when she did not get her way or feel appreciated enough, and a single-minded rather than tough-minded approach to domestic and foreign problems. This determined, but essentially nonanalytical, mode of operation occasionally turned Rankin's statements into self-fulfilling prophecies. This is not to say that her ideas were wrong. Usually they were overly simplistic: war is an inadequate means for settling disputes so it should be outlawed; limitation of armaments is insufficient so the United States should unilaterally disarm.

Rankin attended public schools in Missoula, graduating from the University of Montana in 1902 with a degree in biology. After teaching briefly in country schools at Grant Creek and Whitehall following graduation, she served a short apprenticeship as a seamstress in Missoula. Following her father's death in 1904, Rankin spent several busy but restless years at home. Because of her mother's increasing withdrawal from normal household duties, Rankin assumed full responsibility for the younger children in the family. In 1908 at the age of twenty-eight she left home to study at the New York School of Philanthropy. Returning to the West she practiced for only a few months as a social worker in Montana and Washington. Unhappy with her newly chosen profession because she could achieve few immediate remedial results, Rankin entered the University of Washington in 1909. While a student there she joined the successful Washington state campaign for suffrage in 1910. This experience marked a turning point in her life because she met a New Jersey journalist and former suffrage campaigner in Colorado, Minnie J. Reynolds, who convinced her that the quest for peace should be incorporated into the suffrage question.

Rankin officially launched her own political career in Montana on February 2, 1911, when she urged the state legislature to grant women the right to vote. For the next twelve months she gained valuable organizational and oratorical skills by working for suffrage groups in New York, California and Ohio. During 1913 and 1914, as a field secretary for the National American Woman Suffrage Association (NAWSA), she lobbied for female suffrage in fifteen states. In addition, she made a half dozen trips home helping to win the vote for Montana's women in 1914. By 1916 Rankin faced a serious occupational choice. Should she continue to work for national suffrage; become a lobbyist for social legislation; or take advantage of the opportunity to run for Congress from Montana? Choosing the latter, she campaigned successfully on a progressive Republican platform calling for suffrage, protective legislation for children, tariff revision, prohibition and "preparedness that will make for peace." This began her national career, a career that did not end until her death fifty-seven years later.

From this sketchy biography we learn little about Rankin's motivations. Perhaps there are more subtle personality traits that may help us understand her better. At first glance, for example, it does not seem very significant that she happened to be the oldest of seven children, but the research of psychologists tells us that sibling order in a family can make a difference in the careers of professional women.

First-born girls or only-child females constitute the vast majority of any random sampling of professional women. This is because such girls are raised more like boys; often develop closer relationships with their fathers than younger female siblings; and receive more encouragement from both their mothers and fathers to assume nontraditional female roles inside and outside of the family. At the same time, however, first-born girls frequently find that their powerful sibling position turns out to be a mixed blessing. It can produce a personal sense of insecurity or at least ambivalence in the adult woman because she finds herself engaged in nontraditional activities and is not quite sure how to develop a confident female identity in what is considered an unfeminine role.

Sometimes such first-born or only-child women over-compensate by adopting a style known as the "frilly blouse" syndrome in which they attempt to appear and act as stereotypically feminine as possible while pursing careers normally dominated by men. There are indications that Rankin adopted this defense mechanism by paying excessive attention to her appearance, including wearing carefully coiffured wigs in her later years. Clothes and cosmetics for her many public appearances constituted one of the few examples of extravagance in her otherwise modest lifestyle.

Self-doubt and a sense of inferiority plagued Rankin's entire career, but publicly she demonstrated great self-confidence—partly through impeccable dress. Perhaps she revealed this psychological insecurity most when she repeatedly said in interviews: "I can't stand to be a worm." But like the unprotected worm sunning itself on a warm summer's day, Rankin basked in the limelight during a few historical moments, and gloried in immediate gratification and praise. Thus it seems odd that she did not take the logical step of preserving her own papers to insure lasting interest in, if not approval of, her activities.

In a journal that can no longer be found among her private papers she reportedly wrote the following exhortation to herself upon graduating from college in 1902: "Go! Go! Go! It makes no difference where just so you go! go! go! Remember at the first

*The Rankin family in about 1900. L. to r., John. Mary. Hattie. Jeannette (standing). Edna & Grace. portrait of deceased Phila (d. age 9). Wellington. Olive.*

opportunity go."* Although she could not remember writing this statement, when asked about it in 1972, she expressed the desire in that year to buy a mobile home in order to continue to travel around the country. From the very beginning, therefore, complusive travel characterized Rankin's long life. This personality trait also accounted in large measure for her success as a politician and lobbyist.

Yet for all of her activism and professional contacts, Rankin remained a loner. In contrast, many single and married professional women of her generation participated in extensive female networks. Possibly her reliance on her only brother, continuous travel, and involvement with immediate family members substituted for close personal relationships with other female reformers. Although we will never know for certain because so few of her personal letters to and from other professional women now exist, it appears that Rankin did not receive sustained intellectual or emotional support from women friends. The only career women who corresponded frequently with Rankin were journalist Minnie J. Reynolds, author Katharine Anthony and missionary Harriet Yarrow.

In general, western women remain the orphans of women's history. In Rankin's case this traditional neglect has been reinforced by her own personal aloofness, sense of intellectual inferiority, and absence of intimate male or female friends outside of her immediate family. Since she also believed that her education had been inadequate (her letters and unedited speeches display both grammatical and spelling errors), it is not surprising that she seldom wrote about her career in later years. For these and other reasons, there probably would have been a dearth of personal or reflective information in them.

* All quoted material marked with an asterisk indicates that the original document (or copy of it) cannot be found among Rankin's officially deposited papers.

## Sketchy Biographical Sources

It is surprising that none of the historians who have previously written about Rankin has commented upon the inadequacies or, let's say, the peculiar nature of her private papers, which are now at the Schlesinger Library in Cambridge.[1] In particular there is a lamentable absence of personal information about her formative years up to 1907 when she finally left the family home in Missoula, Montana, and struck out on her own. This is because a journal that she kept during college and many private letters to various members of her family—all of which were made available to at least one researcher in the 1950s—are not in the Schlesinger collection. These documents either were lost or passed into private hands in the early 1960s when Wellington Rankin closed and sold the building that housed his law offices in Helena, Montana.[2] While Jeannette Rankin's letters from 1929 to 1939 to the National Council for the Prevention of War (NCPW) and other peace groups have been preserved,[3] very few of her private letters to close friends or relatives before the Second World War have been. Because she did not type, there are almost no carbon copies of her replies to the many inquiries about American diplomacy that she received over the many years when she was not a

1. Recent cataloging of the Rankin papers has revealed the extent to which they present an incomplete picture of her life, especially for the early years. The sparseness of the Schlesinger collection can only in part be compensated for by the many transcribed interviews of Rankin which exist (see n. 5). In addition to some family and general correspondence, newspaper clippings and scrapbooks, the collection also contains a half-dozen untranscribed tapes with friends in the last years of her life. Brief diary entries she made in 1946, 1955, 1959 and 1962-63 contain no pertinent information.

2. This information about documents missing from officially deposited Rankin papers was confirmed in separate conversations with Harriet Meloy, formerly of the State Historical Society Library, Helena, Montana, February 28, August 19, 1977; with Judge Frances C. Elge of Billings, Montana, March 1, 1977; attorney Louise Rankin Galt of Helena, August 19, 1977; and with Norma Smith of Wenatchee, Washington, January 21, 27, 28, 1977.

3. The bulk of these are located in the Swarthmore College Peace Collection, Swarthmore College, Swarthmore, Pennsylvania. They are located in Boxes 65-74 of the National Council for the Prevention of War (NCPW) collection and contain Rankin's correspondence with Frederick J. Libby and the NCPW staff from 1929 to 1954. There is also a separate Rankin folder containing miscellaneous letters and speeches in addition to those cataloged with the Women's Peace Union and the U.S. Section of the Women's International League for Peace and Freedom at Swarthmore.

member of Congress; there is only the notation "answered", marked on the inquiries. To the thousands of letters Rankin received as a Congresswoman concerning her votes against both world wars she understandably sent out standardized form letters repeating her already public remarks.

To make matters worse, Rankin hastily left her Congressional office in 1943, leaving others to pack up her records. As a result, her second term in Congress from 1941 to 1943 is not as completely documented as it should be. She then proceeded to compound these already haphazard archival habits by allowing what remained of the Congressional papers from her first term, 1917-1919, to grow mouldy in the basement of her brother's ranch outside of Helena. In the 1950s and 1960s she also permitted segments of her papers to be shipped around the country among a few privileged researchers and acquaintances, so there is no telling how much was misplaced or misfiled in this fashion. In 1972 Rankin admitted to having "lost" a number of letters because she sent them to people who neglected to return them. Among those misplaced in this fashion were over a thousand letters defending her against a *Ford Hour* commentator who said in December 1942, that she was "not clear-out American. . . . I have no use for any woman who stands in the place where a man ought to be—the United States House of Representatives."[4]

Consequently, lengthy interviews with Rankin and her friends and relatives from 1963 through 1972 constitute a major source of personal information about her career before World War II. In these interviews she and others are often recalling events and ideas more than a half-century old.[5] From the

4. *Quote can be found in Ted Carlton Harris, "Jeannette Rankin: Suffragist, First Woman Elected to Congress, and Pacifist" (Ph.D. dissertation, University of Georgia, 1972), p.304. Information about her careless attitude toward her own papers came from conversations with Belle Fligelman Winestine of Helena, Montana, February 28, 1977, and with Norma Smith. Also see B. F. Winestine to Hannah Josephson, April 16, 1974, Josephson Papers, Schlesinger Library, Radcliffe College, and "Jeannette Rankin: Activist for World Peace, Women's Rights and Democratic Government," Suffragist Oral History Project, Bancoft Library, University of California, Berkeley, 1974 (hereafter cited as JR: UCB Oral History), p. 12.

5. In addition to JR: UBC Oral History, for a complete listing of personal and public interviews with Rankin and her friends see Harris, "Jeannette Rankin," pp. 361-64, and Doris Buck Ward, "The Winning of Woman Suffrage in Montana" (M.A. thesis, Montana State University, 1974), p. 160.

*Rankin in 1907.*

historian's point of view any individual's memoirs, written or oral, are suspect and should be checked against the private and public records.[6] In Rankin's case even her most sympathetic and conscientious biographers have seldom been able to cite conclusive primary information to confirm that her memories are indeed correct. A recent study, for example, attempts to document what she meant in her 1916 platform when she called for "preparedness that will make for permanent peace." The only source cited to prove that she defined it as "a system of 'coastal defense only' with no preparations that would lead to participation in a war in a foreign country," is a 1969 interview—conducted fifty-three years after the fact.[7] This work also cites the same interview, without confirmation from other sources, to authenticate her initial reactions to the outbreak of war in Europe in 1914.[8] To date, all studies of her have relied excessively and uncritically on interviews conducted in the last ten years of her life.

Added to this paucity of documentary material about the first two-thirds of her long career, is the lack of public or personal information about her views on foreign policy during the crucial Cold War years, 1945-1963. Although Rankin prophetically told a friend in 1942 that she feared FDR would destroy a sound American foreign policy by having the United States assume "responsibility for the rest of the world," she wrote and said little about post-World War II diplomatic events, with exception of the Korean War. In January 1947, the *New York*

6. Memoirs often reflect how a person would like to be remembered, rather than what he or she actually thought or did. This was particularly true of Rankin who by her own admission did not like to think about the past, let alone be too concerned with accurate memories. For confirmation of this see JR: UCB Oral History, p. v, and conversation with Norma Smith. Discrepancies are most evident, for example, in her positive views about the World Court and League of Nations in the 1930s compared to her later criticisms of both when interviewed in the 1960s and 1970s.

7. Harris, "Jeannette Rankin," p. 104. She had earlier defined what she meant by "coastal defense" in a 1942 amendment to the Military Appropriations Bill, but in all likelihood did not develop the concept in detail until some time in the 1930s. See Congressional Record 87 (Part V), p. 4830. This development in her thought can be traced in radio addresses between 1928 and 1939, Folder X, Box 65, NCPW Collection, Legislative Department, Jeannette Rankin Correspondence with Libby and Staff, 1929-1954, Swarthmore College Peace Collection (hereafter cited as NCPW: JR Correspondence).

8. Harris, "Jeannette Rankin," p. 84.

*Herald Tribune* quoted her as saying that the country was "going straight to war unless we change our course . . . as soon as we get another crop of men ready." Privately she expressed "great disappointment" over Korea, which she described as the latest of "our adventures in imperialism." "The [cold] warriors [have] succeeded in getting a good war started," she wrote upon her return from India in 1950. Characteristically she expressed sympathy not only with "the young boys who are having to face this war," but also with the conscientious objectors who opposed it. Believing "there is lots of peace sentiment but they [*sic*] are fed up with all this bla[h] about internationalism," she told the missionary Harriet Yarrow in 1953 that "my heart goes out to the C.O.'s. They can't carry the load alone." In vain she hoped for a dramatic event to rally the forces of peace.[9]

Rankin's comments on American diplomacy during the Cold War are few and far between. She published only one article in the 1950s and it concentrated on justifying her two antiwar votes. Nonetheless, the last paragraph of this 1958 article expressed fear over the country's "being kept in ignorance" and apprehension about another war. Because she credited Eisenhower with ending the Korean conflict, her admiration for him grew as she came to believe that "the military can't put anything over on him." In fact, she voted for him in 1956 and told Yarrow after the election that "we seem to be doing much better about war. Ike seems to be really in ernest [*sic*] about preventing war. It is the only way his name can live in history—and he knows it." Her admiration of Eisenhower led Rankin to support Richard M. Nixon for the presidency in 1960 and 1968 (she voted for Barry Goldwater in 1964 and George McGovern in 1972). Judging from her statements, she simplistically assumed that Nixon's association with Eisenhower had taught him how to avoid war; in the same fashion, she also ignored all the unofficial military incursions and other Cold War

9. *New York Herald Tribune*, January 24, 1947, *Great Falls Tribune*, June 3, 1951, JR to Libby, November 10, 1948, December 13, 1950—all in Folder VII, Box 68, JR: NCPW Correspondence; JR to Harriet Yarrow, January 20, 1953, Yarrow Papers, Schlesinger Library, Radcliffe College.

activities undertaken during Eisenhower's two administrations.[10]

## Influences on Her Thought

Despite these deficiencies in biographical sources, scholars and popular writers have not hesitated to attribute Jeannette Rankin's foreign policy to a variety of personal characteristics, from a sense of rugged individualism and self-reliance she allegedly learned on the family ranch in Montana, to the cooperative, humane and democratic inclinations she supposedly gained from her youth on the frontier. More specifically, the influence of her family, especially the progressive politics of her brother, has often been cited as the primary source of her life-long commitment to sexual equality, aid to the downtrodden, and world peace.[11]

Another influence mentioned by biographers is Rankin's participation in the social justice wing of the Progressive Movement. Social justice Progressives, in contrast to the "scientific" wing which pressed for reform of American political and economic structures, concentrated on providing direct, personal services to the less fortunate through volunteer work and welfare legislation. This work and her early suffrage experiences have been credited with turning her into a humanitarian feminist, an uncompromising pacifist, and an advocate of grassroots or participatory democracy—all by the time she was first elected to Congress in 1916.[12]

10. Jeannette Rankin, "Two Votes Against War, 1917, 1941," *Liberation* March 1958, p. 7; *Great Falls Tribune*, October 5, 1959; JR to Harriet Yarrow, January 20, 1953, December 14, 1956, Yarrow Papers; JR to Grace [Mrs. Thomas E. Kinney] May 29, July 19, August 1, 18, 30, September 3, October 1, 17, 25, 1952, Box 1, Ed Sanders interview of Rankin, February 19, 1971, Box 12—all in Jeannette Rankin Papers, Schlesinger Library, Radcliffe College (hereafter cited as Rankin Papers). More information on Rankin's checkered voting record on presidential candidates will be presented in the second part of this article.

11. Harris, "Jeannette Rankin," pp. 1-38; Ronald Schaffer, "Jeannette Rankin, Progressive-Isolationist" (Ph.D. dissertation, Princeton University, 1959), pp. 1-20; John C. Board, "The Lady from Montana: Jeannette Rankin" (M.A. thesis, University of Wyoming, 1964); idem, "Jeannette Rankin: The Suffrage Years and Before" (seminar paper, n.d.); Hannah Josephson, *First Lady in Congress: Jeannette Rankin: A Biography* (Indianapolis: Bobbs-Merrill Company, 1974), pp. 5-29.

12. Harris, "Jeannette Rankin," pp. 39-124; Schaffer, "Jeannette Rankin," pp. 21-77; Josephson, *First Lady in Congress*, pp. 30-58.

Very little convincing evidence can be found for these generalizations, especially those suggesting that her political, social, economic, or foreign policy ideas had western origins. In later years, for example, Rankin denied one of the frequently quoted tales about how her father's antimilitary attitude, which was supposedly occasioned by his experience during the Nez Perce War in 1877, instilled similar sentiments in her.[13] Apparently her sister Edna, the youngest of the Rankin children, helped to create this story about her father's observations during the Nez Perce excitement. This anecdote was then elevated into a "fact" by historians, one of whom, Hannah Josephson, insisted that her childhood "notions . . . must have been some reflection of your father's ideas," despite Rankin's strong reservations about such an interpretation.[14]

Nonetheless, it is evident from a 1916 article that Jeannette believed that the physical environment of the West had a profound impact on both men and women in their struggle against its hardships. Because they shared frontier burdens equally, men and women in western states accepted sexual equality to a greater degree than their eastern counterparts. Although American historians no longer categorically endorse this interpretation of western influences, Rankin's belief in it was a significant factor in her ideas about sexual equality. Otherwise her views on women appear to have been most influenced by Benjamin Kidd, the English sociologist, although she did not publicly emphasize this intellectual debt until the 1970s.[15]

While campaigning for suffrage in New York, Rankin purchased a book Kidd had written a few years before, entitled *Social Evolution*. In this work he tried to popularize a version of reform Darwinism which argued that individuals could not be held exclusively responsible for their successes or failures.

13. JR. UCB Oral History, pp. 189-90.

14. Wilma Dykeman, *Too Many People, Too Little Love: Edna Rankin McKinnon: Pioneer for Birth Control* (New York: Holt, Rinehart and Winston, 1974), pp. 21-22; Harris, "Jeannette Rankin," pp. 20-21, 27; JR: UCB Oral History, pp. 189-90, 192-93.

15. Rankin, "Why the West Leads in the East in the Recognition of Women," *Chicago Sunday Herald*, December 24, 1916.

Kidd posited this theory in opposition to the popular understanding of social Darwinism that was based on the brutal notion of survival of the fittest. Kidd's reform Darwinism and social justice Progressivism shared an appreciation of the role environment played in individuals' lives.[16]

Although Rankin's temperament did not lend itself to reading and reflection, she was evidently even more impressed by a second book Kidd wrote in 1918 called *The Science of Power*. This was after she had cast her vote against World War I, but the work had a profound impact on her thinking because it made the distinction between "force" and "power." According to Kidd, men exercised the former; women the latter. As Rankin later recalled: ". . . force is something you use in the present . . . but power—it's something you can use in the future, and . . . the greatest power in the world was the emotion of an idea[l]." Kidd had attributed this "Emotion of the Ideal" to women, concluding that "it is in the woman that we have the future center of Power in civilization. . . . She is the . . . being to whom the future is greater than the present."[17] Rankin modified Kidd's theories, insisting that men and women had to work together for peace and freedom, but she never gave up the idea that women were more likely to understand why "working for the future" was so important, especially if "peace habits" were to be substituted for war as a means of settling international disputes.[18]

Rankin's thinking led her to a singular and

---

16 Although Rankin quoted Kidd in at least one radio address in the 1920s ("Peace Through Political Action") and privately recommended an article condensing his views in 1943, the most publicized acknowledgment of his influence on her thinking occured in her 90th Birthday Address on June 11, 1970 (see transcript in Box 10, Rankin Papers). A year earlier she also acknowledged Kidd's influence in an interview (see Harris, "Jeannette Rankin," p. 31) and two years later as well (see JR: UCB Oral History, pp. 2-3), but neither the Schaffer nor Board studies of the late 1950s and early 1960s contains any reference to Kidd. It is conceivable that Rankin overemphasized his influence on her in her later years, but there is no denying how cogently she continued to remember his ideas. Norma Smith to author, September 15, 28, 1977.

17. Benjamin Kidd, *The Science of Power* (New York: Putnam's Sons, 1918), pp. 194, 203, 219; JR: UCB Oral History, pp. 2-3.

18. JR: UCB Oral History, pp. 3, 66, 277-78; Harris, "Jeannette Rankin," pp. 256, 276, 314-16; Jeannette Rankin Interview with Dick Cavett, April 17, 1972, pp. 7-8; "Why I Voted Against War," co-authored by Rankin and John Kirkley in the early 1970s, p. 3, Box 12, Rankin Papers.

powerful conclusion—women and peace were inseparable. For example, when she spoke in support of the most successful disarmament meeting in the interwar years, the Washington Conference on Limitation of Armament (1921-1922), she came directly to the point:

> The peace problem is a woman's problem. Disarmament will not be won without their aid. So long as they shirk . . . something will be radically wanting in the peace activities of the public and the state. . . . I am aware that men are disposed to look down on the temperamental pacifism of women (which in spite of all the exceptions is a psychological fact) as something which the manly man would scorn to imitate. However, there is no other way that I can see in which peace can be realized except through forbearance from fighting on the part of men as well as women. . . . Therefore peace is a woman's job.[19]

In this same speech Rankin astutely noted that it would be more difficult for women to work for peace than it has been for them to work for suffrage because by joining the antiwar movement they would have to face "the most painful consequence of all—the loss of social approval."[20]

Already convinced by Kidd that "women have something special to contribute to the progressive civilization: the belief in the power of a sustained passion for the ideal," she proceeded to equate such passion with motherhood. "Her life is given for her children, not by her death, but by her living, and not only in her working and caring day by day, but also in her looking always to the future, towards the fulfillment of her ideal." Rankin reasoned that because "killing is the antithesis of life and negates the very possibility of growing into fullness" it was this "same passion for the ideal, which a mother expresses in her love for her children, which we must achieve and

19. Rankin. "Peace and the Disarmament Conference," n.d., Box 3, Rankin Papers. Also see radio addresses, "Peace Through Political Action," n.d. [1925 and/or 1928-29] and "Women and Neutrality," July 18, 1935, Folder X, Box 65, NCPW/JR Correspondence.

20. Rankin, "Peace and the Disarmament Conference."

maintain if we want our ideals to mature and flourish in society: self-control, compassion, honesty, integrity, and love must be conceived in our minds, incarnated through our daily actions and living, and patiently sustained in adversity. A dead enemy cannot become our friend. And—just as certainly—the ideal dies within us when we violate it." With this she concluded that "the motherhood of the world must demand that destruction be stopped and the abundance distributed."[21]

It is not surprising, therefore, to find that Rankin viewed women as the best vehicles in her crusade to inculcate "peace habits" throughout western society in order that the stupidity of war as a diplomatic tool would be universally recognized. In 1934, remarking on her own antiwar vote in 1917, she talked about peace habits.

> I voted against war because for 7 years I had been following peace habits and thinking peace.... Now the reason the men voted for war was that they had war habits in their tradition, history and hearts. They think in terms of war, and habit is something you use in any emergency. War is an emergency and consequently they reverted to their war habits.[22]

She believed that "the work of educating the world to peace is the women's job," was "because men have a natural fear of being classed as cowards if they oppose war." She also thought that since women greatly influenced the education of youth, they should be able to change not only public opinion about war, but other societal values as well.

Rankin urged women to eradicate war as an instrument of diplomacy. For her it was the most important message. Over the years she advocated a variety of ways for women to accomplish this task—ranging

---

21. Rankin, "Why I Voted Against War," p. 3, and "Women and Neutrality." These are simply two of many similar statements she made over the years.

---

22. U.S. House of Representatives, Committee on the Judiciary, *Hearings on Amending the Constitution with Respect to Declaration of War* 73rd Cong., 2nd sess., March 1934, p. 11. Also see 90th Birthday Address and JR, UCB Oral History, p. 66.

from female peace organizations to consumer boycotts.[23] It was the futility of war she decried, as she discussed in 1963 when she once again elaborated on her antiwar votes.

> Both of my votes were votes against the war method. They were against war, not against or for the issues that we were told we were fighting for. If you're against war, you're against war regardless of what happens. It is a wrong method of trying to settle a dispute. I can't settle a dispute with a young man by shooting him. And a nation can't settle a dispute with another nation by killing their young men. We kill women and children with bombs, even the land and everything. War is a method, and you can be either for or against it and I'm against it because of its futility, its stupidity and its ultimate destruction of humanity—of civilization.[24]

This statement and others Rankin made over the years clearly indicate the depths of her pacifism, but they do not indicate the origins of such ideas nor exactly when she began to relate them to Benjamin Kidd's concept of women. Unless her college journal and other pre-World War I letters, which were cited in a 1959 study, are relocated, it will remain impossible to trace back any further the origins of her foreign policy views.

In contrast, it is fairly certain that many of her progressive domestic ideas crystallized during the year she studied at the New York School of Philanthropy in 1908-1909. We know who her instructors were, what classes she enrolled in, and, from the school's records and from one letter to her sister Mary written in February 1909, what books she read. The impact of the economic ideas of Simon N. Patten seemed to have impressed her most. In his book, *The New Basis of Civilization*, Patten stressed

23. Harris, "Jeannette Rankin," pp. 182-84, 276, 314-17; JR: UCB Oral History, pp. 31-32, 82, 276-78; John C. Board, "Lady from Montana," *Montana the Magazine of Western History* 17, No. 3 (Summer 1967), p. 17; also see "Peace Through Political Action," and *St. Paul News*, April 9, 1925, for still another reference to peace being a woman's job.

24. Transcript of John C. Board interview with Jeannette Rankin, August 29, 30, 1963, p. 52, Box 12, Rankin Papers.

that poverty and misery were not inevitable conditions of life and could be eliminated through greater efficiency and reform. By accepting this viewpoint, Jeannette Rankin joined the ranks of the social justice wing of the Progressive Movement at its most simplistic level. Her initial attempts to practice social work in Montana, however, ended in frustration.[25]

By her own admission Rankin "didn't enjoy going to school" and considered herself a "very poor student". Although she graduated from the University of Montana in 1902 with a B.S. in biology, she later said she was "not prepared to do anything." It was also evident that she felt intellectually inferior to the "well trained college girls" with whom she attended the New York School of Philanthropy and did not display any marked interest in scholarly pursuits.[26] In this sense she was a fairly typical progressive activist. Whether she systematically continued her formal education on her own after leaving the School of Philanthropy in 1909 is uncertain. It would appear that only accidental encounters with people or books directed her thinking from that time on.

One of these encounters was the writings of Kidd. An even earlier one, but harder to document, was her association with pacifist Minnie J. Reynolds in the Washington state campaign for suffrage, 1909-1910. Until her death in 1935, Reynolds remained Rankin's closest friend and correspondent. Unfortunately no correspondence between them can now be found in the Rankin papers, although some letters reportedly exist in private hands. It is also possible that another friend, Katherine Devereaux Blake, a New York school principal and co-worker with Rankin in the 1914 Montana suffrage campaign, instilled in her antiwar views. In 1915 Blake supervised the collection of over 355,000 signatures of school children against American entrance into

25. Harris, "Jeannette Rankin," pp. 30-35; Schaffer, "Jeannette Rankin," pp. 15-19 (quoting February 1909 letter from JR to Mary Rankin*).

26. JR: UCB Oral History, p. 282; Harris, "Jeannette Rankin," pp. 15-16; B. F. Winestine conversation; Schaffer, "Jeannette Rankin," p. 18 (again quoting material no longer among Rankin's deposited papers*). In 1933 Libby chided Rankin for the fact that she "hate[d] to study." See September 18, 1933, Folder III, Box 68, NCPW: JR Correspondence.

*Rankin accepts bouquet from suffragists in Washington, D.C., in 1917.*

World War I. By this time Rankin had also fallen under the influence of the pacifist faction within the suffrage movement led by Jane Addams—a woman she later thought should have been president. As a result of all these associations, especially the one with Reynolds, Rankin later recalled that "one of the first things we had talked about in woman suffrage [was] that it was women's job to get rid of war."[27]

27. Harris, "Jeannette Rankin," pp. 43, 93, 167; JR: UCB Oral History, pp. 80-81, 199; Board, "Lady from Montana," p. 5; Norma Smith to author, September 28, 1977, and comments by Smith at Montana History Conference, Helena, November 4, 1977.

## Rankin's Vote Against War

Pacifism was not unusual among prewar Progressives. It was only Rankin's later insistence on the crucial role that women instinctively could play in preserving peace that proved unusual in the long run. It is clear that her mentor Minnie J. Reynolds already believed that opposing war was as much a woman's issue as suffrage. While Rankin apparently subscribed to this point of view, she repeatedly said that suffrage, not the war in Europe, prompted her to run for Congress in 1916. Given her single-minded approach to issues, this was probably correct. She also insisted that she had not anticipated the outbreak of war in 1914 during her fight for suffrage in Montana, let alone American entrance during her 1916 campaign for Congress.[28] However, her platform did include a peace plank and a Montana newspaper described her in the summer of 1916 as an advocate of "a preparedness that will make for permanent peace." Forty-seven years later she claimed to have been very suspicious of Woodrow Wilson's 1916 campaign slogan: "He Kept Us Out of War." In contrast hers was "Let the People Know," but reportedly on Wellingtons's advice she did not publicly question the President's sincerity while running for Congress.[29]

Shortly after her election, the *New York Times* quoted Rankin as believing that no war could continue for long without assistance from women. At her first news conference in February 1917, Rankin refused to state whether she was actually a pacifist, although she later indicated that Montanans were well aware of her antiwar position as a result of her campaigning for suffrage and for Congress. Curiously enough, she signed a lecture contract in January 1917, with a clause voiding the agreement if she voted *against* war as a United States Congresswoman. And her first official address under this contract in Carnegie Hall in March did not mention foreign policy at all. Instead, she emphasized

28. Harris, "Jeannette Rankin," pp. 40-43, 84-85; JR: UCB Oral History, p. 79; Rankin, "Two Votes Against War," p. 4; Board, "Lady from Montana," pp.5-6.

29. Harris, "Jeannette Rankin," pp. 104-06; Board, "Lady from Montana," p. 6.

such progressive political reforms as the direct popular vote for President, an absentee voter law, and the principle of what later became known through a Supreme Court decision as "one-man-one-vote."[30]

During these months Rankin appeared unaware that President Wilson was anguishing about whether to recommend to Congress that the United States enter World War I, which had been in progress since 1914. Although the President had first exhorted the American people to be neutral about the European conflict, by the end of 1916 popular sentiment and the international lending policy of the U.S. government clearly favored the coalition of powers led by England over those led by Germany. Following the German return to unrestricted submarine warfare in February 1917, and the disclosure early in March of the infamous Zimmerman note suggesting an alliance between Mexico and Germany, Wilson's cabinet unanimously recommended that he ask Congress for a declaration of war. Still the President hesitated; he was no warmonger. Finally he called a special session of Congress for the evening of April 2. In tense silence the nation's representatives listened to Wilson describe the use of the submarine as "warfare against mankind" and proclaim that "the world must be made safe for democracy." Then they broke into thunderous applause.

Ironically on the morning of that same momentous day, Jeannette Rankin had been introduced on the floor of the House of Representatives as its first female member. Four days later on April 6, 1917, she cast her first ballot in Congress, against American entrance into World War I, saying: "I want to stand by my country, but I cannot vote for war. I vote no." She was joined on that historic occasion by fifty-six

30. *New York Times*, November 19, 1916, *New York Tribune*, March 3, 1917; JR: UCB Oral History, p. 80; Board, "Lady from Montana," pp. 5, 10; Schaffer, "Jeannette Rankin," p. 82 (quoting letter no longer among Rankin's deposited papers*); *Christian Science Monitor*, April 1, 1936.

other members of Congress and, contrary to popular accounts, she did not cry.[31]

The *Washington Post* reported at that time that her public record did not indicate how she would vote. In an era before it became famous for investigative reporting, the *Post* had no way of knowing that as early as December 14, 1914, Rankin had written to Stephen J. Stillwell, a member of the New York legislature, about the "brutal useless . . . great economic war" then raging in Europe.[32] Only left-of-center Progressives viewed war as a struggle for economic advantage and condemned military confrontation as a primitive method for settling international conflicts. Such a position did not reflect mainstream progressivism. Rankin also privately reiterated the same minority sentiment among Progressives in 1918 when, during the negotiation of the Treaty of Versailles, she wrote the only Republican member of the peace delegation that wars were fought to "protect special economic privileges."[33] However, neither letter surfaced to document her early antiwar position until well after World War II.

In retrospect, what is most important about Rankin's vote against World War I is that it became a part of her persona. Four days after the momentous session in Congress she apologized to her brother for disappointing him. It "was the only way I could go," she lamely wrote him, mindful that he had urged her to vote a "man's vote" for war.[34] Then in August 1917, she sent out her first official justification to a

31. *New York Times*, April 7, 1917; Board, 1963 interview with Rankin, pp. 32-33; U.S. House of Representatives, Hearings on Jt. Res. 200, January 27, 1918, p. 204; JR, UCB Oral History, p. 214. No matter how many times Rankin refuted the charge she had cried in casting her vote against war, the story lived on. Typical of the editorials that perpetuated this myth was one which appeared in the *Atlanta Constitution*, April 7, 1917, entitled "The Tears and the Vote," Rankin Folder, CDG-A, Box 130, Swarthmore College Peace Collection (SCPC).

32. *Washington Post*, April 2, 1917; *quote from Schaffer, "Jeannette Rankin," p. 82.

33. JR to Henry White, November 30, 1918, Box 23, Henry White Collection, Library of Congress.

34. *Helena Independent*, April 26, 1917; Harris, "Jeannette Rankin," p. 120 (quoting JR to Wellington Rankin, April 10, 1917, no longer among Rankin's deposited papers*).

Montana constituent. It read in part:

> In the campaign last fall, I judged the sentiment in Montana was overwhelmingly against war. Of course, the situation had changed when the vote was taken and yet the letters and telegrams that came to me were sixteen to one against the war resolution. I tried to let Montana people know that whenever a question arose on which I had received no definite instructions I would vote in accordance with my highest ideals.[35]

This moderate statement became Rankin's standard response to the many inquiries she received about her vote during the war. From the floor of Congress, however, her words were more strident. "I still believe war is a stupid and futile way of attempting to settle international difficulties," she said during the debate over declaring war against Austria-Hungary in December 1917. "I believe war can be avoided and will be avoided when the people . . . have the controlling voice in their government. Today special privileged commercial interests are controlling the world."[36]

Not until the summer of 1935 did Rankin begin to construct a much more elaborate rationalization of her original antiwar vote along these same lines. Obviously she had been influenced in the interim by her work for a variety of peace groups, most notably the NCPW, and the then popular revisionist criticisms of World War I. (Revisionist theories about historical events, especially wars, usually challenge the official explanations of national administrations on the basis of either a reinterpretation of old data or the introduction of newly uncovered facts.) In a private letter written on July 30, 1935, Rankin expressed her growing revisionist viewpoint about World War I.

> I knew that we were asked to vote for a commercial war, that none of the idealistic hopes would be carried out, and I was aware of the falseness of much of the propaganda. It [*sic*] was easy to stand a-

35. *Literary Digest* 55 (August 11, 1917), p. 43.

36. *Congressional Record* 56 (Part I), p. 98.

> gainst the propaganda of the militaris[ts] but very difficult to go against friends and dear ones who felt that I was making a needless sacrifice by voting against war, since my vote would not be a decisive one.[37]

By the end of the 1930s Rankin wrote standard revisionist articles against World War I as a matter of course. To this essentially economic argument she began to add highly subjective reasons. Sometimes she was critical of those House members who ignored statements opposing Wilson's war message. "They were stampeded," she later told John C. Board. "But never for one second could I face the idea that I would send young men to be killed for no other reason than to save my seat in Congress." Having not realized at the time how her negative vote might have given courage to others if she had made her intentions clear, she vowed never again to fail "to let people know ahead what I was going to do." At other times Rankin recalled that she wanted to take a "woman's" stand against war, regardless of its political consequences.[38]

Finally, writing in *Liberation* magazine in 1958, she repeated all of these reasons and tagged on an anecdote from her college days about how repugnant she had found Tennyson's "The Charge of the Light Brigade" because it glorified war and soldiers. In the same article she also insisted that "war had been on everybody's mind" in Montana in 1914, saying: "so we talked about suffrage in relation to war [and] I argued that women should get the vote because that would help keep the country out of war." Moreover, Rankin no longer distinguished between those suffragists who had encouraged her antiwar vote, such as Alice Paul, leader of the militant Woman's Party, and those who had not, such as Carrie Chapman Catt, head of the more moderate National American

37. *Quoted in Schaffer, "Jeannette Rankin," pp. 83-84. Rankin made somewhat similar statements to Harry E. Terrell, May 17, 1935, Folder V, Box 68, NCPW, JR Correspondence, and in a 1935 press release entitled "I Would Vote 'No' Again," Rankin Folder, CDG-A, Box 130, SCPC. This later appeared in the *Christian Science Monitor*, April 1, 1936, and still later in a 1938 radio address.

38. *The Christian Herald*, April 1937; *Washington Daily News*, April 6, 1937; Jeannette Rankin, "Beware of Holy Wars," *World Outlook*, November 1938; Board, 1963 Interview, pp. 30-31.

Woman Suffrage Association (NAWSA).[39] Clearly time and age worked to embellish, even obliterate, her initial apologetic and defensive responses about voting against war.

The passing years never changed Rankin's antiwar sentiments, however. If anything, her pacifism grew stronger toward the end of her life. On May 18, 1967, for example, she addressed a peace group in Atlanta, Georgia, suggesting that 10,000 determined women could end the war in Indochina. This and similar statements led to the creation of the Jeannette Rankin Brigade that organized a Washington protest march in 1968.

"I was thirty-six when I cast my vote [against World War I]," she confidently wrote with John Kirkley in 1972, "and I have not changed my mind." To biographer Norma Smith, Rankin finally concluded: "It was not only the most significant thing I ever did, it as a significant thing in itself."[40] So Jeannette Rankin's original opposition to World War I became a *raison d'etre* for the rest of her career. That one act must have been disproportionately important to reorient her entire career toward professional pacifism, and this is even more a wonder when we consider that consistency and stubbornness were hallmarks of her personality.

## Rankin's Dedication to Pacifism

During the remainder of her first term in Congress, Rankin used her position to try to improve the condition of women and limit the negative effects of war on them as consumers and workers. She supported pensions for dependents of American soldiers, public hygiene legislation and protective labor laws in addition to a federal suffrage amendment. Although she endorsed the President's "vigorous presecution of the war," she campaigned

39. "Two Votes Against War," *Liberation*, March 1958, p. 4; Board, 1963 Interview, pp. 28-29.

40. "Why I Voted Against War," pp. 2-3. That she was clearly aware of the antagonism between Catt and Paul was evident from the fact that she met separately with the two groups on the day of her vote against war. Norma Smith conversation and taped interview with Alice Paul. Also see Harris, "Jeannette Rankin," pp. 131-32, and JR: UCB Oral History, pp. 61-62.

only half-heartedly for Liberty Bond drives.[41] This desultory display of patriotism combined with emotions fanned by government-sponsored prowar propaganda to increase suspicions among Montanans about Rankin's as yet undeclared pacifism.

No longer able to run for the House in a statewide election because the legislature had divided Montana into two Congressional districts, she decided to run for the Senate in 1918 despite her growing unpopularity. When she lost her bid for the Republican nomination, she continued in the general election as a senatorial candidate of the newly organized National party, which represented an amorphous coalition of Non-Partisan League farmers, prowar Socialists, antiwar Progressives, and prohibitionists. From the outset it was a hopeless campaign made even worse when suffragist leader Carrie Chapman Catt supported Thomas J. Walsh, Rankin's Democratic opponent. As president of NAWSA, Catt had supported the war effort from the very beginning and after Rankin's vote against war Catt had written a friend that "our Congress Lady is a sure enough joker. Whatever she has done or will do is wrong to somebody, and every time she answers a roll call she loses us a *million votes.*"[42]

Even before April 1917, however, relations between Catt and Rankin had been poor. The former had thrown her weight behind Wilson in the election of 1916—presumably in return for the President's support of a federal suffrage amendment. And prior to the 1916 election there is evidence of personal rivalry between Catt and Rankin because of the condescension the eastern-based leadership of NAWSA had traditionally exhibited toward western suffragists.[43] Neither Rankin nor Nevada's Anne Henrietta Martin had been enthusiastically endorsed by eastern suffragists in their bids for House and Senate seats in 1916, 1918, and 1920. Martin and

41. "Why I Voted Against War," p. 3. Quote is from Norma Smith's manuscript.

42. 1918 Election Campaign Pamphlet, Rankin Papers; *Helena Independent*, April 18, 27, 29, 1918. More militant suffragists than Rankin supected that Wilson stopped opposing the suffrage amendment to enlist women into the war effort. She was much more enthusiastic about selling Peace Bonds in the 1930s. See: JR to Libby, September 4, October 8, 1935, Folder V, Box 68, NCPW: JR Correspondence.

43. Carrie C. Catt to Mary Gray Peck, April 8, 1917, Catt Papers, Schlesinger Library.

*Carrie Chapman Catt in 1914.*

Rankin both felt that they merited high offices in suffragist and later in national peace organizations.[44]

Jeannette Rankin, like many prewar reformers, remained convinced that the war had killed the Progressive Movement and broken the momentum behind the drive for women's rights. Always skeptical about President Wilson's claim that winning the war would make the world "safe for democracy," Rankin pointedly campaigned in 1918 to "make the world safe for humanity."[45] While this distinction is important, both were overly optimistic. The President

44. Harris, "Jeannette Rankin," pp. 131, 140; Harriett B. Laidlaw to JR, n.d. [1917], Laidlaw Papers, Schlesinger Library; JR, UCB Oral History, p. 37; conversation with Norma Smith; interview with Dorothy Detzer Denny, Monterey, California, December 11, 1976; "Mabel Vernon," Suffragist Oral History Project, Bancroft Library, University of California, Berkeley, 1976 [hereafter cited as MV: UCB Oral History], pp. 43-44.

45. Otis Graham, *The Great Campaigns: Reform and War in America, 1900-1928* (Prentice-Hall, 1971); JR: UCB Oral History, pp. 56-57, 178, untranscribed interview of JR by Marie Sale, n.p., n.d., reel 4 and transcribed interview of JR by Dick Cavett, April 17, 1972, reel 2 or Folder 205—both in Box 12, Rankin Papers; Schaffer, "Jeannette Rankin," p. 144.

tried to compensate with his futile battle over the League of Nations and the former Congresswoman did likewise by turning to the burgeoning postwar peace movement. In the course of the 1920s she became more of a pacifist than a feminist. Both her pacifism and feminism were, however, means to a larger end—humanitarianism.[46]

Beginning in 1915 when she first joined the Woman's Peace Party, Jeannette Rankin's search for peace became a life-long pursuit. She subsequently belonged to the National Committee on the Cause and Cure of War, the Women's Peace Union, the Women's International League for Peace and Freedom (WILPF), and finally the National Council for the Prevention of War (NCPW). With the exception of the Georgia Peace Society, which she founded in 1928, none of these organizations lived up to Rankin's idealistic or organizational standards. In each case either she opposed their top-down organizing tactics or they refused to finance her grassroots approach. In some instances there were ideological differences as well. Thus, she left her position as field secretary with the WILPF in 1925 after it proved impossible to finance her elaborate plan for organizing in the West. Like so many other women who had worked for suffrage in western states, Rankin had difficulty working with the top eastern leadership of the WILPF, especially its strong-minded executive secretary Dorothy Detzer.[47]

The Georgia Peace Society remained her "home base" of pacifist operations from the late 1920s until it languished from lack of funds and support on the eve of World War II. Although she remained a resident of Montana, it was from Georgia that she participated in a number of national projects usually requiring much travel. Between 1921 and 1929, for ex-

46. JR, UCB Oral History, p. 213; conversation with Norma Smith; interview with Dorothy Detzer Denny, Monterey, CA, December 11, 1976. She did not, for example, participate in efforts to obtain international rights for women in the 1920s and 1930s. See Paula F. Pfeffer, " 'A Whisper in the Assembly of Nations': The International Movement for Women's Rights Between the Wars," unpublished paper.

47. Marie Louise Degen, *The History of the Woman's Peace Party* (Baltimore: Johns Hopkins University Press, 1939), p. 38; JR: UCB Oral History, pp. 13, 102-03; Harris, "Jeannette Rankin," pp. 184-85; Schaffer, "Jeannette Rankin," pp. 164-77; interview with Dorothy Detzer Denny.

ample, she supported the activities of the Women's Peace Union, whose sole purpose was to outlaw war through a constitutional amendment. The WPU hired her as an official lobbyist for six months in 1929. She left the job disillusioned with the organization's methods. The WPU wanted her to lobby members of Congress while she wanted to organize people at grassroot levels. So in 1929 she stopped lobbying for this particular constitutional amendment.[48]

That same year Rankin began a ten-year association with the National Council for Prevention of War. Once again she was employed as a lobbyist, but this time for the wider variety of National Council antiwar causes. In 1939 this affiliation also ended in acrimony engendered by disagreement over salary cuts due to declining funds and Rankin's feeling that her local peace work in Georgia against Representative Carl Vinson's perennial naval bills had never been sufficiently appreciated by other NCPW leaders. Although Rankin directed much of her dissatisfaction toward NCPW Executive Director Frederick J. Libby, she finally resigned when a rather petty dispute erupted with Education Secretary Florence Boeckel over the contents of a speech.[49] More important, Rankin conflicted with the National Council after 1936 when she became increasingly critical of the international policies of both Secretary of State Cordell Hull and FDR.[50]

In the late 1930s she came to believe that her associates were not as dedicated to the cause of

48. Rankin, "Working Politically for Peace in Georgia," January 5, 1932 statement; Elinor Byrns to JR, April 1, May 10, 1929, Caroline Lexow Babcock to JR, May 9, 1929, JR to Byrns, April 6, 1929—all in Rankin Folder, CDG-A, Box 130, SCPC; "Teachers and World Peace," July 1, 1929 radio address, untitled September 6, 1929 radio address, "Outlaw War Constitutionally," September 9, 1929 radio address—all in Folder X, Box 65, National Council for Prevention of War [NCPW]; JR Correspondence, SCPC; Harris, "Jeannette Rankin," pp. 185-201; Schaffer, "Jeannette Rankin," pp.173-177.

49. Harris, "Jeannette Rankin," pp. 202-220; Schaffer, "Jeannette Rankin," pp. 229-230. For representative correspondence over tactical and financial disputes see: Libby to JR, September 19, 1931, July 28, 1938, JR to Libby October 2, 1931, October 24, November 29, 1933, September 4, 1935, January 17, July 21, September 12, 1938, August 7, September 20, 1939, Box 68, NCPW: JR correspondence, SCPC; Norma Smith to author, July 12, 1978.

50. Her eariest criticism of FDR began with an October 24, 1933 letter to Libby, but became most evident in 1938. See: JR to Gladys E. Heinrich Knowles, August 22, 1938, JR to Libby, January 17, 1938, NCPW: JR Correspondence, SCPC; JR to Flora Belle Surles, January 15, 1938, uncataloged Surles Papers, Schlesinger Library.

peace as she was. In an absolute sense she *was* more committed to pacificism than some co-workers in these interwar years; the cause of peace dominated her life to the degree that she demonstrated little, if any interest, in other pursuits. It should be remembered, however, that such single-mindedness is still considered a "normal" perspective for today's most committed reformers. It is true that Rankin often justified her frenetic traveling as working for world peace even when it was obvious that sometimes she simply wanted to escape from disagreeable situations. No doubt many of her colleagues had difficulty working with her. Occasionally they complained about her so-called dictatorial methods and suspected that she coveted the limelight too much. But these were common charges levied against practically every outstanding female leader of her generation.[51]

Although these characteristics made Rankin a very effective lobbyist, she, in turn, resented not being able to work at her own intense pace and on her own terms. Often frustrated and unhappy with her treatment at NCPW headquarters, she finally resigned on April 1, 1939. Despite her private conviction that she and the Executive Director were in basic disagreement over tactics and that "neither she nor any woman on the [NCPW] staff was ever accorded equality with the men," Rankin remained on relatively friendly terms with him. Not even the unconscious sexism that emerges in his correspondence prevented Libby from contributing to her successful 1940 campaign for a second term in Congress.[52]

51. Ted C. Harris, "Jeannette Rankin in Georgia," *The Georgia Historical Quarterly* 58 (Spring 1974), p. 70. In turn, Rankin expressed much discouragement, boredom and fatigue to Surles and NCPW leaders between 1935 and 1940.

52. For her decision to run in 1940 and Libby's support see: JR to Libby, June 4, 1940 and Libby to JR, June 6, 1940, NCPW, JR Correspondence, SCPC; JR, UCB Oral History, p. 84 (quote paraphrased by interviewer from off-tape remarks made by Rankin).

## Her View of Foreign Policy

Rankin's difficulties with the NCPW were due, in part, to her particular views on foreign policy. In the interwar years she was a "nationalist," or one who supported very limited American commitments around the world. She was not, however, an isolationist; she did not accept an attitude of isolation from European affairs while accepting the use of force in the Far East or Latin America. Unlike this approach of the isolationists, Rankin was true to her pacifist ideals: she objected to the use of American military force anywhere in the world, except for the defense of the continental United States.[53]

She supported international cooperation, but she opposed American interventionism around the globe. Her views had much to do with her own reactions to the economic changes that took place between the wars. As America became an urban and consumer nation, those who first experienced mass consumerism in the 1920s tended to be more internationally-minded than those who did not. Rankin turned away from the consumer society and led a spartan life in Georgia after World War I. She emerged as an avowed pacifist with strong nationalist leanings, not an isolationist. After 1945, as a pacifist critic of the Cold War, Korea and Vietnam, her foreign policy views became revisionist. She increasingly associated American expansionism with deficiencies in the country's political economy and the power of a conspiratorial military-industrial complex. Characteristically, her nationalism and revisionism remained simplistic and unsophisticated.[54]

53. For a discussion of nationalism versus internationalism and differences between orthodox and revisionist historians on this issue see: Joan Hoff Wilson, *American Business and Foreign Policy, 1920-1933* (Lexington, Ky.: University Press of Kentucky, 1971); idem, *Ideology and Economics: U.S. Relations with the Soviet Union, 1918-1933* (Columbia, Missouri: University of Missouri Press, 1974).

54. Joan Hoff Willson, ed., *The Twenties: The Critical Issues* (Boston: Little, Brown & Co., 1971); JR: UCB Oral History, p. 113; Harris, Rankin in Georgia," pp. 57-59, 72; John Kirkley, "An Afternoon with Jeannette Rankin," in JR: UCB Oral History, p. 149; Rankin, "There is Continuous Want While the Governments of World are Spending Billions for Armaments," *International Disarmament Notes*, January 18, 1932; Rankin, "Can We Afford War?" *Church Woman*, August-September, 1967. The "Georgian" side to her life will be discussed in the second part of this article.

Jeannette Rankin may have been simplistic in her viewpoint, but she consistently pursued a progressive brand of foreign policy that had its roots in Jeffersonian agrarian values, in a nonconsumer oriented life style, in direct, decentralized government, in reform at home before reform of the world, and finally, in the belief that people, especially women, could be educated in the habits of peace. "The only safe way of preventing war and waste and confusion," she repeatedly said, "will be through broadening the base of political control. . . . Peace is coming not through political leaders but through the voter. The great value of political action lies in its power to educate the masses."[55]

Rankin's private and professional life after 1917 symbolize her total commitment to these related concepts of "peace education" and "peace action." Her revisionist views of American foreign policy and her attachment to grassroots political action often put her at odds with large reform organizations. She had ideals. As we shall see, however, it was one thing to hold out such high ideals; it was entirely another matter to convince a majority of the American people to accept them.

JOAN HOFF WILSON, currently on leave from Arizona State University where she is Professor of History, is a noted historian of twentieth-century American foreign policy and the author of *American Business and Foreign Policy, 1920-1933* (1971) and *Ideology and Economics: U.S. Relations with the Soviet Union, 1918-1933* (1974). A native of Butte and a graduate of University of Montana, Prof. Wilson delivered a portion of this article in an address at the Montana History Conference in Helena, November 1977.

55. Transcript of Rankin's 90th Birthday Address, June 11, 1970, Box 11, Rankin Papers. For similar remarks see: "Peace Through Political Action," 1925 and/or 1928-1929 radio address, "I'd Still Vote No," April 6, 1938 radio address—both in Folder X, Box 65, NCPW: JR Correspondence, SCPC.

*Rankin after her first term in Congress.*

**This is part one of Prof. Wilson's study of Jeannette Rankin's foreign policy. The second half will take Rankin from her early involvement in the pacifist movement and her second term in Congress when she voted a second time against war to her last years as a critic of America's course in Vietnam in the 1960s.**

# *"Peace is a woman's job . . ."* Jeannette Rankin and American Foreign Policy: Her Lifework as a Pacifist

by Joan Hoff Wilson

Jeannette Rankin emerged from World War I believing that America could no longer isolate itself from international affairs because the world was becoming too interdependent. "We are living in the world," she repeatedly said in the 1920s. "We are no longer living in a community, state or nation . . . whatever happens in one part of the world affects every other part sooner or later to a greater or less extent." Five years before she joined the National Council for the Prevention of War (NCPW) as a lobbyist Rankin entirely agreed with its 1924 statement which proclaimed: "Isolation is a myth. . . . All nations are entangled now—financially, commercial [*sic*], and agriculturally." While she clearly did not subscribe to isolationism, this belief in international dependency did not turn her into an interventionist, nor into a supporter of Franklin D. Roosevelt's brand of internationalism. Instead, as a pacifist Rankin insisted that "it is not cooperation with the rest of the world that the American people object to. They object, and I believe rightly, to entering into an agreement with other nations which will bind them in advance to use our military or naval forces in coercing or punishing a nation which shall start a war in which we have no interest or at most a remote one."[1]

She dedicated her remaining life, personally and politically, to the pacifist cause. Increasingly she connected the causes of war with the structure of the American economic system. There was profit in war, Rankin told audiences, and the only way to prevent future wars was to disarm and retain only defensive forces to protect the nation itself from invasion. Moving to Georgia in the 1920s, where she lived in a cabin without modern conveniences, Rankin formed the Georgia Peace Society and involved it in Georgia and national politics. Many Georgians thought she was dangerous, that her opinions were treasonous, that she might be a communist. She was not deterred. When Congress considered neutrality legislation in the 1930s, Jeannette Rankin was there to testify, and when the war in Europe threatened to pull America into its maelstrom, she readily re-entered politics as a Representative from Montana. In Washington she voted her principles and always put the pacifist proposition before Congress. Even the shock and tragedy of Pearl Harbor in 1941 did not move her to vote for war, she voted no a second time. Criticized for her action, Rankin continued to press for disarmament in the post World War II era, but she seemed doomed to being the advocate of a losing cause. When she died in 1973, America was still at war in Vietnam and disarmament was little more than a hopeful vision. But the measure of Jeannette Rankin's life was not the failure of her mission to change American foreign policy, it was the example she set as a great crusader against war—a legacy, worth studying in this age of nuclear armaments.

1. Jeannette Rankin, "Peace Through Political Action," 1925 and/or 1928-29 radio address, NCPW *Bulletin*, June 21, 1924, both in Folder X, Box 65, National Council for the Prevention of War Collection, Legislative Department, Jeannette Rankin Correspondence with Libby and Staff, 1929-1954, Swarthmore College Peace Collection [hereafter cited as NCPW: JR Correspondence]; Rankin, n.d. [1922?] untitled speech on the Permanent Court of International Justice and the outlawry of war, Folder 53, Box 3, Jeannette Rankin Papers, Schlesinger Library, Radcliffe College [hereafter cited as Rankin Papers].

Montana Historical Society

*Jeannette Rankin's 1940 campaign portrait.*

The first segment of this essay on Jeannette Rankin's foreign policy attempted to track down the origins of her ideas about suffrage and pacifism, despite the absence of complete documentation. Her biography showed Rankin developing from a strong-willed, yet retiring University of Montana student who was unsure of her intellectual capabilities into an effective suffrage campaigner, progressive politician, and national peace lobbyist. Rankin's two votes against the First and Second World Wars confirmed her pacifism in the minds of most Americans but, in fact, her antiwar activities were much more sustained and systematic than the twenty-four years separating these Congressional ballots indicate.

Again, however, it is difficult to reconstruct all of Rankin's actions because she was such a poor record keeper. To understand the diversity of her efforts on behalf of peace, it is best to divide them into several categories: her life in Georgia; her views on communism, the League of Nations, World Court and the United Nations; her lifelong campaign for disarmament; her attempts to outlaw war; her sporadic recommendations for reform of American monetary and political systems; and finally, her support for neutrality or arms embargo legislation. Rankin, of course, did not compartmentalize her actions in this fashion, but these divisions provide convenient guides to the consistency of her pacifism from 1920 until her death in 1973. While the intensity with which she promoted peace through these various types of activities and attitudes varied over the years, her general commitment to a world without war did not. In that Jeannette Rankin was very consistent.

## Rankin in Georgia

Rankin never limited her pacifism to press statements or public appearances. In 1924, to bring her lifestyle in line with her ideals, she purchased land near Athens, Georgia. Ostensibly this 64-acre farm served as a winter vacation home, but in practice it became a symbol of her commitment to a simple, stoic life and the base from which she launched several peace education and peace action programs. Not surprisingly, Georgia also became the area of the country that most bitterly attacked her pacifism in the 1930s. For example, by 1934 the Atlanta American Legion Post had publicly labeled Rankin a communist and circulated throughout the state a book by Elizabeth Dilling, *The Red Network*, in which the Montanan was listed as one of 1300 leaders of organizations controlled by communists, radicals, pacifists, anarchists, Socialists, or wobblies. "The sum of my radicalism," Rankin asserted in answer to these attacks, "seems to be my opposition to war, to competitive armaments and to predatory interests."[2]

What had she done to arouse the ire of local patriots in Georgia? First, she chose to live unconventionally in a one-room house without electricity, running water or a telephone; a house she designed, built and later expanded. Second, she organized "Sunshine" Clubs for local boys and girls to teach them "peace habits." Third, she established a foreign policy study group for adults in Athens that became the nucleus of the Georgia Peace Society in 1928. One of this group's first priorities became the defeat of the perennial naval appropriation bills of Georgia Congressman Carl Vinson. But the last straw as far a local members of the American Legion were concerned came in 1934 when Brenau College, an exclusive female liberal arts institution in Gainsville, hinted that it wanted to establish a "Chair of Peace" for her.[3]

Although the entire controversy was more the product of publicity than an issue of substance, Rankin filed a libel suit to stop the personal assault upon her character. She also transformed the Georgia Peace Society into one of the first peace action groups in the country, directing the society during its most active years, 1935-1936, in an attempt to

2. JR to H.J. Pearce, Sr., November 22, 1934, Rankin Folder, CDG-A, Box 130, Swarthmore College Peace Collection (SCPC) (quote). Background material on her Georgia lifestyle and run-in with Atlanta American Legion can be found in Ted C. Harris, "Jeannette Rankin in Georgia," *The Georgia Historical Quarterly*, 58 (Spring 1974), pp. 54-78 and Norma Smith, unpublished biography of Jeannette Rankin, Chapters 15 and 16.

3. Ted C. Harris, "Jeannette Rankin: Suffragist, First Woman Elected to Congress, and Pacifist" (Ph.D. dissertation, University of Georgia, 1972), pp. 178-79, 221-55.

defeat Representative Vinson. Ironically, these efforts only served to consolidate support for military appropriations in the state of Georgia and allowed Rankin's enemies to vilify her name. Once the 1936 primary election was over, attacks on her and the peace society subsided. Subsequently she received a belated out-of-court settlement and public retraction of libelous statements by the Macon *Evening News*. Jeannette Rankin made both a private and public commitment to pacifism in Georgia before the Second World War, one that was sincere and energetic, but she did not succeed in changing rank and file opinion of her or the peace movement.[4]

Despite this less than enthusiastic response to pacifism, Rankin continued, for the next half century, to live a good portion of the year near Athens, Georgia. Although she voted in Montana, registered her car there, and rented Montana property that she owned, "home" was Georgia. In 1941, during her second term in Congress, her house burned down. After leaving Washington in 1943 at the age of 63 she returned to Georgia and moved into a three-room share cropper cabin located on thirty acres of land she had purchased some years before. She immediately set about remodeling the place; this time there was electricity and a telephone, but still no running water. From these somewhat more spacious and modern surroundings Rankin entertained guests and relatives and continued to cultivate an image of marginal living despite her obvious ability to travel at will and to afford such luxuries as a car, television, and tastefully expensive clothes. Her final experiment in housebuilding occurred in 1967 when, at the age of 87, she decided to design and build a home for elderly women. Intended to provide semi-communal living for retired women, the home was never completed, but the idea remains a testimony to her life-long interest in social welfare concerns.[5]

4. *Ibid.*; JR to Libby, November 22, 1934, Folder V, Box 68, W.G. Cornett to Harry F. Ward, November 4, 1935 in folder entitled, "Accusations of American Legion, Macon, Georgia and Resulting Libel Suit, 1935-36," Box 69, NCPW: JR Correspondence, SCPC.

5. JR to Ann Denmler, October 11, 1943, JR to Blanche Watson, October 12, 1943, Folder 168, Box 9, Rankin Papers; Norma Smith, unpublished biography of JR, Chapters 19 and 20; Harris, "Jeannette Rankin," pp. 316-317.

Montana Historical Society

Rankin at her Georgia house during the years she led the Georgia Peace Society.

## Rankin and Communism

The charges leveled against her in Georgia accused Rankin of having communist beliefs. Did these charges have any substance? From the limited number of documents in her papers on this subject it is clear that she opposed Bolshevism during the Red Scare following World War I. As she prepared to attend the Second International Congress of Women for Permanent Peace in 1919, along with such prominent pacifists and social workers as Jane Addams, Florence Kelley and Lillian Wald, the *New York Times* reported her saying: "I intend to place the problem of stopping the spread of Bolshevism before the Congress...." Yet at no time did she consider communism a threat to the United States and even in those eastern European countries where communism appeared to be a threatening force she opposed the use of military intervention or blockades of any kind.[6]

There is no documentary evidence of any significant change in her attitude toward Communist Russia prior to World War II. Although she was a close friend and supporter of other aspects of Senator William E. Borah's foreign policy, it does not appear that she consistently advocated recognition of the Soviet Union in the 1920s or that she endorsed the re-establishment of diplomatic relations with the USSR in 1933. In fact, her view of communism in 1941 seems very similar to the one she held in 1920, namely, that the American people were "simply not enthused about saving the Red Menace."[7] As a pacifist, however, Rankin never succumbed to the extreme nationalist position that Hitler's fascism should be supported because it was anticommunist. At the same time, the summers that she spent in Europe from 1931 to 1937 convinced her of fascism's dangerous militaristic character. In 1935, for example, she wrote to Eleanor Roosevelt about the way Hitler's arms build-up

6. *New York Times*, April 10, 1919.

7. Great Falls *Tribune*, July 12, 1941.

was being concealed from both the American and German peoples. In this same letter she urged the President's wife to use her influence to educate public opinion about *defensive* preparedness and Nazi military might. At no time before the end of 1937, however, did she believe even the most militaristic countries like Italy and Germany would "rush into a war in the immediate future."[8]

Despite her fear of German militarism, Rankin probably remained more hostile to communism than to fascism. As was the case with most Americans during the interwar years, there is no evidence that she understood the philosophical and economic differences between the two. And despite the persecution Rankin had experienced at the hands of the American Legion in Georgia, she was not above red-baiting. In her 1940 campaign for a second term in Congress she endorsed a widely distributed radio script that implied her opponent, Democrat Jerry O'Connell, was associated with the Communist Party.[9]

The only discernible softening of her attitude toward communism (outside of her opposition to American participation in the Korean War) came in 1962 during a tour of the Soviet Union when she asked communist party leaders to unilaterally disarm. "We can't do it," Rankin explained to the obviously surprised Russians, "because we're controlled by the army! But you control your army; therefore, you could do it." Nothing concrete came of this forthright suggestion, but in the course of this trip to the USSR Rankin's views on communism seemed to soften because of her favorable impression of Khruschev, a Soviet peace conference that she attended, and the enhanced roles for

8. "Jeannette Rankin: Activist for World Peace, Women's Rights and Democratic Government," Suffrage Oral History Project, Bancroft Library, University of California, Berkeley, 1974 [hereafter cited as JR: UCB Oral History], p. 83; *quote is from Harris "Jeannette Rankin," p. 267, based on material not now in the Rankin papers; Eleanor Roosevelt to JR, August 6, 1935, Folder 56, Box 3, Rankin Papers. In the summer of 1937 Rankin also interviewed the first lady and once again tried to influence the President through her. See: JR to Libby, June 28, 1937, Folder VI, Box 68, NCPW: JR Correspondence.

9. One of the reasons why she underestimated the danger from fascism is that she viewed Hitler as no more than "another Kaiser." See: JR to Libby, September 20, 1939, Folder VII, Box 68, NCPW: JR Correspondence; Harris, "Jeannette Rankin," p. 283.

women that she observed. She also had come to believe that

> You can't shoot an ideology: the only way to control communism is to have a better system at home. We haven't taken care of our children. We haven't educated our people. We haven't done the things necessary to make a happy nation. We must work together to raise not only the general standards of living, for much of our crime comes from poverty, but also "the quality of the people—of their minds," for a free, intelligent, and sensitive people would not allow the toxic conditions in our society to continue.[10]

Like so many former Progressives who became critics of the Cold War, domestic reform was the keystone not only of her battle against communism, but of her foreign policy views in general.

## Rankin and Domestic Reform

Throughout her long public career, Rankin proposed two types of domestic reform: one would have broadened the electoral process; the other would have created a special "profit removing" currency in time of war or other military crises. She associated both with specific foreign events. As early as 1917, for example, during World War I she had advocated proportional representation "as an indispensable instrument of a truly representative government" along with a "direct vote for president." Over the years her belief in the power of the electorate persisted and, if anything, gained in strength as she championed several methods of expanding electoral power. By 1930 she had abandoned her earlier idea about proportional representation in favor of multiple-member Congressional districts, and by the fall of 1952 was once again working on "a new method of selecting a president." Not until the late 1960s did she simultaneously

10. JR: UCB Oral History, p. 262 (first quote), pp. 263-8; John Harris Kirkley, "An Afternoon with Jeannette Rankin," in JR: UCB Oral History, p. 150.

advocate both multiple-member districts and a direct preferential vote for the presidency.[11]

Her attempts to broaden the electoral process had always been rooted in an abiding faith in the American people, a typically progressive belief in the democratic process and its relationship to foreign policy. On her ninetieth birthday her views remained the same:

> ...the President is much more important than he was at the time of the Revolution because today our international relations are just as important as our human relations, and the President has something to say about it. He should have the advice and consent not only of the Senate, but of all the people, and the people should have something direct to say about the selection of President... but we can't elect a President [directly] under present conditions and we don't get a representation of public opinion because the people haven't a choice. I think that making choices is one of the processes in advancement.... You can't make progress without choice.[12]

Rankin's other major domestic reform stemmed from her dissatisfaction with certain aspects of American capitalism. In particular, Senator Gerald Nye's investigation of the role played by the munitions industry in America's entrance into World War I confirmed her worst suspicions about the economic origins of modern warfare. His committee's findings, from 1934 to 1936, proved to her that commercial interests caused wars. Accordingly, in the 1930s she revived her World War I ideas about antiprofit legislation.

As early as 1933 she had testified before the House Foreign Affairs Committee that the American economic system inevitably produced wars because the "militaristic system forces an economic problem upon us. . . ." In 1934 several newspapers

---

11. New York *Tribune*, March 3, 1917; JR to Flora Belle Surles, January 15, 1938, Surles Papers, Schlesinger Library; JR to Grace Rankin Kinney, September 3, 1952, Folder 9, Box 1, Rankin and Kirkley material on multiple-member districts and preferential presidential vote, Folder 197, Box 12, all in Rankin Papers.

---

12. Rankin, 90th Birthday Address, Folder 182, Box 11, Rankin Papers.

quoted her as saying that "we are walking in the direction of war and we can get a war anytime the munition makers and profit makers demand it. . . . If we do not crystallize public opinion we are going directly to war because the munition makers ... must use up their stockpiles." She insisted that it was the right of the American people to have information about those "patriots who are willing to give the life of your son for their profit." At the beginning of 1935, when testifying before the House Committee on Military Affairs in favor of issuing temporary currency that would have value only while the country was at war, Rankin made one of her most famous statements against war. "You can no more win a war than you can win an earthquake," she told one committee member in the course of describing how her emergency currency idea would take the profit out of war-making.[13]

After World War II her economic argument became an attack on the military-industrial complex and its general relationship to the monetary system. "Many of the particular problems of women result from the materialistic values and 'crazy money system'" on which the country operated. "My first interest is to get rid of war," she said in 1972, "but we can't do that until we end military control of our economy and government.... Every time we have a war, the military establishment grows stronger.... To attack and break the control of the military-industrial complex, the people must first become aware that their interests are at stake and are unrequited by the status quo. Then they must organize their energies and pool their resources so that they become a match against the money and organization of the military."[14] Needless to say, Rankin never lived to see either of her major domestic reforms enacted.

13. U.S. House of Representatives, Foreign Affairs Committee, *Hearing on the Exportation of Arms or Munitions of War*, 72nd Congress, 2nd Session [Washington, 1933], pp. 21-23; newspaper quotes from Harris, "Jeannette Rankin," pp. 214-215; U.S. House of Representatives, Committee on Military Affairs, *Hearing on Taking the Profit Out of War*, 74th Congress, 1st Session (Washington, 1935), pp. 307-312; Rankin, "Armistice Day radio address," November 11, 1936, Folder X, Box 65, NCPW.

14. Transcribed interview of JR by John Board, August 29, 1963, Folder 205, Box 12, Rankin Papers; Kirkley, "Afternoon with JR," JR: UCB Oral History, pp. 149, 151; Conversation with Belle Fligelman Winestine of Helena, Montana, February 28, 1977.

## Rankin and Disarmament

Rankin's advocacy of world disarmament was also doomed to failure in her lifetime. During her first campaign for Congress she shocked many Montanans with her idea that the United States should have an army or navy only for self-protection, not for aggression. "No enemy," she reportedly said, "is going to take a fleet of ships up the Mississippi." She continued to insist, both before and after World War II, that the country need not fear a foreign invasion—never fully appreciating the significance of air and missile power in modern warfare.

Throughout the 1930s, Jeannette Rankin lobbied against all increases in military preparedness, particularly the annual naval expenditures proposed by Representative Carl Vinson from Georgia. She viewed the successful arms limitation conferences of 1921-1922 and 1930 as inadequate. Maintaining a strident pacifist position but realizing that people were not ready in the interwar years for complete disarmament, she proposed the less threatening idea of an American "shore defense." Nevertheless, anything short of total disarmament would not satisfy her. Later during the escalation of U.S. involvement in the Vietnamese war, she openly urged unilateral disarmament and withdrawal of American troops "even if the Reds take over," adding: "You don't do the right thing because of the consequences. If you are wise, you do it regardless of the consequences."[15]

"I'm for immediate, total and unilateral disarmament," she told one interviewer in 1970. Shortly before her death she continued to insist that "the quickest way to promote world peace is total unilateral disarmament and though immediate dis-

15. See radio addresses in Folder X, Box 65, NCPW, especially, "Disarmament Conference," December 2, 1929, no title, 1931 and April 10, 1937, "Between War and Peace," December 29, 1937, and no title, February 23, 1938; JR to Libby, July 22, 1936, Folder VI, Box 68; also see her testimony before House and Senate Committees against military appropriations in Folders VIII, IX, Box 65, all in NCPW; JR Correspondence; Harris, "Jeannette Rankin," pp. 104, 214-218; *Newsweek*, February 14, 1966, p. 12 (quote).

armament is not possible for economic reasons we could begin at once and set a reasonable timetable of, say, three to five years, for conversion of war industry to peacetime uses and the resulting shifts of job and labor." The fear of unilateral disarmament, she argued, was illusory because: 1) the United States was immune from ideological or cultural attack from communist nations; 2) the American economy would be strengthened if military production was curbed; 3) the country was immune to military takeover because "a foreign invader could not win a guerrilla war fighting us on our own soil" and because Russia or China would be deterred from making a direct nuclear attack "by public opinion and sentiment among their own peoples as well as within the larger community of nations."[16]

Rankin's commitment to disarmament naturally led her to support all attempts to outlaw war in the 1920s. The culmination of this movement was the Kellogg-Briand Pact of 1928, the agreement signed by world powers to outlaw war. In fact, American approval of this pact stimulated rather than satiated her pacifist activities in both Georgia and throughout the nation. It also strengthened her belief in the power of public opinion, and prompted her to continue advocating a number of constitutional amendments either for outlawing war, like the Frazier Amendment in 1935, or for national referenda to determine popular attitudes about foreign policy issues.[17]

One of the most controversial amendments she supported was the Ludlow Amendment of 1938. It would have required a national vote before the country could enter into war. As a representative of the NCPW, Rankin strenuously campaigned for this war referendum bill. Once in a radio address she asked why farmers were allowed to vote under New Deal AAA legislation on whether or not

16. Harris, "Jeannette Rankin," p. 311; Kirkley, "Afternoon with JR," JR: UCB Oral History, p. 150.

17. Insisting on a literal interpretation of the Kellogg-Briand Pact, Rankin advocated amending the Constitution and changing military policy to bring the U.S. in line with the true intent of this agreement. See: JR to Mary B. Orr, May 25, 1929, Rankin Folder, CDG-A, Box 130, SCPC; radio addresses in Folder X, Box 65, NCPW, especially those for September 13, 1929, December 2, 1929, no title, 1931, July 18, 1935, April 10, 1937, January 16, 1940. Her efforts on behalf of various constitutional amendments in the 1920s and 1930s were discussed in the first segment of this article.

to kill piglets when parents could not "vote on whether they want their sons killed?"[18] Although the Ludlow bill died in a House committee, there was considerable popular support for it and Rankin never forgot Congress' failure to respond to what she considered legitimate public opinion.

In keeping with her belief in public opinion, she recommended to the Women's International League for Peace and Freedom (WILPF) in 1920 that the Council of the League of Nations be elected by peoples of the member states instead of appointed by their respective governments. As a strong critic of the Treaty of Versailles, however, she remained only minimally tolerant of the League, especially after nothing came of her suggestions to make it more responsive to world public opinion.

By the early 1930s she consistently maintained that the sole usefulness of the League was as a "channel for communication between nations" that would hopefully increase international understanding. In Rankin's mind only drastic disarmament by all nations could make the League of Nations effective. She had learned this lesson from the Japanese invasion of Manchuria in 1931-1932 when the League had been unable to stop such a blatant act of aggression. Nonetheless, she reluctantly followed the NCPW's position and recommended American entrance into both the League of Nations and the World Court.[19]

With respect to the Court her views were more specific than usual. She thought it should have the "power to render decisions without the consent [of powerful nations]," but not the "power to enforce decisions." Her reasoning in this case was based on the example of the United States Supreme Court. It did not have the power to enforce its own rulings, yet they were followed "because of public opinion and a general respect for the law." Above all she did not want an international army created to enforce World Court decisions because "mere force would

18. JR to Surles, January 15, 1938, Surles Papers; Harris, "Jeannette Rankin," pp. 257-58; Ronald Schaffer, "Jeannette Rankin, Progressive-Isolationist" (Ph.D. dissertation, Princeton University, 1959), pp. 214-216; Rankin, radio address, April 10, 1937 (quote), Folder X, Box 65, NCPW.

19. Harris, "Jeannette Rankin," pp. 170, 208, 265; Schaffer, "Jeannette Rankin," pp. 167-68.

not be able to save a lawless people from themselves."[20]

Rankin harbored similar reservations about the collective security potential first of the League of Nations and later of the United Nations. She believed that the debates in both bodies were based on "an adversary process and, hence, [were] inimical to the very ends" being espoused. Moreover, her views about the economic origins of modern warfare led to the conclusion that the UN was "controlled by countries with great military interests and expenditures" and so the possibility of peaceful settlement of disputes was rendered even more unlikely than earlier under the League when large power control had been less evident.[21]

## Rankin and Neutrality

Rankin considered the neutrality or arms embargo legislation of the mid-1930s the greatest political victory for pacifism of the interwar years. From her point of view, therefore, the 1934-1936 Nye Committee investigation had done more than cast a shadow over the munitions industry; it had also created additional support for neutrality legislation. There were three schools of thought about such legislation. Internationalists, those who urged cooperative action among nations to prevent war, hoped that the incorporation of presidential discretion into neutrality laws would promote American participation with the League of Nations in support of collective security; nationalists, those who wanted the United States to steer clear of commitments to other nations, wanted laws with no presidential discretion that might allow U.S. involvement in foreign wars; and pacifists who saw the

20. JR: UCB Oral History, pp. 97-99, 151; Schaffer, "Jeannette Rankin," pp. 224-25.

21. JR: UCB Oral History, pp. 150-51.

Schlesinger Library, Radcliffe College

*Rankin testifies before the House Naval Affairs Committee in 1939.*

neutrality legislation primarily as a means to cripple the munitions industry and thus further the cause of peace.[22]

It is not entirely clear from existing documents whether Rankin actually understood the difference between a "discretionary" and "nondiscretionary" arms embargo. Many pacifists seemed either confused or short-sighted on this issue of granting the president power to use discretion in applying neutrality legislation. Without it, the first neutrality bills tied the president's hands and made the United States the silent partner of totalitarian powers because, as in the case of the Spanish Civil War, he could not aid the liberal forces.[23] In this sense non-

22. Robert A. Divine, *The Illusion of Neutrality* (Chicago: University of Chicago Press, 1962), pp. 74-121.

23. *Ibid.*; Rankin, Armistice Day radio address, November 11, 1936, Folder X, Box 65, NCPW.

discretionary neutrality legislation was extremely nationalistic and contradicted many of Rankin's internationalist leanings.

Nonetheless, she and the NCPW were in complete agreement on this question. They both thought that "mandatory [that is, nondiscretionary] neutrality [legislation]" was a step ". . . in the process of passing from our futile 'freedom of seas' position to an ultimate collective system of justice and peace. . . ." Neither Rankin nor the NCPW appeared to understand that in the long run the rigid application of an arms embargo, regardless of the countries or issues involved, would not help them obtain their goal of world peace through international cooperation. Instead, like so many other sincere pacifists of the time, she even regretted that the original act of 1935 did not go further than it did to limit the president's powers of discretion. "It was," Rankin lamented on Armistice Day, 1936, "all that could be secured over the opposition of foreign interests and our own racketeers."[24]

## Rankin's Second Term

The way in which the United States entered World War II influenced many of Rankin's post-war foreign policy ideas. Pacifists of the 1930s feared that England wanted America to help preserve what remained of the British empire, and consequently many of them, including Rankin, opposed FDR's attempts to aid the English before the Japanese attack on Pearl Harbor. Rankin even questioned the possibility of a European war. She returned from Europe in the summer of 1937 convinced that despite the arms build-up in Italy and Germany there would be no war, "barring accidents," because both countries realized "there is nothing to be gained by bloodshed and destruction" and hopefully would "decide to cure their own economic troubles by friendly overtures rather than try to force their unwilling constituents into a much feared war."[25]

24. *Ibid.* (second quote from Armistice Day address); *Peace Action*, May, 1935, p. 1, NCPW, SCPC (first quote).

25. *Quote from Harris, "Jeannette Rankin," p. 267 from material not now in Rankin's papers.

Her pacifism had blinded her to the dangerously deteriorating condition of European diplomatic relations. Therefore she denounced Roosevelt's famous "quarantine" speech of October 5, 1937, as an attempt to condition the American people to accept increased military appropriations and ultimately to participate in "a holy war... by arousing fear of invasion." Such a war "would doubtless meet the favor of the munitions and shipbuilding companies and others because of its effect on the current depression," she wrote to Senator James Pope on October 27.[26]

After defeat of Ludlow's bill in Congress in January 1938, Rankin entered her last and most frantic stage of antiwar activity prior to American entrance into World War II. In quick succession she testified before Congressional committees against further naval appropriations, against recission of the nondiscretionary portions of the neutrality legislation, against the occupation of Greenland and Iceland, against the suggested fortification of Guam, against Lend-Lease, against the use of convoy patrols to protect Lend-Lease goods, against the Atlantic Charter, and finally, against the extension of the draft. During this same three-year period she attacked both President Roosevelt and Secretary of State Cordell Hull personally because of what she perceived to be their commitment to war as a resolution of international disputes.[27]

Frustrated by her lack of success on most of these issues and what she perceived to be lack of personal support for some of them on the part of the NCPW leadership, Rankin resigned from the organization in 1939 and decided to run for a second term in Congress as a Republican pacifist. Capitalizing on support from Senator Burton K. Wheeler, her influential family connections, the considerable peace sentiment in Montana, and the backing of labor and women she won against liberal Democrat

26. JR to Senator James P. Pope, October 27, 1937, Box 68, NCPW: JR Correspondence; Rankin, "Beware of Holy Wars," *World Outlook*, November, 1938.

27. Rankin letters to family members, 1941, Folder 7, Box 1, Rankin Papers; Harris, "Jeannette Rankin," pp. 274-94; Schaffer, "Jeannette Rankin," pp. 231-46.

Jerry J. O'Connell and in open opposition to a third term for Franklin Roosevelt.[28]

Back in Congress after a twenty-two year absence, Rankin found that many things had changed. Among other things, she was no longer the only national female legislator. There were five other women in the House and two in the Senate. Moreover, the tone and reputation of the peace movement had changed dramatically from what it had been before World War I. Instead of being part of a bipartisan Progressive Movement, it was now considered the bastion of reactionary Republicans, largely due to charges levied by New Deal internationalists against the activities of the America First Committee. Although she did not belong to this wealthy, noninterventionist organization, she did address some of its meetings and many of her friends contributed heavily to its treasury.

Ironically Rankin found herself convicted of conservatism, largely through guilt by association, at the very moment in her public career when she was forced to take stock of how far apart on socioeconomic issues she had drifted from her brother Wellington since 1916. Although he supported her second bid for Congress, their views and lifestyles now differed widely. For example, he lived in obvious wealth in Montana as one of the largest land owners in the country, while she cultivated an image of semi-poverty in Georgia. He ignored instances of personal suffering during the depression, while she toyed with the radical cures proposed by Francis E. Townsend and Upton Sinclair. He became a Christian Scientist, while she continued to ridicule all religion. He was embarrassed by their sister Edna's involvement in the birth control movement, while she encouraged such activities. Clearly Wellington had lost his liberal credentials during the interwar years, while Jeannette's had become more and more radical.

Undaunted by such changes on the national scene or in her private life, Rankin began her second term by immediately trying to defeat the pending

---

28. Smith, unpublished biography of Rankin, Chapter 17; Harris, "Jeannette Rankin," pp. 274-86.

Schlesinger Library, Radcliffe College

THE WORLD'S WHIPPING BOY?
The Evening Star, *Washington, D.C., February 11, 1938.*

Lend-Lease bill. Attacking Lend-Lease in the spring of 1941, she introduced one of her old and favorite ideas, the unlimited expenditures for a national defense perimeter extending "roughly from the Aleutian Islands to the Hawaiian Islands, then to the Panama Canal and then up to Maine and Labrador. . . ." Failing in this she attempted to attach an amendment to the Lend-Lease bill stating that

> Nothing in this act shall be construed to authorize or permit the President to order, transfer, exchange, lease, lend or employ any soldier, sailor, marine or aircraft pilot outside the territorial waters of the Western Hemisphere without specific authorization of the Congress of the United States.[29]

Insisting as never before that "people never make war; it is always governments," Rankin even redrafted, but did not actually introduce on the floor of Congress, her concept of eliminating war profits

29. Hollywood *Citizen News*, March 1, 1934, p. 1 (first quote); U.S. House of Representatives, 77th Congress, 1st Session, *Congressional Record*, Vol. 87 (Part One), p. 791.

by issuing emergency currency. She also proposed legislation against the draft and on November 18, 1941, introduced a resolution calling for a national advisory election on whether Americans wanted war. The attack on Pearl Harbor in December and the American declaration of war voided all her pending bills.[30]

Prior to Pearl Harbor her private letters indicate considerable optimism about preventing American entrance into the Second World War despite the passage of Lend-Lease and the proclamation of the Atlantic Charter. When military conscription was extended by only one vote at the beginning of August 1941, she confidently predicted to her mother and sister Mary that "Congress will never vote for war." Following the announcement of the Atlantic Charter later in the month she wrote her sister Harriett: "We have all been very curious to know what happened when Frankie D. and Winnie met in the ocean. While the little boys were playing in the ocean, we almost ruined our President. It required the most terrific political pressure to extend the draft. . . . I am feeling greatly encouraged, although many of the peace people are still anxious regarding the situation."[31]

In this same letter she went on to say that the sentiment in Congress was quite different from what it had been in 1917 "because we have such a large, active peace group and we work together against the war measures. I am one who feels very certain that we not come into this war at all. However, there are some who say they think the President will manage to get us in even if only for a short time." Similarly, a few days earlier she had told Wellington that "some Republicans think Roosevelt's desire to control will cause him to work harder to precipitate a war." As late as November 15, 1941, she wrote to members of her family complaining about the loss of life which would result from the convoy system that Congress had approved by another close vote. Nonetheless she still believed that the "opposition is stronger than

30. Harris, "Jeannette Rankin," pp. 289, 294.

31. JR to family members, Folder 7, Box 1, Rankin Papers.

ever and that on sending an expeditionary force, we can defeat the President.... so it will be some time before the President will decide actually to create the incidents that will get us into war."[32]

Even after the Pearl Harbor attack of December 7, Rankin inexplicably thought there would be a lengthy debate in Congress over whether to go to war, as there had been in 1917. So she left that same day to speak in Detroit only to return when she heard that Roosevelt had called a special session of Congress for the next day. Once again, as in 1917, Wellington urged her to vote for war. She finally stopped accepting his calls. This time she voted no alone and amid much criticism. Right after the vote on December 8 she finally talked with Wellington and he told her what she had not wanted to hear earlier: "Montana is 110% against you." Two days later her brother's secretary, Helena Stellway, wrote to tell her not to worry about his attitude, saying "at first Mr. Rankin was quite disturbed, but not now at all. He [has] said many kind things about you and said your vote was the one thing you could do, and that you would be admired for it."[33]

Such belated and second-hand consolation was of little help to Rankin as she sat in her Morris chair on the evening of her second historic antiwar vote—an act that made her the only member of Congress to oppose U.S. entrance into *both* World Wars. That fateful night of December 8 she simply made a gesture of despair with her hands and blurted out: "I have nothing left now except my integrity." Earlier that same day she had sent out an official explanation to her Congressional district. It read in part:

> I felt there were not enough facts before us...to justify such hasty action....I remembered the promise I had made during my campaign....I was thinking of the pledges I had made to the mothers and fathers of Montana. While I believed ...that the stories [about the attack on Pearl Harbor]...were probably true, still I

32. *Ibid.*

33. Smith, unpublished biography of Rankin, Chapter 18; Harris, "Jeannette Rankin," p. 294. For letters criticizing her second vote against war see: Folders 137-159, Boxes 8-9, Helena Stellway to JR, December 19, 1941, Folder 67, Box 4, all in Rankin Papers.

> believed that such a momentous vote, one which could mean peace or war for our country, should be based on more authentic evidence.... It may be right for us to enter the conflict with Japan, if so, it is my belief that all the facts... should be given to the Congress and the American people. So in casting my vote today, I voted my convictions and redeemed my campaign pledges.[34]

This statement was much less defensive than her 1917 one had been. Now Rankin made no attempt to justify her action in the name of public opinion, although as of the summer of 1941 ninety-five per cent of her mail from Montana constituents had been against going to war. At the time this was contrary to the national trend in public opinion. (Over fifty per cent of Americans polled in the spring and summer months consistently favored going to war against both Japan in the Pacific and Hitler in Europe.) It is possible that by December she realized that Germany's attack on the Soviet Union and Japan's seizures of French bases in Indochina in June and July dramatically transformed attitudes across the nation, even among Montanans, before the attack on Pearl Harbor. Rankins' attitude had not changed, however. On July 12 she insisted that "aid to Russia doesn't have the people's support" and she audibly hissed from the floor of the House when an appeal was made later in the fall for United States intervention when it looked as though the USSR could not withstand the German invasion. Despite Rankin's obdurance, by the beginning of December 1941, seventy per cent of Americans thought it was more important to aid England than to continue to keep out of the European theater. Likewise seventy per cent were willing to risk war with the Japanese

34. Harriet Yarrow to Patricia King, January 3, 1974 (recalling Yarrow's visit to Rankin on the evening of December 8, 1941), Yarrow Papers, Schlesinger Library; remarks by Judge Frances C. Elge at the Montana History Conference, Helena, Montana, November 5, 1977; form letter to constituents, December 7, 1941, Folder 70, Box 4, Rankin Papers.

rather than permit their unabated aggression in the Far East.[35]

From the start, therefore, the Congresswoman from Montana defended her solitary "no" vote on the grounds that "we did not need a declaration of war to defend ourselves and to protect the Phillipines, Guam, Wake and other possessions and to fight, defensively and offensively, any enemy who had attacked us. We DID need a declaration of war to send men to die in Europe, Africa and the Far East." Rankin also quoted a statement Winston Churchill had made to Parliament on January 28, 1942, *after* the United States had entered World War II. In it the Prime Minister made reference to his expectations after the Atlantic rendezvous with Roosevelt that the United States would enter the war in the Far East "even if not herself attacked ...and thus make final victory assured." Most of her responses to inquiries about her vote also included an ambiguous statement about preparing to channel war production "to promote the joy of right living for all the people" once the fighting was over. As during World War I she felt that "if women can become emotionally involved in production, they are going to be better prepared to take their part in planning a society in which satisfying human needs must be the determining factor."[36] Thus, she retained an abiding faith in women's postwar role in determining a more equitable distribution of wealth.

The lasting historical significance of her second vote against war, like the first one, lies in the way she defended it. Allying herself with revisionist historians like Charles Beard, Charles C. Tansill, and Harry Elmer Barnes, Rankin immediately began to build a case against the

35. Great Falls *Tribune*, July 12, 1941; conversation with Judge Frances C. Elge of Billings, Montana, March 1, 1977. Public opinion polls cited in Merrill D. Peterson and Leonard W. Levy, eds., *Major Crises in American History: Documentary Problems, 1865-1953* (New York: Harcourt, Brace and World, 1962), Vol. 2, pp. 448-49.

36. For standard replies by Rankin to those inquiring about her vote against World War II, see: Folders 72-165, Boxes 4-9, Rankin Papers, especially JR to Wilfred S. Ball, April 21, 1942, Folder 163 and JR to Rev. Harry Sutton, February 9, 1942, Folder 162.

administration's "back door" approach to war.[37] With the aid of Ralph Baerman she wrote and inserted a detailed defense into the *Congressional Record* exactly one year after her unpopular antiwar vote. Realizing that she had no chance for re-election, she stated publicly what many Republicans privately suspected.

She accused British imperialists of conspiring to bring the United States into the Second World War by convincing Roosevelt to impose economic sanctions "of ever-increasing severity" upon Japan. Before the Atlantic Conference, Rankin pointed out, FDR had been reluctant to enforce the various embargo provisions of the Neutrality Acts against Japan, but once he met with Churchill, the President no longer procrastinated. Although she never subscribed to the extreme revisionist view that Roosevelt knew in advance about the attack on Pearl Harbor, she did insist that "it [the attack] was anticipated by the administration."[38]

Rankin concluded these remarks in the *Congressional Record* in 1942 by returning to her belief that domestic reform was essential for a successful foreign policy. "The American people are willing to struggle for the 'four freedoms' but we realize that we must retain them at home if we are going to give them to others." Then she asked the question that is now so familiar to Americans in the wake of Vietnam and Watergate: "When are we going to get the full story...?"[39] As late as 1963 she still laid the blame for our entrance into World War II squarely on the British and American military establishment, saying:

> The Second World War vote came with even more of a shock to me than the First

37. Revisionist historians generally challenge official explanations about domestic or foreign events either by reinterpreting old data or by introducing recently uncovered facts. Rankin's revisionist ideas about World War I were discussed in the first segment of this article. For proof of her familiarity with the writings of famous revisionist historians like Beard and Barnes, see: 1963 John Board interview with JR, p. 54, Folder 204, Box 12, Rankin Papers.

38. "Some Questions about Pearl Harbor," *Congressional Record*, December 8, 1942, 77th Congress, 2nd Session, pp. 1-3.

39. *Ibid.*, p. 3.

> World War because I had been living in Washington and I knew that the military and everyone said we were not prepared to go to war. I couldn't see how they would deliberately go to war when they weren't prepared. I knew the military in the United States and England had controlled the military in Japan for years, not actually, but by influence. And, the people in Japan had tried over and over again to get rid of their military dictatorship, but each time they got about ready to get rid of them, in would come England and America to support the militarists. I knew that the militarists in Japan wanted to go to war and the United States and England didn't mind if they went to war.... That's why when they said Japan had dropped bombs ... I couldn't believe that it hadn't been instigated.... For two years after the bombs were dropped, we did absolutely nothing in the Pacific. We didn't send one gun or one boat to protect the Philippines. We did absolutely nothing. Japanese situation [*sic*] was created to force Congress to go to war with Germany. That was done to satisfy England's desire for us to go to war in Europe.[40]

## Her Post-War Views

By the time she recorded these words Jeannette Rankin had been out of the limelight for over two decades. During that time she completed her second term in Congress, alternately expressing boredom and discouragement with "this stupid war" that, in 1942 and 1943, seemed to be proceeding both badly and endlessly, according to her interpretation of Congressional opinion. In numerous letters to family, friends, and constituents Rankin lamented the suppression of antiwar criticism by the administration, the waste of life, especially in sea

40. 1963 Board interview with JR, pp. 52-53.

battles, and most important, the loss of social progress, justice, and democracy at home—all because of the "law of military necessity." In a typically progressive fashion she described war as "a breeder of hate and prejudice," adding: "I certainly feel sorry for the poor Jews, Negroes and colored people after this war."[41]

For a brief period she deluded herself with the hope that the female vote would defeat FDR in 1944 because women at home would see through the New Deal foreign policy more easily than those absentee voters away fighting the war. She also thought that women would respond to the revisionist idea that "we should clean our house at home before we accept responsibility for the rest of the world."[42] At one point in the fall of 1943 she wildly speculated that after "four or five more [such] devastating wars," women would

> get control of industry and not be merely workers at the bottom, but will control, and there will be so few men to protest that maybe by that time women will be willing to assert their primitive instincts for the reponsibility of the protection of the young, and do something about war.[43]

At those moments prior to the 1944 election, when she had to face the fact that American women had not protested the war effort to any great degree, Rankin fell back on her vicarious mentor Benjamin Kidd, whose book, *The Science of Power*, had been recently condensed into an article by a friend of hers. This condensation she recommended re-

---

41. JR to family members, 1942, Folder 7, Box 1, Rankin Papers; JR to Harriet Yarrow, September 25, 1943, Yarrow Papers; JR to Flora Belle Surles, September 5, 1942, Surles Papers.

42. JR to family members, 1943-1944, Folder 7, Box 1, JR to Mrs. Kenneth Hayes, June 19, 1943 (quote), Folder 167, JR to Katherine Blake, August 14, 1943, JR to Arthur Cranston, August 17, 1943, Folder 168, Box 9, all in Rankin Papers. Rankin considered running again in 1944 but did not for three reasons: 1) the war was not over; 2) Wellington opposed her candidacy; and 3) FDR did not withdraw from the presidential race as she thought he would because of bad health. See: JR to Surles, n.d. [probably summer, 1944], Surles Papers; JR to Libby, October 11, 1943, May 5, June 2, 1944, NCPW: JR Correspondence; JR to Abbie Crawford, August 14, 1943, JR to Mary M. Wright and Ann Denmler, October 11, 1943, Folder 168, Box 9, Rankin Papers.

43. JR to Ernestine Evans, October 14, 1943, Folder 168, Box 9, Rankin Papers.

peatedly to male and female correspondents in the summer of 1943 as the best theoretical means for mobilizing women against war. She remained convinced that Kidd's work was "the only thing in this man-made world that indicates that women have anything to contribute to our social organization." Because he flattered women, she thought they could be enticed "to use their power in outlawing war." At least once she facetiously referred to this idea as "gunpowder versus face powder." Months before the election, however, she also expressed serious doubts about mobilizing a female antiwar vote.

> I am still convinced that the women can prevent war if they put their minds on it. If the mothers cared as much for their sons as they do for their social position we would not have war. Alas, the parasitic life they have led has corrupted their emotional life.[44]

And, indeed, the masses of women failed to live up to Rankin's idealistic expectations in the 1944 election. Roosevelt's unprecedented fourth-term re-election made her even more pessimistic. "The Dictator's ... election means a continuation of war and deaths," she wrote on November 30, 1944. "A little longer to wait for a saner attitude of the people. The 'little longer' may be 'too long' for me." In fact, she had already decided that "we have been in continuous war; that we have these armistices; that the wars never settle anything because it [*sic*] is a method which does not settle problems." She also did not have any faith in postwar peace conferences unless they were attended by people who sincerely wanted peace. Her standard list of appropriate peace delegates consisted of the unlikely trio of India's Mohandas Gandhi, Lazaro Cardenas, the President of Mexico, and American labor leader John L. Lewis. Obviously she did not think FDR and other well known heads of state

44. JR to Elmer E.S. Johnson, David Morgan, Mr. and Mrs. Kistner, and Mr. Porter Sargent, all written on June 11, 1943, JR to Mrs. Edward Bixler and Mrs. A.C. Avery, Sr., June 12, 1943 (first two quotes), Folder 167, JR to Rosalie Gardiner Jones, August 17, 1943 (gunpowder quote). Folder 168, JR to Katherine Blake, August 14, 1943 (last quote), Folder 168, all in Box 9, Rankin Papers.

would do anything at such conferences except plan another war.[45]

Increasingly India became her model for obtaining peace and neutrality in the world. As early as March 1942 she had read Jawaharlal Nehru's autobiography, *My India, My America*. Then she became a life-long admirer of Gandhi's passive resistance tactics and before the end of 1942 was convinced that India's freedom was as important as the general outcome of World War II.[46] By the summer of 1943 she had elaborate plans for going to India and writing a work entitled, "India's Contributions to the Peace of the World." She even toyed with the idea of asking the Democratic administration to sponsor her trip in the interest of peace.[47]

In a letter to Ralph B. Baerman of the Institute for Christian Economic Action she detailed ideas that she would retain, but would never write extensively about, although she traveled to India over a half-dozen times between 1946 and 1971. The intervening years did not dampen the ardor Rankin initially expressed about both men and their country in 1942 and 1943 when, for the first time in her life, she felt like writing a "helpful" book.

> My idea was to try . . . to use India to hang my ideas of a peace organization in the U.S. on. As I have worked on the idea I have thought out several chapters. . . . For instance, one on what war is, then one on war in an economy of scarcity and in an economy of plenty, and the effect of scarcity of money, etc. And then in simple, straightforward language discuss neutrality as practised in this war and the necessity for a crystallized public opinion

45. JR to Yarrow, November 11, 30, 1944, Yarrow Papers (all quotes). Throughout the summer and fall of 1943 Rankin privately referred to Churchill and Roosevelt as "dictators" and to their peace conferences as "war conferences." See: JR to Mr. Gerald F. M. O'Grady, August 16, 1943, JR to Frances Sherrill and Arthur Cranston, August 17, 1943, Folder 168, JR to David Morgan, June 12, 1943, JR to Mrs. Edward Bixler, Mrs. Kenneth Hayes, Mr. Clifford J. Bernard, H.F. Tarlin, all June 12, 1943, Folder 167, JR to Rosalie Gardiner Jones, August 17, 1943, Folder 168, all in Rankin Papers.

46. JR to family, especially March 31, 1942, Folder 7, Box 1, Rankin Papers.

47. JR to Harry P. Harrison and Mrs. K.K. Spriggs, June 11, 1943, Folder 167, Box 9, Rankin Papers.

> to create a state of neutrality, and another chapter on the possibilities of defending America, and another on new education for a military establishment for defense only. Comparing Gandhi's organization with the possibility of organization in a country like the United States would make an interesting chapter on how to organize.[48]

Aside from supporting nationalism in India, her most strongly held foreign policy opinion during the course of World War II concerned China. In contrast to FDR, who took every occasion to insist that China was a major, stable ally, she correctly suspected that Chiang Kai-skek often played off the best interests of his own people to further his own. Rankin also firmly believed that the "Big Three" allied powers (England, America and the Soviet Union) should remove their troops from the Far East as soon as possible, because in the long run they would be "just as willing to sacrifice China as they are Japan and India—we must have Asia for the Asiatics."[49] Only then did she believe that peace could come to that part of the world. Following the end of World War II, Rankin did not articulate clear positions in public or private on foreign policy events until Vietnam. There are only passing references in her papers, for example, to the Korean conflict and the Cuban missile crisis.

In the last half of the 1940s she did some ranching in Montana, cared for her mother, who died in 1947, remodeled a second spartan house in Georgia and, most important, began to travel extensively abroad to study pacifist methods in other countries. These travels began in 1945 with a short trip to Mexico and then a world tour in 1946 which took her to India for the first of seven visits. She returned in 1949, 1951, 1956, 1959-1960, 1962,

---

48. JR to Ralph B. Baerman, June 11, 1943, Folder 167, Box 9, Rankin Papers. Although she did not write this book, her letters continue to contain many positive references to Gandhi's peace methods and to Nehru (whom she met in 1946). See: JR to Surles, January 1, 1947, Surles Papers; JR to Yarrow, January 20, 1953, Yarrow Papers; JR to family, 1952-53, especially May 29, June 1, October 1, 1952, Folder 9, Box 1, Rankin Papers; transcribed interview of JR by Hannah Josephson, JR: UCB Oral History, pp. 226-230.

---

49. JR to Yarrow, November 30, 1944 (quote), January 20, 1953, Yarrow Papers; JR to Libby, November 10, 1948, December 13, 1950, Folder VII, Box 68, NCPW: JR Correspondence; Great Falls *Tribune*, June 3, 1951; JR to Surles, June 6, 1961, November 6, 1962, Surles Papers; Harris, "Jeannette Rankin," pp. 311-26.

and for a last time in 1970-1971. She also traveled to Africa and Indonesia in 1953, South America in 1956, Ireland, Russia, and Turkey in 1962, Mexico in 1965, and Czechoslovakia in 1969. "I traveled around the world," she laconically explained in a 1972 interview, "and stayed long enough to know how the Americans were dominating underdeveloped countries."[50]

Once the Vietnamese conflict escalated she gave serious consideration to the idea of running for the House again, telling a close Montana friend and former associate in 1968 that she "wanted to go back to Congress to vote against a third war."[51] Given her checkered voting record following World War II, one can only speculate about which party she would have chosen to affiliate had illness not prevented her from running once again for Congress at the age of 88.

Rankin's intense dislike of FDR's foreign policy led her to support the candidacy of General Douglas MacArthur in 1944 on the grounds that he would give new life to the peace movement by rallying all the antiwar forces in the country. She justified this choice to her former boss and NCPW associate Frederick Libby by saying: "The peace movement must become a war movement before we can direct progress." Dumbfounded, Libby replied that he emphatically disagreed with her "catastrophic theory of progress."[52] In 1952 she expressed the opinion that voters really had no choice. She wrote her family from India that year indicating that although she was intrigued by her brother's support of Dwight D. Eisenhower, she was glad that she was not home because she might express a grudge against Ike for being a military man and thus "spoil Wellington's pleasure." By 1956, however, she had changed her mind about Eisenhower because he had ended the Korean War and seemed to be committed to preventing future conflicts. Since "Nixon has been the closest to Eisenhower and therefore knows the most about avoiding war," she supported him in 1960, expressing vague, un-

50. JR: UCB Oral History, p. 12.

51. Conversation with Judge Frances C. Elge, March 1, 1977.

52. JR to Libby, May 5, 1944, Libby to JR, May 17, 1944, NCPW: JR Correspondence.

Montana Historical Society

*Rankin during the postwar years: clockwise from top left, on her Montana ranch in 1952, as she appeared in the late 1960s, speaking in India in 1949.*

defined suspicions about the "young" John F. Kennedy.[53]

Because Lyndon Johnson was so identified in Rankin's mind with FDR, she voted for Barry Goldwater in 1964. Again, for unstated reasons, she considered Johnson more militaristic than Goldwater, who she appeared to think could not possibly be as reactionary as he had been portrayed by the Democrats. No longer harboring any illusions about Richard Nixon's ability to control the military-industrial complex, and still suspicious of the war-mongering history of the Democrats, she apparently voted for Nixon in 1968, but this is not confirmed. Her first choice had been Eugene McCarthy because "he is the only candidate who recognize[s] the influence of the military on our political situations." For some reason she believed that "the military [had] selected Humphrey as its candidate" and so she was left by this process of elimination with Nixon. When he did not immediately end the war in Vietnam, she accelerated her participation in antiwar demostrations and by 1972 was a staunch supporter of the George McGovern campaign. By this time, however, Rankin privately insisted that there was no difference between the two major parties and that she had never voted for a presidential candidate of whom she had entirely approved since women won the suffrage in 1920—except for Norman Thomas![54]

## Her Last Protest

Her final protest against war would not, therefore, be as a Congresswoman, but as an antiwar demonstrator. She had become a national symbol of the peace movement once again with the

---

53. JR to family, Folder 9, Box 1, especially May 29, July 19, August 1, 18, 30, September 3, October 1, 17, 25, 1952, February 21, 1953 (first quote); Ed Sanders interview of Rankin (on tape), February 19, 1971, Reel 2, Box 12, all in Rankin Papers; Great Falls *Tribune*, October 5, 1959 [second quote]; JR to Yarrow, January 20, 1953, December 14, 1956, December 16, 1961, Yarrow Papers; JR to Surles, June 31, 1961, November 6, 1962, Surles Papers.

---

54. Quotes from Harris, "Jeannette Rankin," p. 324; Merv Griffin interview of Rankin (on tape), February 18, 1971 and Sanders interview, Reel 2, Box 12, Rankin Papers; Kirkley, "Afternoon with Rankin," in JR: UCB Oral History, p. 150.

formation of the Jeannette Rankin Brigade in 1967. The years 1967-1973 were travel years for Rankin. In 1972 alone she crisscrossed the country several times, including once by car, in the company of John Kirkley, a young man who served as her traveling companion in these last years. One of the high points of all these personal appearances and television interviews came on January 15, 1968, when a coalition of 5,000 women under the banner of the Jeannette Rankin Brigade demonstrated against the war. Although the demonstration itself was peaceful, the Brigade later brought suit against the Capitol Police for not allowing them to march on to the Capitol grounds. In 1972 the Supreme Court ruled that the Brigade women indeed had been denied their First Amendment rights under an 1882 law forbidding all kinds of demonstrations on Capitol grounds. This decision now makes peaceful demonstrations possible in that area of Washington, D.C.[55]

It was a rather incongruous amalgamation of feminists, pacifists, hippies, rock bands, antiwar students and assorted radicals who coalesced around this tiny, old lady from Montana toward the end of her life. Never did she appear more happy or fulfilled, despite complaints from women friends of her age that she was being misled and exploited by a number of these various groups and individuals. She also revived her proposals for multiple-member Congressional districts and direct preferential election of Presidents. Rankin campaigned as vigorously for these domestic political reforms as she did for an end to war.[56]

Despite this public adulation by members of the peace and counter-cultural movements in the late 1960s and early 1970s (or perhaps because of it) Rankin privately expressed disillusionment with her life-long struggle for a world without war. "It's

55. Untranscribed conversations between Kirkley and Rankin, April 5, May 19-24, 1972, Reel 3, Box 12; Jeannette Rankin Brigade material, Folder 198, Box 12, all in Rankin Papers.

56. January, 1977 conversation with Norma Smith; Shulamith Firestone, "The Jeannette Rankin Brigade: Woman Power?" *Notes From The First Year: 1968*; JR to editor of the Athens *Banner-Herald* and Athens *Daily News*, November 12, 1971, JR to House to Senate of Georgia, October, 1971, Kirkley and Rankin, "Case for Direct Preferential Vote for President," n.d. (probably 1972), Ralph Nader, "Jeannette Rankin—Pioneer Congresswoman," *The Capital Times*, September 11, 1972, all in JR: UCB Oral History, pp. 156-59, 163, 173.

hard to push and push and push and never get anywhere," she told Norma Smith on April 10, 1971. In 1972 she privately noted that "The Peace movement just talks to itself." Moreover, she did not leave any money in her will to peace institutions or groups of any kind.[57] Publicly, she never let these indications of private doubts surface, but they were there nonetheless.

And so her long career ended as it had begun amidst a flurry of travel, public appearances, and extravagant statements about immediate withdrawal of troops from Vietnam and unilateral disarmament by the United States. Jeannette Rankin's pacifism was anything but passive, static, or moderate. Yet it was also not very sophisticated, as she herself apparently realized toward the end. It was one thing to have kept on the go and to have captured the limelight several times in one's life. It was entirely another matter to effect change. Hence the meaning of Rankin's life and foreign policy was more symbolic than practical. One California junior college professor summed up her importance to him in this way in 1971:

> Miss Rankin, I am much impressed by the fact that you have not lost sight of what really matters in life. You have never fallen prey to all of the nonsense which parades as truth. You are an idealist, an independent, a fighter—a woman of deep conviction, rare courage, and unquestionable honesty....
>
> What delights me about you, Miss Rankin, is that unlike many others who are also concerned with improving and enhancing the quality of life, you are very much aware that there are no enchanted isles to take refuge on; that maybe man will destroy himself within the next few years with the bomb, but as long as there is life there is hope that he will avoid this

57. Quotes are from Smith's unpublished biography of JR. Rankin once told an interviewer that the era in which she would have most liked to live would have been during the American Revolution. See: 1963 Board interview with JR, p. 60. While she refused to pay the tax on her telephone bill as a way of protesting the war she continued to hold stock in such companies that produced modern weapons of war as Boeing. See: financial folders 14, 15, Box 1, and 199, Box 12, Rankin Papers.

> possibility. You realize, as few others do, that man has a splendid future before him if he does not foolishly end it now. The main point, I would suggest, is that rather than resigning yourself to things as they are or lamenting the tragic condition of mankind, you are working for the kinds of social reforms which are needed if we are to revitalize our nation and its institutions. If mankind can be saved, it will be saved by people feeling and thinking and acting exactly as you are . . .
>
> Miss Rankin, your determined efforts to end the war in Vietnam and bring peace to the world, have rekindled in so many of us, a profound sense of faith and hope; your work on behalf of a better world, one free from hunger, poverty, racism, illiteracy, disease, overpopulation, and war, has done wonders to help mobilize the great moral and spiritual resources of people everywhere. As a gallant warrior for peace and justice, a woman troubled by the tragic social ills which blight the mind and spirit of man, you give us reason to believe in the future of America. It is on your ways that nations should be built, on truth first and freedom always.[58]

This junior college professor was twenty-four in 1971; Rankin was ninety-two. Perhaps the difference in their ages is the key to her symbolic significance. She was a member of a generation of women who, like Jane Addams, believed in a global society of peace at the turn of the century—one they conceived of "in terms of community and world housekeeping."[59] There has probably never been such an influential generation of American female pacifists. In retrospect it is obvious that their humanitarian goals far exceeded their means for

58. Jeffrey M. Elliot to JR, July 19, 1971, Folder 186, Box 11, Rankin Papers.

59. Elsie Boulding, *The Underside of History: A View of Women Through Time* (Boulder, Colorado: Westview Press, 1976), p. 657. Rankin once used very similar terms in a radio address on December 2, 1929 saying: "Women are house keepers. Government is house keeping for the nation." Folder X, Box 65, NCPW

achieving them. Nonetheless, they remain a source of inspiration, hope, and even yearning because theirs was a time when peace was perhaps more a reality than it can ever be in an age of escalating nuclear arms.

Montanans can be justly proud of Jeannette Rankin's contribution to this impressive group of women reformers—she added a unique and important western combination of common sense and idealism.

---

*This concludes Joan Hoff Wilson's study of Jeannette Rankin and American foreign policy.*

Schlesinger Library, Radcliffe College

# The Woman's Peace Party and The Moral Basis for Women's Pacifism

Linda Schott

At the beginning of August, 1914, Germany began a march to war that rattled the world for the next four years. At the end of that month in New York City, 1,500 women held a march of their own—a quiet, somber march embellished only by the mournful beat of muffled drums and a large white peace banner.[1] The contrast could not have been greater. Men marched to war; women marched for peace. And although everyone knew that some women accepted war as inevitable and that some men worked unceasingly for peace, society still tended to believe in a dichotomy of peaceful women and belligerent men. This dichotomy seemed so obvious to one group of women, in fact, that it was one of their primary reasons for founding the first separate women's peace organization—the Woman's Peace Party.

In the fall of 1914, two European suffragists, Rosika Schwimmer of Hungary and Emmeline Pethick-Lawrence of England, traveled through the eastern and midwestern United States, urging American women to do whatever they could to stop the European war. The urgency and conviction of their message soon sparked the interest of some of America's most prominent women. Thus as most Americans began to take refuge from the European catastrophe in the warm security of the Christmas season, leading women around the nation turned outward instead and began organizing a national peace demonstration. It was to be a demonstration by women only, not by established peace societies, for as Carrie Chapman Catt wrote Jane Addams, those societies "are very masculine in their point of view" and "have as little use for women . . . as have the militarists."[2] Addams concurred. Generally "men and women work best together on these public measures," she wrote, but in this crisis, "there is no doubt that the women are the most eager for action."[3] In December, Addams, the renowned social reformer and founder of Hull House, called a women's peace meeting.

Addams invited all women's clubs that had standing peace committees to meet in Washington, D.C., on January 10-11, 1915. The affiliations of the 3,000 women who attended reflect the breadth both of her appeal and of women's interest in peace. Both the International Woman Suffrage Alliance and the National American Women's Suffrage Association sent representatives, as did more broadly based women's organizations such as the National Council of Women and the General Federation of Women's Clubs. Also participating were groups defined by religion—the National Council of Jewish Women and the National Conference of Catholic Charities—and groups defined by occupation—the Women's Trade Union League, the International Congress of Farm Women, the National League of Teachers, and the League of American Pen Women. Women came representing the National Federation of Settlements, the Woman's Christian Temperance Union, and the National Association of Colored Women, and peace advocates of long standing came from the American School Peace League, the World Peace Foundation, and the American Peace Society. Even the Daughters of the American Revolution and the Society of Spanish-American War Nurses sent representatives.[4]

The peace meeting that these women attended became the organizational conference of the Woman's Peace Party and marked the beginning of the separate women's peace movement. Women had been active in the American peace movement since its beginning almost 100 years earlier, and though groups such as the WCTU and the National Council of Women had acknowledged peace as a women's issue for at least two decades, never before had women organized for peace separately from men. Why, in 1915, did women decide that working in sexually integrated groups was no longer satisfactory? The outbreak of the war in Europe certainly helps account for the timing of this choice, and the close contacts among professional and well-educated women—in the suffrage movement as well as in the various social reform organizations—probably provided the connections necessary to begin such an organization. Neither of these factors, however, accounted for the pervasive sense that peace was an issue of special concern to women. Why did women define peace as a women's issue, and how did this perspective influence women's activity in the peace movement?

Women's peace activity did not remain encompassed within one organization, but the WPP—especially in its post-1919 form as the United States branch of the Women's International League for Peace and Freedom—remained the heart of the women's peace movement.[5] The WPP-WIL's firm commitment to nonviolence and its equally strong commitment to social justice set it apart from the late nineteenth-century peace groups that emphasized international law and arbitration. The WPP-WIL more closely resembled the early nineteenth-century nonresistance movement that emphasized both peace and social reform. With this emphasis, it became one of the most effective and most thoroughly pacifist organizations during the 1920's and 1930's. Significantly, two of its leaders—Jane Addams and Emily Greene Balch—won Nobel Prizes for Peace.[6]

The leaders of the WPP-WIL were primarily white and middle-class, and the majority had been born in the 1860's, 1870's, and 1880's. They had grown to maturity in a time when women were constantly enlarging the so-called women's sphere—the activities and behavior considered appropriate to women. In the first half of the nineteenth century, women had few opportunities for higher education and usually spent their adult lives as wives and mothers, perhaps participating in women's groups and reform organizations at church. The women who became prominent in the WPP, however, led much less circumscribed lives. Of the leaders of the WPP about one-third did not marry, and almost all had college educations; a large number also had done graduate work.[7]

After finishing their educations, most of these women sought some kind of employment. Educated women as a group usually concentrated in professions that could be seen as extensions of women's traditional domestic occupations. The majority became teachers; of those who pursued other professions, most went into social work. Social work was an amorphous profession that included service in charity organizations, public health and recreational work, civic improvement, and work in social settlements.[8] It was from these two professions—teaching and social work—that most of the leaders of the women's peace movement emerged.

Although these women worked in the public sphere, their choice of profession determined that most of their day to day contact was with other women. Through those contacts they established strong friendships as well as effective networks for political action.[9] It was, then, a logical step for them to turn to these friends and colleagues when they decided to protest the war in Europe.

These contacts facilitated the initial organization process, but they were not the most fundamental reason for organizing separately from men. Rather, these women made this choice because of their overwhelming conviction that women's interest in and dedication to peace differed from men's. The organizers of the WPP based this conviction on their pervasive sense that men and women had fundamentally different moral values. Arguing primarily, although not exclusively, that women's moral values were socially conditioned rather than biologically determined, the leaders of the WPP repeatedly emphasized three basic beliefs: that women best understood the supreme value of preserving human life; that women were committed to providing each individual with the best possible quality of life; and that women insisted on resolving conflicts without severing relationships between individuals or nations. Generally speaking, they believed, men did not share these values.

Although the belief that men and women had different moral values was a standard nineteenth-century conviction, the particular emphases given it by women in the peace movement make it an enlightening historical precedent for the recent work of psychologist Carol Gilligan. In her book *In a Different Voice,* Gilligan shows that because women tend to be concerned more with responsibility, human relationships, and interdependence than with rights, rules, and independence, previous theories of moral development chart women as less developed morally than men. Gilligan hypothesizes not one linear course of moral development but two moral perspectives that eventually merge. The "ethic of care," generally associated with women, "rests on the principle of nonviolence—that no one should get hurt," while the "ethic of justice," generally associated with men, "proceeds from the premise of equality—that everyone should be treated the same." For mature moral development, Gilligan believes, both the male-associated ethic of justice and the female-associated ethic of care must converge "in the realization that just as inequality adversely affects both parties in an unequal relationship, so too violence is destructive for everyone involved."[10]

Gilligan's conception of mature moral development is essentially androgynous. So too was the conception of morality and society held by leaders of the WPP, although they did not use this term. Their policies and programs emphasized both their commitment to nonviolence and their commitment to social, political, and economic equality for all people.[11] They organized as a separate women's group, however, because they believed that at that point in history—the early twentieth century—most women exhibited a greater commitment to nonviolence than most men. However, they did not want to "feminize" morality and society by substituting female values for male values. They wanted instead to "humanize" society by fully integrating women and their distinctive values into the public sphere. If such integration occurred, they argued, society would decrease its reliance on violence.

Their argument differs crucially from—but is probably a logical extension of—the arguments that women in the late nineteenth century had used when criticizing aspects of the male sphere. The Woman's Christian Temperance Union, women's literary clubs, and some suffragists, for example, urged women to participate in the public sphere primarily in order to protect the home.[12] The leaders of the WPP, however, argued that women with their distinctive values must not only participate in the public sphere but also be integrated into it; and the desired outcome of this integration was not protection of the home but the creation of a humane, androgynous society.

In spite of this difference, however, the women of the WPP and the women of previous reform movements had in common a belief in a gender-linked perspective on social problems. Historians have tended to use this belief as evidence that these women fell short of a "genuine" feminism or an egalitarian critique of society.[13] For the women of the WPP, however, a gender-linked critique of society did not preclude a vision of equality. Rather, acknowledgment of, and even emphasis on, the differences between women and men led to a clear vision of a radically revised society based on sexual equality and peaceful human relations.

During the war years, a common theme reverberated among many of the leading women of the United States and Europe: women were a community united by a commitment to the inviolability of human life. Jane Addams introduced this theme at the 1915 organizational conference of the WPP. By organizing for peace separately from men, she told her audience, women "are expressing a conviction that we are sure is grounded in the soul of women all over the world, even in the women of the fighting nations."[14] The women of those fighting nations, as well as women in the United States, echoed Addams' statement. They acknowledged that war threatened their community, but they urged one another to "go beyond" faithfulness and devotion to their respective countries in order to "maintain true solidarity with the women of other belligerent nations." They stressed that women must remain united by their common "love of justice, civilization and beauty which are all destroyed by war" and their common "hatred for barbarity, cruelty and destruction, which accompany every war." And they succeeded. When peace came after four long years of struggle, the sense of community among these women had not diminished. They agreed that women were still "a single humanity." They would continue the struggle for a peaceful world, remaining united, "all women against all wars."[15]

What enabled this community to endure the war? Many of these women had cooperated internationally for women's suffrage, but their fervent and repeated descriptions of this community imply that they were united by more than a history of common action. What further united them was, in part, their moral opposition to war—what Addams called a conviction grounded in the soul of women. Perhaps because it was commonly understood and taken for granted, this moral position was not systematically articulated or examined. From occasional references to it, however, one can determine that it was woven from the three separate but closely related beliefs enumerated above: that nothing was more important than the preservation of human life, that each individual deserved the best possible quality of life, and that conflicts could and must be solved without severing relationships between individuals or countries.

First, many WPP members believed that nothing was of greater importance than the preservation of human life. Social reformer Lillian Wald, for example, stated that men reacted positively to the appeal to "die for their country." Women, on the other hand, saw the same appeal as a call to "go out to kill." Wald also pointed out that men seemed able to fight a war to "protect their homes" and "save their wives and children" without ever realizing that by fighting, they destroyed the homes and lives of other women and children.[16] In Wald's opinion, women could never be as short-sighted as men because they viewed all issues and problems from a perspective that gave the preservation of human life preeminence over all other concerns.

Jane Addams played an interesting variation of Wald's theme at the International Congress of Women in 1915. In her presidential address, Addams suggested that war occurred because "the appeals for the organization of the world upon peaceful lines have been made too exclusively to man's reason and sense of justice." Because reason was only part of the "human endowment," any workable peace plans must also utilize "emotion" and the "human urgings to foster life and protect the helpless." These qualities were not peculiar to women; rather, they were "universal desires" of which women had been the "earliest custodians."[17] Addams thus blurred the dichotomy of rational men and emotional women by deemphasizing emotion's connotation of irrationality, emphasizing instead women's longer experience as nurturers of human life. By doing so, she managed to diminish a distinction that had often been used to exclude women from the supposedly rational arenas of politics and diplomacy without diminishing women's special relationship to peace.

The second tenet in the WPP's opposition to war was the belief that each individual deserved the best possible quality of life. This concern was not new with the WPP. Women's reform activity had almost always focused on humanitarian issues, and WPP members probably brought this concern with them from previous reform work. Lucia Ames Mead, for example, had turned to the peace movement after long experience with the temperance movement. Thus when Theodore Roosevelt labeled the WPP "silly" and "base," Mead responded by vehemently criticizing his fondness for militarism and lack of humanitarianism. Apparently it was up to women, Mead wrote, to teach Roosevelt and other "hysterical critics" the enormous difference between "our theoretical enemies without" and "our very real foes of needless accident and preventable disease."[18] There was no doubt in Mead's mind that providing a decent quality of life should take precedence over preparations for war.

Other WPP members articulated similar indictments of what they saw as the wrong priorities of a society run by men. Jeannette Rankin, the first woman elected to the U.S. House of Representatives, was one of fifty representatives to vote against entry of the United States into World War I. Later, Rankin criticized men for being so concerned about commercial profit that they were unable to think, as women did, "in terms of human needs."[19] The Massachusetts writer Florence Guertin Tuttle also thought that men wrongly placed more value on material goods than on the welfare of their fellow citizens. Thus Tuttle urged women to "rebel against those hydra-headed forces controlling civilization"—men—"to whom motherhood and the preservation of exquisite relationships are as irridescent [sic] bubbles when weighed against material values."[20]

The desire to preserve "exquisite relationships" formed the third strand of the WPP's moral opposition to war. Tuttle, for example, suggested that because of women's relationship to children, they gained insight into how conflicts developed and how they could be resolved. Conflict among nations was no more surprising than conflict among family members; the only question was what method would be used to resolve that conflict. In the case of a family quarrel, one obviously would not sever the family tie. Similarly, Tuttle implied, one should not sever the ties between countries by going to war.[21]

In agreement with Tuttle, most WPP members believed that disputes should be resolved by discussion, not by war. Indeed, the first plank in the WPP's platform was for a "convention of neutral nations." This innovative alternative to war—specifically, to the continuation of the European war—was the creation of Rosika Schwimmer and a Wisconsin professor, Julia Grace Wales. As supported by the WPP, the plan called for representatives of the neutral nations to meet continuously in order to mediate the conflicts among the belligerent nations.[22] It provided a method, never before tried, for restoring and maintaining relations among nations in the face of seemingly irreconcilable conflicts.

These three beliefs formed the moral opposition to war that helped bind women from around the world into a community of pacifists. They were also the basis for the WPP's vision of a peaceful, androgynous society, since the WPP believed that such a society could be created only if women and their values were integrated into the public sphere. This belief reflected two related analyses of society: that a society dominated by men inevitably tended to be violent and destructive; and that for a society to be well-balanced and healthy, both sexes—the complementary male and female forces—must be equally active in public life.

It seemed to many WPP members that men had failed as the leaders of society. The Pennsylvania branch of the WPP, in a message to the women of Germany, noted that the European war had revealed "that our civilization rested on greed, violence and the lust of conquest." Incredulous, they asked, "Was that the best civilization man could build?" If so, "Then let woman awaken and help build the temple of the Future upon the new foundations of human sympathy, brotherly love and goodwill to all mankind."[23] Similarly, the New York City teacher Katherine Devereux Blake angrily demanded that women "be permitted a voice in the government, so that the gigantic folly and stupidity of war may end, and the money now wasted in military operations may be spent on education and works for the comfort of humanity."[24] For these angry, disillusioned women, the civilization created by men was a miserable and dangerous failure. They demanded that women be given an opportunity to rebuild civilization, using their own moral values as the new foundation.

The criticism of men and the society they had created was not always so explicit. WPP members sometimes emphasized that the horror of a society at war had been caused by a so-called sin of omission, not commission. In other words, it was the omission of women from the public sphere, not the conscious commission of error by men, that had led society to war. Although this position was implicitly critical of men—for it was they who limited women's public role—its tone was less condemnatory and more compromising than that of the more explicit criticism. The New Hampshire author Agnes Ryan, for example, wrote, "It is not merely that I believe in women. I believe in men too, that is, I believe in the human race." Society's problems developed, however, because "we have not had the human race dealing with the chief affairs of life at all; we have had only half of it, the fighting, hunting, sporting male half." To balance the characteristics of men, society needed "the other half—the half that has borne in its body the human race and fed it and nursed it and washed it and dressed it . . . the half that has taught it from the cradle to the grave that the strongest thing in the world is love."[25]

Ryan's theme—the complementarity of men and women—was a common one. At the annual conference of the WPP in 1916, Laura Clay, a suffragist and temperance worker from Kentucky, told the applauding audience that "the war in Europe is an evidence of what must happen when the duality of human nature is forgotten, and only the masculine mind, with all of its activities, even the excesses of those good qualities which are developed in man, have been unbalanced and uncorrected by the feminine half of humanity."[26] Florence Guertin Tuttle made the same point even more strongly by using the simile of reproduction. Just as man "cannot produce life alone," she wrote, "so he cannot create a civilized civilization alone. He can effect only a sterility—the familiar abortion of peace."[27] Tuttle cautioned, however, that women were no more able than men to stop war by themselves. The only hope lay in "intelligent cooperation" between the two sexes.[28]

The call for "intelligent cooperation" between women and men necessarily involved support for women's suffrage. The WPP consistently gave that support. The party platform included a plank demanding "the further humanizing of governments by the extension of the franchise to women," and many WPP members belonged to suffrage associations. But the WPP wanted more than voting rights for women. It also demanded that women have a voice in "all courts of high debate—within the home, the school, the church, the industrial order, and the state."[29] The New York City branch, one of the more radical branches of the WPP, articulated these demands most specifically. It demanded that women's citizenship be unaffected by marriage, that women and men have equal opportunities in "industry, professional schools, professions and commerce, including the control of capital and credit," and that wives and husbands share equally the responsibilities of the home, thus "abolishing the common law conception of a wife as a chattel, owing personal services . . . in exchange for her necessaries."[30]

The WPP's demand that women be integrated into the public sphere grew out of the belief that women's approach to a wide variety of social issues as well as their dedication to a peaceful world differed from men's. This persuasion was not based, at least not in any specific way or to any large extent, on the belief that women were "naturally"—that is, biologically—more peaceful and more moral than men.[31] The closest they came to claiming a biological basis for these moral differences was in their discussion of the sacrifices that women made by bearing children. The past president of the National

American Woman Suffrage Association, the Reverend Anna Howard Shaw, for example, poignantly described the risk of death that accompanied every pregnancy and the years of care and attention that mothers devoted to their children. She did not claim, however, that the biological act of giving birth caused women to oppose war. Rather, Shaw believed that women opposed war because it destroyed the products of their labor—their children.[32]

WPP members did emphasize, on the other hand, that the social experiences of women and men had caused them to have different ideas on war and peace. Addams assured the audience at the 1915 organizational conference that "I do not believe that women are better than men—even in the suffrage societies and suffrage debates I have never maintained this." But, Addams added, "there are things upon which women are more sensitive than men, and one of these is the treasuring of human life." Addams did not believe that this greater sensitivity was innate in women, but that women had developed it because they had "been responsible for the care of children and the aged and all that class which needed especial care."[33] In other words, Addams believed that the social role traditionally assigned to women—that of nurturer—had caused them to understand better than men the paramount value of human life.

This belief in women's different moral priorities thus provided much of the motivation for establishing a separate women's peace organization. That organization—the WPP and its successor, the WIL—then developed policies consistent with those moral principles. These policies can be divided into two categories: those relating to peace and those relating to broader issues of social justice.[34]

At the organizational conference, WPP members adopted a platform that formed the general basis of its policies throughout the war. They began by calling for an immediate convention of neutral nations. They hoped that such a convention would open discussion of the differences among the belligerents and lead to a quick, mediated compromise instead of a protracted war with both sides seeking total victory. Although this plan did not receive official support from the United States government, it did attract the backing of auto magnate Henry Ford. Unfortunately, Ford's support—in the form of money, a chartered ocean liner to carry the American delegation to the conference, and a call to "get the boys out of the trenches by Christmas," only a month away—led to ridicule. In spite of these problems, the conference opened on January 26, 1916, in Stockholm. Throughout that year it gradually gained prestige, but when Germany resumed unrestricted submarine warfare in February, 1917, Ford withdrew his financial support and the hope for mediation died in almost everyone.[35]

The WPP also called for "the limitation of armaments and the nationalization of their manufacture."[36] Believing that increased defense spending heightened rather than lowered the risk of war, WPP-WIL members supported plans for gradual and total disarmament—sometimes unilateral—throughout the 1920's and 1930's. They also argued that munitions manufacturers profited from war, and in the 1930's WIL Executive Secretary Dorothy Detzer almost single-handedly prompted the congressional investigations of that industry. The WPP platform also specified that the "economic causes of war" should be removed, thereby acknowledging not only that war is profitable for some individuals but also that economic inequality between nations could actually lead to war. Accordingly, throughout the next two decades, the WPP-WIL opposed economic imperialism as well as trade restrictions.

The other planks in the platform specified various ways to eliminate "militarism" from the United States and the world. These included the "education of youth in the ideals of peace," the "democratic control of foreign policies," extension of the vote to women, the substitution of "Law for War," a "Concert of Nations" to replace the "Balance of Power," and the "substitution of an international police for rival armies and navies."[37] As WPP members became more sophisticated in their understanding of peace, however, the WPP often moved away from these original positions to more thoroughly pacifist ones. For example, although the WPP approved the concept of an international police in January, 1915, by January, 1916, the WPP had completely withdrawn that approval. Fanny Garrison Villard expressed the WPP's new position, "If it is wrong to kill for one purpose, it is wrong to kill for another." The WPP accordingly passed a resolution that opposed the use of force for any reason, even self-defense.[38] This resolution signaled the WPP's commitment to nonviolence—a commitment that remained firm throughout the 1920's and 1930's—

and provided the basis for many WIL members' opposition to membership of the United States in the League of Nations.

In addition to nonviolence, the WPP was also committed to the social and economic equality of all people. Because of their previous involvement in social reform movements, many WPP members brought to the peace movement a complex understanding of the links between violence and inequality. Years before the Great War began, for example, Jane Addams had analyzed the lynching of black men as the result of racial and sexual discrimination and class bias.[39] During the war, WPP members necessarily concentrated primarily on anti-war activities, but they also demonstrated their commitment to equality, especially racial equality. The Pennsylvania branch discussed ways of integrating black women into its organization and recorded its opposition to the racist film *The Birth of a Nation*. And when the WPP-WIL selected its delegates to the International Congress of Women in 1919, Jane Addams insisted that the black writer and activist Mary Church Terrell be retained as a delegate even when the government refused to give passports to any more than thirteen members out of a delegation of thirty-five. At the Congress itself, Terrell testified to the "breadth of view and the generosity of heart manifested by the other delegates" and succeeded in having passed unanimously a resolution that opposed discrimination on the basis of "race, color, or creed."[40] During the 1920's and 1930's, the WIL became even more involved in the struggle for racial equality—constantly supporting anti-lynching legislation, fighting the segregation of public facilities, and protesting the United States' economic imperialism toward nonwhite nations. It also tried to lessen economic inequality through the support of organized labor, with especially close ties to the Women's Trade Union League.

The WPP-WIL policy of promoting racial and economic equality was directly related to its members' moral commitment to providing each individual with a good quality of life; similarly, WPP-WIL pacifism was directly related to its members' belief in the supreme value of preserving human life and human relationships.

The goals of the WPP differed crucially from the goals, as we currently understand them, of other women's reform groups. Those groups urged women to participate in the public sphere in order to reform social conditions that might endanger the welfare of the home. WPP members, on the other hand, worked to integrate women and men and their respective values into the public sphere. They hoped this integration would transform a male-dominated society into an androgynous society that would abjure violence because its use would conflict with the greater value that such a society would place on human life.

The primary reason the WPP developed this more radical vision was the nature of the problem it attacked. The WPP organized to abolish war.[41] To many men and women, war was an internationally accepted means of settling conflict between nations, but to members of the WPP, war was simply the deliberate destruction of human life. Human life was more important than any principle or national interest; therefore war was not an acceptable means of settling international conflicts. Because the WPP identified men with the acceptance of war and women with its rejection, the only logical method of abolishing war was to integrate women into the previously male-dominated public sphere. The WPP believed that its goal, unlike the goal of other women's reform groups, would be achieved only through a basic restructuring of society.

One should not overemphasize the differences between the WPP and other contemporary women's reform organizations, however, because their similarities are more striking. Historians have stressed that most women's reform movements grew out of the particular concerns of women. Barbara Epstein has called women's work for temperance "the politics of domesticity," and Karen Blair has characterized women's club activity as "domestic feminism." Jill Conway and William Chafe have each argued that women's work for peace, suffrage, and other reforms developed out of the traditional view of femininity. Finally, in her work on the WPP, Barbara Steinson has argued that women based their activity on the "ideology of nurturant motherhood."[42]

All of these interpretations, however, point out that women reformers did not advocate women's activity in order to achieve equality between the sexes. Although true, this observation is not comprehensive. Steinson, Chafe, and Conway criticize women reformers for not understanding that basing their activity on a gender-linked view of social problems undermined any possibility of true sexual equality.[43] In the WPP, however, such a gender-linked view did lead to a vision of a humane society in which equality for all people was an integral part. The failure of that vision to materialize was due less to faults in the theoretical basis for women's action and more to the powerful, structural barriers of a patriarchal society.

Blair and Epstein are far less critical of these women reformers, but diminish their importance, probably inadvertently, by interpreting them as moving toward, but not reaching, "genuine" feminism.[44] Such genuine feminists were, however, a definite minority during the late nineteenth and early twentieth centuries. To judge all women reformers against this standard, then, is ahistorical and leads us to oversimplify and underestimate the actual power of their social critique. The women of the WPP—and probably other women reformers as well—were morally committed to the creation of a peaceful and just society. By acting on this commitment as social workers and specifically as pacifists, they mitigated the injustices of an industrializing society and projected an ideal of nonviolence on a belligerent land. To emphasize that these women failed to transcend the traditional ideas of domesticity and womanhood does not do them justice. I feel it is more historically correct to emphasize that they sought the reform of a society that denigrated their moral priorities—the preservation and quality of human life and human relationships.

## NOTES

1. See C. Roland Marchand, *The American Peace Movement and Social Reform, 1898-1918* (Princeton: Princeton Univ. Press, 1972), Ch. 7.

2. Carrie Chapman Catt to Jane Addams, December 14, 1914, Carrie Chapman Catt papers, box 4, Library of Congress, Washington, D.C.

3. Addams to Catt, December 21, 1914, Woman's Peace Party papers (microfilm), reel 12.17, Swarthmore College Peace Collection, Swarthmore, Penn. Hereafter referred to as WPP papers.

4. Compiled from "Roll of Charter Members" and list of the Co-operating Council at the Organizational Conference, January 10-11, 1915, WPP papers, reel 12.17.

5. I shall use the designation WPP-WIL when discussing information or policies of both groups or to identify the group during its transition from the WPP to the WIL in 1919. In 1919, a group of the most radical pacifists, led by Fanny Garrison Villard, split from the WIL to form the Women's Peace Society. In 1921, two members of the WPS—Caroline Lexow Babcock and Elinor Byrns—led the organization of the Women's Peace Union of the Western Hemisphere. Neither of these groups attained much influence. The WPU worked steadily throughout the 1920's and 1930's for a constitutional amendment that would define war for any purpose as illegal and remove the government's ability to prepare for

or wage war. The WPS stressed total nonresistance and spiritual pacifism over political work or economic analysis. In 1924, Carrie Chapman Catt organized the National Committee on the Cause and Cure of War. Catt invited representatives of the major women's organizations to an annual conference on peace, hoping to consolidate the peace sentiment of women who shied away from the reputed radicalism of other women's peace organizations. This group met annually for the next twelve years, but because of its format, it never became much more than a vehicle for discussing theories and strategies and providing mutual support.

6. For a general history of the peace movement between the wars, see Charles Chatfield, *For Peace and Justice: Pacifism in America, 1914-1941* (Knoxville: Univ. of Tennessee Press, 1971).

7. This information is compiled from biographical information on twenty-seven leaders of the WPP-WIL: eight never married, twenty-three attended college or a female seminary, and ten pursued graduate work.

8. Joyce Antler, "The Educated Woman and Professionalization: The Struggle for a New Feminine Identity, 1890-1920," Diss. State University of New York at Stony Brook 1977, pp. 381, 397.

9. For an example of how these friendships and networks operated, see Blanche Wiesen Cook, "Female Support Networks and Political Activism: Lillian Wald, Crystal Eastman, Emma Goldman," *Chrysalis*, No. 3 (1977), pp. 43-61.

10. Carol Gilligan, *In a Different Voice: Psychological Theory and Women's Development* (Cambridge: Harvard Univ. Press, 1982), pp. 173-74.

11. I am using the term "androgynous" here to characterize my interpretation of the beliefs of the WPP leaders: that the sexes had different moral priorities and that they could be integrated into society without destroying the integrity of either priority. It was society, not individuals, that the WPP leaders envisioned as uniting the characteristics of both sexes.

12. On the WCTU, see Ruth Bordin, *Woman and Temperance: The Quest for Power and Liberty* (Philadelphia: Temple Univ. Press, 1981); and Barbara Epstein, *The Politics of Domesticity: Women, Evangelism, and Temperance in Nineteenth-Century America* (Middletown: Wesleyan Univ. Press, 1981). Bordin notes that the WCTU soon moved beyond "home protection" to a more comprehensive social critique. See also Karen Blair, *The Clubwoman as Feminist: True Womanhood Redefined, 1868-1914* (New York: Holmes and Meier, 1980); and Aileen Kraditor, *Ideas of the Woman Suffrage Movement, 1890-1920* (New York: Columbia Univ. Press, 1965).

13. I discuss these historiographical differences in more detail in the last section of this paper (see footnote 42, below).

14. Minutes of the Organizational Conference, WPP papers, reel 12.17.

15. "Address of the French Women to the German Women," *Four Lights* (June 12, 1919), WPP papers, reel 12.19.

16. "Women and War," 1915, Lillian Wald papers, Manuscript Division, New York Public Library, New York, N.Y., pp. 2-3.

17. Report of the International Congress of Women at the Hague, 1915, WPP papers, reel 12.19, p. 6. Addams later blurred the issue further by arguing that men were emotional—easily excited—on the question of preparation for military defense. See Addams' testimony before the Committee on Military Affairs of the House of Representatives, January 13, 1916, WPP papers, reel 12.18, pp. 5-7.

18. "Woman's Peace Party Answers Roosevelt," n.d. [1915], papers

of the Massachusetts Branch of the WPP (microfilm), reel 12.22, Swarthmore College Peace Collection, Swarthmore, Penn.

19. Speech before the House of Representatives, "Woman Suffrage," January 10, 1918, Jeannette Rankin papers (microfilm), reel 78.3, Schlesinger Library, Radcliffe College, Cambridge, Mass., pp. 1-2.

20. "Women and Reconstruction," Chapter 1 of "Women and World Problems," n.d. [pre-1919], Florence Guertin Tuttle papers, Sophia Smith Collection, Smith College, Northampton, Mass., pp. 7-8 of irregularly numbered manuscript.

21. Chapter 1 of "Woman and Peace," n.d. [pre-1919], Tuttle papers, p. 5.

22. Platform of the WPP, reprinted in Marie Louise Degen, *The History of the Woman's Peace Party* (Baltimore: Johns Hopkins Univ. Press, 1939), p. 41. For a description of this conference of neutrals, see Chatfield, pp. 18-19.

23. "Message to our German sisters in their sorrow, sent with a gift of milk," n.d. [1919], Hannah Clothier Hull papers (microfilm), reel 75.1, Swarthmore College Peace Collection, Swarthmore, Penn.

24. Katherine Devereux Blake, *Women and War* (National Women's Suffrage Publishing Co., Inc., 1917), p. 2.

25. "Smouldering Fires," 1918, Agnes Ryan papers, Schlesinger Library, Radcliffe College, Cambridge, Mass., pp. 1-2.

26. Minutes of Mass Meeting, January 9, 1916, WPP papers, reel 12.17, pp. 26-27.

27. "An Omission of Diplomacy," n.d., Tuttle papers, p. 4.

28. "Women and Reconstruction," Tuttle papers.

29. Platform of the WPP, reprinted in Degen, p. 40.

30. Program, New York City Branch, 1919, WPP papers, reel 12.21, p. 1.

31. Patrick Geddes and J. Arthur Thomson had hypothesized such biological differences between the sexes, suggesting that differences between male and female cell structure caused women to be passive and peaceful and caused men to be energetic and belligerent (*The Evolution of Sex* [London, 1889]). Geddes and Thomson were, of course, writing before the scientific community understood genetics and endocrinology. Jane Addams was familiar with this theory; no doubt other WPP members were also. For a summary and evaluation of the work of Geddes and Thomson, see Jill Conway, "Stereotypes of Femininity in a Theory of Sexual Evolution," *Victorian Studies*, 14 (1970), 47-62. I disagree with Conway's belief that Addams totally accepted this biological explanation of women's nature.

32. Minutes of the Organizational Conference, WPP papers, reel 12.17, pp. 28-29. This position was extremely common among WPP members.

33. Minutes of the Organizational Conference, WPP papers, reel 12.17, pp. 17-19.

34. My current work provides a more comprehensive discussion of these policies (doctoral dissertation, in progress, Stanford University).

35. See Chatfield, pp. 18-19. See also Barbara Kraft, *The Ford Peace Ship* (New York: Macmillan, 1978).

36. Platform of the WPP, reprinted in Degen, p. 41.

37. Degen, p. 41.

38. Minutes of Sessions 3 and 4 of Annual Meeting, January 9, 1916, WPP papers, reel 12.17.

39. Jane Addams, "Respect for Law," *The Independent* (January 3, 1901), pp. 23-27.

40. Minutes, 1915-17, Pennsylvania Branch, WPP papers, reel 12.20;

Report on Zurich Conference, 1919, Mary Church Terrell papers (microfilm), reel 21, Library of Congress.

41. Platform of the WPP, reprinted in Degen, p. 40.

42. See Epstein; Blair; Jill Conway, "The Woman's Peace Party and the First World War," in *War and Society in North America*, ed. J. L. Granatstein and Robert D. Cuff (Toronto: Thomas Nelson & Sons, 1971), pp. 52-65; Jill Conway, "Women Reformers and American Culture, 1870-1930," *Journal of Social History*, 5 (Winter 1971-72), 164-77; William Chafe, *Women and Equality: Changing Patterns in American Culture* (New York: Oxford Univ. Press, 1977); Barbara J. Steinson, "The Mother Half of Humanity: American Women in the Peace and Preparedness Movements in World War I," in *Women, War, and Revolution*, ed. Carol R. Berkin and Clara M. Lovett (New York: Holmes and Meier, 1980), pp. 259-84. See also Barbara Steinson, *American Women's Activism in World War I* (New York: Garland, 1982).

43. See particularly Steinson, "Mother Half," p. 276; Chafe, p. 38; Conway, "Woman's Peace Party," p. 52; and Conway, "Women Reformers," p. 174.

44. See particularly Blair, pp. 107-08, and Epstein, pp. 132-33, 147.

# The "Womanpower" Campaign: Advertising and Recruitment Propaganda during World War II

Maureen Honey

> For waging psychological warfare, our informational weapons have not been as highly developed as the fighting machines of the armed forces . . . we, in the information field, are rapidly falling behind the Army. There cannot be total war effort unless the informational weapons at hand are properly used . . . we have the brains, the experience, the coast-to-coast polling machines; we know the people, know how to make them read; know how to plan huge informational efforts . . . and know how to coordinate every form of media.[1]
>
> Chester LaRoche, 1943

This paean to the persuasive abilities of American advertising was made by Chester LaRoche, President of the War Advertising Council (W.A.C.), and it indicates the important role advertisers played in supporting government wartime campaigns, including the drive to bring women into defense jobs. Established to save advertisers from bankruptcy at a time when few consumer goods were available, the W.A.C. formed close ties with the government to promote the war effort.[2] By selling the war to the American public, advertisers could perform an important service both for businesses manufacturing war materials through keeping brand names before the public eye, and for government agencies through persuading the public to make needed sacrifices in wartime. One of the results of their efforts was the creation of an ideological framework for the employment of women in male-identified blue-collar jobs, a framework which simultaneously acknowledged that women were capable of filling jobs requiring "male" characteristics and preserved essential features of the feminine role. While the ways in which wartime ideology mediated this contradiction have been outlined by others, the fact that the war was followed by one of the most reactionary periods in American history is, at first glance, such a puzzling phenomenon that the question of how employment of women in male jobs reinforced traditional gender roles warrants further consideration.[3] By focusing on some key themes used by advertisers to mobilize the civilian population, we can better understand why the war produced a narrowing rather than an expansion of women's sphere.[4]

Images of women war workers in part grew out of government policies which stated that their role as wage earners was a temporary one, a view based on inaccurate assumptions about the motivations of women entering war production and on a more accurate assessment about the desires of businessmen to employ them only for the duration of the war.[5] We find, therefore, many advertisements which implied that female defense workers had not abandoned home responsibilities, nor their aspirations to be full-time homemakers. Women in factory overalls were frequently portrayed in the home doing laundry or cooking meals. Soap and home appliance manufacturers, who devoted much space to the recruitment campaign, were particularly likely to use this image in promoting their products and made it clear that women were bearing a double burden in wartime.[6] A Westinghouse advertisement, for example, congratulated a married aircraft worker for both building planes and running a home (January 1943). Similarly, Eureka Vacuum Cleaners described a soldier's mother making gas masks as "a two-job woman, running a house for Dad O'Rourke of a morning, and making gas masks on Eureka's 4-12 shift" (November 1943).

While such traditional images of women were partially based on the view that war work was an aberration borne out of necessity, much of the conservative impulse that lay behind postwar ideology arose from larger issues with which the propaganda campaign concerned itself. One of these was the decision to build morale through showing women as home front soldiers who could competently manage things and keep the machinery of industry moving smoothly until men returned. As LaRoche counseled Washington: "[We must encourage] the development of a militant spirit—a desire to excel on the Home Front. We want more than just favorable compliance. We want zeal, enthusiasm, and individual

*Figure 1.* *"Molly Pitcher, 1944." Pennsylvania Railroad, October 1944,* Saturday Evening Post.

initiative that will raise the standard of the whole effort. *We Need Home Front Heroes*"[7] [emphasis added]. Because the role of women in the economy was so vital, they became the symbol of this militant spirit and the model for proper civilian attitudes. An advertisement by Kraft is representative of this approach. It shows a mother pitching hay while her daughter drives a tractor with the caption: "Heroines . . . U.S.A." The text reads: "Always on our dairy farms, women and girls have had plenty of chores to do. . . . But what they are doing *now* would amaze you" (July 1944). This advertisement is designed to attract women into farm work,

*Figure 2. "When you've done your bit for Uncle Sam. . . ." Maxwell House Coffee, March 1944,* Saturday Evening Post.

one of the government's major campaigns in the summers of 1943 and 1944. At the same time it glorifies women's work as heroic service to the nation. Other tributes to women praised them for their efficiency, intelligence, and their uncomplaining job performance. Bell Telephone, for instance, labeled its operators "Soldiers of Service"; Crosley referigerators applauded the "resourcefulness and ingenuity of American women" (February 1944); and Eureka proclaimed "You're a Good Soldier Mrs. America" (January 1943). Advertisers identified women's work as female military service, equivalent to the service men were rendering overseas. But rather than viewing women as equally entitled to and qualified for the jobs normally held by men, advertisements portrayed war workers as indispensable helpmates, equally shouldering the burdens of war. Bibb Manufacturing pictured women and men marching with determination toward victory (March 1943); Arvin Manufacturing declared that "Women are doing their part to help win the war . . . working shoulder to shoulder with men" (June 1943); and an optical company praised women who "fight beside their men" (May 1944).

Such figures too evoked an image of strong women who nonetheless stayed within the homemaker role. They represented a capable, supportive, and stoic partner who "kept the home fires burning" until men could resume their rightful place. By working for country,

*Figure 3. "Uniform . . . Slacks . . . or Kitchen Apron." Eureka Vacuum Cleaner Co., April 1943,* Saturday Evening Post.

sweetheart, husband, or brother, women who stepped into men's shoes were doing so as helpmates and thus stayed within the boundaries of acceptable female behavior. If men needed women to rivet airplanes and build bombers, they would obligingly don goggles and overalls. As portrayed by propagandists, then, the motivation for women in war jobs was not money or status or job security, but patriotism and love.[8]

A technique which minimized the threat these egalitarian images posed to traditional feminine norms was the use of historical models which placed war work in a context of female loyalty and support. As a result, Revolutionary War heroines such as Molly Pitcher and Dolly Madison were resuscitated as the foremothers of Rosie the Riveter [Figure 1]. Advertising made it appear that the kind of roles women were playing had a long tradition in American history and were a valuable part of our heritage. For example, an ARMCO advertisement refers to a female truck driver as "a 'covered wagon' girl": "'I got a job driving a truck when Paul went across. I'm hauling the stuff they fight with.' . . . Hers is the spirit of the women who reloaded the long rifles as their men fought off the Indians . . . the courage that helped build the kind of America we have today" (April 1944). By casting war work into patriotic molds, the potentially threatening image of women invading male territory was presented as a normal response to an emergency.

Of even greater import in regard to conservative postwar attitudes towards women in the labor force were the techniques used to motivate civilians to tolerate wartime disruptions of the economy and to support government drives for salvage, rationing, and worker productivity. LaRoche saw the primary role of the W.A.C. as "creat[ing] a background for the specific directives of the government" which would "clear up misunderstandings, overcome irritations, disarm unreasonable criticism, and thus condition the public not only to make required sacrifices willingly but to make more than are actually asked." He was convinced that if the government failed to use such manipulative methods most people would not respond to home front campaigns. He therefore proposed that propaganda be used simultaneously to praise citizens for all the hard work they were doing, and to threaten them with the loss of everything they held dear if they did not make such sacrifices: "The citizen must be convinced that, unless he [or she] cooperates, he personally will pay a penalty, either through loss of the war or through loss of something precious to him—his son in the armed forces, his political rights and social privileges, his future freedom."[9] This strategy was to have a profoundly reactionary impact on the portrayal of women, for advertisers settled on the home as the icon which would arouse the most fervent dedication to the cause. Woman was seen both as the primary defender of the home on the domestic front and as the embodiment of those spiritual and nurturing values which "the home" conjured up in American minds.

Typical of the way advertising used the home as a symbol of American ideals is a Servel Refrigerator advertisement which shows a middle-aged woman stating emphatically to the reader: "My home is at war! Enemies of ours are striking at the roots of everything that has meant security and peace and dignity in human relationships—everything we sum up in that precious word HOME" (April 1943). To help insure that war work would not be perceived as destroying the fabric of American society through removing women from their place as caretakers of the family, advertisements featured women workers in scenes of domestic bliss when the recruitment campaign was at its height in 1943 and early 1944. Maxwell House specialized in featuring Norman Rockwell-like scenes wherein factory workers or servicewomen were surrounded by proud family members. A representative advertisement [Figure 2] is one in which a war worker in her early twenties is resting after a hard day's work at the factory. She is still wearing her coveralls and identification badge, while her lunch bucket is prominently displayed on the dining room table. She is flanked by an older couple, probably her parents, and a little girl, a daughter or younger sister, who snuggles against her in rapt attention while she sips the coffee that her mother has just poured. All three are eagerly listening to her working day tales and are clearly full of respect for what she is doing (March 1944). The subtle message is that war workers are not only respectable members of middle-class homes, but that they bring the family closer together.

Indeed, one of the primary functions of all women according to wartime propaganda was to protect and defend the family on the home front while men fought for it overseas: "I'm glad you haven't turned the old house into just a headquarters, Mom; I'm glad you're keeping it our home, the way it was. That's the way I feel about it out here, that is also part of a woman's war job—keeping up the home, the homes we're fighting for, that some day we want to come back to" (soldier in Office of War Information propaganda film).[10]

Although new images were, of necessity, created to legitimate the employment of women in nontraditional occupations, the work which women did in the home was also glorified as essential to victory because homemakers were providing a stable environment for soldiers, defense workers, and the country as a whole. An advertisement which illustrates this theme well [Figure 3] is one which features three figures with nearly identical faces, representatives of the female soldiers of wartime—

*Figure 4. "Courage, Feminine Gender." Eureka Vacuum Cleaner Co., January 1944,* **Saturday Evening Post.**

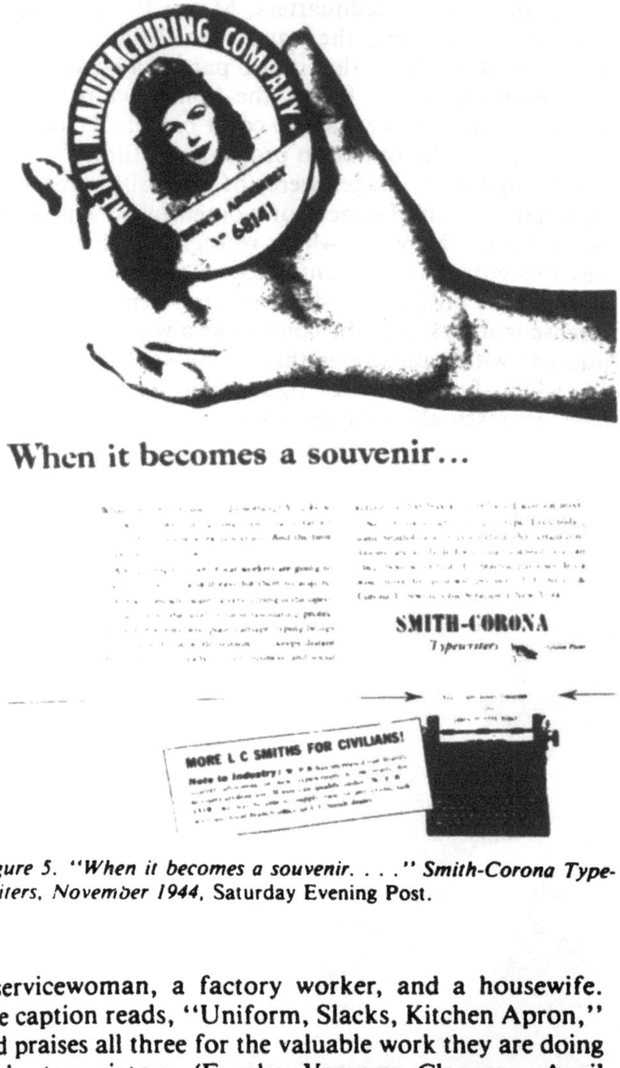


*Figure 5. "When it becomes a souvenir. . . ." Smith-Corona Typewriters, November 1944,* Saturday Evening Post.

a servicewoman, a factory worker, and a housewife. The caption reads, "Uniform, Slacks, Kitchen Apron," and praises all three for the valuable work they are doing to hasten victory (Eureka Vacuum Cleaners, April 1943). While praising housework may seem counterproductive at a time when women were needed in the labor force, it is logical when viewed in the context of an ideology which placed the home at the center of American values. The housewife stood for what made America strong: the family.

The full-time homemaker was an integral part of this American idealization of the family. Thus, two conflicting images of women existed during the war: the strong dependable patriot who could run the nation and the innocent vulnerable homemaker who depended upon soldiers to protect her way of life. In order to dramatize the struggle against the Axis powers, advertising made homemakers into the living embodiment of every value Americans safeguarded; they thus became symbolic of the besieged nation. A good example of this representation is an Adel Manufacturing advertisement which shows a young mother and a little girl gently playing with kittens in a field of flowers. The pastoral scene conveys the beauty, peace, and innocence which war has temporarily obliterated. The advertisement makes clear that this is the way of life which America is trying to preserve: "It's to keep that world and to bring back the birthright of millions of children elsewhere that American men and machines are fighting on every battle front" (June 1944). This advertisement reflects the vulnerable image of women which resulted from focusing on the family as the key element of endangered American beliefs. So too does the following advertisement [Figure 4] which pictures a young mother and baby, and is entitled "Courage . . . Feminine Gender" (Eureka Vacuum Cleaners, January 1944). The simultaneous glorification of women as symbols of America under attack and of soldiers as their champions strengthened traditional gender roles wherein men protected spiritually pure women from a harsh and brutal world.

As it became apparent that the Allies would win, war industries began converting to production of consumer goods and reinstituting prewar hiring patterns. In response, advertisers supported the plans of government and business to move women out of high-paying jobs in durable goods industries into pink-collar jobs or back to the home in order to make way for veterans. The Office of War Information had early disseminated information to the Council concerning the Selective Service requirement that discharged servicemen be given their former jobs if they so desired and asked that publicity be given to relocating soldiers.[11] Advertisements reflected this policy by assuring soldiers that their rightful place was guaranteed and that employers eagerly awaited their return. Mobil Gas, for instance, trumpeted the message: "Yes—your job is waiting for you, Soldier!" (September 1944), while an advertisement for Greyhound pictured a soldier writing home about the good news he had just received: "My old dispatcher at Greyhound writes me that they're planning the finest passenger buses the U.S.A. has ever seen—and he says they'll want me back there to pilot one of 'em" (August 1944).

At the same time, advertisers heralded the channeling of war workers into clerical work and other female fields. A Smith-Corona advertisement [Figure 5] pictures a metal assembly worker contemplating her factory badge and states: "When it becomes a souvenir . . . Like our fighting men, you've earned the right to choose the work you enjoy" (November 1944). While the message supports the notion that one may work where one pleases, it also advises women to enter office work and encourages them to believe that typing will aid the full-time homemaker as well. Similarly, another Smith-Corona advertisement shows several hands and asks the question, "Are *yours* ready for that post-war job?" while urging the reader to "learn to type today and get ahead tomorrow" (September 1944).

Another way advertisers provided public justification for mass firings of women workers was to initiate a hard-sell campaign for home appliances and direct it at the woman earning high wages. These advertisements promised defense workers a utopian life of leisure once they left the grind of the factory. Monsanto Chemicals, for instance, boasted of its new high-technology wares while confidently proclaiming: "There'll come a day . . . when a lot of the good new things of peacetime will become important to Rosie the Housewife" (November 1943). Similarly, a thermos company advertised its product by showing a war worker pouring coffee for herself at the factory in one picture and serving coffee to her husband and friends as a housewife in another as she says: "This is what I'm working for—the carefree home parties we used to have" (July 1944). Thus, returning to the home was billed as Rosie's reward for a job well done.

A more pernicious theme characterizing advertisements in the demobilization period is the portrayal of working mothers' children as suffering from abandonment. As early as the spring of 1944, advertisements dramatized the unhappiness of children whose mothers left them to go to work. An ARMCO ad, for instance, featured a little boy in tears who is being comforted by his mother as she leaves for her factory job: "Chin up soldier . . . just like Daddy said" (March 1944). Another company which manufactured war material used the same idea [Figure 6] when it showed a mother in coveralls and factory badge stopping on her way to work to answer her daughter's plaintive question, "Mother, when will you stay home again?" The text provides an answer for her: "Some jubilant day mother *will* stay home again, doing the job she likes best—making a home for you and daddy, when he gets back" (Adel, May 1944). As defense plants increased their layoffs of female workers, advertisers intensified the attack on working mothers. In one advertisement, a factory worker had to plead for leniency before a judge for her teenage son who is labeled a "Victory Vandal" (Yale and Towne Locks, June 1944), and in another an hysterical girl is carted away to a foster home because her mother has to work (State Farm Insurance, March 1945). In contrast, happy family scenes with war workers at the center disappeared once the recruitment campaign ended in the spring of 1944.

Advertisers played a major role in shaping American ideology to fit the requirements of wartime without seriously challenging sex role stereotypes. Indeed, they strengthened them. By tying national myths and ideals such as the frontier, love of country, and the family to the changing status of women, advertisers avoided the radical implications of women's war work. In addition, the central role played by the family in wartime advertising had a profound effect on the image of women who became symbols of the home-centered values which soldiers and civilians were fighting to preserve. It is this dynamic that most clearly explains why the contradiction posed to patriarchy by the need for women in male roles during the massive removal of men abroad failed to result in a reordering of attitudes toward women's work after the war. We would expect that the demonstrable competence of women in male occupations and the reliance on them as strong home front soldiers would at least seriously weaken, if not destroy an ideology which defines women as weak, nonmechanical, incapable of leadership, and unsuited for the challenges of the public world. However, we find that in the postwar era women were seen as less like men than before the war. What should have encouraged a realignment of gender roles instead produced reactionary views of women as gentle, loving homemakers who had no tools for, nor interest in, taking on the adventures of the world outside the home. The use of women as symbols of the nation's vulnerability to external enemies and as representative of its most cherished institution largely accounts for their enshrinement as wives and mothers. Because the economic need for women in instrumental male-identified roles in wartime coexisted with the propaganda need for an emotional symbol of national unity, wartime ideology did not make permanent changes in our notions of what constitutes suitable behavior for the sexes. Instead, propagandists infused new life into the very image that the glorification of Rosie the Riveter contradicted: the vulnerable homemaker who depended on a man for her livelihood. The successful ploy by advertisers in linking homemaker images with national aspirations for stability, victory, and prosperity—when added to the domestic identities associated with war workers throughout the recruitment campaign—insured the disappearance of strong, competent, wage-earning women from the public mind.

## NOTES

1. Letter from Chester LaRoche to Gardner Cowles (head of the Domestic Branch of the Office of War Information), January 13, 1943. "Young & Rubicam" file, Entry 20, Box 15, National Records Center, Suitland, Maryland.

2. For an excellent description of the role played by advertising in wartime propaganda, see Frank Fox, *Madison Avenue Goes to War: The Strange Military Career of American Advertising, 1941-1945*, Charles E. Merrill Monograph Series (Utah: Brigham Young Univ. Press, 1975).

3. See Leila Rupp, *Mobilizing Women for War: German and American Propaganda, 1939-1945* (Princeton, N.J.: Princeton Univ. Press, 1978); and Susan Hartmann, "Prescriptions for Penelope: Literature on Women's Obligations to Returning World War II Veterans," *Women's Studies*, 5 (1978), pp. 223-39.

4. All advertisements referred to in this paper were taken from the *Saturday Evening Post*. The *Post* enjoyed high circulation during the war and participated extensively in the propaganda activities of OWI. It is a good example of the response made by the magazine industry as a whole to the need for women in the labor force.

5. Eleanor Straub outlines the sexism underlying government and war contractors' policies toward women workers in "United States Government Policy Toward Civilian Women during World War II," Diss. Emory University 1973.

6. Women's Bureau studies confirm that most war workers carried this double burden. See U.S. Women's Bureau, *Women's Wartime Hours of Work: The Effect on Their Factory Performance and Home Life*, Bulletin No. 208 (Washington, D.C.: GPO, 1947). Advertising both reflected the reality of women's lives and distorted them by attri-

buting to war workers motives and class characteristics they did not have. For example, 10 percent of all female workers in war production centers were black, yet advertisements show them as white and middle-class. For an accurate picture of who entered production plants, see Karen Anderson, *Wartime Women* (Conn.: Greenwood Press, 1981).

7. Letter from LaRoche to Cowles, January 13, 1943. "Young & Rubicam" file, Entry 20, Box 15, National Records Center.

8. Rupp comments extensively on this aspect of the recruitment campaign in *Mobilizing Women*, pp. 156-57.

9. Chester LaRoche, "Policy & Plan for the Total War Campaign of the Magazine Publishers Assn.," December 31, 1942. "Young & Rubicam" file, Entry 20, Box 15, National Records Center.

10. "No Exceptions," produced by Twentieth Century Fox, released December 30, 1943 by the War Activities Committee. Script included in "Women in the War" Campaign Guide, January 1944. Records of the Program Manager for the Recruitment of Women, Entry 34, Box 1696, National Records Center.

11. See, for example, the *Magazine War Guide*, September/October, 1943, Entry 345, Box 1700, National Records Center.

*Figure 6. "Mother,when will you stay home again? Adel Manufacturing Corporation, May 1944,* Saturday Evening Post.

# The Working-Class Woman and Recruitment Propaganda during World War II: Class Differences in the Portrayal of War Work

**Maureen Honey**

Researchers have been drawn to the World War II period as a time when women were encouraged to enter nontraditional jobs in manufacturing, white-collar work, and service/trade fields. They have been interested in two primary questions: how war work challenged restrictive notions of the role women ought to play in public life, and why the massive employment of women in male fields did not have a greater impact on discriminatory labor patterns and conventional views of woman's place in the postwar world. In other words, why did the media's legitimation of female entry into male work fail to supplant the traditional image of women as homemakers, unsuited by nature for wielding power outside the domestic province, for competently manipulating the machinery at the heart of our industrial society, and for holding jobs which are normally allocated to male "breadwinners"? Indeed, the great puzzle of the

There are several people who have helped me with revisions of this report, and I would like to thank them warmly for their thoughtful suggestions. Moira Ferguson read two versions and provided invaluable advice for the final revision. Barrie Thorne was instrumental in defining the direction of the research itself, and her careful reading of the manuscript from which this analysis is drawn helped me to understand more clearly the theoretical questions it raised. Karen Anderson made useful criticisms of the significance I was claiming for popular literature when the paper was first read at the Berkshire Conference for Women Historians, Vassar College, June 1981. Sherna Gluck and Karen Skold gave me encouraging feedback on the organization of the material, as did D'Ann Campbell. Finally, I would like to thank the staff of the National Records Center in Suitland, Maryland, for helping me with the archival research, and the editors of *True Story* who allowed me to use their collection and provided office space.

[*Signs: Journal of Women in Culture and Society* 1983, vol. 8, no. 4]

1940s has been the paradoxical spawning of a reactionary postwar feminine mystique by a crisis that necessitated radical revision of traditional views.

To date, these studies have drawn conclusions about the media as a whole and gained considerable insight into the ways in which the contradictory themes of woman as homemaker and woman as competent performer of male roles were meshed during the recruitment campaign.[1] My research continues that inquiry by focusing on the interface between restrictive definitions of femininity and legitimation of egalitarian gender norms in propaganda designed specifically for working-class women. Hoping to determine the impact of class on new images of working women in the media, I designed my study with two specific goals in mind: to describe the popular culture models available to working-class women for forming nontraditional conceptions of women's work during the war and to contrast these models with those propagated for a middle-class audience to see if there were significant differences in recruitment strategies developed for women from the two groups.

To this end, I analyzed the fiction from two magazines with clear class orientations, both of which participated extensively in the government's propaganda campaign and are representative of the magazine industry as a whole. The *Saturday Evening Post* was aimed at a wide group but one that the editors conceptualized as middle-class in orientation. Its editorial direction had been defined long before the war by George Horace Lorimer, who envisioned his readers as successful, enterprising achievers able through hard work and ingenuity to move up the socioeconomic ladder: "The gray-haired President with young brains, the never-say-die salesman, the up-and-coming clerks, the get-ahead cubs . . . the men who win cases and save lives, who fight for clean politics, and a better America . . . the professor who can interest his classes in a dry-as-dust subject . . . and clear-eyed, upstanding women who think in terms of something besides cup custards and sex stories."[2] While it had begun as a man's magazine, by the 1920s the *Post*'s scope had been broadened to include women, and, like all periodicals aimed at a mixed audience, selection of its fiction was heavily weighted toward the tastes of female readers who had been found to be the main consumers of magazine

1. Leila Rupp, *Mobilizing Women for War: German and American Propaganda, 1939–1945* (Princeton, N.J.: Princeton University Press, 1978); Susan Hartmann, "Prescriptions for Penelope: Literature on Women's Obligations to Returning World War II Veterans," *Women's Studies* 5 (1978): 223–39; J. E. Trey, "Women in the War Economy—World War II," *Review of Radical Political Economics* 4 (July 1972): 41–57; Maureen Honey, "The 'Womanpower' Campaign: Advertising and Recruitment Propaganda during World War II," *Frontiers: A Journal of Women Studies* 6, nos. 1/2 (1981): 50–56.

2. John Tebbel, *George Horace Lorimer and the "Saturday Evening Post"* (New York: Doubleday & Co., 1948), p. 226.

stories.[3] With its Norman Rockwell covers and Benjamin Franklin masthead, the *Post* stood for a middle-class, individualistic, family ethic and was the most successful periodical of its type during the early decades of this century.[4]

*True Story*, on the other hand, geared itself to the experiences of a working-class female audience whose concerns were largely ignored by other magazine publishers.[5] In contrast to the *Post*, for instance, which featured stories celebrating the virtues of middle-class life, *True Story* concentrated on the problems which hampered its readers from achieving standard markers of success. While it would be difficult, perhaps impossible, to demonstrate that all readers of the *Post* came from the middle class and all purchasers of confessions like *True Story* were of the working class, we can identify clear editorial directions which allow us to draw conclusions about class-differentiated portrayals of women.

While there are limits to the conclusions that can be drawn from any case study of this sort, recruitment propaganda in these magazines highlights social attitudes toward female capacity to perform male tasks and shows how those beliefs were bifurcated by women's class status during the war.[6] One of the more significant differences between them is that working-class women's fiction presented a far less egalitarian portrait of

3. Martin Martel and George McCall, "Reality-Orientation and the Pleasure Principle: A Study of American Mass-Periodical Fiction (1890–1955)," in *People, Society, and Mass Communications*, ed. Lewis Dexter and David Manning White (New York: Free Press, 1964).

4. Theodore Peterson, *Magazines in the Twentieth Century* (Champaign: University of Illinois Press, 1964), p. 183.

5. The following studies discuss the reasons confession magazines appeal almost exclusively to working-class women and evaluate the impact of the formula on the class consciousness and identities of its readers: Lee Rainwater, Richard Coleman, and Gerald Handel, *Workingman's Wife* (New York: Oceana Pub., 1959); George Gerbner, "The Social Role of the Confession Magazine," *Social Problems* 6 (Summer 1958): 29–40; Cornelia Butler-Flora, "The Passive Female: Her Comparative Image by Class and Culture in Women's Magazine Fiction," *Journal of Marriage and the Family* 33 (August 1971): 435–44; Pamela McCallum, "World without Conflict: Magazines for Working Class Women," *Canadian Forum* 55 (September 1975): 42–44; Patricke Johns-Heine and Hans Gerth, "Values in Mass Periodical Fiction, 1921–1940," *Public Opinion Quarterly* 13 (Spring 1949): 105–13. Documentation for the claim that working-class women do not read middle-class magazines and primarily rely on confessions for leisure reading can be found in Rainwater, Coleman, and Handel, p. 126, and in Paul Lazarsfeld and Rowena Wyant, "Magazines in 90 Cities—Who Reads What," *Public Opinion Quarterly* 1, no. 4 (October 1937): 29–40.

6. I concentrated on magazine fiction because it is formulaic and hence representative of major streams of thought. I am here relying heavily on John Cawelti's pioneering work into the study of popular fantasies as carriers of widespread imaginative constructs which provide meaningful self-images and ways of ordering experience. He points out that though there are a host of story possibilities, only a few standardized plots with conventional characters have emerged with consistent appeal for large numbers of people. Because these formulas have acquired mass appeal, Cawelti postulates that they are a rich source of information of a culture's organizing myths and symbols. Looking at formula fiction, we can find the dreams that make reality tolerable and articulate the cultural

war workers than did middle-class stories. This meant that in *True Story* there was a class rather than a gender emphasis in portrayals of war workers. A host of cultural factors may have been responsible for this difference. Moreover, differing story formulas and differing recruitment strategies led to an emphasis for the two audiences on different aspects of the government's campaign.

As the United States became increasingly involved in the Allied effort to defeat the Axis powers, the editors of mass circulation magazines requested government direction in their treatment of women's new role in the war economy. The publishers of confessions like *True Story* were particularly eager to disseminate propaganda, for they were alarmed, as were all those who published pulp magazines, at the ways in which they were being restricted by federal agencies in paper allocations and transportation priorities. Afraid that they would be forced to cease operating entirely as the war continued, pulp editors presented themselves as key shapers of public opinion for a group not reached by other mass media to those in charge of home-front campaigns.[7] The govern-

assumptions that glue a society together (John Cawelti, *Adventure, Mystery, and Romance: Formula Stories as Art and Popular Culture* [Chicago: University of Chicago Press, 1976]). Because formula stories are expressions of culturally shared ideas and myths, I felt that they were revealing maps of consciousness and guides for piecing together the disparate values that shaped images of women during the war years. Of course there are limitations in a study of this sort. Representative as these magazines are of their type, some idiosyncratic elements undoubtedly set them apart from other publications. The *Ladies Home Journal*, for instance, was probably governed by slightly different editorial principles than was the *Post* since it concentrated on domestic life. Similarly, the confessions group carves out different segments of the market by emphasizing a certain kind of story, some more sexually explicit than others. *True Story* tends to aim for the mature reader, the family woman, while others are directed at teenagers. Such variation cannot be captured in a case study, nor can it determine to what degree propaganda was affected by this variation. This portrait of two magazines fails also to identify all of the popular culture to which their readers were also exposed. Surely working-class women who bought confession magazines, for example, also saw government posters and heard radio programs which provided different models of war workers. Finally, and most seriously, such a study ignores the popular culture of minority women upon whom war work had a dramatic effect. The way in which propaganda, class, and gender interacted with race on a cultural level has yet to be explored.

7. These concerns are expressed in records of the Office of War Information's Magazine Bureau ("Magazine Publishers' Protest against Discrimination by the Government," memo from Dorothy Ducas to Gardner Cowles, November 12, 1942, OWI Magazine Bureau Organization file, Entry 339, Box 1695, Record Group 208, National Archives, Suitland, Maryland; all subsequent reference to OWI records will be to Record Group 208). When the future chief of the Magazine Bureau made visits to magazine editors in the spring of 1942, she found the most enthusiastic responses to the government's plan for distributing thematic guidelines to be from pulp editors. They were already trying to slant their material for propaganda purposes but were hampered by lack of cooperation from Washington and asked that they be given clearer direction on what attitudes the government wanted them to encourage in their readers ("First Visits to Editors," memo from Dorothy Ducas to Ulric Bell, May 11, 1942, OWI Magazine Bureau Organization file, Entry 339, Box 1695).

ment's main avenue of communication with the media, the Office of War Information (OWI), persuaded that their services would be of value in securing the cooperation of workers in home front activities, distributed a *Magazine War Guide* to most magazine publishers, along with a special supplement for confessions, which gave writers and publishers thematic directions that Washington agencies considered useful to the war effort.[8] The OWI's Magazine Bureau provided writers skilled in popular formulas with plot suggestions that would, in the words of one government official, present "emotionally, the story of democracy's fight, the attitudes of good Americans, the stakes of all of us in the war."[9] Since it was considered especially critical to enlist the support of blue-collar workers in meeting high production goals for military equipment, the readiness of pulp editors to slant their material for propaganda purposes was seen as a boon to the mobilization program. Leo Rosten, Deputy Director of OWI, expressed these sentiments when he addressed a meeting of pulp editors brought together to discuss the ways they could help the government: "Pulp magazines reach one of the largest and most important audiences in America. Propaganda is aimed to hit the readers of pulp magazines more than any other group."[10]

8. The *Magazine War Guide* and supplement for fiction writers were published from July 1942 until April 1945. Published and circulated three months in advance of magazine publication deadlines, the *Guide* gave editors time to contact writers who could put together an appropriate piece. This wartime agenda specified propaganda timetables and goals as well as themes the government wanted stressed to the population. It reached the editors of 400–600 magazines with a combined readership of over 140 million, while over 1,000 copies were mailed to free-lance writers. While circulation figures collected by the Magazine Bureau do not include totals for the confessions as a group, it did estimate that 30 million people were reached through working-class popular magazines (memos from Dorothy Ducas to F. Girardot, September 17, 1943, December 11, 1943, and March 3, 1943, OWI Magazine Bureau Organization file, Entry 339, Box 1695). OWI's campaign to reach workers through pulp fiction was made easier by the activities of a group of writers who worked closely with the Magazine Bureau—the Writers' War Board—which was formed in January 1942 to put the talents of popular writers at the service of the government. The board established over a dozen committees which handled special propaganda needs, including a Confessions Committee. It is clear that the Board saw itself as a tool for shaping public opinion in ways that supported government policies. Its first annual report stated these intentions very clearly: "[Members of the Board] are of differing political views, but are united in the belief that the Board should furnish whole-hearted support of any measures which the government considers necessary to a speedy and complete victory over the Axis" ("First Annual Report," December 9, 1942, OWI Writers' War Board file, Entry 339, Box 1695). Though this group was a voluntary organization of writers from the Authors' League, it worked so closely with OWI that it was frequently mistaken for a government agency and, indeed, it received subsidies from both OWI and the Office of Civil Defense. For a detailed account of its operations, see Robert Howell, "The Writers' War Board: Writers and World War II" (Ph.D. diss., Louisiana State and Agricultural and Mechanical College, 1971).

9. Memo from Dorothy Ducas to Ulric Bell, July 15, 1942, OWI Historical Records file, Entry 339, Box 1695.

10. "Editors Conference Report," April 5, 1943, OWI Meetings for Magazine Editors file, Entry 339, Box 1695.

The major campaign conducted by OWI was the one to recruit women into the labor force. Thus both the *Post* and *True Story* devoted much space to propaganda encouraging women to enter male fields that were short of workers: manufacture of aircraft and electrical equipment, work in shipping, and metal trades. To make war jobs look attractive, both magazines published romances in which women who entered defense industries found fulfillment in performing important work for the nation. War worker heroines were featured prominently from March 1943 to June 1944, the months of intensive government recruiting, and were rewarded for their dedication to difficult jobs with admiration from their communities and love from desirable men. One of the most important similarities in the images of war workers produced by both magazines is that working women were portrayed more positively than they had been in the immediate prewar years.[11] They were praised for bravery, loyalty to soldiers, intelligence, steadfastness, and competence. Negative images persisted, in characterizations of women as slackers or as driven to their downfall by ambition or bitterness, but these were counteracted by characters with positive qualities. To a significant degree, negative stereotypes of women gave way to images that showed them possessing strength, dependability, and compassion.

Another characteristic of wartime female images with egalitarian potential was that women's sense of identity as workers received more attention. The feelings of heroines toward their jobs were more likely to surface than they did before the war, and work was often the subject of the story. Women obtained great satisfaction from employment, and in both magazines war jobs heightened the self-esteem of heroines. A *True Story* aircraft worker, for instance, expresses an enthusiasm for her new career as a welder that is typical in such pieces: "I was so thrilled to be learning aircraft production that I didn't know anything else existed. The big Comanche Training Center . . . was the most glamorous place in the world to me. I thought nothing could be more deeply satisfying than to shape a piece of shining aluminum—carefully, conscientiously—knowing that a man's life might depend on the skill of my hands. . . When my class finished the basic training I was so proud I thought I'd burst" ("Each Moment a Memory," March 1943). Such feel-

11. My total sample consisted of 122 lead and 133 nonlead *Saturday Evening Post* stories from the full years 1941, 1943, 1944, and 1945, and from January through March 1946, and of sixty-six lead supplemented by twenty-two nonlead stories from the January 1941 through March 1946 issues of *True Story*. To ensure a fair sampling of the fiction I based my analysis largely on lead stories. The assumption behind this strategy was that lead stories were likely to be read by most readers and were featured prominently because editors judged them to have wide appeal. They were thus both a good reflection of editorial policy and representative of what many people were told about war workers. I also used this method to avoid possible selection bias, so that I would not select stories that appeared to support my thesis. As it turned out, however, the nonlead stories which I read to give the study more depth were not thematically different from the lead pieces.

ings were in dramatic contrast to those described in prewar fiction when work created problems for married women and, in the confessions, played a minor role in heroines' lives. Writers from both magazines also made war jobs look attractive by dramatizing the transformation of women into heroines who enjoyed a keener sense of their importance because they were performing a crucial service for the country. The theme of moral regeneration through war work was a major one: women in factories developing into mature strong adults through meeting the challenge of long hours and hard physical labor. Such themes reflect the Magazine Bureau's suggestion for portraying war workers as enthusiastic defenders of democracy: "Fiction should bring out the . . . spiritual satisfaction of serving the common cause."[12] In addition to these positive portrayals of working women, both magazines modified the career-marriage conflict of prewar fiction in order to recruit married women into war work. Whereas employed married women of the 1930s and early 1940s were presented as selfish and destructive to their families, wartime fiction contained many heroines who successfully coped with both family and work responsibilities.

These were all ways in which the imperatives of the recruitment campaign resulted in a positive image of employed women in both the confessions and middle-class family magazines. However, there are telling differences between the confessions war worker and the national symbol of female strength and power found in magazines such as the *Post* with a middle-class orientation. One of these is that *Post* war workers, while they were certainly motivated by patriotism, were portrayed primarily as adventurous trail blazers, determined to prove that they could handle any job a man could. They clearly enjoyed the challenge of the work itself, apart from whatever significance it had for achieving victory. *True Story* women, on the other hand, experienced job satisfaction primarily because they felt part of the mobilization effort and identified much more closely with working-class people as a whole than with their achievements as women. Whereas *Post* stories frequently supported egalitarian ideals, such as acceptance by male coworkers of women in nontraditional roles, those in *True Story* failed to include feminist themes, focusing instead on war workers' pride in being part of the working class that was leading the country to victory.

The following stories illustrate the way in which writers for the confessions portrayed war workers as self-abnegating patriots with a strong class identification while *Post* authors showed women proving that they were men's equals. The heroine of "Young Girl's Secret" (*True Story*, October 1943) is a disgruntled secretary at an aircraft plant who resents her transfer from a well-paying assembly line job to the office. Because

12. "Supplement for Love Story and Western Love Magazines," September 11, 1942, OWI *Magazine War Guide* file, Entry 345, Box 1700.

her new job is less interesting and less well paid than her previous one, she finds it difficult to feel much enthusiasm for her work. Gradually, however, her supervisor's appreciation of her efficiency at clerical tasks makes her feel important again, and her excitement mounts as she comes to feel part of the company: "All the world seemed filled with high endeavor; the noise of the factory an articulate voice, saying: more planes, more planes, more planes—we're making them, we're building them, we're sending them out. I looked with pride at the lists which came into my hands, and often I would glance up and see the pride in Courtney Atwell's eyes." As a result, she adopts a willingness to do whatever she is asked in order to help her country: "Wherever I'm most needed, wherever I can be the most help—that's all I want." Pleased with her subordination of her own wishes to those of the company, the supervisor approvingly replies: "That's the spirit. . . . That will win this war."

A similar transformation occurs in "The Education of John Manley by a Girl" (*True Story*, September 1943), which features the daughter of a working-class family in a boom town. Initially dubious about giving up her college plans to take a war job, she quickly finds that her duties on an aircraft assembly line clarify where her energies should go: "Suddenly the patriotism that John had publicized awoke in me and flamed in a flower of radiance. When I stood beside a machine, the machine achieved not only vitality but immortality, and gadgets that I passed to the operator of the machine became the food with which it was nourished, and I told myself that when it had been fed sufficiently it would have the strength to gobble up opposition—yellow opposition with slanted eyes, square-headed, ruthless opposition that spoke in gutturals. As I felt muscles tightening in my grease-covered arms, I felt something intangible tightening in the arms of my spirit." In addition, she chastizes her mother for urging her to dress in a way that will hide her working-class origins, reminding her that it is the workers who are primarily responsible for producing weapons that will defeat the enemy. Confessions war workers served as models of dutiful, diligent employees who took pride in the achievements of a blue-collar class that they or others had mistakenly devalued.

Although many *Post* stories used soldiers as figures of inspiration for insufficiently patriotic women, its heroines failed to follow the lead of their bosses and coworkers as did those in *True Story*. Rather, they commanded respect from such men and took the initiative in making a place for women in male-dominated occupations. For example, in "Rough Turn," a *Post* story by Ray Millholland published in August 1943, the manager of a steam engine factory manufacturing guns for the Navy has been forced to hire women machinists by the War Manpower Commission. Within two weeks, he is at his wits' end because, as a result of friction with the new workers, two men have quit and a superintendent is threatening to leave. In desperation, he puts one of the women in charge of the others. She informs him that the women are uncooperative because they are angry that men have been assigned the most skilled work and "get to have all the fun." She convinces him not only that women are capable of performing such jobs but that they desire them. When he accedes to the women's demands, the problems come to an end. Frequently, moreover, *Post* heroines are portrayed as replacing the male head of a war industry when he is drafted or temporarily disabled. "Dangerous Ways" by Robert Pinkerton, published in January 1943, features a heroine who manages a shipyard after the owner has met with a bad accident. Previously the shipyard secretary, she has a vast technical knowledge of shipbuilding and a good head for business, which enable her to handle the operation competently despite the presence of saboteurs. In the April 1945 piece "Taxi! Taxi!" by Clarence Budington Kelland, the shrewd, sardonic sister of a taxi fleet owner takes over the business when her brother is drafted, hires brawny female drivers who have no trouble subduing rowdy fares, and makes the office more efficient. Kelland also used this formula in "Heart on Her Sleeve" (May 1943), when the owner of a plywood company that makes bomb noses becomes incapacitated, and his daughter is propelled into the head executive position.

The self-confidence and authoritative demeanor toward men that are found in *Post* war workers contrast sharply with the self-abnegating subordination characteristic of their *True Story* counterparts, who have trouble acting decisively and occupying positions of power. The principle characteristic of the confessions heroine is that her moves toward independence or power in the male world lead her to make unwise decisions, to behave insensitively to those she loves, and to become increasingly selfish. In short, her desire to participate as an equal in the world of men causes her to make disastrous errors and to lose their love. *Post* heroines, on the other hand, garner male affection through their independent pursuit of excellence; female autonomy is equated with dependability, not egocentricity. In "Nine Days Leave," published in August 1943, we see how problematic wielding power even temporarily is for women in the confessions. The narrator is a secretary in a small printing establishment who is promoted to assistant manager after it blossoms into a large-scale enterprise that prints war posters and pamphlets for the government. We get early indications that this heroine is not meant to be a positive figure when we see that she is unfaithful to her childhood sweetheart, who is not only of princely character and totally in love with her, but is a soldier. Her symbolic betrayal of her country is a sign that she is not to be trusted with the authority she has acquired in her new position. The central scene of the story takes place when the narrator is sent to New York to place an order for the company. There she is propositioned by a high-level executive. At first she is thrilled to be treated as an important person in her business dealings, but the affair with this sophisticated heartbreaker leaves her desolate and repentant. The heroine has been punished for her hubristic exercise of power, and we see that she was wrong to reject the sweet home life offered by her boyfriend in favor of the tantalizing prospects of a career as a businesswoman.

This dramatic difference in attitude toward female authority meant that the *Post* ran recruitment stories that glamorized women with power over men while *True Story* failed to cast war workers in such roles. Two stories which were published as part of the campaign to get women into the armed forces illustrate this difference. Stanley Washburn, Jr.'s, "The Lady and the Flat-Top," published in the *Post* in March 1945, exemplifies that magazine's tendency to place women in command of male subordinates and in dangerous situations where they cope admirably with crisis. Lt. Childs is a member of the Army Air Evacuation Nurse Corps stationed in a combat area in the Pacific. Her position as senior ward nurse in battle zones requires that she be able to make fast decisions under stress and that she inspire a great deal of respect. Her responsibilities are so extensive that she sometimes performs the tasks of chief surgeon. Childs's ability to act appropriately in a crisis is clearly evident in the climax of the story, which occurs when a plane filled with wounded soldiers develops engine trouble over the ocean. The pilot has already angered her by flying at such a high altitude that one of her patients dies (the first soldier she has lost), but when he tells her that it is impossible to avoid a crash landing, she explodes: "'Impossible,' she spoke contemptuously. 'We've been doing the impossible out here for eight months.'" We see further indications of the lieutenant's strength as she talks the pilot into landing aboard a carrier that his plane can reach: "She spoke as if she were forcing fate aside by sheer will power alone." Ultimately convinced that her plan is worth the risk, the pilot makes the landing, thereby saving all on board, and extends to her his admiration and gratitude.

*True Story*'s "One Hour" (March 1944) also concerns a servicewoman who is faced with a critical life-or-death situation and who similarly deals with a combat pilot forced to make a crash landing. Although she is a WAVE air traffic controller, a job with much responsibility, and is described as "disciplined," "calm," and "efficient," the story does not cast the narrator in a heroic role. She is, for one thing, not in the middle of combat as is Lt. Childs; the story takes place on an air base in the United States where pilots are testing planes and acquiring training. The second element which makes this a nonheroic role for the narrator is the nature of the crisis and her part in it. As is typical of the confessions formula, the narrator suffers from a mistake she has made: in this case, she has hesitated to accept the pilot's marriage proposal even though she is strongly attracted to him. The catastrophic event that shows her the choice she should have made occurs in this story when the pilot's plane has a mechanical breakdown while she is guiding it in for a landing. The narrator watches helplessly as the plane flies out of control, and her horrified reaction makes her aware of how grievous her error was. Unlike the *Post* nurse who acts decisively to resolve a similar crisis, the *True Story* character passively awaits the outcome and can only hope that her dreams will not be shattered before her very eyes. While women are praised in *True Story* for their fortitude and dependability as part of the recruiting effort, the prohibition on assertiveness means that strength is defined as perseverance, not as female ability to assume a man's leadership position.

Finally, one of the most striking differences between the two magazines is that few heroines in *True Story* are in nontraditional occupations, while the *Post* regularly features women as police, taxi drivers, engineers, welders, riveters, executives, and servicewomen. Women in *True Story* are concentrated in female occupations such as office work, sales, teaching, nursing, and semiskilled factory work. During the years of the recruitment campaign, the proportion of characters from stories of the *Post* in nontraditional occupations was 28 percent in 1943 and 36 percent in 1944, while those in female occupations (including homemaking) made up 33 percent and 21 percent of the total, respectively. These figures represented a dramatic increase in the number of nontraditional work roles from 1941 when a mere 15 percent of all characters were in atypical wage work and 44 percent were cast as teachers, office workers, and housewives, or placed in other categories identified as female work. In contrast, the proportion of *True Story* characters in male jobs from stories of 1944 was 23 percent with 47 percent in the traditional roles. While this was a significant increase over the number of women in such occupations in 1941 (5 percent), it was nevertheless much lower than one would expect, given the impact of propaganda on the *Post.* Only in 1943, the peak year of the womanpower campaign, did the number of *True Story* heroines in nontraditional occupations approximate that of the *Post,* and even these figures are misleading since characters featured as factory workers were mostly in semiskilled assembly line jobs, whereas *Post* women were in skilled ones (see table 1). In short, *Post* heroines were far more likely to be shown in high-wage or high-status work while those in *True Story* were concentrated in "pink-collar" jobs even when working in war industries.

There are a number of possible explanations for the less egalitarian portrait of war workers in *True Story.* One is that *True Story*'s audience was traditionally young, and since many school-age women who entered the labor force went into clerical work, the large number of office worker

*Table 1*

Occupations of Female Characters in the *Saturday Evening Post* and *True Story* (%)

| | Nontraditional Occupations[1] | | Traditional Occupations[2] | | No Paid Occupation[3] | | Other[4] | |
|---|---|---|---|---|---|---|---|---|
| Year | *Post* | *TS* | *Post* | *TS* | *Post* | *TS* | *Post* | *TS* |
| 1941. . . | 15 | 5 | 44 | 58 | 29 | 21 | 12 | 16 |
| 1943. . . | 28 | 27 | 33 | 45 | 29 | 20 | 10 | 8 |
| 1944. . . | 36 | 23 | 21 | 47 | 29 | 24 | 14 | 6 |

[1]Business executive, journalist, servicewoman, psychologist, factory worker, pilot, policewoman, commercial artist, farm owner, college teacher, taxi driver, engineer, shipyard worker, gas station attendant, doctor.

[2]Nurse, nurse's aide, housewife, high school teacher, office worker, clerk, waitress, maid, housekeeper, stewardess, cashier, dress designer.

[3]No occupation mentioned, volunteer war worker, student, retiree.

[4]Entertainer, detective, spy, writer, resistance fighter, employed but work not specified.

heroines reflected the labor-force activity of the readers.[13] On the other hand, nearly as many women left school to take jobs in factories, and yet they were underrepresented.[14] The relatively low visibility of women as welders and shipyard workers, as well as of women in male jobs within trade and transportation, however, did not mirror the fact that such jobs were actually accessible to working-class women and were sought by them in record numbers. Then, too, if we are going to posit that the magazines reflected the occupations of their readers, how do we account for the large number of *Post* characters in factory work, when labor statistics show that women war workers were predominantly from the working class, while the *Post's* audience was largely middle-class?

One explanation for the failure of *True Story* to feature as many women in authoritative, nontraditional roles is that its readers were extremely unlikely to find managerial or professional positions in the real

13. There are no available data on the age of wartime readers. Before the war, the typical *True Story* reader was between the ages of eighteen and twenty-four (Johns-Heine and Gerth [n. 5 above]). There is evidence from the magazine, however, that readers spanned a wider age range than is indicated in the Johns-Heine and Gerth study. The readers featured in a regular column concerning home problems, for instance, ranged from eighteen to thirty-five. By 1945, 54 percent of women between twenty and twenty-four years old were in the labor force, and one-third of those working women were between fourteen and nineteen (U.S. Women's Bureau, *Employment of Women in the Early Postwar Period,* Bulletin 211 [Washington, D.C.: Government Printing Office, 1946]). Of all women working in April 1945, 54 percent fell between the ages of fourteen and thirty-four (Mary Pidgeon, "Women Workers and Recent Economic Change," *Monthly Labor Review* 65, no. 6 [December 1947]: 666–71).

14. In the ten major war production centers, almost half of the former students who entered the labor force went into clerical work, whereas almost one-third took jobs as machine operatives. Equal numbers of this group found jobs in manufacturing industries and service/trade fields (U.S. Women's Bureau, *Women Workers in Ten War Production Areas and Their Postwar Employment Plans,* Bulletin 209 [Washington, D. C.: Government Printing Office, 1946], pp. 10–11).

world. Their fantasies of upward mobility, therefore, depended on male authority figures who could lift them through marriage out of their clerical or sales jobs into a higher socioeconomic bracket. Thus, we find many romances in which bosses fall in love with their secretaries. If the readers were to fantasize about professional success, the only realistic avenues open to them would have to be the traditional female fields of teaching, dress designing, or nursing, all of which were regularly featured in fiction of the war years.

Second, propagandists in OWI worked toward two major goals in the womanpower campaign, each of which was given differential emphasis in the two magazines because of the strategies used to reach each audience and the constraints of the story formulas upon which they depended. One of these was to recruit women into male fields by giving them role models for filling jobs unfamiliar to them. The Magazine Bureau, for instance, informed writers that it would provide photographs of women who had entered the shipbuilding and aircraft trades, the armed forces, and other nontraditional areas in order to encourage female readers to consider taking such jobs. The other goal was to discourage absenteeism, work slowdowns, high turnover rates, and dissatisfaction in key defense industries through stories on patriotic workers who stoically stuck to their posts despite hardships and who felt a sense of partnership with management. The Magazine Bureau urged that editors emphasize "the contributions of labor to victory" and "a new kind of teamwork between labor unions and industry"; resentful or incompetent job performance was to be portrayed as the work of saboteurs.[15]

Both of these approaches were incorporated into *Post* romances and *True Story* confessions but, because recruitment strategies for attracting the two audiences to factory work differed, they translated into a more powerful figure for the *Post.* Middle-class women needed to be persuaded that it was worth their while to take a step down and enter the blue-collar world, one which carried less status than the bourgeois lifestyle to which people in a capitalist society aspire. One of the recommendations made to the Magazine Bureau by poll takers investigating sources of female resistance to government pleas to take war jobs was that propagandists build up the prestige of factory work because women who did not have to work for economic reasons were reluctant to associate themselves with blue-collar occupations: "The type of work [the war worker] does and the conditions under which he works are too often regarded as characteristic of the lower classes."[16] To do this, *Post* writers placed war-worker heroines in managerial and supervisory positions or

15. OWI *Magazine War Guide* file, September–October 1943, and Supplement II, October 15, 1942, Entry 345, Box 1700.

16. "Resistance to Taking War Jobs in 3 New England Cities," Special Memorandum no. 62, June 24, 1943, OWI Special Services Bureau, Entry 118, Box 706.

in blue-collar jobs requiring technical skill, thus enhancing the appeal of factory work for a middle-class audience. Women were thus featured in the most prestigious blue-collar fields and in roles where they wielded power over men, especially working-class men. Such a portrayal maintained middle-class superiority despite the loss of social status inherent in entering blue-collar occupations.

We can speculate that working-class women, on the other hand, would have been put in a more problematic situation by such a strategy because it would have made them compete for power with men of their own class.[17] In addition, war work for them meant social advancement, since it provided higher wages than did the traditionally female occupations, and it garnered praise for them as leaders of the production front. Two primary themes used in the campaign appear to address these issues. One conveyed the message that all confessions readers, no matter how trouble-filled their lives, had something valuable to contribute to the war effort and would personally benefit from participation in it: "Fictional treatment should be directed towards emphasizing the angle that the womanpower question is one for *every* reader, that it reaches into *every* stratum of society, that it touches, poignantly and personally, *every* woman and girl no matter what her position in life, her environment, her history of work or leisure."[18] Hence many confession stories show war work as a redeeming influence on the heroine rather than as an opportunity to exercise power over men. The other theme strengthened the connection between readers, the working class as a whole, and the interests of the country by featuring war workers who placed national or company goals before their own and whose self-esteem arose from feelings of solidarity with a strong working-class army rather than from pride in the achievements of women. Both approaches avoided exacerbating the tensions between working-class men and women while encouraging confident, energetic, and enthusiastic attitudes toward war work in women.

17. A recent analysis of the impact of new labor patterns on family relations indicates that the entry of working-class women into male occupations exerted stress on working-class marriages when husbands felt their authority threatened. Middle-class men, however, were not faced with the same threat: "The hostility of male workers where women intruded into their work world reflected an attempt not only to protect their prerogatives in the labor force but to preserve the ideological and cultural bases for their family authority as well. Men of the middle class, by contrast, did not experience a comparable incursion into the jobs traditionally allocated to them because the expansion of white-collar jobs for women occurred in traditional 'women's' fields" (Karen Anderson, *Wartime Women: Sex Roles, Family Relations, and the Status of Women during World War II* [Westport, Conn.: Greenwood Press, 1981], p. 83). The relatively greater tension produced in men and women of the working class by the influx of women into nontraditional blue-collar fields may have been reflected in the absence of powerful roles assumed by war workers in *True Story*.

18. War Guide Supplement III for Confession Magazines, October 30, 1942, OWI *Magazine War Guide* file, Entry 345, Box 1700.

In addition, propagandists were forced to operate within the constraints of different, already established formulas. The confession formula was based on the fantasy of personal renewal through exorcism of one's inner demons with domestic happiness as the reward. The confession heroine was usually a battered victim of cruel forces beyond her control, dependent upon a strong male leader for strength and ultimate salvation. Such a story-line was largely incompatible with the potentially feminist aspects of the recruitment campaign. While confession writers showed war workers as strong moral beings, they portrayed them as followers rather than leaders or even equals of men. Such writers were able to support the OWI goals by encouraging stoicism, dedication to the job, and the combining of marriage with wage work, but their attempts to demonstrate that women could perform a man's role were rather unsuccessful.

The *Post*, in contrast, relied on a formula expressing the fantasy that all obstacles can be overcome through wit, pluck, and determination. The adventures it portrayed were not erotic ones, as they were in *True Story*, but forays into the world of business and glamorous careers. Heroines were trailblazers who proved that anyone could overcome obstacles and achieve worthy goals even if she were a woman with sexual prejudice working against her. The fantasy was one of self-actualization through confident tackling of problems rather than the confessions object lesson in self-immolation with eventual rebirth into a safe world. This framework was much more compatible with the propaganda goal of providing home front heroes and eliminating prejudice against women in nontraditional work. As a result, the confessions heroine became a representative of the patriotic blue-collar worker who found self-esteem through a man appreciative of her class background and good work habits, while the *Post* war worker represented her gender, demonstrating that men could rely on women to get the job done.

Paradoxically, then, the audience for whom the labor shortage gave the greatest opportunities for advancement were provided the least egalitarian role models. Material from these two magazines suggests that the redefining of female abilities necessitated by the war produced in middle-class popular fiction strong female characters who could defeat an enemy agent, run a drill press, work eighty-hour weeks, or build a bomber. However, working-class literature for women failed to show war workers in leadership roles and tended not to show them in skilled blue-collar work. While propaganda imperatives produced a more self-respecting, class-conscious heroine in the confessions, the most clearly heroic and strong-minded workers were found in the *Post*. The wartime employment of women, therefore, led to a redefinition of female roles for an audience more likely to have remained in the home, but the real Rosie the Riveter found little affirmation of her ability to do a man's work in magazines aimed at her, nor did she see any indication that the war was a historic opportunity for escaping segregation into traditionally female occupations. Ultimately, of course, the message that women are capable of handling male roles was superseded in the *Post* by "the feminine mystique," as it was in popular culture as a whole, and there are elements in the middle-class portrayal of war workers that foreshadow this development. One of the major points I see emerging from this study, however, is that we cannot speak of a single wartime model of women in nontraditional occupations. For us to view the war period as a time when women were encouraged to believe themselves capable of replacing male workers is to ignore the ways in which working-class women were discouraged from developing identities as nontraditional workers.

During World War II, economic, social, and political forces combined to produce a need for new images of women, those that showed wage work as a normal, vital part of female lives and that conveyed the message that women could and should occupy all types of jobs. The opportunity thus arose for women to be provided with a picture, a word, a name for conceptualizing themselves as nontraditional workers. Fiction of the *Post,* which is perhaps representative of much middle-class magazine literature, did just that. The working-class fiction of confessions, however, failed to encourage readers fully to enter a realm from which they had been actively barred. We cannot measure the impact such a message would have had on any woman's life plans, yet certainly it would have helped protect those who entered man's sphere from self-doubt or the censure of friends, relatives, or male workers. That this permission was not forthcoming in a periodical with high circulation among the group most likely to benefit from it was a loss, not only to working women at the time but to the following female generation that grew up without the social supports to train for occupations other than secretaries, nurses, waitresses, or housewives.

*Department of English*
*University of Nebraska at Lincoln*

# WOMEN WORKERS IN WORLD WAR II: MICHIGAN AS A TEST CASE

By ALAN CLIVE*

Scholars have devoted increasing attention to the American home front during World War II. Studies by Richard Polenberg, John Morton Blum, Geoffrey Perrett, Richard S. Kirkendall, and others have illuminated this neglected period of national history. They have assessed the impact of the war in terms of change and continuity in society, often reaching conflicting conclusions on much the same evidence. "World War II radically altered American society and challenged its most durable values," Polenberg asserts. By ending the depression, the war made it possible for liberals to turn to other pressing but long-ignored social issues, such as medical care, federal aid to education, and most significantly, civil rights. For Kirkendall, the principal theme of the 1939-1945 era is the persistence of continuity despite the disruptions of war. He writes that "many old parts of American life, including the basic political and economic institutions, remained in place [during the war]. American leaders had, in fact, deliberately preserved those institutions, protecting them against serious challenges at home and abroad, and the American people had resisted as well as demanded change."[1]

The war's impact on working women reveals much about the scope and limits of change in American society. The most ob-

* This article is an adapted chapter from Alan Clive's forthcoming book, *State of War: Michigan in World War II*, copyright 1980 by the University of Michigan.

[1] John Morton Blum, *V Was for Victory: Politics and American Culture during World War II* (New York: Harcourt Brace Jovanovich, 1976); Geoffrey Perrett, *Days of Sadness, Years of Triumph: The American People, 1939-1945* (New York: Coward, McCann & Geoghegan Inc., 1973); Richard S. Kirkendall, *The United States, 1929-1945: Years of Crisis and Change* (New York: McGraw-Hill, 1974), 289; Richard Polenberg, *War and Society: The United States, 1941-1945* (Philadelphia: Lippincott, 1972), 5, 36, 56, 76, 92, 94, 97-98, 103, 130-131, 133, 135-138, 145, 153, 184, 187, 213-214, 237.

vious indicator of the wartime change is the great increase in female employment that took place during the conflict. From 14,600,000 in 1941, the number of employed women in the United States had increased by 1944 to 19,370,000, far more than a third of the labor force. Women took jobs of all descriptions and skills in war industry.[2] But what did the rise in the female labor force signify, beyond the fact that more women were at work? Did the war experience generate new attitudes toward women and their status?

Chester W. Gregory declares affirmatively that "women employed in defense plants demonstrated such skill and praiseworthy performance that a kind of social, economic, and psychological equality between men and women which had not existed before in American society was evolved. . . . As a result of the war crisis . . . women were able to emancipate themselves socially and psychologically and to establish a greater degree of social and economic independence than they had ever known before." Looking back at the 1940s, William Chafe notes somewhat less optimistically: "There was no question that economic equality remained a distant goal but the content of women's lives had changed, and an important new area of potential activity had opened up to them, with side effects which could not yet be measured." Eleanor Straub flatly asserts that "World War II permanently altered concepts of welfare, industrial technology . . . the relationship of the individual to the state, and the role of interest and minority groups in politics, but no comparable changes in the status of women in American society are visible."[3]

These discussions of women and World War II, with their contradictory findings, are based on surveys at the national level. An examination of women and war in a single state affords the opportunity of testing national-level generalizations on a specific test community. Few states better qualify for such a study than Michigan. With 4 per cent of America's population, the state obtained better than 10 per cent of the nearly two hun-

[2] William Henry Chafe, *The American Woman: Her Changing Social, Economic, and Political Roles, 1920-1970* (New York: Oxford University Press, 1972), 137-144.

[3] Chester W. Gregory, *Women in Defense Work during World War II: An Analysis of the Labor Problem and Women's Rights* (Jericho, NY: Exposition Press, 1974), xii; Chafe, 195; Eleanor Straub, "Government Policy toward Civilian Women during World War II" (unpublished PhD diss. Emory Univ., 1973), 358.

dred billion dollars in prime war supply and facilities contracts awarded by the US government and the Allies from 1940 to 1945. Only New York state outranked Michigan in this category. Hundreds of companies in dozens of other communities across the state fashioned every conceivable item required by an embattled nation. The automobile industry, which had made the name of Detroit world-famous in a more peaceful era, naturally led all Michigan manufacturers in the output of war goods. Most of the automakers' national total of twenty-nine billion dollars worth of vehicles, engines, guns, shells, and additional assorted material was produced in such prewar industry centers as Detroit, Pontiac, Flint, Lansing, Saginaw, and Muskegon.[4]

Manpower constituted an essential element in Michigan's industrial triumph. State manufacturing employment peaked at 1,226,000 persons in November 1943, a 60 per cent rise over the annual average of 721,000 industrial workers employed statewide in 1940. Total employment in the Detroit labor market area obtained a wartime high during the same month in 1943, more than doubling to 867,000 persons from the 396,000 at work three years earlier. The size of Michigan's labor force gradually declined during the last twenty months of war, but as late as December 1944, 1,075,000 people—one out of every five inhabitants of the state—were directly engaged in war production.[5]

The extent to which women might figure in this enormous manpower increase was in part conditioned by bitter depression experience. Female emancipation had received a severe setback during the 1930s, when mass unemployment lent new emphasis to the long-cherished belief that the woman's place was in the home, not in the office or on the assembly line, where her pres-

[4] U. S. Department of Commerce, Bureau of the Census, *County Data Book, 1947* (Washington: U. S. Government Printing Office, 1947), xii-xiii, 199, 207, 213, 277; Harvey Klemmer, "Michigan Fights," *National Geographic*, 86 (December, 1944), 677-715; War Production Board, *State Listing of Major War Supply Contracts Active as of December 31, 1944* (Washington: U. S. Government Printing Office, 1945), 347-366; Francis Walton, *Miracle of World War II: The Story of American War Production* (New York: Macmillan, 1956), 225-240; Automobile Manufacturers Association, *Freedom's Arsenal: The Story of the Automotive Council for War Production* (Detroit: The Association, 1950), *passim.*

[5] William Haber, *How Much Does it Cost? A Report to the Michigan Economic Security Commission on Long-Range Unemployment Insurance Financing and Fund Solvency in Michigan* (Lansing: The Commission, 1951), 304; U.S. Congress, Senate, Special Committee Investigating the National Defense Program, *Hearings*, 79 Cong., 1 sess. (Washington: U. S. Government Printing Office, 1945), Part XXVIII, 13,542, 13,543; *Detroit News*, December 4, 1944.

ence might deny work to a man supporting a family. The 1932 Michigan state legislature requested that local governments fire all but one member of a family where more than one member worked in a department, a measure clearly aimed at removing married women from payrolls. The proportion of women in the Michigan labor force rose from 18.7 per cent in 1930 to 21.5 per cent in 1940, but females remained clustered in the occupations traditionally reserved to them—storeclerk, stenographer, maid, and so forth. The notion of additional female employment in industry had been discussed at the outset of the defense program but had not been implemented to any great extent. Few women entered defense training courses, and an October 1941 analysis of sixteen major industrial groups in the state found that defense work "still is predominantly a man's job."[6]

But the increasing labor demands of Michigan war industry after Pearl Harbor, combined with the exactions of the draft, compelled the hiring of women workers in great number. The proportional rise of female employment in the state ultimately was more striking than that for the nation; from 391,600 in March 1940 (24.8 per cent of the nonfarm workforce), the number of employed women in Michigan more than doubled by the war peak in November 1943 to 799,100 (34.8 per cent of the nonfarm workers). The proportion of males employed in manufacturing in the Detroit labor market area rose from 56 per cent to 71 per cent between 1940 and 1943, but the percentage of Detroit women in industry increased from 22 per cent to 53 per cent of all employed females in the area during the same period. In October 1940 there were only 5.7 women per one hundred production workers in the automobile industry; four years later, the rate reached 24.4. Examining Detroit war plants in March 1943 investigators for the United Automobile Workers (UAW) found that women composed 30 per cent of the workforce at Briggs, 32 per cent at Bendix's Wayne division, and 27 per cent of all persons employed at Willow Run.[7]

[6] Chafe, 135-136; *Journal of the Senate of the State of Michigan* (Lansing: Senate of Michigan, 1932), 224-225; U. S. Department of Commerce, Bureau of the Census, *Sixteenth Census of the United States, 1940 Population* (Washington: U.S. Government Printing Office, 1943), III, Part III, 593-595, 606-630; Thelma McKelvey, *Women in War Production* (New York: Oxford University Press, 1942), 16; *Detroit News*, December 16, 1941.

[7] Haber, 149, 224; Senate Special Committee Investigating the National Defense

A Women's Bureau survey disclosed that fully 51 per cent of the 387,000 women at work in Detroit during late 1944 and early 1945 had been employed before Pearl Harbor. They had shifted from jobs as waitresses, sales clerks, and maids into manufacturing and, to a lesser extent, into government work. The war years also witnessed the emergence of a new female worker: the same study reported that 28 per cent of the Detroit female labor force were housewives, and 18 per cent had been students prior to the declaration of war (the remaining 3 per cent were then seeking work). The demographic balance of the female labor force altered radically with the entrance of these new workers in vast numbers. Once dominated by single women under thirty years of age, the female labor force now contained substantially larger proportions of older and married women. The Women's Bureau found Detroit's female workers evenly divided at 45 per cent each between single and married women, the remaining 10 per cent being widowed or divorced. Only 44 per cent of the women were in the prime employment age group of twenty-nine years, in contrast to the 41 per cent of women workers over thirty.[8]

A complex set of trends and demands dictated the shape of the wartime women's workforce. Long-term demographic tendencies within the national female population resulted in a reduction of the age at marriage and an increase in the number of older women in relation to all women. The coming of war provided a further stimulus to marriage; the number of Michigan weddings performed in December 1941 set a state record for a single month. The marriage rate declined during the next four years, but rose sharply again with the coming of peace. Seeking a perspective on wartime changes in female employment, Chafe observes: "At the turn of the century, the young, the single and the poor had dominated the female labor force. Fifty years later, the majority of women workers were married

Program *Hearings*, Part XXVIII, 13,527 13,528, 13,542, 13,543; UAW Research Department, "Notes on Women Workers in UAW Plants," March, 1943, 1, UAW Research Department Collection, Archives of Labor History and Urban Affairs, Wayne State University, Detroit, Box 14 (unprocessed) (cited hereafter as UAW Research Collection).

[8] U. S. Department of Labor, Women's Bureau, *Women Workers in Ten War Production Areas and Their Postwar Employment Plans. Women's Bureau Bulletin No. 209* (Washington: U. S. Government Printing Office, 1946), 29-30, 35-49.

and middle-aged, and a substantial minority came from the middle class. In the story of that dramatic change, World War II represented a watershed event."[9]

Government manpower policy also influenced the nature of the female labor force, but that policy left much to be desired both in conception and execution. At no time did the War Manpower Commission (WMC) give women more than an advisory voice in decision-making, and usually the Commission ignored proffered advice. At first paying little attention to the potential of women workers, the WMC abruptly plunged into an unproductive round of female recruitment drives at the end of 1942, nowhere more fruitlessly than in Detroit.[10]

The genesis of the drive was Detroit's surprisingly poor performance in the early months of the war. Conversion was taking longer than had been predicted, and munitions output lagged in many areas. A serious labor shortage also contributed to the problem. By mid-year, local industrialists had grown fearful that Detroit might lose additional contracts and that the War Manpower Commission might step in to take control of hiring practices. Business and union representatives met with government officials at the Detroit office of the War Production Board on June 26 to discuss the manpower crisis. Frederick Harbison, economist and consultant to the WPB's Labor Supply Branch, put the matter bluntly to the assembled group: "If you start to meet some of your problems, you are going to be in the position to tell the Manpower Commission what Detroit is going to do . . . to meet its labor shortage, and you will not be in the position of having policies dictated to you by people who may know nothing about Detroit or the particular . . . problems that affect Detroit. . . ."[11]

---

[9] Valerie Oppenheimer, *The Female Labor Force in the United States: Demographic and Economic Factors Governing its Growth and Changing Composition. Population Monographs Series No. 5* (Berkeley and Los Angeles: University of California Press, 1970), 163-189; *Detroit News*, April 6, 1942; Michigan Department of Public Health, *Michigan Public Health Statistics* (Lansing: The Department, 1951), 13; Chafe, 195.

[10] Eleanor Straub, "United States Government Policy toward Civilian Women during World War II," *Prologue*, 5 (Winter, 1973), 254; Straub, "Government Policy," 144.

[11] Alan Clive, "The Society and Economy of Wartime Michigan, 1939-1945" (unpublished PhD diss., Univ. of Michigan, 1976), 159-172; War Production Board, "Minutes of a Meeting on Labor Supply and Future Labor Requirements," June 26, 1942, 7-8, File 525.11, Records of the War Production Board, Record Group 179, National Archives (cited hereafter as WPB Records, RG 179).

The solution both to the problem of contract removal and to the threat of federal interference, Harbison suggested, lay in the employment by Detroit industry of upward of eighty thousand women, a figure that would have approximately doubled the number of women then employed in local manufacturing. The June 26 meeting approved a program for the recruitment of women into Detroit industry. Of the some two score persons who attended this conference largely concerned with female employment, only one person, Irene Murphy—the Wayne County Office of Civilian Defense's specialist on the day care of children—was a woman.[12]

On August 10, mailmen delivered some 650,000 postcards to households in Wayne, Oakland, Macomb, and Washtenaw Counties; area women, whether interested in factory employment or not, had been asked to fill out and return the cards to the Detroit branch of the United States Employment Service (USES). The USES classified the applications according to availability, experience, and potential work capacity, and, as production demands warranted, the agency scheduled interviews with those women who had offered their services. An encouraging 265,009 cards were returned, but by January, 1943 only 2,290 women had been placed in jobs, and only 1,742 in factory positions. Manpower planners had failed to reckon with female resistance to industrial employment. Many women had not yet decided whether to work and others did not comprehend the seriousness of the labor supply problem. Employers, moreover, persisted in their customary reluctance to utilize the services of the USES.[13]

During 1943 the WMC largely failed in its efforts to persuade Michigan women to take vital but low-paying civilian service jobs in stores and other businesses. Throughout the war, the Michigan state government refused to allow substantial changes in the regulations governing hours of employment and working conditions for female labor. No Michigan manufacturer could employ a woman for more than nine hours a day or for more

---

[12] WPB Records, RG 179, 1-2, 28.

[13] *Detroit News*, August 10, 1942; Michigan USES, "Cumulative Summary Report on Voluntary Registration of Women for War Work," January 9, 1943, Michigan File 533.183, Records of the War Manpower Commission, Record Group 211, National Archives (cited hereafter as WMC Records, RG 211); Straub, "Government Policy," 144.

than fifty-four hours a week, nor could a woman work in a variety of hazardous occupations, especially those that endangered her "capacity for motherhood." Thus women poured into the war plants as often as not in spite of, rather than because of, government policy.[14]

Women worked for many reasons. Some responded to propaganda that stressed the link between their jobs and the lives of their men in combat. "Since I have found the place where I can serve my country best, I should feel as if there were blood on my hands—his blood—if there were no oil on my hands today," a begrimed woman worker proclaimed from a 1943 recruiting advertisement.[15]

Women took jobs out of patriotism or as a way of escape from the tedium of separation from husband or fiancé. They sought to enlarge their economic opportunities, but in many instances, women worked simply to maintain a standard of living equivalent to or even lower than that to which they had become accustomed before the war. Service wives often experienced long delays in receiving government allotment checks or found that the monthly stipend did not stretch far enough. The Women's Bureau estimated that more than 70 per cent of Detroit's married female workers contributed at least 50 per cent of their earnings toward the maintenance of a family group. The majority of the women worked to live.[16]

Despite the declared manpower emergency, Michigan industry welcomed women with something less than enthusiasm. Lansing employers, confronted in late 1942 with a dwindling labor pool, refused to admit the need to recruit female workers, and Flint industry did not undertake mass hiring of women until August 1943. Manufacturers insisted that women simply were not the equal of men in factory work. Women did not understand machinery and were not trainable. Employers complained of the added costs of adjusting equipment used by women and of pro-

---

[14] *Detroit News*, October 1, 1943; January 17, June 18, 1942, February 11, 1943, May 16, 1945.

[15] *Ibid.*, September 8, 1943. On women and wartime propaganda, see Leila J. Rupp, *Mobilizing Women for War: German and American Propaganda, 1939-1945* (Princeton: Princeton Univ. Press, 1978).

[16] Phyllis Aronson, "Adequacy of the Family Allowance System as It Affects the Wives and Children of Men Drafted into the Armed Forces" (MA essay, Wayne Univ., 1944), 20, 67; Women's Bureau, *Women Workers*, 51, 53.

viding such facilities as separate washrooms and the like.[17]

Such negative attitudes, however, could not bar the new female workers from the shop floor, and once the women arrived, recalcitrant employers discovered that the necessary accommodations did not bring on bankruptcy and often promoted productivity. Observers noted that women's absentee rate was generally lower than that of men and that female motivation was generally higher. Briggs and Packard were among the many firms that hired women to act as counselors to the female workers. The counselor's mandate varied from plant to plant, but her duties usually included advising women of company policy and assisting them with personal or work-related problems. The UAW trained female stewards to take on similar responsibilities in several factories. Experience convinced management that women, after all, could learn quickly and well. Much was made of the ability of tiny feminine hands to deal with intricate components and of women's presumed aptitude for dull, repetitive tasks. "There isn't a thing women can't do here when we divide a job into small parts," said a superintendent at Cadillac. Such an assessment, of course, applied to many a raw male recruit as well, and not infrequently the praise bestowed by management on women workers carried a condescending undertone implying that women would never match men in industrial competition.[18]

Employers made no secret of their unwillingness to hire black women, whom management often regarded as so many refugees from *Porgy and Bess* or Harlem's Cotton Club. The first major breakthrough in black female hiring in Detroit did not come until the end of 1942, when, after a vigorous campaign by black protest organizations, token numbers of black women began work at Willow Run, Kelsey-Hayes, and Murray Body. The total black female labor force in the four-county Detroit metro-

[17] Ernest B. Harper, "Day Care for Children of Working Mothers: A Study of the Need for Day Care in Lansing, Michigan," December 1, 1942, 13, Administrative Records Relating to Nursery Schools, Record Group 70-49, Michigan State Archives, Lansing, Box 4 (cited hereafter as Nursery School Records, RG 70-49); Bureau of Labor Statistics, "Effects on Selected Communities of War Contract Cutbacks and Cancellations," 1944, 2, Headquarters Records, Records of the President's Committee on Fair Employment Practice, Record Group 228, National Archives; Walton, 372-383.

[18] Chafe, 138, 151-152; WMC-Michigan, "Female Counseling," May, 1944, Michigan File 533.18, WMC Records, RG 211; *Detroit News*, May 13, 1943; *Ford Times*, 1 (September 3, 1943), 3.

politan area rose from 20,170 in 1940 to 50,215 in 1944, a rise of 150 per cent and a rate of increase triple that of white female workers. Thousands of black domestics abandoned their positions as household servants for more lucrative factory work. Black women eventually constituted between 35 and 75 per cent of the workforce in certain small Detroit plants. Black females, however, remained concentrated in such low-wage positions as janitors, sweepers, and material handlers. And employer discrimination continued: in early 1944 a Detroit firm hired black females in order to demonstrate their incompetence as industrial employees, only to discover that the new workers were equal to their tasks.[19]

Women workers of all races faced a variety of discriminatory practices. Industry upgraded and promoted women much more slowly than men. Separate seniority lists often confined a woman's upward occupational mobility within a single all-female department. It was the wage issue, however, that caused the most controversy. Manufacturers customarily placed women in the lowest-paying jobs and paid them less for the performance of work traditionally done by men. Michigan state law guaranteed women equal pay for "similar" work, but the statute was so vague that it was virtually unenforceable. "In the plant I come from, we have thousands of women who in the past have been working on jobs that are practically identical with men's work, and yet because there was the word 'similar' in there, we have never been able to break this thing down," complained Irene Young, a worker from the General Motors (GM) Ternstedt plant in Detroit, in 1942. In late September of that year, the War Labor Board (WLB) ruled against GM in an equal-pay case brought by the UAW and the United Electrical Workers,

---

[19] U. S. Department of Agriculture, Bureau of Agricultural Economics, "The Social Dynamics of Detroit," December 3, 1942, 34-35, Records of the Office of Government Reports, Record Group 44, Washington National Records Center, Suitland, Maryland (cited hereafter as OGR Records, RG 44); Lloyd Bailer, "Negro Labor in the Automobile Industry," (unpublished PhD diss., Univ. of Michigan, 1943), 353-359; Catherine Blood, *Negro Women War Workers, Women's Bureau Bulletin No. 205* (Washington: U. S. Government Printing Office, 1945), 7; Robert Weaver, *Negro Labor, A National Problem* (New York: Harcourt, Brace & Co., 1946), 80-81; "Employment of Women as of April 1, 1943," UAW Research Department Collection, Box 3 (unprocessed); George Kirshner, "Government Agencies in Detroit in the Work of Overcoming Discrimination against the Negro in Private Employment" (MA Essay, Wayne Univ., 1945), 49-50.

and WLB General Order 16, issued in November, permitted companies to equalize male and female pay on a voluntary basis without reference to Washington.[20]

The voluntary clauses of the WLB's order, together with qualifications later placed on the original GM decision, vitiated the Board's original initiative. Organized labor failed to mount a sustained campaign on the equal-pay issue. Employers proved adept in maintaining the sexual pay differential by such means as giving different titles to similar jobs or by changing job classifications from skilled to semi-skilled. The Michigan Regional WLB issued a murky directive in August 1944 forbidding employers to pay lower rates to women because of slight changes in job content, but the same ruling stated that women were not entitled to equal pay *per se*, especially when costs were increased in order to hire them. Despite government laxity, union indifference, and employer evasion, women's average weekly wages in Michigan rose $14.40 between October 1942 and August 1944, while male wages increased only an average of $9.90 per week. By August 1944 women in the state's engine turbine industry earned 94.3 per cent as much as men, and female in the automobile industry had closed to within 89 per cent of the male wage average. But the weekly wage gap at that time favored males by $15.22, or more than seven hundred dollars a year.[21]

Male workers and union leaders did not go out of their way to welcome women employees. Men vociferously protested and sometimes went on strike against policies favorable to women, such as the movement of women to better shifts that they were not entitled to by strict seniority. Speaking before a New York City meeting of female unionists in October 1943, UAW president R. J. Thomas scored women for an alleged inability to think through problems; for their "ingratitude" in refusing to support unions, which were responsible for their high wages; and for their dependence on men for leadership.[22]

---

[20] Straub, "Government Policy," 242-43; "Equal Pay: Resolution and Discussion . . ., Chicago, Illinois, August, 1942," 1-2, Acc. 56-850, Records of the Women's Bureau, Record Group 86, Washington National Records Center (cited hereafter as Women's Bureau Records, RG 86).

[21] Straub, "Government Policy," 180-185, 244-250; Chafe, 155-158; *Lansing State Journal*, August 24, 1944; *Detroit News*, December 6, 1944; "Hours and Earnings of Men and Women in Factories: Michigan, August, 1944," *Monthly Labor Review*, 60 (January, 1945), 159-161.

[22] Straub, "Government Policy," 197-199, 203-204; *Decisions of the Impartial Um-*

Many women, however, undoubtedly agreed with May McKernan, a delegate to the 1942 UAW convention from a Detroit Plymouth local, who told her fellow unionists: "I should [not] like for the brothers to forget that when the subject of women comes up, they shouldn't say, 'Well, that's the woman's problem.' We are getting tired of men saying, 'Well, that's the woman's problem.'" In his 1943 scolding of women, Thomas had described the equal-pay issue as "a woman's problem," forgetting that much hung on the issue: the pay of thousands of returning veterans who might be forced to accept a "woman's wage" in order to reclaim jobs temporarily held by women; and the ability of the UAW to convince its members that it could win critical tests against management.[23]

Belatedly, the UAW took steps to bring itself into closer touch with its estimated 250,000 dues-paying female workers. In early 1944 the union established a Women's Bureau within its War Policy Division to offer counseling and other forms of aid. Mildred Jeffrey, an experienced organizer in the clothing industry serving at the time on the staff of the War Production Board (WPB) in Washington, was chosen to head the new department. Under the Bureau's auspices, a group of women delegates held the UAW's first Women's Conference on December 8-9, 1944 in Detroit. The conferees voted against special seniority rights for women, followed the CIO line by denouncing the Equal Rights Amendment then pending in Congress, and prodded the UAW International Executive Board to take more vigorous action on the equal-pay issue. The establishment of the Women's Bureau and the calling of the Women's Conference indicated a willingness on the part of Michigan's largest union to assist its female workers; the extent to which they were accepted, however, is indicated by the fact that R. J. Thomas began his 1944 annual report to a union one-fifth female in membership with the customary salutation, "Dear Sirs and Brothers."[24]

The woman worker may not have been the beloved of labor

---

*pire under the October 19, 1942 Agreement between General Motors Corporation and International Union, United Automobile, Aircraft, and Agricultural Implement Workers of America, CIO.* 2 vols. (Detroit: The Corporation, 1945), I, 465-466, 573-576; *The New York Times*, October 23, 1943.

[23] "Equal Pay," 2, Women's Bureau Records, RG 86.

[24] *United Automobile Worker*, March 1, 1944, September 15, 1944, January 1, 1945; *Detroit News*, December 10, 1944.

and management, but she was the undoubted darling of the press and public. According to a typically gushing newspaper report of mid-1943, every Rosie who riveted at Detroit's N. A. Woodworth Company looked "like a cross between a campus queen and a Hollywood starlet." The press closely scrutinized "the girls," their parties, and their late-night meetings with male coworkers at local bars. Such glamorization may have served a useful purpose insofar as it attracted women to war work by assuring them that they would not lose their "feminine" qualities in so doing. But some of the publicity, with its constant emphasis on beauty and its sexual innuendo, deprecated the woman worker as a person.[25]

Much of the excitement surrounding women workers was created by their special wearing apparel. For safety, industry forbade most female production workers to wear jewelry, nail polish, makeup, dresses, or Veronica Lake hairstyles. Snoods, low-heeled shoes, and slacks were "in." In the early 1940s, however, slacks were still garments to be worn only by a Marlene Dietrich or by the most chic of society trendsetters. In 1941 the *Detroit News*'s fashion writer had cautiously suggested to her readers: "If you have a truly adventurous spirit, you might pioneer in introducing slacks on city streets. Try wearing them around your neighborhood. . . . Report to us how the neighbors take to the idea."[26]

On the right figure, a pair of slacks could cause a sensation; supervision at the Ford Highland Park plant docked a young woman a half-hour's pay for wearing a pair of red slacks. The article of clothing in question, management claimed, created safety and production hazards because of the potential for distraction of male workers. The case ultimately reached Harry Shulman, the umpire of grievances under the Ford-UAW contract, who decided in favor of the woman in June 1944. Noting the absence of a company rule against vividly colored garments, Shulman opined, "It is common knowledge that wolves, unlike bulls, may be attracted by colors other than red and by various other enticements in the art and fit to female attire."[27]

Management often feared that the introduction of women

[25] *Detroit News*, January 25, August 17, 1943.
[26] *Ibid.*, April 25, 1941.
[27] Harry Shulman, *Opinions of the Umpire, Ford Motor Company and UAW-CIO, 1943-1946* (Detroit: n.p., 1946), A-117.

workers would set off a sexual explosion. General Motors adopted a strict policy of firing any male supervisor and female employee who were discovered to be "fraternizing." The company justified its position on the grounds that improper sexual conduct by either party could impair labor-management relations and might expose the policy of hiring women to unfair criticism. In a 1944 decision, the GM contract arbitrator upheld the dismissal of two women and two foremen from the Flint AC plant who had been seen together in after-hours spots. Unions sometimes proved as puritanical as management on the subject of sex; Flint UAW Local 599 voted in April 1943 to instruct committeemen to ignore grievances brought by any woman "indecent in her wearing apparel or actions." The minutes of the meeting offer no clue as to how the female members of the local divided on the issue. Here and there, a woman gained a nickel an hour more with a sultry glance, and a foreman conditioned the promotion of a woman on sexual considerations, but despite rumors of illicit affairs and illegitimate pregnancies, moral standards in war industry remained remarkably impervious to propinquity.[28]

The working woman of World War II was concerned with far more than the decency of her dress. An employee in plant or office, she was, in many instances, also the manager of a household. She shared with other citizens the discomforts of crowded housing and transportation, but manpower and supply shortages particularly frustrated her efforts to maintain a home. Too often, she found empty shelves or locked doors at neighborhood groceries. A WPB study of August 1943 estimated that 75 per cent of female absenteeism in one plant could be attributed to inadequate laundry service. The Detroit WPB office announced in February 1943 the appointment of local socialite and Presidential in-law Dorothy Kemp Roosevelt as special coordinator for both female recruitment and for women's out-of-plant problems; little, however, was ever heard from her. In seeking to solve war-related community problems, the federal government rarely distinguished between matters of concern to the entire community and those that impinged especially upon women. This attitude

[28] *Decisions of the Umpire* (GM), I, 735-736; "Minutes of the Meeting, Local 599," April 11, 1943, 5, Local 599 Collection, Archives of Labor History, Series 3, Box 2.

was described by Mary Anderson, one of the wartime directors of the Women's Bureau, who noted "a great tendency among governmental officials to speak about 'the people' as a whole, but when they spoke of 'the people,' they meant the men."[29]

The sudden entrance of thousands of women into industrial life raised many issues, and none carried more far-reaching social implications than the question of whether mothers should work, and the subsidiary problem of care for their children. Some mothers had always worked outside the home, but *Detroit News* women's advisor Nancy Brown stated the prevalent opinion about the practice in a 1940 reply to a woman undecided about seeking a job: "Your children are still of school age. In spite of your assertion to the contrary, they do need you. It would not be possible for you to carry on two jobs, one outside your home and one inside."[30]

Throughout the war, government agencies, social workers, educators, and politicians echoed this sentiment in varying words. Mothers who worked, it was maintained, might do enormous psychic harm to their young children and irreparable damage to the family, the primary social unit. The WMC released its first official statement on the working-mother question during the spring of 1942: "The first responsibility of women with young children in war, as in peace, is to give suitable care in their own homes to their children."[31]

Even when the state reached the height of its manpower demand in November 1943, Governor Harry Kelly observed: "I have yet to find any emergency that should call mothers away from home to the detriment of our youth. For the good of the Michigan of tomorrow, I ask mothers of young children to pause and consider before they seek outside employment. . . . Consider your children."[32]

Among the arguments mustered on behalf of working mothers was the contention that their employment in war industry might

---

[29] WPB, "Problems of Women War Workers in Detroit," August 20, 1943; 1-2, Regional Classified Files, Region V-Michigan, Records of the Office of Community War Services, Record Group 215, National Archives (cited hereafter as OCWS Records, RG 215); *Detroit News*, February 25, 1943; Straub, "United States Government Policy," 244-245.

[30] *Detroit News*, April 11, 1940.

[31] Straub, "Government Policy," 260-261; Chafe, 163-164.

[32] *Detroit News*, November 14, 1943.

reduce migration into congested areas (there is no evidence, however, that such a relationship actually developed). The economic imperative certainly weighed heavily upon the woman who had to support her family while her husband was in the service. Even the 1942 WMC directive cited above insisted that no bar to employment be placed in the way of mothers with young children and that "the decision as to gainful employment should, in all cases, be an individual decision made by the woman herself. . . . When certain Michigan factories attempted to exclude younger mothers, management invariably discovered that many women lied about their family status rather than lose the chance for work. Since women workers were being recruited and since an increasingly large number of mothers intended to work in spite of pleas to the contrary, something had to be done about their children, from whom they would be separated for a large part of each working day.[33]

A few isolated schools and centers had pioneered the concept of day care. Detroit's Merrill-Palmer School, founded in 1920 to instruct young women in home management and child development techniques, opened the state's first nursery school in 1922. During the depression the Federal Emergency Relief Administration and the Works Progress (later the Work Projects) Administration (WPA) introduced day care on a nationwide basis by opening centers for the children of mothers receiving government assistance. The WPA centers were closed to regularly employed women.[34]

With the onset of the defense boom in the spring of 1941, officials in the Michigan Department of Social Welfare (DSW) grew anxious about the "haphazard and undesirable day nurseries" that were springing up. State welfare officials began to plan for the establishment of a committee to coordinate day care service in hard-hit Wayne County. Such a committee began work in Detroit in January 1942, its leadership and expertise supplied

---

[33] Irene Murphy, "Detroit's Experience in the Wartime Care of Children," in Cordelia Trimble, ed., *Proceedings of the National Conference of Social Work* (New York: Columbia Univ. Press, 1943), 133-134; Straub, "Government Policy," 261-263; Clarence Young, *Foundation for Living: The Story of Charles Stewart Mott and Flint* (New York: McGraw-Hill, 1963), 161-162.

[34] Robert Bremner, ed., *Children and Youth in America: A Documentary History*, 3 vols. (Cambridge, MA.: Harvard Univ. Press, 1971-1973), III. Part I. 677-678; Merrill-Palmer Institute, 1976-1977 *Catalogue* (Detroit: Merrill-Palmer, 1975), 6-7.

in large part by Irene Murphy, a social worker and lecturer at Wayne University, and Dr. Edna Noble White, for twenty years director of Merrill-Palmer. Thirty-seven communities across the state eventually organized more or less active counterparts of the Wayne County body. There was a need for a complementary state organization and in November 1942 the Michigan government asked Dr. White to chair a State Day Care Committee (SDCC) under the sponsorship of the MCD.[35]

Although Michigan took the initiative in setting up an administrative structure for day care, no network of nursery centers could be organized without federal assistance. Various government agencies, including the United States Children's Bureau (USCB) and the Federal Works Agency (FWA), examined the day care question throughout 1941, and in February, 1942 the FWA received permission to use Lanham Act funds for the construction and maintenance of child care centers for the children of working mothers. Enacted in 1940, the Lanham Act authorized federal aid to defense-impacted communities. The first such project, however, did not win final certification until August 31, 1942. The FWA could pay all expenses for nursery projects under certain circumstances, but it generally adhered to the standard Lanham funding formula that required localities to contribute half of all costs. Washington eventually spent nearly fifty-three million dollars for hundreds of day care centers, established primarily in major production areas. Shortly after Pearl Harbor, the WPA opened its centers to children of working mothers and to youngsters with a parent in the armed forces, and this expanded program continued until the agency's demise in mid-1943.[36]

The Detroit, Highland Park, and Hamtramck boards of education agreed to supervise separate federally sponsored nursery programs, and the necessary documents were sent to Washington for

[35] Gladys Cook to Dr. Edna Noble White, June 6, 1941, Nursery School Records, RG 70-49, Box 2; Irma Unruh to Cook, November 6, 1941, *ibid.*; Cook to Unruh, November 13, 1941, *ibid.*; Irene Murphy "Day Care in Wayne County: Its Past and Future," November 30, 1945, 1, *ibid.;* Michigan Department of Social Welfare, "Proposed State Plan for Day Care in Michigan," October 29, 1942, 1, *ibid.*, Box 1; *Detroit News*, November 13, 1942.

[36] Straub, "Government Policy," 264, 265-271, 274; Chafe, 165-166; Elsie M. Bond to Chairmen, Local War Service Committees et al, November, 1942, 5-6, Nursery School Records, RG 70-49, Box 2.

approval in October 1942. The FWA assented to the plans in March 1943, agreeing further to take over the twenty-three Wayne County WPA centers, which were due to close within a matter of weeks. By the end of January 1945 twenty-eight Michigan communities, most of them in the four-county Detroit area, were sponsoring 179 child care centers at an estimated cost for the first six months of the year of $1,694,828, 60 per cent of which was provided by the FWA.[37]

The most popular type of facility was the day nursery for two-to-five year-old children. Practices varied from area to area, but most centers operated continuously for twelve hours, from six-thirty or seven o'clock in the morning onward. They served three meals a day, offered organized recreation directed by nursery teachers and volunteers, and provided cots or beds for afternoon naps. Extended school services allowed mothers to leave children six to fourteen years of age for care immediately before and after school. These centers or "canteens" usually were located within the school building itself. A center for night care proved unsuccessful in Detroit, but similar centers apparently worked well in Ypsilanti and Saginaw. Several communities sought to obtain care for infants by encouraging nonworking women to become foster mothers, taking perhaps three or four infants into their homes for more individualized attention. In addition to sponsoring such programs, four Michigan cities ran counseling services to guide mothers to the best available child care, and the Wayne County committee organized an elaborate information clearinghouse, the Children's War Service (CWS), in April 1943.[38]

Day care advocates supported their demands with a flood of statistics suggestive of a great unmet need. The Wayne County committee estimated in early 1943 that local war plants and civilian industry employed some sixty thousand mothers, who had forty-five thousand children potentially in need of care. On the

[37] *Detroit News*, January 3, February 24, March 14, June 30, 1943; "Programs in War-Impacted Areas to which FWA Assistance is Being Provided," 1945, 1, Records of the Executive Office, Harry F. Kelly, Governor, 1943-1946, Record Group 42, State Archives, Box 114 (cited hereafter as Executive Records, RG 42).

[38] DSW, "Day Care in Michigan," February 3, 1944, Nursery School Records, RG 70-49, Box 1; Murphy, "Day Care in Wayne County," 1, *ibid.*, Box 2; Ruth C. Rogers, "A Report on Children's War Service," June 16, 1943, *ibid.*; Region V OCWS, "Composite Report on Health, Welfare, and Related Activities in the Detroit, Michigan, War Area," December 22, 1943, 54, OCWS Records, RG 215.

basis of this and other surveys, the Michigan WMC devised a formula that calculated that one child required day care for every seven women employed in Michigan industry (the ratio was projected to be 1:5 for women entering manufacturing for the first time). The friends of day care also noted many pathetic instances of individual deprivation. Thousands of children roamed the streets of industrial communities unable to enter homes locked for the day by their war-worker parents. More fortunate youngsters carried the house key on a string fastened around the neck.[39]

A need clearly existed, yet day care centers were strikingly underutilized both in Michigan and across the country. Nationally, Lanham Act programs served a mere hundred thousand children, perhaps a tenth of those eligible, and far fewer than the total of youngsters served by Great Britain's more elaborate system of child care. To be sure, the number of day care children in Michigan steadily increased, reaching 6,024 in early 1945 (4,501 in metropolitan Detroit), while the number of employed women steadily declined. But the same surveys that seemed to affirm the necessity for day care consistently reported that no more than 5 to 10 per cent of the presumably needy youngsters were actually enrolled in nursery school programs.[40]

An analysis of the Michigan day care failure casts light on the underlying forces in society that actively or unwittingly placed limits on wartime change. Bureaucratic in-fighting and political opposition at the national level hobbled the day care program from the outset. The Children's Bureau, the Office of Education, and the Federal Security Administration (FSA) waged guerrilla war against the FWA for control of day care policy and funds. On the one hand, the FSA and its allies favored a state-controlled program that placed emphasis on foster homes and a high quality of care; the FWA, on the other hand, looked upon a federally

[39] Region V OCWS, "Composite Report," 56, OCWS Records, RG 215; *Grand Rapids Press*, July 1, 1943; SDCC, "Report of the State Day Care Committee to Donald S. Leonard," November 23, 1943, 3-4, Executive Records, RG 42, Box 88; Ruth C. Rogers, "Care of Children of Working Mothers in Michigan," April 28, 1944, 2, Nursery School Records, RG 70-49, Box 1; DSW, "Day Care Bulletin," January 13, 1944, 1, *ibid.*; DSW, "Day Care in Michigan," February 3, 1944, *ibid.*; DSW, "Report on Day Care in Michigan," June, 1943, 4-5, *ibid.*

[40] Chafe, 170; "Programs in Impacted Communities," 1, Executive Records, RG 42, Box 114; SDCC, "Report of the State Day Care Committee," 3-4, *ibid.*, Box 88; Rogers, "Care of Children of Working Mothers," 2, Nursery School Records, RG 70-49, Box 1; DSW, "Day Care in Michigan," *ibid.*; DSW, "Report on Day Care," 4-5, *ibid.*

controlled system of rapidly constructed group centers as the best answer to the problem of child care in a temporary crisis. The struggle came to a climax when the contending parties clashed over a day-care bill introduced in Congress earlier that year by Senator Elbert Thomas of Utah. The Thomas bill gave the Children's Bureau final jurisdiction over day care and revamped the entire program to suit foster-care proponents. Passed by the Senate, the measure died in a House committee. Neither the Lanham Act nor its supplementary titles mentioned day care, and the entire nursery program was generally unpopular on Capitol Hill. President Roosevelt finally arranged a cease-fire in August, 1943 that left the FWA's authority intact.[41]

Bickering and buckpassing concerning Michigan day care rivalled the fighting in Washington. In several communities, the local Council of Social Agencies, which favored day care, fought with the county MCD committee, which did not. During a special session in 1944 the state legislature defeated a program sponsored by the State Day Care Committee to establish counseling centers and to provide state-funded child care services in war-impacted areas wherever local initiative failed to do so. State lawmakers enacted bills authorizing boards of education to set up nursery facilities and bringing private day care centers under state licensing authority, but these statutes did not represent a fundamental state commitment to day care. Charged with the major responsibility for the financing and operation of day care centers, local school boards, usually strapped for cash, objected to paying for a program so costly and so socially questionable.[42]

Administrative and legal problems also dogged day care in Michigan. A federal regulation prohibited school districts from asking for Lanham Act funds until schoolbuildings reached 200 per cent of capacity, by which time most such schools no longer

[41] Howard Dratch, "The Politics of Child Care in the 1940s," *Science and Society*, 38 (Summer, 1974), 176-186; Chafe, 166-170; Straub, "Government Policy," 271, 280-284.

[42] Leroy Peterson to Joseph Wilson, July 20, 1944, Records Relating to the Operation of Field Offices, Records of the President's Committee for Congested Production Areas, Record Group 212, National Archives; DSW, "Report on Day Care," 1, Nursery School Records, RG 70-49; Gunnar Dybwad to Monica Owen, November 19, 1945, *ibid.*, Box 2; *Day Care News*, April, 1945, 1, Lanham Act Records, Records of the United States Office of Education, Record Group 12, National Archives (cited hereafter as Education Records, RG 12).

had room for a day care center. Once a locality applied for government assistance, it had to surmount seven separate state and federal reviews before approval was granted. A 1943 study of Detroit day care needs revealed that many of the centers were poorly located (it was not unusual for waiting lists to lengthen at one nursery while other centers remained half-empty), improperly staffed, and inadequately administered. A cumbersome Detroit licensing ordinance made it all but impossible for individual women to offer foster care in their homes. Illegal foster homes inevitably appeared, and the press reported that a three-month old baby had suffocated at one such home in Detroit and that children had been beaten in others.[43]

The statistics of need the day care defenders cited were subject to wild fluctuations: the Census Bureau's sample survey of the Detroit-Willow Run area in 1944 counted only half as many children eligible for day care as previous compilations had indicated, and the state WMC thereafter revised its ratio of needy children to employed mothers upward to one to nine. Reflecting on the vicissitudes that beset the state's child-care effort, the supervisor of the DSW's Children's Division, Gunnar Dybwad, concluded in a November 1945 letter that "Michigan has no reason to be particularly proud of its day care program."[44]

Michigan industry did little to accommodate the working mother. As the great Detroit female recruitment drive began in the fall of 1942, local manufacturers stated that they had no plans to provide day care facilities. A UAW woman told the Senate Education and Labor Committee considering the Thomas bill in June 1943 that many mothers had been forced to quit war jobs for lack of adequate nursery centers. It was not until September 1943 that the Automotive Council for War Production began to circulate information throughout Detroit war plants publicizing available facilities. Hudson established a center for the children of mothers employed in all three of its Detroit plants, but nowhere in Michigan were there day care services equal to the

[43] Region V OCWS, "Composite Report," 54, OCWS Records, RG 215; Betty Heliker, "The Need for a Day Care Program in Detroit" (MA Essay, Univ. of Michigan, 1943), 19, 22, 40-53; *Detroit News*, February 21, March 13, September 19, October 3, November 21, 1943.

[44] *Day Care News*, September 27, 1944, 1, Education Records, RG 12; Dybwad to Owen, November 19, 1945, Nursery School Records, RG 70-49; Box 2.

highly publicized programs in the West Coast shipbuilding industry. Although Michigan organized labor generally supported day care and Irene Murphy credited the UAW as the driving force behind her Wayne County committee, the unions apparently allowed their female members to carry on alone the battle for expanded child care services, the struggle being seen as only another "woman's problem." Neither labor nor management seemed eager to take the steps, admittedly complex, required to assign working mothers with young children to convenient shifts.[45]

Day care specialists spent most of the war years attempting to explain the seeming maternal indifference that even the minimal use of day care appeared to signify. The UAW claimed, with much justification, that many women simply could not afford to pay the fees charged for day care. Weekly costs for day care in Detroit varied from six dollars at a city-run center to sixteen dollars for a foster home, no small sums for that majority of working women who made less than the average of $47 per week earned by Detroit female employees in 1943. Other observers emphasized the apathy of working mothers or their lack of knowledge. The Detroit Board of Education discovered that a three-month lag existed between the time a center opened and the generation of a large-scale response from the nursery's expected clientele. Women often resented having to deal with social workers and counselors; middle-class mothers especially perceived day care, with its WPA antecedents, to be a welfare measure and shied away from mixing their children with youngsters from the lower classes.[46]

At base, most women rejected day care services because they preferred to have their children cared for by relatives, neighbors, or friends—or not at all—rather than by strangers in a nursery or a canteen. Despite the horror stories about "latch-key" children, most mothers were able to make arrangements that the mothers

[45] *Detroit News*, September 2, 1942; Sept. 19, 26, 1943; U. S. Congress, Senate, Committee on Education and Labor, *Hearings*, 78 Cong., 1st sess. (Washington: U.S. Government Printing Office, 1943), Part I, 451; Murphy, "Detroit's Experience," in Trimble, 136-137; Dratch, "Politics of Child Care," 184-185.

[46] Senate Committee on Education and Labor, *Hearings*, Part I, 91, 93; DSW, "Day Care in Michigan," February 3, 1944, 1, Nursery School Records, RG 70-49, Box 1; Straub, "Government Policy," 292-294; SDCC, "Report to Governor Harry F. Kelly on the Need for a State Day Care Program," December 3, 1943, 9, Executive Records, RG 42, Box 86.

apparently regarded as satisfactory. The Women's Bureau 1944-1945 survey reported that 92 per cent of Detroit working women with children under fourteen years of age claimed to have made some provision for regular care, with only a meager 2 per cent relying on day nurseries. When an interviewer asked a group of Detroit working mothers why they did not avail themselves of the local day care program, she received such replies as the following: "I wouldn't have a stranger"; "No one could be better than my mother"; and, "The baby might catch a disease in a nursery."[47]

With the exception of a few lay activists, it was the child welfare professional, not the mother, who demanded day care in World War II. Social workers and psychologists were convinced that many children suffered grave emotional harm because mothers provided insufficient nurture on the spurious grounds that self-care was "good experience" and that youngsters could "fend for themselves." Irene Murphy told a 1943 meeting of the SDCC that the necessity for day care had long existed and that the war simply had brought the need into sharper focus. Yet the child-care experts probably confused and distressed some mothers by constant arguments over such issues as the desirability of foster care as opposed to group care or the merits and deficiencies of the Lanham Act program. Day care advocates, moreover, undercut their case by agreeing with opponents that the working mother could pose a threat to the child. "Experiences in established child-care agencies show that the war has had some effect on parents' relationship with their children," noted Charlene Schiland, chairwoman of the Kent County (Grand Rapids) child care committee; "mothers in many instances seemingly have become independent of domestic ties and are seeking an opportunity to get out of the home into employment. . . . A number of broken homes are the result of extremes of this feeling."[48]

The Michigan day care program faced termination with the approach of victory and the general decline in war-related em-

[47] Women's Bureau, *Women Workers*, 55-56; Aronson, "Adequacy of Dependency," 69-70.

[48] *Day Care News*, January, 1945, 1, Education Records, RG 12; Straub, "Government Policy," 292-294; "Minutes of the Meeting of the State Day Care Committee," September 28, 1944, 3, Nursery School Records, RG 70-49, Box 2; DSW, "Day Care for Children," 3, *ibid.*, Box 4; *Grand Rapids Press*, July 2, 1943.

ployment. Since all Lanham Act authorizations were scheduled to expire on June 30, 1945 the Wayne County committee organized a letter-writing campaign to persuade the Federal government to extend funding. During the summer and fall the FWA granted several reprieves, agreeing in October to finance a curtailed operation through July 1946. A group of two hundred mothers led by Irene Murphy petitioned the Detroit Board of Education in late August to maintain a skeleton system of twenty-five centers, and on September 26 after the Common Council guaranteed the necessary funding, the Board approved the mothers' proposal. Although the State Day Care Committee lingered on, the Wayne County panel, the most vigorous proponent of child care in Michigan, wound up its affairs on November 30, 1945.[49]

Day care centers constituted what might have been, in Eleanor Straub's words, "the most significant social experiment of the war years." Child welfare specialists learned through their wartime experience much about the aims and realities of day care. A sufficient number of Detroit mothers became interested in the service to support a small program into the late 1940s, and the DSW reappointed a state day care consultant in 1947, the post having been vacant since the legislature's rebuff of the SDCC's statewide nursery plan three years earlier. Limited, well-run nursery schools gained a measure of acceptance among the postwar middle class, but the concept of large-scale day care for the children of working mothers never caught on. Nothing happened during World War II to warrant abandonment of the belief that the mother—and the mother alone—bore the principal responsibility for the upbringing of her children.[50]

The failure of working mothers to make sufficient use of nursery facilities eventually relegated the question of day care to a position of secondary importance. A problem of greater import, and one that could not be swept aside, was the postwar status of

[49] *Detroit News*, June 7, 27, August 28, 29, Sept. 26, 1945; "Minutes of the Meeting of the State Day Care Committee," July 24, 1945, 1-10, Nursery School Records, RG 70-49, Box 2; R. C. Ashton to F. F. Fauri, October 22, 1945, *ibid.*; Alice May to Gunnar Dybwad, August 26, 1945, *ibid.*; Murphy, "Day Care in Wayne County," 1, *ibid.*

[50] Straub, "Government Policy," 263, 296; Michigan Social Welfare Commission, *Fourth Biennial Report, July, 1944-June, 1946* (Lansing: The Commission, 1946), 57; Chafe, 158-159.

working women. Even as Detroit manpower officials readied postcards for distribution to area women in the opening phase of the August 1942 recruitment drive, the author of a letter to the *Detroit News* mused: "We have quite a number of intelligent men devising ways and means of getting women in on all the factory and war jobs so we boys can go knock off a Jap and a Heinie, but I really want to meet the chap who is intelligent enough to get them out again when we boys come back."[51]

The army of newly employed women added greater uncertainty to already uncertain postwar economic calculations, as evidence accumulated to document female intentions of remaining at work. The Women's Bureau reported in May 1945 that 75 per cent of all Detroit working women desired some form of postwar employment. The percentage rose to 80 per cent among women employed before Pearl Harbor and fell to no less than 60 per cent among former housewives.[52]

Such surveys, of course, indicated only what women wished to do, not what they would do after V-J Day. Many female workers probably wanted to remain in their high-paying industrial jobs but did not really expect to do so. A large number of women declared against future employment if their husbands could support them or if men were in need of work. A national consensus, moreover, developed rapidly and strongly in support of the contention that women should not remain at work in their wartime numbers once peace returned. Opinion polls found solid majorities opposed to female employment that jeopardized jobs for men. The Federal government took pains to emphasize the temporary nature of war work and did nothing to encourage women in their aspirations for peacetime jobs. A spate of books and articles appeared, increasing in volume as victory neared, picturing a happy future for women in wedded bliss and in homes chock-a-block with long-unavailable consumer goods.[53]

Betty Allie, chairwoman of the Michigan Unemployment Compensation Commission, spoke for the majority when she said in November 1943: "When the period of postwar adjustment comes, and their men come home, . . . you will see women returning

[51] *Detroit News*, August 2, 1942.
[52] *Ibid.*, February 10, May 9, 23, 1945; "Women's Postwar Job Plans," *Monthly Labor Review*, 58 (May, 1944), 1030; Women's Bureau, *Women Workers*, 40-48.
[53] Straub, "Government Policy," 141-143, 323; Chafe, 175-179.

naturally to their homes. A woman's first interests are her home, her husband, and their children. . . ." Women without family ties or who had lost husbands during the war were entitled to employment, Allie continued, "but there need be no fear that all [women] will compete for the postwar job. They will look on this period in their lives as an interlude. . . . Women will always be women."[54]

When production cutbacks accelerated during the spring and summer of 1945, women were severed from employment at a rate approximately double that of men. Women composed one of the largest elements in the low-seniority pool ordinarily laid off first, but management had other ways of ridding itself of unwanted females. A government survey of conditions in Michigan as of September noted that some employers were shuffling work assignments to give women the sort of heavy-lifting jobs that they were either legally barred from performing or that they might not want. One GM plant in Flint violated seniority altogether to put all women on the midnight shift.[55] The majority of women who worked prior to the war could return to being waitresses, shop clerks, or maids, but they could not remain in industry.

Those women who turned for help to their unions found little comfort. The UAW was preoccupied with assimilating the returning veterans and with its forthcoming confrontation with General Motors. Walter Reuther warned the Women's Conference in 1944 that women could expect no "special privilege" to enable them to hold on to their jobs; rather, they must fight for a full employment economy. By November 1945 Michigan's nonfarm female workforce stood at 525,000, a quarter of a million less than the wartime peak, but still higher both proportionately and absolutely than in 1940. Female manufacturing employment in Detroit, however, fell from 124,000 in March 1945 to sixty-six thousand by year's end, one-quarter of the wartime high and a mere twenty thousand more than in 1940. Only a handful of women workers protested the treatment accorded them.[56]

---

[54] *Detroit News*, November 26, 1943.

[55] Straub, "Government Policy," 338-343; Sheila Tobias and Lisa Anderson, "Whatever Happened to 'Rosie the Riveter'?," *Ms*, 1, (June, 1973), 92-97.

[56] *United Automobile Worker*, January 1, 1945; Haber, 149, (shortly after V-J Day a small group of women picketed UAW headquarters in Detroit, demanding that the Women's Bureau within the union be upgraded, an all-female staff be pro-

When America entered the war, leaders of some of the prominent women's organizations expressed cautious optimism that the nation would respond to the female contribution to victory with the grant of equality. As V-J Day dawned, however, it was difficult to determine the actual extent of change. The volume of female employment had risen, but women's status had not. The government, so generous in its praise of female America, still evinced no willingness to grant women an effective voice in political or economic decision-making. Neither business, labor, nor any other major organized segment of society supported a significant change in women's role based on wartime accomplishments. There had been no revolution in attitudes, only a series of expedient measures, often implemented grudgingly in the face of national emergency. The genteel club leaders and lady college presidents who functioned as spokeswomen for their sex submitted, with more or less grace, to male notions of women's place.[57]

Women of other nations made no more progress toward equality during the war than did their American sisters. British women had received the vote in partial reward for their contributions during World War I but secured no comparable concession after 1945. Since Nazi ideology enshrined women as childbearers, Hitler vetoed plans put forth in 1942 for the increased employment of German-born women in munitions plants, preferring slave labor. Thomas R. H. Havens found that the status of Japanese women rose little between 1937 and 1945. Despite enormous strains placed on the Japanese economy by mobilization and American aerial assault, the tradition-bound military regime opposed the utilization of large numbers of women in war industry. "It is moot," Havens concludes, "whether total war more greatly ossifies or transforms a people in response to national crisis."[58]

This observation was no less true of the United States than of its enemies, especially in light of the objectives for which

vided for the Bureau, and female representation be increased on the staff of other UAW divisions [*Michigan Chronicle*, August 18, 1945]).

[57] Leila J. Rupp, "A Reappraisal of American Women in a Man's War, 1941-1945" (paper delivered at the Second Annual Berkshire Conference on Women's History, Radcliffe College, October, 1974), 1-5, 20-21.

[58] Angus Calder, *The People's War: 1939-1945* (New York: Pantheon, 1969), 400; Albert Speer, *Inside the Third Reich* (New York: Avon Books paperback, 1971), 294-295; Thomas R. H. Havens, "Women and War in Japan, 1937-45," *American Historical Review*, 80 (October, 1975), 913-933.

America fought. Save for the Four Freedoms address and the Atlantic Charter, both of which predated Pearl Harbor, President Roosevelt shied away from the high-flow patriotic rhetoric that marked World War I. At one point, he recorded his wish that the new global conflict be known simply as "the Survival War." What Roosevelt and the American people wished to see survive was the existing social and political order. The depression of the 1930s had caused millions to question the justice of that order. The New Deal had tinkered with the problem of economic collapse for years without satisfactory solution. Dictators abroad and doubters at home sneered at American institutions and saw the nation sliding toward social catastrophe.[59]

The war offered Americans the chance to vindicate their system. Michigan's governor, Murray D. Van Wagoner, expressed a belief held by many when he told his fellow state chief executives in August 1942:

> When Hitler sneered at democracy, and when we ourselves began to wonder if perhaps we were incapable of uniting to do the job that had to be done, the war gave us the chance to prove to ourselves that America still has the best economic and political system on earth, a system that creates, that offers hope for a better and more prosperous world tomorrow, . . . a system that we can all believe in and work for, and fight and die for.[60]

Americans wanted affirmation, not change. The pride of the nation before 1929 had been its industrial machine, exemplified best by the automotive factories of Detroit and Michigan. To that machine, and not to a transforming doctrine, the nation turned in 1941 for the key to victory. Among the most hallowed of American institutions to be protected and affirmed was the traditional concept of womanhood. It was during World War II that the apotheosis of the unliberated woman, Miss America, rose to national prominence and respect. At times it appeared that every nubile young woman was competing for a place in the pin-up parade. Most women failed to grasp whatever opportunity for

[59] Jerome S. Bruner, *Mandate from the People* (New York: Duel, Sloan and Pearce, 1944), 28-29; Eric Goldman, *Rendezvous with Destiny: A History of American Reform* (New York: Random House, 1956), 301; William E. Leuchtenburg, *Franklin D. Roosevelt and the New Deal, 1932-1940* (New York: Harper and Row, 1963), 275-276.

[60] Murray D. Van Wagoner, "Operating the Tool Shop of America," *Vital Speeches*, 8 (August, 1942), 664; Perrett, 440-442.

emancipation the war afforded. As Straub observes, they "saw it as a matter of production and military strategy rather than a contest of values and ideals." Women perceived World War II very much as men did, and by and large, expected no more than a better life for themselves and their families in a nation renewed and once more confident.[61]

[61] Frank Deford, *There She Is: The Life and Times of Miss America* (New York: Viking, 1971), 153-160; Straub, "United States Government Policy," 242-243, 254.

# Last Hired, First Fired: Black Women Workers during World War II

**Karen Tucker Anderson**

As a result of the increasing demand for workers in all categories of employment, and especially in the high-paying manufacturing sector, the full employment economy of World War II posed the most serious challenge in American history to the traditional management preference for white male labor in primary-sector jobs. The war years were especially important for blacks, who benefited from an expanding labor force, changing racial values, a revitalized migration out of the rural South, and the attempted enforcement of equal employment opportunity under a presidential executive order. Although scholars have given some attention to the labor-force fortunes of blacks in the war economy, few have considered the impact of the wartime expansion on black women, who constituted 600,000 of the 1,000,000 blacks who entered paid employment during the war years. Those who have focused on black women have stressed the degree to which the war opened new job categories and fostered mobility. William Chafe, for example, contends that the opportunities generated by the wartime economy and the long-term changes they fostered constituted a "second emancipation" for black women. According to Dale L. Hiestand, occupational shifts by black women workers during the 1940s promoted substantial income improvement.[1]

Karen Tucker Anderson is assistant professor of history at the University of Arizona.

[1] Robert C. Weaver, *Negro Labor: A National Problem* (Port Washington, N.Y., 1969); Herbert Hill, *Black Labor and the American Legal System: Race, Work, and the Law* (Washington, 1977); Philip S. Foner, *Organized Labor and the Black Worker, 1619-1973* (New York, 1974), 238-74; Harvard Sitkoff, "Racial Militancy and Interracial Violence in the Second World War," *Journal of American History*, 58 (Dec. 1971), 661-81; Richard R. Lingeman, *Don't You Know There's A War On! The American Home Front, 1941-1945* (New York, 1970), 195-201; Charles C. Killingsworth, *Jobs and Income for Negros* (Ann Arbor, Mich., 1968), 20-48; Herbert R. Northrup, *Negro Employment in Basic Industry: A Study of Racial Policies in Six Industries* (Philadelphia, 1970), 11-18, 26-30, 61-64, 145-49; Ray Marshall, *Negro Employment in the South* (3 vols., Springfield, Va., 1973), I, 8-10; Philip S. Foner, *Women and the American Labor Movement: From World War I to the Present* (New York, 1980), 344-48; William Chafe, *The American Woman: Her Changing Social, Economic, and Political Roles, 1920-1970* (New York, 1972), 142-43; Daniel O. Price, *Changing Characteristics of the Negro Population* (Washington, 1969), 6; Dale L. Hiestand, *Economic Growth and Employment Opportunities for Minorities* (New York, 1964), 35; "War and Post-War Trends in Employment of Negroes," *Monthly Labor Review*, 60 (Jan. 1945), 1.

A careful examination of the labor-force status of black women during the 1940s brings into question such sanguine pronouncements. Focusing on the wartime experiences of black women provides insight into the nature of prejudice as manifested and experienced by women and into the sources and mechanisms of labor-force discrimination in a particular historical context. It also facilitates an examination of the relative importance of managerial intransigence and coworker prejudice in perpetuating discriminatory employment practices. In addition, it gives an indication of the importance of tight labor markets in fostering economic mobility for minority group women.[2]

Labor force statistics support the contention that the war marked an important break with the historic allocation of work by race and sex. Between 1940 and 1944 the proportion of employed black women engaged in domestic service declined from 59.9 percent to 44.6 percent, although their share of jobs in this field increased because white women exited from private household work in even greater proportions. In addition, the percentage of the black female labor force in farm work was cut in half, as many from the rural South migrated to urban areas in response to the demand for war workers. The shift of large numbers of black women from work in farms and homes to work in factories resulted in the proportion of black females employed in industrial occupations rising from 6.5 percent to 18 percent during the war. A comparable expansion also occurred in personal service work outside of the private household, which claimed 17.9 percent of black women workers in 1944.[3]

To stress only the improvement wrought during the war, however, is to understate the extent to which discrimination persisted and to ignore the fact that the assumptions of a historically balkanized labor force continued to determine the distribution of the benefits of a full employment economy. When faced with a shortage of white male workers, employers had various options. They could seek workers from other areas of the country, hoping that this would enable them to minimize the changes produced by the wartime expansion, or they could rely on underutilized elements of the local labor supply—workers in nonessential employment, women, blacks, and older and younger workers. If unable to secure large numbers of white male in-migrants and unwilling to modify hiring patterns too dramatically, they could limit production, sacrificing output to prejudice.[4]

Those who decided to employ substantially increased numbers of women and/or minorities established a complex hierarchy of hiring preferences based

[2] Marshall, *Negro Employment*, I, 8–45; Ronald L. Oaxaca, "Theory and Measurement in the Economics of Discrimination," in *Equal Rights and Industrial Relations*, ed. Leonard J. Hausman et al. (Madison, Wis., 1977), 1–30; Marcus Alexis, "The Political Economy of Labor Market Discrimination: Synthesis and Exploration," in *Patterns of Racial Discrimination: Employment and Income*, ed. George M. von Furstenberg, Ann R. Horowitz, and Bennett Harrison (Lexington, Mass., 1974), 63–83; Duran Bell, Jr., "The Economic Basis of Employee Discrimination," in *ibid.*, 121–35.

[3] "War and Post-War Trends," 1–5.

[4] "Employment of Minority Workers during Current Period of Intensive War Production," [1945], box 378, Records of the President's Committee on Fair Employment Practice, RG 228 (National Archives); "Labor Market Problems in Selected Firms Manufacturing Machine Guns, War Manpower Commission," March 5, 1943, box 408, *ibid.*; "Macon, Georgia—Group 1," [1943], *ibid.*; Foner, *Organized Labor*, 243.

on the composition of the local labor force and the nature of the work to be done. In light industries, women workers became the first recourse of employers unable to recruit large numbers of white males. In the airframe industry, for example, women constituted 40.6 percent of the employees by November 1943, while blacks claimed only 3.5 percent of airframe jobs. Employers in heavy industries, by contrast, sought minority males as a preferred source of labor, with the result that the level of utilization of women depended on the minority population of an area. In Baltimore, for example, blacks comprised up to 20 percent of the shipbuilding workers while women represented only 4 percent. Seattle, which had only a small black population, relied on women for 16 percent of its shipyard employees.[5]

Whatever the hierarchy of preference, however, black women could always be found at the bottom. The dramatic expansion of jobs for women did not necessarily mean the opening up of new categories of employment for minority group women. A survey conducted by the United Auto Workers (UAW) in April 1943 found that only 74 out of 280 establishments that employed women in production work were willing to hire black women. Similarly, a 1943 study by the National Metal Trades Association revealed that only twenty-nine out of sixty-two plants that used women workers had black women in their employ. Moreover, most of them used black women only in janitorial positions. Even some employers willing to hire white women and black men in large numbers balked at including black women in their work forces. At the Wagner Electric Corporation in Saint Louis, for example, 64 percent of the employees were white women, 24 percent were black males, and 12 percent were white males. The company refused to hire black women throughout the war, even in the face of a January 1945 order from the President's Committee on Fair Employment Practice (FEPC) to cease all discrimination.[6]

Because of the mobilization of large numbers of young men by the military, the availability of white women for aircraft and munitions work, the nature of the jobs being created during the war, and the depth of the prejudice against black women, the male labor force proved to be more racially flexible than the female labor force. While the number of all blacks employed in manufacturing increased 135 percent between April 1940 and January 1946, the number of black women in such work rose only 59 percent. Blacks made their greatest wartime gains in heavily male-employing industrial fields; by January 1945 they constituted 25 percent of the labor force in foundries, 11.7 percent in

[5] The wartime allocation of jobs thus supports to some extent Albert Szymanski's contention that sexism and racism operate as functional substitutes in the American economy. Albert Szymanski, "Racism and Sexism as Functional Substitutes in the Labor Market," *Sociological Quarterly*, 17 (Winter 1976), 65–73; Weaver, *Negro Labor*, 17, 19–20, 81, 125; "Women in the Wartime Labor Market," August 30, 1943, box 1536, Records of the Women's Bureau, RG 86 (National Archives); "Labor Market Developments Report, Baltimore," March 1943, box 161, Records of the Bureau of Employment Security, RG 183 (National Archives).

[6] Lloyd H. Bailer, "The Negro Automobile Worker," *Journal of Political Economy*, 51 (Oct. 1943), 426; "Negro Women War Workers," *Women's Bureau Bulletin* (No. 205, 1945), 1, 19; Decision, Case No. 58, Wagner Electric Corporation, Jan. 19, 1945, box 342, Records of the President's Committee on Fair Employment Practice; Alonzo Nelson Smith, "Black Employment in the Los Angeles Area, 1938–1948" (Ph.D. diss., University of California, Los Angeles, 1978), 34.

shipbuilding, and 11.8 percent in blast furnaces and steel mills. By contrast, nonwhites accounted for only 5.8 percent of employees in aircraft and 2.7 percent of those in electrical equipment production. In the traditional female fields of clerical and sales, the gains of black women were negligible—their share of female clerical jobs rose from 0.7 percent to 1.6 percent while their proportion in the female sales force declined from 1.2 percent to 1.1 percent.[7]

One of the most important and obdurate of the industries that fought the employment of black women during the war was the auto industry. Led by the negative example of the Ford Motor Company, which refused to hire nonwhite women in any but token numbers, the auto companies persisted in rejecting trained black female applicants or in limiting their employment to a few work categories until very late in the war. When referred to the automakers by the United States Employment Service (USES) in response to calls for women workers, black women found that the white women accompanying them would be hired immediately while they would be told to await a later call, a call that would never come. When Samella Banks, along with five white women, applied to Cadillac Motor Company in November 1942, she was told that there might be a janitress opening in a day or two while they were hired as welder trainees. As a result, much of the expansion of the female labor force in industrial work occurred before economic or political pressures necessitated the hiring of black women. By February 1943 nonwhite women had claimed only 1,000 of the 96,000 jobs held by women in major war industries in Detroit. Consequently, most nonwhite females were confined to work in low-paying service and other unskilled categories, and those who landed industrial jobs had so little seniority that their postwar fate was guaranteed.[8]

As was generally the case with wartime racial discrimination in employment, the most frequent employer rationale for excluding nonwhite women was the fear that white opposition to the change might cause work slowdowns or strikes. An examination of the nature and goals of coworker prejudice during the war years provides some possible answers to the question of whether such prejudice is rooted in an aversion to social contact in a context of equality or is primarily a calculated attempt on the part of whites to maintain an exploitative economic advantage. When the former issue is the basic concern, it is manifested in a desire to exclude blacks altogether or to segregate them on the job. When the latter is the wellspring of white workplace prejudice, it is evidenced, not in a wish to segregate black workers, but in an attempt to pre-

[7] Committee on Fair Employment Practice, *Final Report, June 28, 1946* (Washington, 1947), 63; "Employment of Minority Workers during Current Period of Intensive War Production," box 378, Records of the President's Committee on Fair Employment Practice; "War and Post-War Trends," 1-5; "Negro Women War Workers," 1, 19; Weaver, *Negro Labor*, 80-81.

[8] Weaver, *Negro Labor*, 77, 285-86, 294; Bailer, "Negro Automobile Worker," 426-27; "A Statement About the Ford Motor Company Based on Employment Service Records, Experiences, and Observations," March 17, 1943, box 659, Records of the President's Committee on Fair Employment Practice; "Ford Motor Company: Hiring Practices and Labor Shortage," Feb. 19, 1943, *ibid.*; Josephine A. Blackwell to G. James Fleming, Feb. 14, 1943, box 678, *ibid.*; Complaint, Samella Banks, Feb. 10, 1943, *ibid.*; U.S. Employment Service, Detroit Central Placement Office, Report of Discriminatory Hiring Practices, Nov. 9, 1942, box 659, *ibid.*

vent the hiring of blacks or to limit them to particular low-paying job categories.[9]

During the war years, white male hostility to expanded job opportunities for black men focused primarily on the issue of promotion rather than on hiring or segregation. Although some strikes occurred when black men were admitted to entry-level jobs or over the issue of integrating the workplace, most white-male hate strikes took place when black male workers were promoted into jobs at higher skill and pay levels. This was a product of the fact that black men had been employed as janitors and unskilled laborers in many defense industries prior to the war and sought promotions as opportunities expanded. White males thus seemed to be concerned primarily with maintaining their advantaged economic position. Moreover, their resistance to the elimination of discrimination was more tenacious and more effective than was the opposition of white women to the opening of opportunities for black women. Control over labor unions, whose opposition to black entry into previously white jobs proved an effective barrier to change in many cases, gave white males more power to translate prejudice into employer discrimination.[10]

For women workers, on the other hand, the desire to maintain social distance, rather than a wish to safeguard economic prerogatives, seemed to be the dominant motivation in many cases. White female workers frequently objected to working closely with black women or sharing facilities with them because they feared that blacks were dirty or diseased. Work stoppages occurred in several places after the introduction of black women into the female work force. More than 2,000 white women employed at the U.S. Rubber plant in Detroit walked off the job in March 1943, demanding separate bathroom facilities. A similar walkout occurred at the Western Electric plant in Baltimore in summer 1943. In both cases management refused to segregate the facilities and appealed to patriotic and egalitarian values to persuade the striking workers to return to their jobs. Significantly, the one hate strike by white women workers that focused on upgrading as well as integration, the Dan River strike in 1944, was in a traditional female-employing industry.[11]

The different kinds of labor-force prejudice evidenced by men and women during the war indicate that women workers in nontraditional jobs felt a

[9] Marshall, *Negro Employment*, I, 8–45; Oaxaca, "Theory and Measurement," 1–30; Alexis, "Political Economy," 63–83; Bell, "Economic Basis," 121–35.

[10] In the railroads, where blacks had historically worked as porters and firemen, white opposition surfaced over their entrance into previously white job categories. Malcolm Ross, *All Manner of Men* (New York, 1948), 125–41. The same pattern prevailed in the auto industry. Weaver, *Negro Labor*, 61–77. For further evidence on male resistance to upgrading of blacks, see Foner, *Organized Labor*, 238–68; Allan M. Winkler, "The Philadelphia Transit Strike of 1944," *Journal of American History*, 59 (June 1972), 73–89. Herbert Hill contends that unions were even more resistant to FEPC efforts to improve the labor force status of blacks than management. Hill, *Black Labor*, 181.

[11] Alan Gale Clive, "The Society and Economy of Wartime Michigan, 1939–1945" (Ph.D. diss., University of Michigan, 1976), 443; Fleming to Lawrence Cramer, March 25, 1943, box 678, Records of the President's Committee on Fair Employment Practice; Jack B. Burke to Fleming, March 24, 1943, *ibid.*; Weaver, *Negro Labor*, 201–02. A walkout over integration occurred at the Edgewood Arsenal near Baltimore, and many others were threatened. *Baltimore Afro-American*, July 31, April 17, 1943.

weaker sense of job entitlement than male workers and that women were more threatened by the diminution of social distances than were men. Sociological studies corroborate the fact that women of all social groups express a stronger wish to avoid social contact with members of other groups than do men. According to Emory S. Bogardus, this can be attributed to the infrequency of social contacts experienced by women as a result of their confinement to homemaking, to the fact that women's contacts are more likely to be personal while men's are professional, and to the customary constraints on women's interracial contacts.[12]

Although coworker bias undoubtedly contributed to job discrimination against black women, many managers shared the racist beliefs of their white employees and used the threat of walkouts as a subterfuge for continuing their own discriminatory behavior and abdicating their responsibility for educating their employees as to the necessity and justice of equal hiring practices. When an Oakland hospital refused to hire trained black women as dietitians' aides, its representatives explained their conduct to the USES with the assertion that "Negroes couldn't pass Wasserman tests." Such an attitude, shared by many in management, deterred employers from abandoning discriminatory practices. The ease with which many employers counteracted employee resistance to the hiring of black women testifies to the centrality of managerial resolve in facilitating integration. When faced with the alternative of losing their unusually high wartime wages or acquiescing in integration, the vast majority of white women returned quickly and peacefully to work. The fact that many companies persisted in their exclusion of black women despite examples of the harmonious integration of similar industries within their own communities also attests to the importance of management actions.[13]

As a result of the idiosyncratic nature of employer practices during the war, some areas and some employers offered greater employment opportunities for black women than others. Aircraft plants in the Los Angeles area, for exmaple, began hiring black women for production work relatively early by comparison with similar operations in other areas of the country. As a result, by 1945 black women could be found doing industrial work in all Los Angeles aircraft plants; 2,000 were employed by North American Aviation alone. Among the automakers, the Briggs plant in Detroit deviated from industry patterns and hired

[12] Emory S. Bogardus, "Race Reactions by Sexes," *Sociology and Social Research*, 43 (July–Aug. 1959), 439–41; Judson R. Landis, Darryl Datwyeler, and Dean S. Dorn, "Race and Social Class as Determinants of Social Distance," *ibid.*, 51 (Oct. 1966), 81. Black women also score higher on social distance tests. John B. Edlefsen "Social Distance Attitudes of Negro College Students," *Phylon*, 17 (No. 1, 1956), 83. White desires to maintain social distance increased, 1926–1946, but information on attitudes by sex was not provided. Emory S. Bogardus, "Racial Distance Changes in the United States during the Past Thirty Years," *Sociology and Social Research*, 43 (Nov.–Dec. 1958), 132.

[13] Committee on Fair Employment Practice, *Final Report*, 80; Clive, "Society and Economy of Wartime Michigan," 443; Decision, Case No. 59, Bussman Manufacturing Company, Jan. 10, 1945, box 342, Records of the President's Committee on Fair Employment Practice; Weaver, *Negro Labor*, 81–82. Saul Pleeter has suggested that resistance to hiring blacks may be a function of managerial avoidance of risk taking as much as managerial racism. Saul Pleeter, "Uncertainty and Discrimination," in *Employment and Income*, ed. von Furstenberg, Horowitz, and Harrison, 96.

substantial numbers of black women. In Saint Louis, where defense industry discrimination against black women was the general rule, the Curtiss-Wright Company and the U.S. Cartridge Company eased the situation somewhat by providing industrial jobs for hundreds of nonwhite women. These examples, however, were not typical of employer response; restrictive hiring and segregation remained the rule, even in industries faced with severe labor shortages. Nowhere was this truer than in the South, where traditional practices remained virtually unchanged.[14]

Even when defense employers broke with tradition and hired nonwhite women, they generally segregated them from other women workers and employed them only for certain kinds of work, usually that which was arduous, dirty, hot, or otherwise disagreeable. A cursory study of black women workers done by the Women's Bureau of the United States Department of Labor in 1945 revealed that in many cases nonwhite women were disproportionately represented among women employed in outside labor gangs, in foundries, and in industrial service work. On the ore docks of the Great Lakes, for example, the survey found women, predominantly black, shoveling the leavings of ore from the bottoms of ships onto hoists. According to the USES, the meat-packing industry in Detroit resorted to black women in large numbers during the war years to take jobs others had spurned. On the railroads minority group women found employment in substantial numbers as laborers, loaders, car cleaners, and waitresses. The city of Baltimore first broke with its policy of hiring only whites for street-cleaning work in the immediate prewar period when it began hiring black males; by 1943, when the black male labor force was completely exhausted, the city turned to the only labor reserve left—the large numbers of unemployed and underemployed black females.[15]

The insistence by some employers on segregated work arrangements and facilities served as a rationale for excluding black women altogether or limiting their numbers to conform to physical plant requirements. The Glenn Martin Aircraft Company, for example, hired the same proportion of nonwhite women for its integrated plant in Omaha, where the black population was quite small, as it did for its Baltimore operations, where black women constituted a substantial proportion of the local labor supply. In Baltimore, however, their numbers were limited because they had to be assigned only to a small separate subassembly plant. A small aircraft parts firm in Los Angeles asserted that it could not hire black women because it separated workers by sex as well as by race and could not further complicate its managerial and supervisory difficulties. At the Norfolk Navy Yard, management excluded black women from most production jobs on the grounds that women workers

[14] Helen M. Gould, "The Negro and the CIO," *Common Ground*, 5 (Winter 1945), 73–75; Richard R. Jefferson, "Negro Employment in St. Louis War Production," *Opportunity*, 22 (Summer 1944), 117; Bailer, "Negro Automobile Worker," 428; "Employment of Negroes in War Industries," May 31, 1943, box 409, Records of the President's Committee on Fair Employment Practice.

[15] "Negro Women War Workers," 5, 6, 9; "Labor Market Developments in the Detroit Area," Nov. 5, 1943, box 17, Records of the Bureau of Employment Security; *Baltimore Afro-American*, April 24, 1943.

had to be segregated by race, although the racial integration of male workers was an accomplished fact. As a result, black men worked in a wide variety of jobs at all skill levels in the yard while the jobs assigned to women were virtually monopolized by whites.[16]

In the major woman-employing industry in a peacetime economy, the textile industry, black women registered only tentative gains late in the war. As late as January 1943, a survey of 188 woolen mills revealed that only 40 employed blacks, including 12 out of 20 southern mills and that the numbers used were quite small in most plants. By May 1944 some barriers had been toppled in southern cotton textile operations with the result that 5.3 percent of their employees were nonwhite, although most were limited to certain unskilled jobs and employed only on third shifts. Coworker opposition to the hiring of blacks in the mills was not overcome, although the strength of managerial resolve is difficult to assess. In a Dan River cotton mill in rural Virginia, management agreed to fire the black women it had recently hired after white women in the plant struck in protest.[17]

Even major employers of women outside of the manufacturing sector, who had considerable difficulty recruiting and retaining women workers as a result of competition from war industries, retained racial restrictions to a surprising extent. Despite considerable pressure from the FEPC, the Bell system eased racial barriers only very slowly during the war years. The greatest gains came in opening up jobs as elevator operators and cafeteria workers and in other service work. In white-collar categories, small numbers of clerical positions were made available to black women, but positions as telephone operators remained limited to whites in all but a few locations. American Telephone and Telegraph Company (ATT) justified its continued discrimination in that area on the grounds that operators worked in close proximity to one another, often leaning across each other's boards. According to "Ma Bell," breaching taboos regarding social integration would provoke serious coworker resistance.[18]

ATT's willingness to hire black women for clerical work, which paid better than did switchboard work, in order to accommodate the desire of some whites to maintain social distance presaged the long-term patterns by which blacks would integrate the white-collar sector of the female labor force. In general, employers preferred to hire blacks for clerical, stock-handling, packing, and wrapping work rather than for sales positions that involved public contact.

[16] Weaver, *Negro Labor*, 125; Smith, "Black Employment," 253; Memo by Cramer, Daniel R. Donovan, and Elmer W. Henderson, Sept. 29, 1942, box 64, Records of the President's Committee on Fair Employment Practice.

[17] "Labor Market Problems in the Woolen and Worsted Textile Industry," Jan. 5, 1943, box 408, Records of the President's Committee on Fair Employment Practice; Will Maslow to All Regional Directors, Sept. 13, 1944, *ibid.*; "Details of Strike at the Riverside Division of Dan River Cotton Mills as related to C. K. Coleman by Mary Lumpkin on Saturday, June 24, 1944," box 338, General Office file, Records of the National Association for the Advancement of Colored People (Library of Congress); *Norfolk Guide*, June 10, 1944.

[18] Evelyn N. Cooper to Committee Members, March 7, 1945, box 303, Records of the President's Committee on Fair Employment Practice; Clarence M. Mitchell to Cooper, July 21, 1945, *ibid.*; Final Disposition Report, Michigan Bell Telephone Company, June 23, 1944, box 674, ibid.; Committee on Fair Employment Practice, *First Report, July 1943–December 1944* (Washington, 1945), 44.

Although some small gains were registered during the war years, the process of integrating clerical and sales work did not really begin until the late 1940s, spurred by demographic change and black protests in many urban areas.[19]

As a result of the serious shortage of nurses during the war and of the government's efforts to encourage the training of nurses, black women experienced an appreciable improvement in their access to nursing education programs and to hospital employment as nurses. In order to increase the supply of nurses, the federal government provided scholarships through the United States Public Health Service and the Cadet Nurse Corps, which paid for tuition and books and provided monthly allowances for those agreeing to remain in essential nursing work for the duration of the war. Largely because of this program, black enrollment in nursing schools jumped from 1,108 in 1939 to 2,600 in 1945. Moreover, the number of nonwhite nurses and student nurses doubled between 1940 and 1950.[20]

Beginning in the immediate prewar period, the National Association of Colored Graduate Nurses (NACGN) worked to end the imposition of quotas and segregation on black nurses in the Army Nurse Corps. Although the American Nurses' Association had supported the NACGN on this issue, it made it a higher priority in January 1943, when it created a special unit within its National Nursing Council for War Service (NNCWS) to foster the integration of black nurses into all war work. This unit, which was headed by Estelle Massey Riddle, a past president of the NACGN, worked to encourage black schools to create or upgrade nursing education programs and to participate in the Cadet Nurse Corps, to persuade white schools to admit blacks to their programs, and to fight discrimination against black nurses by public and private hospitals. In response to these efforts, the number of integrated nursing programs grew from fourteen to thirty-two, and numerous hospitals, including twenty-six in New York City, agreed to employ blacks as nurses for the first time. Under pressure from the NNCWS, the NACGN, and other civil rights groups, the federal government integrated the Army and Navy Nurse Corps late in the war.[21]

Whether in white-collar or blue-collar work, many of the new wartime opportunities for blacks came from government rather than private-sector employment. Even within the civil service, however, the black woman found her gains limited and her position tenuous. Most of the industrial work available to blacks in government-owned shipyards and arsenals was in hot, heavy jobs

[19] Gordon F. Bloom, F. Marion Fletcher, and Charles R. Perry, *Negro Employment in Retail Trade: A Study of Racial Policies in the Department Store, Drugstore, and Supermarket Industries* (Philadelphia, 1972), 39–40; Smith, "Black Employment," 55.

[20] "Negro Women War Workers," 13; Estelle Massey Riddle and Josephine Nelson, "The Negro Nurse Looks Toward Tomorrow," *American Journal of Nursing*, 45 (Aug. 1945), 628–29; U.S. Department of Commerce, Bureau of the Census, *Sixteenth Census of the United States: 1940. Population: The Labor Force (Sample Statistics), Occupational Characteristics* (Washington, 1943), 21; U.S. Department of Commerce, Bureau of the Census, *United States Census of Population: 1950*, vol. IV: *Special Reports: Part 1, Chapter B, Occupational Characteristics* (Washington, 1956), 1B–29.

[21] Riddle and Nelson, "Negro Nurse Looks Toward Tomorrow," 627–29; Mabel Keaton Staupers, "The Negro Nurse," *Opportunity*, 20 (Nov. 1942), 332–33; Mabel Keaton Staupers, *No Time for Prejudice: A Story of the Integration of Negroes in Nursing in the United States* (New York, 1961), 99–121.

usually reserved to men. Despite this, black women did claim some industrial positions within the government. In addition, they broke into some white-collar categories in federal agencies for the first time. Most of these gains occurred in departmental offices in the Washington, D.C., area rather than in field offices, where racial barriers persisted. The expansion of work opportunities in the federal government offered few prospects for permanent gain, however. Most black workers concentrated in war agencies and defense production work. Moreover, most new wartime appointments were made under the Civil Service Commission's War Service Regulations and conferred no permanent civil service status.[22]

When confronted with employer discrimination, black women turned for help primarily to civil rights groups and the FEPC rather than relying on the Women's Bureau or other women's organizations. Given the powerlessness and lack of responsiveness of women's groups to the problems of nonwhite women workers, such a choice is understandable. As Susan M. Hartmann has pointed out, the Women's Bureau refused to hire a black woman to investigate the employment situation for nonwhites, indicating the low priority it accorded the question. Although the Women's Bureau lacked the legal authority to prohibit employment discrimination on the basis of race or sex, it could have provided the informational basis for a sustained campaign on the part of the War Manpower Commission (WMC) and the FEPC. Instead, in 1945, it issued a short, vague report filled with anonymous examples of expanding job opportunities, ignoring the persistence of discrimination, and giving the impression of considerably greater mobility than was actually occurring.[23]

To the extent that it concerned itself with employment issues of importance to black women, the Women's Bureau directed most of its attention to upgrading the pay, security, and working conditions of domestic servants. In order to minimize employer-employee conflict over standards and expectations and to prepare women more adequately for work in household service, the Women's Bureau considered promoting a nationwide training system funded under federal vocational education programs in the public schools. The agency also lobbied for the inclusion of domestic service in the social security system and for legal standards for hours, wages, and working conditions for household workers. Not surprisingly, the bureau seemed as concerned with insuring a sufficient supply of willing workers for middle-class women as with improving the circumstances of the women who performed such work.[24]

[22] "The Facts about Negro Employment in the Federal Government," [1944], box 396, Records of the President's Committee on Fair Employment Practice; "Tables and Summary of Employment of Negroes in the Federal Government," Dec. 1943, box 405, *ibid.*; Alexander J. Allen to Regional Director, U.S. Civil Service Commission, Region IV, April 11, 1944, box 448, *ibid.*

[23] "Negro Women War Workers," 1–23; Susan M. Hartmann, "Women's Organizations during World War II: The Interaction of Class, Race, and Feminism," in *Woman's Being, Woman's Place: Female Identity and Vocation in American History*, ed. Mary Kelley (Boston, 1979), 317. According to Hartmann, the actions of the Women's Bureau reflected the class and race bias of white middle-class women's organizations at the time.

[24] "Women's Bureau, Old-Age Insurance for Household Workers," Nov. 1945, box 1718, Records of the Women's Bureau; boxes 1718 and 1719 of the Records of the Women's Bureau contain much information on wartime shortage of domestic servants; Hartmann, "Women's Organizations," 319–20.

The major agency charged with enforcing equal opportunity in employment regardless of race, religion, or national origin was the FEPC, an agency created in 1941 by executive order of President Franklin D. Roosevelt in response to a threatened march on Washington by civil rights groups protesting discriminatory policies by war contractors. Although the FEPC could theoretically recommend the removal of war contracts from those who continued to discriminate and the WMC could restrict work permits to enforce federal hiring policies, the federal government was not inclined to hamper the production of essential war materials in order to foster racial equity. As a result, the agency had to rely on behind-the-scenes negotiations and the possibility of adverse publicity generated by public hearings. Although effective in some cases, such tools proved ineffectual against recalcitrant violators, whose ranks included some major war industries. The large volume of complaints and the bureaucratic delays inherent in the situation facilitated evasion, even on the part of blatant violators officially ordered to cease restrictive hiring practices. Moreover, the reliance on individual, documented complaints rather than on employer hiring patterns as the basis for action hampered effective enforcement.[25]

The decision by Roosevelt to place the FEPC under the jurisdiction of the WMC in July 1942 also handicapped the agency in its efforts to end employment discrimination. WMC head Paul McNutt, never enthusiastic regarding the FEPC's goals and afraid that they were incompatible with his agency's responsibility for allocating scarce manpower within war industries, canceled scheduled FEPC hearings on discrimination by the railroads and generally made racial equity a low priority within WMC. Even after the FEPC was removed from the WMC in May 1943, it was hampered in its efforts to enforce the law by the unwillingness of southern representatives of the WMC and the USES to cooperate in reporting and seeking to change discriminatory practices. Although the USES had agreed in September 1943 to refuse to fill employer requests for workers when they included racial restrictions, its agents in the South frequently disregarded this directive. Thus, when blacks with defense training applied for appropriate work, they were often referred to jobs outside the area. The persistence of discrimination, despite a federal commitment to eliminate it, hampered the ability of all blacks, male and female, to find industrial employment in the region that still claimed a majority of the black population.[26]

In its official policies the FEPC treated discrimination against black women

[25] Richard Polenberg, *War and Society: The United States, 1941-1945* (Philadelphia, 1972), 117-23; Louis Coleridge Kesselman, *The Social Politics of FEPC: A Study in Reform Pressure Movements* (Chapel Hill, 1948), 15-24; Herbert Garfinkel, *When Negroes March: The March on Washington Movement in the Organizational Politics for FEPC* (New York, 1969); Louis Ruchames, *Race, Jobs, and Politics: The Story of the FEPC* (New York, 1953); Foner, *Organized Labor*, 238-43; Hill, *Black Labor*, 173-84; Winkler, "Philadelphia Transit Strike," 75-76.

[26] Rough Draft, Part 1: Wartime Experience, [1943], box 66, Records of the President's Committee on Fair Employment Practice; Garfinkel, *When Negroes March*, 111; Ruchames, *Race, Jobs, and Politics*, 46-56, 149, 158, 190-91.

as seriously as discrimination against black males, although its rate of success in enforcing compliance in women's cases lagged somewhat behind the rate for men. After its 1944 hearings in St. Louis, the FEPC ruled that a company that hired black males while discriminating against black women was still in violation of the executive order, noting that "partial compliance is partial violation." Despite pressure from civil rights groups on behalf of black women workers and occasional threats of strikes by black male workers, the equal opportunity machinery of the government proved unable to aid minority women in any substantial way. By the time the agency had investigated, negotiated, or held hearings, much valuable time had been lost. For women, this could be especially damaging because it meant that anything beyond token conformity could be jeopardized by employer unwillingness to expand the female work force late in the war.[27]

The Carter Carburetor Company in Saint Louis, for example, managed a minimal compliance with an FEPC order to cease discriminating when it came to black men, but refused in April 1944 to hire any black women on the grounds that it had no intention of hiring any more women. Although the government continued to pressure the company, it stood by its policies. The Allied Tent Manufacturing Company in New Orleans claimed to have instituted a nondiscriminatory policy regarding women workers when it announced its intention in June 1945 to replace all its women machine operators with men (white and black), having decided that women workers had proved themselves "unsatisfactory." Federal enforcement officials thus found that labor-market forces late in the war provided a rationale and a means for continued resistance by those employers intent on circumventing federal hiring policies regarding black women.[28]

The organization that was most cognizant of persisting discrimination against black women and most active in fighting against it was the National Association for the Advancement of Colored People (NAACP). As early as August 1942, Detroit NAACP officer Gloster Current wrote to McNutt of the WMC, complaining that the Ford Motor Company was discriminating against black females as it hired thousands of whites for work at the Willow Run Bomber Plant. In March 1943 the Detroit NAACP cooperated with the United Auto Workers Inter-Racial Committee in staging a large rally to protest continued discrimination against black women in hiring and black men in promotion on the part of Detroit's war industries. Thereafter both groups continued to pressure employers and government officials at all levels on the issue. In a statement prepared for presentation to the House manpower committee, the NAACP evinced its awareness that the situation was not unique to Detroit but

[27] Committee on Fair Employment Practice, *First Report*, 43; Decision, Case No. 64, McQuay Norris Manufacturing Company, Dec. 16, 1944, box 344, Records of the President's Committee on Fair Employment Practice.

[28] Theodore E. Brown to Roy A. Hoglund, April 29, 1944, box 342, Records of the President's Committee on Fair Employment Practice; Decisions on Exceptions, Case No. 60, March 1945, *ibid.*; Bi-Weekly Report, June 23, 1945, Region XIII, box 403, *ibid.*

was a national problem resulting in the serious underutilization of black womanpower.[29]

By contrast, the National Urban League seemed not to have discovered the particular difficulties encountered by black women until after the FEPC hearings in Saint Louis in August 1944. In an April 1943 issue of *Opportunity* dedicated to "brown American womanpower," several articles pointed to the widening of opportunities for black women, who, it claimed, faced many fewer problems of discrimination than black men and thus shared more fully in the benefits of the full employment economy. Charles C. Berkley concluded, for example, that "midst the problems of racial discrimination. . . Negro women have forged ahead and have welded themselves into the semi-skilled and skilled brackets of war production work." After the Saint Louis hearings, however, the organization took note of the systematic discrimination faced by nonwhite women in the war industries there. The National Urban League's position on the issue seems to have stemmed from a lack of adequate information, rather than from a lack of concern, for the employment prerogatives of black females, suggesting that it relied on impressionistic data to support an erroneous assumption.[30]

The major organization of black women, the National Council of Negro Women (NCNW), was especially sanguine about the opportunities fostered by wartime changes. In summer 1943, the *Aframerican Women's Journal* predicted that "neither caste nor class will operate to keep us in kitchens and laundries and other service occupations in the months to come." Although it cooperated in the wartime coalition dedicated to strengthening the FEPC and making it permanent, the NCNW focused its wartime efforts primarily on a "Keep your Job" campaign directed at black women workers. Through its publications and clinics, the NCNW sought to facilitate the integration and retention of black women in production jobs by helping them adjust to the imperatives of industrial work—and by encouraging conformity to white-middle-class specifications regarding dress, behavior, and attitudes appropriate for women. Thus, the NCNW publication entitled "Wake Up! Your Job Is in Danger: A Message to Negro Women Workers" served, not as a call to organization and action to safeguard their employment rights, but rather as a warning to be careful regarding personal appearance, to avoid loud and boisterous behavior on the job, and to be prompt and hardworking. By focusing on the problem of job retention rather than that of job acquisition and by directing its efforts to changing employee behavior rather than employer policies, the NCNW adopted an accommodationist posture out of step with the growing

[29] Gloster B. Current to Paul McNutt, Aug. 26, 1942, box 659, *ibid.*; Tentative Draft of NAACP Statement to be Submitted to Pepper Manpower Committee, [1944], box 651, General Office file, Records of the National Association for the Advancement of Colored People; "Along the N.A.A.C.P. Battlefront," *Crisis*, 49 (Dec. 1942), 390; "20,000 Members in 1943," *ibid.*, 50 (May 1943), 154.

[30] Charles C. Berkley, "War Work—A Challenge to Negro Womanpower," *Opportunity*, 21 (April 1943), 58; Jefferson, "Negro Employment in St. Louis," 117–18.

militance of black organizations during the war and revealed a certain naïveté regarding the real problems faced by black women at that time.[31]

Job retention was a serious issue for those women who landed industrial work during the war. The persistence of discrimination and the late entry of black women into production work, rather than their on-the-job conduct, meant that nonwhite females were more likely than others to experience layoffs resulting from contract completions or seasonal cutbacks. Once fired, they faced great difficulties in finding comparable work. According to an official of the Baltimore Urban League, white women there with industrial experience were easily reabsorbed by war industries while black women were being referred by the USES to work as maids, counter girls, and laundry pressers. As would be the case for all unemployed women after the war, those who turned down such jobs faced the possibility of losing their unemployment benefits for refusing suitable work. Black women thus experienced a much greater degree of job discontinuity than others during the war, hampering their ability to accumulate seniority.[32]

Once the war was over and American industry began its postwar contraction, those black women who had held industrial jobs during the war found that their concentration in contracting industries, their low seniority, and their sex contributed to employment difficulties in the postwar period. American women, black and white, were overrepresented among those experiencing layoffs in durable good industries. When management began rehiring workers in the reconversion period, it reinstituted most prewar discriminatory policies regarding working women, even to the point of disregarding their seniority rights, a practice facilitated by union acquiescence. USES officials reinforced employer policies by denying unemployment benefits to those women who refused referrals to jobs in traditional female-employing fields. To a greater extent than white women, black women were victimized by the postwar eviction of women from jobs in durable goods industries.[33]

[31] The posture of the National Council of Negro Women (NCNW) was probably shaped by its middle-class membership and by the facts that it was headquartered in Washington, D.C., and directed many of its efforts at black women recently integrated into clerical work in the federal civil service. Marjorie McKenzie, "Against the Lean Years," *Aframerican Women's Journal* (Summer 1943), 6; NCNW News Release, Sept. 10, 1943, box 11, series 5, Records of the National Council of Negro Women (National Archives of Black Women's History, Washington); "Wake Up! Your Job Is In Danger: A Message to Negro Women Workers, [1943], *ibid*; "Wartime Employment Clinics" [1943], *ibid.*; Garfinkel, *When Negroes March*, 179–80; Richard M. Dalfiume, "The 'Forgotten Years' of the Negro Revolution," *Journal of American History*, 55 (June 1968), 90–106; Sitkoff, "Racial Militancy," 679–81 stresses the growing conservatism of civil rights activities toward the end of the war.

[32] Allen to Lawrence B. Fenneman, May 5, 1944, box 448, Records of the President's Committee on Fair Employment Practice; A. G. Mezerik, "Getting Rid of the Women," *Atlantic*, 175 (June 1945), 82.

[33] Mary Pidgeon, "Employment of Women in the Early Postwar Period with Background of Prewar and War Data," *Women's Bureau Bulletin* (No. 211, 1946); "Detroit," [1946], box 66, Records of the President's Committee on Fair Employment Practice; Marjorie McKenzie Lawson to Jeanetta Welch Brown, Oct. 23, 1945, box 11, Series 5, Records of the National Council of Negro Women; Committee on Fair Employment Practice, *Final Report*, 62.

Even the UAW, which had been in the vanguard of those working for widened industrial opportunities for black women workers during the war, ignored the seniority rights of women in the postwar period and allowed management to determine how many women workers there would be and who they should be. Such policies proved especially detrimental to black women workers, for whom management had little enthusiasm. The union allowed the auto companies to hire inexperienced male workers in preference to women with wartime seniority despite union-management contract provisions to the contrary. In the postwar period, the UAW and some automakers jointly agreed that local unions would no longer be required to recognize the seniority of a worker who had not been recalled within a specified period of time. Because black women had been largely excluded from postwar rehiring, the arrangement served to lock in the discriminatory policy. Although several protested to the union regarding the discriminatory effects of the agreements, they had no success in changing the situation.[34]

The postwar situation at the General Cable Corporation in Saint Louis typified the patterns affecting the opportunities of black women workers. Under pressure from the FEPC, management at the company had sponsored a belated introduction of black women into production work. After the war, the cord assembly department, where the company had assigned most of its women production workers, was closed and only women with several years seniority were retained. No black women survived the cutbacks, By contrast, black men, who benefited from their ealier integration into production work and the postwar bias in favor of male workers, constituted 16 percent of male employees in 1947 and could be found working in every job classification.[35]

In other work categories black women fared somewhat better in the postwar years. Although some apparently lost employment in service, sales, and clerical work as a result of competition from displaced white women, most managed to maintain their hold on lower-level jobs in the female work force. Despite attempts by USES officials in some local offices to force black women to return to domestic service work by threatening to withhold unemployment compensation benefits, enough job opportunities in other categories remained available to prevent a massive return to household work. Even so, domestic service remained the primary occupation of black women, providing employment to 782,520 in 1950, 40 percent of the black female work force.[36]

[34] William H. Oliver to Lillian Hatcher, May 4, 1948, box 5, Fair Practices Department—Women's Bureau Records of the United Auto Workers (Wayne State University Archives of Labor History and Urban Affairs, Detroit, Mich.); Summary of Minutes, National United Auto Workers-Congress of Industrial Organizations Advisory Council on Discrimination Meeting, April 2, 1947, box 2, *ibid.*; *Detroit News*, Nov. 8, 1945; *New York Times*, Nov. 9, 1945; *Detroit Free Press*, Nov. 9, 1945; Nancy Gabin, "Women Workers and the UAW in the Post-World War II Period: 1945-1954," *Labor History*, 21 (Winter 1979-1980), 5-30.

[35] Ross, *All Manner of Men*, 302.

[36] Committee on Fair Employment Practice, *Final Report*, 54; Lawson to Jeanetta Welch Brown, Oct. 23, 1945, box 11, series 5, Records of the National Council of Negro Women; U.S. Department of Commerce, Bureau of the Census, *United States Census of Population: 1950*, Vol. IV: *Special Reports: Part 1, Chapter B, Occupational Characteristics*, 1B-34.

As a result of the wartime experience, black women made substantial progress in the operatives occupational category, although their position in this area deteriorated somewhat in the late 1940s. One of the most important areas of expansion for nonwhite women was the apparel industry, which witnessed a 350 percent increase in black female employment during the 1940s. By 1950, it offered employment to 56,910 black women and ranked second in the operatives category behind laundry and dry cleaning establishments, where 105,000 black females were employed. Other major sources of industrial work for women, including textiles, remained virtually closed to blacks during the 1940s. In the durable goods industries, which had experienced the greatest wartime expansion, black women were a rarity in the postwar period. In 1950, only 60 black women held jobs as operatives in aircraft plants, while 2,730 claimed similar positions in the auto industry.[37]

In the long run, the greatest benefit of the wartime experience for black women workers derived from their movement in large numbers out of the poverty of the rural South to the possibilities provided by an urban, industrialized economy. The extent to which those possibilities were realized in the decade of the 1940s can be overstated, however. Both during and after the war, black women entered the urban female labor force in large numbers only to occupy its lowest rungs. Largely excluded from clerical and sales work, the growth sectors of the female work force, black women found work primarily in service jobs outside the household and in unskilled blue-collar categories. Although many experienced some upward mobility during the war, their relative position within the American economy remained the same.

Wartime circumstances illustrate the extent to which an economic system that had historically allocated work according to race and sex could tolerate a high level of unemployment and underemployment even in a time of labor shortage in order to minimize the amount of change generated by temporary and aberrant conditions. By stressing the modification of traditional patterns fostered by rapid economic growth, scholars ignore the degree to which prejudices inhibited change and constrained the rate of economic expansion even in the face of strong patriotic, political, and economic incentives favoring expanded output at all cost. For black women, especially, what is significant about the war experience is the extent to which barriers remained intact.

[37] U.S. Department of Labor, Bureau of Labor Statistics, *Negroes in the United States: Their Employment and Economic Status* (No. 1119, 1952), 15, 17; U.S. Department of Commerce, Bureau of the Census, *Sixteenth Census of the United States: 1940. Population: The Labor Force (Sample Statistics). Occupational Characteristics*, 21; U.S. Department of Commerce, Bureau of the Census, *United States Census of Population: 1950*. Vol. IV: *Special Reports: Part 1. Chapter B. Occupational Characteristics*, 1B-33, 1B-34.

# WORKING WOMEN AND WORLD WAR II

MARC MILLER

WORLD WAR II has been customarily studied as an international event. Recently, social historians have cited the impact of the war years on American domestic life, including women's work, but none has attempted to examine the details of women's wartime life. This essay is concerned with the domestic effects of World War II by focusing on occurrences in the American city of Lowell, Massachusetts. The kind of work women performed, the conditions under which they worked, and how they viewed their role as workers, reflect the influence of a major global conflict.

## I

The war led to a dramatic rise in the number of women working in the United States; from 10.8 million in March, 1941, to more than 18 million in August, 1944, reversing a downward trend attributed to the depression. Although many women entered the labor force for the first time, 29 percent of American women workers in 1944-1945 had over ten years of experience; another 19 percent had worked for over five years.[1]

In Lowell, prior work experience was even more widespread. The 1940 census listed 38 percent of Lowell's 35,000 women over age twenty in the labor force, double the national figure.[2] A survey of women workers in the Springfield-Holyoke district, a similar Massachusetts textile region, showed signifi-

1 Joan Ellen Trey, "Women in the War Economy," *Review of Radical Political Economics*, IV, 44 (1972); United States Bureau of the Budget, Committee of Records of War Administration, War Records Section, *The United States at War* (New York, 1946), p. 174; United States Department of Labor, Women's Bureau, *Women Workers in Ten War Production Areas and Their Postwar Employment Plans*, Bulletin no. 209 (Washington, 1946), p. 30.

2 City of Lowell, "Record of Votes 1937 to 1943"; United States Department of Commerce, Bureau of the Census, *Population, Fourth Series, Characteristics by Age, Marital Status, Relationship, Education and Citizenship: Massachusetts* (Washington, 1943), p. 31; United States Department of Labor, Women's Bureau, *Changes in Women's Employment During the War*, Special Bulletin no. 20 (Washington, 1944), p. vi.

cantly more women than the national average working before the war and fewer who were solely housewives. The *Lowell Sun* reported that "working wives have been the rule rather than the exception in Lowell for a long time."[3]

Lowell's history partially explains why so many of the city's women considered it normal to work. Women supplied the labor force for Lowell's textile industry when it commenced production in the 1820's; by 1848 the population was five-eighths female. With immigration, the balance of men and women in the city equalized, but women continued to provide a significant proportion of the labor force for Lowell's mills. At the outset of World War II, almost half the non-skilled textile positions were held by women although they comprised only about a third of the city's total labor force. Women filled the basic mill positions, holding only about 5 percent of the jobs as craftsmen and foremen.[4]

For both men and women, mill work in Lowell was a family tradition. When Lowell women entered the labor force after 1941 and in new jobs, it did not mean they hadn't wished to work previously; they simply had had no choice. In the 1930's, "there was nothing." It was fortunate for those who needed work that, in the view of *Redbook* magazine, "Women are needed almost as much as men, in modern war, to serve their countries."[5]

During World War II, two types of companies employed the women of Lowell. As always, the textile mills—principally the Merrimack, Boott, Ames, and Wannalancit mills—were major

[3] Women's Bureau, *Women Workers in Ten War Production Areas*, p. 29; *Lowell Daily Sun*, March 24, 1943, p. 4.

[4] *Handbook for the Visitor to Lowell* (Lowell, 1848), p. 30; United States Department of Commerce, Bureau of the Census, *Sixteenth Census of the United States, 1940, Population, Third Series, The Labor Force: Occupation, Industry, Employment, and Income: Massachusetts* (Washington, 1943), pp. 31, 32.

[5] Interview with Yvonne Hoar, May 6, 1975. All interviews for this essay were conducted in Lowell and surrounding communities by the author between 1974 and 1976. Significantly, only two people interviewed out of seventy cited World War II as the period when wives began working at the same time as their husbands, and both sources were middle-class men.

sources of employment. The other type of employer was new: the war-based industries—principally Atlantic Rayon Company (Parachute Division), Remington Arms, General Electric, and United States Rubber.

For Lowell's larger mills—notably the Merrimack—need of workers meant hiring proportionately more women than previously when the draft monopolized available men. In the biggest boom year, beginning in July, 1942, textile employment of women in Lowell reached 53 percent.[6] By mid-1943, the female proportion of the work force had risen from 35 percent in 1940 to just over 50 percent. Both the Boott and the Newmarket Manufacturing companies had employed 40 percent women before the war; by 1943, they employed 60 percent and the proportion was still rising. The Atlantic Parachute Company began hiring women as power stitchers in early 1942, assembling a force of 300 within a few months and 1,000 by year's end.[7]

On the other hand, women rapidly abandoned textile work after 1943. Although the demand for cotton products continued, textile employment in the nation declined steadily after 1943 until and beyond V-E Day as women moved to work in war-based industries. Many of the Lowell textile companies were forced by a tight labor market to operate at half strength. Merrimack's velvet-cutting department had employed highly skilled women, but these quickly abandoned the textile industry for higher paying, unskilled work at Remington and other war industries.[8]

New occupations provided different routines, albeit rou-

[6] United States War Production Board, *Production Wartime Achievements and the Reconversion Outlook*, WPB Document no. 334 (n.p., Oct. 9, 1945), p. 81; United States Employment Service, Massachusetts and Massachusetts Division of Employment Security, *Joint Quarterly Statistical Bulletin*, April, 1943-June, 1943, p. 5; nationally, employment of men and women in the cotton mills rose steeply from 396,000 in 1939 to 510,000 in 1942.

[7] *Lowell Daily Sun*, March 24, 1943, p. 4; U.S.E.S., *Joint Quarterly Statistical Bulletin*, April, 1943-June, 1943, p. 5; U.S.E.S., Massachusetts, *Monthly Labor Market Report*, March 16, 1942-April 15, 1942, p. 15; oversize volume 9, Edith Nourse Rogers Papers, Schlesinger Library, Cambridge, Mass.

[8] WPB, *Production Wartime Achievements*, p. 81; interview with Hazel Fiske and Frank Fiske, Dec. 3, 1974.

tines, for Lowell's working women. The biggest employer, Remington—with an estimated payroll of 5,000; 70 percent female and 90 percent from Lowell—created headaches for the mill owners who lost thousands of low-paid workers first to Remington, which closed on December 31, 1943, and then to Remington's successors: GE, U. S. Rubber and others.[9] A Textile Workers Union of America postwar report summed up the situation:

Decades of mismanagement had resulted in a disinclination to work in textile mills. Wages were low, so the workers sought other industries. Mills were physically unattractive and management continued ancient practices; accordingly, they could not attract enough workers to their mills.[10]

Remington produced .50 caliber armor-piercing cartridges and was "the biggest thing that has happened to this city since the Cartridge Shop was going full blast during the last war." The tasks women performed ranged from "grease-monkey" for the machines to "floor ladies." Most worked on the assembly line. With "key skilled workers . . . transferred from the parent company" in Connecticut, women's tasks proved fully as tedious as they had been in the mills.[11]

There was a conveyor belt and we'd sit here with big boxes—a big box of bullets—and we'd have to inspect the bullets to see if they were all smooth and the tips were right and everything and pack them in a box. I believe there was a dozen to a box. And we'd have to put them on a conveyor belt and there was a girl at the end of the conveyor belt that would seal them and count them. Then they'd be packed into cartons and shipped from there. . . . There was quite a few of us on the conveyor belt. There must have been a dozen or more girls on just one short belt. I would say it was [about 50 feet]. And, of course, when the belt broke down, well then, we'd have to keep packing the bullets and pile them on

[9] *Lowell Daily Sun,* March 4, 1943, p. 1; Dec. 31, 1943, p. 1; Rogers Papers.

[10] Textile Workers of America, CIO, *Executive Council Report, Fourth Biennial Convention* (n.p., 1946), p. 13.

[11] *Lowell Daily Sun,* March 4, 1943, p. 1; U.S.E.S., *Monthly Labor Market Report,* March 16, 1942-April 15, 1942, p. 13.

a table aside and then, when the belt started again, we'd have to keep putting them on. [The workers] didn't like it [when the belt broke down] because it doubled their work. We'd have to keep packing them, and then taking them off when the belt broke down, and when the belt started we'd have to put them back on again. And people were kind of resentful of that; they didn't like the idea too well. And it broke down quite often, too.[12]

While textile mills were once famous for their mechanized production, technological progress had passed Lowell by; the modern assembly line had not yet reached the mills in the early 1940's. Power stitchers at the parachute factory—essentially textile work, although a child of the war—needed training; Remington work required little skill and, unlike assembly lines work in the highly efficient automobile industry, work at Remington could continue even when the line broke down.

The Boston Navy Yard, within a 35-mile commuting distance, and other government operations provided the most varied tasks for Lowell women. The image of Rosie the Riveter remains famous, and some women performed male jobs at the Navy Yard; far more women, however, worked in traditionally female occupations. Even some of these—especially the government jobs—meant welcome variety for the Lowell women accustomed only to mill routines. One woman, for example, did accounting and bookkeeping at the Navy Yard for several years in an office of 150 people, mostly female. She then transferred to a navy office in Lawrence, Massachusetts, where she worked in a personnel office while being trained for a job at the War Labor Board. Another Lowell woman worked first in the Navy Yard's typing pool, and eventually as secretary to a production officer. By war's end, she was supervising thirty women at the Boston Separation Center.[13]

To a city that had suffered depression for fifteen years,

12 Interview with Yvonne Hoar.

13 Interview with Claire Contardo, Sept. 16, 1975; interview with Doris Poisson, May 15, 1975, *Boston Herald Traveler*, Jan. 30, 1944.

World War II meant the opportunity to earn a decent income. In Lowell, the standard prewar wage against which to compare wartime income is simple to establish and remarkably uniform. Before the effects of the war and the Fair Labor Standards Act of 1938 began to be felt, most women started in the mills at $13 per week. "Everybody got $13." The average weekly salary of $18.65 for Lowell women in 1941 was not much higher than the $ .40 per hour legal minimum reached in 1942 under the Fair Labor Standards Act. There were few increases or promotions beyond this minimum.[14]

Competition for workers from Remington—offering women a minimum of $ .55 to start—caused mill wages to rise steadily in spite of a semi-rigid wage freeze nationally. Lowell wages rose to $23.60 within a year and to $29.10 by 1943. Women recall wartime wages ranging from a low of $20 per week through $30-$40 per week to $50-$70 on piecework. The most common experience seems to have been pay starting at $30 with steady increases. Remington paid women up to $37 for a normal 48-hour work week in mid-1943.[15]

Increased income for mill women came partly in the form of overtime hours and fringe benefits. The Merrimack Mill followed the Remington policy of paid holidays and time-and-a-half for overtime and Saturdays in an effort to retain its workers. Nationally, women's wages in Lowell's predominant industries increased about 50 percent from 1941 to 1944. As a city with old industries, however, the rise in wages for Lowell's leading industries lagged behind for all manufacturing.[16]

Just as significant as the absolute wage for women is their wage compared with that of men. Comparing national ratios of women's to men's wages is interesting in light of a WLB

[14] Interview with Yvonne Hoar; interview with Frank Fiske and Hazel Fiske; *Lowell Daily Sun*, March 24, 1943, p. 4.

[15] *Lowell Daily Sun*, March 24, 1943, p. 4; National Archives Record Group, 202, "Records of the National War Labor Board," interview with Alice Swanton, June 4, 1975.

[16] International Labor Office, *The War and Women's Employment:...* (Montreal, 1946), pp. 207, 210; interview with Hazel Fiske and Frank Fiske; Remington Arms Co., Inc., Lowell Ordnance Plant, *Information for Employees* (n.p., n.d.), p. 10.

order allowing employers to grant increases to women to help equalize pay and after passage of equal-pay legislation in Massachusetts (and four other states) during the war.[17] Considering all industries, the ratio of women's weekly wages to men's rose from .54 in 1941 to .60 in 1944. The same ratio only for Lowell's principal industries, however, reveals a worsening position for women. For example, in textiles the women earned 72 percent of what men received in 1941; by 1944 they received only 62 percent of what men were paid. The same pattern is found in the boot and shoe industry and in silk, rayon, and wool mills.[18] Even at Remington the minimum wage for women was below that for men until complaints brought an adjustment a few months after the plant opened.[19]

Contrary to myth, women workers, especially during the war, used their paychecks not as "pin money," but to support themselves and their families. This was especially true in working-class cities like Lowell. Figures compiled by the Department of Labor's Women's Bureau for Springfield and Holyoke again suggest the case in Lowell where 87 percent of the pay of a married woman went to support her family, compared to 77 percent nationally. Over half the women contributed their entire paychecks to family expenses, compared to a third nationally.[20]

Along with higher wages on an hourly basis went increased hours of work. Nationally, the average weekly hours for women increased from 38.1 in 1941 to 41.2 in 1944. A Remington survey of thirteen Lowell companies in January, 1943, showed that three had increased hours for women and eight had a standard work week for women of 46-48 hours.[21]

17 Chester W. Gregory, *Women in Defense Work During World War II: An Analysis of the Labor Problem and Women's Rights* (New York, 1974), pp. 180-181.

18 ILO, *War and Women's Employment*, pp. 207, 210.

19 National Archives, Record Group, 202, "NWLB Records."

20 Women's Bureau, *Women Workers in Ten War Production Areas*, pp. 50-53.

21 Trey, "Women in the War Economy," p. 45; National Archives, Record Group, 202, "NWLB Records."

This does not, however, reveal fully the change in women's working hours. Prior to the war, law and custom limited women to the first shift in the mills, even when the mills would run two (rare after 1925) or three (almost unheard of after 1925) shifts each day.[22] Early in 1942, "Lowell cotton goods manufacturers . . . received a waiver permitting women over thirty years of age to work on the third shift." The Massachusetts legislature passed a law allowing the Commissioner of Labor and Industries to suspend any regulations pertaining to women and minors "as he deems necessary to supply any deficiency in manpower." Further legislation allowed the governor to suspend rules regarding Sunday and holiday work if "necessary to expedite the production, processing or transporting of war materials." Similar acts allowed suspension of seating laws for women, weight-lifting laws, and lunch-period laws for women. Dressing room, rest room, and toilet regulations were unaffected, as were prohibited work periods during pregnancy.[23] Twenty-three other states passed similar legislation. These changes "for the duration" represented a step away from protective labor legislation, but also tended to equalize—at the lowest common denominator—working conditions for men and women.

Changes in the law affected all areas in which women worked. Women found jobs on all three shifts at the Merrimack, and all the mills shortened the standard lunch period from forty-five to thirty minutes, ostensibly to make the shifts more efficient. After the war, women continued to work until 11:00 P.M. (instead of 6:00 P.M. prior to the war) and the

[22] According to Massachusetts law, women could work only nine hours per day, six days per week and forty-eight hours per week. The law also required a 45-minute lunch period in any six-hour period and prohibited women from working between 10:00 P.M. and 6:00 A.M. In practice, women did not work in the mills after 6:00 P.M.

[23] U.S.E.S., *Monthly Labor Market Report*, March 16, 1942-April 15, 1942, p. 14; United States Department of Labor, Women's Bureau, *State Labor Laws for Women with Wartime Modifications, December 15, 1944*, Bulletin no. 202 (Washington, 1945), part I, pp. 36-39, 108; part II, pp. 4, 19, 34; part III, pp. 2, 10; part V, pp. 27, 44; Commonwealth of Massachusetts, *Sessions Laws 1943*, chapter 382.

shortened lunch period remained in effect. To accommodate night workers both at Remington and other mills, public bus service was extended to serve the late shifts. By 1944, cotton manufacturers were expected by the federal government to keep all women—except those "with bona fide household responsibilities which made them available for part-time work only"—at work forty-eight hours per week.[24]

The net effect of these changes is an open question. Of course, more workers working more hours meant more production. No one in Lowell reported problems with women becoming less efficient as they worked increased hours, although the *Lowell Sun,* quoting a management source, reported higher absenteeism in the textile mills. Evidence from other parts of the country varied. A *Bulletin* of the Women's Bureau stated that "as the months of war work lengthened into years during World War II, reports of increasing fatigue among employees became numerous; absenteeism occasioned much comment; and in the summer of 1943 the War Production Board reported a slowing down of production." Richard Polenberg, in *War and Society,* appears to contradict Anderson's report: "As long as the work week did not exceed forty-eight hours, there was no difference in either the productivity or efficiency of men and women." It appears (with reservations) that the latter statement best describes Lowell. In woolen, worsted, and cotton goods, fewer workers made far more products in 1945 than in 1940. Production per dollar of wages stayed relatively constant, in spite of any increase in fatigue or absenteeism, and the proportion of manufacturing costs represented by workers' wages declined in all Lowell industries.[25]

24 Interview with Hazel Fiske and Frank Fiske; interview with Yvonne Hoar; report to members of the National Association of Cotton Manufacturers, May 2, 1944, Northern Textile Association Papers, Merrimack Valley Textile Museum, North Andover, Mass.

25 *Lowell Daily Sun,* March 24, 1943, p. 4; United States Department of Labor, Women's Bureau, *Women's Wartime Hours of Work: The Effect on Their Factory Performance and Homelife,* Bulletin no. 208 (Washington, 1947), p. 1; Richard Polenberg, *War and Society: The United States 1941-1945* (Phila-

## II

The war conditions led to a great emphasis on "security" in the workplace. Ostensibly intended to prevent sabotage, these measures reinforced the already authoritarian atmosphere of the factory or mill.

As a war production plant, Remington had more security regulations than did the mills. Guards were posted at the gate and employees had to show a badge in order to enter. With each paycheck came an entry pass for the following week. The instructions in the employees' handbook included numerous rules governing different aspects of security: the carrying of weapons was prohibited, visitors had to be authorized, passes were required in order to carry out any packages, and cameras were banned.[26]

The reality of security at Remington, however, did not always match the theory. "It didn't seem worth a darn. You had to have your picture taken and you couldn't go in unless you had your picture and number. Then if you tell them you forgot it, you'd just walk in and that was it." Even more surprising is the experience of photographer Dow Case from the *Lowell Sun*. Case wanted to tour the plant, but no one was at the gate to direct him to the office where he intended to get permission and a guide. He then decided to go through the gate and start snapping pictures, assuming it was the quickest way to get to the office. After half an hour of waiting, Mr. Case gave up and returned to the newspaper.[27]

The Boston Navy Yard observed its security regulations with greater strictness. For example, Ms. Poisson learned that her brother's ship had just arrived. When she sent him a note arranging for them to meet, he was called before an inspection board for telling her about the ship's docking. In another

delphia, 1972), p. 146; Commonwealth of Massachusetts, Department of Labor and Industries, Division of Statistics, "Census of Manufactures—1950—Lowell, Mass.," mimeographed (n.p., 1950), pp. 2-3.

[26] Remington, *Information for Employees*, pp. 10, 16, 20-22.

[27] Interview with Yvonne Hoar; interview with Dow Case, Dec. 12, 1974.

instance, Ms. Poisson got in trouble for speaking in French to a friend about a movie they planned to see after work: one of the security rules at the Yard admonished workers always to speak English. Similarly, another woman at the Navy Yard recalls that employees' telephone calls were monitored as part of standard procedure.[28] The same rationale for increased security led to increased discipline over workers' lives in matters unrelated to security. Here, too, the official regulations and the reality of discipline did not always correspond.

The Remington employee handbook included instructions on smoking, eating, phone calls, address regulations, cursing, raffle selling, and the "passing of papers of any nature." It stated: "Employees may be transferred from one Area to another when it is considered for the good of the employee or the Company." This last rule was often invoked when there was a lack of work in one department, and a woman could be temporarily transferred to another.[29]

Women enjoyed work at Remington more than they had at the mills, but the atmosphere was more strict. "You couldn't loaf. If you loafed, they'd send somebody to the house to find out why you were loafing, if you were sick or not. . . . It was like playing hookey from school." When returning to work after being ill, an employee needed "clearance" from the Medical Department. And "there was a load [of supervisors]. Everybody had a title in them days." This same worker "ignored most of [the supervisors]. I didn't pay no attention. As long as I got in and done all my work, I figured that's all that mattered."[30]

Several factors contributed to lack of respect for discipline in spite of the psychological and social pressures of the war effort. There was an understandable resentment of a paternalism and supervision reminiscent of Lowell's origin as a com-

[28] Interview with Doris Poisson; interview with Claire Contardo.

[29] Remington, *Information for Employees*, pp. 8, 20-22; interview with Yvonne Hoar.

[30] Interview with Yvonne Hoar; Remington, *Information for Employees*, p. 13.

pany town. Most of the Remington bosses were civilian males, and open to the accusation of avoiding the armed services. "Men bosses couldn't really control the help. . . . They [got] quite a good roughing over from the women." There were persistent rumors that all of Remington's Lowell production was defective.[31]

While the war meant increased limitations due to security, it also brought the increased freedom of job and geographical mobility. During World War II, Margaret Mead observed that an "important experience women have had, while the men were away, is moving about."[32] Undoubtedly, many Lowell women would have deserted the mills sooner had alternatives been available; the war created the alternatives. Nationally, the separation rate for textiles reached a phenomenal high of 89 per 100 workers in 1943. "They were paying better money, so everybody was leaving the mills to go there and make bullets, ammunition and all."[33]

Women didn't leave the mills only for new permanent work at Remington. New types of women's jobs opened both in the mills and elsewhere. At the Boott Mill, women performed at least eight distinct jobs previously reserved for men. A local bank replaced men with women as tellers. The *Lowell Sun* carried a regular feature, "Women at War," which portrayed women in previously all-male occupations. Throughout the war, the women changed jobs in search of better conditions, more money, and, perhaps, variety. This was especially true in Lowell. Without the threat of the draft, women quit their jobs twice as often as did men.[34]

31 Interview with Alice Swanton.

32 Jack Goodman, Editor, *While You Were Gone: A Report on Wartime Life in the United States* (New York, 1946), p. 284; Richard R. Lingeman, *Don't You Know There's A War On: The American Home Front, 1941-1945* (New York, 1970), p. 148.

33 T.W.U.A., *Fourth Executive Council Report*, p. 16; interview with Yvonne Hoar.

34 *Lowell Daily Sun*, March 24, 1943, p. 4; U.S.E.S., *Joint Quarterly Statistical Bulletin*, Jan. 1944-March, 1944, p. 7; *Lowell Daily Sun*, Feb. 11, 1943; Feb. 23, 1943, p. 1; interview with Yvonne Hoar; interview with Alice Swanton.

In addition to creating new and better paid jobs for Lowell's working women, World War II also helped to overcome traditional limitations based on ethnic backgrounds. The Merrimack, for instance, had refused to hire Catholics to work in the front office. The fight by workers against such bigotry continued until the war: strikers against the Merrimack in early December, 1941, cited ethnic prejudice by the owners as one of their principal grievances. The arrival of Remington aided the fight as the new company, with its great demand for workers, quickly won a reputation for hiring people of many national backgrounds. There was "a different attitude at the defense plants. . . . That turned the tide on [prejudice]" as people refused to accept the discrimination they might have overlooked during the depression.[35]

The 1941 strike at the Merrimack reflected the increasing organized activity of Lowell workers which began in the late 1930's and reached fruition during the war. By 1943, the Merrimack and Boott mills—the two largest in Lowell—had become organized as the companies preferred to avoid conflicts while government orders were pouring in. Women played a major role in the organizing efforts, although one organizer believed that the "confusion of such large numbers of women" in the labor force weakened unions, and some unions—such as the plumbers—continued their all-male membership.[36] The paid organizers at the Merrimack were male, but the fight succeeded largely because of the participation of the women in the mill. Said one woman of the Merrimack drive, "Mrs. Hoar did it. . . . That woman took on the whole Merrimack, and she fought them to a standstill. . . . She had the heart of a lion. . . . It was something to see that woman at a meeting [with management]."[37] Union organizing extended beyond the factories: Lowell's high school teachers—almost all women

[35] *Lowell Daily Sun*, Dec. 7, 1941; interview with Yvonne Hoar; interview with Alice Swanton.

[36] Interview with John Mullen, June 16, 1975; interview with Everett Harris, Sept. 17, 1975.

[37] Interview with Alice Swanton.

—finally overcame intense opposition and won equal pay for women teachers. Nationally, over 800,000 women joined labor unions, increasing their union membership to over three million.[38]

The war also introduced new limitations on job mobility. With labor scarce, employers and planners pushed for government controls over where people could work and when they could change jobs. Although a "labor draft" never developed, hiring controls announced on February 5, 1943, were intended to direct workers into essential industries and reduce the high turnover in industries like textiles. To be hired by a new employer in an essential industry, a worker had to present a certificate of availability from the previous employer or the U. S. Employment Service. When one woman decided to leave the Waltham Watch Company after a pay cut, she had to get an official release. That controls were not drastic is indicated by the fact that the release to go to nonwar work was granted despite opposition from the Waltham Watch superintendent. Controls "depended entirely on voluntary compliance by employers" and were laxly applied to workers.[39]

As was the case with many aspects of women's work during World War II, job mobility reflected positive and negative effects at the same time. On the positive side were the jobs which had been opened up and the removal of some ethnic limitations. Knowing jobs were available and that some choice existed made women feel secure enough to refuse the worst jobs and to challenge their employers. On the other hand, these nonfundamental changes rarely conflicted with a business point of view. No rational reason existed to keep women out of certain occupations; movement was generally horizontal, not vertical, and any threat women posed to the male monopoly on supervisory jobs was temporary. And while old

[38] ILO, *War and Women's Employment*, p. 237.

[39] United States Civilian Production Administration, Bureau of Demobilization, *Industrial Mobilization for War: History of the War Production Board and Predecessor Agencies 1940-1945* (Washington, 1947), p. 702; Committee on Records of War Administration, *United States at War*, pp. 435-436; interview with Alice Swanton.

ethnic divisions in Lowell were being buried—and had become obsolete as a method of dividing and controlling workers—the city would in the coming years have a new "outgroup": the blacks and Puerto Ricans.

Hiring controls had much greater potential for limiting the freedom of workers. First, although rarely exercised, the power inherent in their existence must have had a threatening effect, thus discouraging workers from changing jobs more frequently. Second, the introduction of hiring controls set a precedent, just as a precedent was set of increased corporate control for alleged security reasons. Indeed, many of the aspects of discipline described here remain in effect today in plants with no relation to defense production. Similarly, the potential for government intrusion into the lives of individuals was again increased.

## III

What the women liked and disliked about wartime work is a summary of the conditions under which they worked. When considering both pleasures and displeasures, the narrow range of jobs and opportunities available to all workers and, most especially, to women workers—during wartime and during peacetime—must be remembered. While working through the war years, women were bombarded with propaganda extolling home life reminding them they would have to return to their homes when "the boys came back."

Undoubtedly, the feeling that she made a contribution to the war against Fascism made a woman's work more enjoyable, but patriotic motives were cited by very few Lowell women. "A lot of them [those who went to work for Remington Arms] said it was patriotism, but it really wasn't; it was more money."[40] But money does not provide a complete answer: wages, of course, brought economic subsistence and created a measure of security and even luxury after fifteen years of depression; but unanswered is what else money represented to

[40] Interview with Yvonne Hoar.

women. It could have meant new independence, self-respect, power, or all that work is expected to bring to men or women. Clearly, "confidential" government work offered excitement and a feeling of importance impossible in the mills.

The novelty of having a choice of work beyond the mill tradition and the confines of Lowell meant a great deal. Many women felt themselves freed of limitations—both official and cultural—on where they could work and what they could do at work. Relationships with other workers and participation in unions provided a social network at the job. Working outside Lowell exposed them to new ideas about themselves and about their work. "Among the coworkers, everything was beautiful."[41]

On the negative side, women saw many farcical aspects of their work. Discipline and security measures annoyed the women at the Navy Yard and complaints resulted when telephone calling and other social contacts were arbitrarily stopped. Remington was abused for its extreme security measures, for the lax enforcement of rules, and for rumors that its products were useless. Resented most were the "truant officers" Remington sent to the homes to check on absent workers. These invasions of workers' privacy and the distrust they symbolized by employers run counter to rumors of dedicated patriotism. Moreover, the need corporations felt for increased control implied that workers were resisting the combined dictates of a war effort and their employers.

Significantly, there seems to have been little complaint on the surface about the temporary nature of many jobs. Most women were either content or resigned about having men return home and resume the old economic hierarchies. Part of this may have been resignation to conditions that would return to prewar standards. It was common knowledge that the Remington plant, symbolic of the increased options for women, had been built to last from only five to ten years.[42] In

[41] Interview with Doris Poisson.

[42] *Lowell Daily Sun*, March 4, 1943, p. 1.

addition, while women's work roles did change somewhat, the changes rarely altered the relationships between men and women either in the home or at work. Yet, over three-quarters of women workers in 1944-1945 indicated they planned to continue working after the war.[43]

## IV

Just as the onset of war brought a great swelling in the number of women active in the labor force, so the winding down meant a decline in the number of women working. This decline began even before the war ended: from June to September, 1945, one out of every four women in United States factories lost her job. Immediately after V-J Day, 175 out of every 1,000 women employed in manufacturing were laid off, a rate twice that of men. By August, 1946, the proportion of women in the American labor force had declined from 36 percent to 29 percent, but remained significantly above the 1940 level of 15.5 percent. Despite this decrease, official figures for unemployment among women remained small; women reportedly left the labor force entirely as economic conditions stayed above the depression figures of the 1930's.[44]

The Lowell case supports these national figures and answers some of the questions they pose. Some Lowell women gladly left their work after their husbands returned and found employment; these women had seen work only as an option "for the duration." Others left as the postwar baby boom began. As one woman recalled, she had intended to find work in Lowell after her government office closed, but found herself "in the family way" and didn't return to work.[45]

Many women simply left the labor force when defense

[43] Women's Bureau, *Women Workers in Ten War Production Areas*, p. 31.

[44] United States Department of Labor, Women's Bureau, *Employment of Women in the Early Postwar Period with Backgrounds of Prewar and War Data*, Bulletin no. 211 (Washington, 1946), p. iv; United States Department of Labor, Bureau of Labor Statistics, *Monthly Labor Review*, 64, no. 3 (1947), p. 411; Lingeman, *Don't You Know There's A War On*, p. 158; Women's Bureau, *Employment of Women in the Early Postwar Period*, p. iv.

[45] Interview with Claire Contardo.

plants and several textile mills ceased operations between 1945 and 1948. Other companies such as Waltham Watch lost their lucrative contracts and reduced their wages, leading many employees to seek work closer to home or to stop working entirely. Fortunately, for the first few years until a new long-term depression began for Lowell, work existed for most of the women who sought it, albeit at lower wages. This availability of work is partly attributable to the large numbers not seeking employment. The U. S. Employment Service reported that "elderly and other marginal workers" in Massachusetts left the labor market rather than accept "necessary wage and occupational adjustments."[46]

In spite of wartime threats to the contrary, Merrimack rehired many skilled women who had left the company to work at Remington. Other women who had been hired by the Merrimack during the war stayed on, but moved to less desirable slots as the men returned and resumed their hold on the favored positions. Some workers found employment in Lowell's shoe factories or in new or expanded war-related factories such as Sylvania, Raytheon, and AVCO. The state actually had a reported excess of men in the 1946 labor market and a lack of women to fill the jobs reserved for the "marginal" workers.[47]

The memory of the 1930's helped women workers to accept ideas that today often appear dubious. First, many women may have desired to hold their jobs—or find new ones—but faced with a resignation founded upon prewar conditions coupled with propaganda sending them back into the home, they withdrew silently from the postwar labor market. Although little stigma attached to working-class women who worked, both sexes continued to believe and to act as though it were preferable for the husband to be the sole wage earner should only

[46] U.S.E.S., *Joint Quarterly Statistical Bulletin*, April, 1946-June, 1946, pp. 3-4.

[47] U.S.E.S., pp. 3-4; interview with Alice Swanton; interview with Doris Poisson; interview with Hazel Fiske and Frank Fiske; interview with Yvonne Hoar.

one job be available per family. Women may have resented this, but they either moved to inferior jobs, or "voluntarily" left the labor market. Only slight protest greeted the preference given to returning servicemen over women with seniority.

Male-dominated unions, perhaps also fearing a new depression, fought to protect their newly acquired organizational strength by concentrating on bread-and-butter issues; the rights of their female members ranked low on the scale of priorities. As a result, employers could look upon women as a continued source of plentiful, cheap, unprotected workers. In Lowell, women worked in the increasingly marginal textile industry until, by the mid-1950's, the major mills had all closed, moved South, or out of the country—a change the unions were powerless to prevent. The depression had conditioned Lowell women to accept "the inevitable"; indeed, it was obvious in Lowell that only the war had provided a respite from depression and the narrowing choices for workers.

## V

The case of Lowell produced divergent interpretations of the meaning of the war years for American women. On the one hand, it has been said that World War II changed little, that reconversion brought a renewal of prewar standards in terms of the absolute number of women working and in their status.[48] This view points to the still strong ideology prohibiting women from working. Fundamental to this position is the assertion that conditions were no different from what would have been the case had the depression ended without war. But in Lowell no strong ideology had ever kept women out of the factories; only local custom resisted their competing with men when the labor market tightened. Lowell was a working-class city; ideologies which frowned on working women were peculiar to the small middle class and the rich. The ideology did not change; conditions did. When work appeared, women

[48] See Mary McKinney Schweitzer, "Women in the Labor Force, 1940-1947," MA Dissertation, University of North Carolina, Chapel Hill (1977), and Eleanor F. Straub, "U. S. Government Policy Toward Civilian Women During World War II," *Prologue*, v, 240-254 (Winter, 1973).

grabbed it; when prewar depression became postwar recession, some women left the labor market. Because ideology played a relatively minor role in such decisions by Lowell's working-class women, the crucial point in determining the domestic impact of 1941 through 1945 becomes not war, but the economic effect of war: the end of the Great Depression.

On the other hand, World War II has been viewed as the turning point in the role of women in the labor force.[49] Masses of women who would never have thought of seeking employment entered the labor force; they took jobs previously forbidden to the "weaker sex." With the experience of work—both novel and traditional—women would continue to assert their rights after 1945, although they had to give up some ground. This attitude denies what was—at least in Lowell, and probably in many regions—the experience of working-class women; given the availability of work, household economics dictated that all able members of a family bring home a wage. Further, this interpretation flies in the face of current conditions: women continue to earn less than men in equal jobs; women continue to be shut out of "men's" work; women rarely have the opportunity to find "equal" work. Again, the change was not ideology, but in the fact that employment became a real possibility during and after World War II.

In other words, interpretations of the long- and short-term effects of war on women have focused on ideology, mystiques, and cults. This approach tends by its nature to focus on intellectual history and, therefore, on the elites. Focusing on Lowell workers seems exceptional at first glance because of the city's peculiar history. But that history only appears peculiar: it is a case of a history focused on the working class, a history in which individual lives are more clearly and closely limited by day-to-day economic reality. For Lowell women, ideology as it has been used in relation to women's work would have been a largely unaffordable luxury.

[49] See William Chafe, *The American Woman: Her Changing Social, Economic, and Political Roles, 1920-1970* (New York, 1972), and Chester W. Gregory, *Women in Defense Work During World War II: An Analysis of the Labor Problem and Women's Rights* (New York, 1974).

# Riveters, Volunteers and WACS: Women in Mobile During World War II

Patricia G. Harrison

> Demand for women to staff vital war services has become so urgent that we are appealing to every woman in Mobile to register ... this week.
>
> Civilian Volunteer Office
> March 1942

> We do not believe that you Women of Mobile will shirk your responsibility...we believe you will rally to the call, now.
>
> War Manpower Commission
> February 1943

World War II, with its symbolic figure of "Rosie the Riveter," is considered by some historians to be a watershed in women's history and women's roles. [1] The experience of women in Mobile, Alabama, during World War II provides one of the most striking examples in the country of the changes which affected American women during this period. An indication of the degree of change in the city can be seen in the fact that three times as many women were working outside the home in 1944 as in 1940. [2] However, in Mobile, as in many other defense cities, "Rosie the Riveter" was joined by "Virginia the Volunteer" and "Wanda the WAC." Some resumed the pattern of their lives after the war, many did not, but all Mobile women's lives were affected by the experience. The direct and indirect impact of World War II can be seen in many areas. Women were involved in volunteer activities, in defense work, in other wartime jobs, and in the military service.

As might be expected, volunteer work was one of the first areas in which they became personally involved in the war effort. By early 1942 there were numerous ads and announcements in the Mobile papers describing the need for volunteers. Women were often pictured wearing the uniform of one volunteer organization or another. Appeals for volunteers came from many agencies and organizations, one of the most important being the Red Cross. In the Red Cross Cross one could serve in the motor corps, as a nurses' aide, do canteen work, be a staff assistant, or help with production. By January 4, 1942, seven hundred women had registered for the Red Cross Motor Corps. As part of their training they received instruction on servicing automobiles and making emergency repairs on their vehicles. The course included twenty hours of first aid work and six hours of auto mechanics—enough of the latter to keep a car moving. The volunteers learned to install

Mobile Press Register, *February 1943* *USA Library*

"jumper" wires on faulty ignition systems, clean out gas lines, change tires and make other repairs to cars and trucks. [3] The primary duty of the motor corps was to provide transportation service for regular Red Cross chapter activities, but in emergencies members were to be prepared to drive ambulances and to help in various other ways. The women carried emergency medical passes to be used when their services were needed. By 1942 the Red Cross Motor Corps had 110 automobiles at its disposal and was offering free transportation to the men and officers of the air depot at Brookley Field.

Many women volunteered to serve as Red Cross Nurses' Aides and completed the eighty hour, five week course required to qualify for the position. [4] In March 1942 the chapter directors announced that the development of a nurses' aide corps was the task of first importance facing the volunteer services of the Mobile County Red Cross Chapter. [5] In the same month the *Mobile Register* contained an article which began:

> Attention, women of Mobile! If you wish to serve your country, and are able to meet the qualifications necessary to enlist for training, the Mobile Nurses Aid [*sic*] Corps is asking for 300 volunteers to register next Monday, Tuesday, and Wednesday ...

*Nurses and Red Cross Volunteers, War Bond Parade 1943, ADDSCO Collection, USA Photo Archives*

The article stated that Mobile was confronted with a steady depletion of the nursing services of hospitals and health departments, partially due to the requirements of the military. [6] As thousands of workers poured into the city looking for defense jobs, hospitals were desperately in need of auxiliary staff to relieve their overburdened registered nurses.

Another Red Cross activity which depended upon female volunteers was canteen work. Although several hundred women had already registered by March 1942, this announcement appeared in the *Mobile Press Register:*

> MOBILE WOMEN GIVEN OPPORTUNITY TO LEARN TO COOK FOR LARGE CROWDS Can you cook? Do you enjoy watching people eat? If so, you will want to start classes in Red Cross Canteen work beginning Tuesday. [7]

Red Cross volunteers were instructed in canteen organization, nutrition, the preparation and serving of food in large quantities, and improvising equipment. The training course lasted forty hours. By June 1942 volunteers in the canteen were providing lunch for servicemen working in downtown offices. They were open between 12:00 and 2:00 each day except Sunday at 159 St. Michael Street. Plans were made to keep the facility open until 8:00 p.m. in order for men stationed at Brookley Field to get coffee and doughnuts when they came to town. On a more somber note, in the event of disaster, canteen workers expected to be called to feed civilians in the stricken areas. Photographs often appeared in the *Mobile Press Register* featuring women involved in canteen activities. A number of volunteers served on the staff of the Red Cross as typists and clerks or assisted the Red Cross program in various other ways. Many women and women's organizations produced a variety of articles for the Red Cross including knitted sweaters, caps, mufflers, and socks. Others sewed and made surgical dressings.

*Red Cross Worker Soliciting Contributions at ADDSCO, ADDSCO Collection, USA Photo Archives*

The Junior Red Cross made rugs and afghans to be used in the dayrooms and sunrooms of military and naval hospitals.[8] Mobilians' ideas and designs for the afghans were so well received by the national Red Cross headquarters that they were featured in several national ladies' magazines including *Harper's Bazaar*, *Good Houskeeping*, and *Women's Home Companion*.[9] The afghans were adopted as the official project of the Junior Red Cross.

Although Mobile's women volunteered in large numbers early in the war, demand consistently outpaced the supply. For example, on March 24, 1942, the Civilian Volunteer Office issued this statement.

> The Civilian Volunteer Office needs volunteers and must have them. Demand for women to staff vital war services has become so urgent that we are appealing to every woman in Mobile to register this week.[10]

One organization which received many volunteers was the USO (United Service Organizations). It provided many services to military personnel and defense workers through its member organizations. In March 1942 the national board of the Young Women's Christian Association (YWCA) sent an emergency worker, June Donahue, to the Mobile USO area.[11] She was to cooperate with other USO officials who were operating under the supervision of the National Catholic Community Services. She said that in sending her, the YWCA national board showed that it "regarded Mobile as one of the largest centers of defense industry in the country."[12] As a member agency of the USO, the YWCA directed its work primarily toward the problems

*Government Street USO Club, McNeely Collection, USA Photo Archives*

of girls and women affected by the defense program. It attempted to meet the needs of both female defense workers and the female family members of the defense workers and military personnel who were arriving in Mobile in increasing numbers. Miss Donahue felt that one of the YWCA's major services was to "help maintain a nearly normal social life among women in defense areas, with health, relaxation, and recreation stressed." [13]

The USO's attempt to provide a social life for the servicemen in Mobile included sponsoring many dances. Hostesses were available at the USO centers to play table games with servicemen and at the train depot to serve refreshments. By April 1942 the USO had established a club for industrial and defense workers at 307 Conti Street. [14] At the USO Service Men's Club located at 602 Government Street, activities included boxing instruction, bridge, photography, dances, and "home hospitality," or the Sunday dinners, another task assumed by Mobile's women. In the black community, female volunteers staffed the Davis Avenue Service Center which had been established for black military personnel.

Other groups also sponsored dances for servicemen. The Mars Girls (Mobile Army Recreation Service) were well known and were referred to as Mobile's dancing girls. Asking Mobilians to volunteer to serve with the Mars Girls, one officer pointed out that "recreational service is an important national defense project." [15] Organized in April 1941 the Mars Girls had sponsored nearly thirty dances by February 1942. By February 1944, 1500 volunteers had served with the organization. [16]

A Downtown Service Men's Center, sponsored by twelve Mobile churches, was established at the St. Francis Street Methodist Church located at St. Francis and Joachim Streets. Activities included ping pong, darts, horseshoes, movies, reading, table games, and suppers. Soldiers and sailors who visited the center were asked to list their interests and hobbies so that it could determine what they most wanted to do. It was open daily from 2:00 p.m. to 10:00 p.m. There were evening programs, games, and music, and on Sunday nights, a men's song service. The Government Street Presbyterian Church kept a "Browsing Room" open every day from 9:00 a.m. to 10:00 p.m. It actually consisted of several rooms—a lounging room, a date room, a writing room, and a ping pong room. Three pianos, a phonograph, and a radio were all provided by the church.

In March 1942 the Civilian Defense Volunteer Office issued a plea for six hundred female volunteers for Air Raid Warning Service. The *Mobile Register* urged Mobilians to perform the important function

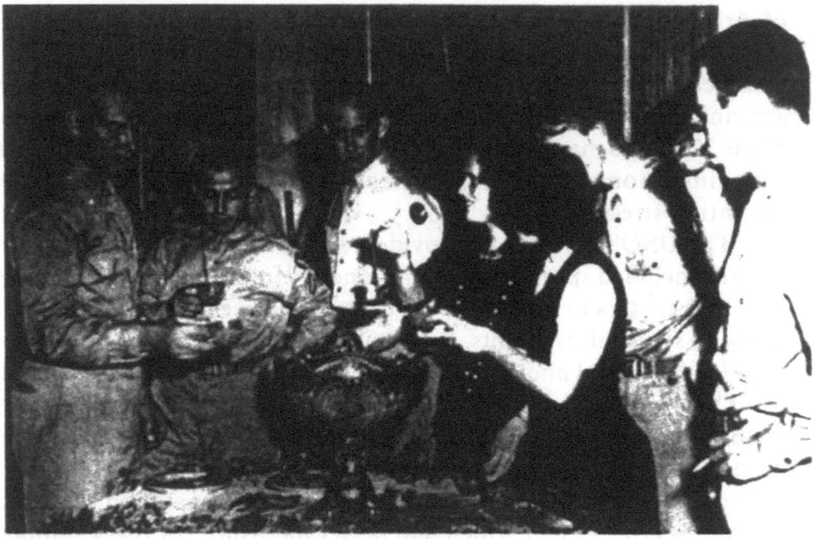

*Hostesses at Downtown Servicemen's Center, Archives, St. Francis Street United Methodist Church*

of defending this major industrial center from enemy raids. Some women had almost completed air raid warning training and there was a need for additional help. The *Register* stressed that since Mobile was such an important industrial center, her women should be eager to serve, and since the war might last for a number of years, they should receive appropriate training. The article also noted that a good way for newcomers to meet other women was to become involved in war work. [17] Evidently many did not heed the call, for two weeks later the headline read, "Mobile's Women Slow to Proffer Services in War." [18] Only one hundred fifty people had responded to the newspaper's earlier plea.

For those who were more traditionally minded, the Information Center and the Sunday Dinners provided opportunities for women to serve their country in the wartime crisis. They could volunteer to work in the Information Center which was opened in Bienville Square in June 1942. It was designed to assist servicemen, war workers, and the general public, using competent and well trained volunteers. However, an even more traditional way of serving one's country was to invite a serviceman to dinner on Sunday. Committees were formed which worked with the USO to provide opportunities for servicemen to be Sunday dinner guests in the homes of Mobilians. Soldiers or sailors registered on the Saturday preceding the Sunday they wished to come to dinner.

Many of the established or traditional women's clubs and organizations participated actively in volunteer work or urged their members to do so. They regularly had defense-related topics for their monthly programs. [19] At the January 1942 meeting of the Virginia Cavalier Chapter of the Daughters of the American Revolution (DAR), reports were given on Red Cross work and the group donated a box of clothes to Britain. The Bonnie Blue Flag Chapter of the United Daughters of the Confederacy officially joined defense classes and organized a first aid class for members of the chapter. In the same month the Wisteria Study Club's guest speaker was the chairman of civilian defense in Mobile. He stressed the important role women had to play in that activity while urging club members to do what they could to help. Members of the Mobile Business and Professional Women's Club, representing those who were gainfully employed outside their homes, pledged their talents and efforts in the nation's war effort. In February the speaker for that organization evaluated the accomplishments of female workers in the volunteer defense effort in Mobile. The Forum Club's topic for their March meeting was "Air Raid Precautions." By May 1942 the Junior League had started a scrap drive. It placed a bin at Government and Broad Streets in which the public could deposit rags, rubber, worn-out tires, old newspapers, boxes, and scrap metal. Younger women also got involved. Mobile Girl Scouts began collecting books for servicemen as part of a nationwide drive. They collected adventure and mystery stories, and all sorts of books considered suitable for soldiers and sailors. Thus by early 1942, Mobile clubwomen were either being made aware of, or actively participating in, some phase of war-related activity. The war intruded and changed the routines of Mobile's women and girls. Through club activities and volunteer work, they developed new skills, broadened their circle of acquaintances, and widened the range of their daily activities.

However, the most striking and obvious changes World War II brought to women's lives, not only in Mobile but throughout the country, were the changes in work patterns. Many women who had never worked outside the home began doing so during World War II. Patriotic ads encouraging women to join the war effort could be seen in Mobile as well as in other parts of the country. A typical example appeared in the *Mobile Press Register* in February 1943.

TO THE WOMEN OF MOBILE
Uncle Sam Says:
I NEED YOU

The full page advertisement, sponsored by forty-five Mobile businesses and signed by the War Manpower Commission of the United

States Employment Service, declared "there is an acute shortage of workers for both Mobile's War Industries and for Essential Civilian Services." It stated:

> Thousands of new residents have come in and taken up a lot of the slack, but they have not proved to be enough. We Mobilians must pitch in and help to overcome this shortage...and at once! Practically all available manpower has been exhausted, so the solving of the problem *rests with the women.* Uncle Sam, through Mobile's office of the War Manpower Commission is asking that you step up and volunteer to take a job either in a War Industry or in some store, office, or other essential civilian business. *We do not believe that you Women of Mobile will shirk your responsibility* ... we believe you will rally to the call, now. [20]

In the same issue of the *Mobile Press Register* an Alabama Dry Docks and Shipbuilding ad was captioned: WOMEN CAN BUILD SHIPS, YET NEVER SEE A SHIPYARD. It continued:

> We are building ships faster than they have ever been built before on the Gulf Coast. But we must employ many more workers if we are to reach peak production. *Many of the new workers must be women.* Jobs are open now for women who have finished training courses.

It then went on to describe how they could receive training. However, it was stressed that women were needed in jobs beyond the shipyard as well:

> BUT WOMEN CAN BUILD SHIPS, yet never see a shipyard. Our workers must have food, clothing, and housing. Many businesses are essential to shipbuilding even though they are not directly connected with shipyards. Their service to shipyards must not be reduced by lack or workers. In the words of the War Manpower Commission, every Mobile woman who isn't in a war job or an essential civilian job and isn't needed in her home is urged to take an essential job or training which will prepare her for a job. [21]

In addition to civilian jobs such as grocery store clerks, stenographers, waitresses and salesclerks, they were needed to fill numerous positions at the Mobile Air Depot (Brookley Field). Women were encouraged to receive training to become welders, mechanics, and war plant workers. A representative for the War Manpower Commission stated:

> perhaps a housewife can work only part time in say, for example, a department store. But that little aid will help enormously. If every woman will do something towards winning this war, the task won't be such a long, hard one. [22]

Mobile Press Register, *February 1943*

Mobile Register, *February 1943*

The week of February 22-27, 1943, was designated as WOMEN'S RECRUITMENT WEEK IN MOBILE. Registration booths were open in all public schools and at several downtown locations. More than two thousand Mobile women registered for jobs in the war industries and essential civilian industries during the week. [23] The War Manpower Commission had hoped for six thousand registrations but the drive was considered a success since it was expected that others would take jobs later.

By February 1943 significant changes can be seen in the Mobile newspapers. At the beginning of the war, they had contained many references to the *male* workers at the shipyards and there were occasional stories featuring the women or wives behind these men. But by February 1943 the war industries in Mobile were actively recruiting women for defense jobs. There were other examples of this change. In June 1942 women had been advised not to come to Mobile looking for jobs. At that time the Information Center volunteers in Bienville Square said that women and girls from out-of-town were pouring into Mobile, "expecting to find jobs plentiful and for the asking." The volunteers noted that "in almost every case, the visitors were short of money and had not paid their board very far in advance." [24] They urged them not to come to Mobile unless they had relatives or enough money to return home. Just eight months later the positions were reversed. The female workers were being actively courted by industry.

Because of the boom in defense and other war related work, many women changed jobs during World War II. The teaching profession offers a striking example, for although there was a tremendous growth in the school age population, many teachers resigned their positions. They left to work in the war industries or for the government where they could earn much more money. The maximum annual salary for teachers with college degrees at the beginning of 1943 was $1300 while the maximum annual salary without a degree was $1200. [25]Women in the war industries could earn over $2000 a year. [26] Although patriotism may have been a factor, many teachers simply left their overcrowded classrooms for better paying jobs.

*ADDSCO Woman Welder ADDSCO Collection, USA Photo Archives*

By February 1944 there were over two thousand women employed at the Alabama Dry Dock and Shipbuilding Company (ADDSCO), most of them as welders. There were also female firemen on almost every shipyard crane, and at least one female rigger. ADDSCO's Women's Counseling Service Supervisor headed a staff of nine women, some of whom had been shipyard workers themselves. Their duty was "to keep the girl workers happy, healthy, and on the job." [27]

The Counseling Supervisor, Mrs. Mary McMullan Roberts, observed that

> when women first came to the shipyards, the shipyards were not quite ready for them. At first, therefore, they came into only a few crafts. As the manpower shortage increased, more women were needed, and they began to spread into a greater variety of jobs. [28]

The counseling service helped working women plan for the care of their children. Mrs. Roberts pointed out that a large number of the workers had children and that that nurseries were important to them. She tried to insure that mothers took advantage of the available nurseries and the extended day care program at the the public schools. The service also made arrangements for women to participate in local activities in their time off the job. It maintained contact with the the USO, the YWCA, and the city recreation units. Mrs. Roberts emphasized that every effort was being made to make the shipyard women part of the community through local church and recreational activities. She noted, "After all, by the time this war is over the so-called 'newcomers' will be Mobilians." She emphasized that people shouldn't think that after the war these workers would pull up their stakes and go home. "Remember," she said, "many of them have been here several years already, and they should feel they're a part of Mobile."

Mrs. Roberts also faced problems fitting people who were not used to working regular hours to the mold of shipyard life. She stated that most of the new workers had farm backgrounds and were accustomed to working ten hours one day and perhaps going fishing the next. The counseling department stressed to them that ADDSCO expected eight hours of work from them each day, but no more. Roberts also hoped to spend more time scouting for new job possibilities for women in the shipyard, explaining their needs to the community, and attacking the causes of absenteeism. The counseling service had round the clock duty—four counselors worked at night and five during the day.

At Brookley Field the civilian work force increased dramatically. By July 1943 it was estimated that approximately fifty per cent of the civilians employed at the Mobile Air Service Command (MOASC) were women. [29] Local publications highlighted the many jobs they held at Brookley. They worked as secretaries, typists, and clerks—white collar jobs which some had held before the war. Others did skilled work on aircraft, repairing engines, working on fuselages, welding or soldering parts, operating precision machines, and shearing, tacking, or riveting sheet metal. One observer noted that "one immediately

*Counselor and Shipyard Worker*

*ADDSCO Workers* *ADDSCO Collection, USA Photo Archives*

perceives that the majority of repair work on airplane instruments is being done by girls, for experience has proven them to be more adept than men at handling the intricate parts." [30] Women also worked in the supply warehouses getting material ready for shipment overseas or to a sub-depot. Some of them worked on high ladders getting supplies from shelves while others loaded packages on warehouse wagons. Still others were drivers or chauffeurs, civilian guards, nurses, radio mechanic helpers, parachute packers, mail handlers, telephone operators, and inspectors. One woman who was an operating engineer at the water treatment plant was responsible for purifying Brookley's water supply. A Brookley Field publication noted that she was the only member of her sex in the United States to hold down this "strictly man-sized job." [31] A group of physically handicapped women, some deaf mutes and some totally blind, also worked at MOASC. Women of all ages worked at Brookley Field. Seventeen and eighteen year olds were joined by matrons in their fifties and sixties. Several articles in the Brookley Field publications and in the Mobile papers highlighted the facility's working grandmothers. One headline read: "No Rockers Wanted: Grandmothers Far from Old Fashioned at MOASC." [32]

In addition to defense work, many took what had been non-traditional jobs. By April 1942 the senior interviewer for the U.S. Employment Service in Mobile outlined jobs recently opened to women including work at service stations, groceries, banks, radio stations, and as elevator operators and mechanics. Local papers were filled with pictures and articles on working women—butchers, telegraph messengers, gas company draftsmen, bank tellers, elevator operators, service station attendants, and gas company dispatchers. They also had milk routes, repaired meters for the electric power company, and by 1943 drove Mobile city buses. During 1944 female sheriff's deputies directed traffic in front of Mobile schools. The sheriff announced that a shortage in manpower made this program necessary. [33]

The Women's Bureau of the Department of Labor conducted a study of women workers in ten war production centers including the Mobile metropolitan area. The Bureau conducted interviews for this project in Mobile in November 1944. The report described Mobile as a "Southern city where comparatively few women in peacetime are employed in manufacturing and where the mushroom growth was due to demand for women workers in shipyards and air service installations." It added that the "area [is] also representative of the employment opportunities of Negro women workers in the South." [34] It should be noted, however, that the female workers interviewed in each

*ADDSCO Workers* *ADDSCO Collection, USA Photo Archives*

*Telephone Operators, 1944* *ADDSCO Collection, USA Photo Archives*

area were representative of all industries and occupations except household employment. It was considered too difficult to interview household employees in the homes of their employers. [35] Thus the data included in the bulletin generally excluded household employment and the many Mobile black women working as domestics.

The Women's Bureau survey is revealing and indicates the degree of change the war brought to the lives of many Mobile women. [36] Indeed, the study found that of the ten cities surveyed, the relative increase in employment was most marked in Mobile. Discounting household help or domestics, three times as many women were working outside the home in 1944 as in 1940. In-migrants, or those coming into Mobile, represented 47 per cent of the women employed in war-time Mobile. Eighty per cent or more of those surveyed said that they intended to continue working after the war. About two and one-half times as many wanted to continue working in the Mobile area as had been employed in 1940. There were more females employed by government during the war than in all the city's trade and service industries in 1940. Employment in those industries also increased substantially from 1940 to 1944. Although Mobile ranked just below the three highest paying areas in war manufacturing earnings (Detroit, San Francisco, and Seattle), it was the lowest paying area in three of the other five industrial groups. It also contained a higher proportion of black working women (31 per cent) than any of the other areas. However, not one black female was found working as an operative in the war factories in November 1944. Of all the women who worked outside the home during the war period, 40 percent were single, 47 per cent were married, and 13 per cent were widowed or divorced.

In Mobile the weekly take-home earnings of female operatives averaged $43.45 in war factories while the weekly take-home earnings of their counterparts in consumer installations was $22.90. Wages in other categories of civilian work were even lower. The take-home earnings in retail and wholesale trade averaged $21.25 per week while the equivalent pay of women employed in restaurants and taverns was $13.95. The lure of employment in wartime industries was obvious.

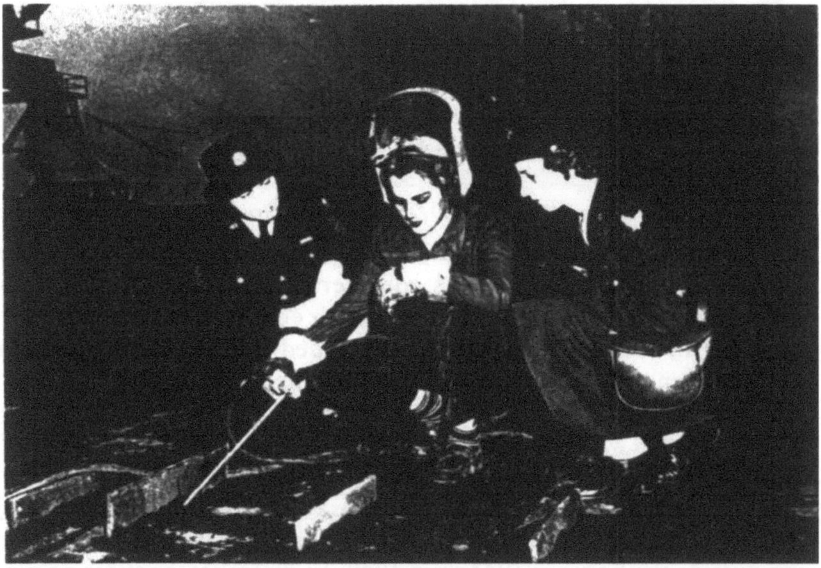

*WACS Visit ADDSCO, 1943 ADDSCO Collection, USA Photo Archives*

While many Mobile women were working in volunteer agencies and in defense industries to support the war effort, others joined the armed forces. In May 1942 several took the first steps toward joining the WACS (Women's Army Corps). Others later joined the WAVES, the SPARS, and the Marines. Stories appeared in the local papers about young women in the services, and the regular feature "Men in Our Armed Forces" was sometimes captioned "Men and Women in Our Armed Forces." Many local businesses sponsored recruiting ads for the WACS showing women in uniform driving, typing, or involved with photography, the mail, and supply services. WACS were stationed at the Brookley Field headquarters of the Mobile Air Service Command. Most had office assignments but they also served in a variety of other positions including aircraft mechanics, drivers, map readers, flight dispatchers, dental assistants, and nurses' aides. By February 1945 there were WACS at Brookley representing forty-one states. [37]

The war affected the daily lives of all Mobile women. The city suffered an acute housing shortage when thousands of people seeking jobs in the war industries or at Brookley, plus military personnel, poured into the city. In an effort to meet the newcomers' housing needs, women conducted door to door canvasses to find housing and to monitor conditions. Figures tell the city's story. Mobile had a population of 114,906 in the 1940 census; by May 1942 the estimated population of the Mobile metropolitan area was 175,000; and by February 1944 the estimate was 250,000. [38] The Chamber of Commerce called upon Mobilians to list any suitable living quarters for these newcomers. The Chamber asked for a "patriotic sacrifice" by residents to meet the situation. [39] During these years many of the large old homes were chopped up into several apartments or even into single rooms.

Schools were also terribly overcrowded even though many children did not attend regularly. In April 1943 it was reported that the rate of absenteeism at Murphy High School was increasing to an alarming figure. According to a school spokesman, the war was the major cause as older boys who expected to be called up for the military service did not take school seriously, country children were attracted by the city and its activities, and working mothers did not know if their children were in school or not. [40]

*Washington Avenue Nursery, 1943* *ADDSCO Collection, USA Photo Archives*

Day care for pre-schoolers was also a pressing problem for working mothers. By the end of the war eleven nurseries and kindergartens were operating in the city with Lanham Act funds. [41] The Lanham Community Facilities Act was designed to supplement local efforts in areas where war industries had brought about crowded conditions. These nurseries and kindergartens in Mobile, administered by the Board of School Commissioners, cared for children of women employed in war work. The minimum age for children in the nurseries was two years. In the spring of 1945, 530 children were enrolled and plans were being made for a twelfth center. [42] Nevertheless, access to child care represented a major problem for many. ADDSCO's counseling supervisor was aware of the problem. The Women's Bureau of the Labor Department found in its survey that even though a number of arrangements were made regarding child care, such as leaving them with relatives or friends, that sixteen per cent of the city's children had no care while the worker was absent. [43]

The war was a daily fact of life for all Mobile women whether or not they were war workers or volunteers. In March 1942 the city experienced its first blackout. Sugar and gasoline were rationed and home milk deliveries were eventually stopped due to restricted tire usage. Women were encouraged to grow victory gardens. Housewives were asked to shop between 10:00 a.m. and 3:00 p.m. to help alleviate Mobile's severe traffic congestion. Stores were kept open on Monday

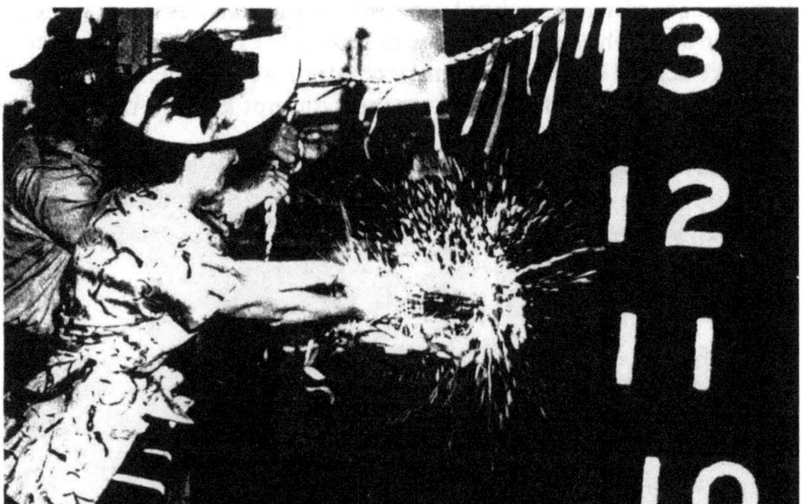


*Christening the "Carib Queen", Gulf Shipbuilding Company.* *S. Blake McNeely Collection, USA Photo Archives*

nights so female defense workers could shop. Women from one end of the economic and social scale to the other were affected. Ladies christened the many ships built at the shipyards. Female prisoners helped the sheriff prepare defense booklets. [44]

Newspaper advertisements are good mirrors of the changes in lifestyles. In 1942 a large Mobile Gas Service Corporation ad pictured a pretty woman in a Red Cross nurses' aide uniform, referred to her as a "Lucky Lady," and described how she organized her work at home so that she had precious free hours to devote to the nation's war effort. [45] Later ads showed women in military uniforms.

Yet in some ways life went on as before. Throughout the war years the department stores ran ads featuring the latest fashions and the society pages continued to chronicle events in the lives of the socially prominent. Marriages took place, but increasingly the young men were in the military service. Babies were born and most children went to school. Nevertheless, the effects of World War II on Mobile women were profound. Before the war Mobile had been a small Southern city in which most women filled traditional roles. During the course of the war, they were recruited for new jobs and undertook new responsibilities. Women grew and changed during the war, and if many returned to their traditional roles after V-J Day, they never forgot their wartime lives. Former shipyard workers still tell their grandchildren about their experiences as welders during the war; former volunteers and members of the armed forces still recount their wartime years with a sense of satisfaction. Women continued to work after 1945, holding on to the opportunities the war had brought in private business or at Brookley Field. Many who had come to the city seeking employment in war-related work remained in Mobile after the war. Whether the newcomers worked outside the home or not, they

*Hammel's Advertisement,* Mobile Press Register, *February 1943,*

brought new attitudes and values to the city they now called home. As in other parts of the country, the war changed the lives of Mobile's women, and for many, their lives would never be the same again.

Patricia G. Harrison is a member of the history faculty at Spring Hill College and the University of South Alabama. She is the book review editor of the *Gulf Coast Historical Review*.

## Notes

[1] William H. Chafe, *The American Woman: Her Changing Social, Economic, and Political Roles, 1920-1970* (New York, 1972). However, some historians maintain that the changes brought about by World War II were only temporary since many women resumed their former traditional roles after the war.

[2] United States Department of Labor. Women's Bureau, *Women Workers in Ten War Production Areas and Their Postwar Employment Plans.* Bulletin of the Women's Bureau, No. 209 (Washington, D.C., 1946), 3. In 1940, 7,800 women were employed compared to 27,000 in November 1944. This does not include household help.

[3] *Mobile Press Register*, January 4, 1942, 11.

[4] *Mobile Register*, March 6, 1942, 22.

[5] *Mobile Register*, March 11, 1942, 2.

[6] *Mobile Register*, March 6, 1942, 22.

[7] *Mobile Press Register*, March 15, 1942, 4B.

[8] *Mobile Press Register*, April 19, 1942, 5.

[9] *Mobile Press Register*, May 3, 1942, 1.

[10] *Mobile Register*, March 24, 1942, 1.

[11] *Mobile Press Register*, March 1, 1942, 5. Miss Donahue was from Little Rock, Arkansas.

[12] *Mobile Register*, March 13, 1942, 15.

[13] *Mobile Press Register*, March 1, 1942, 5.

[14] *Mobile Press Register*, April 12, 1942, 7.

[15] *Mobile Register*, February 13, 1942, 10.

[16] *à la MOAD*, February 28, 1944, 13. *à la MOAD* was published by the Mobile Air Service Command, Brookley Field.

[17] *Mobile Register*, March 17, 1942, 2.

[18] *Mobile Register*, March 28, 1942, 12.

[19] Accounts of the following meetings can be found in these issues: *Mobile Register*, 1942: January 15, 10; January 9, 10; January 10, 5; February 19, 9; March 13, 15; February 15, 5. *Mobile Press Register*, 1942: January 4, 5; May 17, 1.

[20] *Mobile Press Register*, February 21, 1943, 3B. (Italics mine.)

[21] Ibid., 9. (Italics mine.)

[22] Ibid., 1B.

[23] *Mobile Press*, March 1, 1943, 7.

[24] *Mobile Register*, June 18, 1942, 18.

[25] *Mobile Press Register*, May 16, 1943, 10.

[26] Women's Bureau, *Women Workers in Ten War Production Areas*, 15-16.

[27] *Mobile Press Register*, February 13, 1944, 7A.

[28] Excerpts and quoteş from the interview contained in these two paragraphs can be found in the *Mobile Press Register*, February 13, 1944, 7A.

[29] *à la MOAD*, July 5, 1943, 8.

[30] Ibid.

[31] *The Welfarer*, July 18, 1945, 9. *The Welfarer* was published for the civilian personnel of the Mobile Air Service Command at Brookley Field.

[32] *The Welfarer*, November 3, 1944, 5.

[33] *Mobile Register*, January 8, 1944, 5.

[34] Women's Bureau, *Women Workers in Ten War Production Areas*, 27.

[35] Ibid., 2.

[36] The information contained in these two paragraphs can be found in: Women's Bureau, *Women Workers in Ten War Production Areas*, 3-5, 8, 14-16, 44-45.

[37] *The Welfarer*, February 18, 1945, 1.

[38] *Mobile Press Register*, May 10, 1942, 1; *Mobile Register*, May 8, 1942, 1; *Mobile Press Register*, February 13, 1944, 1.

[39] *Mobile Press Register*, April 12, 1942, 1.

[40] *Mobile Register*, April 14, 1943, 5.

[41] *Mobile Press Register*, April 29, 1945, 1B.

[42] *Mobile Register*, March 11, 1945, 1.

[43] Women's Bureau, *Women Workers in Ten Production Areas*, 56.

[44] *Mobile Press Register*, March 15, 1942, 1.

[45] *Mobile Register*, February 18, 1942, 5.

# Japanese American Women During World War II

Valerie Matsumoto

> The life here cannot be expressed. Sometimes, we are resigned to it, but when we see the barbed wire fences and the sentry tower with floodlights, it gives us a feeling of being prisoners in a "concentration camp." We try to be happy and yet oftentimes a gloominess does creep in. When I see the "I'm an American" editorial and write-ups, the "equality of race etc."—it seems to be mocking us in our faces. I just wonder if all the sacrifices and hard labor on [the] part of our parents has gone up to leave nothing to show for it?
>
> —Letter from Shizuko Horiuchi,
> Pomona Assembly Center, May 24, 1942

Thirty years after her relocation camp internment, another Nisei woman, the artist Miné Okubo, observed, "The impact of the evacuation is not on the material and the physical. It is something far deeper. It is the effect on the spirit."[1] Describing the lives of Japanese American women during World War II and assessing the effects of the camp experience on the spirit are complex tasks: factors such as age, generation, personality, and family background interweave and preclude simple generalizations. In these relocation camps Japanese American women faced severe racism and traumatic family strain, but the experience also fostered changes in their lives: more leisure for older women, equal pay with men for working women, disintegration of traditional patterns of arranged marriages, and, ultimately, new opportunities for travel, work, and education for the younger women.

I will examine the lives of Japanese American women during the trying war years, focusing on the second generation—the Nisei—whose work and education were most affected. The Nisei women entered college and ventured into new areas of work in unfamiliar regions of the country, sustained by fortitude, family ties, discipline, and humor. My understanding of their history derives from several collections of internees' letters, assembly center and relocation camp newspapers, census records, and taped oral history interviews that I conducted with eighty-four Nisei (second generation) and eleven Issei (first generation). Two-thirds of these interviews were with women.

The personal letters, which comprise a major portion of my research, were written in English by Nisei women in their late teens and twenties. Their writing reflects the experience and concerns of their age group. It is important, however, to remember that they wrote these letters to Caucasian friends and sponsors during a time of great insecurity and psychological and economic hardship. In their struggle to be accepted as American citizens, the interned Japanese Americans were likely to minimize their suffering in the camps and to try to project a positive image of their adjustment to the traumatic conditions.

## Prewar Background

A century ago, male Japanese workers began to arrive on American shores, dreaming of making fortunes that would enable them to return to their homeland in triumph. For many, the fortune did not materialize and the shape of the dream changed: they developed stakes in small farms and businesses and, together with wives brought from Japan, established families and communities.

The majority of Japanese women—over 33,000 immigrants—entered the United States between 1908 and 1924.[2] The "Gentlemen's Agreement" of 1908 restricted the entry of male Japanese laborers into the country but sanctioned the immigration of parents, wives, and children of laborers already residing in the United States. The Immigration Act of 1924 excluded Japanese immigration altogether.

Some Japanese women traveled to reunite with husbands; others journeyed to America as newlyweds with men who had returned to Japan to find wives. Still others came alone as picture brides to join Issei men who sought to avoid army conscription or excessive travel expenses; their family-arranged marriages deviated from social convention only by the absence of the groom from the *miai* (preliminary meeting of prospective spouses) and wedding ceremony.[3] Once settled, these women confronted unfamiliar clothing, food, language, and customs as well as life with husbands who were, in many cases, strangers and often ten to fifteen years their seniors.

Most Issei women migrated to rural areas of the West. Some lived with their husbands in labor camps, which provided workers for the railroad industry, the lumber mills of the Pacific Northwest, and the Alaskan salmon canneries.[4] They also farmed with their husbands as cash or share tenants, particularly in California where Japanese immigrant agriculture began to flourish. In urban areas, women worked as domestics[5] or helped their husbands run small businesses such as laundries, bath houses, restaurants, pool halls, boarding houses, grocery stores, curio shops, bakeries, and plant nurseries. Except for the few who married well-to-do professionals or merchants, the majority of Issei women unceasingly toiled both inside and outside the home. They were always the first to rise in the morning and the last to go to bed at night.

The majority of the Issei's children, the Nisei, were born between 1910 and 1940. Both girls and boys were incorporated into the family economy early, especially those living on farms. They took care of their younger siblings, fed the farm animals, heated water for the *furo* (Japanese bath), and worked in the fields before and after school—hoeing weeds, irrigating, and driving tractors. Daughters helped with cooking and cleaning. In addition, all were expected to devote time to their studies: the Issei instilled in their children a deep respect for education and authority. They repeatedly admonished the Nisei not to bring disgrace upon the family or community and exhorted them to do their best in everything.

The Nisei grew up integrating both the Japanese ways of their parents and the mainstream customs of their non-Japanese friends and classmates—not always an easy process given the deeply rooted prejudice and discrimination they faced as a tiny, easily identified minority. Because of the wide age range among them and the diversity of their early experiences in various urban and rural areas, it is difficult to generalize about the Nisei. Most grew up speaking Japanese with their parents and English with their siblings, friends, and teachers. Regardless of whether they were Buddhist or Christian, they celebrated the New Year with traditional foods and visiting, as well as Christmas and Thanksgiving. Girls learned to knit, sew, and embroider, and some took lessons in *odori* (folk dancing). The Nisei, many of whom were adolescents during the 1940's, also listened to the *Hit Parade*, Jack Benny, and *Gangbusters* on the radio, learned to jitterbug, played kick-the-can and baseball, and read the same popular books and magazines as their non-Japanese peers.

The Issei were strict and not inclined to open displays of affection towards their children, but the Nisei were conscious of their parents' concern for them and for the family. This sense of family strength and responsibility helped to sustain the Issei and Nisei through years of economic hardship and discrimination: the West Coast anti-Japanese movement of the early 1920's, the Depression of the 1930's, and the most drastic ordeal—the chaotic uprooting of the World War II evacuation, internment, and resettlement.

## Evacuation and Camp Experience

The bombing of Pearl Harbor on December 7, 1941, unleashed war between the United States and Japan and triggered a wave of hostility against Japanese Americans. On December 8, the financial resources of the Issei were frozen, and the Federal Bureau of Investigation began to seize Issei community leaders thought to be strongly pro-Japanese. Rumors spread that the Japanese in Hawaii had aided the attack on Pearl Harbor, fueling fears of "fifth column" activity on the West Coast. Politicians and the press clamored for restrictions against the Japanese Americans, and their economic competitors saw the chance to gain control of Japanese American farms and businesses.

Despite some official doubts and some differences of opinion among military heads regarding the necessity of removing Japanese Americans from the West Coast, in the end the opinions of civilian leaders and Lieutenant General John L. DeWitt—head of the Western Defense Command—of Assistant Secretary of War John McCloy and Secretary of War Henry Stimson prevailed. On February 19, 1942, President Franklin Delano Roosevelt signed Executive Order 9066, arbitrarily suspending the civil rights of American citizens by authorizing the removal of 110,000 Japanese and their American-born children from the western half of the Pacific Coastal States and the southern third of Arizona.[6]

During the bewildering months before evacuation, the

Japanese Americans were subject to curfews and to unannounced searches at all hours for "contraband" weapons, radios, and cameras; in desperation and fear, many people destroyed their belongings from Japan, including treasured heirlooms, books, and photographs. Some families moved voluntarily from the Western Defense zone, but many stayed, believing that all areas would eventually be restricted or fearing hostility in neighboring states.

Involuntary evacuation began in the spring of 1942. Families received a scant week's notice in which to "wind up their affairs, store or sell their possessions, close up their businesses and homes, and show up at an assembly point for transportation to an assembly center."[7] Each person was allowed to bring only as many clothes and personal items as he or she could carry to the temporary assembly centers that had been hastily constructed at fairgrounds, race tracks, and Civilian Conservation Corps camps: twelve in California, one in Oregon, and one in Washington.

The rapidity of evacuation left many Japanese Americans numb; one Nisei noted that "a queer lump came to my throat. Nothing else came to my mind, it was just blank. Everything happened too soon, I guess."[8] As the realization of leaving home, friends, and neighborhood sank in, the numbness gave way to bewilderment. A teenager at the Santa Anita Assembly Center wrote, "I felt lost after I left Mountain View [California]. I thought that we could go back but instead look where we are."[9] Upon arrival at the assembly centers, even the Nisei from large urban communities found themselves surrounded by more Japanese than they had ever before seen. For Mary Okumura, the whole experience seemed overwhelming at first:

> Just about every night, there is something going on but I rather stay home because I am just new here & don't know very much around. As for the people I met so many all ready, I don't remember any. I am not even going to try to remember names because its just impossible here.[10]

A Nisei from a community where there were few Japanese felt differently about her arrival at the Merced Assembly Center: "I guess at that age it was sort of fun for me really [rather] than tragic, because for the first time I got to see young [Japanese] people. . . . We signed up to work in the mess hall—we got to meet everybody that way."[11]

Overlying the mixed feelings of anxiety, anger, shame, and confusion was resignation. As a relatively small minority caught in a storm of turbulent events that destroyed their individual and community security, there was little the Japanese Americans could do but shrug and say, "*Shikata ga nai,*" or, "It can't be helped," the implication being that the situation must be endured. The phrase lingered on many lips when the Issei, Nisei, and the young Sansei (third generation) children prepared for the move—which was completed by November 1942—to the ten permanent relocation camps organized by the War Relocation Authority: Topaz, Utah; Poston and Gila River, Arizona; Amache, Colorado; Manzanar and Tule Lake, California; Heart Mountain, Wyoming; Minidoka, Idaho; Denson and Rohwer, Arkansas.[12] Denson and Rohwer were located in the swampy lowlands of Arkansas; the other camps were in desolate desert or semi-desert areas subject to dust storms and extreme temperatures reflected in the nicknames given to the three sections of the Poston Camp: Toaston, Roaston, and Duston.

The conditions of camp life profoundly altered family relations and affected women of all ages and backgrounds. Family unity deteriorated in the crude communal facilities and cramped barracks. The unceasing battle with the elements, the poor food, the shortages of toilet tissue and milk, coupled with wartime profiteering and mismanagement, and the sense of injustice and frustration took their toll on a people uprooted, far from home.

The standard housing in the camps was a spartan barracks, about twenty feet by one hundred feet, divided into four to six rooms furnished with steel army cots. Initially each single room or "apartment" housed an average of eight persons; individuals without kin nearby were often moved in with smaller families. Because the partitions between apartments did not reach the ceiling, even the smallest noises traveled freely from one end of the building to the other. There were usually fourteen barracks in each block, and each block had its own mess hall, laundry, latrine, shower facilities, and recreation room.

Because of the discomfort, noise, and lack of privacy, which "made a single symphony of yours and your neighbors' loves, hates, and joys,"[13] the barracks often became merely a place to "hang your hat" and sleep. As Jeanne Wakatsuki Houston records in her autobiography,

*Farewell to Manzanar*, many family members began to spend less time together in the crowded barracks. The even greater lack of privacy in the latrine and shower facilities necessitated adjustments in former notions of modesty. There were no partitions in the shower room, and the latrine consisted of two rows of partitioned toilets "with nothing in front of you, just on the sides. Lots of people were not used to those kind of facilities, so [they'd] either go early in the morning when people were not around, or go real late at night. . . . It was really something until you got used to it."[14]

The large communal mess halls also encouraged family disunity as family members gradually began to eat separately: mothers with small children, fathers with other men, and older children with their peers. "Table manners were forgotten," observed Miné Okubo. "Guzzle, guzzle, guzzle; hurry, hurry, hurry. Family life was lacking. Everyone ate wherever he or she pleased."[15] Some strategies were developed for preserving family unity. The Amache Camp responded in part by assigning each family a particular table in the mess hall. Some families took the food back to their barracks so that they might eat together. But these measures were not always feasible in the face of varying work schedules; the odd hours of those assigned to shifts in the mess halls and infirmaries often made it impossible for the family to sit down together for meals.

Newspaper reports that Japanese Americans were living in luxurious conditions angered evacuees struggling to adjust to cramped quarters and crude communal facilities. A married woman with a family wrote from Heart Mountain:

> Last weekend, we had an awful cold wave and it was about 20° to 30° below zero. In such a weather, it's terrible to try going even to the bath and latrine house. . . . It really aggravates me to hear some politicians say we Japanese are being coddled, for *it isn't so*!! We're on ration as much as outsiders are. I'd say welcome to anyone to try living behind barbed wire and be cooped in a 20 ft. by 20 ft. room. . . . We do our sleeping, dressing, ironing, hanging up our clothes in this one room.[16]

After the first numbness of disorientation, the evacuees set about making their situation bearable, creating as much order in their lives as possible. With blankets they partitioned their apartments into tiny rooms and created benches, tables, and shelves as piles of scrap lumber left over from barracks construction vanished; victory gardens and flower patches appeared. Evacuees also took advantage of the opportunity to taste freedom when they received temporary permits to go shopping in nearby towns. These were memorable occasions. A Heart Mountain Nisei described what such a trip meant to her in 1944:

> for the first time since being behind the fences, I managed to go out shopping to Billings, Montana—a trip about 4 hours ride on train and bus. . . . It was quite a mental relief to breathe the air on the outside. . . . And was it an undescribable sensation to be able to be dressed up and walk the pavements with my high heel shoes!! You just can't imagine how full we are of pent-up emotions until we leave the camp behind us and see the highway ahead of us. A trip like that will keep us from becoming mentally narrow. And without much privacy, you can imagine how much people will become dull.[17]

Despite the best efforts of the evacuees to restore order to their disrupted world, camp conditions prevented replication of their prewar lives. Women's work experiences, for example, changed in complex ways during the years of internment. Each camp offered a wide range of jobs, resulting from the organization of the camps as model cities administered through a series of departments headed by Caucasian administrators. The departments handled everything from accounting, agriculture, education, and medical care to mess hall service and the weekly newspaper. The scramble for jobs began early in the assembly centers and camps, and all able-bodied persons were expected to work.

Even before the war many family members had worked, but now children and parents, men and women all received the same low wages. In the relocation camps, doctors, teachers, and other professionals were at the top of the pay scale, earning $19 per month. The majority of workers received $16, and apprentices earned $12. The new equity in pay and the variety of available jobs gave many women unprecedented opportunities for experimentation, as illustrated by one woman's account of her family's work in Poston:

> First I wanted to find art work, but I didn't last too long because it wasn't very interesting . . . so I worked in the

> mess hall, but that wasn't for me, so I went to the accounting department—time-keeping—and I enjoyed that, so I stayed there. . . . My dad . . . went to a shoe shop . . . and then he was block gardener. . . . He got $16. . . . [My sister] was secretary for the block manager; then she went to the optometry department. She was assistant optometrist; she fixed all the glasses and fitted them. . . . That was $16.[18]

As early as 1942, the War Relocation Authority began to release evacuees temporarily from the centers and camps to do voluntary seasonal farm work in neighboring areas hard hit by the wartime labor shortage. The work was arduous, as one young woman discovered when she left Topaz to take a job plucking turkeys:

> The smell is terrific until you get used to it. . . . We all wore gunny sacks around our waist, had a small knife and plucked off the fine feathers.
>
> This is about the hardest work that many of us have done—but without a murmur of complaint we worked 8 hours through the first day without a pause.
>
> We were all so tired that we didn't even feel like eating. . . . Our fingers and wrists were just aching, and I just dreamt of turkeys and more turkeys.[19]

Work conditions varied from situation to situation, and some exploitative farmers refused to pay the Japanese Americans after they had finished beet topping or fruit picking. One worker noted that the degree of friendliness on the employer's part decreased as the harvest neared completion. Nonetheless, many workers, like the turkey plucker, concluded that "even if the work is hard, it is worth the freedom we are allowed."

Camp life increased the leisure of many evacuees. A good number of Issei women, accustomed to long days of work inside and outside the home, found that the communally prepared meals and limited living quarters provided them with spare time. Many availed themselves of the opportunity to attend adult classes taught by both evacuees and non-Japanese. Courses involving handcrafts and traditional Japanese arts such as flower arrangement, sewing, painting, calligraphy, and wood carving became immensely popular as an overwhelming number of people turned to art for recreation and self-expression. Some of these subjects were viewed as hobbies and leisure activities by those who taught them, but to the Issei women they represented access to new skills and a means to contribute to the material comfort of the family.

The evacuees also filled their time with Buddhist and Christian church meetings, theatrical productions, cultural programs, athletic events, and visits with friends. All family members spent more time than ever before in the company of their peers. Nisei from isolated rural areas were exposed to the ideas, styles, and pastimes of the more sophisticated urban youth; in camp they had the time and opportunity to socialize—at work, school, dances, sports events, and parties—in an almost entirely Japanese American environment. Gone were the restrictions of distance, lack of transportation, interracial uneasiness, and the dawn-to-dusk exigencies of field work.

Like their noninterned contemporaries, most young Nisei women envisioned a future of marriage and children. They—and their parents—anticipated that they would marry other Japanese Americans, but these young women also expected to choose their own husbands and to marry "for love." This mainstream American ideal of marriage differed greatly from the Issei's view of love as a bond that might evolve over the course of an arranged marriage that was firmly rooted in less romantic notions of compatibility and responsibility. The discrepancy between Issei and Nisei conceptions of love and marriage had sturdy prewar roots; internment fostered further divergence from the old customs of arranged marriage.

In the artificial hothouse of camp, Nisei romances often bloomed quickly. As Nisei men left to prove their loyalty to the United States in the 442nd Combat Team and the 100th Battalion, young Japanese Americans strove to grasp what happiness and security they could, given the uncertainties of the future. Lily Shoji, in her "Fem-a-lites" newspaper column, commented upon the "changing world" and advised Nisei women:

> This is the day of sudden dates, of blind dates on the up-and-up, so let the flash of a uniform be a signal to you to be ready for any emergency. . . . Romance is blossoming with the emotion and urgency of war.[20]

In keeping with this atmosphere, camp newspaper columns like Shoji's in *The Mercedian*, *The Daily Tulean Dispatch*'s "Strictly Feminine," and the *Poston Chronicle*'s "Fashionotes" gave their Nisei readers countless suggestions on how to impress boys, care for their complexions, and choose the latest fashions. These evacuee-authored columns thus mirrored the mainstream girls' periodicals of the time. Such fashion news may seem incongruous in the context of an internment camp whose inmates had little choice in clothing beyond what they could find in the Montgomery Ward or Sears and Roebuck mail-order catalogues. These columns, however, reflect women's efforts to remain in touch with the world outside the barbed wire fence; they reflect as well women's attempt to maintain morale in a drab, depressing environment. "There's something about color in clothes," speculated Tule Lake columnist "Yuri"; "Singing colors have a heart-building effect. . . . Color is a stimulant we need—both for its effect on ourselves and on others."[21]

The evacuees' fashion columns addressed practical as well as aesthetic concerns, reflecting the dusty realities of camp life. In this vein, Mitzi Sugita of the Poston Sewing Department praised the "Latest Fashion for Women Today—Slacks," drawing special attention to overalls; she assured her readers that these "digging duds"[22] were not only winsome and workable but also possessed the virtues of being inexpensive and requiring little ironing.

The columnists' concern with the practical aspects of fashion extended beyond the confines of the camps, as women began to leave for life on the outside—an opportunity increasingly available after 1943. Sugita told prospective operatives, "If you are one of the many thousands of women now entering in commercial and industrial work, your required uniform is based on slacks, safe and streamlined. It is very important that they be durable, trim and attractive."[23] Women heading for clerical positions or college were more likely to heed Marii Kyogoku's admonitions to invest in "really nice things," with an eye to "simple lines which are good practically forever."[24]

## Resettlement: College and Work

Relocation began slowly in 1942. Among the first to venture out of the camps were college students, assisted by the National Japanese American Student Relocation Council, a nongovernmental agency that provided invaluable placement aid to 4,084 Nisei in the years 1942-46.[25] Founded in 1942 by concerned educators, this organization persuaded institutions outside the restricted Western Defense zone to accept Nisei students and facilitated their admissions and leave clearances. A study of the first 400 students to leave camp showed that a third of them were women.[26] Because of the cumbersome screening process, few other evacuees departed on indefinite leave before 1943. In that year, the War Relocation Authority tried to expedite the clearance procedure by broadening an army registration program aimed at Nisei males to include all adults. With this policy change, the migration from the camps steadily increased.[27]

Many Nisei, among them a large number of women, were anxious to leave the limbo of camp and return "to normal life again."[28] With all its work, social events, and cultural activities, camp was still an artificial, limited environment. It was stifling "to see nothing but the same barracks, mess halls, and other houses, row after row, day in and day out, it gives us the feeling that we're missing all the freedom and liberty."[29] An aspiring teacher wrote: "Mother and father do not want me to go out. However, I want to go so very much that sometimes I feel that I'd go even if they disowned me. What shall I do? I realize the hard living conditions outside but I think I can take it."[30] Women's developing sense of independence in the camp environment and their growing awareness of their abilities as workers contributed to their self-confidence and hence their desire to leave. Significantly, Issei parents, despite initial reluctance, were gradually beginning to sanction their daughters' departures for education and employment in the Midwest and East. One Nisei noted:

> [Father] became more broad-minded in the relocation center. He was more mellow in his ways. . . . At first he didn't want me to relocate, but he gave in. . . . I said I wanted to go [to Chicago] with my friend, so he helped me pack. He didn't say I could go . . . but he helped me pack, so I thought, "Well, he didn't say no."[31]

The decision to relocate was a difficult one. It was compounded for some women because they felt obligated to stay and care for elderly or infirm parents, like the Heart Mountain Nisei who observed wistfully, "It's getting so more and more of the girls and boys are leaving camp, and I sure wish I could but mother's getting on and I just can't leave her."[32] Many internees worried about their acceptance in the outside world. The Nisei considered themselves American citizens, and they had an allegiance to the land of their birth: "The teaching and love of one's own birth place, one's own country was . . . strongly impressed upon my mind as a child. So even though California may deny our rights of birth, I shall ever love her soil."[33] But evacuation had taught the Japanese Americans that in the eyes of many of their fellow Americans, theirs was the face of the enemy. Many Nisei were torn by mixed feelings of shame, frustration, and bitterness at the denial of their civil rights. These factors created an atmosphere of anxiety that surrounded those who contemplated resettlement: "A feeling of uncertainty hung over the camp; we were worried about the future. Plans were made and remade, as we tried to decide what to do. Some were ready to risk anything to get away. Others feared to leave the protection of the camp."[34]

Thus, those first college students were the scouts whose letters back to camp marked pathways for others to follow. May Yoshino sent a favorable report to her family in Topaz from the nearby University of Utah, indicating that there were "plenty of schoolgirl jobs for those who want to study at the University."[35] Correspondence from other Nisei students shows that although they succeeded at making the dual transition from high school to college and from camp to the outside world, they were not without anxieties as to whether they could handle the study load and the reactions of the Caucasians around them. One student at Drake University in Iowa wrote to her interned sister about a professor's reaction to her autobiographical essay, "Evacuation":

> Today Mr.—, the English teacher that scares me, told me that the theme that I wrote the other day was very interesting. . . . You could just imagine how wonderful and happy *I* was to know that he liked it a little bit. . . . I've been awfully busy trying to catch up on work and the work is *so* different from high school. I think that little by little I'm beginning to adjust myself to college life.[36]

Several incidents of hostility did occur, but the reception of the Nisei students at colleges and universities was generally warm. Topaz readers of *Trek* magazine could draw encouragement from Lillian Ota's "Campus Report." Ota, a Wellesley student, reassured them: "During the first few days you'll be invited by the college to teas and receptions. Before long you'll lose the awkwardness you might feel at such doings after the months of abnormal life at evacuation centers."[37] Although Ota had not noticed "that my being a 'Jap' has made much difference on the campus itself," she offered cautionary and pragmatic advice to the Nisei, suggesting the burden of responsibility these relocated students felt, as well as the problem of communicating their experiences and emotions to Caucasians.

> It is scarcely necessary to point out that those who have probably never seen a nisei before will get their impression of the nisei as a whole from the relocated students. It won't do you or your family and friends much good to dwell on what you consider injustices when you are questioned about evacuation. Rather, stress the contributions of [our] people to the nation's war effort.[38]

Given the tenor of the times and the situation of their families, the pioneers in resettlement had little choice but to repress their anger and minimize the amount of racist hostility they encountered.

In her article "a la mode," Marii Kyogoku also offered survival tips to the departing Nisei, ever conscious that they were on trial not only as individuals but as representatives of their families and their generation. She suggested criteria for choosing clothes and provided hints on adjustment to food rationing. Kyogoku especially urged the evacuees to improve their table manners, which had been adversely affected by the "unnatural food and atmosphere" of mess hall dining:

> You should start rehearsing for the great outside by bringing your own utensils to the dining hall. Its an aid to normality to be able to eat your jello with a spoon and well worth the dishwashing which it involves. All of us eat much too fast. Eat more slowly. All this practicing should be done so that proper manners will seem natural to you. If you do this, you won't get stagefright and spill your water glass, or make bread pills and hardly dare to eat when you have your first meal away from the centers and in the midst of scrutinizing caucasian eyes.[39]

Armed with advice and drawn by encouraging reports, increasing numbers of women students left camp. A postwar study of a group of 1,000 relocated students showed that 40 percent were women.[40] The field of nursing was particularly attractive to Nisei women; after the first few students disproved the hospital administration's fears of their patients' hostility, acceptance of Nisei into nursing schools grew. By July 1944, there were more than 300 Nisei women in over 100 nursing programs in twenty-four states.[41] One such student wrote from the Asbury Hospital in Minneapolis: "Work here isn't too hard and I enjoy it very much. The patients are very nice people and I haven't had any trouble as yet. They do give us a funny stare at the beginning but after a day or so we receive the best compliments."[42]

The trickle of migration from the camps grew into a steady stream by 1943, as the War Relocation Authority developed its resettlement program to aid evacuees in finding housing and employment in the East and Midwest. A resettlement bulletin published by the Advisory Committee for Evacuees described "who is relocating":

> Mostly younger men and women, in their 20s or 30s; mostly single persons or couples with one or two children, or men with larger families who come out alone first to scout opportunities and to secure a foothold, planning to call wife and children later. Most relocated evacuees have parents or relatives whom they hope and plan to bring out "when we get re-established."[43]

In early 1945, the War Department ended the exclusion of the Japanese Americans from the West Coast, and the War Relocation Authority announced that the camps would be closed within the year. By this time, 37 percent of the evacuees of sixteen years or older had already relocated, including 63 percent of the Nisei women in that age group.[44]

For Nisei women, like their non-Japanese sisters, the wartime labor shortage opened the door into industrial, clerical, and managerial occupations. Prior to the war, racism had excluded the Japanese Americans from most white-collar clerical and sales positions, and, according to sociologist Evelyn Nakano Glenn, "the most common form of nonagricultural employment for the immigrant women (issei) and their American-born daughters (nisei) was domestic service."[45] The highest percentage of job offers for both men and women continued to be requests for domestic workers. In July 1943, the Kansas City branch of the War Relocation Authority noted that 45 percent of requests for workers were for domestics, and the Milwaukee office cited 61 percent.[46] However, Nisei women also found jobs as secretaries, typists, file clerks, beauticians, and factory workers. By 1950, 47 percent of employed Japanese American women were clerical and sales workers and operatives; only 10 percent were in domestic service.[47] The World War II decade, then, marked a turning point for Japanese American women in the labor force.

Whether they were students or workers, and regardless of where they went or how prepared they were to meet the outside world, Nisei women found that leaving camp meant enormous change in their lives. Even someone as confident as Marii Kyogoku, the author of much relocation advice, found that reentry into the Caucasian-dominated world beyond the barbed wire fence was not a simple matter of stepping back into old shoes. Leaving the camps—like entering them—meant major changes in psychological perspective and self-image.

> I had thought that because before evacuation I had adjusted myself rather well in a Caucasian society, I would go right back into my former frame of mind. I have found, however, that though the center became unreal and was as if it had never existed as soon as I got on the train at Delta, I was never so self-conscious in all my life.

Kyogoku was amazed to see so many men and women in uniform and, despite her "proper" dining preparation, felt strange sitting at a table set with clean linen and a full set of silverware.

> I felt a diffidence at facing all these people and things, which was most unusual. Slowly things have come to seem natural, though I am still excited by the sounds of the busy city and thrilled every time I see a street lined with trees, I no longer feel that I am the cynosure of all eyes.[48]

Like Kyogoku, many Nisei women discovered that relocation meant adjustment to "a life different from our former as well as present way of living"[49] and, as such, posed a challenge. Their experiences in meeting this challenge were as diverse as their jobs and living situations.

"I live at the Eleanor Club No. 5 which is located on the west side," wrote Mary Sonoda, working with the American Friends Service Committee in Chicago:

> I pay $1 per day for room and two meals a day. I also have maid service. I do not think that one can manage all this for $1 unless one lives in a place like this which houses thousands of working girls in the city. . . . I am the only Japanese here at present. . . . The residents and the staff are wonderful to me. . . . I am constantly being

entertained by one person or another.

The people in Chicago are extremely friendly. Even with the Tribune screaming awful headlines concerning the recent execution of American soldiers in Japan, people kept their heads. On street cars, at stores, everywhere, one finds innumerable evidence of good will.[50]

Chicago, the location of the first War Relocation Authority field office for supervision of resettlement in the Midwest, attracted the largest number of evacuees. Not all found their working environment as congenial as Mary Sonoda did. Smoot Katow, a Nisei man in Chicago, painted "another side of the picture":

> I met one of the Edgewater Beach girls. . . . From what she said it was my impression that the girls are not very happy. The hotel work is too hard, according to this girl. In fact, they are losing weight and one girl became sick with overwork. They have to clean about fifteen suites a day, scrubbing the floors on their hands and knees. . . . It seems the management is out to use labor as labor only. . . . The outside world is just as tough as it ever was.[51]

These variations in living and work conditions and wages encouraged—and sometimes necessitated—a certain amount of job experimentation among the Nisei.

Many relocating Japanese Americans received moral and material assistance from a number of service organizations and religious groups, particularly the Presbyterians, the Methodists, the Society of Friends, and the Young Women's Christian Association. One such Nisei, Dorcas Asano, enthusiastically described to a Quaker sponsor her activities in the big city:

> Since receiving your application for hostel accommodation, I have decided to come to New York and I am really glad for the opportunity to be able to resume the normal civilized life after a year's confinement in camp. New York is really a city of dreams and we are enjoying every minute working in offices, rushing back and forth to work in the ever-speeding sub-way trains, counting our ration points, buying war bonds, going to church, seeing the latest shows, plays, operas, making many new friends and living like our neighbors in the war time. I only wish more of my friends who are behind the fence will take advantage of the many helpful hands offered to them.[52]

The Nisei also derived support and strength from networks—formed before and during internment—of friends and relatives. The homes of those who relocated first became way stations for others as they made the transition into new communities and jobs. In 1944, soon after she obtained a place to stay in New York City, Miné Okubo found that "many of the other evacuees relocating in New York came ringing my doorbell. They were sleeping all over the floor!"[53] Single women often accompanied or joined sisters, brothers, and friends as many interconnecting grapevines carried news of likely jobs, housing, and friendly communities. Ayako Kanemura, for instance, found a job painting Hummel figurines in Chicago; a letter of recommendation from a friend enabled her "to get my foot into the door and then all my friends followed and joined me."[54] Although they were farther from their families than ever before, Nisei women maintained warm ties of affection and concern, and those who had the means to do so continued to play a role in the family economy, remitting a portion of their earnings to their families in or out of camp, and to siblings in school.

Elizabeth Ogata's family exemplifies several patterns of resettlement and the maintenance of family ties within them. In October 1944, her parents were living with her brother Harry who had begun to farm in Springville, Utah; another brother and sister were attending Union College in Lincoln, Nebraska. Elizabeth herself had moved to Minnèapolis to join a brother in the army, and she was working as an operative making pajamas. "Minn. is a beautiful place," she wrote, "and the people are so nice. . . . I thought I'd never find anywhere I would feel at home as I did in Mt. View [California], but I have changed my mind."[55] Like Elizabeth, a good number of the 35,000 relocated Japanese Americans were favorably impressed by their new homes and decided to stay.

The war years had complex and profound effects upon Japanese Americans, uprooting their communities and causing severe psychological and emotional damage. The vast majority returned to the West Coast at the end of the war in 1945—a move that, like the initial evacuation, was a grueling test of flexibility and fortitude. Even with the assistance of old friends and service organizations, the transition was taxing and painful; the end of the war meant not only long-awaited freedom but more battles to be fought in social, academic, and economic arenas.

The Japanese Americans faced hostility, crude living conditions, and a struggle for jobs. Few evacuees received any compensation for their financial losses, estimated conservatively at $400 million, because Congress decided to appropriate only $38 million for the settlement of claims.[56] It is even harder to place a figure on the toll taken in emotional shock, self-blame, broken dreams, and insecurity. One Japanese American woman still sees in her nightmares the watchtower searchlights that troubled her sleep forty years ago.

The war altered Japanese American women's lives in complicated ways. In general, evacuation and relocation accelerated earlier trends that differentiated the Nisei from their parents. Although most young women, like their mothers and non-Japanese peers, anticipated a future centered around a husband and children, they had already felt the influence of mainstream middle-class values of love and marriage and quickly moved away from the pattern of arranged marriage in the camps. There, increased peer group activities and the relaxation of parental authority gave them more independence. The Nisei women's expectations of marriage became more akin to the companionate ideals of their peers than to those of the Issei.

As before the war, many Nisei women worked in camp, but the new parity in wages they received altered family dynamics. And though they expected to contribute to the family economy, a large number did so in settings far from the family, availing themselves of opportunities provided by the student and worker relocation programs. In meeting the challenges facing them, Nisei women drew not only upon the disciplined strength inculcated by their Issei parents but also upon firmly rooted support networks and the greater measure of self-reliance and independence that they developed during the crucible of the war years.

## NOTES

For their invaluable assistance with this paper, I would like to thank Estelle Freedman, Mary Rothschild, and members of the women's history dissertation reading group at Stanford University—Sue Cobble, Gary Sue Goodman, Yukiko Hanawa, Gail Hershatter, Emily Honig, Susan Johnson, Sue Lynn, Joanne Meyerowitz, Peggy Pascoe, Linda Schott, Frances Taylor, and Karen Anderson.

1. Miné Okubo, *Miné Okubo: An American Experience*, exhibition catalogue (Oakland: Oakland Museum, 1972), p. 36.

2. The very first Japanese women to arrive in the United States before the turn of the century were the *ameyuki-san*—prostitutes—of whose lives little is known. For information, see Yuji Ichioka, "Ameyuki-san: Japanese Prostitutes in Nineteenth Century America," *Amerasia Journal*, 4, No. 1 (1977). A few references to the *ameyuki-san* appear in Mildred Crowl Martin's biography, *Chinatown's Angry Angel, The Story of Donaldina Cameron* (Palo Alto: Pacific Books, 1977).

3. In Japan, marriage was legally the transfer of a woman's name from her father's registry to that of the groom's family. Even through the Meiji Era there was enormous diversity in the time period of this formalization; it might occur as early as several days before the wedding ceremony or as late as seven or more years later, by which time the bride should have produced several sons and proven herself to be a good wife and daughter-in-law. For a detailed cross-cultural history of the Issei women, see Yukiko Hanawa, "The Several Worlds of Issei Women," Thesis California State University at Long Beach 1982.

4. Yuji Ichioka, "*Amerika Nadeshiko*: Japanese Immigrant Women in the United States, 1900-1924," *Pacific Historical Review*, 69, No. 2 (May 1980), 343.

5. Evelyn Nakano Glenn has examined the lives of Issei and Nisei domestic workers in the prewar period in her study, "The Dialectics of Wage Work: Japanese-American Women and Domestic Servants, 1905-1940," *Feminist Studies*, 6, No. 3 (Fall 1980), 432-71.

6. Sources on evacuation: Robert A. Wilson and Bill Hosokawa, *East to America, A History of the Japanese in the United States* (New York: William Morrow, 1980); Audrie Girdner and Anne Loftis, *The Great Betrayal: The Evacuation of the Japanese-Americans During World War II* (Toronto: Macmillan, 1969); Daisuke Kitagawa, *Issei and Nisei: The Internment Years* (New York: Seabury Press, 1967); Roger Daniels, *The Decision to Relocate the Japanese Americans* (Philadelphia: J. B. Lippincott, 1975).

7. Wilson and Hosokawa, p. 208.

8. Bettie to Mrs. Jack Shoup, June 3, 1942, Mrs. Jack Shoup Collection, Hoover Institution Archives (hereafter referred to as HIA), Stanford, California.

9. May Nakamoto to Mrs. Jack Shoup, November 30, 1942, Mrs. Jack Shoup Collection, HIA.

10. Mary Okumura to Mrs. Jack Shoup, May 30, 1942, Mrs. Jack Shoup Collection, HIA.

11. Miye Baba, personal interview, February 10, 1982, Turlock, California.

12. Many of the Japanese community leaders arrested by the FBI before the evacuation were interned in special all-male camps in North Dakota, Louisiana, and New Mexico. Some Japanese Americans living outside the perimeter of the Western Defense zone in Arizona, Utah, etc. were not interned.

13. Miné Okubo, *Citizen 13660* (New York: Columbia Univ. Press, 1946), p. 66.

14. Chieko Kimura, personal interview, April 9, 1978, Glendale, Arizona.

15. Okubo, *Citizen 13660*, p. 89.

16. Shizuko Horiuchi to Henriette Von Blon, January 24, 1943, Henriette Von Blon Collection, HIA.

17. Shizuko Horiuchi to Henriette Von Blon, January 5, 1944,

Henriette Von Blon Collection, HIA.

18. Ayako Kanemura, personal interview, March 10, 1978, Glendale, Arizona.

19. Anonymous, *Topaz Times*, October 24, 1942, p. 3.

20. Lily Shoji, "Fem-a-lites," *The Mercedian*, August 7, 1942, p. 4.

21. "Yuri," "Strictly Feminine," September 29, 1942, p. 2.

22. Mitzi Sugita, "Latest Fashion for Women Today—Slacks," *Poston Chronicle*, June 13, 1943, p. 1.

23. Sugita.

24. Marii Kyogoku, "a la mode," *Trek* (February 1943), p. 38.

25. From 1942 to the end of 1945 the Council allocated about $240,000 in scholarships, most of which were provided through the donations of churches and the World Student Service Fund. The average grant per student was $156.73, which in that era was a major contribution toward the cost of higher education. Source: National Japanese American Student Relocation Council, Minutes of the Executive Committee Meeting, Philadelphia, Pennsylvania, December 19, 1945.

26. Robert O'Brien, *The College Nisei* (Palo Alto: Pacific Books, 1949), p. 73-74.

27. The disastrous consequences of the poorly conceived clearance procedure have been examined by Wilson and Hosokawa, pp. 226-27, and Girdner and Loftis, pp. 342-43.

28. May Nakamoto to Mrs. Jack Shoup, November 20, 1943, Mrs. Jack Shoup Collection, HIA.

29. Shizuko Horiuchi to Henriette Von Blon, December 27, 1942, Henriette Von Blon Collection, HIA.

30. Toshiko Imada to Margaret Cosgrave Sowers, January 16, 1943, Margaret Cosgrave Sowers Collection, HIA.

31. Ayako Kanemura, personal interview, March 24, 1978, Glendale, Arizona.

32. Kathy Ishikawa to Mrs. Jack Shoup, June 14, 1942, Mrs. Jack Shoup Collection, HIA.

33. Anonymous Nisei nurse in Poston Camp to Margaret Finley, May 5, 1943, Margaret Finley Collection, HIA.

34. Okubo, *Citizen 13660*, p. 139.

35. *Topaz Times*, October 24, 1942, p. 3.

36. Masako Ono to Atsuko Ono, September 28, 1942, Margaret Cosgrave Sowers Collection, HIA. Prior to the war, few Nisei had college experience: the 1940 census lists 674 second-generation women and 1,507 men who had attended or were attending college.

37. Lillian Ota, "Campus Report," *Trek* (February 1943), p. 33.

38. Ota, pp. 33-34.

39. Kyogoku, "a la mode," p. 39.

40. O'Brien, p. 84.

41. O'Brien, pp. 85-86.

42. Grace Tanabe to Josephine Duveneck, February 16, 1944, Conard-Duveneck Collection, HIA.

43. Advisory Committee for Evacuees, *Resettlement Bulletin* (April 1943), p. 2.

44. Leonard Broom and Ruth Riemer, *Removal and Return, The Socio-Economic Effects of the War on Japanese Americans* (Berkeley: Univ. of California Press, 1949), p. 36.

45. Glenn, p. 432.

46. Advisory Committee for Evacuees, *Resettlement Bulletin* (July 1943), p. 3.

47. 1950 United States Census, Special Report.

48. Marii Kyogoku, *Resettlement Bulletin* (July 1943), p. 5.

49. Kyogoku, "a la mode," p. 39.

50. *Poston Chronicle*, May 23, 1943, p. 1.

51. *Poston Chronicle*, May 23, 1943.

52. Dorcas Asano to Josephine Duveneck, January 22, 1944, Conard-Duveneck Collection, HIA.

53. Okubo, *An American Experience*, p. 41.

54. Ayako Kanemura, personal interview, March 24, 1978, Glendale, Arizona.

55. Elizabeth Ogata to Mrs. Jack Shoup, October 1, 1944, Mrs. Jack Shoup Collection, HIA.

56. Susan M. Hartmann, *The Home Front and Beyond, American Women in the 1940s* (Boston: Twayne Publishers, 1982), p. 126. There is some debate regarding the origins of the assessment of evacuee losses at $400 million. However, a recent study by the Commission on Wartime Relocation and Internment of Civilians has estimated that the Japanese Americans lost between $149 million and $370 million in 1945 dollars, and between $810 million and $2 billion in 1983 dollars. See the *San Francisco Chronicle*, June 16, 1983, p. 12.

# Copyright Information

Cometti, Elizabeth. "Women in the American Revolution." *New England Quarterly* 20:1 (March 1947): 329-346. ©*The New England Quarterly*, Northeastern University, Boston, Massachusetts, USA.

Norton, Mary Beth. "Eighteenth-Century American Women in Peace and War: The Case of the Loyalists." *The William and Mary Quarterly* 33:3 (July 1976): 386-409. ©Professor Mary Beth Norton, Cornell University, Ithaca, New York, USA.

Crow, Terrell Armistead. "'As Thy Days, So Shall Thy Strength Be': North Carolina Planter Women in War and Peace." *Carolina Comments* 28:1 (January 1980): 24-31. ©*Carolina Comments*, North Carolina Division of Archives and History, Department of Cultural Resources, Raleigh, North Carolina, USA.

Racine, Philip N. "Emily Lyles Harris: A Piedmont Farmer during the Civil War." *The South Atlantic Quarterly* 79:4 (Autumn 1980): 386-397. "Reprinted with permission from *The South Atlantic Quarterly*, Vol. 79:4 (Autumn 1980), pp. 386-397. Copyright ©1980 by Duke University Press," Durham, North Carolina, USA.

Wood, Ann Douglas. "The War within a War: Women Nurses in the Union Army." *Civil War History* 18 (September 1972): 197-212. ©*Civil War History*, Kent State University Press, Kent Ohio, USA.

Kondert, Nancy T. "The Romance and Reality of Defeat: Southern Women in 1865." *Journal of Mississippi History*: 35:2 (May 1973): 141-152. "Reprinted with permission of the Mississippi Department of Archives and History, the Mississippi Historical Society," and the author, Jackson, Mississippi, USA.

Breen, William J. "Black Women and the Great War: Mobilization and Reform in the South." *The Journal of Southern History* 44:3 (August 1978): 421-440. ©The Southern Historical Association, Athens, Georgia, USA.

Breen, William J. "Southern Women in the War: The North Carolina Woman's Committee, 1917-1919." *North Carolina Historical Review* 55:3 (July 1978): 251-283. ©*North Carolina Historical Review*, Department of Cultural Resoures, Raleigh, North Carolina, USA.

Conner, Valerie J."'The Mothers of the Race' in World War I: The National War Labor Board and Women in Industry." *Labor History* 21:1 (Winter 1979-1980): 31-54. ©1980 The Tamiment Institute, New York, New York, USA.

Graebner, William. "Notes and Documents: 'Uncle Sam Just Loves the Ladies': Sex Discrimination in the Federal Government, 1917." *Labor History* 21:1 (Winter 1979-1980): 75-85. ©1980 The Tamiment Institute, New York, New York, USA.

Greenwald, Maurine Weiner. "Women Workers and World War I: The American Railroad Industry, A Case Study." *Journal of Social History* 9:2 (Winter 1975), 154-177. ©*Journal of Social History*, Carnegie-Mellon University Press, Pittsburgh, Pennsylvania, USA.

Benson, Ronald M. "Searching for the Antecedents of Affirmative Action: The National War Labor Board and the Cleveland Women Conductors in World War I." *Women's Rights Law Reporter* 5:4 (Summer 1979): 271-283. ©Professor Ronald Benson, Millersville University of Pennsylvania, Millersville, Pennsylvania, USA.

Hoff Wilson, Joan. "'Peace is a Woman's Job...' Jeannette Rankin and American Foreign Policy: The Origins of Her Pacifism." *Montana The Magazine of Western History* 30:1 (Winter 1980): 28-41. ©Joan Hoff Wilson, Bloomington, Indiana, USA. Reprinted with permission of the Montana Historical Society, Helena, Montana, and the author.

Hoff Wilson, Joan. "'Peace is a Woman's Job...' Jeannette Rankin and American Foreign Policy: Her Lifework as a Pacifist." *Montana The Magazine of Western History* 30 (Spring 1980): 38-53. ©Joan Hoff Wilson, Bloomington, Indiana, USA. Reprinted with permission of the Montana Historical Society, Helena, Montana, and the author.

Schott, Linda. "The Woman's Peace Party and the Moral Basis for Women's Pacifism." *Frontiers* 8:2 (1985): 18-24. ©1985 Frontiers Editorial Collective, Women's Studies Program, University of Colorado at Boulder, Boulder, Colorado, USA. Reprinted with permission of the journal and the author.

Honey, Maureen. "The 'Womanpower' Campaign: Advertising and Recruitment Propaganda during World War II." *Frontiers* 6:1 (1981): 50-56. ©1981 Frontiers Editorial Collective, Women's Studies Program, University of Colorado at Boulder, Boulder, Colorado, USA. Reprinted with permission of the journal and the author.

Honey, Maureen. "The Working-Class Woman and Recruitment Propaganda during World War II: Class Differences in the Portrayal of War Work." *Signs: Journal of Women in Culture and Society* 8:4 (Summer 1983): 672-687. "©1983 by The University of Chicago. All rights reserved." Chicago, Illinois, USA.

Clive, Alan. "Women Workers in World War II: Michigan as a Test Case." *Labor History* 20:1 (Winter 1979): 44-72. ©1979 The Tamiment Institute, New York, New York, USA.

Anderson, Karen Tucker. "Last Hired, First Fired: Black Women Workers during World War II." *The Journal of American History* 69:1 (June 1982): 82-97. ©Organization of American Historians, Indiana University, Bloomington, Indiana, USA.

Miller, Marc. "Working Women and World War II." *The New England Quarterly* 53 (March-December 1980): 42-61. ©The New England Quarterly, Inc., The Colonial Society of Massachusetts, Northeastern University, Boston, Massachusetts, USA.

Harrison, Patricia G. "Riveters, Volunteers and WACS: Women in Mobile during World War II." *Gulf Coast Historical Review* 1:2 (Spring 1986): 33-54. ©*Gulf Coast Historical Review*, University of South Alabama, Mobile, Alabama, USA.

Matsumoto, Valerie. "Japanese American Women during World War II." *Frontiers* 8:1 (1984): 6-14. ©1984 Frontiers Editorial Collective, Women's Studies Program, University of Colorado at Boulder, Boulder, Colorado, USA. Reprinted with permission of the journal and the author.

# Index

Bei Fragen zur Produktsicherheit wenden Sie sich bitte an:
If you have any questions regarding product safety,
please contact:

Walter de Gruyter GmbH
Genthiner Straße 13
10785 Berlin
productsafety@degruyterbrill.com